SUNDAYS

AND

SEASONS

2001

Augsburg Fortress

ABOUT THE ART

The most significant Christian symbol is the cross, reflecting the mystery of God's sacrificial love of creation given through Christ Jesus. The cover cross for *Sundays and Seasons* is meant to represent this mystery in a primal, direct, and rugged way. Exploding off the cover edges, this cross symbolizes the boundless and powerful life it gives while its metallic quality represents the sacred and precious nature of the Christian way.

The images in *Sundays and Seasons* symbolize the various and many beliefs and practices of the church. Some symbols are from of old, some newer. Some symbolize Christian truths, some Christian festivals, and still others Christian rituals. Primal and rugged in style, all the symbols form a family of imagery that, whatever their source or place, speaks anew of the power, beauty, and wonder of Christ Jesus and the church.

Nicholas T. Markell is a liturgical artist from Minneapolis, Minnesota. In 1984 he earned a bachelor of visual arts degree at the University of Saint Thomas in Saint Paul, Minnesota, and in 1987 chose to respond more fully to his religious yearnings by studying for Christian ministry, earning a master of arts degree in theology and a master of divinity degree from the Washington Theological Union in Washington, D.C. Among his many studies was that of ancient Christian art and symbolism. Working in a variety of media and recognized for his artistic excellence, Nicholas's original art has won national awards and has been published, exhibited in shows, galleries, academic institutions, and installed in numerous churches across the country.

SUNDAYS AND SEASONS

2001, Cycle C

ACKNOWLEDGMENTS

Scripture quotations are from the New Revised Standard Version Bible © 1989 Division of Christian Education of the National Council of the Churches of Christ in the United States of America. Used by permission.

The prayers (printed in each Sunday/festival section) may be reproduced for one-time, congregational use, provided copies are for local use only and the following copyright notice appears: From *Sundays and Seasons*, copyright © 2000 Augsburg Fortress. May be reproduced by permission for use only between December 3, 2000, and November 25, 2001.

Art: Markell Studios, Minneapolis, MN
Book Design: The Kantor Group, Inc., Minneapolis, MN

Editors: Dennis Bushkofsky, Eric Vollen

Manufactured in the U.S.A.   0-8066-3627-0   3-1205

1   2   3

CONTRIBUTORS

Annual Materials
A Pastoral Overview of Luke's Gospel, Dennis Creswell; The Ministry of Healing, Paul R. Nelson; Presiding and Assisting Ministers, Theodore Asta; Worship for All Generations, John Sippola; Introduction, Keeping the Christian Sabbath, Worship Planning Checklist, Dennis Bushkfosky.

Seasonal and Weekly Materials
Images of the Season: Susan Palo Cherwien, Robert Buckley Farlee, James Frazier, Jay Rochelle, Jeffrey Truscott, Ronald Roschke, Mons Teig, Brad Schmeling, Margaret Spring. Environment and Art for the Season: Foy Christopherson, Walter Huffman, Susan Palo Cherwien. Preaching with the Season and Images for Preaching: Donald Kreiss, Galen Knutson, William Greeley, Carol Tomer. Shape of Worship for the Season: Dennis Bushkofsky. Alternate/seasonal liturgical texts: Julie Ryan, Rhoda Schuler, Dennis Bushkofsky, Martin Seltz. Introductions to the day and the readings: Ronald Roschke. The prayers: Mark Briehl, Kent Burreson, Karen Parker, Karen Ball. Worship Matters: Dennis Bushkofsky, Mark Hoffman, Craig Satterlee, Brenda Peconge. Let the Children Come: Martha Fisher, David Olson, Melissa Maxwell-Doherty. Festivals and commemorations: Mark Strobel.

Music Materials
Assembly Song for the Season, Linda Kempke; mainstream hymnody, Timothy Guenther; mainstream choral, Michael Krentz; classic choral, James Bobb; childrens music, Dorothy Christopherson; popular song, David Ellison; popular choral, Marshall Bowen; handbell, William Mathis; organ, Wayne Wold.

Contributing Editors
Norma Aamodt-Nelson, Suzanne Burke, Carol Carver, Linda Parriott, Martin A. Seltz, Frank Stoldt

RELATED RESOURCES

Worship Planning Calendar, 2001, Cycle C (AFP 23-2010)
Words for Worship, 2001, Cycle C (AFP 3-4029)

INTRODUCTION

ADVENT

CHRISTMAS

EPIPHANY

LENT

THE THREE DAYS

EASTER

SUMMER

AUTUMN

NOVEMBER

INTRODUCTION

Thanks to you, the user of *Sundays and Seasons*, this volume has continued to grow and expand into its sixth year! Readers continue to affirm this project and to suggest ways in which it might still evolve in the years to come.

The key to the success of *Sundays and Seasons* seems to be its usefulness for many different types of worship leaders. While few persons will be interested in reading every line of this book, nearly all people who plan and lead worship will find several things here that are useful. Those who preach will find the images for preaching helpful in bringing weekly lectionary passages into focus. Musicians will discover an incredibly rich variety of hymnic, choral, and instrumental possibilities that are ready for exploration. Few congregations will be able to use all of the musical genres that are represented here, but nearly everyone will discover something new or old as we move through the weeks and seasons of the church year.

New alternate worship texts, new suggestions for dealing with the environment for worship, and new ways to consider the shape or order of worship each season make this volume indispensable for thousands of worship planners. A word of caution though: do not attempt to try all of these new things at once! Use your own discretion in determining what is right for your setting at this time. Let this volume unleash some of your own creative skills, too, and feel free to make your own adaptations as you go. The possibilities are limitless.

This year, the year of Luke (cycle C), gives us an opportunity to explore aspects most characteristic of the third gospel. "A Pastoral Overview of Luke" and "The Ministry of Healing" in the introductory pages are especially intended for this Lukan year. Other articles in the annual section explore keeping the Christian sabbath, the use of assisting ministers and worship for all generations.

For those who have not yet discovered it, *Sundays and Seasons* actually stands as the cornerstone of an array of worship planning resources and may be used most profitably when it is combined with several of them. Lectionary passages, introductions to the day and readings, prayers, and alternate texts for worship are all reprinted in *Words for Worship,* an annual CD-ROM product that makes it much easier for congregations to customize their own worship folders through the use of computer technology. New to *Words for Worship* this year are the same background comments for each of the lesser festivals that appear here.

Worship Planning Calendar serves as a kind of workbook for *Sundays and Seasons.* It is a place for worship planners to record selections for each Sunday and major festival. The book also serves as a devotional tool and appointment book.

Meanwhile, with the production of Life Together, a new lectionary-based curriculum, worship planners and educational leaders have the ability to work together more harmoniously. If you have not yet done so, check out *Faith Life Weekly,* a set of reproducible take-home activity and devotional sheets; *LifeSongs,* a major set of children's musical resources that can be used in worship, educational, and fellowship settings; and *Kids Celebrate,* reproducible children's worship bulletins.

Using many of these tools that connect to the lectionary means that your congregation's total ministry may be coordinated more fully—not just on Sunday, but throughout the week as well.

One of the strengths of this book may not be apparent to the casual reader. Well over fifty people are involved in writing, editing, and reviewing the contents of this volume. New people are brought into this team every year, ensuring that the book always continues to be fresh and exciting. May that same excitement be yours in the coming year as well.

—Dennis Bushkofsky, editor

5

A PASTORAL OVERVIEW OF LUKE

Preaching on the Gospel of Luke is both challenging and delightful. The challenge comes from trying to be faithful to Luke's understanding of what God is doing in the world through Jesus' life, teaching, suffering, death, and resurrection. The delight comes from hearing again Luke's own affirmations of God's activity through Jesus.

According to most contemporary scholars, the Gospel of Luke and its companion volume, the Acts of the Apostles, were written between A.D. 80 and 90. The indications are that the first generation Christians who walked and talked with Jesus were almost all dead. Preserving the story of Jesus for the future is a concern for Luke, as explained in the introductions to both the gospel and the book of Acts: "I...decided...to write an orderly account..." (Luke 1:3); "I wrote about all that Jesus did and taught..." (Acts 1:1).

The writer of Luke appears to be a Gentile Christian with strong ties to Paul. Luke is concerned with witnessing to the unity of the Christian church in the first century. His account of the meeting between Paul and the leaders of the church in Jerusalem, and his complete silence about the confrontation between Peter and Paul in Antioch (Acts 15 and Gal. 1:15—2:14), seem to point to a desire to downplay any differences within the community of faith and to present the church to the world as a united entity with one purpose—to proclaim the gospel of Jesus.

FOUR IMPORTANT ASPECTS OF LUKE'S GOSPEL

Here are four important themes to keep in mind while preparing to preach on any text in Luke.

First, Luke is insistent that the story of Jesus is firmly planted in history. "In the days of King Herod of Judea, there was a priest named Zechariah..." (1:5); "In the sixth month [of Elizabeth's pregnancy]..." (1:26); "In those days a decree went out from Emperor Augustus.... This was the first registration and was taken while Quirinius was governor of Syria" (2:1-2). In these three instances, Luke ties his narrative into the larger fabric of history, even though the dates are not always exact.

Pay attention to what happens when the ministry of John the baptizer begins: "In the fifteenth year of the reign of the Emperor Tiberius, when Pontius Pilate was governor of Judea, and Herod was ruler of Galilee, and his brother Philip ruler of the region of Ituraea and Trachonitis, and Lysanias ruler of Abilene, during the high priesthood of Annas and Caiaphas, the word of God came to John..." (3:1ff). Here Luke wants the reader to know that the ministry of John the baptizer, and the subsequent ministry of Jesus, did not happen off in a corner of heaven somewhere, but the word of God came to John at a specific time in history and during the lifetimes of certain people whose lives and deeds can be verified by sources outside of the gospel. The importance of this documentation for Luke is to show that God is active in the events and people of history, and God's works may be seen in them. God does not simply act in heaven and then send the results to us, but God acts within our history, among human beings to accomplish God's will. In this historical context Jesus is baptized (3:21ff), and begins his ministry at about thirty years of age (2:23).

Second, in addition to believing that God acts in the history of humankind and brings about God's will through historical events, Luke also wants to say that what happens in Jesus of Nazareth is a unique historical event, one through which all of history needs to be interpreted. For Luke, Jesus is the centerpiece of history. In his book *The Gospel of Luke,* Hans Conzelmann makes this case. His conclusion is pointed out by the German title of this work, *Die Mitte der Zeit,* literally translated *The Middle of Time.* So the events of Jesus do not just *happen* for Luke, but they are "the events that *have been fulfilled* among us" (1:1; emphasis by the author). Jesus is not just a child of Abraham, as the genealogy of Matthew shows (Matt. 1:1-17), but his ancestry is traced all the way back to "Adam, son of God" (3:38). As early as the message of Gabriel to Zechariah, which speaks of the work of John the baptizer (1:16-17), it is obvious that something new is happening. When Mary questions Gabriel about how she could have a child when she is still a virgin, the response—"The Holy Spirit will come upon you and the power of the Most High will overshadow you; therefore the child to be born will be holy; he will be called Son of God" (1:35)—indicates that this child is to be the Messiah, a new beginning for God's people. The message of the angel to the shepherds ("to you is born this day in the city of David a Savior, who is the Messiah, the Lord" in 2:11); the responses of Simeon (the Nunc dimittis in 2:29-32) and Anna (2:36-38); and Jesus' response to Mary and Joseph when they found him in the temple ("Did you not know that I must be in my father's house?" in 2:49) all indicate that something different is happening here, an act of God centered in the person of Jesus. The voice of God speaking from the cloud at Jesus' baptism (3:22) and on the Mount of Transfiguration (9:35), the voices of the demons that he cast out (4:41), Peter's response to the miraculous catch of fish ("Go away from me, Lord, for I am a sinful man!" in 5:8), Peter's confession of the identity of Jesus (9:20), and Jesus' proclamation of his ministry and identity (for example, 4:18f) all point to this person and event as the most important thing to have happened since the creation of the world. So while Luke ties Jesus tightly to history, he also presents Jesus as one through whom the whole of history has to be interpreted. Everything that has happened from creation up to Jesus is in preparation for Jesus' incarnation. Everything that has happened since Jesus' death and resurrection is affected by and interpreted through that event. Jesus is the center of history, the center of God's work in our world.

Third, more than any other New Testament writer, Luke seems to have a sense of the place of women in the life of Jesus and the church. For example, while Matthew records the appearance of Gabriel only to Joseph (Matt. 1:20f), Luke records two appearances: one to a man, Zechariah, the father of John the baptizer (1:11-20); and one to a woman, Mary, the mother of Jesus (1:26-38), and none to Joseph. The song Zechariah sings at the circumcision of John (the Benedictus in 1:67-79) is paralleled by the song Mary sings when she is greeted by Elizabeth, Zechariah's wife (the Magnificat in 1:46-55). In the temple, when Joseph and Mary

come to make the sacrifice of cleansing for Mary, not only is Simeon there to praise God (2:25-35), but Anna, the prophet, is there also and tells others about what was happening.

Even though not all of the stories in Luke's gospel are paired, Luke does relate several stories together, so that a story about a man or a boy follows or precedes one about a woman or a girl. The healing of the man with the withered hand on the Sabbath (6:6-11), parallels the healing of a crippled woman on the Sabbath (13:10-17), and in both cases Jesus is reviled by religious authorities for healing on the Sabbath. The healing of the centurion's slave (7:1-10) is followed immediately by the raising of the son of the widow of Nain (7:11-16). The plea of Jairus to heal his daughter (8:40-42, 49-56) is followed closely by the plea of a man to heal his son who is possessed by a demon (9:37-43). The placement of the parable of the good Samaritan (10:25-37) with its message of "Don't just listen—Do something!" right before the story of Mary and Martha (10:38-42) with its message of "Don't just do something—Listen!" does not appear to be merely accidental. The fact that the one features a man who is a foreigner and an outcast (the Samaritan) and the other features two women (who were considered second-class citizens at the time) emphasizes the idea that what God is doing in Jesus is being done for everyone. When Jesus tells parables of the way God works, we find parallel stories, such as in chapter 15, where the story of the lost sheep is paired with the story of the lost coin (15:3-7, 8-10). In the stories about prayer, the persistent woman is paralleled with the tax collector, as a picture of what prayer is supposed to be like (18:2-8, 9-14).

In addition to these parallel stories, Luke presents more stories that hold up women as the object of God's love and as examples of faith than does any other gospel. The woman who ministers to Jesus at Simon the Pharisee's house (7:36-50); the naming of the women who travel with Jesus (8:2f); the healing of the woman with the hemorrhages (8:43-48); the statement "mother against daughter and daughter against mother," as a parallel to "father against son and son against father" (12:53); the equality of women in marriage (16:18); the image of "two women grinding meal together; one will be taken and the other left" when talking about the coming day of the Lord (17:35; also

Matt. 24:40ff); the use of the persistent woman and the poor widow as pictures of the life of faith (18:2-8; 21:1-4); the women who were there with Jesus in his crucifixion and death (23:27-31, 49, 55-56); and the women (named) who went to the tomb on Sunday and discovered it empty, and who returned to tell the disciples about it (24:1-11) all point to Jesus as one who has a strong concern for women and to the church of Jesus also as a community concerned about the place of women in that community.

Fourth, the Gospel of Luke has a strong commitment to justice for the poor, the needy, and the outcast. The shepherds, who were considered to be "unclean" because of the work they did and unacceptable because of their shady reputations, were the first to hear about the birth of the Messiah (2:8ff) and were the first to worship God in praise of this great gift (2:20). Mary's song about the work of God in bringing Jesus into the world includes a reversal of position between the powerful and the lowly, the rich and the poor, the full and the hungry (1:51-53). John the baptizer's ministry ("Every valley shall be filled, and every mountain and hill be made low" 3:4) and his warning to the children of Abraham, to the crowds, and to the soldiers (3:7-14) indicate a concern that faith also be shown with justice and equity among people.

When he preaches in his home synagogue in Nazareth, Jesus declares his ministry of justice when he reads from Isaiah, "The spirit of the Lord is upon me, because he has anointed me to bring good news to the poor. He has sent me to proclaim liberty to the captives and recovery of sight to the blind, to let the oppressed go free, to proclaim the year of the Lord's favor," and then declares, "Today, this scripture has been fulfilled in your hearing" (4:18-19, 21). In his ministry, Jesus touches and heals lepers (5:13); proclaims that feeding the hungry and healing the sick are more important than observing the Sabbath (6:1-11); preaches blessings to the poor, the hungry, the mourning, and the hated, while at the same time preaching woe to the rich, the full, those who laugh, and the well-respected (6:20-26). Jesus has compassion for the widow and raises her only son from the grave (7:13ff); tells John's disciples that he is fulfilling the work of the Messiah by healing and preaching (7:22ff); recognizes a prostitute as a more fit object of God's love than Simon the Pharisee (7:40ff);

takes pity on the woman who has suffered for twelve years with hemorrhages (8:43-48); speaks of true treasure that comes not from the world, but from God (9:25f); points to a child as the greatest in the kingdom (9:46ff); and speaks of internal righteousness in addition to external, and contends that justice and the love of God are served both in listening to God and God's messengers, and in loving the neighbor (11:41-52). He also points out that the wealth and trappings of this world can indeed be a trap for the faithful, for disciples are to rely on God alone for the things they need for life in the world (12:15-34).

In many other places in the Gospel of Luke, Jesus shows a concern for justice for sinners (15:2ff); the returning prodigal (15:25ff); women facing divorce (16:18); the poor, hungry, and beggars (16:19-31); lepers (17:11ff); tax collectors (19:1-10); the ones who reject him (19:41); the ones who are being defrauded in the temple market (19:45f); and widows (20:46f). The final act of his life—his crucifixion—is a miscarriage of justice (23:13-24), but still he prays for those who crucify him (23:34), and takes time to assure the thief on the cross next to his that he would have a share of paradise that day (23:42f). It is impossible to preach on the Gospel of Luke and not speak of how our unjust actions negatively affect our neighbor and how love toward our neighbor includes working for justice with those who are not able to help themselves.

FOR FURTHER READING

Conzelmann, Hans. *The Theology of St. Luke,* trans. G. Buswell. New York: Harper and Row, 1960.

Just Jr., A. A. *The Concordia Commentary: A Theological Exposition of Sacred Scripture: Luke 1:1—9:50* (St. Louis: Concordia Publishing House, 1996) and *The Concordia Commentary: A Theological Exposition of Sacred Scripture: Luke 9:51—24:53* (1997).

"The Gospel of Luke and the Acts of the Apostles: The Idea of Salvation History," in *The New Testament: An Introduction,* 2d ed. Norman Perrin and Dennis C. Duling, eds. New York: Harcourt Brace Jovanovich, 1982.

"The Gospel According to Luke," in *The New Oxford Annotated Bible.* New York: Oxford University Press, 1991.

Juel, Donald. *Luke–Acts: The Promise of History.* Atlanta: John Knox Press, 1983.

Tannehill, Robert C. *The Narrative Unity of Luke–Acts.* Philadelphia: Fortress Press, 1986.

THE MINISTRY OF HEALING

The year of Luke presents a special opportunity to explore and deepen the liturgical ministry of healing. This ministry can take place in congregations, clinical settings, and other places where Christians assemble for worship around word and sacrament.

Saint Luke has long been associated in the church's mind with the ministry of healing. The church's tradition identifies him as the author of the third gospel and the Acts of the Apostles. Tradition also identifies him as a Gentile. Colossians 4:14 describes him as a physician. Saint Paul includes him as a companion on two of his missionary journeys. He accompanies Paul on his final trip to Rome. Luke is often pictured as a painter or iconographer. He is patron of both artists and physicians. The church celebrates Luke's ministry in a lesser festival on October 18 each year.

Luke's gospel includes important accounts of healing. Among the lectionary readings for 2001 the following healing (sometimes exorcism) stories are included:

- Third Sunday after the Epiphany: Luke 4:14-21—Jesus identifies "recovery of sight to the blind" with his ministry.
- Fourth Sunday after the Epiphany: Luke 4:21-30—The admonition, "doctor cure yourself," and the reference to Elijah's healing of Naaman touch the healing theme.
- Sixth Sunday after the Epiphany: Luke 6:17-26—This passage identifies healing as one reason that people came to Jesus.
- The Transfiguration of Our Lord: Luke 9:28-43 (longer reading)—Jesus heals the possessed boy after his disciples had failed.
- Second Sunday in Lent: Luke 13:31-35—Jesus describes his ministry as including "performing cures."
- Proper 6: Luke 7:36—8:3—Women Jesus had healed join in proclaiming and bringing the good news of the kingdom of God.
- Proper 7: Luke 8:26-39—Jesus ends the possession of the Gerasene demoniac.
- Proper 9: Luke 10:1-11, 16-20—Jesus identifies healing the sick with the nearness of the kingdom.

- Proper 10: Luke 10:25-37—The good Samaritan is described as bandaging wounds and caring for the injured traveler.
- Proper 16: Luke 13:10-17—Jesus cures the crippled woman.
- Proper 21: Luke 16:19-31—Lazarus is described as "covered with sores."
- Proper 23: Luke 17:11-19—Jesus heals the ten lepers.

HEALING, RECOVERY, OR CURE

The scriptures contain diverse stories of miraculous cures. These stories occur in both the New Testament and the Hebrew Scriptures. None of these stories of miraculous cure takes place in what we would call a liturgical setting. When set within an assembly for worship—especially in Holy Communion—the church's expectation is for healing, not miraculous cure. What is the difference? In the scriptures, curing the sick is a gift from God given to some but not to all believers. Caring for the sick is a responsibility laid on all believers and a special commitment of officials of the community, the "elders" in the Letter of James. The liturgical ministry of healing seems more closely related to caring for the sick than to miraculous cures. Persons in our culture who struggle with addictions understand their need for *recovery* and carefully avoid the use of *cure* as an expectation associated with their disease. Healing can apply to virtually every human person and need not be limited in a strict sense to those seeking remedy for a particular illness or injury. It is an appropriate category for use in a liturgical assembly where various needs for healing may be present among those gathered.

MISUNDERSTANDINGS

Because of the long, and often unfortunate, tradition of identifying illness with divine punishment or retribution, we must be clear about the church's expectations of the ministry of healing. Persons who do not receive a

9

miraculous or immediate cure must be helped to understand that their circumstance is not a negative judgment on their worth or relationship to God. This responsibility falls in a special way to pastors when they are the liturgical ministers of healing for the church.

The Christian tradition also holds a close link between illness and sinfulness, forgiveness and cure. This close link can also be seen between the ministries of confession and forgiveness and of healing. Expecting cure can result in feeling condemnation and judgment when cure does not result from the liturgical ministry of laying on of hands and anointing.

The ministry of healing begins in the assurance of forgiveness, often in spite of illness and its apparent judgment. The important account of the liturgical ministry of healing in the New Testament in James is clear: the assurance of forgiveness is an important obligation of the elders who are called to the sick person. Note that it is not a call for more confession or penitence on the part of the sick person, but for clear declaration of forgiveness on the part of the ministers.

CHRONIC AND ACUTE ILLNESS

Distinguishing between the needs of the acutely ill and the chronically ill as well as those who are caregivers is useful in the context of healing ministry. The ministry of healing also reaches out to persons whose illness does not lead them to expect a cure. Today Christians and others in North American cultural contexts have come to a special understanding of chronic illness. Persons living with chronic diseases may long for healing but without anticipating such healing in terms that may apply to injuries or acute diseases. A person living with a chronic arthritic condition does not live with that illness in the same way that a person whose arm was broken in a playground accident. The injured anticipates healing, improvement, and even cure. A chronic sufferer may hold none of these expectations. Yet healing is a hope and expectation associated with the restoration of the created order and the coming of the kingdom of God, which all people can share.

HEALING AND CAREGIVERS

Caregivers of those who are ill also often ask for anointing in the context of healing, which may rightly be done because they too participate in the care of the sick. They may wish to identify more closely with those they care for and see anointing as a gesture of that solidarity as they see the close connections it traditionally has with forgiveness. Their work with those who are ill may also make them acutely conscious of their own need for healing and forgiveness.

THINGS TO CONSIDER

Consider the possible liturgical contexts for the celebration of healing in your congregation. Among those contexts are occasions when the liturgical assembly is gathered for worship: the liturgy of Holy Communion (a basic resource is the *Saint Luke's Day Service*—see list of resources that follows); the Service of the Word for Healing (a basic resource is *Occasional Services,* 1982); Morning Prayer and Evening Prayer. In addition, liturgical assemblies apart from the congregation may include clinical settings: extended care facilities, residential facilities, nursing homes, or hospital chapels. The form of liturgy used in these settings will differ from the administration to a single person in a private home, in a semiprivate room, or another clinical setting.

Consider the possible times for the celebration of healing in your congregation's liturgical life: Sunday morning; Saturday evening; weekdays or weekday evenings. Choose Sundays with readings that raise up healing themes (see the preceding list and also the list in each of the seasonal sections titled "Shape of Worship for the Season" in this book). Consider the appropriateness of special days in the calendar of lesser festivals and commemorations: October 18, St. Luke; and other lesser festivals and commemorations associated with healing such as January 27, Lydia, Dorcas, and Phoebe; February 25, Elizabeth Fedde, deaconess; July 22, St. Mary Magdalen; July 29, Mary, Martha, and Lazarus; August 13, Florence Nightingale and Clara Maass, renewers of the church; September 4, Albert Schweitzer, missionary to Africa.

CONSIDER THE BASIC GESTURES USED

The basic context for the ministry of healing among Christians is prayer. James 5:14-15 is the basic manual in scripture for this ministry. Prayer is clearly the context here. This context of prayer also includes a close link to the forgiveness of sin as a healing gift. James also makes it clear that this ministry is one that rightly belongs to "the elders" of the congregation. James also continues the use of oil for the anointing of the sick and its application by the hands of the elders.

Consider the gestures used: laying on of hands; sign of the cross; anointing with oil.

The chief gestures associated with the ministry of healing are located in scripture: the touch of a hand or hands (laying on of hands); anointing with oil; speaking a word of personal address ("Little girl, get up!"); a word of forgiveness, or rebuke to evil. These gestures can be found in many healing stories in the New Testament and Hebrew Scriptures. To this list of scriptural gestures, the early Christians added the sign of the cross, a gesture that has come down to the present day in many liturgical contexts. Rather than constituting a separate gesture, the sign of the cross has become one of the ways in which Christians carry out the anointing with oil.

THE OIL ITSELF

Where does this oil come from today? Olive oil is traditionally used for anointing. This oil is readily available and need not be expensive. It was, and continues to be, a basic staple of the diet in many parts of the world. Anointing oil may be set apart by prayer at the time of its use or in a special preparatory liturgy. Several synods now celebrate an annual liturgy in which the bishop blesses oil for use in congregations that desire to use it. Oil that is set apart for use with the sick has no scent or other matter added to it. In the Roman Rite, three oils are prepared and blessed by the bishop in the Chrism Mass: chrism (used in baptism and confirmation and ordinations), oil of catechumens (used in the rites associated with encouraging those preparing for baptism and sometimes identified with exorcism), and oil of the sick (used with those who are ill). The rite of Dedication of Worship Furnishings in *Occasional Services* provides a specific prayer for oil.

The medieval practice for distribution of oil was to place a few drops of oil on some cotton or other fibre and keep it in a covered "stock." An oil stock was usually made of silver or gold and often equipped with a small ring so that it could be held conveniently in the hand of the minister doing the anointing. Using a stock can still be convenient in clinical settings such as homes, sick rooms, nursing homes, or hospitals. Today, the visual sign of the oil is being recovered in liturgical settings. A glass cruet or other vessel that allows the oil to be seen may be used. Oil may then be poured into a small glass bowl for use during anointing.

How is it administered? The minister performing anointing may lay his or her hands on the person receiving the sign. Then, dipping a thumb into the oil, the minister makes the sign of the cross with the oil on the forehead of the person and speaks the formula prescribed in the service. When all have received the anointing who desire to do so, the minister will use a clean cloth to wipe off any oil remaining on his or her hands, which is especially important if the minister will be distributing communion later in the service.

WHO ANOINTS?

Who should administer the laying on of hands and anointing for those who are ill? Ordained pastors and bishops are the traditional ministers of laying on of hands and anointing in the name of the church, particularly in settings of public worship. The calling in the New Testament for "the elders" to come and pray and lay on hands and anoint those who are ill seems to be the origin of this practice. This tradition also clearly indicates it is a liturgical ministry of the church. It is not a further obligation or tool for caregivers in the family or persons involved in clinical ministry.

AN ALTERNATIVE FORMULA FOR ADMINISTERING ANOINTING

The words that accompany a ritual gesture, such as laying on of hands or anointing with oil, need to fulfill two important criteria. First, they must link the gesture or physical element to a biblical promise. Second, they must link that gesture or element specifically to the person to whom it is being administered either by speaking the name or by first person address (for examples, see the baptismal formula of administration in *LBW*, p. 123, either "Richard, I baptize you…" or "Sue is baptized…").

The setting for the celebration also affects the character of these words. In a clinical or home setting it is appropriate to use a rich and full formula of administration. This can also be appropriate in settings where only a few members of the gathered assembly receive laying on of hands and or anointing with oil. However, if many people will come for anointing, a shorter formula can be useful. In such circumstances, one of the following might serve:

P Receive this oil ✝ as a sign of forgiveness and healing in Jesus Christ.

C **Amen**

OR

P Receive the promise of forgiveness and healing in Jesus Christ.

C **Amen**

FOR FURTHER READING

Gusmer, Charles. *And You Visited Me: Sacramental Ministry to the Sick and the Dying.* Collegeville: Liturgical Press.

Kinast, Robert L. *Sacramental Pastoral Care: Integrating Resources for Ministry.* New York: Pueblo Publishing Company, 1988.

Occasional Services: A Companion to Lutheran Book of Worship. Minneapolis: Augsburg Publishing House; Philadelphia: Board of Publication, Lutheran Church in America, 1982.

"Rito de Sanación" in *Libro de Liturgia y Cántico.* Minneapolis: Augsburg Fortress, 1998.

Saint Luke's Day Service. Chicago: Evangelical Lutheran Church in America, 1996.

KEEPING the CHRISTIAN SABBATH

With the increasing use of telecommunications technology, it is not uncommon to have pagers beeping, watches chirping, or cell phones ringing during public worship on Sunday mornings. We have in fact become so accustomed to being attached to these modern devices that a recent television news program offered a segment on how some young people will no longer wait beyond one or two rings for another party to answer a phone call. Time is important; saving time even more so.

So where do we disconnect from this fast-paced life? Can we disconnect from it at all? These questions are important. They are not unrelated to our spirituality or worship practices. Rightly or wrongly, the clock has often guided our worship lives.

For several decades, congregations of worshipers and their leaders have often agreed to an unwritten contract of an hour for worship each Sunday morning. While this sacred hour might be extended for special occasions or festival seasons, it is remarkable how most congregations have determined that one hour is appropriate for weekly worship. Certainly this allotment was not always the case. We can read of services in past generations where the sermon alone might have lasted an hour. Congregational hymns, liturgical music, and the celebration of one or both sacraments might have ex-tended a typical

service to two or three hours. But services of this length are exceptional for most of us these days.

We could debate whether an hour is appropriate (either too much or too little) for our chief weekly liturgy, but let us assume for now that it is a satisfactory amount of time for the contemporary worshiper. What happens during that hour?

VERBAL CLUTTER

In many congregations the gathering portion of the liturgy may last up to a quarter of an hour. Frequently parish announcements take up a good amount of that time—two or three minutes of explanation regarding items that are already included in bulletins or newsletters. How much needs to be said about items already covered elsewhere? Brief reminders to read about an event in a worship folder or on a bulletin board can cover a variety of parish activities. Announcements of this type might best be saved for the end of the service rather than the beginning.

The remainder of the gathering time might be used for a prelude, an order for confession and forgiveness, an entrance hymn, the Kyrie, a hymn of praise, a prayer of the day, and even a choral anthem. All these things happen as "preliminaries" before a congregation finally sits down to hear the first reading. Congregations looking for ways to free up some time might think about whether the gathering rite is too long. Are all components needed every week?

Despite the use of worship folders and hymn boards, many presiding ministers seem compelled to announce every page or hymn number. If such announcements cannot be eliminated entirely, at least they can be limited to those service junctures that are especially challenging to negotiate.

Various options for confession and forgiveness do exist. Seasonal forms for confession and forgiveness are printed in this book; many are shorter than standard orders provided in our worship books. Many congregations use an order for confession and forgiveness only during Lent and Advent. Some make a special attempt to place petitions of confession in the prayers. When a specific order for confession is determined to be necessary, it might in fact be used as a preparatory order, the way that it is laid out in *Lutheran Book of Worship* (p. 56). The order could be used prior to a prelude, thereby allowing the service itself to start with the entrance hymn. The order might begin before the announced time of the service.

Although many congregations will begin worship with an entrance hymn, it is not necessary to use both a Kyrie and a hymn of praise as well. One or both of these may be omitted. The hymn of praise is customarily omitted during Advent and Lent. The Kyrie might be omitted during festival seasons. After Pentecost, especially during hot uncomfortable summers, both the Kyrie and the hymn of praise might be omitted. The gathering rite then moves swiftly from the entrance hymn to the apostolic greeting and the prayer of the day.

SAVE TIME FOR THE MAIN THING

Congregations are often tempted to save time by omitting one or more of the readings for a given Sunday or festival. Be realistic—how much time does a given reading usually take? One minute? Two minutes at the most? Those wanting to shave time will not save much by cutting here. The lectionary has been assembled in such a way that the readings are intended to be heard together. The first reading often links to the day's gospel in a particular way. The psalm is frequently a way for the congregation to respond to something articulated in the first reading. Meanwhile the second reading may provide a different thread for comparison or contrast to the other readings for the day. A liturgical preacher will take into account the varied richness of this scriptural resource each week, rather than simply choosing one of the readings as a "sermon text."

Finally, the congregation sings the hymn of the day, which is intended to bring the liturgy of the word to a climax. On most occasions, readings, sermon, hymns, and prayers should fit together in such a way that they expound on one another. The weekly materials in *Sundays and Seasons* are intended to provide linkages all rooted in the lectionary and the celebration of the liturgical seasons.

How much time should be devoted to a sermon? This question is tricky because much depends on cultural and congregational expectations. In some communities where preaching is a dialogical exercise, the congregation interjects spontaneous responses ("Amen" or "Hallelujah") throughout the sermon. In a large majority of North American congregations, the sermon is akin to a monologue, perhaps punctuated by laughter, silence, or smiles on worshipers' faces, but generally not a true dialogical event. It is the rare preacher who can hold the attention of worshipers for longer than ten to fifteen minutes in our contemporary context. Preachers who are gifted storytellers can often exceed this limit, but this gift is not shared by all. Nor is a lengthy sermon usually necessary. Interpreting the day's readings to contemporary hearers and applying those interpretations to some aspect of daily life does not need to take twenty minutes. Some of the most famous speeches and sermons are brief (Abraham Lincoln's Gettysburg Address, for example). Preachers need to learn the art of judicious trimming. Not everything the preacher knows needs to be said in any given sermon. One powerful point will be remembered better than three.

Congregations that try to save time by drastically cutting or entirely eliminating the prayers have forgotten that prayer should not be primarily about getting anything. Prayer cultivates the relationship we have with our creator. It is, to borrow the title of Marva Dawn's recent book, *A "Royal" Waste of Time*. Prayer is an important part of our whole gathering for worship in the

13

first place. Led by a variety of voices from the congregation (including assisting ministers as prayer leaders), prayers need not be verbose, but instead remind us of our absolute dependence on God for life and of our connections to the church at large, the natural and civil orders, those in need, and those who have died. Short petitions, with appropriate silences in between, can open our spirits as the place where God dwells.

SUNDAY DINNER STARTS IN CHURCH

Though the Evangelical Lutheran Church in America and its predecessor church bodies have articulated a vision of weekly communion for more than two decades (see *The Use of the Means of Grace*, principle 35), a majority of congregations still have not begun this practice. Growing numbers of congregations have discovered the centrality of word *and* sacrament for the primary weekly gathering of the congregation and not just at one service or the other for those congregations with multiple services.

What are the reasons given for not communing every week? Two of those most commonly heard are that it takes too long or that it would lose its meaning if celebrated every week. Let's be clear about the facts. Communion services can and do take place within the sanctified hour in congregations around the globe. Communities must determine what is important during that time. Are five minutes of announcements worth not being able to commune each week? Are rambling twenty-minute sermons better than going without the eucharist for an entire month? Weekly, even daily reading of scripture has not decreased the Bible's importance for Christians who follow such patterns. Why would weekly reception of communion decrease its meaning? Congregations that celebrate communion weekly have discovered benefits from this sacrament that can only be experienced by those who receive it frequently.

ATTENTION TO THE MAIN THING

If we will allow ourselves to scrutinize our worship patterns, we may find that we have provided time for doing many things but we are not doing the main things with regularity nor are we doing them well. If we do not use full prayers of thanksiving during our weekly communion liturgies (see "Praying at the Eucharist," pp. 19–21 in *Sundays and Seasons 2000*), we are depriving ourselves of what it is that we have come together to do each week. If we cannot set aside time to hear all the readings, pray prayers, and celebrate the sacraments generously, what *are* we doing when we come together each week?

We may be trimming time in many aspects of our lives, but are we using our time for the main things? It's a tough question, one that has no simple answers. But it is a question we should be asking ourselves regularly.

SABBATH REST

One beloved nineteenth-century hymn text lives as almost an anachronism in hymnals of this generation. The third stanza of John G. Whittier's "Dear Lord and Father of Mankind" goes like this:

> Oh, Sabbath rest by Galilee,
> Oh, calm of hills above;
> Where Jesus knelt to share with thee
> The silence of eternity,
> Interpreted by love! (*LBW* 506)

As the Sabbath has grown to become one more frenzied day like all the others, dare the church sound a prophetic—even countercultural—note and try to restore some rest into this day? Dare we open up our Sunday morning schedules for the centrality of word and sacrament? Can we even risk putting away the watches for a time and really enter into a place filled with the "silence of eternity"?

Dare we clear our chancels of their visual clutter and provide wide and open spaces for God's word and for the sacramental presence in water, bread, and wine? Dare we clear time (personal schedules and congregational calendars) to meet for what is truly our center and our source of life?

Indeed, time will tell.

PRESIDING AND ASSISTING MINISTERS

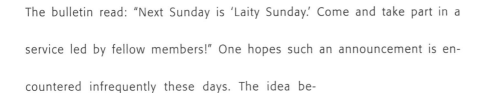

The bulletin read: "Next Sunday is 'Laity Sunday.' Come and take part in a service led by fellow members!" One hopes such an announcement is encountered infrequently these days. The idea behind such a service is well-intentioned. It betrays the fact, however, that the normal liturgy in such a congregation on a Sunday morning is understood not as the liturgy of the people, but of the ordained leader. Indeed, every Sunday—every celebration of word and sacrament—is a liturgy of the people, as the word *liturgy* connotes. If all those gathered for worship on a given day are appropriately involved in worship, a special day need not be set aside for laypersons to take the parts normally done by the pastor.

In truth, "Laity Sundays" do just the opposite of what they intend to accomplish. By having the non-ordained members of the assembly take the roles of the ordained, it looks as if the only truly important role in the liturgy is that of the ordained leader. Nothing could be further from the truth!

For this reason recent Lutheran worship books provide for presiding and *assisting* roles in the leadership of the eucharistic assembly. This model takes seriously the baptismal priesthood of *all* the faithful who gather for worship, bringing their various gifts to be offered in worship for the sake of the assembly and in thanksgiving for God's grace in Jesus Christ.

For several important reasons, the one who presides at the eucharistic assembly's worship is an ordained minister, usually a pastor of the congregation. First, the ordained pastor is trained and called by the church to oversee and care for the life of God's people in a particular congregation. Besides being prepared to lead worship appropriately, the ordained pastor is the one who is held accountable to the church as the *public* servant of the word. Such accountability helps to ensure that the preaching of the word will be biblically sound and the sacraments will be administered according to the gospel. To the ordained ministers of the church is given the responsibility to relay the apostolic faith in accordance with the teaching and practice of the church through the ages. Such responsibility and authority are given to pastors at their ordination, not as a power *over* the church, but for the sake of the unity and catholicity of the church.

Once the liturgy has been prepared (with the consultation and collaboration of various members of the community), the presiding minister and other worship planners need to consider how the service will be carried out. What aspects of the liturgy will be different this day? How will these various elements affect the usual way the liturgy is conducted in this place? How will the various parts of the service connect to one another? What movement or gesture will serve as the appropriate transition? Are all the necessary elements for the baptism set out? These questions are just a few of the issues worship planners might have to consider in order for the liturgy to flow gracefully and reverently.

Every presiding minister will have her or his own style. This uniqueness is one of the gifts of each pastor. Central to the role of presiding minister, however, is a heart that reflects the love, mercy, and grace of Christ. To preside with a sense of warmth and love for the assembly, to exude the joy of the life of faith, and to imitate the open arms of Christ is to help the worshipers recognize Christ present among us in word and sacraments.

Part of the role of the presiding minister is to enable members of the assembly to use their individual gifts for the edification of the community. The worship of the assembly should be a reflection of the lives and talents of those who belong to it. For the liturgy of a community to be fully authentic, worshipers need to use their talents to praise God, hear their spiritual struggles addressed in the sermon, and recognize their hopes and hurts lifted up in prayer. In order to accomplish these things, worship leaders need to be called forth from the congregation to serve as cantors, prayer leaders, communion assistants, acolytes, ushers, greeters, gift bearers, singers, and lectors. Of course the list can go on and is shaped by the particular needs and circumstances of each assembly.

Even as people serve in various assisting roles in worship, it is particularly important that at least one person from the congregation serve with the presiding minister as an assisting minister of the liturgy. The parts appropriate to that role are marked in Lutheran worship books with an **A**. Such a distinction of roles conveys the fullness of the eucharistic community and the ministries of those whose priesthood is lived out predominantly in the world.

The person assisting at the altar—historically called the deacon—should be vested in an alb, the baptismal garment of the people of God. Presiding ministers are also vested in albs with the addition of the stole as a sign of the pastoral office and possibly also a chasuble to designate the eucharistic presider. Use of the same foundational garment by both presiding and assisting ministers makes it clear that the one priesthood is shared by all the baptized in different ways. Wearing a colored choir robe or a black gown does not convey this same clear message. Likewise, if the assisting minister does not vest, though the presiding minister does, the equality of all the baptized before God is again poorly presented. Other assisting ministers—acolytes, servers, choir members, lectors—can also be vested in albs for the same purpose.

No member of the assembly ought to be expected to be a leader of worship without proper preparation. Normally conducted by a pastor or other trained person, such preparation shows concern and respect for the gifts of the person serving in this role as well as for the congregation aided in its worship by ministers who are confident and comfortable in their ministry. Such training should involve actually walking through aspects of the service for which the assisting minister is responsible, especially for acolytes, crucifers, book/torch/banner bearers, ministers of communion, and those directly assisting at the altar. It is much easier to communicate such actions by doing them than by merely speaking about them.

The use of gestures in liturgical leadership ought not be restricted to the ordained. Gestures serve to communicate beliefs that are important to our faith and worship. The *orans* (prayer) position of arms uplifted is appropriate during the offertory prayer and at the post-communion prayer, two prayers specifically assigned to an assisting minister in *LBW*. Arms moving outward as the words of the dismissal ("Go in peace. Serve the Lord.") are spoken help signal that all of the assembly is sent out into the

world to be the body of Christ. Gestures that serve as directions for standing, sitting, and kneeling can be kept to a minimum. Encouraging the congregation simply to follow the posture of its leaders or to observe directions in a service folder encourages all to take responsibility for their worship and to claim their central place in the assembly. When assisting ministers, acolytes, and choir members know recommended postures, they can also assist the rest of the assembly in a natural way.

"I always wanted to be an assisting minister, but I can't sing!" If this comment is frequently heard from members of the congregation, the problem is easily remedied so that one who desires to serve in this way can do so. Parts of the liturgy that require an assisting minister to sing need not be done by the same person who does the other assisting parts. Let a sung portion of the liturgy be sung by the choir or by a cantor, and let the nonsinger serve as she or he is able. The more voices (sung or spoken) heard within the assembly, the stronger is the reflection of the communion of saints.

The assisting minister also has the important role of leading the prayers of the people. In the ancient church the deacon, whose ministry was to the sick and the poor, would have been the leader of the prayers as the one personally in touch with the needs and concerns of the community. These concerns would be brought to voice in the assembly's prayers. The deacon was seen as the extension of the community itself, offering its petitions of praise, thanksgiving, and intercession to God for itself and for the world.

Having a lay member of the community lead these prayers in our contemporary setting makes clear the connection between the daily life of the people and the prayer ministry of the faith community. The ideal situation is to have the lay minister compose the prayers. Many resources are available to aid in this purpose, including this volume. If the prayers are used directly from preprinted sources, they need to be updated according to current events and the specific needs of the local congregation.

Though the first two readings and the psalm are normally proclaimed by people other than the presiding minister, the preacher (or pastor) is usually the most appropriate person to read the gospel and break open the word in the sermon.

The presiding minister offers only two prayers during the eucharistic liturgy, but they are central to her or his role as presiding minister of the assembly. The first is the prayer of the day. This prayer gathers the central thoughts of the liturgy for the day in a tersely worded prayer. It is appropriate that this prayer serve as the introduction to the liturgy of the word, because it gathers ("collects") the congregation while frequently giving voice to themes that will be heard shortly in the scriptural readings.

The prayer of the day functions as a way for the presiding minister "to call the meeting to order." Much may have happened in the gathering rite (though we hope not *too* much), and the congregation is now ready to turn its attention to the liturgy of the word. The presiding minister is the best one to signal this change in focus. Though congregations are frequently asked to speak the prayer of the day together, it is not generally a good thing for them to do. For one thing, not everyone can read large portions of text easily. The assembly speaks best through short, patterned responses.

The second prayer reserved for the presiding minister is the great thanksgiving, the eucharistic prayer. This prayer thanks God for the creation of all things, for our redemption in Christ Jesus, and for the Spirit's work through the church. It is spoken by the ordained presiding minister as the one who is called by the church to be the steward of God's mysteries on behalf of all. The one who offers the prayer of the whole church to God is one who stands in the long line of those who have been set aside for this ministry of word and sacrament since the earliest days of the apostles.

It is no more appropriate for the lay ministers of the assembly to take to themselves the prayer of the day and the prayer of thanksgiving than it is for ordained ministers to take the prayers of the church to themselves. Just as it portrays a lack of valuing of the ministry of the laity to have an ordained minister take the leadership of the entire liturgy, so it portrays a lack of connection of this assembly to those of all the saints of all times and places when the pastor's leadership over the central prayers of the liturgy of the word and the liturgy of the meal is obscured.

The purpose of using members of the assembly as assisting ministers is not an issue of power or status, but in order to include the fullness of the community at prayer. Hypothetically, all active members of the assembly ought to serve as assisting ministers as they are able. Such a practice makes clear the "(baptismal) priesthood we all share in Christ Jesus" (*LBW*, liturgy of Holy Baptism, p. 124), a priesthood whose ministry is normally carried out in the world of daily life but that is also brought into the worship assembly in thanksgiving for the grace of God in Jesus Christ.

17

WORSHIP FOR ALL GENERATIONS

In a culture that tends to isolate generations from one another, many congregations have become more intentional about developing relationships across generational lines. Search Institute research shows that one key variable supporting the health of youth is the presence of three or more caring adults, other than parents, in the life of each young person. Furthermore, kids who interact with adults in meaningful service activities tend to take those important servant values into adult life. These findings remind us that the kind of learning we call spiritual formation is best transmitted through relationships where spiritual disciplines and values are modeled consistently within and across generational boundaries.

The church continues to be a natural gathering place for old and young. The primary context is, of course, the weekly gathering for worship. In a culture that tends to separate age groups from one another, how can we leverage weekly worship of the congregation to further the development of relationships among generations?

Luke points us in the right direction by painting powerful pictures of faithful interactions among generations. When Mary discovers she is pregnant she hurries to the house of a relative. There she finds refuge, acceptance, and encouragement from an older female mentor. Through song Mary invites all generations to respond in grateful, enthusiastic worship. Weeks after Jesus is born, an elderly man takes Jesus in his arms and in the presence of the parents sings a radiant hymn of peace. Twelve years later the boy Jesus is drawn into adult discussion in the temple, where teachers affirm qualities that will eventually make him a gifted teacher. Over and over again Luke demonstrates how strong, faith-filled interactions among generations are fundamental for the faith life of the church.

INTERGENERATIONAL WORSHIP

These kinds of interactions have always been important connective tissue that keeps communities healthy. On any given Sunday morning you can still see moms and dads, grandpas and grandmas holding their babies and young children and singing songs of hope. Today, more than ever, young people need safe places where they can experience wisdom, affirmation, and support in conversation with caring adults. Yet at this time churches find themselves in an odd situation. One of the last places left in our culture where all generations gather on a weekly basis may be the church. This reality is significant. In a culture that separates and isolates people, the weekly gathering for worship has become an oasis of intergenerational hope. What a gift we have to offer!

Or look at it this way: "Assembly itself, when that assembly is an open invitation to all peoples to gather around the truth and presence of Jesus Christ, is a witness in the world" (*Use of the Means of Grace,* background 51A).

Dietrich Bonhoeffer pointed out the relational significance of the weekly gathering for worship when he wrote, "The whole common life of the Christian fellowship (koinonia) oscillates between word and sacrament, it begins and ends in worship." Intentional intergenerational ministry nurtures the gift of Christian community by using our prime time together to accent interaction between generations. These interactions, set in the context of God's reconciling and forgiving love in Jesus Christ through word and sacrament, bring healing and hope.

In any congregation a few people have a rich supply of significant relationships. Many people in our society and in our churches experience relational poverty, however. Certainly a few symbolic moments of interaction on Sunday morning will not make up for separation and loneliness that is experienced throughout a person's week. Depending on a person's circumstances and skills, interaction may be awkward. Nevertheless, in most congregations, usually a few people, both young and old, are comfortable and even adept at communicating across generational lines. When the congregation becomes a place where healthy relationships are consistently modeled and supported, its gathering can have a positive impact on other relationships outside of the church.

INTERGENERATIONAL EVENTS

Intergenerational activity does not mean that people have to stop gathering in age-related groups. The tendency for people to gather with people their own age is healthy, and these groups provide the kind of support and challenge one can only get from a generational cohort. In addition, age-related groups form the backbone of many congregations. Don't get rid of them. Rather, invite groups such as women's circles, youth groups, and men's groups to join in an intergenerational event on occasion or just once a year. This coming together can raise people's awareness of intergenerational relationships in a helpful, nonthreatening way. In this way intergenerational work can simply add value to what is already working well.

Some families come to church only to be separated into age-related groups. The only time they may be together is in the car—that is, if they do not arrive in separate cars. Although all generations may gather in the same space, there may be little or no interaction among age groups. As congregational leaders, we can ask how we might redeem this critical time to support healthy relationships among generations.

AN UNDERSTANDING OF GENERATIONS

Before careful intergenerational work can be pursued, it is important that leaders agree on a common working definition of the generations. One set of definitions that many have found helpful in bringing generations together is posited by William Strauss and Neil Howe (*Generations: The History of America's Future 1584–2016.* New York: William Morris, 1991.) Strauss and Howe developed the five generational types around the premise that human values are formed around the age of adolescence, somewhere between the ages of eight and thirteen.

The oldest living generation—those born before 1931—is called the Civic or GI Generation. The GIs developed their approach to the world in the Depression and World War II. Some of their siblings and some of their children were born between 1932 and 1944, into the generation called the Adaptives. They grew up in a world of war and economic devastation.

The much-talked about Boomers (born between 1945 and 1963) were formed in an age of abundance and rapid cultural and sociological change. Some of their siblings and some of their children were born between 1964 and 1981 into the Diversity Generation, or what marketers have dubbed Generation X. Their formative years were colored by Watergate, the AIDS epidemic, high inflation, divorce, and the devastating employment contractions of an emerging global economy.

The newest generation, the Millennials (born between 1982 and 2003), are coming of age at the end of the Cold War. The Berlin wall is down, the explosion of the Internet has linked the globe, and society is harboring a new concern for the welfare of children and a growing if not speculative economy.

Strauss and Howe invite us to picture one long life cycle railroad track, with birth the place of origin and death the destination. Along the way are "Phase of Life Stations" from childhood to elderhood. Now picture a series of generational trains, all heading down the track at the same speed. While the GI train is moving from one station to the next, other trains are also rolling down the same track. If we picture ourselves sitting at any given train station watching one train go and the other arrive, we have a sense of how to view each of the living generations and a sense of their interaction.

In 1996 Lutheran Brotherhood convened an intergenerational think tank composed of representatives from each of the five generations. They expanded the five generational types already described to include the Saints and the Unborn. The resulting seven-generation framework symbolically represents all generations, past, present, and future. They are listed here along with key generational strengths. The colors listed are suggestions based on color schemes some groups have used to help identify the different generations.

The Unborn represent all the generations not yet born, the future. Color: White

In a society that often makes plans only with the short run in view, it is important that the churches reinstate the kind of long-range prayer and planning that respects and cares for generations yet unborn. It is not difficult to predict that health and even survival of the human species will depend on wisdom and stewardship that has thus far eluded us. The historic heart of intergenerational wisdom is that the living generations have always sought to improve the life and lot of succeeding generations.

Millennials were born between 1982 and 2003. Color: Green

The Millennials are also sometimes called the optimistic generation. This generation has come of age during one of the most sophisticated scientific and technological times in human history. They are a service-oriented generation that tends to value working with other generations on local issues. They shy away from political parties. Yet many believe that the significant leaders of the postmodern society will come from the Millennial generation.

The Diversity Generation, sometimes called Baby Busters or Generation X, includes those born between 1964 and 1981. Color: Red

The Diversity Generation came of age in a society with rapidly increasing divorce rates, experimental education practices, latchkey programs, an AIDS infected dating-scene, birth control, kids with weapons, increasing numbers of young people committing suicide, and more proficiency with technology than any other generation. They get along very well with elders but often not as well with their Adaptive and Boomer parents, who also happen to be their bosses in the workplace. The Diversity Generation is a storehouse of wisdom regarding multicultural and multiracial relations, because many have actually lived out the experiment of integration that was initiated by previous generations.

Baby Boomers include those born between 1945 and 1963. Color: Purple

The Boomers were the first generation in American history raised in a culture of abundance and influenced by a plethora of media dominated by television. They were the babies of optimism and hubris, often idealistic in their values and seemingly intensely self-immersed.

19

Work is an important measure of who you are as a person. They ask "Does my work have meaning?" unlike the GIs who saw their jobs and personal life as separate. The sheer size and economic power of this generation will ensure its historical center stage position for the next twenty-five years.

Adaptive Generation includes those born between 1932 and 1944. Color: Orange

This generation represents the majority of men and women who came of age too late for World War II. A small number served in Korea but were born too early to feel the pressures and burdens of the war in Vietnam. This generation created the corporate system, expanded American myths, made dress and appearance an important value, changed work from the personal to the organizational, developed the concept of career and loyalty to one's employer. Unlike their GI counterparts, they view issues as much more complex. They dominate the helping professions, civil rights organizations, and public interest law. They are also some of America's finest arbitrators and mediators.

Members of the GI Generation or Civics were born before 1931. Color: Blue

The first GI babies were born in 1901, and those born in 1931 will have turned 69 in the year 2000. This generation came out of an agricultural economy and accepted many American myths. They lived as young adults through the Great Depression. They were heroes in their hour of crisis, World War II. Their lives coincide with an "American Century" of general economic growth, technological progress beyond anyone's expectations, and military dominance. Tom Brokaw calls them the "Greatest Generation"—a generation that brought optimism, teamwork, a clear-cut sense of right and wrong, and civic pride to every problem they encountered.

The Saints represent all generations past, including the scriptures and the traditions. Color: Gold

The Saints is a grand, all-inclusive term. This generational grouping represents the saints recognized in the lesser festivals, the scriptures, doctrine, the traditions, and the legacy of the church and the congregation. To personalize this term, imagine your spiritual lineage tracing from your baptism in Christ and, like Luke's genealogy, symbolically back to God, the fount and source of all life.

Taken together, the symbolic seven generations represent the entire past, present, and future of the church.

HOW CAN AN AWARENESS OF GENERATIONS HELP?

The seven-generation framework can be used as leaders and planners assess generational balance and emphasize an intergenerational face and feel during the weekly gathering of the congregation. To assess generational and gender balance, tally the ages and genders of all those assisting in worship over the course of a typical month. Include preachers, readers, acolytes, assistants, ushers, greeters, and so on, in your calculations. Place them on the generational grid under their usual role. The results will give you a rough picture of the generational composition of key participants in worship for that month and may highlight areas in which you want to grow.

Many congregations are giving spiritual gifts a much higher profile in their traditional time and talents surveys. Use the generational grid in conjunction with gifts and talents to affirm and use the gifts of all ages. Wise planners will intentionally seek to improve generational balance. For congregations that already have intentional mentoring partnerships, strategic partnering during the worshiping assembly based on spiritual gifts can become yet another opportunity to cultivate relationships across generational lines.

Meaningful, enthusiastic participation during worship does not happen by itself. People need to be invited and trained to participate. In Psalm 148:12-13 (the first Sunday after Christmas), the songwriter nests this intergenerational snapshot in the context of cosmic worship: "Young men and women alike, old and young together! Let them praise the name of the Lord, for his name alone is exalted; his glory is above earth and heaven." Worship leaders in liturgical churches recognize that they need to be intentional about passing the church's liturgical tradition from generation to generation, or they will lose continuity with riches of the past.

LITURGICAL CATECHESIS AND PREPARATION FOR ALL AGES

Liturgical catechesis provides one of the best opportunities for intergenerational learning. Appreciation for the liturgy and worship is more caught than taught. People, young and old, learn to appreciate and participate enthusiastically when they are mentored by enthusiastic and appreciative worshipers. The primary context for this kind of mentoring is through the actual worship service itself. Some congregations are also experimenting periodically with well-planned intergenerational catechesis. Depending on what is being taught, the catechesis may take anywhere from fifteen to forty-five minutes of instructional time. What is learned is then immediately reinforced in the worship that follows. Here are some examples that work well as intergenerational liturgical instruction:

- Practicing a procession with the choir
- Learning a new song or refrain
- Experiencing scripture readings as drama or radio theater
- Learning about baptism or holy communion
- Learning how to share the peace more mindfully

Cross-generational learning in this kind of context can be profound, especially as children come to appreciate the elaborate ritual language of the church through the positive reinforcement of parents and elders.

The catechumenate presents yet another model for intergenerational liturgical instruction. The apprenticeship approach to the catechumenate is similar to the mentoring style that undergirds intergenerational learning (see Robert Hofstad, "How does the catechumenal process work?" in *Welcome to Christ: A Lutheran Introduction to the Catechumenate*, Augsburg Fortress, 1997). Catechesis for worship often begs for an integenerational approach, particulary when candidates for baptism or those affirming their baptism have children who are also being introduced to the church.

Key opportunities for liturgical catechesis occur immediately before or after the rites that punctuate the catechumenate (see *Welcome to Christ: Lutheran Rites for the Catechumenate*, Augsburg Fortress, 1997). Many of the concrete elements of the rites hold interest for young people: the signing of the cross, the presentation of a Bible, hands-on blessings, the enrollment of names, the presentation of a book of worship, the presentation of the creed, not to mention the rich symbolism throughout the Easter Vigil. Transformation in faith always means change. The wisdom patterned in the rites of the church can also help young and old better negotiate those changes together. After every period of liturgical catechesis is the added bonus of a solid core of people who can help teach, model, and lead the rest of the congregation as they learn to worship together.

ONE IDEA FOR PREACHERS

Consider convening an intergenerational group whose task is to help you develop two or three sermons designed to reach an intergenerational audience. Convene ten people, two from each generational group. If you are having trouble finding a representative from a specific generation, ask someone outside the congregation to participate. When you convene them, present them with the scripture readings, your key ideas, and a draft of your sermon. Invite their suggestions. Have the group tell you what works or doesn't work for their generation. As the group develops, trust you might invite them to submit generation-specific illustrations and stories that you might weave into one of your sermons. Convening an intergenerational sermon group has many benefits. It can give both preacher and participants a firsthand experience of intergenerational sharing. Significant relationships have a chance of developing. The effort can even have a snowball effect on the rest of the congregation. Try it!

The texts of many songs support intergenerational work. Listen to stanza two of Fred Kaan's "Let us talents and tongues employ" (*WOV* 754):

> Christ is able to make us one,
> at the table he sets the tone,
> teaching people to live to bless,
> love in word and in deed express.

Songs such as this one remind us that Christ is the heart of all intergenerational efforts, and the appropriate response is for all generations to join in the celebration!

As stewards of the communal life, pastors, worship planners, and leaders in the church are called to wise and attentive care of the weekly gathering for worship. Most healthy communities of faith have a strong intergenerational covenant that permeates every area of community life: playing, planning, praying, problem solving, learning, worshiping, and serving together. What happens in the weekly assembly is fundamentally important, though, because it "sets the tone." The barriers that separate are not insurmountable. When the weekly gathering reflects an intergenerational face and feel, it encourages all other intergenerational efforts in the congregation. Remember, skillful and enthusiastic worship practice not only supports communal reality, it generates it!

21

WORSHIP PLANNING CHECKLIST

ADVENT

- Purchase materials needed for the Advent wreath (four candles and enough greens to cover the wreath. Perhaps more than one wreath will be desired for your congregation if Sunday school openings and other groups gather for worship in multiple locations during the season.
- Arrange for setting up the Advent wreath one or two days prior to the first Sunday in Advent (December 3 this year).

CHRISTMAS

- Arrange for purchase/donation of a Christmas tree.
- Locate any decorations in storage from previous years for the Christmas tree, crèche, the chancel, other interior and/or exterior areas. Repair or replace decorations as needed.
- Decide on a date and time for Christmas decorating, and solicit volunteer help needed.
- Prepare for extra communion elements and communionware that may be needed for additional worshipers at Christmas services.
- Prepare a sign-up list for additional flowers or poinsettia plants to be sponsored at Christmas.
- Plan for removal of Christmas decorations following the twelve days (on or near January 6).
- If handheld candles are used by worshipers on Christmas Eve, determine how many candles and holders can be used from previous seasons and how many new candles and holders will be needed.
- Order special bulletin covers if needed for services on Christmas Eve and/or Christmas Day.

EPIPHANY

- Determine what (if any) Epiphany decorations are needed.
- If incense is to be used for a service on the festival of the Epiphany, purchase a small quantity of it (along with charcoal).
- If the Baptism of Our Lord (January 9) is to be observed as a baptismal festival, publicize the festival through congregational newsletters and bulletins in advance; arrange for baptismal preparation sessions with parents, sponsors, and candidates; and when the day arrives set out the following:

- Towel (baptismal napkin) for each person baptized
- Baptismal candle for each person baptized
- Shell (if used)
- Oil for anointing (also lemons and a towel for removing oil from the presiding minister's hands)
- Baptismal garment for each person baptized (if used)
- Fresh water in a ewer (pitcher) and/or the font

LENT

- If ashes are used on Ash Wednesday, arrange for someone (perhaps one or two altar guild members) to burn palms from the previous Passion Sunday. (Ask members to bring in their own if they also saved them at home.) Or contact a church supply store for a supply of ashes. (A small quantity of ashes mixed with a small amount of olive oil will go a long way).
- Determine whether any Lenten decorations are to be used other than Lenten paraments.
- If crosses or images are draped in purple during the Lenten season, recruit volunteers to do this between the Transfiguration of Our Lord (February 25) and Ash Wednesday (February 28).
- Order enough palm branches to distribute to worshipers on Passion Sunday. (Additional palm branches or plants may be used as decorations that day.) Palm branches also need to be prepared ahead of time. Make sure that they are fresh.
- Do worshipers know where to gather for a procession with palms liturgy? Have signs been prepared to direct them? How will those with physical disabilities participate in the procession (or be seated ahead of time)?
- Reserve leftover palm branches to be burned for ashes next Ash Wednesday.
- Order worship participation leaflets if used for the

22

Ash Wednesday liturgy and/or Passion Sunday processional liturgy.

- Order additional bulletin covers if needed for any special Lenten services (especially midweek liturgies).

THE THREE DAYS

- Schedule special rehearsals for the liturgies on these days. The liturgies in this week hold enough unique characteristics to warrant intentional preparation on the part of all worship leaders, even those who have been involved in previous years.
- Be sure that altar guild members are well equipped and informed about their tasks for these busy days.
- Locate one or more sets of basin and pitcher to be used for the Maundy Thursday liturgy. Towels are also needed for drying the feet of participants.
- How will participants be recruited for the footwashing? Even if all in the congregation are invited, key people should also be prepared to participate.
- If the altar and the rest of the chancel is to be stripped on Maundy Thursday, recruit helpers (perhaps an altar guild, or even children) for this task.
- If you have bells that are rung to announce services or chimes that mark times of the day, consider silencing them from the beginning of the Maundy Thursday liturgy until the hymn of praise at the Easter Vigil (or the first celebration of Easter).
- Keeping in mind that all of the liturgies of the Three Days are considered to be as one, do not plan a procession of worship leaders for Good Friday. All worship leaders simply find their own way to their respective places in advance of the service.
- If procession/adoration of the cross is to be used on Good Friday, find or construct a rough-hewn cross, and determine how it will be placed in the chancel ahead of time or carried in procession.
- Prepare to have a thorough cleaning of the worship space sometime between the Maundy Thursday liturgy and the Easter Vigil.
- If handheld candles are to be used by worshipers at an Easter Vigil, determine how many candles and holders can be used from previous seasons, and how many new candles and holders will need to be purchased.
- Purchase a paschal candle (or arrange to make one) prior to the Easter Vigil. Several days before the

Easter Vigil, make sure that the paschal candle fits its stand.

- Prepare materials needed to start a fire at the beginning of the Easter Vigil (kindling, wood, brazier, matches, etc.). Also, recruit someone to start and extinguish the fire properly.
- Place the paschal candle stand in the chancel prior to the Easter Vigil for use throughout the fifty days of Easter.
- Do worshipers know where to gather for the service of light at the Easter Vigil? If you plan to gather outside, what arrangements have been made for inclement weather?
- How will assisting ministers and lectors see to read during the Easter Vigil service? What kind of lighting level is desirable for participation by all members of the congregation during this liturgy? Practice setting lighting levels (at night) with the person who will be responsible for this during the vigil.
- How will the readings of the Easter Vigil be proclaimed? Consider having readers for each reading to enliven the readings for the assembly.
- Prepare for extra communion elements and communionware that may be needed for additional worshipers at Holy Week and Easter services.
- Order worship participation leaflets if used for the Maundy Thursday, Good Friday, or Easter Vigil liturgies.
- Order bulletin covers if needed for any Holy Week liturgies.
- It is helpful to prepare printed materials for worship leaders for the Three Days. Consider placing all the texts and musical resources needed by worship leaders into three-ring binders (half-inch binders purchased at office supply stores work well). Highlight speaking parts and instructions for all worship leaders in their own individual copies.
- If the Easter Vigil (or Easter Sunday) is to be observed as a baptismal festival, publicize the festival through congregational newsletters and bulletins; arrange for baptismal preparation sessions with parents, sponsors, and candidates; and when the day arrives set out the following:
  - Towel (baptismal napkin) for each person baptized
  - Baptismal candle for each person baptized
  - Shell (if used)

23

- Oil for anointing (also lemons and a towel for removing oil from the presiding minister's hands)
- Baptismal garment for each person baptized (if used)
- Fresh water in a ewer (pitcher) and/or the font
- Evergreen branches for sprinkling

EASTER

- Prepare a sign-up list for Easter lilies or other flowers to be sponsored on Easter Day (and throughout the season of Easter).
- Order extra bulletin covers for additional worshipers on Easter Day.
- Determine whether special flowers are to be used on Pentecost. (Some churches order several red geraniums to be placed around the church grounds or given away following Pentecost services.)
- If Pentecost is to be observed as a baptismal festival, publicize the festival through congregational newsletters and bulletins; arrange for baptismal preparation sessions with parents, sponsors, and candidates; and when the day arrives set out the following:
  - Towel (baptismal napkin) for each person baptized
  - Baptismal candle for each person baptized
  - Shell (if used)
  - Oil for anointing (also lemons and a towel for removing oil from the presiding minister's hands)
  - Baptismal garment for each person baptized (if used)
  - Fresh water in a ewer (pitcher) and/or the font
- On Pentecost, seven votive candles in red glass holders may be lit and placed on or near the altar to recall the gifts of the Spirit.

SUMMER

- If the worship schedule changes, notify local newspapers and change listings on exterior signs and church answering machines.

- Consider ways to make worshipers cooler during warm weather.
- If the congregation worships outside one or more times during the summer, how will worshipers know where to gather? How will they be seated?

AUTUMN

- For worship schedule changes, notify local newspapers and change listings on exterior signs and church answering machines.
- If a harvest festival is scheduled, determine what (if any) additional decorations are to be used and who is to do the decorating.
- If one or more food collections are to be received, notify the congregation about them in advance, and also arrange to deliver food to the appropriate agency within a day or two after the collection.

NOVEMBER

- Provide a book of remembrance or another way to collect the names of those who have died and who are to be remembered in prayers this month (or just on All Saints Sunday).
- If All Saints is to be observed as a baptismal festival, publicize the festival through congregational newsletters and bulletins; arrange for baptismal preparation sessions with parents, sponsors, and candidates; and when the day arrives set out the following:
  - Towel (baptismal napkin) for each person baptized
  - Baptismal candle for each person baptized
  - Shell (if used)
  - Oil for anointing (also lemons and a towel for removing oil from the presiding minister's hands)
  - Baptismal garment for each person baptized (if used)
  - Fresh water in a ewer (pitcher) and/or the font

KEY TO MUSIC PUBLISHERS

ABI	Abingdon	ECS	E. C. Schirmer	MEA	Meadowgreen
AFP	Augsburg Fortress	EV	Elkan-Vogel	MFS	Mark Foster
AG	Agape (Hope)	FLA	Flammer (Shawnee)	MSM	Morning Star Music
AGEHR	AGEHR Inc.	GAL	Galaxy	NGP	New Generation (ColorSong)
ALF	Alfred	GIA	GIA Publications	NMP	National Music Publishers
AMC	Arista	GS	GlorySound	NOV	Novello (Shawnee)
AMSI	AMSI	GSCH	G. Schirmer	NPH	Northwestern Publishing House
AUR	Aurole	GVX	Genevox	NPM	National Association of Pastoral
BBL	Broude Brothers	HAL	Hal Leonard: G. Schirmer		Musicians
BEC	Beckenhorst	HIN	Hinshaw	OCP	Oregon Catholic Press
BEL	Belwin (Warner)	HOP	Hope	OXF	Oxford University Press
BNT	Brentwood–Benson Music	HWG	H. W. Gray (Warner)	PAR	Paraclete
B&H	Boosey & Hawkes	INT	Integrity (Word)	PET	Peters
BOR	Bornemann	ION	Ionian Arts	PLY	Plymouth
BRD	Broadman	JEF	Jeffers	PRE	Presser
BRE	Breitkopf	KAL	Kalmus	PVN	Pavanne (Intrada)
BRN	Bourne	KIR	Kirkland House	RIC	Ricordi
BST	Boston	KJO	Kjos	RME	Randall M. Egan
CAL	Calvary Press	LAK	Lake State	SCH	Schott (European American)
CCF	Changing Church Forum	LAW	Lawson-Gould Publishing	SCM	Shattinger
CEL	Celebration Press	LB	Lutheran Brotherhood	SEL	Selah
CFI	Carl Fischer	LED	Leduc	SGM	Stained Glass Music
CFP	C. F. Peters	LEM	Lemoine (Presser)	SHW	Shawnee
CG	Choristers Guild (Lorenz)	LIL	Lillenas (Royal Marketing)	SMP	Sacred Music Press (Lorenz)
CHA	Chantry (Augsburg Fortress)	LIN	Lindsborg Press	VIV	Vivace
CHE	Chester	LOH	Live Oak	WAL	Walton
CLP	Warners: CCP/Belwin	LOR	Lorenz	WAR	Warner (Plymouth)
CPH	Concordia	LUD	Ludwig	WJK	Westminster John Knox
DOV	Dover	MAR	Maranatha	WLP	World Library
DUR	Durand (Presser)	MCF	McAfee Music Corp. (Warner)	WRD	Word Music

25

MUSIC FOR WORSHIP KEY

acc	accompaniment	hc	handchimes	qrt	quartet
bar	baritone	hp	harp	rec	recorder
bng	bongos	hpd	harpsichord	sax	saxophone
bsn	bassoon	hrn	horn	sop	soprano
cant	cantor	inst	instrument	str	strings
ch	chimes	kybd	keyboard	synth	synthesizer
cl	clarinet	M	medium	tamb	tambourine
cong	congregation	MH	medium high	tba	tuba
cont	continuo	ML	medium low	tbn	trombone
cym	cymbal	mxd	mixed	timp	timpani
DB	double or string bass	narr	narrator	trbl	treble
dbl	double	ob	oboe	tri	triangle
desc	descant	oct	octave	tpt	trumpet
div	divisi	opt	optional	U	unison
drm	drum	orch	orchestra	vc	violoncello
eng hrn	English horn	org	organ	vcs	voices
fc	finger cymbals	perc	percussion	vla	viola
fl	flute	picc	piccolo	vln	violin
glock	glockenspiel	pno	piano	ww	woodwind
gtr	guitar	pt	part	xyl	xylophone
hb	handbells	qnt	quintet		

KEY TO HYMN AND PSALM COLLECTIONS

ASG *As Sunshine to a Garden: Hymns and Songs by Rusty Edwards.* Mpls: Augsburg Fortress, 1999.

BAS *Bach for All Seasons Choirbook.* Mpls: Augsburg Fortress, 1999.

BH *Baptist Hymnal.* (Southern Baptist Convention). Nashville, TN: Convention Press, 1991.

CC *Chantry Choirbook: Sacred Music for All Seasons.* Mpls: Augsburg Fortress, 2000.

CW *Christian Worship: A Lutheran Hymnal* (Wisconsin Evangelical Lutheran Synod). Milwaukee: Northwestern Publishing House, 1993.

DH *Dancing at the Harvest: Songs of Ray Makeever.* Mpls: Augsburg Fortress, 1997.

GS2 *Global Songs 2: Bread for the Journey.* Mpls: Augsburg Fortress, 1997.

H82 *The Hymnal 1982* (Episcopal). New York: The Church Pension Fund, 1985.

HS98 *Hymnal Supplement 98.* St. Louis: Concordia Publishing House, 1998.

LBW *Lutheran Book of Worship.* Mpls: Augsburg; Philadelphia: Board of Publication, LCA, 1978.

LLC *Libro de Liturgia y Cántico.* Mpls: Augsburg Fortress, 1998.

LS *LifeSongs.* Mpls: Augsburg Fortress, 1999.

LW *Lutheran Worship* (Lutheran Church–Missouri Synod). St. Louis: Concordia Publishing House, 1982.

NCH *The New Century Hymnal* (United Church of Christ). Cleveland: The Pilgrim Press, 1995.

OBS *O Blessed Spring: Hymns of Susan Palo Cherwien.* Mpls: Augsburg Fortress, 1997.

PCY *Psalms for the Church Year.* 8 vol. Chicago: GIA Publications.

PH *The Presbyterian Hymnal* (PC-USA). Louisville: Westminster John Knox Press, 1990.

PS *Psalm Songs.* 3 vol. Mpls: Augsburg Fortress, 1998.

PsH *Psalter Hymnal* (Christian Reformed). Grand Rapids, MI: CRC Publications, 1987.

PW *Psalter for Worship.* 3 vol. (Cycles A, B, C.) Mpls: Augsburg Fortress.

REJ *Rejoice in the Lord* (Reformed Church in America). Grand Rapids, MI: William B. Eerdmans Publishing Co., 1985.

RS *RitualSong: A Hymnal and Service Book for Roman Catholics.* Chicago: GIA Publications, Inc., 1996.

SPW *Songs for Praise and Worship.* Nashville: Word Music, 1992.

STP *Singing the Psalms.* 3 vol. Portland: OCP Publications.

TFF *This Far by Faith.* Mpls: Augsburg Fortress, 1999.

TP *The Psalter: Psalms and the Canticles for Singing.* Louisville: Westminster/John Knox Press.

TWC *The Worshiping Church.* Carol Stream, IL: Hope Publishing Company, 1990.

UMH *The United Methodist Hymnal.* Nashville: The United Methodist Publishing House, 1989.

VU *Voices United.* The Hymn and Worship Book of the United Church of Canada. Etobicoke, Ontario, Canada: United Church Publishing House, 1996.

W3 *Worship: A Hymnal and Service Book for Roman Catholics.* Third ed. Chicago: GIA 1986.

WOV *With One Voice.* Mpls: Ausgburg Fortress, 1995.

W&P *Worship & Praise.* Mpls: Augsburg Fortress, 1999.

SELECTED PUBLISHERS

AMSI
3706 East 34th Street
Minneapolis MN 55406
612/724-1258 General
612/729-4487 Fax

ABINGDON PRESS
201 8th Avenue South
PO Box 801
Nashville TN 37202
800/251-3320 Customer Service
800/836-7802 Fax

AGEHR, INC.
1055 E. Centerville Station Road
Dayton OH 45459
800/878-5459
937/438-0085

ALFRED PUBLISHING CO., INC.
Box 10003
16380 Roscoe Boulevard
Van Nuys CA 91410-0003
800/292-6122 Customer Service
800/632-1928 Fax
818/891-5999 Direct

AMERICAN LUTHERAN PUBLICITY
BUREAU
PO Box 327
Delhi NY 13753-0327
607/746-7511General

ARISTA MUSIC
PO Box 1596
Brooklyn NY 11201

AUGSBURG FORTRESS
PO Box 1209
Minneapolis MN 55440-1209
800/328-4648 Ordering
800/421-0239 Permissions
612/330-3300 General

BECKENHORST PRESS
PO Box 14273
Columbus OH 43214
614/451-6461 General
614/451-6627 Fax

BOOSEY & HAWKES, INC.
35 East Twenty-first Street
New York NY 10010
212/358-5300 General
212/358-5301 Fax

BOSTON MUSIC CO.
172 Tremont St.
Boston, MA 02111
617/426-5100 Retail
617/528-6199 Fax

BOURNE COMPANY
5 West 37th Street
New York NY 10018
212/391-4300 General
212/391-4306 Fax

BRENTWOOD-BENSON MUSIC, INC.
Order from: Provident Music
741 Cool Springs Boulevard
Franklin TX 36067
800/333-9000 ext 3300

BROUDE BROTHERS LTD.
141 White Oaks Road
Williamstown MA 01267
413/458-8131

BROADMAN HOLMAN GENEVOX
Customer Accounts Center
127 Ninth Avenue North
Nashville TN 37234
800/251-3225 General
615/251/3870 Fax

C F PETERS CORPORATION
Building 36, Atlas Terminal
70-30 80th Street
Glendale NY 11385
718/416-7800 General
718/416-7805 Fax

CHANGING CHURCH FORUM/
PRINCE OF PEACE PUBLISHING
200 E. Nicollet Blvd.
Burnsville, MN 55337
800/874-2044

CHESTER MUSIC
Contact Hal Leonard Corp
Music Dispatch

CHURCH PUBLISHING
445 5th Avenue
New York NY 10016-0109
800/223-6602 General
800/242-1918 Customer Service
212/592-1800 General
212/779-3392 Fax

CONCORDIA PUBLISHING HOUSE
3558 South Jefferson Avenue
Saint Louis MO 63118
800/325-3391 Sales
800/325-3040 Customer Service
314/268-1329 Fax
314/268-1000 General

E. C. SCHIRMER MUSIC CO.
138 Ipswich Street
Boston MA 02215
800/777-1919 Ordering
617/236-1935 General
617/236-0261 Fax
614/236-1935

EUROPEAN AMERICAN MUSIC DIST.
Note Service Department
15800 Northwest 48th Avenue
Miami FL 33014
800/628-1528

CARL FISCHER, INC.
65 Bleaker Street
New York, NY 10003
800/762-2328 General

GIA PUBLICATIONS, INC.
7404 South Mason Avenue
Chicago IL 60638
800/442-1358 General
708/496-3800 General
708/496-3828 Fax

GALAXY COMMUNICATIONS
Contact E.C. Schirmer Music Co

HINSHAW MUSIC CO, INC.
PO Box 470
Chapel Hill NC 27514-0470
919/933-1691 General
919/967-3399 Fax

HAL LEONARD CORP
PO Box 13819
7777 West Bluemound Road
Milwaukee WI 53213
414/774-3630 General
800/637-2852 Music Dispatch

HOPE PUBLISHING CO.
380 South Main Place
Carol Stream IL 60188
800/323-1049 General
630/665-3200 General
630/665-2552 Fax

ICEL (INTERNATIONAL COMMISSION
ON ENGLISH IN THE LITURGY)
1275 K Street Northwest
Suite 1202
Washington DC 20005-4097
202/347-0800 General

IONIAN ARTS, INC.
PO Box 259
Mercer Island WA 98040-0259
206/236-2210 General

THE LITURGICAL CONFERENCE
8750 Georgia Avenue
Suite 123
Silver Spring MD 20910-3621
800/394-0885 Ordering
301/495-0885 General
901/495-5945 Fax

THE LITURGICAL PRESS
St. John's Abbey
PO Box 7500
Collegeville MN 56321-7500
800/858-5450 General
800/445-5899 Fax
320/363-2213 General
320/363-3299 Fax

LITURGY TRAINING PUBLICATIONS
1800 North Hermitage Avenue
Chicago IL 60622-1101
800/933-1800 Ordering
800/933-4779 Customer Service
800/933-7094 Fax

LIVE OAK HOUSE
3211 Plantation Rd.
Austin TX 78745-7424
512/282-3397

THE LORENZ CORPORATION
PO Box 802
Dayton OH 45401-0802
800/444-1144 General

LUDWIG MUSIC PUBLISHING CO.
557 East 140th Street
Cleveland OH 44110-1999
800/851-1150 General
216/851-1150 General
216/851-1958 Fax

MARANATHA!
30230 Rancho Viejo Rd
San Juan Capistrano CA 92675
800/245-7664 Retail

MASTERS MUSIC PUBLICATIONS, INC.
PO Box 810157
Boco Raton FL 33481-0157
561/241-6169 General
561/241-6347 Fax

MORNINGSTAR MUSIC PUBLISHERS
1727 Larkin Williams Road
Fendon MD 63026
800/647-2117 Ordering
314/305-0121 Fax

MUSICA RUSSICA
27 Willow Lane
Madison CT 06443
800/326-3132

NEW GENERATION PUBLISHERS
Box 321
Waverly IA 50677
319/352-4396

NORTHWESTERN PUBLISHING HOUSE
1250 North 113th Street
Milwaukee WI 53226-3284
800/662-6093

OREGON CATHOLIC PRESS
5536 Northeast Hassalo
Portland OR 97213
800/547-8992 General
800/462-7329 Fax

OXFORD UNIVERSITY PRESS
2001 Evans Road
Cary NC 27513
800/451-7556 General
919/677-1303 Fax

PARACLETE SOCIETY INTERNATIONAL
1132 Southwest 13th Avenue
Portland OR 97205

PLYMOUTH MUSIC CO.
170 Northeast 33rd Street
Fort Lauderdale FL 33334
954/563-1844 General
954/563-9006 Fax

RANDALL M. EGAN, PUBLISHERS
2024 Kenwood Parkway
Minneapolis MN 55405-2303
612/377-4450 General
*51 Fax

SHAWNEE PRESS
PO Box 690
49 Waring Drive
Delaware Water Gap PA 18327-1699
800/962-8584 General
570/476-0550 General
570/476-5247 Fax

THEODORE PRESSER CO.
1 Presser Place
Bryn Mawr PA 19010
610/527-4242 Retail
610/527-7841 Fax

WARNER BROTHERS PUBLICATIONS
15800 Northwest 48th Avenue
Miami FL 33014
800/327-7643 General
305/621-4869 Fax

WESTMINSTER/JOHN KNOX PRESS
100 Witherspoon Street
Louisville KY 40202-1396
800/523-1631 General
800/541-5113 Fax

WORD MUSIC CO.
3319 West End Avenue, Suite 201
Nashville TN 37203
888/324-9673

WORLD LIBRARY PUBLICATIONS
3825 North Willow Road
Schiller Park IL 60176
800/621-5197 General
847/678-0621 General
847/671-5715 Fax

29

ADVENT

The hope toward which we move

is the fullness of Christ

IMAGES OF THE SEASON

Even though the church year does have a beginning, in a way the church year is also a circle with no beginning or ending. Although many other times during the year could well be called times of beginning, times of ending, now is a time that we in the church have for centuries called the beginning of the church year: Advent, meaning "coming."

As one looks at the season of Advent, its assigned readings and images, one could ask just what is beginning here. The end-time themes from November carry on uninterrupted. The Advent images of one appearing on the clouds, one who refines with fire, one who promises to come, are the same images as those of the last days after Pentecost. So what is beginning here?

What is beginning is a new spiral into the life of Christ, a new encounter with the mysteries of God, and a further journey into the transforming story of God in Christ. Advent serves as a bridge into this renewed encounter, a bridge into this deeper journey.

Advent bridges the overlapping circle of the year as worshipers move from contemplating the ending and fulfillment of all creation at Christ the King, to contemplating the beginning of Jesus' role in that fulfillment at the Nativity of Our Lord. The story of salvation proclaimed, sung, and enacted throughout the preceding year is reentered. The circle continues. So the church takes branches that are always green with vitality and life; shapes them into a circle, the eternal round of God's time; and suspends this circle of life in the worship space to be a reminder of the journey we take. Eternally surrounded by God's gift of life, we journey into the life of Christ, a journey into seasons of darkness and times of light, always encircled by the love of God.

Advent bridges the past and the future and brings them into the present. Advent is the time of the Christ who was, who is, and who is to come. Christ is seen not only as the child born of Mary, crucified and resurrected, nor as the fulfillment of all things, but as an active presence here and now. Christ stirs power from the past and hope from the future to begin his Messianic reign in the present, which begins in the hearts of those who follow the Christ.

Advent bridges the "what is not" and "what shall be," as Mary did when she burst forth in song at Elizabeth's greeting: "He *has* brought down the powerful… *lifted* up the lowly… *filled* the hungry with good things" (Luke 1:52-53). Mary, transformed by hope and joy, sang the future as if it were already the past, already completed—so full was her trust. So Advent has the color of hope—a deep blue. It is the color associated in art with this handmaid of the Lord, the color of possibility and of depth.

The visit of the archangel Gabriel to Mary bridged the world of the divine and the world of humans, culminating in the mystery of the incarnation. To this joining, Mary answered, "Let it be with me according to your word." With the four Sundays in Advent, the church celebrates heaven's coming to earth, for four is the number of the earth: four winds, four corners, four directions, four elements (earth, air, fire, water), four bases that form the DNA spiral, thus four candles on the circle of evergreens. God intends to be present on earth. It is for us to reply, "Let it be with me according to your word."

Advent is that silver-blue hour between night and day, between deep darkness and the light, when we know in our hearts that indeed "the dawn from on high will break upon us" (Luke 1:78). It is the messenger before the day of God, as John the baptizer was the messenger before Jesus, calling people in darkness to increase in the light of love and to bear fruit worthy of repentance. Advent bridges night and day as the forerunner and beginning of the golden dawn.

The holy day that breaks in to conclude Advent leads to the destination of this spiral journey: the Nativity of Our Lord. The future we draw to us is the reign of Christ. The hope toward which we move is the fullness of Christ. The dawn for which we yearn is the day of Christ—in all things, through all things, beginning in our own earthly hearts.

ENVIRONMENT AND ART FOR THE SEASON

In the incarnational cycle of the liturgical year, the promises of God are extended to the whole inhabited world. The promise that God's chosen people will be a blessing to the whole world is fulfilled in the birth of David's heir: Jesus of Nazareth,

who will write a new covenant for all people the world over. We proclaim this Jesus to be the Christ. Also present throughout this time are those who are marginalized, seen in the persons of Mary, the Holy Innocents, the homeless, pilgrims, and travelers.

A PBS video documentary quotes Frank Lloyd Wright: "Every house is a missionary. Space that is transformative changes the people who live there." When the House of Commons was rebuilt, Winston Churchill said, "We shape our buildings and afterwards our buildings shape us" (*Where We Worship*, p. 4). We are quite simply products of our environments.

In the spirit of the incarnation we are called to use worship spaces and the arts to assist people to touch, taste, feel, see, and meet Jesus. When seekers, the unbaptized, the uncatechized, those preparing for baptism, the bruised or weak in faith come to us, we need to be prepared to use every tool at our disposal so that they may respond in faith. That is the task and promise of arts that are truly incarnational.

A SITUATIONAL EXAMPLE

The altar guild invited its new pastor to come to its November meeting to talk to them about Advent. Edith led the devotions and read from a book that talked about the love, hope, faith, and joy candles of the Advent wreath. In the discussion that followed, Sophia was sure that she used to teach the Sunday school that the candles stood for Mary, Joseph, the shepherds, and the angels. Who was right, pastor? And what's the deal with that pink one?

In the discussion that followed, the new pastor was careful to acknowledge that both explanations had often been used in ascribing meaning to candles of the Advent wreath but that neither one necessarily precluded the other. In fact, the candles best served as primarily a

counting device throughout the weeks of Advent. Their meaning came more through their use, rather than through any allegorical interpretation. As darkness deepens in the northern hemisphere, the growing light of the Advent wreath proclaims the intensity of Christ's light.

PRIMARY SYMBOLS

Let us look at two related symbols for Advent: the color blue and the growing intensity of light. The blue of Advent comes out of the darkness; think of its origin as the color of the night sky just before the sun rises. It holds the promise of the light. The images of sun and moon of Advent suggest the relationship of John and Jesus, central to the weeks of Advent. As the lesser moon sets, the sun rises and outshines it. In this daily occurrence the church witnesses the retreat of the forerunner and the coming reign of the Messiah. It is no accident that John's birth is celebrated June 24, as the nights begin to overtake the days, and Jesus' birth is celebrated six months later as the light begins to overtake the long nights of winter. In the growing light, we see the growing reign of Jesus.

The garland crown of the advent wreath points to Jesus' fulfillment of all things. The endless circle of the wreath brings to mind Jesus' eternal reign. Each week the wreath glows a little brighter. So the wreath is also about waiting. Its candles mark the passage of time—not the shepherds and the angels, not hope, love, peace, and joy. Just waiting. We can abandon that pink candle too—once associated with "Rejoice" *(Gaudete)* in the second reading of Advent 3, cycle B, but few remember that any more.

Our Advent emphases have changed. No longer a purple season of penitence, Advent for us is more about preparation—preparation for embarking upon concrete paths of action in the world. Four white candles or four blue candles will do just fine. If they must mean anything, Advent candles are about waiting. They

33

are a visual reminder, a countdown. We are waiting for the fulfillment of promises, waiting for birth, waiting and watching for the Lord, for the bridegroom, for the reign of God to break in again and again.

Waiting is an important discipline. The candles simply help us to wait, like the tick of a clock. When they are given names or linked too closely with the Christmas story, their power is diminished. The multivalent symbolic value of these Advent candles is lost. So, how do we construct a waiting environment? Does the environment develop and change weekly along with the light of the Advent wreath?

Where is the word proclaimed in this season of waiting? At the door, from the food shelf, in the aisle, and on the wreath. Plan how you use your space. Consider both location and scale when preparing your wreath. Although the use of the Advent wreath began as a devotion for the home, its scale must change when brought into the worship assembly. A wreath scaled for use in the home will be ineffective in a large worship space.

Use Advent as an opportunity to simplify the worship environment. Do not obstruct the primary places of the word, meal, bath, and assembly. Plan a night for the whole community to come and help decorate for these incarnation seasons. An intergenerational opportunity where people can create art and environment for celebration together will be faith forming for everyone. Give people ideas about how they can link their seasonal art at home to the art of the congregation in order to help carry the themes of the season throughout the week. Both home and church can have a wreath. The church might have paraments and the home a blue Advent tablecloth. Help people to make the connections with art.

Think also of social implications for the environment in the incarnation cycle. Create spaces that allow for a mitten tree, the food pantry basket, or the homeless shelter donations in your environment planning. As we wait, we also reach out to those on the road with us who travel hungry or homeless.

PREACHING WITH THE SEASON

The difficulty with Advent is time. This notion will not come as a shock to those who annually must cope with the struggle imposed by our calendars and our culture as the year draws to a close. On the one hand, this year at least, we have had one Sunday of grace: we did not need to bolt from the Thanksgiving table in order to begin Advent preparations. Christ the King Sunday, with its burden of humility and majesty, offers much needed punctuation to the end of the liturgical year.

On the other hand, this means Advent begins on December 3rd, and once again the church has the challenge and opportunity of trying to make its voice heard over the sound of Christmas carols that play in every store and mall throughout most of North America.

While the blending of pagan and religious elements is a tradition as venerable as our faith, the public broadcast of carols with explicitly Christian texts is a cultural holdover from the days when it was assumed that the vast majority of folks listening were either believers or unlikely to bring attention to the fact that they were not. That this assumption no longer holds seems not to matter. The songs and carols are a part of the season, as are the colored lights and the decorations along main street. Who could object to that, when it all looks and sounds so festive?

But the season of Advent is not yet Christmas. While it is and remains the time of hope and new beginning, Advent is not properly "festive." Or at least it is not festive as the world would have us acknowledge it, with a premium placed on frenzied consumerism and mandated cheer.

Here is where the church comes in, with a word that is different from all of that. Here is where preaching in the Advent season is most challenging, as we try to engage our folk in something deeply countercultural: to live in expectation, to hold fast to a promise deferred, to wait for the arrival of the one who has already come.

It is hard for us not to be busy at this time and hard for us not to add still another item to our list of December obligations. We have grown increasingly unfamiliar with expectations because we thrive on immediate gratification. We hate to wait in lines at banks and gas stations and grocery stores, because we almost always have something else that we know we should be doing. And even when we have nothing urgent to do, to be forced to wait on someone or something beyond our control rankles. We are a part of a culture that celebrates our ability to have and get things now. We charge what we cannot afford, order on-line to avoid the crowds at the stores, and carry cell phones and pagers so that we can always be in touch with others, lest something happen and we not know about it instantly.

Advent is a promise deferred. We are inheritors of the prophecy from of old. Like the Israelites we look for a leader who will free us from bondage, a guide who can lead us safely back to the place that belongs to us. We have grown weary of headlines that speak of more tragedy and suffering. We labor under the weight of hearts heavy with grief. We eagerly anticipate God's redemption of the world through his Son Jesus Christ, and pray that the day will come soon.

It is living in the meantime that is difficult. God's promise remains, but we have so little experience with fidelity that doubts may sometimes creep around the edges of even the most steadfast soul. Advent is God's guarantee renewed in the darkest, shortest days of winter (for us in the Northern Hemisphere, anyway). It is a guarantee that we are not forgotten, that God so loved and continues to love the world, and that God's Son will come again to bind up every broken heart and to wipe away every tear.

Finally, Advent is an invitation to wait. It is a chance to keep a watch at the door and a light in the window for the one whose arrival is long expected. Our peculiar position in the world is that even as we wait, we know that Jesus is already present in and with us and that the Holy Spirit offers both counsel and comfort to those who will receive it. As Christians, it is our privilege to know both the beginning and the end of the story of all creation. The middle part still needs some working out, but it is not, thank God, left to our hands alone. The season of Advent reminds us that we are not responsible for our own salvation and that we will never be.

The candles of the Advent wreath burn with a single flame, a symbol of all the light and warmth contained in God's promise that Christ will come again. By that flickering light, even with the darkness all around us, we can look to remember who we are and where we have been, and to see the promises that bind us together from place to place and generation to generation. By that light we will watch and wait for the coming Messiah.

SHAPE of WORSHIP for the SEASON

BASIC SHAPE OF THE EUCHARISTIC RITE

- Confession and Forgiveness: see alternate worship text for Advent in *Sundays and Seasons*

GATHERING

- Greeting: see alternate worship text for Advent in *Sundays and Seasons*
- Use the Kyrie
- Omit the hymn of praise

WORD

- Use the Nicene Creed
- The prayers: see alternate forms and responses for Advent in *Sundays and Seasons*

MEAL

- Offertory prayer: see alternate worship text for Advent in *Sundays and Seasons*
- Use the proper preface for Advent
- Eucharistic prayer: in addition to the four main options in *LBW*, see "Eucharistic Prayer A: The Season of Advent" in *WOV* Leaders Edition, p. 65
- Invitation to communion: see alternate worship text for Advent in *Sundays and Seasons*
- Post-communion prayer: see alternate worship text for Advent in *Sundays and Seasons*

SENDING

- Benediction: see alternate worship text for Advent in *Sundays and Seasons*
- Dismissal: see alternate worship text for Advent in *Sundays and Seasons*

OTHER SEASONAL POSSIBILITIES

BLESSING OF THE ADVENT WREATH

The gathering rite for either the first week or all the weeks in Advent may take the following form of lighting the Advent wreath. Following the entrance hymn and the greeting, one of the prayers of blessing in the seasonal rites section may be spoken. A candle on the wreath may then be lit during the singing of an Advent hymn, such as "Light one candle to watch for Messiah" (WOV 630). The service then continues with the prayer of the day. On the remaining Sundays in Advent, the number of candles lit prior to the service would be the total number lit the previous week. One new candle is then lit each week during the service.

Alternatively, candles of the Advent wreath may simply be lit before the service, without any special prayer of blessing. Candles may also be lit during the singing of an entrance hymn, the Kyrie, or the psalm for the day, without any special accompanying prayers or music.

EVENING PRAYER FOR ADVENT

Consider holding an evening prayer service one weeknight each week throughout the Advent season. All the events might take place in a fellowship hall around tables. A possible format for the gatherings:

- Light candles placed at tables as worshipers begin singing a hymn of light ["Joyous light of glory" (*LBW*, p. 143), "O Trinity, O blessed Light" (LBW 275) "Light one candle to watch for Messiah" (WOV 630), "O Light whose splendor thrills" (WOV 728), among others]. Follow with a table prayer.
- Have a simple meal, perhaps consisting only of soups, breads, and salads.
- Prepare gifts to be given to homebound persons or others in need.
- Close with an abbreviated form of evening prayer:
  - a psalm (especially 141)
  - a short scripture reading
  - the Song of Mary [Canticle 6 in *LBW*, or "My soul now magnifies the Lord" (LBW 180), or "My soul proclaims your greatness" (WOV 730)]
  - brief prayers of intercession
  - the Lord's Prayer
  - dismissal

Try to focus on things that people of all ages can do together, so that families are brought together during this time of year.

ASSEMBLY SONG for the SEASON

Advent would have us wait for the Lord. Waiting will be especially difficult this Advent because December 24 falls on a Sunday. There will be the temptation to make the fourth Sunday in Advent into a morning Christmas celebration. Our waiting quotient will surely be tested. Let Advent be a full four weeks of waiting. Use the morning liturgy to focus on Mary's patient waiting for her Lord.

GATHERING

One way to mark the new church year is by beginning the service with the singing of "The Litany" (*Lutheran Book of Worship*, pp. 168–73) on the first Sunday in Advent. The petitions can be sung by different cantors in an entrance procession or stationed at different places in the nave. Have children chant some of the shorter petitions. The litany is lengthy (about seven minutes), but the prayer is all-inclusive. When singing the litany, the prayers of the church might be brief for that day. The remaining Sundays in Advent could also begin with a Kyrie in place of an entrance hymn. The Kyrie from *With One Voice,* setting 4, captures the mood of Advent well. The hymn of praise is generally not sung during Advent, being reserved for the Christmas celebration.

WORD

The Magnificat, Mary's song of faith and praise, portrays many of the themes of the gospel of Luke. "Canticle of the turning" (W&P 26) offers many different possibilities for use during Advent. At the lighting of the Advent wreath and following the appropriate prayer, the song could be used with a different stanza sung each week. Another option would be to have the assembly sing the refrain to frame the proper verse for the day, with a cantor singing the verse to a psalm tone.

Another option for a seasonal psalm antiphon is "Lift up your heads" (TFF 4), which has an accompanying psalm tone. The refrain of "The King of glory" (W&P 136) or "Oh, come, oh, come, Emmanuel" (LBW 34) could also serve as an antiphon and be used with an psalm tone. Sing "Oh, come, oh, come, Emmanuel" unaccompanied, and use handbells to punctuate the phrases.

MEAL

Meter and tempo can be helpful in expressing a joyful waiting during this season. "Prepare the royal highway" (LBW 26), "Comfort, comfort now my people" (LBW 29), and "Fling wide the door" (LBW 32) can be interpreted in a duple meter (strong feeling of two beats to the measure) with crisp articulations to express sprightly, dance rhythms. The addition of a tambourine can enhance this interpretation.

Choose a new Advent hymn and sing it every week during communion distribution. On the fourth Sunday in Advent, the use of hymns with texts such as "The angel Gabriel from heaven came" (WOV 632) and "People, look east" (WOV 626) can help to satisfy that Christmas urge and yet keep us expectant and waiting.

SENDING

An appropriate post-communion hymn for the season is "Come, thou long-expected Jesus" (LBW 30) or "The King shall come" (LBW 33). On the fourth Sunday in Advent consider using a sending hymn in addition to the post-communion canticle. Sing "Lo! He comes with clouds descending" (LBW 27) as the sending hymn. The text of stanzas one and four can intensify our waiting on this morning, while stanzas two and three help us to connect the crib with the cross. Begin learning these hymns early in Advent or even earlier. Teach them to Sunday school children and other groups during the month of November.

37

MUSIC FOR THE SEASON

VERSE AND OFFERTORY

Cherwien, David. *Verses for the Sundays in Advent.* MSM 80-001.
U, org, opt hb.

Hillert, Richard. *Verses and Offertory Sentences, Part 1: Advent–Christmas.*
CPH 97-5501. U, kybd. Acc. ed. 97-5509.

Krentz, Michael. *Alleluia Verses for Advent.* AFP 11-02564. SAB, org.

Weber, Stephen. *Verses for Advent.* CPH 98-2886. U, kybd.

Wetzler, Robert. *Verses and Offertories: Advent I through Baptism of Our
Lord.* AFP 11-09541. SATB, kybd.

Willan, Healey. "Rejoice Greatly, O Daughter of Zion."
CPH 98-1113. SA.

CHORAL

Bach, J. S. "Savior of the Nations, Come" in BAS. SATB, org.

Bausano, William. "Advent Carol." OCP 10831. SATB.

Distler, Hugo. "Maria Walks amid the Thorn" in CC. SAB.

Distler, Hugo. "O Savior, Rend the Heavens Wide" in CC. SATB.

Gieseke, Richard. "Lift Up Your Heads." CPH 98-2959. 2 pt, kybd.

Larkin, Michael. "Comfort, Comfort, Now My People."
MSM 50-0025. SATB, kybd.

Nicolai/Christiansen. "Wake, Awake." AFP 102. SSAATTBB.

Ratcliff, Cary. "Savior of the Nations, Come." KAL K-13.
2 pt, kybd, drum.

Sirett, Mark. "In Night's Dim Shadows Lying." AFP 11-10729.
SATB, T solo.

CHILDREN'S CHOIRS

Hopson, Hal H. "Dance and Sing, for the Lord Will Be with Us."
CG CGA749. U/2 pt, kybd, opt tamb.

Kemp, Helen. "A Waiting Carol." CG CGA-555. U, kybd, hd, opt
rec/fl.

McRae, Shirley W. "A Litany for Advent." CG CGA-570. U/2 pt, sop
rec/fl, sop/alto glock, kybd.

Schalk, Carl. "Light the Candle." MSM-50-6. U, org.

Taulé, Alberto, setting. Thomas Keesecker. "All Earth Is Hopeful."
AFP 11-10877. U/2 or 3 pt, pno.

KEYBOARD/INSTRUMENTAL

Augsburg Organ Library: Advent. AFP 11-11034. Org.

Cherwien, David. *Seasonal Interpretations: Advent–Christmas.*
AMSI SP-110. Org.

Hopson, Hal H. "Prelude on 'O Come, O Come, Emmanuel.' "
HWG GSTC 1015. Org.

Kickstadt, Paul. *Six Advent Chorales for Manuals.* MSM-10-03. Kybd.

Pachelbel, Johann. *Fugues on the Magnificat.* Kistner & Siegel 28366 or
DOV 0-486-25037-7. Kybd.

Pinkham, Daniel. *O Come, Emmanuel.* PRE 493-00065. Org.

HANDBELL

Afdahl, Lee J. "Prepare the Royal Highway." AFP 11-10723. 3-5 oct.

Bach/McFadden. "Pastorale on 'Lo, How a Rose.' " AFP 11-10522.
3-5 oct, fl.

Dobrinski, Cynthia. "Comfort, Comfort Ye My People." AG 1861.
3-5 oct, opt fl and hand drm.

Garee, Betty B. "Holy Manna." FLA HP 5230. 3-5 oct.

Keller, Michael R. "Alleluia, He Comes to Us" (a medley of three
Advent hymns). AG 1263. 3 oct.

Kinyon, Barbara B. "Let All Mortal Flesh." AG 1659. 2 oct.

PRAISE ENSEMBLE

Armstrong, Matthew. "Comfort, Comfort, These My People."
CPH 98-3155. SATB, C inst, pno.

Bridges, David, and Carol Poston. "Savior of the Nations, Come."
CPH 98-3100. SAB, kybd.

Haugen, Marty. "Now in This Banquet." GIA 2918. U/2 pt, kybd,
opt gtr, 2 ww, cong.

ALTERNATE WORSHIP TEXTS

CONFESSION AND FORGIVENESS

In the name of the Father, and of the ✠ Son, and of the Holy Spirit.
Amen

The Sun of righteousness shall rise
with shining beams of healing.
Let us gather under the wings of God's mercy.

Silence for reflection and self-examination.

Gracious God,
we acknowledge that we are sinners
and we confess our sins—
those known to us that burden our hearts,
and those unknown to us but seen by you.
We know that before you nothing remains hidden,
and in you everything is revealed.
Free us from the slavery of sin;
liberate us from the bondage of guilt;
work in us that which is pleasing in your sight;
for the sake of Jesus Christ our Lord.
Amen

With a heart full of mercy and compassion,
God saves us and forgives us all our sins.
Christ, the dawn from on high, shines upon us,
and by the light of the Holy Spirit
guides our feet into the way of peace.
Amen

GREETING

From the one who is and who was
and who is to come, the Almighty:
grace, light, and peace be with you all.
And also with you.

OFFERTORY PRAYER

O Mighty One,
you have done great things for us,
and holy is your name.
Bless all we offer you—
our selves, our time, and our possessions—
that through us your grace and favor
may be made known to all the world;
for the sake of Jesus Christ, our Redeemer. Amen

INVITATION TO COMMUNION

Surely God is our salvation;
great in our midst is the Holy One of Israel.

POST-COMMUNION PRAYER

O God,
in this eucharist you give us a foretaste of that day
when all the hungry will be fed with good things.
Send us forth to make known your deeds,
and to proclaim the greatness of your name.
Grant this through the one whose advent is certain,
whose day draws near, your Son, Jesus Christ our Lord.
Amen

BENEDICTION

The peace of God, which surpasses all understanding,
guard your hearts and your minds in Christ Jesus;
and the blessing of almighty God,
the Father, the ✠ Son, and the Holy Spirit,
be among you and remain with you always.
Amen

DISMISSAL

The coming of the Lord is near.
Go in peace. Serve the Lord.
Thanks be to God.

39

SEASONAL RITES

BLESSING OF THE ADVENT WREATH

FIRST SUNDAY IN ADVENT

We praise you, O God, for this evergreen crown
that marks our days of preparation for Christ's advent.
As we light the first candle on this wreath,
rouse us from sleep, that we may be ready to greet our Lord
when he comes with all the saints and angels.
Enlighten us with your grace,
and prepare our hearts to welcome him with joy.
Grant this through Christ our Lord,
whose coming is certain and whose day draws near.
Amen

Light the first candle.

SECOND SUNDAY IN ADVENT

We praise you, O God, for this circle of light
that marks our days of preparation for Christ's advent.
As we light the candles on this wreath,
kindle within us the fire of your Spirit,
that we may be light shining in the darkness.
Enlighten us with your grace,
that we may welcome others as you have welcomed us.
Grant this through Christ our Lord,
whose coming is certain and whose day draws near.
Amen

Light the second candle.

THIRD SUNDAY IN ADVENT

We praise you, O God, for this victory wreath
that marks our days of preparation for Christ's advent.
As we light the candles on this wreath,
strengthen our hearts as we await the Lord's coming in glory.
Enlighten us with your grace,
that we may serve our neighbors in need.
Grant this through Christ our Lord,
whose coming is certain and whose day draws near.
Amen

Light the third candle.

FOURTH SUNDAY IN ADVENT

We praise you, O God, for this wheel of time
that marks our days of preparation for Christ's advent.
As we light the candles on this wreath,
open our eyes to see your presence in the lowly ones of this earth.
Enlighten us with your grace,
that we may sing of your advent among us in the Word made flesh.
Grant this through Christ our Lord,
whose coming is certain and whose day draws near.
Amen

Light the fourth candle.

LESSONS AND CAROLS FOR ADVENT

Stand

ENTRANCE HYMN

LBW 32	Fling wide the door
LBW 34	Oh, come, oh, come, Emmanuel
WOV 631	Lift up your heads, O gates

DIALOGUE

The Spirit and the church cry out:

Come, Lord Jesus.

All those who wait his appearance pray:

Come, Lord Jesus.

The whole creation pleads:

Come, Lord Jesus.

OPENING PRAYER

The Lord be with you.

And also with you.

Let us pray.

Eternal God, at the beginning of creation you made the light that scatters all darkness. May Christ, the true light, shine on your people and free us from the power of sin and death. Fill us with joy as we welcome your Son at his glorious coming; for he lives and reigns with you and the Holy Spirit, one God, now and forever.

Amen

Sit

LESSONS AND CAROLS

First Reading: Isaiah 40:1-11

LBW 29	Comfort, comfort now my people
LBW 556	Herald, sound the note of judgment
WOV 629	All earth is hopeful

Second Reading: Isaiah 35:1-10

| LBW 384 | Your kingdom come, O Father |
| WOV 633 | Awake, awake, and greet the new morn |

Third Reading: Baruch 4:36--5:9

| WOV 626 | People, look east |

Fourth Reading: Isaiah 11:1-9

| LBW 87 | Hail to the Lord's anointed |
| WOV 762 | O day of peace |

Fifth Reading: Isaiah 65:17-25

| LBW 33 | The King shall come |
| WOV 744 | Soon and very soon |

Sixth Reading: 1 Thessalonians 5:1-11, 23-24

LBW 31	Wake, awake, for night is flying
WOV 630	Light one candle to watch for Messiah
WOV 649	I want to walk as a child of the light

Seventh Reading: Luke 1:26-38

| LBW 28 | Savior of the nations, come |
| WOV 632 | The angel Gabriel from heaven came |

Stand

RESPONSIVE PRAYER

Blessed is the one who comes in the name of the Lord.

Hosanna in the highest.

Show us your mercy, O Lord,

and grant us your salvation.

Give peace, O Lord, in all the world;

for only in you can we live in safety.

Let not the needy, O Lord, be forgotten,

nor the hope of the poor be taken away.

Shower, O heavens, from above,

and let the skies rain down righteousness.

Come, O Lord, at evening, with light,

and in the morning, with your glory,

to guide our feet in the way of peace.

THE LORD'S PRAYER

BLESSING AND DISMISSAL

Let us bless the Lord.

Thanks be to God.

May Christ, the Sun of righteousness, shine upon you and scatter the darkness from your path. Almighty God, Father, ✝ Son, and Holy Spirit, bless you now and forever.

Amen

SENDING HYMN

| LBW 26 | Prepare the royal highway |
| LBW 27 | Lo! He comes with clouds descending |

41

DECEMBER 3, 2000

FIRST SUNDAY IN ADVENT

INTRODUCTION

Like an expectant mother, the church in Advent prepares for an arrival: we anticipate the celebration of Jesus' birth and look forward to Christ's coming again at the end of history. But here and now—in scripture and preaching, in water and bread and wine—God comes to us. Today the church remembers the life of Francis Xavier, a sixteenth-century missionary who played a part in Jesus' arrival in India and Japan. Christ's arrival in today's world is furthered through our witness: like the Advent wreath, we also are to bring light into the darkness.

PRAYER OF THE DAY

Stir up your power, O Lord, and come. Protect us by your strength and save us from the threatening dangers of our sins, for you live and reign with the Father and the Holy Spirit, one God, now and forever.

READINGS

Jeremiah 33:14-16

In the Hebrew scriptures, righteousness is not so much a moral virtue as the fulfillment of the responsibilities of a relationship among people or with God. God acts righteously in speaking against Israel's faithlessness and in working salvation for them. In today's reading, Jerusalem's future name—"The LORD is our righteousness"—serves as a sign that the Lord is even now working salvation for the people.

Psalm 25:1-9 (Psalm 25:1-10 [NRSV])

To you, O LORD, I lift up my soul. (Ps. 25:1)

1 Thessalonians 3:9-13

From Timothy, Paul hears about the faithful congregation in Thessalonica and is moved to express his thanks to God. He prays that the congregation may grow in love and holiness until "the coming of our Lord Jesus with all the saints."

Luke 21:25-36

When God brings the creation to fulfillment, there will be dismay, perplexity, fright, and shaking heavens. But with this vision also come words of assurance: for the faithful, it will be a time not to cower in fear, but to stand boldly and receive God's promised redemption.

COLOR Blue *or* Purple

THE PRAYERS

With longing for the fullness of redemption, let us pray for the church, the world, and all people according to their needs.

A BRIEF SILENCE.

For all the baptized, that our eyes may be alert to Christ's presence, and our hearts make a home for his word: God of hopefulness,

hear our prayer.

For leaders of government, and especially those newly elected, that they may walk humbly with God, doing justice and loving kindness: God of hopefulness,

hear our prayer.

For those who, like Francis Xavier, have spread the gospel to people in distant lands: God of hopefulness,

hear our prayer.

For those who are sick and for those recovering from illness (especially...), that they may know the healing love of Christ: God of hopefulness,

hear our prayer.

For our guests at worship, that the grace and love of Jesus Christ may keep them now and in the coming week: God of hopefulness,

hear our prayer.

HERE OTHER INTERCESSIONS MAY BE OFFERED.

In thankfulness for loved ones and all who have gone before us, with whom we await the great heavenly feast: God of hopefulness,

hear our prayer.

God of salvation, hear the prayers we make in the name of Jesus Christ, whose coming is certain and whose day draws near.

Amen

IMAGES FOR PREACHING

Just as we move into the full swing of the secular Christmas season, just after we have cleared up the last leftovers from Thanksgiving, we begin the season of preparation. The color for the day is blue, the color of

42

hope and faithfulness. But on this first Sunday in Advent it would be helpful if the blue that adorns our altars and pulpits were the dark blue of outer space. After all, the Lord's coming will be an event of celestial significance.

The gospel for the day begins ominously enough: signs in the sun, the moon, and the stars will be seen. Not only that, even as we are tempted to look forward to Christmas, we hear a different word here, now. "[A]nd on the earth" the promise of peace and goodwill is yet to come to those who know "distress among the nations." It is time for serious events, and it is a good thing to hear those words at the beginning of Advent.

For this day, this season is a reminder that Christ will come again, and not only into lives and places that have managed to pull themselves together for the holiday season. As we await the coming of the Lord, it is important to remember that the one who came as a baby born in a manger in Bethlehem has promised to return in different guise. We expect the return of the king, and with his return will be a reckoning.

What then, must we do? How is it that we might prepare ourselves for the events that are to come? "Be on guard," Jesus says, "be alert." We are commanded to live in a state of readiness and not to withdraw from the world, but to separate ourselves from the worries that grow from a life that is too worldly. Jesus' words offer no brief for a Christian survivalist movement. It may not be possible, Jesus goes on to say, to escape from the disturbance and turmoil that will attend the Lord at his return. And still this message ought not to be a cause for despair, for with Christ's return comes the promise of redemption.

WORSHIP MATTERS

How do we remain alert at all times to God's presence? Certainly one way is by keeping the practice of daily prayer. This discipline helps many people to be aware of faith in the midst of everyday life. Congregations that provide resources for daily prayer, whether through daily devotional booklets or even occasional gatherings for prayer throughout the week (possibly even in workplace settings), find that members are strengthened for their faith journey in those times and places where they need it the most. How might the worship planners in your congregation strengthen daily prayer practices? Consider using one or more of the daily prayer re-

sources listed in the bibliography at the back of this volume.

LET THE CHILDREN COME

Today is the New Year's Day of the church year. It is another new beginning of telling the story of Jesus—a story told each week in church. Children need to be present for consecutive weeks to hear the story unfolding. Advent is time to prepare: to prepare for Christmas and to prepare for Jesus to come again. Focus on some of the environmental changes: blue or purple paraments, four candles to be lighted each Sunday in Advent. It is a quiet and thoughtful time. Throughout this time we pray, watch, and wait for God's presence through Jesus.

MUSIC FOR WORSHIP

SERVICE MUSIC

See "Assembly Song for the Season" in the seasonal materials at the beginning of this section for service music suggestions that can be carried throughout the season of Advent.

GATHERING

LBW 27   Lo! He comes with clouds descending
WOV 631   Lift up your heads, O gates

PSALM 25:1-9

Artman, Ruth. "Psalm 25" in *Sing Out! A Children's Psalter*. WLP 7191.

Balhoff, M., G. Daigle, and D. Ducote. "Psalm 25" in PCY, vol. 6.

Haas, David. "To You, O Lord" in PCY, vol. 9.

Jennings, Carolyn. PW, Cycle C.

"Psalm 25: To You, O Lord" in *Forty-one Grail Gelineau Psalms*. GIA G-4402.

Soper, Scott. "Psalm 25: To You, O Lord" in STP, vol. 1.

See Proper 10.

HYMN OF THE DAY

LBW 33   The King shall come
            CONSOLATION

VOCAL RESOURCES

Busarow, Donald. "The King Shall Come When Morning Dawns." CPH 98-2449. SAB, kybd.

Ramseth, Betty Ann. "The King Shall Come" in *LifeSongs* Leader Book. AFP 11-10939. U, Orff.

43

INSTRUMENTAL RESOURCES

Burkhardt, Michael. "Consolation" in *Five Advent Hymn Improvisations*, Set 1. MSM 10-004. Org.

Held, Wilbur. "Awake, Awake to Love and Work" (Consolation) in *Hymn Preludes for the Autumn Festivals*. CPH 97-5360. Org.

Oliver, Curt. "Consolation" in *Advent Keyboard Seasons*. AFP 11-10724. Pno/kybd.

Pelz, Walter L. "Consolation" in *Hymn Settings for Organ and Brass*, Book 2. AFP 11-7626. Org, brass.

Read, Gardner. "Consolation" in *Eight Preludes on Old Southern Hymns*. HWG GB 293. Org.

ALTERNATE HYMN OF THE DAY

LBW 31	Wake, awake, for night is flying
WOV 626	People, look east

COMMUNION

LBW 28	Savior of the nations, come
WOV 705	As the grains of wheat

SENDING

LBW 25	Rejoice, rejoice, believers
WOV 744	Soon and very soon

ADDITIONAL HYMNS AND SONGS

ASG 38	Stir up your power
PsH 330	O Christ! Come back to save your folk
TFF 198	When the storms of life are raging
W&P 70	I will call upon the Lord
W&P 136	The King of glory

MUSIC FOR THE DAY

CHORAL

Bach, J. S. "Wake, Awake, for Night Is Flying" in BAS. SATB, opt kybd.

Burkhardt, Michael. "I Lift My Soul." MSM 50-5552. U/2 pt, pno, opt ob, cl, vc.

Farrant, Richard. "Call to Remembrance." ECS 1639. SATB, org.

Hopson, Hal H. "Advent Prayer." AFP 11-10950. 2 pt mxd, kybd.

Larkin, Michael. "O Child of Promise Come." AFP 11-10952. SATB, kybd.

Manz, Paul. "E'en So, Lord Jesus, Quickly Come." MSM 50-0001. SATB.

Pelz, Walter. "Show Me Thy Ways." AFP 11-642.

Rossi, Richard Robert. "Conditor Alme Siderum." GIA G-4725. SATB, 11 hb.

Schalk, Carl. "As the Dark Awaits the Dawn." AFP 11-10951. SATB, org.

Thiman, Eric H. "Hark! A Thrilling Voice Is Sounding." NOV M.T. 993. SATB, org.

Walter, Johann. "Rise Up, Rise Up" in CC. SATB.

CHILDREN'S CHOIRS

Handel, G. F./arr. Hal H. Hopson. "Lord, I Lift My Soul to You." CG CGA-440. 2 pt mxd (SA/TB), kybd.

Hopson, Hal H. "A Star, A Song." CG A-167. U, pno/org.

Lindh, Jody W. "Lift Up Your Heads." CG CGA-420. U/2 pt, kybd, opt perc.

Walker, Christopher. "Stay Awake, Be Ready" in LS.

Wold, Wayne L. "Watch for Messiah" in *Three Songs for Advent*. AFP 11-9949. U, kybd.

KEYBOARD/INSTRUMENTAL

Bach, J. S. "Nun komm, der Heiden Heiland." BWV 659 ("Great 18" or "Leipzig" Chorales), various editions. Org.

Sedio, Mark. "Comfort, Comfort, Now My People" (Suo-Gan) in *A Global Piano Tour*. AFP 11-10977. Pno.

Wood, Dale. "People, Look East" in *Wood Works on International Folk Hymns*. SMP 70/1070S. Org.

HANDBELL

Garee, Betty B. "God with Us for All Time." FLA HP5099. 5 oct.

Honoré, Jeffrey. "Maranatha!" LOR HB262. 3 oct.

PRAISE ENSEMBLE

Crouch, Andraé, adapted William F. Smith/Kevin Keil. "Soon and Very Soon." OCP 10265. SATB, desc, opt cong.

Handel, G. F. "To You, O Lord, I Lift My Soul" in *Borning Cry*. NGP.

Monroe, Charles. "Unto Thee, O Lord" in *Praise Hymns and Choruses*, 4th ed. MSM.

SUNDAY, DECEMBER 3

FRANCIS XAVIER, MISSIONARY TO ASIA, 1552

Francis Xavier was born in the Basque region of northern Spain. Francis's native Basque language is unrelated to any other, and Francis admitted that learning languages was difficult for him. Despite this obstacle he became a missionary to India, Southeast Asia, Japan, and the Philippines. At each point he learned the local language and, like Martin Luther, wrote catechisms for the instruction of new converts. Another obstacle Francis overcame to accomplish his mission work was a propensity to seasickness. All his travels to the Far East were by boat. Together with Ignatius Loyola and five others, Francis formed the Society of Jesus (Jesuits). Francis spoke out against the Spanish and Portuguese colonists when he discovered their oppression of the indigenous people to whom he was sent as a missionary.

Pray for churches and missionaries in Asia, spiritual heirs to Francis Xavier. Consider singing "Lord your hands have formed" (WOV 727, Philippine traditional) to honor the work of Francis.

WEDNESDAY, DECEMBER 6
NICHOLAS, BISHOP OF MYRA, C. 342

Though Nicholas is one of the church's most beloved saints, little is known about his life. In the fourth century he was a bishop in what is now Turkey. Legends that surround Nicholas tell of his love for God and neighbor, especially the poor. One famous story tells of Nicholas secretly giving bags of gold to the three daughters of a father who was going to sell them into prostitution because he could not provide dowries for them. Nicholas has become a symbol of anonymous gift giving.

In some countries gifts are given on this day, and may include a visit from Nicholas himself. One of the ways Nicholas can be remembered is to have the congregation or families within it gather to prepare gifts that will be given anonymously as a way to remind us of the tradition of giving gifts as a sign of God's love given freely to all.

THURSDAY, DECEMBER 7
AMBROSE, BISHOP OF MILAN, 397

Ambrose was a governor of northern Italy and a catechumen when he was elected bishop of Milan. He was baptized, ordained, and consecrated a bishop all on the same day. While bishop he gave away his wealth and lived in simplicity. He was a famous preacher and is largely responsible for the conversion of St. Augustine.

He is also well known for writing hymns. On one occasion, Ambrose led people in a hymn he wrote while the church in which they were secluded was threatened by attack from Gothic soldiers. The soldiers turned away, unwilling to attack a congregation that was singing a hymn. Ambrose's hymn "Savior of the nations come" (LBW 28) could be sung during these first weeks in Advent when the apocalyptic readings on Sundays encourage believers to stand firm in their faith.

45

DECEMBER 10, 2000

SECOND SUNDAY IN ADVENT

INTRODUCTION

During this second week of Advent, John the Baptist walks onto the stage and calls people to a new beginning. Our baptism is also a new beginning. Day after day, as we are renewed in our baptism, God who began a good work in us continues to prepare us for the day of Jesus Christ.

PRAYER OF THE DAY

Stir up our hearts, O Lord, to prepare the way for your only Son. By his coming give us strength in our conflicts and shed light on our path through the darkness of this world; through your Son, Jesus Christ our Lord, who lives and reigns with you and the Holy Spirit, one God, now and forever.

READINGS

Malachi 3:1-4

The Lord announces a covenant with Israel. A messenger like Malachi (his name means "my messenger") shall prepare a way for the sudden coming of the Lord, who will purify and refine God's people for the offering of pleasing sacrifices.

or Baruch 5:1-9

The return of scattered Israel

Luke 1:68-79

In the tender compassion of our God, the dawn from on high shall break upon us. (Luke 1:78)

Philippians 1:3-11

Paul exhorts Christians to experience love that grows "richer in knowledge and insight of every kind" until the day of Christ Jesus. On that day, the good work begun in them will be flawless, a "full harvest of righteousness."

Luke 3:1-6

Luke takes care to place John in secular history. Yet John's arrival also heralds a new age of salvation. John refers to the words of the prophets, but with a vigorous immediacy: Now is the time to prepare for Christ through a "baptism of repentance for the forgiveness of sins."

COLOR   Blue *or* Purple

THE PRAYERS

With longing for the fullness of redemption, let us pray for the church, the world, and all people according to their needs.

A BRIEF SILENCE.

For preachers, teachers, and missionaries, that with bold and compassionate words they may prepare the way of the Lord: God of hopefulness,

hear our prayer.

For all places where people are divided by sin, that God's gift of reconciliation may enter in: God of hopefulness,

hear our prayer.

For those who are ill and who look to God's healing light to restore them (especially...): God of hopefulness,

hear our prayer.

For *this community of faith* and for our mission, that the good news of Jesus Christ may direct our planning and decision making throughout the coming year: God of hopefulness,

hear our prayer.

HERE OTHER INTERCESSIONS MAY BE OFFERED.

We offer thanks for all who have loved God, and who now rest from their labors. Preserve us with them in faith until the day we see you face to face: God of hopefulness,

hear our prayer.

God of salvation, hear the prayers we make in the name of Jesus Christ, whose coming is certain and whose day draws near.

Amen

IMAGES FOR PREACHING

They were important people, the ones included in Luke's cast of characters. They were men charged with a great deal of authority. They ruled empires and kingdoms. They controlled regions and cities. They were the high priests chosen to offer sacrifices on behalf of the entire nation.

And of course they all had their niche in the scheme of things: they all had establishments, followers, or palaces. They all had responsibilities that come with any kind of political, religious, or military power. But most of all they had *places* and *positions.* As men of authority and power, they were a little bit like the planets themselves, moving in a fixed orbit, predictable, dependable, regular, and unlikely to do anything really out of the ordinary. So Luke catalogs them by name and place, all neat and organized.

But what about the person at the end of the list? After carefully laying out the organized patterns of leadership, after he identifies each of the stars in the constellation of political authority during the fifteenth year of the reign of Tiberias Caesar, Luke throws in a wild card. It was at that particular time that the word of God came to John. John had no place, no secure base of power from which to hold forth. John knew only the wilderness and the people who wandered in it.

Yet it was to John that the word of the Lord came. It was John who proclaimed the baptism of repentance for the forgiveness of sins.

The world that seemed so neatly organized and carefully arranged for the convenience of Tiberias and the others was going to be turned upside down. Things were no longer what they seemed. The Lord was coming! And the messenger sent to prepare the way and to share the word with the emperor and rulers and high priests and all who cared to listen was a relative nobody named John, who had no place other than the wilderness around the Jordan.

WORSHIP MATTERS

Christians prepare for worship in many ways. We can encourage people to enter into the weekly worship of the congregation by reading scripture passages for upcoming Sundays at home. We can provide lists of the readings in bulletins, calendars, or monthly newsletters. Use these same readings for meetings of the congregation throughout the week. Corporate worship then serves as the culmination of communal reflection and deliberation. Spoken and written announcements about the changing liturgical seasons throughout the year also help to prepare people for the central event in the church's life each week.

LET THE CHILDREN COME

Some of us put on special clothing to get ready for worship. A chorister may put on a choir vestment to demonstrate, or an acolyte may dress in an alb and fasten a cincture. Choirs warm up to get ready for worship, and often a prelude prepares us for worship. The table is set with communion vessels and cloth coverings. Flowers are brought in, and candles are lit. All these things show that we are preparing for something important: our worship. We pray and prepare our hearts and minds as we light two candles to show the way.

MUSIC FOR WORSHIP
GATHERING

| LBW 29 | Comfort, comfort now my people |
| WOV 626 | People, look east |

PSALMODY: LUKE 1:68-79

LBW 2	Blessed be the Lord
RS 7	Now bless the God of Israel
WOV 725	Blessed be the God of Israel
W&P 20	Blessed be the Lord God of Israel

Jennings, Carolyn. PW, Cycle C.

Makeever, Ray. "Blessed Are You, Lord" in DH.

HYMN OF THE DAY

| LBW 36 | On Jordan's banks the Baptist's cry |
| | PUER NOBIS |

VOCAL RESOURCES

Bisbee, B. Wayne. "On Jordan's Banks the Baptist's Cry" in *Assist Us to Proclaim.* AFP 10597. SATB, org.

Busarow, Donald. "On Jordan's Banks the Baptist's Cry." CPH 98-2639. SAB, ob, kybd, cong.

INSTRUMENTAL RESOURCES

Dahl, David P. "Puer Nobis" in *Hymn Interpretations for Organ.* AFP 11-10972. Org, opt inst.

Engel, James. "Puer Nobis" in *Nine Easy Chorale Preludes for the Christmas Season.* MSM 10-119. Org.

Heller, David. "Puer Nobis" in *Augsburg Organ Library: Advent.* AFP 11-11034.

Oliver, Curt. "Puer Nobis" in *Advent Keyboard Seasons.* AFP 11-10724. Pno.

Young, Jeremy. "Puer Nobis" in *Gathering Music for Advent.* AFP 11-10798. Kybd, inst, bass/cello.

ALTERNATE HYMN OF THE DAY

| LBW 418 | Judge eternal, throned in splendor |
| WOV 631 | Lift up your heads, O gates |

COMMUNION

| LBW 224 | Soul, adorn yourself with gladness |
| WOV 629 | All earth is hopeful |

SENDING

| LBW 35 | Hark, the glad sound! |
| WOV 725 | Blessed be the God of Israel |

ADDITIONAL HYMNS AND SONGS

PH 409	Wild and lone the prophet's voice
TFF 46	Freedom is coming
W&P 56	He who began a good work in you
W3 362	City of God, Jerusalem
W3 640	Thou whose purpose is to kindle

MUSIC FOR THE DAY
CHORAL

Dietterich, Philip R., arr. "Carol of the Advent." HOP APM-216. SATB, org.

Ellingboe, Bradley. "Soul Adorn Yourself with Gladness" (Vengo a ti, Jesús amado). AFP 11-10949. SATB.

Farlee, Robert. "Song of Zechariah" in *Three Biblical Songs.* AFP 11-10604. U, kybd.

Ferguson, John. "Advent Processional." AFP 11-10448. SATB.

Goudimel, Claude. "Comfort, comfort ye my people." GIA G-2893.

Handel, G. F. "And the Glory of the Lord" from *Messiah.* SATB, acc.

Rotermund, Donald. "Blessed Be the Lord." CPH 98-3380. U/solo/ 2 pt, org, opt hb.

Shute, Linda Cable. "On Jordan's Banks." AFP 11-10953. SATB, pno.

White, David Ashley. "Comfort, Comfort Ye My People." SEL 405-152. SATB.

CHILDREN'S CHOIRS

Beck, John Ness. "Every Valley." BEC BP1040. SATB, org/pno.

French carol. "People, Look East" in LS.

Hopson, Hal H. "Prepare the Royal Highway." MSM 50-0301. U/2 pt, kybd.

White, David Ashley. "Zechariah's Song." CG CGA-590. 2 pt, kybd.

47

KEYBOARD/INSTRUMENTAL

Carter, John. "Rejoice Greatly" in *Handelbars.* HOP 1949. Pno.

Lind, Robert. "Prepare the Royal Highway" in *Organ Music for Advent.*
CPH 97-6192. Org.

Wold, Wayne L. "The King of Glory Comes" in *God With Us.*
AFP 11-10975. Org.

HANDBELL

Allured, Donald E. "Sleepers, Wake." NMP HB-409. 3-5 oct.

Moklebust, Cathy. "People, Look East." AFP 11-10805. 3-5 oct.

PRAISE ENSEMBLE

Beck, John Ness. "Every Valley." BEC BP1040. SATB, kybd.

Berthier, Jacques. "Wait for the Lord" in *Gather.* GIA.

Collins, Dori Erwin. "A Story for All People" in W&P.

MONDAY, DECEMBER 11
LARS OLSEN SKREFSRUD, MISSIONARY TO INDIA, 1910

Lars Olsen Skrefsrud was born in Norway in 1840. When he was nineteen years old, he and some friends robbed a bank. In prison he began to read religious books. Visits with a pastor who came to the prison revived Skrefsrud's earlier desire to become a pastor. In 1863 he began work among the Santals of northern India. His work among them included providing a written language, translating the gospels and the Small Catechism, and writing hymns in that language. He also taught agriculture and carpentry methods to raise the Santal's standard of living. The Christian community he founded there continues to flourish.

Consider ways in which Skrefsrud's life echoes the prophetic work of Isaiah and John the Baptist, who prepared the way of the Lord. In what ways can a congregation's proclamation of the gospel and its work for justice point the way to the coming Christ?

TUESDAY, DECEMBER 12
OUR LADY OF GUADALUPE

Many Mexican and Mexican American Christians, as well as many others of Central and South America, commemorate Mary, mother of our Lord, on this day. In a famous painting found on the cloak of Juan Diego, a sixteenth-century Mexican Christian, Mary is depicted as an indigenous native, head bowed in prayer and preg-

nant with the Word of God. As a sign of the blending of the Aztec and European culture, as a sign of God's identification with the poor and powerless, and as an evangelical sign of the coming of the gospel to the new world, Our Lady of Guadalupe can be a powerful symbol of Advent longing for the Word of God among the poor in this hemisphere. Images for preaching on this day might arise from Revelation 12, Luke 1:39-56, or Luther's *Commentary on the Magnificat.*

THURSDAY, DECEMBER 14
JOHN OF THE CROSS, RENEWER OF THE CHURCH, 1591
TERESA OF AVILA, RENEWER OF THE CHURCH, 1582

John and Teresa were both members of the Carmelite religious order. John met Teresa when she was working to reform the Carmelite Order and return it to a stricter observance of its rules, from which she believed its members had departed. John followed Teresa's lead and encouraged others to follow her reform. He was imprisoned when he encountered opposition to the reform. Both John and Teresa's writings reflect a deep interest in mystical thought and meditation. Their emphasis on contemplation can guide us in our Advent worship as we watch for the coming Christ.

Both John and Teresa believed that authentic prayer leads to greater love of neighbor and service to those in need. Teresa wrote, "Christ has no body now but yours…yours are the eyes through which he looks in compassion on the world." In one of John's poems, *The Spiritual Canticle,* he cried, "Oh, that my griefs would end! Come, grant me thy fruition full and free!"

SATURDAY, DECEMBER 16
LAS POSADAS

Las Posadas, "lodgings," is celebrated in homes of Mexican heritage and is becoming a popular parish practice as well. Families or groups of people wander through the neighborhood to mark the journey of Mary and Joseph to Bethlehem. They knock on doors, asking to come in, but a rude voice says that there is no room. The visitors either respond that Mary is about to give birth to the king of heaven, or they sing an Advent carol foretelling his birth. Eventually the door is opened, and everyone is welcomed into a great party of traditional Mexican holiday food and singing.

The traditional songs of this celebration are included in *Libro de Liturgia y Cántico* (284–86). Prepare a special package or offering for a shelter or halfway house. Las Posadas can be a strong reminder of Christ's humble birth among the poor and the importance of extending hospitality.

DECEMBER 17, 2000

THIRD SUNDAY IN ADVENT

INTRODUCTION

The arrival is fast approaching; the light from the Advent wreath is growing. How shall we prepare for God's coming among us? With joy! With resolute action! With prayer and thanksgiving! The Lord is near.

PRAYER OF THE DAY

Almighty God, you once called John the Baptist to give witness to the coming of your Son and to prepare his way. Grant us, your people, the wisdom to see your purpose today and the openness to hear your will, that we may witness to Christ's coming and so prepare his way; through Jesus Christ our Lord, who lives and reigns with you and the Holy Spirit, one God, now and forever.

or

Lord, hear our prayers and come to us, bringing light into the darkness of our hearts; for you live and reign with the Father and the Holy Spirit, one God, now and forever.

READINGS

Zephaniah 3:14-20

The prophet Zephaniah's message is mostly one of judgment for sin. This reading, however, which comes from the conclusion of the book, pictures the new people of God (3:12-13). Judgment has brought repentance and salvation, and now is the time of celebration.

Isaiah 12:2-6

In your midst is the Holy One of Israel. (Isa. 12:6)

Philippians 4:4-7

The theme of joy sounded in the first reading continues in Paul's confident words to the Philippians. Although he writes from prison, Paul finds hope in the assurance that hearts and minds are guarded securely by the peace of God.

Luke 3:7-18

Before he begins his account of Jesus' ministry, Luke describes the work of John the Baptist, who proclaimed the good news in startling images. Radical generosity and faithfulness in vocation are among the fruits of repentance John identifies.

COLOR   Blue *or* Purple

THE PRAYERS

With longing for the fullness of redemption, let us pray for the church, the world, and all people according to their needs.

A BRIEF SILENCE.

For the whole Christian church, that we might bear fruits worthy of repentance: God of hopefulness,

hear our prayer.

For our stewardship of creation, that it may reflect faithful partnership with you and benefit those who will come after us: God of hopefulness,

hear our prayer.

For all who hunger or lack basic necessities of life, that our sharing may encourage them in hope: God of hopefulness,

hear our prayer.

For those who are hospitalized or ill (especially...), that their worries might be given over to you: God of hopefulness,

hear our prayer.

For the children of this community, whose hearts are at

49

home in God, that this might be a safe and nurturing place for them: God of hopefulness,

hear our prayer.

HERE OTHER INTERCESSIONS MAY BE OFFERED.

With thanksgiving we remember all our friends and relatives who have died and rest securely in your arms. May your presence bring comfort to those who grieve: God of hopefulness,

hear our prayer.

God of salvation, hear the prayers we make in the name of Jesus Christ, whose coming is certain and whose day draws near.

Amen

IMAGES FOR PREACHING

It is not what you expect to hear so close to Christmas, is it? This is not the sort of text you could fit into a greeting card, with pictures of angels or stars or wise men, or even of a baby in a manger. Nothing about this text is charming or quaint or picturesque.

Instead, it is filled with vipers and axes, and loaded with the threat of fire at both ends. "[E]very tree therefore that does not bear good fruit is cut down and thrown into the fire" and "[T]he chaff he will burn with unquenchable fire." Snakes and axes and fire! Flames before and behind us—the fire that consumes, the fire that clears away all the rubbish, all the refuse, and leaves behind a bareness that is filled with nothing but expectation, a charred landscape that can support nothing but hope. And so we, like the crowds that followed John out to the Jordan River only to be immersed in fire instead of water, turn and ask, "What then should we do?"

It is a dangerous question to ask anyone, especially one who claims to be a prophet of God—most especially one who *is* a prophet of God—for John has an answer. John has come to the water spouting talk of snakes, axes, and fire, and he comes prepared to tell the people how to start, where to begin, and what they should do. The answers are spoken with a clarity at least as frightening as anything he has said before.

"Whoever has two coats must share with anyone who has none; and whoever has food must do likewise." In short, practice stewardship and justice. From John's perspective, you cannot separate the two: stewardship and justice are good fruits that hang on the same stem.

It is not the word we expect this close to Christmas, but it certainly may be the word we need.

John speaks of still another fire and a flame that warms the cold words until they become words of gospel. "I baptize you with water," John said. "He will baptize you with the Holy Spirit and with fire!" Let us, then, warm our hands and hearts at the fire of the Holy Spirit.

WORSHIP MATTERS

Congregations have a variety of ways in which the prayers reflect the requests and needs of their members. Many congregations place a book of intercessions in the narthex or other gathering areas for people to use as they arrive for worship. A book of intercessions may simply be a blank book with each Sunday's date written at the top of the page. Spaces may be designated for thanksgivings, those who are ill, and those who have died, as well as other concerns. Anyone having a need may write a name or a request in the book during the gathering for worship. The assisting minister who leads the prayers during the service may then incorporate these names.

LET THE CHILDREN COME

When we pray, we are to ask for what we need. God hears our prayers and sometimes sends us answers that are not what we expect or when we expect them. Sometimes what we ask for is given in a different way; only after some time goes by do we understand God's answer. Advent is a time to practice waiting—waiting for answers to our prayer requests.

MUSIC FOR WORSHIP

GATHERING

| LBW 36 | On Jordan's banks the Baptist's cry |
| WOV 633 | Awake, awake, and greet the new morn |

PSALMODY: ISAIAH 12:2-6

WOV 635 Surely it is God who saves me

Haugen, Marty. "With Joy You Shall Draw Water" (Isaiah 12) in PCY, vol. 2.

Lindh, Jody. "Behold, God Is My Salvation." CPH 98-3193. U.

Mealy, Norman. "Canticle of Thanksgiving" in TP.

White, Jack Noble. "The First Song of Isaiah." HWG CMR 3347. SATB, cong, kybd, opt gtr, opt hb, opt perc, opt dance.

HYMN OF THE DAY

WOV 715   Open your ears, O faithful people
           YISRAEL V'ORAITA

VOCAL RESOURCES

Hobby, Robert A. "Open Your Ears, O Faithful People." AFP 11-10752.
U, opt desc, fl, fc, tamb, hb.

INSTRUMENTAL RESOURCES

Albrecht, Mark. "Open Your Ears, O Faithful People" in *Three for
Piano and Sax*. AFP 11-10929. Pno, sax or inst.

Burkhardt, Michael. "Torah Song" in *Ten Hymn Introductions*.
MSM 10-719. Org.

Hassell, Michael. "Yisrael V'Oraita" in *Folkways*. AFP 11-10829.
Pno, inst.

ALTERNATE HYMN OF THE DAY

LBW 32   Fling wide the door
WOV 635   Surely it is God who saves me

COMMUNION

LBW 23   O Lord, how shall I meet you
WOV 706   Eat this bread, drink this cup

SENDING

LBW 171   Rejoice, the Lord is king!
WOV 627   My Lord, what a morning

ADDITIONAL HYMNS AND SONGS

REJ 171   The voice of God goes out
           to all the world
TFF 257   I've got the joy, joy, joy
W&P 93   Lord, my strength
W&P 95   Make me a channel of your peace

MUSIC FOR THE DAY

CHORAL

Anon. Sixteenth century. "Rejoice in the Lord Always." OXF 43.243.

Bach, J. S. "Zion Hears the Watchmen Singing" in BAS. U, kybd.

Byrd, William. "Laetentur coeli." NOV 16006.

Hopson, Hal H. "Advent Prayer." AFP 11-10950. 2 pt mxd, kybd.

Jean, Martin. "Advent Hymn." AFP 11-10801. SATB.

Lovelace, Austin. "Come, Thou Long-Expected Jesus." AFP 11-10244.
SA(T)B, org.

White, David Ashley. "Surely It Is God Who Saves Me." AFP 11-2357.
2 pt, kybd, opt fl.

CHILDREN'S CHOIRS

Bach, J. S./arr. Michael Burkhardt. "Prepare Thyself, Zion."
MSM 50-0415. U, kybd, opt cello/bsn.

Christopherson, Dorothy. "The Lord Is My Salvation." AFP 11-10254.
U, fl, opt fc, opt choreography.

Walker, Christopher. "Stay Awake, Be Ready" in LS.

KEYBOARD/INSTRUMENTAL

Organ, Anne Krentz. "Rejoice, Rejoice Believers" in *Advent
Reflections*. AFP 11-10864. Pno, inst.

Walcha, Helmut. "Macht hoch die Tür" in *Chorale Preludes*, vol. I.
CFP 4850. Org.

HANDBELL

Mathis, William H. "Oh, Come, Oh, Come, Emmanuel." FBM BG0947.
3-6 oct, opt hc.

Moklebust, Cathy. "Savior of the Nations, Come." CG CGB-173.
2-3 oct, opt perc.

PRAISE ENSEMBLE

Roth, John. "Rejoice, Rejoice!" CPH 98-3229. U, kybd, opt solo,
cong, inst.

Tarner, Evelyn. "Rejoice in the Lord Always" in *All God's People Sing!*
CPH.

51

THURSDAY, DECEMBER 21

ST. THOMAS, APOSTLE

Thomas is perhaps best remembered as "Doubting
Thomas." But alongside this doubt, the gospel of John
shows Thomas as fiercely loyal: "Let us also go, that we
may die with him" (John 11:16). And John's gospel
shows Thomas moving from doubt to deep faith.
Thomas makes one of the strongest confessions of faith
in the New Testament, "My Lord and my God!" (John
20:28). From this confession of faith, ancient stories tell
of Thomas's missionary work to India where Christian
communities were flourishing a thousand years before
the arrival of sixteenth-century missionaries.

Though we hear about Thomas each year on the
second Sunday of Easter, Thomas can also serve as an
Advent saint. He watched for the risen Christ and
looked for the signs of Christ's incarnation. In Advent
we, too, watch. We look for the coming of Christ in our
lives, his risen presence in the sacraments, and his incarnation soon to be celebrated at Christmas.

DECEMBER 24, 2000

INTRODUCTION

We come to the threshold of the celebration. The time is right; the place, Bethlehem of Judah, is identified; Mary's song announces the great things God is doing. A new day is being birthed into existence, and we are meant to be a part of it. This final day of preparation leads to the darkness tonight and the dawn of tomorrow, where the mystery unfolds again.

PRAYER OF THE DAY

Stir up your power, O Lord, and come. Take away the hindrance of our sins and make us ready for the celebration of your birth, that we may receive you in joy and serve you always; for you live and reign with the Father and the Holy Spirit, now and forever.

READINGS

Micah 5:2-5a

Many years before the time of Micah, God promised David that his dynasty would last forever. Although prophets such as Micah warned that judgment would come from unfaithfulness, Micah foresees a restoration beyond that judgment.

Luke 1:47-55

The Lord has lifted up the lowly. (Luke 1:52)

or Psalm 80:1-7

Show the light of your countenance and we shall be saved. (Ps. 80:7)

Hebrews 10:5-10

The author of Hebrews uses the image of religious sacrifice to convey the significance of Christ's coming. Through obedient acceptance of God's will, Christ allows his own body to become the greatest sacrifice of all, one through which we are made a holy people.

Luke 1:39-45 [46-55]

Luke presents Elizabeth, the mother of John the Baptist, and Mary, the mother of Jesus, as women who are filled with the Holy Spirit and with faith. We hear Elizabeth's inspired greeting and Mary's song of praise: God is among the lowly and the hungry.

COLOR   Blue *or* Purple

THE PRAYERS

With longing for the fullness of redemption, let us pray for the church, the world, and all people according to their needs.

A BRIEF SILENCE.

For the church in every place, that with Mary and Elizabeth we would be prepared for your arrival into our lives: God of hopefulness,

hear our prayer.

For peace among nations, and especially for peacekeeping forces serving in regions of conflict *(names),* that human divisions might be overcome: God of hopefulness,

hear our prayer.

For those who are poor and homeless in our community, that the church may assist them in meeting their needs: God of hopefulness,

hear our prayer.

For the sick and all who suffer (especially...), that they might find relief: God of hopefulness,

hear our prayer.

For greeters and readers, for ushers and nursery keepers, and for all whose serving enables our praise today we give thanks: God of hopefulness,

hear our prayer.

HERE OTHER INTERCESSIONS MAY BE OFFERED.

We remember those who have died and are at rest in your arms of mercy. Bring us with them to joyous life in your presence: God of hopefulness,

hear our prayer.

God of salvation, hear the prayers we make in the name of Jesus Christ, whose coming is certain and whose day draws near.

Amen

IMAGES FOR PREACHING

"In those days" is how Luke begins this story, but it is a story told in marked contrast to the one we heard earlier (Advent 2), the one with all the kings and princes. This story is not about worldly greatness at all, but instead is the recounting of a meeting between cousins, women who suddenly and beyond all expectation find themselves filled with the promise of new life.

In a way they are mirror opposites of each other, their lives at different ends of the trajectory of human experience. Elizabeth had been married for years to her husband, Zechariah, and for all those years had waited for a child. She had reached the age when they could expect to remain childless but to her great surprise found that at long last she was expecting. It was an astonishing event, connected somehow to an episode that had left her husband—quite literally—speechless. Eager for conversation, eager for the sound of another human voice, she greeted Mary and discovered that the world is changed.

Mary's youth was a counterpoint to Elizabeth's age, and though betrothed, she was still single. Nonetheless, she was expecting a child, a child whose conception was even more astonishing than Elizabeth's. The child that Mary bore was the Son of God, the one whom the Lord had promised the children of Israel during all the long years of their exile and oppression. He had come to deliver them as both Elizabeth and Mary would in time deliver their children.

The story of the meeting of these women is a story filled with miracles great and small. It holds the promise of new life, a promise made real despite the fact that it was impossible. It holds the power of love, the power to bring two lives together so that one's joy quickly spills over into another, revealing that love shared is not divided but increased.

Finally, it offers the presence of Jesus, a presence that may be sensed, felt, or apprehended with the heart. It is a belief that comes with its own blessing.

WORSHIP MATTERS

For centuries the church has sung Mary's song (Luke 1:46-55) as a canticle at evening prayer. Mary personifies the faith of the whole Christian church that is always ready to answer God's call to service. Far from being words of mere submission though, Mary's song gives witness to a God of justice who brings down the powerful and fills hungry people with good things. Consider using various forms of Mary's song throughout the year to give expression to the full range of emotions present in this great canticle. Two hymn paraphases of this canticle are "My soul now magnifies the Lord" (LBW 180) and "My soul proclaims your greatness" (WOV 730). How do each of these settings express one or more aspects of the canticle?

LET THE CHILDREN COME

Talk about the words that Mary sang when the angel announced that she would be the mother of God's Son. For centuries the church has sung Mary's song in our evening prayer (Luke 1:46-55). Mary is also a special part of the church's Advent and Christmas celebrations. We can use this song of Mary every day in our prayers. She understood that she had a special job to do and that God is strong and will help us always. These words of Mary are suitable for us to use as we seek to learn God's will for us and then to complete what God has set before us.

MUSIC FOR WORSHIP
SERVICE MUSIC

A musical setting of the Magnificat may be used to proclaim the conclusion of today's gospel. If this is done, the alternate psalm may be used (80:1-7).

GATHERING

LBW 34	Oh, come, oh, come, Emmanuel
WOV 643	Once in royal David's city

PSALM 80:1-7

Callahan, Mary David. PW, Cycle B.

Cox, Joe. "Restore Us, O God" in *Psalms for the People of God.* SMP 45/1037 S.

Haugen, Marty. "Lord, Make Us Turn to You" in PCY, vol. 2.

Kogut, Malcolm. "Lord, Make Us Turn to You" in PCY, vol. 10.

Schoenbachler, Tim. "Psalm 80/85: Maranatha" in STP, vol. 1. OCP 9926.

LUKE 1:47-55

LBW 6	My soul proclaims the greatness of the Lord
LBW 180	My soul now magnifies the Lord
TFF 168	My soul does magnify the Lord
WOV 730	My soul proclaims your greatness
W&P 26	Canticle of the turning

Haugen, Marty. "My Soul Proclaims Your Greatness" in PCY, vol. 2.

Jennings, Carolyn. PW, Cycle C.

HYMN OF THE DAY

LBW 41	O little town of Bethlehem
	St. Louis
	(*alternate tune:* Forest Green, WOV 725)

53

VOCAL RESOURCES

Laster, James. "O Little Town of Bethlehem" in *Carol Fest*.
CPH 98-3166. SATB, opt brass, kybd.

Leavitt, John. "O Little Town of Bethlehem." AFP 11-2507, inst pts
11-2508. SATB, kybd or opt 2 vln, 2fl, vla, cello, kybd.

INSTRUMENTAL RESOURCES

Fruhauf, Ennis. "Forest Green" in *Ralph Vaughan Williams and the
English School*. AFP 11-10826. Org/kybd.

Haan, Raymond. "Prelude on Forest Green." MSM 20-197A. Org, inst.

Leavitt, John. "Forest Green" in *Christmas Suite*. AFP 11-10857. Org.

Sedio, Mark. "Forest Green" in *Dancing in the Light of God*.
AFP 11-10793. Pno.

ALTERNATE HYMN OF THE DAY

| LBW 86 | The only Son from heaven |
| WOV 730 | My soul proclaims your greatness |

COMMUNION

| LBW 198 | Let all mortal flesh keep silence |
| WOV 711 | You satisfy the hungry heart |

SENDING

| LBW 315 | Love divine, all loves excelling |
| WOV 797 | O God beyond all praising |

ADDITIONAL HYMNS AND SONGS

NCH 106	My heart sings out with joyful praise
PsH 204	Little Bethlehem of Judah
TFF 54	That boy-child of Mary
W&P 19	Bless his holy name
W&P 36	Emmanuel

MUSIC FOR THE DAY

CHORAL

Bach, J. S. "Savior of the Nations, Come" in BAS. SATB, kybd.

Brahms, Johannes. "A Dove Flew Down from Heaven" in CC. SATB.

Eccard, Johannes. "Over the Hills Maria Went." GSCH 8420. SSATB.

Hassler, Hans Leo. "Magnificat" in CC. SATB.

Hopson, Hal. "O Day of Peace." AFP 11-10495. SAB, kybd, opt hb.

Prower, Anthony. "The Angel Gabriel from Heaven Came."
CPH 98-2853. SATB, org.

Willcocks, David, arr. "Gabriel's Message" in *Carols for Choirs 2*. OXF.

Zacharia, Cesare de. "Magnificat." AFP 11-10508. SATB.

CHILDREN'S CHOIRS

Ahner, Sally. "Light One Candle: Christ Is Coming" in LS.

Haugen, Marty. "The Magnificat" in *Holden Evening Prayer*.
GIA G-3460. U, pno.

Howell, John Raymond. "The Angel Gabriel." B&H OCTB6256.
U/2 pt trbl, kybd.

Sleeth, Natalie. "Oh, Come, Oh, Come, Emmanuel." CG CGA-273.
U, desc, kybd.

KEYBOARD/INSTRUMENTAL

Osterlund, Karl. "Gabriel's Message" in *I Wonder as I Wander*.
AFP 11-10858. Org.

Pepping, Ernst. "A Solis Ortus Cardine" in *Hymns for Organ*.
Bärenreiter 2747 or KAL K09968. Org.

Uehlein, Christopher. *Four Variations on Carols for Advent*, vol. 12. OCP.

HANDBELL

Hopson, Hal H. "Variations on Kingsfold." AFP 11-10703. 3-5 oct.

Morris, Hart. "The Promise Fulfilled." RRM HB0027. 3-6 oct.

PRAISE ENSEMBLE

Fettke, Tom. "The Majesty and Glory of Your Name" in *Sing & Rejoice*. BNT.

Hommerding, Alan J. "Sing, My Soul (Mary's Song Of Praise)" in
Renew. HOP.

Larkin, Michael. "Savior of the Nations, Come." AFP 11-10731.
SATB, kybd.

CHRISTMAS

At last the time has come

to celebrate our Lord's birth

IMAGES OF THE SEASON

At last the time has come to celebrate our Lord's birth. The world around us may have almost worn out the celebration already, but commercial interests only play around the edges, while the church has the duty and delight of moving to the very heart of this festival.

Our festivities mark the incarnation of God. *Incarnation* is one of those clinical-sounding, Latin-derived words literally meaning "taking on flesh." In order to keep the meaning in mind, we might substitute the word *embodiment*. At Christmas, then, we celebrate God's embodiment, God's taking on a body—a *human* body. It is the central miracle of this season—not the angels or the star or even the virgin birth, but the simple yet astounding fact that almighty God would love us unworthy creatures enough to become one of us, to take on a mortal life directed toward the cross.

It is difficult for us to make sense of that divine embodiment. In trying to do so, we often tend to help God bridge the gap by downplaying the complete otherness of God, as if God were a sort of enhanced human to begin with, so taking on human flesh and blood is no big surprise, no great leap. We freely ascribe human emotions, impulses, and even shortcomings to God. We take the metaphor of God the Father literally, picturing a grandfatherly human male sitting on a heavenly throne. The reality, of course, is that God is the holy one from whom Hebrew patriarchs and prophets hid lest they catch a devastating glimpse of the divine countenance. And now this source of all life, all being, has been born as one of us?

That central truth is so unbelievable, so incomprehensible, that we tend to focus on more manageable facets, even inventing details as we go along. Babies are both cute and helpless, so we spend a lot of time on the baby aspect of Jesus' birth, even though two of the gospels did not find that aspect important enough to mention. Shepherds were low-class citizens of their day, and their presence in Luke's account stresses the humility of the incarnation. Yet we have romanticized their role, adding snow, pipes and drums, and the mythical shepherd boy. Even the mighty cherubim have been domesticated into some sort of baby angels.

One could say that all of this embellishment comes with the territory. We are, after all, made in God's creative image, and therefore God should have expected that we would take creative liberties with the script. And in reality, it is doubtful whether God is much troubled with the way we embroider Christmas.

Heaven may not mind, but it is we who lose out if we stop with the merely cute facets of Christmas. Yes, we get the warm fuzzies, and, yes, the people who crowd the pews are pleased, but in the process, are we missing the whole point of the festival, God's embodiment? After all, it is when we move beyond the somewhat artificial happiness of family gatherings, cards, gifts, and into the postholiday realities that the true value of Jesus' birth comes home to us.

When illness, unemployment, the breaking of a relationship, or any of life's tragedies are visited upon us, mere happiness will not help us—not enough. The sentiment that pervades the air at Christmas is a fragile thing, easily crushed. The terrible mistake we make, then, if we lean too heavily on secondary frills is to give the impression to those who are strangers to the faith that it is all we have to offer, this mere happiness, however sanctified. They can find something at least as helpful as that in any self-help book. How much better, though, if what we find in church at Christmas is a Savior God who is fully human—born, yes, but in humble circumstances that point to a life lived for others, for *us*.

Whereas a sentimental view will often try to deny humanity's less savory aspects, a God who cares enough to take on our shape, our body, is a God who will not be disgusted or repelled by the human body or the troubles our embodied selves can get into. God honors our whole being by taking our form. In an era when the "unimproved" body is never good enough, that divine acceptance alone can be valuable. But there is more: in baptism our bodies are washed in saving water and we are claimed as God's beloved. Go another step farther, to the eucharistic level. When we gather at the table for the "Christ-mass," the great Christmas feast, we eat of the body that was born in Bethlehem, *and we become* that body of which Christ is the head.

Just as Jesus' embodiment was only the beginning of his ministry for us, so our embodiment as Christ's people is only the beginning for our ministry. At Christmas *we* are born into the real world, ready to serve the real people in it. Yes, we may occasionally indulge in a bit of sweet sentimentality, but we will never mistake it for anything other

than the frosting it is. The real, created world, full of grit and glory, is our natural habitat. There we find humanity (ourselves included) in need of salvation, and there, thanks to Christ's embodiment, we find the needed salvation.

> Behold, the world's creator wears
> the form and fashion of a slave;
> our very flesh our maker shares,
> his fallen creatures, all, to save.
>
> —Coelius Sedulius (LBW 64)

ENVIRONMENT AND ART FOR THE SEASON

White, the color of full-spectrum light, is the color of all the festivals of our Lord. It is often blended with gold for Easter. For Christmas and the other incarnational festivals, white may be blended with other colors as well. Though our consumer culture

likes to celebrate Christmas much more than Easter, the church's challenge is to keep the Christmas environment in proper relationship to whatever we have planned for our Easter environment. Hold the festivals of Easter and Christmas in tension. We are always tempted to make Christmas bigger than Easter. Another challenge for a seasonal planning team is to address this question: How can the environment help maintain the celebration of Christmas for twelve days when the culture may be done with Christmas by the afternoon of December 25?

Art that forms Christian faith does not transport us back to "Bibleland." Remember the request made to Philip, "Sir, we wish to see Jesus" (John 12:21)? Worshipers come to meet Jesus in their lives today. Even on Christmas Eve worshipers come seeking the whole Christ, not a romanticized baby. They come seeking for someone worthy to be Lord of their lives. Help them meet the Lord this season.

LIGHTING

While contemplating the festive lighting associated with this season, remember that every candle used in worship should always be in relation to the paschal candle, the

primary candle that burns throughout the fifty-day celebration of the resurrection. This candle should be the largest, most beautiful, and central candle in the community's life as a symbol of the risen Christ. It traditionally burns for every worship service throughout the Easter season and for any baptism or funeral throughout the year. All other candles used in the worship space should be in relative proportion to the paschal candle.

The so-called Christ candle is a quite recent innovation in the Protestant tradition. This candle is confusing because its use competes with the paschal candle. The Advent wreath needs no fifth candle. What happens to the wreath at Christmas? It may be removed prior to the Christmas Eve celebration. Or if you wish to have the wreath remain along with other Christmas decorations, try building a large wreath that will span the entirety of the Advent and Christmas seasons (see *Sundays and Seasons 2000*, pp. 36, 62). Such a wreath need not be limited to four candles or exclusively to Advent symbolism.

A great nativity tradition is that of lining the church exterior with luminaria. The preparation and arrangement of these candle lanterns can be a great intergenerational project. They can be purchased as kits or created from inexpensive lunch bags (or white bakery bags), sand, and votive candles. If you live in a cold climate, try making luminaria out of ice. Fill five-quart pails completely with water and leave them outside until they are partially frozen. While the center core is still liquid, remove the ice from the pails and drill through the center of either the top or bottom end to drain the water out of the core. Repeat the process until enough ice crystal luminaria are created. They are absolutely fireproof and windproof. Votive candles drop in the hole in the center and form a lovely crystal lighted path to worship.

If a tree appeared sometime in the Advent season, how is it different for the celebration of the nativity? Following the principle of ever-increasing light, a tree that may have been unadorned in Advent now has plain white lights.

Does your parish have a crèche? Is it in the gathering space or the worship area? Is it scaled in proportion to the size of the room and assembly? Is it child-friendly? If so gather the children there for a story.

SOCIAL IMPLICATIONS FOR THE ENVIRONMENT

We often hear the assembly referred to as the body of Christ, but when was the last time you heard the assembly referred to as the word of the Lord? How can the environment for worship this Christmas season help the assembly (and the lectors especially) to see themselves as the word of the Lord in this incarnational season?

How will the glad tidings announced at Christmas be true for others in your community? Consider how you literally make room for guests who may not be regular worshipers. How will seasonal exterior displays announce a welcome to neighbors and passersby? How can your congregation's festivity turn outward to serve those who are most in need of God's saving grace in your community? Might a portion of the funds collected to decorate your space with festive flowers be used to help decorate (or even entirely furnish!) one or more rooms in a homeless shelter?

58

PREACHING WITH THE SEASON

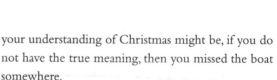

If a member of the congregation asked you to write down the "true meaning of Christmas" on one side of an index card, could you do it? Could you do it in one word? A sentence? Both sides of the card in small print?

The "true meaning of Christmas" is a phrase that crops up frequently this time of year, appearing in all sorts of media and every kind of setting. The difficult thing about it is that little general agreement surrounds what that meaning is.

As society's problems go, this lack of consensus seems unimportant. It is, however, a matter for legitimate concern, for as we are increasingly divided by things such as class, race, and gender (not to mention politics, philosophy, or religion), my claim to possess and to understand the true meaning of Christmas suggests that unless you possess and understand the same meaning, then what you claim is false. No matter how warmhearted, no matter how generous, no matter how nice

your understanding of Christmas might be, if you do not have the true meaning, then you missed the boat somewhere.

But that conclusion cannot be the whole story. Can the true meaning of Christmas be an exclusive property, something we could use to put labels on other folks and to dismiss them for their lack of understanding? Definitely not. Though we may not all agree, though we may never agree entirely, we could rule out anything that involves a lot of sneering at or judging of others.

But where are we left as we struggle to preach once more from these so familiar and beloved texts? How do we fill out the index card? Several options are available. Try this answer: the true meaning of Christmas is giving. That is short and to the point, which is a good thing during this season when you already have to remember so many other things. And giving is an appropriate gesture, because it directs our attention beyond ourselves and beyond our own needs, which is another good thing. We even have scriptural authority for it. Though they do not arrive yet, all during the Christmas season wise men are on their way to Bethlehem, each of them carrying a gift of great value to place at the feet of the Christ child.

Of course, the true meaning of Christmas is certainly more than a gift exchange, no matter how thoughtful, no matter how precious the gifts. We often find it difficult to offer with open hands, keeping one finger on the calculator and trying to figure out whether what we got was equal to what we spent. The other trap is that the meaning of Christmas may become instead the meaning of what we choose to give. So we try again.

The true meaning of Christmas is wonder. It appeals to one's poetic streak. Wonder! Sheer amazement at God's decision to enter the world, the awe you feel when face to face with Niagara Falls or the Grand Canyon. You knew that such a place existed but had no idea it would be so overwhelming. The wonder of Christmas is the wonder we experience at God's breaking into the world God had created. Confronting the truth of that, recognizing our insignificance in relationship to God's greatness, is cause enough for wonder all through the Christmas season and for the rest of our lives. But is it enough?

The problem with wonder is that we hardly know what to do with it. Wonder should have something a little raw about it, something that takes your breath away by its grandeur alone. Wonder is difficult; it resists neat packages or being broken into smaller pieces for easy consumption. When we meet it head on, it can knock us to the ground under the sheer weight of glory. It can leave us breathless, motionless, aimless. Another choice?

Consider this: the true meaning of Christmas is vulnerability. It is the lowering of walls, the removal of the defenses and the boundaries that separate us from one another, the barriers that are the cause of so much suspicion, fear, doubt, and mistrust. To be vulnerable is to be open to the wounds and chance hurts that happen simply because the world is filled with those things. It is to put oneself forward without being at all certain of what is waiting ahead, over the next hill, or around the next corner. To be vulnerable is to be open to the possibility of being touched by hands that are rough or gentle, knowing that you cannot experience one without also experiencing the other.

What we do at Christmas is celebrate the gift of God's Son to the world. That in itself is cause for wonder, amazement, and deep humility. It is a sign of great and abiding love. But the gift is more amazing, the wonder more profound, the love more precious when we think how it was that Jesus came to us: not as a mighty king, not as the ruler of nations and leader of armies, but as a human baby. Jesus was a creature of flesh just as we are flesh, born to ordinary parents who found out firsthand what the rest of us must never forget: the Messiah will not wait until everything in our lives and the world is perfect. The Christ does not wait for our convenience, but comes, ready or not, into the midst of our lives and meets us there.

But remember and treasure this also: The Son of God came to us not as a judge but as a baby, needing the care and protection of a mother and father, shelter from the cold, and the compassionate, vulnerable love that one human heart can give to another. It is that vulnerability, given freely in spite of the danger, in spite of the fear, the cost, and finally the pain, that is the true meaning of Christmas. Immanuel—God with us! The Son of God came to us in vulnerability, willing that we should touch and be touched by him, to change the ordinary into the holy and our darkness into light.

SHAPE OF WORSHIP FOR THE SEASON

BASIC SHAPE OF THE EUCHARISTIC RITE

- Confession and Forgiveness: see alternate worship text for Christmas in *Sundays and Seasons*

GATHERING

- Greeting: see alternate worship text for Christmas in *Sundays and Seasons*
- Use the Kyrie, particularly for the most festive liturgies during this season
- Use the hymn of praise ("Glory to God")

WORD

- Use the Nicene Creed
- The Prayers: see alternate forms and responses in the daily materials of *Sundays and Seasons*

MEAL

- Offertory prayer: see alternate worship text for Christmas in *Sundays and Seasons*
- Use the proper preface for Christmas
- Eucharistic prayer: in addition to the four main options in *LBW*, see "Eucharistic Prayer B: The Season of Christmas" in *WOV* Leaders Edition, p. 66
- Invitation to communion: see alternate worship text for Christmas in *Sundays and Seasons*
- Post-communion prayer: see alternate worship text for Christmas in *Sundays and Seasons*

SENDING

- Benediction: see alternate worship text for Christmas in *Sundays and Seasons*
- Dismissal: see alternate worship text for Christmas in *Sundays and Seasons*

OTHER SEASONAL POSSIBILITIES

PROCLAMATION OF THE BIRTH OF CHRIST

The services on Christmas Eve may begin with the proclamation of the birth of Christ (see text in the section Seasonal Rites), taken from the ancient martyrology. The proclamation should be understood as the announcement of the incarnation within human history rather than a literal counting of years. The lights may be turned down, and, following a period of silence, the proclamation is preferably sung or read (the proclamation may be sung on one note). The congregation may face the reader/cantor at the entrance to the church.

Following the proclamation the lights are turned on as the musician(s) introduce the entrance hymn. "Oh, come, all ye faithful" (LBW 45) is an appropriate hymn following the proclamation. The congregation turns to the front as the cross passes in procession. "Glory to God in the highest" is the most appropriate hymn of praise for the Christmas season.

CANDLELIGHTING OPTIONS FOR CHRISTMAS EVE

OPTION 1

- The liturgy may begin with a service of light as at evening prayer. The congregation may face the entrance to the church, and handheld candles may be lit. As the procession passes during the Christmas versicles, all turn to face forward.
- Christmas versicles (from "Propers for Daily Prayer," *LBW*, p. 175; these may be sung to the tones given in evening prayer, *LBW*, p. 142)
- Hymn of light (LBW 45, 56, or WOV 638)
- Thanksgiving for light (see *LBW*, p. 144)
- The service may then continue with the greeting, followed by the hymn of praise and the prayer of the day. Electric lights may be turned on gradually as the hymn of praise is begun (though a rather subdued level of lighting may be desired throughout the service, in order not to overwhelm tree lights and candles). Handheld candles may be extinguished at this time.

OPTION 2

Another option for the lighting of handheld candles is to use them at the reading of the gospel. A hymn, such as "The first Noel" (LBW 56) or "Angels, from the realms of glory" (LBW 50), may be sung as handheld candles are lit. The gospel may be read from the midst of the people. "Silent night, holy night!" (LBW 65) may be sung following the gospel, after which the handheld candles would be extinguished. Another way to use this hymn is by singing it together with "Night of silence" (W&P 101; notes on how to combine it with "Silent night" are printed there as well).

OPTION 3

- A final option for the lighting of handheld candles is at the close of the service. Following the post-communion canticle (or at a service without communion, following the offering and the prayers), handheld candles are lit. Instrumental or choral music may accompany the candlelighting.
- Hymn: "Silent night, holy night!" (LBW 65:1–2; or another hymn of light, as listed in option 1)
- Reading from John 1:1-14 (especially fitting if the gospel earlier in the service was from Luke 2). A

gospel procession may move to the midst of the assembly.

- LBW 65:3 (or the final stanza of another·hymn of light)
- Benediction and dismissal

BLESSING OF A NATIVITY SCENE

The text for the blessing of a nativity scene may be used after the sermon or after the communion of the people on Christmas Eve. See the seasonal rites section.

NEW YEAR'S EVE

Though gathering for worship on New Year's Eve may not be a common experience for most congregations, those wishing to observe the passing into the year 2001 this year might use the New Year's Eve suggestions in the seasonal rites section.

61

ASSEMBLY SONG FOR THE SEASON

How difficult it is to keep the song of Christmas alive after December 25. Let the love of God be fully sung by the assembly throughout the twelve days of Christmas. Find additional opportunities to gather and sing the hymns and carols of the season.

GATHERING

See "Shape of Worship for the Season" for a number of musical options for use with candlelighting on Christmas Eve.

On Christmas Eve use familiar gathering music so that the assembly can sing it well. On Christmas Day consider substituting "Angels we have heard on high" (LBW 71) or "Angels, from the realms of glory" (LBW 50) for the hymn of praise. On the first Sunday after Christmas have a Christmas hymn sing during the gathering time. Why not let the assembly choose their favorite hymns and carols and sing them as a prelude? Because there is only one Sunday after Christmas this year, be sure to include some of the carols and hymns that were not used at liturgies on December 24 or 25.

WORD

Use "Let the heavens rejoice" (TFF 10) as a psalm antiphon and psalm tone for the season. Phrases of Christmas hymns also work well as psalm refrains. The first phrases of "Joy to the world" (LBW 39) and "Hark! The herald angels sing" (LBW 60) are two examples of hymns that work well as refrains.

If it is not your normal practice, consider using a gospel procession during this season to emphasize God in our midst. Sing a gradual hymn to frame the gospel reading, such as stanzas 1 and 2 of "Good Christian friends, rejoice" (LBW 55) before the gospel reading and stanza 3 after the gospel reading.

Use the hymn of the day creatively, especially those with numerous stanzas. On Christmas Eve sing all the stanzas of "From heaven above" (LBW 51), for it tells a complete story. Many settings of the hymn are available.

Let every voice in the assembly take its part by alternating between cantors, choirs, children, organ, instruments, and assembly. Let the assembly have the opportunity to reflect on the text as each voice takes its part in the hymn. During the singing of the hymn have the assembly seated until stanza 14 or consider singing the first half of the hymn before the sermon and the second half afterwards. Let the word be sung to its fullest during the season.

On Christmas Day, "Of the Father's love begotten" (LBW 42) may be combined with "Holy Child within the manger" (WOV 638). One plan might be choir/cantor/children singing "Holy Child" and the assembly singing "Of the Father's love." Have the assembly sing stanzas one and two of "Of the Father's love," and then have the choir sing stanza one of "Holy Child." Continue alternating to the end. Sing "Of the Father's love" unaccompanied or with a single instrument on the melody line and punctuate the phrases with handbells.

MEAL

Stanza 3 of "What child is this" (LBW 40) is fitting as an offertory hymn. The text of "What feast of love" (WOV 701) has images from both the beginning and the end of the church year. Its use can be especially effective if it was sung on the festival of Christ the King.

Sing familiar carols and hymns continuously during distribution this season. The texts of many Christmas carols are in the public domain and may be easily printed in the bulletin. (Be sure to check the acknowledgments section of the hymnal from which you copy them, though.)

SENDING

On Christmas Day and the first Sunday after Christmas, sing a seasonal hymn as the post-communion canticle. Possibilities include "Go tell it on the mountain" (LBW 70 and TFF 52), "Let our gladness have no end" (LBW 57), and "Jesus, the light of the world" (TFF 59).

MUSIC FOR THE SEASON

VERSE AND OFFERTORY

Boehnke, Paul. *Festive Verse Settings for Christmas, Epiphany and Transfiguration.* MSM 80-100. SATB, opt kybd.

See also the Advent seasonal listing.

CHORAL

Bouman, Paul, arr. "A Babe Is Born." CPH 98-1058.

Carter, Andrew, arr. "A Maiden Most Gentle." OXF X266. SATB, kybd.

Kellermeyer, David. "Angelic Gloria." MSM 50-1405. 2 pt, 9 hb.

Lawler, Tom. "The Long-Awaited One." GIA G-4802. U, desc, gtr, pno, 2 C inst.

Leavitt, John. "The Virgin Mary Had a Baby Boy." AFP 11-2545. SATB, opt perc.

Schalk, Carl. "Before the Marvel of This Night." AFP 11-2005. Also in *The Augsburg Choirbook.* AFP 11-10817. SATB, org.

Schalk, Carl. "Where Shepherds Lately Knelt." AFP 11-2456. SATB, kybd.

CHILDREN'S CHOIRS

Bedford, Michael. "Hodie Christus Natus Est." CG CGA-421. U/2 pt, kybd.

Bisbee, B. Wayne. "While Angels Sing." CG CGA-556. U, C trbl inst, kybd, opt fc.

Christopherson, Dorothy. "The Virgin Mary Had a Baby Boy." CPH 98-3094. U, pno, perc.

Hruby, Dolores. "Norwegian Dance Carol." AFP 11-2453. U, kybd, tamb.

Kern, Philip. "What Child Is This?" ALF 7783. SSA, kybd, opt 2 oct hb.

Proulx, Richard. "A Radiant Light." GIA G-4351. Trbl vcs, fl, ob, cello, org, opt hp.

Stroope, Z. Randall. "Sans Day Carol." CG CGA-549. 2 pt, hp/pno.

KEYBOARD/INSTRUMENTAL

Augsburg Organ Library: Christmas. AFP 11-11074.

Callahan, Charles. *The Christmas Tree.* RME EO-315. Org.

Weston, Matthew. *Five Christmas Hymns for Piano.* MSM-15-821. Pno.

Farlee, Robert Buckley. *Five Carols for Oboe and Organ.* MSM-20-161. Inst and org.

Fedak, Alfred V. *An Advent Christmas Suite.* SEL 160-112. Org.

HANDBELL

Behnke, John H. "Mary Had a Baby." RRM BL5012. 3-5 oct, opt conga drm.

Hilty, Everett J. "Bring a Torch, Jeanette, Isabella." CPH 97-6794. 3-5 oct, opt hc.

Moklebust, Cathy. "A Christmas Fiesta." CG CGB206. 3-5 oct, perc.

Morris, Hart. "Manger Lullaby." RRM HB0021. 3-5 oct, opt fl.

Sherman, Arnold B. "Christmastide" (6 Carols). RRM HB00024A (2-3 oct), HB0024B (4-5 oct).

Thompson, Martha Lynn. "'Twas in the Moon of Wintertime." AG 2100. 3-5 oct.

Wagner, Wayne L. "From Heaven Above to Earth I Come." AGEHR AG4041. 4 oct.

PRAISE ENSEMBLE

Henkelmann, Brian. "As a Child." CPH 98-3304. SATB, kybd, fl, opt children, hand drm.

Hunnicutt, Judy. "Now Tell Us, Gentle Mary." AFP 11-1659. U, fl, hb.

Larson, Lloyd. "Song of the Stars." BEC 1507. SATB, kybd.

Shaw, Kirby. "Rock Him in the Manger." HAL 08666017. SAB.

ALTERNATE WORSHIP TEXTS

CONFESSION AND FORGIVENESS

In the name of the Father, and of the ✚ Son, and of the Holy Spirit.
Amen

Amid the shadows of this world, let us confess our sin
and welcome the light of God's forgiveness.

Silence for reflection and self-examination.

God of grace and truth,
in Christ Jesus you come among us
as light shining in the darkness.
We confess that we have not welcomed the light,
nor trusted the good news of great joy.
Forgive us and renew our hope,
so that we may live in the fullness of your love,
trusting in the grace of Christ our Lord. Amen

The angel said, You shall call his name Jesus
for he will save his people from their sins.
With great joy, I announce to you
the entire forgiveness of your sins,
in the name of the Father, and of the ✚ Son, and of the Holy Spirit.
Amen

GREETING

The grace and lovingkindness of our Savior Jesus Christ,
Word made flesh, born of the virgin Mary,
be with you all.
And also with you.

OFFERTORY PRAYER

God of wonder,
we offer you these humble gifts,
signs of your goodness and mercy.
Receive them with our gratitude,
that through us all people may know
the riches of your love
in Jesus Christ our Lord. Amen

INVITATION TO COMMUNION

Always be thankful;
and let the word of Christ dwell in you richly.

POST-COMMUNION PRAYER

God of light,
with our eyes we have seen your salvation
in this holy feast you have prepared for us.
Send us forth into the world to be your holy people,
revealing your glory made known to us
in Jesus Christ our Lord.
Amen

BENEDICTION

May Christ, born into time to bring endless peace,
guide your days and years in righteousness
from this time onward and forevermore.
The Lord bless you and keep you.
The Lord's face shine on you with grace and mercy.
The Lord look upon you with favor and ✚ give you peace.
Amen

DISMISSAL

Filled with the joy of Christ's birth,
go in peace to love and serve the Lord.
Thanks be to God.

SEASONAL RITES

BLESSING OF THE NATIVITY SCENE

This blessing may be used after the sermon or after the communion of the people on Christmas Eve.

O Lord our God, with Mary and Joseph, angels and shepherds, and the animals in the stable, we gather around your Son, born for us. Bless us with your holy presence, and inspire us to help those who have no place to dwell. Be with us that we might share Christ's love with all the world, for he is our light and salvation. Glory in heaven and peace on earth, now and forever.
Amen

LESSONS AND CAROLS FOR CHRISTMAS

This service may be used during the twelve days of Christmas.

Stand
ENTRANCE HYMN
LBW 45   Oh, come, all ye faithful
WOV 643   Once in royal David's city

DIALOG
The people who walked in darkness have seen a great light.
The light shines in the darkness,
and the darkness has not overcome it.
Those who dwelt in the land of deep darkness,
on them light has shined.
We have beheld Christ's glory,
glory as of the only Son from the Father.
To us a child is born, to us a Son is given.
In him was life, and the life was the light of all people.

OPENING PRAYER
The Lord be with you.
And also with you.
Let us pray.
Almighty God, you have filled us with the new light of the Word who became flesh and lived among us. Let the light of our faith shine in all we do; through your Son, Jesus Christ our Lord, who lives and reigns with you and the Holy Spirit, one God, now and forever.
Amen

Sit
LESSONS AND CAROLS
First Reading: Isaiah 9:2-7
LBW 58   Lo, how a rose is growing
TFF 45   Emmanuel

Second Reading: Micah 5:2-5a
LBW 41   O little town of Bethlehem
TFF 58   Rise up, shepherd, and follow

Third Reading: Luke 1:26-35, 38
LBW 40   What child is this
WOV 634   Sing of Mary, pure and lowly
TFF 51   Jesus, what a wonderful child

Fourth Reading: Luke 2:1-7
WOV 642   I wonder as I wander
WOV 644   Away in a manger
TFF 53   The virgin Mary had a baby boy

Fifth Reading: Luke 2:8-16
LBW 44   Infant holy, infant lowly
WOV 636   Before the marvel of this night
TFF 55   May had a baby

Sixth Reading: Luke 2:21-36
LBW 184   In his temple now behold him
May also be sung to REGENT SQUARE, LBW 50.
TFF 54   That boy-child of Mary

Seventh Reading: Matthew 2:1-11

LBW 56	The first Noel
WOV 646	We three kings of Orient are
TFF 60	Sister Mary

Eighth Reading: Matthew 2:13-18

| WOV 639 | Oh, sleep now, holy baby |
| LLC 310 | Oh, Mary, gentle poor Mary (María, pobre María |

Ninth Reading: John 1:1-14

LBW 42	Of the Father's love begotten
LBW 57	Let our gladness have no end
TFF 37	He came down

Stand

RESPONSIVE PRAYER

Glory to God in the highest,

and peace to God's people on earth.

Blessed are you, Prince of peace.

You rule the earth with truth and justice.

Send your gift of peace to all nations of the world.

Blessed are you, Son of Mary. You share our humanity.

Have mercy on the sick, the dying, and all who suffer this day.

Blessed are you, Son of God.

You dwell among us as the Word made flesh.

Reveal yourself to us in word and sacrament

that we may bear your light to all the world.

THE LORD'S PRAYER

BLESSING AND DISMISSAL

Let us bless the Lord.

Thanks be to God.

May you be filled with the wonder of Mary, the obedience of Joseph, the joy of the angels, the eagerness of the shepherds, the determination of the magi, and the peace of the Christ child. Almighty God, Father, ✛ Son, and Holy Spirit bless you now and forever.

Amen

SENDING HYMN

| LBW 60 | Hark! The herald angels sing |
| TFF 59 | Jesus, the Light of the world |

PROCLAMATION
OF THE BIRTH OF CHRIST

Today, the twenty-fifth day of December,
unknown ages from the time when God created the heavens
and the earth and then formed man
and woman in his own image.

Several thousand years after the flood,
when God made the rainbow shine forth
as a sign of the covenant.
Twenty-one centuries from the time of Abraham and Sarah;
thirteen centuries after Moses led the people of Israel out of Egypt.

Eleven hundred years from the time of Ruth and the Judges;
one thousand years from the anointing of David as king;
in the sixty-fifth week according to the prophecy of Daniel.

In the one hundred and ninety-fourth Olympiad;
the seven hundred and fifty-second year from the foundation
of the city of Rome.

The forty-second year of the reign of Octavian Augustus;
the whole world being at peace,
Jesus Christ, the eternal God and Son of the eternal Father,
desiring to sanctify the world by his most merciful coming,
being conceived by the Holy Spirit,
and nine months having passed since his conception,
was born in Bethlehem of Judea of the Virgin Mary.

Today is the nativity of our Lord Jesus Christ according to the flesh.

SERVICE FOR NEW YEAR'S EVE

During the evening of December 31, which is the eve of the Name of Jesus and also the eve of the civil New Year, the following service may be used.

This order for worship may begin with the service of light, pp. 142-45 in LBW. The prayer of the day for New Year's Eve may replace the prayer of thanksgiving on p. 144 of LBW.

After the service of light, two or more of the following readings are used, each followed by a psalm, canticle, or hymn, and a prayer. The last reading would normally be from the New Testament.

THE HEBREW YEAR
Exodus 23:9-16, 20-21
Psalm 111 or Psalm 119:1-8
Hymn: Of the Father's love begotten (LBW 42)

Let us pray.
Silence
O God our creator, you have divided our life into days and seasons, and called us to acknowledge your providence year after year. Accept your people who come to offer their praises, and, in your mercy, receive their prayers; through Jesus Christ our Lord.
Amen

THE PROMISED LAND
Deuteronomy 11:8-12, 26-28
Psalm 36:5-10 or Psalm 89:1-18
Hymn: Lift every voice and sing (LBW 562)

Let us pray.
Silence
Almighty God, the source of all life, giver of all blessing, and savior of all who turn to you: Have mercy upon this nation; deliver us from falsehood, malice, and disobedience; turn our feet into your paths; and grant that we may serve you in peace; through Jesus Christ our Lord.
Amen

A SEASON FOR ALL THINGS
Ecclesiastes 3:1-13
Psalm 90 or Psalm 8
Hymn: Day by day (WOV 746)

Let us pray.
Silence
In your wisdom, O Lord our God, you have made all things and have allotted to each of us the days of our life. Grant that we may live in your presence, be guided by your Holy Spirit, and offer all our works to your honor and glory; through Jesus Christ our Lord.
Amen

REMEMBER YOUR CREATOR
Ecclesiastes 12:1-8
Psalm 130
Hymn: O God, our help in ages past (LBW 320)

Let us pray.
Silence
Immortal Lord God, you inhabit eternity and have brought us your unworthy servants to the close of another year. Pardon, we entreat you, our transgressions of the past, and graciously abide with us all the days of our life; through Jesus Christ our Lord.
Amen

MARKING THE TIMES AND WINTER
Sirach 43:1-22
Psalm 19 or Psalm 148
Hymn: 'Twas in the moon of wintertime (LBW 72)

Let us pray.
Silence
Almighty Father, you give the sun for a light by day and the moon and the stars by night. Graciously receive us, this night and always, into your favor and protection, defending us from all harm and governing us with your Holy Spirit, that every shadow of ignorance, every failure of faith or weakness of heart, every evil or wrong desire may be removed far from us; so that we, being justified in our Lord Jesus Christ, may be sanctified by your Spirit and glorified by your infinite mercies in the day of the glorious appearing of our Lord and Savior Jesus Christ.
Amen

THE ACCEPTABLE TIME

2 Corinthians 5:17—6:2

Psalm 63:1-8

Hymn: Greet now the swiftly changing year (LBW 181)

Let us pray.

Silence

Most gracious and merciful God, you have reconciled us to yourself through Jesus Christ your Son and called us to new life in him. Grant that we, who begin this year in his name, may complete it to his honor and glory; who lives and reigns now and forever.

Amen

A THOUSAND YEARS AS ONE DAY

2 Peter 3:8-15a

Psalm 119:89-96

Hymn: The Lord will come and not be slow (LBW 318; *alternate tune:* CAROL, LBW 54)

Let us pray.

Silence

O God, through your Son you have taught us to be watchful and to await the sudden day of judgment. Strengthen us against Satan and his forces of wickedness, the evil powers of this world, and the sinful desires within us; grant that, having served you all the days of our life, we may finally come to the dwelling place your Son has prepared for us; who lives and reigns forever and ever.

Amen

NEW HEAVENS AND NEW EARTH

Revelation 21:1-6a

LBW Canticle 21

Hymn: O Christ the same (WOV 778)

Let us pray.

Silence

Almighty and merciful God, through your well-beloved Son Jesus Christ, the King of kings and Lord of lords, you have willed to make all things new. Grant that we may be renewed by your Holy Spirit and may come at last to that heavenly country where your people hunger and thirst no more and the tears are wiped away from every eye; through Jesus Christ our Lord.

Amen

A homily, sermon, or instruction may follow the readings.

An affirmation of baptism may follow, using the form provided on pp. 198–201 of LBW. Begin with 12 on p. 199 and continue to the end of that order.

The service may conclude in either of the following ways: with the singing of a hymn of praise, followed by the Lord's Prayer, the prayer of the day for the Name of Jesus, and benediction (see LBW, p. 152); or with communion, beginning with the offering.

Adapted from *The Book of Occasional Services,* 1994 edition, Church Hymnal Corporation.

68

DECEMBER 24, 2000

THE NATIVITY OF OUR LORD
CHRISTMAS EVE (I)

INTRODUCTION

The miracle happens in the dark. A cold stable, inky night, and tired shepherds—all is jolted to a new awakening when God comes among us! We, too, are greeted with angel song as Christ makes his way among us in an old story, in miracles of bread and wine, in the wondrous fellowship of flesh-and-blood people called together to be a body for Christ.

PRAYER OF THE DAY

Almighty God, you made this holy night shine with the brightness of the true Light. Grant that here on earth we may walk in the light of Jesus' presence and in the last day wake to the brightness of his glory; through your only Son, Jesus Christ our Lord, who lives and reigns with you and the Holy Spirit, one God, now and forever.

READINGS

Isaiah 9:2-7

Originally this poem was written to celebrate either the birth or the coronation of a new king in David's line. After the fall of Jerusalem, this poem came to be viewed as an expression of the hope that eventually God would raise up a new ruler who would possess the qualities described in the text.

Psalm 96

Let the heavens rejoice and the earth be glad. (Ps. 96:11)

Titus 2:11-14

The appearance of God's grace is an invitation for God's people to live a life worthy of the new age inaugurated in Jesus.

Luke 2:1-14 [15-20]

Luke tells the story of Jesus' birth with reference to rulers of the world because his birth has significance for the whole earth, conveying a divine offering of peace.

COLOR   White

THE PRAYERS

As we celebrate the mystery of the Word made flesh, let us place our needs before the Creator of heaven and earth.
A BRIEF SILENCE.

Let us pray that the light of Christ will shine brightly in the words and deeds of Christians throughout the world. Lord, in your mercy,
hear our prayer.

Let us pray for artists and musicians who reveal the presence of the Word made flesh, that their ministry will enrich our worship and help us offer thanksgiving to God. Lord, in your mercy,
hear our prayer.

Let us pray for the rulers of every land, that they protect and uphold justice for those who are poor and in need. Lord, in your mercy,
hear our prayer.

Let us pray that Christ, born for our health and salvation, will enlighten those who are sick (especially…). Lord, in your mercy,
hear our prayer.

Let us pray for visitors and travelers who join us in worship, that they be welcomed as Christ and return to their homes in safety. Lord, in your mercy,
hear our prayer.

HERE OTHER INTERCESSIONS MAY BE OFFERED.

On this holy night, let us remember with thanksgiving our beloved dead who, marked with the sign of Christ, now rest in God's eternal mercy. Lord, in your mercy,
hear our prayer.

Receive our prayers, gracious God, and fill us with hope as we behold your presence among us in Jesus Christ our Lord.
Amen

IMAGES FOR PREACHING

Can you imagine if you had been one of the shepherds out on the hillside keeping watch over your sheep when an angel appears to you saying not to be afraid? And as if that is not enough, a whole choir of angels suddenly appears, praising God with sounds and sights beyond your experience.

Perhaps the story would have ended right there had the angel choir only appeared to one solitary shepherd out in the field. Just how many shepherds saw the sight,

69

we do not know, but enough shepherds for them all to have figured out that it was not a strange dream or the result of being a bit inebriated.

So, naturally, the shepherds ran like mad into Bethlehem, where the angel had told them a miracle would be found. When they got there they saw with their own eyes the Son of God lying in a simple manger. All of those gathered around were amazed by the shepherds' story.

We can imagine the shepherds days later trying to explain the whole incident to others. "But it *was* real, I tell you. We all saw and heard the same thing with our own eyes. It was simply the most amazing thing that ever occurred."

Yes, it was the most amazing thing that ever happened. And God kept appearing to even more folks along the way. Nearly everywhere Jesus went he caused a bit of a stir with his words, miraculous healings, and powerful signs of God's presence.

Because of the faith of shepherds and the faith of a handful of disciples, the church came into being decades later. The strange and unusual beginning of an appearance to shepherds, on a lonely hillside outside of Bethlehem, eventually turned into one of the farthest reaching stories of all time.

The church continues to grow because people come together to listen to one another's stories like this one. We encourage one another to go on and tell them, even in the midst of those who do not believe us.

WORSHIP MATTERS

At Christmas we join in singing the song of the angels: "Glory to God in the highest heaven. . . ." It is a song that many congregations sing weekly in the liturgy. As we come into Christ's presence in word and sacrament, we stand back with awe and amazement and sing this ancient angelic hymn. Is "Glory to God" something that your congregation sings with joy the year around, and especially during this season? How might the majesty of this grand song enter into even the humblest places?

LET THE CHILDREN COME

In one of the liturgy's hymns of praise we celebrate Christmas. "Glory to God in the highest" is the song of the angels at Jesus' birth. We remind ourselves of their song and the joy of Christmas every time we sing these words. It is a celebration of God's Son coming to earth,

and the awe of the shepherds as they saw the sky lit by angels. So celebrate Christmas with the angels tonight and every Sunday.

MUSIC FOR WORSHIP
GATHERING

LBW 45	Oh, come, all ye faithful
WOV 643	Once in royal David's city

PSALM 96

TFF 10   Let the heavens rejoice

Christopherson, Dorothy. "The Lord Is King." AFP 11-10173. U, opt cong, kybd.

Daw, Carl P. Jr., and Kevin R. Hackett. *A Hymn Tune Psalter.* Church Publishing Inc.

Haugen, Marty. "Today Is Born Our Savior" in PCY, vol. 2. U/SATB, kybd, solo, opt cong, gtr.

Hobby, Robert. PW, Cycle C.

Inwood, Paul. "Psalm 96: Today Is Born Our Savior" in STP, vol. 1.

Marchionda, James V. *Psalms for the Cantor, vol. III.* WLP 2504.

HYMN OF THE DAY

LBW 47	Let all together praise our God
	LOBT GOTT, IHR CHRISTEN

VOCAL RESOURCES

Gieseke, Richard. "Let All Together Praise Our God." CPH 98-2640. SATB, tpt, kybd, cong.

Kosche, Kenneth. "Let All Together Praise Our God" in *Hymn Stanzas for Choirs, Set 2.* CPH 97-6814. SAB, kybd.

INSTRUMENTAL RESOURCES

Elmshauser, Dale. "Let All Together Praise Our God." LOH 446-0123. Brass.

Manz, Paul. "Let All Together Praise Our God" in *Improvisations for the Christmas Seasons, Set 3.*

Sampson, David. "Let All Together Praise Our God" in *Trumpet Descants for Christmas Hymns.* CPH 97-5780. Org, tpt.

Schein/ed. Thomas. "Lobt Gott, ihr Christen" in *The Praise of Christmas,* vol. 1. CPH 97-5050. Kbd, 2 inst.

ALTERNATE HYMN OF THE DAY

LBW 51	From heaven above
WOV 636	Before the marvel of this night

COMMUNION

LBW 61	The hills are bare at Bethlehem
WOV 636	Before the marvel of this night

SENDING

LBW 65	Silent night, holy night!
WOV 638	Holy Child within the manger

ADDITIONAL HYMNS AND SONGS

ASG 32	One sacred moment
REJ 222	To us in Bethlehem city
TFF 56	Hush, little Jesus boy
W&P 57	Hear the angels

MUSIC FOR THE DAY

CHORAL

Bach, J. S. "From Heaven Above to Earth I Come" in BAS. SATB, kybd.

Bach, J. S. "Gloria in excelsis Deo" in BAS. SATB, kybd, opt C inst.

Brandvik, Paul. "What Is This Fragrance." AFP 11-10954. SATB.

Distler, Hugo. "Lo, How are Rose E'er Blooming" in CC. SATB.

Eccard, Johann. "Raise a Song, Let Praise Resound" in CC. SATB.

Hassler, Hans Leo. "Cantate Domino" in CC. SATB.

Hyslop, Scott M. "The Christmas Candles Glow." AFP 11-10956. SATB, org, fl.

Praetorius, Michael. "Psallite" in CC. SATB.

Schalk, Carl. "Before the Marvel of This Night." AFP 11-2005. SATB, kybd.

Schalk, Carl. "The Child Lay in the Cloth and Hay." AFP 11-2434. SATB, org, opt str.

CHILDREN'S CHOIRS

Colvin, Tom. "That Boy-Child of Mary" in LS.

Grotenhuis, Dale. "Lullaby, Sleep in Peace." MSM-50-1404. SA, pno.

Lindh, Jody W. "The Snow Lay on the Ground." CG CGA636. U/SATB, kybd.

Rutter, John. "Angels' Carol." HIN HMC-986. 2 pt, hp/pno.

KEYBOARD/INSTRUMENTAL

Osterlund, Karl. "A la ru" in *I Wonder As I Wander.* AFP 11-10858. Org.

Walcha, Helmut. "Von Himmel hoch da komm ich her" in *Chorale Preludes,* vol. II. PET 4871. Org.

Wold, Wayne L. "Once in Royal David's City" in *God with Us.* AFP 11-10975. Org.

HANDBELL

Beck, Theodore. "O Sleep Now, Holy Baby" and "O Come, Little Children." AFP 11-10521. 2 oct.

McFadden, Jane. "A la ru." AGEHR AG35119. 3-5 oct, opt gtr.

Page, Anna Laura. "Once in Royal David's City." ALF 12417. 3-5 oct.

Page, Anna Laura. "Fanfare for Christmas." RRM. 3-5 oct, brass, org.

Young, Philip M. "Sussex Carol." BEC HB38. 4-5 oct.

PRAISE ENSEMBLE

Armstrong, Matthew. "Wondrous Night." CPH 98-3303. SATB, kybd.

James, Stephen. "Sing, Sing, Sing to the Lord" in *Worship Songs.* HOP.

Kantor, Daniel. "Night of Silence" in W&P.

Kee, Ed. "Come, Give Glory to the Lord" in *Sing & Rejoice.* BNT.

DECEMBER 25, 2000

THE NATIVITY OF OUR LORD

CHRISTMAS DAWN (II)

INTRODUCTION

The miracle happens in the dawn. "Glory to God in the highest!" the angels sing. We echo their song in our hymn of praise. The light that springs upon us at God's arrival invites us to greet this new day with joy. Christ the Savior is born—and in baptism we too are born into eternal life.

PRAYER OF THE DAY

Almighty God, you have made yourself known in your Son, Jesus, redeemer of the world. We pray that his birth as a human child will set us free from the old slavery of our sin; through Jesus Christ our Lord, who lives and reigns with you and the Holy Spirit, one God, now and forever.

READINGS

Isaiah 62:6-12

When Israel returned from exile and Jerusalem still lay in ruins, the prophet invited God's people to imagine the city's restoration.

Psalm 97

Light has sprung up for the righteous. (Ps. 97:11)

Titus 3:4-7

Salvation is a free and gracious gift from God. In baptism, God's people have a new birth with Christ.

Luke 2:[1-7] 8-20

The darkness of the world is shattered by the light of God's new day. Shepherds not only come to the manger to see what has happened; they also return to share the good news with others.

COLOR   White

THE PRAYERS

As we celebrate the mystery of the Word made flesh, let us place our needs before the Creator of heaven and earth.
A BRIEF SILENCE.

Let us pray that we will eagerly welcome the dawn of God's justice and peace in Christ Jesus our Savior. Lord, in your mercy,
hear our prayer.

Let us pray for our children, that they will always be guided in life by the light of Christ's word and holy supper. Lord, in your mercy,
hear our prayer.

Let us pray for the poor and powerless people of this world, that they will be welcomed at the manger of the Lord and know his great love. Lord, in your mercy,
hear our prayer.

Let us pray for those ignored by society, that like the shepherds they will hear the good news of Christ and discover in him their eternal dignity. Lord, in your mercy,
hear our prayer.

Let us pray for those who dwell in the shadows of death and all who suffer (especially . . .), that they will receive Christ's unfailing light and abiding mercy. Lord, in your mercy,
hear our prayer.
HERE OTHER INTERCESSIONS MAY BE OFFERED.

Let us remember with thanksgiving all our beloved dead who have revealed to us the light of Christ and now dwell in the brightness of his glory. Lord, in your mercy,
hear our prayer.

Receive our prayers, gracious God, and fill us with hope as we behold your presence among us in Jesus Christ our Lord.
Amen

IMAGES FOR PREACHING

In one way or another, most of us have seen evidence of Christ's appearance in our lives. Maybe we have not actually seen angels with their wings flapping, but we have seen signs nonetheless. We have seen signs for ourselves of God's miraculous salvation. We have seen how even in the most difficult of times, someone can reach out to us and say something that gives us strength.

The church has often provided us with a place where we can say to one another, "Did you see that? Have you seen God acting in your life as God has been acting in mine?" And so it is that God often comes to us. No, it may not be as dramatic as God's coming with the presence of an angel choir on a hillside outside of Bethlehem. But God is made known to us in many ways, and we need to be able to talk about those occurrences with one another.

So we come together to check out the story we have all heard in one way or another. We come together essentially to ask one another, "Did you see what I've seen? Have you heard the great news that I've heard too?"

If we were left alone in our faith, it might be too difficult for any of us to believe. The only way we are going to spread peace and goodwill to the rest of the world is if we hang together. If we are going to succeed in believing the miracle of God's presence with us, day after day we must keep reminding one another of the peace and goodwill that comes only from Christ. "Have you seen what I've seen?" Good! Now let us get to work sharing this message, so that others may also come to believe in the miracle we have all seen with our own eyes.

WORSHIP MATTERS

As the shepherds returned to their homes glorifying and praising God, so we return from our worship telling the good news of what we have seen and heard. The Christmas gospel contains a story that must be told to others. In what ways do we announce this good news to our communities? In what ways have our congregations invited others to join us? Encourage members of the congregation to invite neighbors and acquaintances to attend worship services and other gatherings throughout the year. Be especially prepared to welcome guests during this season as well.

LET THE CHILDREN COME

The shepherds were scared, doubting, and unbelieving, but they were finally convinced. What an amazing message the angels brought to them! Maybe it is true; maybe they should go to Bethlehem and look for this Messiah. They went to the barn and bowed before the baby. Then they returned to their hillsides, to their jobs watching sheep. We too go out from worship and tell the good news: a savior is born to humankind. Use a cardboard cutout of a shepherd's crook to remind us of this shepherd's story.

MUSIC FOR WORSHIP
SERVICE MUSIC

Hymn paraphrases of portions of the service music are useful at an early Christmas day service. Consider "Glory to God, we give you thanks" (WOV 787) or "Angels we have heard on high" (LBW 71) as the hymn of praise. "Rejoice, rejoice this happy morn" (LBW 43) can be a brief and fitting offertory or post-communion song.

GATHERING

| LBW 60 | Hark! The herald angels sing |
| LBW 73 | All hail to you, O blessed morn! |

PSALM 97

Cooney, Rory. "The Lord Is King" in STP, vol. 4.

Haas, David. "Psalm 97: Our God Is Here" in PCY, vol. 9.

Hobby, Robert. PW, Cycle C.

Hopson, Hal H. "Psalm 97" in *Psalm Refrains and Tones for the Common Lectionary*. HOP 425.

Marcus, Mary. "The Nativity of Our Lord/Christmas Day" in *Psalm Antiphons 2*. MSM 80-722.

See also the seventh Sunday of Easter.

HYMN OF THE DAY

| WOV 643 | Once in royal David's city |
| | IRBY |

VOCAL RESOURCES

Proulx, Richard. "Once in Royal David's City." AFP 11-1754. SATB, org, fl.

Willcocks, David. "Once in Royal David's City" in *100 Carols for Choirs*. OXP ISBN 0-19-353227-1. SATB, desc, org.

INSTRUMENTAL RESOURCES

Albrecht, Timothy L. "Once in Royal David's City" in *Grace Notes VII*. AFP 11-10975. Org.

Wold, Wayne L. "Once in Royal David's City" in *God with Us*. AFP 11-10975. Org.

Wolff, S. Drummond. "Irby" in *Hymn Descants, Set I*. CPH 97-6051. Org, inst.

ALTERNATE HYMN OF THE DAY

| LBW 66 | Come rejoicing, praises voicing |
| WOV 638 | Holy Child within the manger |

COMMUNION

| LBW 40 | What child is this |
| LBW 52 | Your little ones, dear Lord |

SENDING

| LBW 70 | Go tell it on the mountain |
| WOV 645 | There's a star in the East |

ADDITIONAL HYMNS AND SONGS

H82	Christians, awake, salute the happy morn
TFF 59	Jesus, the Light of the world
UMH 235	Rock-a-bye, my dear little boy
W&P 73	I will sing, I will sing

MUSIC FOR THE DAY
CHORAL

Bach, J. S. "Break Forth, O Beauteous Heavenly Light" in BAS. SATB.

Oliver, Curt. "Born Is the Babe." MSM 50-1110. SAB.

Pergolesi, G. B. "Glory to God in the Highest." LOR 7380. SAB, org.

Proulx, Richard. "From Bethlehem Fair City." GIA G-4155. SATB.

White, Nicholas. "Poor Little Jesus." AFP 11-10955. SATB.

Willan, Healey, arr. "What Is This Lovely Fragrance?" OXF 42.171. SATB, kybd.

CHILDREN'S CHOIRS

African American spiritual. "Go Tell It on the Mountain" in LS.

Cherwien, David. "On This Day Earth Shall Ring!" CPH 98-3208. 2 pt, org, opt 3 oct hb.

Ferguson, John. "Angels We Have Heard on High" in *Two Carols*. AFP 11-2080. SATB, opt hb.

Scholz, Robert. "Listen, Hear the News." MFS YS 302. U/SA, kybd, opt inst.

KEYBOARD/INSTRUMENTAL

Drischner, Max. *Partitas on Two Christmas Songs* ("Es ist ein Ros" and "In Dulci Jubilo"). C. L. S. Schultheiss CLS 170. Org or kybd.

Ireland, John. "The Holy Boy" in *Organ Music of John Ireland*. NOV. Also in *The Oxford Book of Christmas Organ Music*, ed. Robert Gower. OXF. Org.

Reger, Max. "Weihnachten." Breitkopf & Härtel, 2270. Org, fl, vc.

HANDBELL

McFadden, Jane. "Pastorale on 'Lo, How a Rose E'er Blooming.'" AFP 11-10522. 3-5 oct.

PRAISE ENSEMBLE

Cain, Robin, and Phil Kadidlo. "Hear the Angels" in W&P.

Courtney, Craig, and Pamela Martin. "The Gift." BEC BP1558. SATB, kybd.

Hanson, Handt, and Paul Murakami. "Jesus Is Born" in *Spirit Touching Spirit*. CCF.

73

DECEMBER 25, 2000

INTRODUCTION

The miracle happens in the bright light of day. Where God is, it is day. The light shining in the darkness is a sign of new creation, and the Word that is flesh is among us also in bread and wine and even in our own humanity born anew from God.

PRAYER OF THE DAY

Almighty God, you wonderfully created and yet more wonderfully restored the dignity of human nature. In your mercy, let us share the divine life of Jesus Christ who came to share our humanity, and who now lives and reigns with you and the Holy Spirit, one God, now and forever.

READINGS

Isaiah 52:7-10

Changing events in Babylon inspire this announcement of hope and joy to the people of Judah near the end of their exile. "Your God reigns," says the prophet. It is not some Babylonian god who rules. It is the dawn of comfort, redemption, and the salvation of our God.

Psalm 98

All the ends of the earth have seen the victory of our God. (Ps. 98:4)

Hebrews 1:1-4 [5-12]

The letter to the Hebrews begins with a strong affirmation of Jesus as the Son of God. To call Jesus God's Son is to recognize that he is superior even to prophets and angels.

John 1:1-14

The poetic opening words of John's gospel refer to Jesus as the Word that became flesh—that is, the one whose human existence incorporates God's very self.

COLOR   White

THE PRAYERS

As we celebrate the mystery of the Word made flesh, let us place our needs before the Creator of heaven and earth.

A BRIEF SILENCE.

O God, maker of all that is, fill your church with grace, that in word and deed we may proclaim your gospel to the ends of the earth. Lord, in your mercy,
hear our prayer.

O God, ruler of the universe, send your holy gift of peace upon our world, that all people might sing your praise. Lord, in your mercy,
hear our prayer.

O God, source of all life, comfort those who suffer with sickness (especially...). Heal them of anything that would prevent them from trusting in your saving power. Lord, in your mercy,
hear our prayer.

O God, guardian of the poor, strengthen us in our service to those who are homeless and hungry. Lord, in your mercy,
hear our prayer.

HERE OTHER INTERCESSIONS MAY BE OFFERED.

O God, redeemer of the world, nourish us with your living word and holy meal, and bring us to endless life with all the saints. Lord, in your mercy,
hear our prayer.

Receive our prayers, gracious God, and fill us with hope as we behold your presence among us in Jesus Christ our Lord.
Amen

IMAGES FOR PREACHING

Service people who make house calls in today's world seem to be a dying breed. More often than not we may need to call several different places before we find the right person who has the time to help us have something fixed in our own home or workplace.

Was not Jesus' birth really about God coming to visit our broken world in order to fix it and make it work as good as new? The despair of our world has been given an elaborate fix in the person of Jesus Christ. In a world where no one seems to make house calls the way they used to, here is Jesus, coming into our lives. And on a holiday, no less!

As you can imagine, it takes an incredible army of

helpers to pull off such an operation. People need to be trained and encouraged to do this work. Every neighborhood needs folks who are skilled in caregiving and offering their love to persons in need.

Being able to enter into all the places where people are hurting and in need of comfort is no small task. Thousands—even millions—of technicians are needed everywhere to be placed into action whenever a call comes in.

People will always have a need for the visiting nurse and the caring friend or church member who enters into their world and deals with their problems in their own home. When people are no longer able to come to church, the church is able to come to them. We have wheels. We are flexible. We can go wherever we are needed.

We now are sent to shed that same light into all of the dark corners of our world. This mission is kind of an anomaly in what many think is an increasingly impersonal world. That is also why, more than ever before, the world needs Jesus and the ministry that his church brings.

WORSHIP MATTERS

Taking our cue from the opening lines of John's magnificent gospel, Christians celebrate Jesus as God's incarnate Word. Consequently the *Word* means much more to us than simply the Bible or words that are spoken about God. How do we honor the presence of the Word of God in our midst? Are we mindful that our readings from scripture, our preaching, and in fact all of our public worship gathers us around God's Word? Do we treat symbols of that presence of Christ, especially Bibles or lectionaries used in proclaiming the readings, with reverence? Do we take care in the training of lectors and all worship leaders who guide people into an experience with God's Word made flesh?

LET THE CHILDREN COME

God loves us so much that God sent Jesus to help us love. Jesus, as a human, tells us the words of God's love, and the story is in the Bible. Make three-inch construction paper hearts with "God's love" printed on them; then add stickers of a manger. Explain that through the words of the Bible Jesus brought us the story of God's love.

MUSIC FOR WORSHIP

SERVICE MUSIC

Even though Christmas morning comes early for those who have attended a late night service, people love to "hear the bells on Christmas Day." Crown festive portions of the service music (hymn of praise, gospel acclamation, Sanctus) with a random ring of handbells. Even the tower bells (if you are blessed to have them) could join on the Sanctus.

GATHERING

LBW 39	Joy to the world
LBW 46	Once again my heart rejoices

PSALM 98

Colgan, Tobias. "Psalm 98: Joyfully Give Praise To God" in STP, vol. 2.

Haugen, Marty. "All the Ends of the Earth" in PCY, vol. 1.

Hobby, Robert. PW, Cycle C.

Hruby, Dolores. *Seasonal Psalms for Children with Optional Orff.* WLP 7102.

Smith, Timothy R. "Ps. 98: The Lord Has Revealed" in STP, vol. 4.

LBW 39   Joy to the world

HYMN OF THE DAY

LBW 42	Of the Father's love begotten
	DIVINUM MYSTERIUM

VOCAL RESOURCES

Kosche, Kenneth T. "Of the Father's Love Begotten" in *Hymn Stanzas for Choirs, Set 2*. CPH 97-6814. SAB, kybd.

INSTRUMENTAL RESOURCES

Cherwien, David. "Divinum mysterium" in *Gotta Toccata: Three Toccatas for Organ*. AFP 11-11008. Org.

Fedak, Alfred V. *Divinum Mysterium*. SEL 160-116. Org.

Hyslop, Scott M. "Divinum mysterium" in *Six Chorale Fantasias for Solo Instrument and Piano*. AFP 11-10799. Pno, inst.

Owens, Sam Batt. "Divinum mysterium" in *Six Meditations on Plainsong Melodies*. MSM-10-531. Org.

Rose, Richard. "Divinum mysterium" in *Hymnal Companion for Woodwinds, Brass and Percussion, Series 1*. CPH 97-6710. Inst.

ALTERNATE HYMN OF THE DAY

LBW 48	All praise to you, eternal Lord
WOV 633	Awake, awake, and greet the new morn

COMMUNION

LBW 62	The bells of Christmas
WOV 701	What feast of love

75

SENDING

| LBW 70 | Go tell it on the mountain |
| LBW 53 | Cold December flies away |

ADDITIONAL HYMNS AND SONGS

LLC 297	Glory in the highest
TFF 53	The virgin Mary had a baby boy
VU 57	Oh, how joyfully
W&P 39	For God so loved
W&P 138	The trees of the field

MUSIC FOR THE DAY

CHORAL

Bach, J. S. "O Little One, Sweet" in *100 Carols for Choirs*. OXF ISBN 0-19-353277-1.

Distler, Hugo. "Now to Us a Child Is Born" in CC. SATB.

Manz, Paul. "Peace Came to Earth." MSM 50-1020. SATB, opt cong, org.

Praetorius, Michael. "To Us Is Born Emmanuel" in CC.

Roberts, Paul. "The Word Became Flesh" in *The Augsburg Choirbook*. AFP 11-10817. SATB, fl.

Schalk, Carl. "Where Shepherds Lately Knelt." AFP 11-2456. SATB, org.

Sedio, Mark. "There Is No Rose of Such Vertu." AFP 11-10784. SATB, org.

CHILDREN'S CHOIRS

Burkhardt, Michael. "Sing We Now of Christmas" in LS.

Grotenhuis, Dale. "Infant Holy, Infant Lowly." MSM-50-1402. SA, fl, org.

Jacobson, Borghild. "Oh, Mary, Rock the Word Made Flesh" in *Five Christmas Songs, Set I*. MSM-50-1800. U, kybd.

Marshall, Jane. "Psalm 98." CG CGA-427. U antiphonal, kybd.

Shute, Linda Cable. "He Is Born." AFP 11-10461. 2 pt, kybd.

KEYBOARD/INSTRUMENTAL

Corelli/Mitchell-Wallace & Head. "Suite from Christmas Concerto" in *Christmas Majesty*. HOP 313. Org, tpt.

Visser, Larry. *Four French Couplets on "Angels We Have Heard on High."* ECS WL600077. Org.

Yon, Pietro A. "Gesu Bambino." Fischer 4518-4. Org.

HANDBELL

Buckwalter, Karen. "Infant Holy." BEC HB-174. 3-5 oct, kybd.

Gramann, Fred. "Sing We All Noel." HOP Agape 1608. 3-4 oct.

Helman, Michael. "Rise Up, Shepherd." AFP 11-10721. 2-3 oct.

McChesney, Kevin. "Joy to the World." AFP 11-10472. 3-5 oct.

Page, Anna Laura. "In Dulci Jubilo." CG CGB198. 3-5 oct, opt hc.

PRAISE ENSEMBLE

Haas, David. "God Has Done Marvelous Things" (W&P 51). GIA G-4731.

Hanson, Handt, and Paul Murakami. "Jesus Is Born" in *Spirit Touching Spirit*. CCF.

Smith, Michael W. and Amy Grant/arr. David T. Clydesdale. "Praise to God, Whose Love Was Shown." MEA 3100004167. SATB, kybd.

TUESDAY, DECEMBER 26
ST. STEPHEN, DEACON AND MARTYR

St. Stephen was a deacon and the first martyr of the church. He was one of those seven upon whom the apostles laid hands after they had been chosen to serve widows and others in need. Later, Stephen's preaching angered the temple authorities, and they ordered him to be put to death by stoning.

The Christmas song "Good King Wenceslas" takes place on the feast of Stephen. The king sees a peasant gathering wood near the forest and sends his page to invite the peasant to a feast. The song, with its theme of charity to the poor, can be a way to remember St. Stephen, who cared for widows and those in need. Congregations and families within them can be invited to include gifts to charitable organizations during these days of Christmas in honor of St. Stephen.

WEDNESDAY, DECEMBER 27
ST. JOHN, APOSTLE AND EVANGELIST

John, the son of Zebedee, was a fisherman and one of the twelve. John, his brother James, and Peter were the three who witnessed the light of the Transfiguration. John and James once made known their desire to hold positions of power in the kingdom of God. Jesus' response showed them that service to others was the sign of God's reign in the world. Though authorship of the gospel and the three epistles bearing his name has often been attributed to the apostle John, this tradition cannot be proven from scriptural evidence.

John is a saint for Christmas through his proclamation that the Word became flesh and dwelt among us, that the light of God shines in the darkness, and that we are called to love one another as Christ has loved us. According to an early story about John, his enemies once tried to murder him with poisoned wine. On this day, many Christians in Europe will toast one another with the words "I drink to the love of John."

THURSDAY, DECEMBER 28
THE HOLY INNOCENTS, MARTYRS

In a culture where Christmas is overcommercialized and sentimentalized, the commemoration of the Holy Innocents, Martyrs on the fourth day of Christmas must come as something of a shock. How could the birth of a baby be the occasion for the death of anyone? Yet these martyrs were the children of Bethlehem, two years old and younger, who were killed by Herod, who worried that his reign was threatened by the birth of a new king. St. Augustine called these innocents "buds, killed by the frost of persecution the moment they showed themselves." Those linked to Jesus through their youth and innocence encounter the same hostility Jesus encounters later in his ministry.

Remembering all innocent victims and taking up the words of the prayer of the day, which ask God to "frustrate the designs of evil tyrants and establish your rule of justice, love, and peace," can mark this commemoration.

DECEMBER 31, 2000
FIRST SUNDAY AFTER CHRISTMAS

77

INTRODUCTION

During Christmastide, our attention is drawn to the holy family: Jesus, Mary, and Joseph. We, too, are God's children and part of a holy family, set apart through the baptismal waters in which we have been washed. As we end one year and begin another, we ask how God's likeness in Christ may become more visible in us, God's new offspring.

PRAYER OF THE DAY

Almighty God, you have made yourself known in your Son, Jesus, redeemer of the world. We pray that his birth as a human child will set us free from the old slavery of our sin; through Jesus Christ our Lord, who lives and reigns with you and the Holy Spirit, one God, now and forever.
or
Almighty God, you wonderfully created and yet more wonderfully restored the dignity of human nature. In your mercy, let us share the divine life of Jesus Christ who came to share our humanity, and who now lives and reigns with you and the Holy Spirit, one God, now and forever.

READINGS

1 Samuel 2:18-20, 26

Like Mary and Joseph in the gospel text, Hannah and Elkanah were faithful parents. At the time of their annual pilgrimage to visit their son, the high priest blesses them with a prayer for more children in return for the dedication of Samuel.

Psalm 148

The splendor of the LORD is over earth and heaven. (Ps. 148:13)

Colossians 3:12-17

Just as newly baptized Christians in the early church were clothed with white robes upon arising from the baptismal waters, so all who have received God's gift of life in Jesus Christ are clothed with those qualities that reflect the Lord's presence.

Luke 2:41-52

Jesus grew up in a family that went to the Passover festival each year. Their faithful adherence to the law provided a healthy environment for the young Jesus to grow into spiritual maturity.

COLOR   White

THE PRAYERS

As we celebrate the mystery of the Word made flesh, let us place our needs before the Creator of heaven and earth.
A BRIEF SILENCE.
For the leaders of nations, that they follow in the path of the Prince of Peace, let us pray to the Lord.
Lord, have mercy.
For bishops, pastors, and all who serve in the church, that they guide and support the flock of Christ with humility and compassion, let us pray to the Lord.

Lord, have mercy.

For teachers, that they lead our children to the riches of Christ's wisdom and love, let us pray to the Lord.

Lord, have mercy.

For Christian homes where Christ is welcomed in the stranger and the poor, let us pray to the Lord.

Lord, have mercy.

For those who mourn the loss of children and look for strength and healing, let us pray to the Lord.

Lord, have mercy.

For those who struggle with illness (especially . . .) and all who seek God's wisdom amid their suffering, let us pray to the Lord.

Lord, have mercy.

HERE OTHER INTERCESSIONS MAY BE OFFERED.

For this community of faith that rejoices in the birth of the Savior and looks for the day of his final coming, let us pray to the Lord.

Lord, have mercy.

Receive our prayers, gracious God, and fill us with hope as we behold your presence among us in Jesus Christ our Lord.

Amen

IMAGES FOR PREACHING

"Now the boy Samuel continued to grow both in stature and in favor with the Lord and with the people" (1 Sam. 2:26).

"And Jesus increased in wisdom and in years, and in divine and human favor" (Luke 2:52).

We find both Samuel and Jesus in the house of the Lord. Samuel is ministering before the Lord; Jesus is instructing the elders. With Jesus, it is clear that nothing is more important than the work he is doing in his Father's house.

How can these stories speak of the birth of Christ among us in these Sundays after Christmas? Can these youths be images of Christmas for us now that the celebration of Christmas has come and gone for many people? Colossians exhorts us today to continue to praise God and teach one another. "Let the word of Christ dwell in you richly; teach and admonish one another in all wisdom; and with gratitude in your hearts sing psalms, hymns, and spiritual songs to God."

Perhaps Paul is inviting us to let the stories of the boy Samuel and the boy Jesus become our story as well.

Though the busyness of these holy days may diminish, still is anything more important for us than to be in the house of Jesus' Father, teaching and ministering to one another? For Christ, the Word, has come to dwell with us. And, like Samuel and Jesus, as we dwell with him in the house of God's people we too may discover that together we grow in the wisdom of the Lord.

WORSHIP MATTERS

Children learn to pray through a pattern of daily prayer in the home. Meal times and bed times are the most obvious moments for prayer, but other occasions invite prayer as well—a prayer of thanksgiving for creation after an enjoyable walk outdoors, prayer upon learning of a relative's illness, prayer after seeing a troubling story in the news. All these spontaneous opportunities for prayer yoke daily life events to faith. Simple words used on these occasions can also teach that prayer is much like talking to a friend.

LET THE CHILDREN COME

Light some candles in your house. It will remind us of God's presence among us at this holiday season. Light a candle on the kitchen or dining room table. Before eating, say "The Lord be with you." Respond with "And also with you." Then comes the blessing of the meal. Establish this simple worship sequence to remind children that we can "do church" in any time and place, even in our own homes.

MUSIC FOR WORSHIP

SERVICE MUSIC

Because the jubilee year of the second millennium A.D. comes to an end on this Sunday, hymns and other music may appropriately acknowledge the Christ who is both Lord of time and born into time.

GATHERING

| LBW 47 | Let all together praise our God |
| LBW 170 | Crown him with many crowns |

PSALM 148

LBW 242	Let the whole creation cry
LBW 540	Praise the Lord! O heavens
LBW 541	Praise the Lord of heaven!

Gelineau, Joseph. "Psalm 148." GIA G-2245. 2 pt mxd, cant, cong.

Haas, David. "Praise in the Heights" in PCY, vol. 9.

Hobby, Robert. PW, Cycle C.

Marcus, Mary. "First Sunday after Christmas" in *Psalm Antiphons-2*.
   MSM 80-722.

"Psalm 148" (refrain based on "Lasst uns erfreuen") in UMH.

See also Fifth Sunday of Easter.

HYMN OF THE DAY

LBW 417   In a lowly manger born
          MABUNE

INSTRUMENTAL RESOURCES

Cherwien, David. "In a Lowly Manger Born" in *Interpretations,* vol. 7.
   AMSI SP-104. Org, opt fl.

ALTERNATE HYMN OF THE DAY

LBW 53   Cold December flies away
WOV 638   Holy Child within the manger

A SUGGESTION FOR THE ALTERNATE HYMN OF THE DAY (LBW 53)

Intonation   C inst only plays cantus firmus on mea-
               sures one through four; kybd (and guitar)
               join on measure five
Stanza one   All
Stanza two   Soloist, slightly slower
Stanza three   All

COMMUNION

LBW 52   Your little ones, dear Lord
WOV 642   I wonder as I wander

SENDING

LBW 181   Greet now the swiftly changing year
WOV 790   Praise to you, O God of mercy

ADDITIONAL HYMNS AND SONGS

LW 80   Within the Father's house
RS 967   The God of all eternity
TFF 141   Come and go with me
          to my Father's house
W&P 18   Bind us together

MUSIC FOR THE DAY

CHORAL

Averitt, William. "He Is Born the Divine Christ Child." CPH 98-2953.
   SATB.

Britten, Benjamin. "A Boy Was Born." OXF 84.092.

Joubert, John. "Torches" in *Carols for Choirs 1*. OXF. SATB, org.

Sedio, Mark. "To Thee with Joy I Sing." CPH 98-3443. SATB.

CHILDREN'S CHOIRS

Horman, John D. "When Jesus Was a Growing Lad." CG CGA772.
   U/2 pt, opt desc, kybd, opt fl, opt hb.

Mozart, Wolfgang Amadeus/arr. Austin C. Lovelace. "Hallelujah
   Round of Praise." CG CGA-423. U/SATB, pno.

Robb, John Donald. "Oh, Sleep Now, Holy Baby" in LS.

KEYBOARD/INSTRUMENTAL

Callahan, Charles. "Cold December Flies Away" in *The Christmas Tree*.
   RME EO-315. Org.

Ferguson, John. "Cold December Flies Away" in *A Christmas Triptych*.
   MSM-10-103. Org.

Neswick, Bruce. "Fantasia on Adeste Fideles." PAR PPMO 9719. Org.

Sedio, Mark. "Forest Green" in *Dancing in the Light of God*.
   AFP 11-10793. Pno.

HANDBELL

Gramann, Fred. "Good Christian Friends, Rejoice." BEC HB159.
   4-6 oct.

Kinyon, Barbara B. "Go, Tell It on the Mountain." CG CGB143. 2 oct.

Turner, Ronald. "Of the Father's Love Begotten." CG CGB197. 2 oct.

PRAISE ENSEMBLE

Hurd, Bob. "I Want to Praise Your Name" in *Glory & Praise*. OCP.

Smith, Henry. "Give Thanks" in W&P.

Unknown. "Let the Peace of Christ Rule in Your Heart" in *Sing &
   Rejoice*. BNT.

MONDAY, JANUARY 1
THE NAME OF JESUS

The observance of the octave (eighth day) of Christmas has roots in the sixth century. Until the recent
past, Lutheran calendars called this day "The Circumcision and Name of Jesus." The emphasis on circumcision is the older emphasis. Every Jewish boy was cir-
cumcised and formally named on the eighth day of his
life. Already in his youth, Jesus bears the mark of a
covenant that he makes new through the shedding of
his blood, now and on the cross. That covenant, like
Jesus' name, is a gift to us and marks us as children of
God. Baptized into Christ, we begin this new year in
Jesus' name. Sustained by the gift of his body and
blood, we will find that this year, too, we will be sustained by the gift of Christ's body and the new
covenant in Christ's blood.

TUESDAY, JANUARY 2
JOHANN KONRAD WILHELM LOEHE, PASTOR, 1872

Loehe was a pastor in nineteenth-century Germany. From the small town of Neuendettelsau he sent pastors to North America, Australia, New Guinea, Brazil, and the Ukraine. His work for a clear confessional basis within the Bavarian church sometimes led to conflict with the ecclesiastical bureaucracy. Loehe's chief concern was that a parish finds its life in the eucharist, and from that source evangelism and social ministries would flow. Many Lutheran congregations in Michigan, Ohio, and Iowa were either founded or influenced by missionaries sent by Loehe, and the chapel at Wartburg Theological Seminary is named in his honor.

Loehe's vision to see the eucharist at the center of parish life can lead us on to think about ways that the incarnate presence of Christ in holy communion sends us out in a life of ministry and mission.

FRIDAY, JANUARY 5
KAJ MUNK, MARTYR, 1944

Munk, a Danish Lutheran pastor and playwright, was an outspoken critic of the Nazis who occupied Denmark during the Second World War. His plays frequently highlighted the eventual victory of the Christian faith despite the church's weak and ineffective witness. The Nazis feared Munk because his sermons and articles helped to strengthen the Danish resistance movement. In one of his sermons for New Year's Day he wrote, "The cross characterizes the flags of the North [Nordic countries]. . . . Lead us, thou cross in our flag, lead us into that Nordic struggle where shackled Norway and bleeding Finland fight against an idea which is directly opposed to all our ideals" (*Four Sermons*, trans., J. M. Jensen. Blair, Neb: Lutheran Publishing House, 1944).

Munk's life and death invite us to ponder the power of the gospel in the midst of social and political conflicts. Offer prayers for those who face persecution and for those who resist and challenge tyranny.

EPIPHANY

The world is charged with the grandeur of God

IMAGES of the SEASON

Along with Easter and Pentecost, the festival of the Epiphany was one of the

early church's most important festivals. Its significance is surprising when we

realize that today most North American congrega-

tions observe the festival of the Epiphany with

little of the fanfare that we associate with Christmas, Easter, or even Pentecost. One of the reasons is that the feast of the Epiphany has a complex history. The season that follows it features biblical events and theological realities that are more subtle than the dramatic raising of a man from the dead, for instance, or an invasion by the Spirit through wind, flame, and tongues. Why was the Epiphany such an important festival in the early centuries of the church?

The festival originated in the East, where it was celebrated from the third century as a commemoration of the Lord's baptism. Later on it came to include an observance of the nativity as well. The festival was introduced into the West in the fourth century as an observance of the manifestation of Christ to the Gentiles in the persons of the magi; it was not an observance of the Lord's baptism. No matter which of these three events from the life of Jesus was observed on the Epiphany, the common theme was the appearance of God in the world in one form or another.

Notice that the church designates the Sundays that follow Epiphany as Sundays *after* the Epiphany. By contrast, the Sundays in Lent are identified as Sundays *in* Lent, and the Sundays following Easter are designated as the Sundays *of* Easter. Epiphany is not a season in the same way that Lent is. And Easter, the day of all days, is not so much a season as it is a day that lasts fifty days, Pentecost being the culmination of that day. These distinctions help the church to maintain the relative importance of these three liturgical periods.

In the churches of the West today, the Epiphany is the observance on January 6 of the manifestation of Christ to all the nations of the world, which the gospel represents in the persons of the magi who found Jesus in Bethlehem. In this liturgical year the festival occurs on a Saturday. In the Sundays that follow, we see his

glory revealed at a river, a wedding, in a synagogue, beside a lake, on a plain, and on a mountain.

What these scriptural images and stories have to say to us, in the end, is that if we look with discerning eye and listen with discriminating ear, we can perceive God behind, above, within, around, and below the world all about us. We can contemplate an infant lying in a manger, for instance, and have a vision of God.

When we approach all of creation this way, we find it more difficult to abuse our environment, to treat it casually, to hoard it, or to use it in destructive ways. Living responsibly in the world then becomes less a question of merely doing good and avoiding evil, less a question of moral imperatives or obeying the Ten Commandments, and more an active partnership with God in transfiguring creation until it becomes a place increasingly fit for the kingdom.

For these reasons and many others, Epiphany and the Sundays that follow are critical occasions for the church to address the secularization of society and the world, giving answer to, or at least declaring solidarity with, those who struggle with lingering doubts about the reality of God in our troubled, violent world. Is God important in the world or not? Can we see any real evidence in the life of the average person around us that God really matters?

Certainly the average unchurched person is capable of living a completely secular life that is at once good, socially responsible, generous, and loving. At its most obvious, the world is truly a satisfying place to be. We can take it seriously and manage to live a life that appears rich and full, even without "interference" from God. What does the church have to say to those who dismiss the practice of religion as irrelevant to a life lived well in this modern, high-tech world of ours?

The church's answer is that behind the evidence of things seen, there lurks evidence of things unseen. A recovery of Epiphany would sharpen our eyesight, attune our ears, indeed develop all our senses, so that we are receptive to the glimpses of God's glory all around us. Can we, even at our frantic pace, capture a craving for that glory, freshen our yearning for incomprehensible light and incomparable music? Or have commerce and entertainment so deadened us to the subtle reality of God hidden behind the appearance of things that the appearances themselves suffice?

This kind of sensual deadness has no place among a eucharistic people who claim that words uttered, bread broken, and wine poured out have a meaning far beyond the mere words, the mere bread and wine. The word preached and the eucharist shared are, after all, the church's greatest assurance that the material world holds more than our senses at first tell us. The words we hear, are they now the very Word of God made flesh? And the bread and wine we share, are they not a communion in the body and blood of Christ? These material things, are they not transfigured for us in faith when two or three of us gather in Jesus' name?

And what do we say we believe? In the Nicene Creed we describe Christ as light from light. In the evening we identify Christ as the light that dispels our darkness. The prayer for the fifth Sunday after the Epiphany says, "Almighty God, you sent your only Son as the Word of life for our eyes to see and our ears to hear." When the prophet Simeon took the infant Jesus in his arms, what he saw, at last, was his salvation revealed.

Physicists say that if you strike clay with a hammer and look at it with a low-level infrared camera, you will see that it emits light. Quantum physics has led some scientists to believe that one day, everything will exist in the form of light. Some of the world's great luminaries, spending solitary time in deserts or canyons, have beheld an illuminated earth. Who has not heard music when a crystal goblet is tapped?

As the poet Gerard Manley Hopkins wrote:

The world is charged with the grandeur of God.
It will flame out, like shining from shook foil;
It gathers to a greatness, like the ooze of oil
Crushed.

ENVIRONMENT AND ART FOR THE SEASON

Epiphany speaks of liminality. It helps us cross borders and boundaries, transitions and changes, portals, gates, and doorways. The Epiphany brought Easterners to the place of Christ's birth.

The transfiguration was a different kind of liminal experience for everyone involved, less a liminality of geography than a liminality of time. To be removed from the ordinary, transformed by experience, and returned to the ordinary somehow different is liminality.

Maintain the incarnational theme of light to the world though the use of candles throughout these Epiphany days. Sconces, hanging votives, and mobiles all provide safe locations for Epiphany lights. Send chalk home for marking front doors on Epiphany as part of a house blessing (see "Blessing of a Home" in the Epiphany seasonal rites section).

Pay special attention to the baptismal environment in your space this season. With the celebration of the Baptism of Our Lord comes a great opportunity for a baptismal celebration. Some congregations set aside this festival as one of four primary days to schedule baptisms (the Easter Vigil, Pentecost Day, and All Saints Day are the others). Adorn the baptismal space with white, because the Epiphany light, the festivals of the Lord, and the baptismal garment all reflect the bright robe of Christ.

The Baptism of Our Lord is a fitting time to celebrate baptismal renewal, even if no baptism is scheduled for this day. Modify the Affirmation of Baptism liturgy for use with the entire congregation (eliminate those parts designated for confirmation or for particular groups of affirmers). It may also be a good occasion for Recognition of Ministries in the Congregation (*Occasional Services,* pp. 143–46), especially if members begin new responsibilities at the beginning of a calendar year.

As this season celebrates God's light moving to those outside of our faith tradition, ultimately encompassing the whole world, find ways to symbolize the outward movement through the worship environment and art. Consider using artistic elements from other cultures, particularly those that were instrumental to the founding of the congregation or that are related to contemporary mission relationships of your own congregation or synod.

In many parts of the world, the weeks between the Baptism of Our Lord and Ash Wednesday are marked by carnival, a time of midwinter celebration before the simple and austere character of Lent begins. If you celebrate Carnival or Shrove Tuesday, or consider the Epiphany season itself as a time of carnival, why not link the global dimension of the church's mission with such celebrations? A great multicultural party can follow a festival evening prayer that gently and appropriatly incorporates songs from around the world. In one parish that holds such a celebration, members come in costumes from their ancestral lands, bringing a diverse array of foods that are an echo of eucharistic hospitality.

Christmas decorations typically remain through the celebration of the Epiphany. The "green" Sundays after Epiphany call for more ordinary decorations until Lent begins. It is not necessary to bring visual importance to Sundays intervening between the Epiphany and Lent.

PREACHING WITH THE SEASON

From the outset, the stories we hear during the Epiphany season draw us again and again to the revealing of an identity. Who is this person born in Bethlehem, "a light to reveal [God] to the nations"?

The magi bring gifts of identity: gold for a king, frankincense for a priest, myrrh for the embalming of an ordinary mortal body. As the light poured from the opened heavens above Jesus' baptism, a voice said, "You are my Son, my Beloved." At the wedding in Cana, John records that Jesus did the first of his signs, the changing of water into fine wine, "and revealed his glory." On through the stories of Jesus' reading from the Isaiah scroll to the wondrous catch of fish on Galilee, to his radiant appearance on the mountain with Moses and Elijah, Jesus' identity is revealed.

But the "appearing" in the meaning of the word *epiphany* is not only an appearing of the identity of the light who came into the world. Light shines on its surroundings, giving them a reflected glow, which in turn brings light to other surroundings. "All of us, with unveiled faces, seeing the glory of the Lord as though reflected in a mirror, are being transformed into the same image from one degree of glory to another" (2 Cor. 3:18). The appearing of Epiphany is also about our identity as children of the light. The glory of the Lord arisen upon us causes us also to shine with light. We are called today in a manner no different from the way the sons of Zebedee were called two thousand years ago. Not only is Paul transformed by the grace of God, but we also are transformed by the coming of the light. Arise, shine, we are told.

When we live as people upon whom the light has shined, we see differently. We become aware. Like Isaiah, we become aware that the whole earth is full of God's glory. Like the psalmist we become aware of those precious in God's sight, the weak and needy. Like Jesus, we become aware that the poor, the hungry, the mourning, the hated are blessed in God's sight. Like Paul, we become aware that the glory of God reflects from us as love. The light shines and draws our attention outside of ourselves. The light shines, and we become aware of the faces around us. The light shines, and we live as images of that light, radiating love.

As the magi brought gifts to Jesus for the living out of his identity, so too are we given gifts for the living out of our lives as children of the Most High. Diverse gifts. Gifts of the Spirit. Gifts to be used for the common good. "Common," with the same root as "community" and "communion," implies a sharing among equals. No hierarchy gauges the gifts here: the gifts of the rich are not of greater worth than the gifts of the poor, nor are those of the poor greater than those of the rich. The gifts of the scholar are not greater than those of the deckhand, nor are those of the bishop greater than those of the custodian. As children of the light, all have been given gifts for the living out of this identity, for the common good. And all have their source in the light that has arisen upon us.

The baptism of the Lord reminds us that when we pass through the waters, God is with us, we need not fear. Jesus' baptism heralds him as the beloved Son in whom God is well pleased. It is one of the three times in scripture in which God speaks to Jesus: here at the baptism, at the transfiguration, and in a clap of thunder in which God tells Jesus he has been glorified during his entry into Jerusalem (John 12:28). The proclamation at the baptism is central in recognizing Jesus' identity and our identity as his baptized and communing followers.

The wedding at Cana follows immediately as Jesus shows himself in his works of power and compassion. This event ends the classical Christmas cycle, twelve or forty days of celebration, depending on the tradition one follows. One classical terminal moment was the Epiphany itself, and the other, on February 2, was the presentation of Jesus in the temple.

The Sundays following the Epiphany of the Lord set forth a number of images. The third Sunday begins the promise of the Spirit as the Isaian prophecy is fulfilled with the blind seeing, the lame walking, and the dead rising. What the reader should note is that Jesus surpasses the Isaian text. In short, he is going beyond anyone's expectation of salvation. The extremity of the prophecy creates a backlash in Jesus' hometown of

Nazareth as people try to throw him out. Yet Jesus continues with signs such as the great catch of fish and teaching of the new order. The Sundays following Epiphany are about life in the new order and the demands of discipleship.

The Transfiguration culminates the season. It is the second time we hear God's voice acclaiming the Son. Yet now is added a sense of destiny: to die on the cross. The two great prophets standing at Jesus' side serve as a foil for the two thieves at the cross. Here humanity is exalted. In a real sense this festival is our feast, a time in which we see God's promise that all creation will be transfigured in the risen Christ. Like the festival of the Lord's baptism, it is a moment of God's choice. It is equally a time of renewal for the community, a commitment to the new humanity. We see where Lent will lead us: to the death and resurrection of Christ in which our graves become the gate to Paradise.

The light has come, and it is now given to us to shine. The glory of the Lord is risen upon us, and it is now given to us to arise and follow. Christ has revealed his glory, and it is now given to us to be transfigured by the light of this love.

85

SHAPE of WORSHIP for the SEASON

BASIC SHAPE OF THE EUCHARISTIC RITE

- Confession and Forgiveness: see alternate worship text for Epiphany in *Sundays and Seasons*

GATHERING

- Greeting: see alternate worship text for Epiphany in *Sundays and Seasons*
- Consider omitting the Kyrie on Sundays after the Epiphany, but use the Kyrie on the festivals of the Epiphany, the Baptism of Our Lord, and the Transfiguration of Our Lord
- Use the hymn of praise throughout Epiphany ("Glory to God")

WORD

- Use the Nicene Creed for festival days and Sundays in this season; use the Apostles' Creed for the Sundays after the Epiphany
- The Prayers: see alternate forms and responses in the daily material of *Sundays and Seasons*

BAPTISM

- Consider having a baptismal festival on the Baptism of Our Lord (January 7)

MEAL

- Offertory prayer: see alternate worship text for Epiphany in *Sundays and Seasons*
- Use the proper preface for Epiphany
- Eucharistic prayer: in addition to the four main options in *LBW*, see "Eucharistic Prayer C: The Season of Epiphany," *WOV* Leaders Edition, p. 67
- Invitation to communion: see alternate worship text for Epiphany in *Sundays and Seasons*
- Post-communion prayer: see alternate worship text for Epiphany in *Sundays and Seasons*

SENDING

- Benediction: see alternate worship text for Epiphany in *Sundays and Seasons*
- Dismissal: see alternate worship text for Epiphany in *Sundays and Seasons*

OTHER SEASONAL POSSIBILITIES

- Celebrate the festival of the Epiphany (January 6) with evening prayer or with Holy Communion. It is a fitting occasion to use incense. *Worship Wordbook* (pp. 103–104) or *Manual on the Liturgy* (pp. 279–82) are two possible resources to consult for instructions on using incense.

ECUMENICAL SERVICES DURING THE WEEK OF PRAYER FOR CHRISTIAN UNITY (JANUARY 18–25)

- One way to observe this week is by using the service in the seasonal rites section. For Lutherans celebrating with one or more congregations of the Reformed family, "Guidelines and Worship Resources for the Celebration of Full Communion," available from Augsburg Fortress (code 69-4519), may be consulted. A similar resource is available for Lutheran–Moravian celebrations (code 69-4524). Resources for interim sharing of the eucharist are available from denominational offices for Lutheran and Episcopal congregations worshiping together.
- The blessing of homes is customary in the season after the Epiphany. See "Blessing of a Dwelling," *Occasional Services*, pp. 186–91, or "Blessing of a Home" in the Epiphany seasonal rites section of *Sundays and Seasons*.

ASSEMBLY SONG FOR THE SEASON

Epiphany reveals who Jesus is while proclaiming the power of the new creation. The song of the assembly needs to point to this truth of God in Christ Jesus—the intersection of the divine and human. The song needs to clothe the assembly in the story of Jesus, so that the people may be dismissed to proclaim the reign of God. Epiphany is a time of action and mission for Christians. Epiphany requires faith, faithfulness, and vision. Action verbs abound in the lectionary, bringing (good news), binding (brokenhearted), proclaiming (liberty), overcoming (weaknesses of sin). If you do not already do so, consider having an Epiphany service this year. Join with a neighboring congregation, and use the opportunity as a time for fellowship. Have a potluck supper, and sing Christmas and Epiphany hymns and carols.

GATHERING

Sing the hymn of praise "Glory to God" at every service this season. If the assembly knows *Lutheran Book of Worship* settings of this canticle well, then explore other settings, especially those of other cultures. "Glory to God, glory in the highest" (WOV 788) is easily learned because of its call and response pattern. Have a different cantor each week to sing the leader's part. Remember to include the voices of youth. The use of percussion instruments such as tambourine (used lightly and sparingly), guiro, and shakers gives a festive flavor to this Peruvian melody and affords the opportunity to involve more people in the song. Have the sounds come from different parts of the assembly by asking different people if they would be willing to play the percussion instruments that day. Teach them the rhythms by rote. "Gloria" (LLC 189) has both English and Spanish texts and also works well with the assembly singing the antiphon and a cantor singing the proper text. Another possibility based on Luke 2:14 is "Gloria, gloria, gloria" (WOV 637) with cantor or choir singing the proper text.

WORD

Use "Open your ears, O faithful people" (WOV 715) as a gradual hymn at the reading of the gospel. Use selected stanzas, and vary them weekly. Stanza 2 is especially appropriate to the third Sunday after the Epiphany, and stanza 3 is appropriate to the fifth Sunday after the Epiphany. Repeat the refrain after the gospel reading. A tambourine can enhance the accompaniment of this Hasidic tune.

MEAL

Epiphany is a time of mission for the church. Hymns from other cultures, such as "Grains of wheat" (WOV 708 and LLC 392), might be used at the offertory during this season. "Now in this banquet" (W&P 104) or "United at the table" (LLC 408) would be good distribution hymns to learn and sing for the season.

SENDING

"Lord, now you let your servant" is especially appropriate as a seasonal post-communion canticle. A Spanish and English text setting of this canticle is "Has cumplido tu palabra/ Now, Lord, you let your servant go in peace" (LLC 248). This setting could be very effective accompanied by a guitar. Some variations that emphasize the theme of light are "We are called" (W&P 147), "Ahora, Señor/At last, Lord" (LLC 247) with English and Spanish texts, and "Jesus, the light of the world" (TFF 59).

87

MUSIC for the SEASON

VERSE AND OFFERTORY

Boehnke, Paul. *Festive Verse Settings for Christmas, Epiphany, and Transfiguration.* MSM 80-100. SATB, opt kybd.

Cherwien, David. *Verses for the Epiphany Season.* MSM 80-200. U, hb, org.

Hobby, Robert. A. *Offertory for the Transfiguration of Our Lord.* MSM 80-225. Mxd vcs, hb, org.

Johnson, David N. *Verses and Offertories for Epiphany 2 through Transfiguration.* AFP 11-9544. U, kybd.

Martinson, Joel. "Arise, Shine!" (Offertory) AFP 11-10450. SATB, org.

"Now the Silence" (LBW 205) may be used as an offertory hymn throughout the Epiphany season.

Schack, David, Henry Gerike, and Barry Bobb. *Verses and Offertory Sentences, Part II: Epiphany through Transfiguration.* CPH 97-5502. Acc. 97-5509. U/SATB, kybd.

Shephard, Richard. "The Baptism of the Lord" in *Gospel Acclamations.* Kevin Mayhew 1400050. U, org.

Werning, Daniel J. *Verse Settings for Festival Days.* CPH 97-5787. SATB.

Wetzler, Robert. "Ascribe to the Lord." CPH 98-3109. CPH 98-3163 (parts). SATB, org; opt fl, str, ob.

CHORAL

Attwood, Thomas. "Teach Me, O Lord, the Way of Thy Statutes." ECS 169. SATB, org.

Burroughs, Bob. "Christ, Whose Glory Fills the Skies." CPH 98-3015. SATB.

Candlyn, T. Frederick H. "Christ, Whose Glory Fills the Skies." CFI C. M. 622. SATB, org.

Christiansen, F. M., arr. "Beautiful Savior." AFP 11-0051. SSAATTBB.

Handel, G. F. "O Thou That Tellest Good Tidings to Zion" in *Messiah.* GSCH. Solo, chorus.

Hassell, Michael. "This Little Light of Mine." AFP 11-10889. SATB, pno.

Lovelace, Austin C. "Song of Simeon." SEL 410-852. U, org or SATB.

Neswick, Bruce. "Epiphany Carol." AFP 11-10511. Also in *The Augsburg Choirbook.* AFP 11-10817. U, org.

Powell, Robert J. "The Great Creator of the Worlds." AFP 11-10883. SATB, org.

CHILDREN'S CHOIRS

Hopson, Hal. H. "We Are Singing for the Lord Is Our Light." AG HH 3949. U/SATB, kybd.

Kemp, Helen. "God's Great Lights." CPH 98-3072. U, opt cong, narr.

Kemp, Helen. "Set the Sun Dancing!" CG CGA780. U, kybd, 3-4 oct hb.

Neswick, Bruce. "Epiphany Carol." AFP 11-10511. U, org.

Schalk, Carl. "Jesus, Jesus, Light from Light." AFP 11-2438. 2 pt, flu/ob, 8 hb.

KEYBOARD/INSTRUMENTAL

Augsburg Organ Library: Epiphany. AFP 11-11073.

Behnke, John. *Three Global Songs.* HOP 8057. Org.

Gade, Niels W. "Prelude on 'Wie schön leuchtet' " in *Organ Works.* Wilhelm Hansen 4158. Org.

Jones, Philip. *Asian Praise.* VIV 308. Org.

Wold, Wayne L. "I Want to Walk as a Child of the Light" in *Child of the Light: Preludes on Hymntunes by Women.* AFP 11-10938. Org.

HANDBELL

Dobrinski, Cynthia. "Go, Tell It on the Mountain." AG 2119. 3-5 oct, opt cl, tbn.

Gramann, Fred. "Prelude on 'Divinum mysterium.' " LOR HB332. 4 oct.

Kinyon, Barbara B. "O Morning Star." AG 1690. 3 oct.

Kinyon, Barbara B. "What Star Is This That Beams So Bright?" CG CGB 111. 2 oct.

Larson, Katherine Jordahl. "Celestia." AFP 11-10622. 3-4 oct.

PRAISE ENSEMBLE

Haas, David. "Arise, Shine Out!" GIA G-4868. 2 pt, kybd, opt cong, 2 C inst, gtr.

Johnson, Ralph M. "Listen! You Nations of the World." CPH 98-3157. SATB, solo, pno.

Kendrick, Graham, and Tom Fettke. "Shine, Jesus, Shine." LIL AN-8079. SATB, kybd, opt orch.

ALTERNATE WORSHIP TEXTS

CONFESSION AND FORGIVENESS

In the name of the Father, and of the ✝ Son, and of the Holy Spirit.
Amen

Through water and the Spirit God gives us new life.
Let us confess our sin,
that we may be renewed in the covenant of baptism.

Silence for reflection and self-examination.

Strong and faithful God,
we confess that we have not lived
as the body of Christ in the world.
We have veiled our hearts from your light.
We have resisted your call to follow.
We have failed to exercise your gift of love.
Forgive us for the sake of Christ,
heal us with your abundant grace,
and help us walk as children of light. Amen

In the mercy of almighty God,
Jesus Christ came among us
to proclaim release to the captives,
to let the oppressed go free.
Today the promise is fulfilled:
God forgives you all your sins.
May the Holy Spirit strengthen you
to follow Christ in newness of life.
Amen

GREETING

May the light and love of God,
who wonderfully made you,
who graciously redeemed you,
who calls you each by name,
be with you all.
And also with you.

OFFERTORY PRAYER

God of all creation,
all you have made is good,
and your love endures forever.
You bring forth bread from the earth
and fruit from the vine.
Nourish us with these gifts,
that we might be for the world
signs of your gracious presence
in Jesus Christ our Lord. Amen

INVITATION TO COMMUNION

Come, feast on the abundance God provides;
drink from the river of God's delights.

POST-COMMUNION PRAYER

Holy God,
in this eucharist you reveal your faithfulness
to us, your beloved children.
Anoint us with your Spirit,
that we may be signs of your grace
and compassion for the world.
Grant this through Christ our Lord.
Amen

BENEDICTION

May Christ, whose epiphany
revealed God's glory to the world,
deepen your faith and make your hearts glad.
Almighty God, Father, ✝ Son, and Holy Spirit,
bless you now and forever.
Amen

DISMISSAL

Go in peace.
The joy of the Lord is your strength.
Thanks be to God.

89

SEASONAL RITES

ECUMENICAL SERVICE DURING THE WEEK OF PRAYER FOR CHRISTIAN UNITY

CONFESSION AND FORGIVENESS

We gather as the people of God
to offer our repentance and praise,
to pray for the unity of the church
and the renewal of our common life.
Trusting in God's mercy and compassion,
let us ask for the forgiveness of our sins.

Silence for reflection and self-examination.

Lord Jesus, you came to reconcile us
to one another and to the Father:
Lord, have mercy on us.
Lord, have mercy on us.
Lord Jesus, you heal the wounds
of pride and intolerance.
Christ, have mercy on us.
Christ, have mercy on us.
Lord Jesus, you pardon the sinner
and welcome the repentant.
Lord, have mercy on us.
Lord, have mercy on us.
May almighty God grant us pardon and peace,
strengthen us in faith,
and make us witnesses to Christ's love.
Amen

HYMN OF PRAISE

PRAYER OF THE DAY

God our Father, your Son Jesus prayed that his followers might be
one. Make all Christians one with him as he is one with you, so that
in peace and concord we may carry to the world the message of
your love; through your Son, Jesus Christ our Lord, who lives and
reigns with you and the Holy Spirit, one God, now and forever.
Amen

THE WORD OF GOD

Isaiah 2:2-4
Psalm 133
Ephesians 4:1-6
John 17:15-23

SERMON

HYMN OF THE DAY

THANKSGIVING FOR BAPTISM

*The people remain standing after the hymn as the minister(s)
gather at the font. After the prayer, the people may be sprinkled
with water from the font. Or at the conclusion of the service, they
may be invited to dip their hands in the font and trace the sign of
the cross over themselves.*

The Lord be with you.
And also with you.
Let us give thanks to the Lord our God.
It is right to give our thanks and praise.
Holy God and mighty Lord, we give you thanks,
for you nourish and sustain us and all living things
with the gift of water.
In the beginning your Spirit moved over the waters,
and you created heaven and earth.
By the waters of the flood you saved Noah and his family.
You led Israel through the sea out of slavery
into the promised land.
In the waters of the Jordan
your Son was baptized by John and anointed with the Spirit.
By the baptism of his death and resurrection
your Son set us free from sin and death
and opened the way to everlasting life.

We give you thanks, O God,
that you have given us new life in the water of baptism.
Buried with Christ in his death,
you raise us to share in his resurrection
by the power of the Holy Spirit.
May all who have passed through the water of baptism
continue in the risen life of our Savior.
To you be all honor and glory, now and forever.
Amen

CONFESSION OF FAITH

There is one Lord, one faith, and one baptism.
United in Christ, let us confess the faith we hold in common.

The people recite the Apostles' Creed

THE PRAYERS

After the conclusion of the prayers, the people are invited to pray the Lord's Prayer.

GREETING OF PEACE

The Lord Jesus prayed for the unity of his disciples.
We look for the day when the church will shine forth
in unity at his holy supper.
The peace of the Lord be with you always.
And also with you.

The people exchange a sign of Christ's peace.

BLESSING AND DISMISSAL

SENDING HYMN

LESSONS AND CAROLS FOR EPIPHANY

Stand
ENTRANCE HYMN

| LBW 55 | Good Christian friends, rejoice |
| LBW 56 | The first Noel |

DIALOG

The people who walked in darkness have seen a great light.
The light shines in the darkness,
and the darkness has not overcome it.
Those who dwelt in the land of deep darkness,
on them light has shined.
We have beheld Christ's glory,
glory as of the only Son from the Father.
For to us a child is born, to us a Son is given.
In him was life, and the life was the light of all people.

OPENING PRAYER

See prayer of the day for Epiphany (LBW, p. 15 or WOV Leaders Edition, p. 78).

Sit
LESSONS AND CAROLS
First Reading: John 1:1-14

LBW 42	Of the Father's love begotten
LBW 45	Oh, come, all ye faithful
LBW 57	Let our gladness have no end
TFF 37	He came down

Second Reading: John 1:18-25

LBW 44	Infant holy, infant lowly
LBW 67	Away in a manger
WOV 644	Away in a manger
TFF 59	Jesus, the light of the world

Third Reading: Matthew 2:1-12

LBW 75	Bright and glorious is the sky
WOV 645	There's a star in the East
WOV 646	We three kings of Orient are
LLC 317	The magi who to Bethlehem did go
TFF 60	Sister Mary

Fourth Reading: Matthew 2:13-23

LBW 177	By all your saints in warfare (st. 9)
WOV 639	Oh, sleep now, holy baby
LLC 310	Oh, Mary, gentle poor Mary

Fifth Reading: Luke 2:41-51

LBW 417	In a lowly manger born
WOV 634	Sing of Mary, pure and lowly
WOV 643	Once in royal David's city
TFF 53	The virgin Mary had a baby boy

Sixth Reading: Matthew 3:13-17

LBW 85	When Christ's appearing was made known
LBW 88	Oh, love, how deep
WOV 647	When Jesus came to Jordan
TFF 114	Wade in the water

Seventh Reading: John 2:1-11

| LBW 205 | Now the silence |
| WOV 648 | Jesus, come! for we invite you |

Stand
RESPONSIVE PRAYER

Glory to God in the highest,
and peace to God's people on earth.
Blessed are you, Prince of Peace.
You rule the earth with truth and justice.
Send your gift of peace to all nations of the world.
Blessed are you, Son of Mary. You share our humanity.
Have mercy on those who are sick, dying,
and all who suffer this day.
Blessed are you, Son of God.
You dwell among us as the Word made flesh.
Reveal yourself to us in word and sacrament,
that we may bear your light to all the world.

THE LORD'S PRAYER

BLESSING AND DISMISSAL

Let us bless the Lord.

Thanks be to God.

May you be filled with the wonder of Mary, the obedience of Joseph, the joy of the angels, the eagerness of the shepherds, the determination of the magi, and the peace of the Christ child. Almighty God, Father, ✛ Son, and Holy Spirit bless you now and forever.

Amen

SENDING HYMN

LBW 90   Songs of thankfulness and praise

TFF 61   The Lord is my light

BLESSING OF THE HOME AT EPIPHANY

Matthew writes that when the magi saw the shining star stop overhead, they were filled with joy. "On entering the house, they saw the child with Mary his mother" (2:10-11). In the home, Christ is met in family and friends, in visitors and strangers. In the home, faith is shared, nurtured, and put into action. In the home, Christ is welcome.

Twelfth Night (January 5) or another day during the season of Epiphany offers an occasion for gathering with friends and family members for a blessing of the home, using the following as a model. Someone may lead the greeting and blessing, while another person may read the scripture passage. Following an eastern European tradition, a visual blessing may be inscribed with white chalk above the main door; for example, 20+CMB+01. The numbers change with each new year. The three letters stand for either the ancient Latin blessing Christe mansionem benedica, which means, "Christ, bless this house," or the legendary names of the magi (Caspar, Melchior, and Blather).

GREETING

May peace be to this house
and to all who enter here.
By wisdom a house is built
and through understanding it is established;
through knowledge its rooms are filled
with rare and beautiful treasures.
See Proverbs 24:3-4.

READING

As we prepare to ask God's blessing on this household,
let us listen to the words of scripture.
In the beginning was the Word,
and the Word was with God, and the Word was God.
He was in the beginning with God.
All things came into being through him,
and without him not one thing came into being.
What has come into being in him was life,
and the life was the light of all people.
The Word became flesh and lived among us,
and we have seen his glory,
the glory as of a father's only son, full of grace and truth.
From his fullness we have all received, grace upon grace.
See John 1:1-4, 14, 16.

INSCRIPTION

This inscription may be made with chalk above the entrance:

20 + C M B + 01

The magi of old, known as

C Caspar,

M Melchior, and

B Balthasar

    followed the star of God's Son who came to dwell among us

    20 two thousand

    21 and one years ago.

✛ Christ, bless this house,

✛ and remain with us throughout the new year.

PRAYER

O God, you revealed your Son to all people
by the shining light of a star.
We pray that you bless this home and all who live here
with your gracious presence.
May your love be our inspiration,
your wisdom our guide,
your truth our light
and your peace our benediction;
through Christ our Lord. Amen

Then everyone may walk from room to room, blessing the house with incense or by sprinkling with water, perhaps using a branch from the Christmas tree.

Adapted from Come, Lord Jesus: Devotions for the Home (Augsburg Fortress, 1996).

JANUARY 6, 2001

THE EPIPHANY OF OUR LORD

INTRODUCTION

The Epiphany of Our Lord brings the twelve days of Christmas to an end and begins a season that will focus on God's revelation in Jesus. The day is filled with surprises, mysterious visitors, and exotic gifts. God's story leads us through unexpected twists and turns, and the mission of God's people introduces us to faith partners we have never expected.

PRAYER OF THE DAY

Lord God, on this day you revealed your Son to the nations by the leading of a star. Lead us now by faith to know your presence in our lives, and bring us at last to the full vision of your glory, through your Son, Jesus Christ our Lord, who lives and reigns with you and the Holy Spirit, one God, now and forever.

READINGS

Isaiah 60:1-6

The long years of darkness are over. The prophet announces the end of exile in Babylon and looks forward to the restoration of the city of Jerusalem. God's light, reflected in Israel, will draw caravans bearing treasure from all the nations who freely come to praise the Lord.

Psalm 72:1-7, 10-14

All kings shall bow down before him. (Ps. 72:11)

Ephesians 3:1-12

Though it had been hidden for years, Paul now reveals the secret that has shaped his apostolic witness: in Jesus Christ, God's salvation extends beyond the Jews to include all people. The light of Christ shines upon Jew and Gentile alike.

Matthew 2:1-12

The rich symbolism of this story—the magi, a star in the East, Herod's plots—announces the prophetic hope for an epiphany, the revelation that God has entered into our history as one of us.

COLOR   White

THE PRAYERS

Let us pray for all people upon whom the light of Christ shines with grace and mercy.

A BRIEF SILENCE.

For missionaries, translators of the Bible, and all whose work proclaims good news of Christ for the nations. Lord, in your mercy,

hear our prayer.

For leaders of nations and for all governing authorities, that they may be responsive to your will in all that they seek to do for the public good. Lord, in your mercy,

hear our prayer.

For those who are ill (especially . . .), that they may rejoice in your gift of wholeness and know the healing touch of your hands. Lord, in your mercy,

hear our prayer.

For all who minister in this congregation, that our daily service at home, in the workplace, and in our community may reveal the light and life of Jesus Christ. Lord, in your mercy,

hear our prayer.

HERE OTHER INTERCESSIONS MAY BE OFFERED.

For all who have died, that with them we may come to the brightness of your dawn. Lord, in your mercy,

hear our prayer.

All these things and whatever else you see that we need, grant us, O God, for the sake of your Son, Jesus Christ our Lord.

Amen

IMAGES FOR PREACHING

Matthew's story about the magi seems to suggest that the matter over who exactly was included in the people of the promise had long ago been decided. These wise men from East who came to worship and pay homage to Jesus had seen a sign from afar and followed it. They followed that sign across deserts and mountains, and across national barriers. Finally they came to the place where the newborn king lay.

This newborn baby was given by God to be a king of a different sort for all the people who come to him. All people the world over have been called to be part of God's covenant of love and peace—the promise of God given through the birth, death, and resurrection of Jesus.

93

We are called, just as the magi were, to cross all barriers in our world today in order to come to him ourselves and to bring others with us.

Not many of us have had to arrive on camelback to worship Jesus, but we do have to transcend other barriers of our time. We have to transcend our self-centeredness and recognize that we are not alone here. Other strangers and sojourners in our world seek light and truth, the love of God and the peace of Christ. The door to the place where God is revealed is always open to all.

WORSHIP MATTERS

The star pointed the way for the wise men to the child Jesus at Bethlehem. Light in our worship often points the way to Christ as well. The custom of lighting two or more candles at the altar for communion services indicates Christ's presence in the sacrament. The paschal candle, lit for the first time each year at the Easter Vigil, is a special sign of the risen Christ when it is lit during Easter's fifty days, and throughout the rest of the year when it is placed near the baptismal font. Candles given to the newly baptized proclaim the presence of Christ in their lives. While originally serving a primarily utilitarian function, candles flanking an ambo or lectern, or accompanying a gospel procession, also proclaim the presence of Christ in the reading of the scriptures. The star still guides the way for us today.

LET THE CHILDREN COME

We all love candles on our birthday cakes. We receive a baptismal candle at our baptism. This candle should be lit every year at the anniversary of the person's baptism. It reminds us of our spiritual birthdays. If your church has a hanging star (perhaps a "Moravian star"), point out to children that the star is also a light, and that it reminds us of the story of the wise men following the light of the star. Make a cutout of a candle from poster board. The flame could be a star shape. Decorate with glitter glue.

MUSIC FOR WORSHIP

SERVICE MUSIC

Appropriate throughout Christmastide, "What child is this" (LBW 40) is especially fitting as an offertory hymn on this day.

GATHERING

| LBW 56 | The first Noel |
| WOV 652 | Arise, your light has come! |

PSALM 72:1-7, 10-14

LBW 87   Hail to the Lord's anointed

LBW 530   Jesus shall reign

Daw, Carl P. Jr., and Kevin R. Hackett. *A Hymn Tune Psalter*. Church Publishing Inc.

Haugen, Marty. "Every Nation on Earth Will Adore You" in PCY.

Hobby, Robert. PW, Cycle C.

Schoenbachler, Tim. "Psalm 72: Justice Shall Flourish" in STP, vol. 3.

HYMN OF THE DAY

WOV 649   I want to walk as a child of the light

                HOUSTON

VOCAL RESOURCES

Erickson, Richard. "I Want to Walk as a Child of the Light." AFP 11-10957. SATB, org.

INSTRUMENTAL RESOURCES

Organ, Anne Krentz. "I Want to Walk as a Child of the Light" in *Woven Together*. AFP 11-10980. Pno, inst.

Wasson, Laura. "I Want to Walk as a Child of the Light" in *A Piano Tapestry, vol. II*. AFP 11-10978. Pno.

Wold, Wayne L. "I Want to Walk as a Child of the Light" in *Child of Light*. AFP 11-10938.

ALTERNATE HYMN OF THE DAY

| LBW 76 | O Morning Star, how fair and bright! |
| LBW 84 | Brightest and best of the stars of the morning |

COMMUNION

| LBW 518 | Beautiful Savior |
| WOV 648 | Jesus, come! for we invite you |

SENDING

| LBW 82 | As with gladness men of old |
| WOV 646 | We three kings of Orient are |

ADDITIONAL HYMNS AND SONGS

HFG 201	The star carol
LLC 317	The magi who to Bethlehem did go
TFF 60	Sister Mary
TWC 186	Wise men, they came to look for wisdom
W&P 57	Hear the angels

MUSIC FOR THE DAY

CHORAL

Bach, J. S. "O Morning Star, How Fair and Bright" in BAS. SATB, opt kybd, C inst.

Jennings, Kenneth. "Arise, Shine, for Thy Light Has Come" in *The Augsburg Choirbook* 11-10817. SATB.

Keesecker, Thomas. "The Silent Stars Shine Down on Us." AFP 11-10958. 2 pt mxd, kybd.

Lovelace, Austin. "Rise Up and Shine." GIA G-4431. SAB, kybd.

Mendelssohn, Felix. "Behold a Star from Jacob Shining." ECS 987. Also in CC. SATB, kybd.

Owens, Sam Batt. "He Shall Come Down." MSM 50-0202. SAB, org.

Praetorius, Michael. "O Morning Star, How Fair and Bright" in CC. SATB.

Shute, Linda. "The Magi Who to Bethlehem Did Go." AFP 11-10960. SATB, pno, perc.

Willan, Healey. "Arise, Shine, for Thy Light Is Come." CPH 98-1508. SATB, org.

CHILDREN'S CHOIRS

Christopherson, Dorothy. "The Night of the Star." AFP 11-10890. U, opt desc and 2nd pt, kybd, fl, perc.

Gullickson, Karen Nelson. "See the Star." AFP 11-2530. 2 pt trbl, pno.

Kemp, Helen. "Follow the Star." CG CGA-484. U, kybd, perc.

Thomerson, Kathleen. "I Want to Walk as a Child of the Light" in LS.

KEYBOARD/INSTRUMENTAL

Linker, Janet. "Brightest and Best" in *Three Epiphany Pieces.* AFP 11-10974. Org.

McIntyre, John. "We Three Kings" in *Christmas Brass.* AMSI B-13.

Wold, Wayne L. "Brightest and Best" in *God with Us.* AFP 11-10975. Org.

HANDBELL

Moklebust, Cathy. "Meditation on Beautiful Savior." CG CGB175.

Rogers, Sharon Elery. "As with Gladness." AMSI HB-31.

PRAISE ENSEMBLE

Haugen, Marty. "Arise, Shine" in *Gather.* GIA.

Haugen, Marty. "Bring Forth the Kingdom." GIA 3592. 3 pt, solo, kybd, opt cong, gtr, C ww.

Richards, Noel, and Tricia Richards. "Our Confidence Is in the Lord" in W&P.

95

JANUARY 7, 2001

THE BAPTISM OF OUR LORD

FIRST SUNDAY AFTER THE EPIPHANY

INTRODUCTION

Baptism is the beginning of a new story. It was for Jesus; it is for us. God claims us as sons and daughters, fills us with the Holy Spirit, and promises to travel the path with us—a path that will bring us home.

PRAYER OF THE DAY

Father in heaven, at the baptism of Jesus in the River Jordan you proclaimed him your beloved Son and anointed him with the Holy Spirit. Make all who are baptized into Christ faithful in their calling to be your children and inheritors with him of everlasting life; through your Son, Jesus Christ our Lord, who lives and reigns with you and the Holy Spirit, one God, now and forever.

READINGS

Isaiah 43:1-7

Near the end of Israel's exile in Babylon, God promises to bring them home. They need no longer fear, because the one who formed, created, and called them by name now claims and redeems them.

Psalm 29

The voice of the LORD is upon the waters. (Ps. 29:3)

Acts 8:14-17

Peter and John are sent by the church to the Christians in Samaria, a group that had been converted through the preaching of Philip. Here the Samaritans received the gift of the Holy Spirit in the laying on of hands.

Luke 3:15-17, 21-22

The last of the prophets of Israel, John the Baptist points ahead to "the one mightier than I [who] is coming." Although John baptizes with water, Jesus will baptize with the Spirit and fire. In Luke's version of this story, the focus is not on John, however. God is the actor, causing the Spirit to descend upon Jesus and inaugurating his mission with the proclamation that he is the "beloved Son."

COLOR   White

THE PRAYERS

Let us pray for all people upon whom the light of Christ shines with grace and mercy.

A BRIEF SILENCE.

For all the baptized, that we might be daily renewed by your Spirit. Lord, in your mercy,

hear our prayer.

For the earth and its created goodness, that we may use its resources wisely. Lord, in your mercy,

hear our prayer.

For those who are sick and infirm (especially . . .), that your Spirit's gifts of peace, love, and hope may be multiplied in their lives. Lord, in your mercy,

hear our prayer.

For this new year in mission, that Christ may be seen in our praising, giving, teaching, and witnessing. Lord, in your mercy,

hear our prayer.

HERE OTHER INTERCESSIONS MAY BE OFFERED.

We praise you for the faithful departed and their witness to Christ, and we pray that we may serve faithfully in our time. Lord, in your mercy,

hear our prayer.

All these things and whatever else you see that we need, grant us, O God, for the sake of your Son, Jesus Christ our Lord.

Amen

IMAGES FOR PREACHING

Disney's *The Lion King* opens with the sun dawning over the African plain. All the animals were traveling to observe the birth of King Mufasa's son. Rafiki, a wise, old baboon, came up to King Mufasa and Queen Sarabi. He opened a gourd, put his finger into its juice, and placed a mark on the infant lion cub's forehead. Cheers rang out from the gathered throng as Rafiki held the newborn lion high.

Was the scene anything like that at Jesus' baptism? The crowds had gathered around. Our gospel today says that they were filled with expectation. They were questioning among themselves whether John the Baptist might be the messiah—*their* long-awaited king. John's announcement that, no, he was not the messiah must certainly have disappointed many.

But then the heaven opened, and the Holy Spirit descended upon Jesus. A voice came from heaven, "You are my Son, the Beloved; with you I am well pleased."

Maybe that day was not all that different from days we know after our children are born. We are so proud of them. We show pictures or our newest children or grandchildren, whether or not anyone asks to see them. God proclaims about this new daughter or son, "Child of God, you have been sealed by the Holy Spirit, and marked with the cross of Christ forever."

Child of God, we say. This young life is not just anybody, this is God's child—signed with oil, the mark of anointing of kings and queens. Then we welcome this king or queen into our midst. With this mark and this welcome, and through our baptism into Christ, we become little Christs. Our lives are a tangible witness of what Christ came to accomplish in our world.

WORSHIP MATTERS

Some of our most significant occasions in life are also moments when God calls us by name through the liturgy. In baptism we are called children of God. Prayers for the sending of the Spirit are made specifically on our behalf at baptism and confirmation. We specifically name husbands and wives in the prayers of the marriage liturgy. People who receive laying on of hands and anointing hear their names addressed to God. Finally, at death, we commend each Christian to God by name in the burial liturgy. Worship leaders should take great care in pronouncing names during these and other occasions, because in these moments we come to understand that our names are important to God.

LET THE CHILDREN COME

John the Baptist baptized Jesus in the river. Our baptisms are generally quite different from Jesus' going to the river. But God is speaking the same word of love. God spoke at Jesus' baptism and said how much God loved Jesus. In baptism we also are loved by God and named to be children of God as we are washed in the water. We remember our own baptisms whenever we participate in a baptism in our worship services.

MUSIC FOR WORSHIP

GATHERING

| LBW 550 | From all that dwell below the skies |
| WOV 797 | O God beyond all praising |

PSALM 29

Haas, David. "The Lord Will Bless All People" in PCY, vol. 8.

Hobby, Robert. PW, Cycle C.

Marshall, Jane. *Psalms Together*, vol. 2. CG CGC-21.

Psalms for the Cantor, vol. 3. WLP 2504.

HYMN OF THE DAY

LBW 194   All who believe and are baptized
             Es ist das Heil

INSTRUMENTAL RESOURCES

Behnke, John. "Es ist das Heil" in *Variations for Seven Familiar Hymns*.
      AFP 11-10702. Org.

Kolander, Keith. "Es ist das Heil" in *All Things Are Thine*.
      AFP 11-10931. Org.

Oliver, Curt. "Variations on 'Salvation unto Us Has Come.' "
      MSM 15-813. Pno.

ALTERNATE HYMN OF THE DAY

LBW 85   When Christ's appearing
             was made known

WOV 647   When Jesus came to Jordan

COMMUNION

LBW 486   Spirit of God, descend upon my heart

WOV 710   One bread, one body

SENDING

LBW 90   Songs of thankfulness and praise

WOV 721   Go my children, with my blessing

ADDITIONAL HYMNS AND SONGS

H82 121   Christ, when for us you were baptized

TFF 115   I'm going on a journey

VU 100   When Jesus comes to be baptized

W3 412   When John baptized by Jordan's River

W&P 158   You are mine

MUSIC FOR THE DAY

CHORAL

Bach, J. S. "The Only Son from Heaven" in BAS. SATB, opt kybd,
      C inst.

Gardner, John. "Tomorrow Shall Be My Dancing Day." OXF 40.107.
      SATB, kybd, opt perc.

Plery, James. "The Waters of Life." AFP 11-10902. SATB, org.

Proulx, Richard. "Jesus Went to Jordan's Stream." AFP 11-10649. 2 pt
      mxd, org.

Uhl, Dan. "This Is My Beloved Son." AFP 11-2416. Also in *The Augsburg Choirbook*. 11-10817. SATB, org.

Wyton, Alec. "When Jesus Went to Jordan's Stream." PAR PPM0806.
      SATB, fl, hb, org.

CHILDREN'S CHOIRS

Burkhardt, Michael. "Go, My Children, With My Blessing."
      MSM 50-9416. U, opt 2-3 pt, pno.

Callahan, Charles. "The Baptism of Our Lord." MSM- 50-2003.
      U, opt desc, org.

Gaelic tune. "Baptized in Water" in LS.

Rotermund, Donald. "Children of the Heavenly Father."
      CPH 98-2572. 2 trbl vcs, opt C inst, org.

KEYBOARD/INSTRUMENTAL

Pachelbel, Johann. "Christ, unser Herr, zu Jordan kamm." Various editions, including KAL K03762. Org.

Sedio, Mark "Oh, Blest the House" ("When Christ's Appearing Was Made Known") in *How Blessed This Place*. AFP 11-10934. Org.

HANDBELL

Holst/Buckwalter. "In the Bleak Midwinter." FLA HP5317. 3-5 oct.

Stephenson, Valerie W. "Waters in the Wilderness." Gentry Publications
      JG0707. 4-5 oct.

PRAISE ENSEMBLE

Chapman, Morris, and Claire Cloninger. "Jesus, Your Name" in *Praise Hymns and Choruses*, 4th ed. MAR.

Hanson, Handt. "Waterlife" in W&P.

Nystrom, Martin J., and Don Harris. "You Called Me by Name" in *Hosanna! Music* 11. INT.

TUESDAY, JANUARY 9
ADRIAN OF CANTERBURY, TEACHER, C. 710

African by birth, Adrian (or Hadrian) worked with Theodore, archbishop of Canterbury, in developing the church in England, particularly through his direction of an influential school where many church leaders where instructed.

The growing awareness of the multicultural life of the church leads many to discover surprises in the church's history; for example, that an African missionary such as Adrian would have been influential in the development of the church in England, a church sometimes perceived only as Western and European in its history. Within parish groups, use the example of Adrian to explore the cross-cultural influence within the ancient church.

SATURDAY, JANUARY 13
GEORGE FOX, RENEWER OF SOCIETY, 1691

Fox severed his ties among family and friends in search of enlightenment. He found no comfort in the traditional church, and he became an itinerant preacher. His preaching emphasized the abiding inward light given by God to believers as the real source of comfort and authority. His preaching led to the establishment of preaching bands of women and men known as the "Publishers of the Truth." In time, these preachers established local communities that came to be known as the Society of Friends, or Quakers. During visits to the Caribbean and North America, Fox witnessed the evil of the slave trade, and he founded the abolitionist movement in England.

Quakers are known for the long period of silence in their meetings. Consider growing into the practice of silence in worship. Be mindful of the ways that silence breaks the hectic pace of life and leads us to attend to the wisdom of God in spoken word and through service to others.

JANUARY 14, 2001

SECOND SUNDAY AFTER THE EPIPHANY

INTRODUCTION

Scenes from familiar life and landscapes of disappointment become the setting where God intends to perform miracles. A wedding is about to happen between God and people, joining the predictable with the extraordinary. Today the church remembers in thanksgiving Bishop Eivind Berggrav, who resisted Nazism and worked for church renewal. This weekend also commemorates the life and ministry of Martin Luther King Jr., who called his nation to a new vision of justice.

PRAYER OF THE DAY

Lord God, you showed your glory and led many to faith by the works of your Son. As he brought gladness and healing to his people, grant us these same gifts and lead us also to perfect faith in him, Jesus Christ our Lord.

READINGS

Isaiah 62:1-5

The people's return to their homeland after the exile was not the glorious event announced earlier by the prophet. Nevertheless, the prophet declares hope. Jerusalem receives a new name as it becomes God's bride; the people are called to the celebration.

Psalm 36:5-10

We feast on the abundance of your house, O LORD. (Ps. 36:8)

1 Corinthians 12:1-11

The Corinthian congregation experienced division as various factions each claimed to have superior spiritual gifts. Paul invites this fractured community to discover a deeper unity from the Spirit who binds us together.

John 2:1-11

John's gospel describes Jesus' first miracle as an epiphany, a "sign" that reveals God's presence and power in and through Jesus.

COLOR Green

THE PRAYERS

Let us pray for all people upon whom the light of Christ shines with grace and mercy.

A BRIEF SILENCE.

For chaplains and all who proclaim your glory in military settings, hospitals, and homes for the aged, that people may have new life in Christ. Lord, in your mercy,
hear our prayer.

For those who guide policies of international trade, that the world's rich resources may be a blessing to all. Lord, in your mercy,
hear our prayer.

For all who are ill (especially...), that they might look to you as a source of strength in their struggles. Lord, in your mercy,

hear our prayer.

For the many gifts in this community we give you thanks, and we ask that you bless their use in Christ's saving mission. Lord, in your mercy,

hear our prayer.

HERE OTHER INTERCESSIONS MAY BE OFFERED.

We give thanks for loved ones who have died in the faith, remembering especially Eivind Josef Berggrav (*and those we name before you now...*). We pray that your comforting presence might be upon all who grieve their absence. Lord, in your mercy,

hear our prayer.

All these things and whatever else you see that we need, grant us, O God, for the sake of your Son, Jesus Christ our Lord.

Amen

IMAGES FOR PREACHING

What are we to make of this miracle? Does Jesus offer his catering services to us in order to help us host better parties, to make sure that food and drink never run out? Not likely. In this story and in other miraculous feeding stories of the New Testament, we learn that Jesus himself becomes the gift.

Jesus provided the choicest wine of the banquet. Jesus used the water set aside for the Jewish rites of purification as a way to proclaim that the new age had now come. No longer are those ritual washings necessary. No more do people have to worry about the kinds of actions they must perform in order to cleanse themselves. God gives the wine freely to all.

God often appears to be in the business of blessing us beyond our need. In our congregations we are often encouraged in the face of worries and difficulties. It is there that we receive God's limitless grace. When we eat and drink the body and blood of Christ, our pain and sorrow are overcome. Our fear is transformed into hope. We are bound again to Christ. We are one with him and with his future.

Of course, we often try to limit God. We may revel in abundance for our private needs, but we seem to believe that if God is generous to some folks, God cannot be generous to others. We think that someone else's

blessings will come out of what had been intended for us. But God does not work that way. God wills full and abundant life for all people—even those whom we may think have not earned it. The wedding at Cana proclaimed God's rich and abundant grace for everyone.

WORSHIP MATTERS

Worship is not a time to hold back. It is a time to celebrate the generosity of God. Hearty communion breads, pools of baptismal water, and a genuine book for the reading of the scriptures communicate God's lavish grace for us. These things are not necessarily expensive, but they do proclaim God's generosity with us. This week when we hear about the extravagance of Jesus' miracle at Cana might be a good time to watch Liturgy Training Publication's video *This Is the Night,* which shows how a Roman Catholic parish in Texas welcomes its newest members lavishly through sacramental signs.

LET THE CHILDREN COME

Jesus was a gift from God to humankind at Christmas. At Epiphany we celebrate the coming of the wise men and remember the gifts they brought to Jesus. Every time we come to worship, we receive gifts from God: gifts of bread and wine, gifts of love, gifts of learning and understanding, and shared experiences from our worship together. We receive more than we need as it is poured out to us in an unlimited flow (think of the miracle at Cana). God loves us so much and gives all that we need.

MUSIC FOR WORSHIP

GATHERING

| LBW 76 | O Morning Star, how fair and bright! |
| WOV 755 | We all are one in mission |

PSALM 36:5-10

"Psalm 35 (36)" in *The Grail Gelineau Psalter.* GIA G-1703.

Haas, David. "The Fountain of All Life" in PCY, vol. 9.

Hopson, Hal H. *Psalm Refrains and Tones.* HOP 425.

Isele, David Clark. TP.

Kallman, Daniel. PW, Cycle C.

HYMN OF THE DAY

| WOV 748 | Bind us together |
| | BIND US TOGETHER |

A SUGGESTION FOR THE HYMN OF THE DAY

Children sing stanzas from LS 127. All sing the refrain.

INSTRUMENTAL RESOURCES

Hammerly, Tornquist, Wolaver & Wyrtzen. "Bind Us Together" in *Weddings and Worship: Contemporary Christian Songs for Solo Piano.* WRD 301 0137 311. Pno, opt inst.

Rogers, Harlan. "Bind Us Together" in *Easy Piano Praise.* WRD 301 0092 318.

ALTERNATE HYMN OF THE DAY

LBW 224	Soul, adorn yourself with gladness
WOV 648	Jesus, come! for we invite you

COMMUNION

LBW 205	Now the silence
WOV 789	Now the feast and celebration

SENDING

LBW 216	For perfect love so freely spent (*alternate tune:* ST. PETER, LBW 345)
WOV 769	Mothering God, you gave me birth

ADDITIONAL HYMNS AND SONGS

HS98 817	Come, join in Cana's feast
LW 252	Lord, when you came as welcome guest
TFF 299	Holy God, you raise up prophets
W&P 139	The trumpets sound, the angels sing

MUSIC FOR THE DAY

CHORAL

Bach, J. S. "The Only Son from Heaven" in BAS. SATB, kybd.

Byrd, William. "Surge illuminare." NOV TM 6.

dePrez, Josquin. "O Mighty Word of God Come Down" in CC. SATB.

Handel, G. F. "All My Spirit Longs to Savor" in CC. SATB, org.

Jennings, Kenneth. "Arise, O Zion." KJO 5135.

Schalk, Carl. "This Touch of Love." MSM 50-8301. SATB, cong, org.

Sedio, Mark. "Each New Day/*Al despuntar en la loma el día.*" AFP 11-10968. SATB, pno, 2 C inst, perc.

Zipp, Friedrich. "Soul, Adorn Yourself with Gladness" in CC. SATB, kybd, opt 3 inst.

CHILDREN'S CHOIRS

Foley, John/arr. Jack Schrader. "One Bread, One Body." HOP A709. 3 pt mxd, pno.

Wold, Wayne. "To the Banquet Come" in LS.

KEYBOARD/INSTRUMENTAL

Brahms, Johannes. "Schmücke dich" in *Organ Works* (various editions).

Hancock, Gerre. "Meditation on 'Draw Us in the Spirit's Tether.'" OUP 386052-X. Org.

Rotermund, Melvin. "Draw Us in the Spirit's Tether" in *The Living God.* CPH 97-6762. Org.

HANDBELL

Geisler, Herbert. "Now the Silence." CPH97-6732. 3-5 oct, opt hc.

Honoré, Jeffrey. "Shine, Jesus, Shine." CPH 97-6633.

PRAISE ENSEMBLE

Dresie, Deborah. "All This and More." BEC BP1540. SATB, kybd.

Hurd, Bob. "Come unto Me" in *Glory & Praise.* OCP.

Willard, Kelly, and Paul Baloche. "Most Holy One" in *Praise Hymns and Choruses,* 4th ed.

SUNDAY, JANUARY 14

EIVIND JOSEF BERGGRAV, BISHOP OF OSLO, 1959

In 1937, Berggrav was elected bishop of Oslo and primate of Norway. In 1940, he was asked to negotiate with the Nazi regime in order to ascertain its intentions regarding the social and religious life of the Norwegian people. Rejecting any compromise with the occupation forces, he left the negotiations and demanded that the Nazis recognize the rights of the Jews and the autonomy of the church. Deprived of his episcopal title in 1943, he was placed under arrest, only to escape and remain in hiding in Oslo until the end of the war.

During the season of Epiphany, the life of Berggrav is another witness to the light of Christ. His life raises questions for believers today about the readiness to risk title, power, and prestige to speak for victims of injustice and seek truth in the midst of evils that face us in the world.

MONDAY, JANUARY 15
MARTIN LUTHER KING JR., RENEWER OF SOCIETY, MARTYR, 1968

Martin Luther King Jr. is remembered as an American prophet of justice among races and nations, a Christian whose faith undergirded his advocacy of vigorous yet nonviolent action for racial equality. A pastor of churches in Montgomery, Alabama, and Atlanta, Georgia, his witness was taken to the streets in such other places as Birmingham, Alabama, where he was arrested and jailed while protesting against segregation. He preached nonviolence and demanded that love be returned for hate. Awarded the Nobel Peace Prize in 1964, he was killed by an assassin on April 4, 1968. Congregations may choose to remember King by singing "We shall overcome" (TFF 213) or "Holy God, you raise up prophets" (TFF 299).

WEDNESDAY, JANUARY 17
ANTONY OF EGYPT, RENEWER OF THE CHURCH, C. 356

Antony was born in Qemen-al-Arous, Upper Egypt, and was one of the earliest Egyptian desert fathers. Born to Christian parents from whom he inherited a large estate, he took personally Jesus' message to sell all that you have, give to the poor, and follow Christ. After making arrangements to provide for the care of his sister, he gave away his inheritance and became a hermit. Later, he became the head of a group of monks that lived in a cluster of huts and devoted themselves to communal prayer, worship, and manual labor under Antony's direction. The money they earned from their work was distributed as alms. Antony and his monks also preached and counseled those who sought them out.

Antony and the desert fathers serve as a reminder that certain times and circumstances call Christians to stand apart from the surrounding culture and renounce the world in service to Christ.

THURSDAY, JANUARY 18
THE CONFESSION OF ST. PETER
WEEK OF PRAYER FOR CHRISTIAN UNITY BEGINS

The Week of Prayer for Christian Unity is framed by two commemorations, today's Confession of St. Peter and next week's Conversion of St. Paul. Both apostles are remembered together on June 29, but these two days give us an opportunity to focus on key events in each of their lives. Today we remember that Peter was led by God's grace to acknowledge Jesus as "the Christ, the Son of the living God" (Matt. 16:16).

This confession is the common confession that unites us with Peter and with all Christians of every time and place. During these weeks of Epiphany, with their emphasis on mission, consider holding an ecumenical worship service with neighboring congregations to embody the unity we share in our confession of Christ, a unity granted us in our one baptism, a unity we yearn to embody more fully. The hymn "We all are one in mission" (WOV 755) could be sung at this service.

FRIDAY, JANUARY 19
HENRY, BISHOP OF UPPSALA, MISSIONARY TO FINLAND, MARTYR, 1156

Henry, an Englishman, became bishop of Uppsala, Sweden, in 1152 and is regarded as the patron of Finland. He traveled to Finland with the king of Sweden on a mission trip and remained there to organize the church. He was murdered in Finland by a man whom he had rebuked and who was disciplined by the church. Henry's burial place became a center of pilgrimage. His popularity as a saint is strong in both Sweden and Finland.

Today is an appropriate day to celebrate the Finnish presence in the Lutheran church. Consider singing "Lost in the night" (LBW 394), which uses a Finnish folk tune. During Epiphany we celebrate the light of Christ revealed to the nations, and martyrs such as Henry continue to reveal that light through their witness to faith.

101

JANUARY 21, 2001

INTRODUCTION

Preaching is powerful, and the power is in the word of God. That word can convict us of sin and raise us to new life. That word can heal divisions in Christ's body and help us appreciate the gifts of others. And that Word has become flesh in Jesus of Nazareth. In this week of prayer for Christian unity, we join with other Christians to pray that we can come together in Christ.

PRAYER OF THE DAY

Almighty God, you sent your Son to proclaim your kingdom and to teach with authority. Anoint us with the power of your Spirit, that we, too, may bring good news to the afflicted, bind up the brokenhearted, and proclaim liberty to the captive; through your Son, Jesus Christ our Lord.

READINGS

Nehemiah 8:1-3, 5-6, 8-10

The exiles have returned. Under Nehemiah they have rebuilt the city of Jerusalem and its walls. Now the people ask Ezra, the priest, to read the law of Moses to them in the public square. When they hear it they weep for their sins, for the long years in exile, and for the joy of the Lord that was their strength.

Psalm 19

The law of the LORD revives the soul. (Ps. 19:7)

1 Corinthians 12:12-31a

Paul writes to the divided congregation in Corinth to tell them what it means for the church to be the one body of Christ.

Luke 4:14-21

Near the beginning of Jesus' public ministry, he visits his hometown of Nazareth. In the words of Isaiah, he clearly states his purpose and mission.

COLOR   Green

THE PRAYERS

Let us pray for all people upon whom the light of Christ shines with grace and mercy.

A BRIEF SILENCE.

For the church in every place, that we may embody Jesus' love for those who are poor, oppressed, or held captive. Lord, in your mercy,

hear our prayer.

For the newly inaugurated president and administration, that they may be strengthened for the tasks ahead and lead the nation in honoring the justice and dignity of every living creature. Lord, in your mercy,

hear our prayer.

For those struggling in the wilderness of despair, loneliness, or sickness (especially . . .), that you would sustain them with life in Christ. Lord, in your mercy,

hear our prayer.

For this community, that by the gifts of the living Word we may grow strong in the body of Christ. Lord, in your mercy,

hear our prayer.

HERE OTHER INTERCESSIONS MAY OFFERED.

We give thanks for Martin Luther King Jr. and all who have died proclaiming the new creation and the freedom of eternal life with God. Lord, in your mercy,

hear our prayer.

All these things and whatever else you see that we need, grant us, O God, for the sake of your Son, Jesus Christ our Lord.

Amen

IMAGES FOR PREACHING

The apostle Paul was writing to a congregation in a city that had a wide diversity of people and religious practices. These differences ultimately contributed to a division in the church at Corinth.

Paul likened the church to the human body. Just as a single body is one and yet is composed of many parts, so it is with those who are in Christ. "For in the one Spirit we were all baptized into one body—Jews or Greeks, slaves or free—and all were made to drink of one Spirit."

Paul urged Christians not to value any person less than another. Everyone is needed in the body, despite their many different talents or functions. The body must remain together if it is to survive.

Christ's church is a place where every person's gifts are honored. It is also a place where everyone's spiritual and physical needs are fulfilled. We all have our imperfections, but we are all drawn together by the one who shall make each of us perfect in the coming kingdom.

That we with all our differences can be drawn together in word and sacrament, in service and in witness, can mean only that God is truly present in our midst.

And this is our mission to the rest of the world: Having lived together despite our differences and disagreements, we can proclaim to others that it is only through God's power that we have true unity. There is a place and a function for all of us. We are the body of Christ and individually members of it.

WORSHIP MATTERS

The gospel today reminds us that God's word is good news to everyone in need. How do we receive these words as *good*? One way certainly is by responding "Thanks be to God" following each reading (or "Praise to you, O Christ" following the gospel). Another way we receive them as good is through our attentiveness to the words. Lectors who have examined a passage for the good news will help worshipers be attentive to these words at the moment of proclamation. Preachers who know that their central task is to proclaim God's good news are a gift to the church.

LET THE CHILDREN COME

Everyone likes to hear the good news. We hear the news from friends and relatives. We share good words with friends at school. The story of Jesus and God's love for us is too exciting to keep to ourselves. We listen in worship as someone reads the words of the Bible to us. Week by week we hear of the joy of Jesus' life. It is too good a story to miss even one chapter. Thus, we go to church every week to hear every part of the good news of God's word.

MUSIC FOR WORSHIP

SERVICE MUSIC

Today's first reading is a marvelous story of the people's acclamation at the reading of the word of God. How might our musical acclamations (at the gospel reading, especially) reflect a similar eager awe? "What a mighty Word God gives!" (W&P 155) is a new text based on a

traditional song that can serve as an acclamation before and after the gospel reading.

GATHERING

| LBW 233 | Thy strong word |
| WOV 756 | Lord, you give the great commission |

PSALM 19

Cox, Joe. "The Heavens Are Telling the Glory of God" in *Psalms for the People of God*. SMP 45/1037 S.

Haas, David. "Lord, You Have the Words" in PCY.

Hruby, Dolores. *Seasonal Psalms for Children with Optional Orff Instruments*. WLP 7102.

Inwood, Paul. "Psalm 19: You, Lord, Have the Message" in STP, vol. 2.

Kallman, Daniel. PW, Cycle C.

HYMN OF THE DAY

| LBW 87 | Hail to the Lord's anointed |
| | FREUT EUCH, IHR LIEBEN |

VOCAL RESOURCES

Bender, Mark. "Hail to the Lord's Anointed." CPH 98-2888. SAB, tpt, kybd, cong.

INSTRUMENTAL RESOURCES

Burkhardt, Michael. "Freut euch, ihr lieben" in *Five Christmas Hymn Improvisations, Set 1*. MSM 10-111. Org.

Wolff, S. Drummond. "Freut euch, ihr lieben" in *Hymn Descants, Set I*. CPH 97-6051. Org, inst.

ALTERNATE HYMN OF THE DAY

| LBW 35 | Hark, the glad sound! |
| WOV 755 | We all are one in mission |

COMMUNION

| LBW 225 | Lord Jesus Christ, we humbly pray |
| WOV 710 | One bread, one body |

SENDING

| LBW 559 | Oh, for a thousand tongues to sing |
| WOV 723 | The Spirit sends us forth to serve |

ADDITIONAL HYMNS AND SONGS

LW 78	Jesus has come and brings pleasure eternal
NCH 273	Praise with joy the world's creator
TFF 214	In Christ there is no east or west
W&P 111	One bread, one body

MUSIC FOR THE DAY

CHORAL

Bender, Jan. "O God, O Lord of Heaven and Earth." AFP 11-10481. Also in *The Augsburg Choirbook*. AFP 11-10817. SATB, opt cong, org, opt tpt.

Elgar, Edward. "The Spirit of the Lord Is Upon Me." NOV. SATB, org.

Englert, Eugene. "Awake, Arise, Go Forth in Faith." GIA G-2747. SATB, org, kybd.

Mendelssohn, Felix. "How Lovely Are the Messengers" in CC. SATB, org.

Rotermund, Melvin. "O God of Light." CPH 98-3375. SATB, kybd.

CHILDREN'S CHOIRS

Bach, J. S./arr. Michael Burkhardt. "The Heavens Declare Thy Glory." MSM-50-7503. U, 2 trbl inst, kybd, opt bass.

Smale, Marcelyn. "One Lord, One Faith." CG CGA-363. 2 pt, Orff inst.

Van Oss, Richard L. "Jesus, Jesus, Let Us Tell You" in LS.

Young, Philip M. "I Will Greatly Rejoice in the Lord." CPH 98-3093. U, desc, opt cong, kybd.

KEYBOARD/INSTRUMENTAL

Bach, J. S. "Liebster Jesu" BWV 730 & 731 (various editions). Org.

Gieschen, Thomas. "Dearest Jesus, at Your Word" in *Four Quiet Hymn Settings*. CPH 97-5839. Org.

Pinkham, Daniel. "Pastorale on 'The Morning Star.'" Galaxy. Org.

Wood, Dale. "Nyland" (Kuortane) in *Seven Folk Tune Sketches*. HWG GB357. Org.

HANDBELL

Behnke, John A. "I Want to Walk as a Child of the Light." CPH 97-6611. 3-5 oct.

Sherman, Arnold B. "Acclamation on 'Azmon.'" HOP Agape 1363. 3-5 oct.

PRAISE ENSEMBLE

Balhoff, Mike, Gary Daigle, and Darryl Ducote. "He Has Anointed Me" in *Gather*. GIA.

Foley, John. "One Bread, One Body." OCP 9494. SATB, kybd, gtr, opt cong.

Kendrick, Graham. "Make Way" in *Worship Songs*. HOP.

Ylvisaker, John. "The Heavens Are Telling" in *Borning Cry*. NGP.

Young, Jeremy. "God Has Spoken, Bread Is Broken." AFP 11-10733. SAB, kybd, opt cong.

THURSDAY, JANUARY 25
THE CONVERSION OF SAINT PAUL
WEEK OF PRAYER FOR CHRISTIAN UNITY ENDS

Today the Week of Prayer for Christian Unity comes to an end. The church remembers how a man of Tarsus named a Saul, a former persecutor of the early Christian church, was led by God's grace to become one of its chief preachers. The risen Christ appeared to Paul on the road to Damascus and called him to proclaim the gospel. The narratives describing Paul's conversion in the Acts of the Apostles, Galatians, and 1 Corinthians inspire this commemoration, which was first celebrated among the Christians of Gaul.

The entire Week of Prayer for Christian Unity gives us a chance to consider our calling in light of Paul's words in Galatians that all are one in Christ. The hymn "Bind us together" (WOV 748) can be used to pray that Christ will continue to hold us in our baptismal unity.

FRIDAY, JANUARY 26
TIMOTHY, TITUS, AND SILAS

Following the celebration of the Conversion of Paul, we remember his companions. Today, we remember Timothy, Titus, and Silas. They were missionary coworkers with Paul. Timothy accompanied Paul on his second missionary journey and was commissioned by Paul to go to Ephesus, where he served as bishop and overseer of the church. Titus was a traveling companion of Paul, accompanied him on the trip to the council of Jerusalem, and became the first bishop of Crete. Silas traveled with Paul through Asia Minor and Greece, and was imprisoned with him at Philippi, where they were delivered by an earthquake.

This festival invites the church to remember Christian leaders, bishops, pastors, and teachers—both men and women—who have been influential in the lives of individual members as gospel signs of the light of Epiphany.

SATURDAY, JANUARY 27
LYDIA, DORCAS, AND PHOEBE

Today we remember three women in the early church who were companions in Paul's ministry. Lydia was Paul's first convert at Philippi in Macedonia. She was a merchant of purple-dyed goods, and because purple dye was extremely expensive, it is likely that Lydia was a woman of some wealth. Lydia and her household were baptized by Paul, and for a time her home was a base for Paul's missionary work. Dorcas is remembered for her charitable works, particularly making clothing for needy widows. Phoebe was a *diakonos,* a deacon in the church at Cenchreae, near Corinth. Paul praises her as one who, through her service, looked after many people.

Today provides an opportunity for congregations to reflect the ministry of women, ordained and lay, wealthy and poor, who have given of themselves in service to the church and to the ministry of the gospel in their congregations.

JANUARY 28, 2001
FOURTH SUNDAY AFTER THE EPIPHANY

INTRODUCTION

An epiphany ought to be a surprise. The prophet Jeremiah is surprised that God would call a youth, but Jeremiah has been in God's sight for a long, long time. Jesus is popular in many places but maybe not at home. And love, which seems so familiar, is really a radical invitation to care for others on their terms. How will love surprise us this day?

PRAYER OF THE DAY

O God, you know that we cannot withstand the dangers which surround us. Strengthen us in body and spirit so that, with your help, we may be able to overcome the weakness that our sin has brought upon us; through Jesus Christ, your Son our Lord.

READINGS

Jeremiah 1:4-10

Today's reading relates Jeremiah's call and commission as a prophet in the years before the Babylonian exile. His task was to preach God's word in the midst of the difficult political realities of the time. He was to make God known, not just among the Israelites, but also among the nations.

Psalm 71:1-6

From my mother's womb you have been my strength. (Ps. 71:6)

1 Corinthians 13:1-13

Some at Corinth prided themselves on their spiritual gifts. Paul reminds them that God gives us many gifts through the Holy Spirit, but the most important of these is love, the kind of love that allows us to live and work in cooperation with one another, the kind of love that God showed us particularly in Christ.

Luke 4:21-30

People in Jesus' hometown are initially pleased when he says that God will free the oppressed. Their pleasure turns to rage, however, when he reminds them that prophets often bring God's blessings to those who are regarded as outsiders.

COLOR Green

THE PRAYERS

Let us pray for all people upon whom the light of Christ shines with grace and mercy.

A BRIEF SILENCE.

For bishops, pastors, associates in ministry, deaconesses, and diaconal ministers, that their work may be a joy to them and a blessing to the people they serve. Lord, in your mercy,

hear our prayer.

For peace among nations and for the diplomatic efforts of those serving in troubled places. Lord, in your mercy,

hear our prayer.

105

For all enduring a time of crisis or illness (especially…), that they may cast their burdens on you. Lord, in your mercy,

hear our prayer.

For those who founded this congregation, we praise you. Help us continue that mission with joyful purpose, that others may build their lives on Christ. Lord, in your mercy,

hear our prayer.

HERE OTHER INTERCESSIONS MAY BE OFFERED.

For those who loved the Lord and now rest from their labors, we give thanks. May we share God's presence with them in the world to come. Lord, in your mercy,

hear our prayer.

All these things and whatever else you see that we need, grant us, O God, for the sake of your Son, Jesus Christ our Lord.

Amen

IMAGES FOR PREACHING

The opening verses of the book of Jeremiah record how the prophet was called by God. The call came to Jeremiah in much the same way it had come to others before him: "I appointed you a prophet to the nations." And Jeremiah responded, "Ah, Lord God! Truly I do not know how to speak, for I am only a boy."

When faced with the prophetic charge ourselves, our first response might well be to run or to offer some excuse: "But I'm too young!" or "I'm too old!" or "I've done my share—let someone else." In all truthfulness, we prefer to avoid God's call, rather than to heed it.

When we read about all of the prophets who answered God's call, finally none of them took the easy way out. They did what they did not want to do. They met with people they did not want to see. They went to places where they had never before thought of going.

We can do all the things God calls us to do because, as with Jeremiah, the Lord has put his words into our mouths. We have been "set over nations and over kingdoms, to pluck up and to break down, to destroy and to overthrow, to build and to plant."

It is God working in and through us who gives us the ability to do these things. And so like all of God's faithful who have been called before, we do not have to make up excuses when we are called ourselves. We know that God will give us the strength to do the task. We can heartily respond, "Here I am, send me!"

WORSHIP MATTERS

While it is a laudable goal to make many of the mechanics of worship as easy as possible for worshipers (well-designed bulletins, signs for the benefit of newcomers, attentive ushers and greeters), the meaning of much of what we do in worship may not make much sense to first-time worshipers. Today's second reading reminds us that we can only enter into God's mystery partially. Yet we can help people become more acclimated to our liturgy with its seemingly coded language and learned behaviors. Are regular opportunities to meet with newcomers offered, so that they might ask questions (inquirer's classes or informal gathering times after services)? Make sure that those who are new to the Christian tradition may ask any question (there are no dumb questions) without fear or ridicule.

LET THE CHILDREN COME

Ask children, "Do you know that many of the grownups here do not understand all of the things we say in our worship services?" We may hear things that we do not always understand, but we continue to listen despite our lack of understanding, knowing that one day we may understand better. In the meantime, we are building lifelong traditions that help us through troubled times. Our worship serves as a guide to help us along the way.

MUSIC FOR WORSHIP

GATHERING

| LBW 487 | Let us ever walk with Jesus |
| WOV 718 | Here in this place |

PSALM 71:1-6

Barrett, James/Hal H. Hopson. TP.

Currie, Randolph. "Psalm 71: I Will Sing" in RS.

Haas, David. "I Will Sing" in PCY, vol. 3.

Kallman, Daniel. PW, Cycle C.

HYMN OF THE DAY

| LBW 397 | O Zion, haste |
| | ANGELIC SONGS |

INSTRUMENTAL RESOURCES

Sedio, Mark. "O Zion, Haste" in *Praises of Zion*. CPH 97-6728. Org.

ALTERNATE HYMN OF THE DAY

LBW 237	O God of light
WOV 768	He comes to us as one unknown

COMMUNION

LBW 406	Take my life, that I may be
WOV 665	Ubi caritas et amor

SENDING

LBW 315	Love divine, all loves excelling
WOV 721	Go, my children, with my blessing

ADDITIONAL HYMNS AND SONGS

PH 531	Not for tongues of heaven's angels
TFF 213	We shall overcome
UMH 408	The gift of love
VU 193	Gracious Spirit, Holy Ghost
W&P 161	You are the rock of my salvation

MUSIC FOR THE DAY

CHORAL

Cherwien, David "O Radiant Christ, Incarnate Word." GIA G-3882. SATB, cong, org, opt fl.

Hopson, Hal H. "Canticle of Love." AFP 11-10911. SATB, org.

Hopson, Hal H., arr. "The Gift of Love." HOP HH 3922. SATB, kybd.

Mendelssohn, Felix. "See What Love" in CC. SATB, kybd.

CHILDREN'S CHOIRS

Haugen, Marty. "Love Is Never-Ending" in LS.

Hopson, Hal H. "The Gift of Love." HOP CF 148. U/2 pt, kybd.

Pote, Allen. "The Greatest Is Love." CG CGA781. SAT(B), pno, opt fl.

KEYBOARD/INSTRUMENTAL

Behnke, John A. "Prelude on 'How Clear Is Our Vocation, Lord/He Comes to Us as One Unknown'" in *Five Preludes of Praise.* CPH 97-6753. Org.

Powell, Robert. "Repton" in *Sing a New Song.* AFP 11-10766. Org.

HANDBELL

Kinyon, Barbara B. "All Things Bright and Beautiful." HOP Agape 1733. 2-3 oct.

Thompson, Martha Lynn. "God of Grace." CPH 97-5628. 4-5 oct.

PRAISE ENSEMBLE

Schutte, Daniel. "Before The Sun Burned Bright" in *Glory & Praise.* OCP.

Shaw, Kirby. "Rock Me in the Cradle of Love." HAL 08662432. SAB, kybd.

FRIDAY, FEBRUARY 2
THE PRESENTATION OF OUR LORD

Forty days after the birth of Christ we mark the day Mary and Joseph presented him in the temple in accordance with Jewish law. There in the temple, a prophet named Anna began to speak of the redemption of Israel when she saw the young child. Simeon also greeted Mary and Joseph. He responded to the presence of the consolation of Israel in this child with the words of the Nunc dimittis. His song described Jesus as a "light for the nations."

Because of the link between Jesus as the light for the nations, and because an old reading for this festival contains a line from the prophet Zephaniah, "I will search Jerusalem with candles," the day is also known as Candlemas, a day when candles are blessed for the coming year. If no service is planned to celebrate this day in the congregation, be sure to read the story about the presentation when congregational groups meet and include a setting of the Song of Simeon (such as LBW 339 or 349).

SATURDAY, FEBRUARY 3
ANSGAR, ARCHBISHOP OF HAMBURG, MISSIONARY TO DENMARK AND SWEDEN, 865

A traditional emphasis during the weeks of Epiphany has been the mission of the church. Ansgar was a monk who led a mission to Denmark and then later to Sweden, where he built the first church. His work ran into difficulties with the rulers of the day, and he was forced to withdraw into Germany, where he served as a bishop in Hamburg. Despite his difficulties in Sweden, he persisted in his mission work and later helped consecrate Gothbert as the first bishop of Sweden. Ansgar also had a deep love for the poor. He would wash their feet and serve them food provided by the parish.

Ansgar is particularly honored by Scandinavian Lutherans. The Church of Sweden honors him as an apostle. His persistence in mission and his care for the poor invite congregations to reflect on their own ministry of bearing the light of Christ during the days of Epiphany.

107

FEBRUARY 4, 2001

INTRODUCTION

We are part of God's epiphany. In baptism God calls us. In the eucharist Christ feeds us and sends us to the world—just as God called Isaiah, and just as Jesus sent Simon, James, and John. The good news handed down to us is meant to be passed on to others.

PRAYER OF THE DAY

Almighty God, you sent your only Son as the Word of life for our eyes to see and our ears to hear. Help us to believe with joy what the Scriptures proclaim, through Jesus Christ our Lord.

READINGS

Isaiah 6:1-8 [9-13]

Today's reading recounts Isaiah's commission as a prophet in Jerusalem during the second half of the eighth century B.C. Isaiah's intense experiences were part of his credentials to announce God's judgment and warn God's people.

Psalm 138

I will bow down toward your holy temple. (Ps. 138:2)

1 Corinthians 15:1-11

Paul stresses that the proclamation of the resurrection is not a novelty. Along with the story of Jesus' crucifixion and burial, this resurrection witness has shaped the whole church from the time of the apostles to the present. The Christian church is solidly founded upon this good news.

Luke 5:1-11

Near the beginning of Jesus' ministry, his words and signs have powerful and surprising effects: crowds press upon him, a great and unexpected number of fish fill the nets, and a fisherman becomes an apostle.

COLOR   Green

THE PRAYERS

Let us pray for all people upon whom the light of Christ shines with grace and mercy.

A BRIEF SILENCE.

O God, enlarge our vision, so that we may recognize your saving power at work in your Son and join the prophets as heralds of your life-giving word. Lord, in your mercy,

hear our prayer.

O God, bless us with the mind of Christ, so that we may be his partners in welcoming others into the wide net of your mercy and forgiveness. Lord, in your mercy,

hear our prayer.

O God, come to those who are separated from your love and the love of family and friends. Gently lead them by your grace, and help them walk on the path of understanding, forgiveness, and peace. Lord, in your mercy,

hear our prayer.

O God, stretch out your saving hand to those who are sick (especially...). With your strong love, comfort the lonely, the oppressed, and all who suffer. Lord, in your mercy,

hear our prayer.

O God, we pray for this community of faith: Teach us to use the many gifts you have given us for the common good. Lord, in your mercy,

hear our prayer.

HERE OTHER INTERCESSIONS MAY BE OFFERED.

O God, hear us who sing your praise on earth, and lead us with all your children through this life until we join the angels and saints in heaven. Lord, in your mercy,

hear our prayer.

All these things and whatever else you see that we need, grant us, O God, for the sake of your Son, Jesus Christ our Lord.

Amen

IMAGES FOR PREACHING

Many of us have often heard today's gospel and have probably wondered how we could simply drop what we were doing and leave everything behind to follow Jesus. We have responsibilities to our families. We have mortgages and car payments that we cannot simply walk away from. How could we possibly leave it all behind to serve Christ's mission?

Indeed, some people have taken Jesus' words quite literally and have sold all their possessions, leaving a house and its contents behind in order to serve. Still others have altered the direction of their lives without getting rid of all other commitments.

Some have changed careers or moved into new neighborhoods. Some people have simplified their lives in order to become more focused on answering God's call, rather than just searching for personal rewards.

Following Christ does have an impact on the kind of work we do. Following Christ must affect how we act toward our neighbors. All of the various relationships we have in life should be viewed from Christ's call to come and follow him. If something in our lives is blocking the way for us to serve Christ, then we ought to leave it beside the shore along with the disciples' fishing nets in order to follow Christ.

This week, as in every week, we have the opportunity to follow Jesus. The choice is ours. Will we try to avoid him and be content with business as usual? Or will we strike out behind Jesus, leaving our boats at the shore in order to follow him?

WORSHIP MATTERS

The regular highpoint of the liturgy for many worshipers throughout the centuries has been the singing of the Sanctus ("Holy, holy, holy Lord"). Isaiah's vision of the six-winged seraphs in today's reading is the source for this ancient hymn. It is a hymn that proclaims the grandeur of God while affirming our humility. How does your congregation sing this liturgical song? Is it a hymn that they can *belt* out? Can they literally make the rafters ring? Consider how choirs and instruments might embellish this hymn through festival settings of the liturgy that are available.

LET THE CHILDREN COME

Angels sang a great song in the first reading from Isaiah. "Holy, holy, holy Lord" is a great song that we also sing in our communion services. We believe that it is a time when God's glory appears to us. In loud and happy voices, we celebrate Jesus' presence among us in the sharing of bread and wine among us. Sing of the power and glory of God. Sing "Holy, holy, holy Lord, God of power...."

MUSIC FOR WORSHIP
SERVICE MUSIC

Martin Luther's paraphrase of the Sanctus, "Isaiah in a vision did of old" (LBW 528), echoes today's first read-

ing. One way of using it in the liturgy is to choose LBW eucharistic prayer IV, which is intended to be prayed without the Sanctus, and then to let this hymn be the first hymn during communion (perhaps sung by the choir, with the congregation joining at "Holy...").

GATHERING

| LBW 247 | Holy majesty, before you |
| WOV 750 | Oh, praise the gracious power |

PSALM 138

Cooney, Rory. "On the Day I Called" in STP, vol. 4.

Haas, David. "The Fragrance of Christ" in PCY, vol. 3.

Kallman, Daniel. PW, Cycle C.

Stewart, Roy James. "Lord, Your Love Is Eternal" in PCY, vol. 5.

See proper 12.

HYMN OF THE DAY

| LBW 403 | Lord, speak to us, that we may speak |
| | CANONBURY |

INSTRUMENTAL RESOURCES

Ferguson, John. "Canonbury" in *Hymn Preludes and Free Accompaniments*, vol. 17. AFP 11-9413. Org.

Galetar, Charles. "Canonbury" in *Contemporary Hymn Accompaniments*. FLA HF-5173. Org.

ALTERNATE HYMN OF THE DAY

| LBW 432 | We worship you, O God of might |
| WOV 752 | I, the Lord of sea and sky |

COMMUNION

| LBW 506 | Dear Lord and Father of mankind |
| WOV 708 | Grains of wheat |

SENDING

| LBW 529 | Praise God. Praise him |
| WOV 723 | The Spirit sends us forth to serve |

ADDITIONAL HYMNS AND SONGS

TFF 289	Holy, holy
UMH 581	Whom shall I send?
W&P 120	Rejoice in the mission
W&P 153	We see the Lord

109

MUSIC FOR THE DAY

CHORAL

Bach, J. S. "Jesu, Joy—My Joy Forever" in BAS. SATB, org.

Williams, David McKinley. "In the Year That King Uzziah Died."
HWG. SATB, org.

Mendelssohn, Felix. "Heilig/Holy." HAL 12005. SSAATTBB.

Powell, Kathy. "To Be Fishers of Women and Men." GIA G-4486.
SATB, cong, gtr, kybd, fl.

Schutte, Daniel/arr. Ovid Young. "Here I Am, Lord." AFP 11-10747.
SSATB, kybd.

Shepperd, Mark. "Balm in Gilead." AFP 11-10923. SATB, kybd.

Willan, Healey. Hymn anthem on the tune "Picardy," PET 6262.
SATB, org.

CHILDREN'S CHOIRS

Dietterich, Philip R. "Come One, Come All, Come Follow."
CG CGA-553. U, kybd.

Larson, Sonia. "Simon Peter" in *Three for the Children.* AMSI CC-8.
U, opt desc, kybd.

Sleeth, Natalie. "Carol of the Fishermen." AMSI 249. 2 pt, kybd.

Zorzin, Alejandro. "Jesus Brings a Message" in LS.

KEYBOARD/INSTRUMENTAL

Linker, Janet. "Here I Am, Lord" in *Laudate! Volume 4.* CPH 97-6665.
Org.

Hassell, Michael. "Here I Am, Lord" in *More Folkways.* AFP 11-10866.
Inst, pno.

HANDBELL

Afdahl, Lee J. "You Have Come Down to the Lakeshore" in *Two
Spanish Tunes for Handbells.* AFP 11-10874. 3-5 oct, opt tamb.

Bohr, Jodi Acker. "Meditation on 'Forest Green.'" FLA HP-5321.
2-3 oct, fl.

PRAISE ENSEMBLE

Fettke, Tom. "I Saw The Lord" in *Master Chorus Book.* LIL.

Prince, Nolene. "Holy, Holy, Holy Is the Lord of Hosts" in *Praise &
Worship.* MAR.

Schutte, Dan/Craig Courtney. "Here I Am, Lord" (Isaiah 6).
BEC BP1403. SATB, kybd.

MONDAY, FEBRUARY 5
THE MARTYRS OF JAPAN, 1597

In the sixteenth century, Jesuit missionaries, followed by Franciscans, introduced the Christian faith in Japan. But a promising beginning to those missions—there were perhaps as many as 300,000 Christians by the end of the sixteenth century—met complications from competition between the missionary groups, political difficulty between Spain and Portugal, and factions within the government of Japan. Christianity was suppressed. By 1630, Christianity was driven underground.

Today we commemorate the first martyrs of Japan, twenty-six missionaries and converts, who were killed by crucifixion. Two hundred and fifty years later, when Christian missionaries returned to Japan, they found a community of Japanese Christians that had survived underground. The Martyrs of Japan are a somber reminder of the cost of Christianity and discipleship. Their witness invites us to pray for the church's own witness to the gospel and encourages us to trust that the church is sustained in times of persecution.

FEBRUARY 11, 2001

INTRODUCTION

A fundamental decision is placed before us this day: Will we choose the way of blessing or the way of woe? The death and resurrection of Jesus is the pivot on which the decision turns. To be in Christ means that we get planted by streams of water and are rooted among those who thirst for God's reign. The eucharistic acclamation points the path to life: "Christ has died. Christ is risen. Christ will come again."

PRAYER OF THE DAY

Lord God, mercifully receive the prayers of your people. Help us to see and understand the things we ought to do, and give us grace and power to do them; through your Son, Jesus Christ our Lord.

READINGS

Jeremiah 17:5-10

These verses compose a poem that is part of a larger collection of wisdom sayings contrasting two ways of life. Life with God brings blessing; the power and vitality of God is active in our life. Life without God brings a curse, the power of death.

Psalm 1

They are like trees planted by streams of water. (Ps. 1:3)

1 Corinthians 15:12-20

For Paul, the resurrection of Christ is the basis for Christian hope. Because Christ has been raised, those who are in Christ know that they too will be raised to a new life beyond death.

Luke 6:17-26

After choosing his twelve apostles, Jesus teaches a crowd of followers about the nature and demands of discipleship. He begins his great sermon with surprising statements about who is truly blessed in the eyes of God.

COLOR Green

THE PRAYERS

Let us pray for all people upon whom the light of Christ shines with grace and mercy.

A BRIEF SILENCE.

O God, nourish the life of your church with the word and sacraments of your Son's life so that your people may continue to bear the fruits of justice and peace. Lord, in your mercy,

hear our prayer.

O God, teach us to use earth's abundant gifts wisely and to respect every living thing you have created. Lord, in your mercy,

hear our prayer.

O God, bless with your comfort and healing those who are sick (especially . . .). Help us respond to their needs with compassion and generosity. Lord, in your mercy,

hear our prayer.

O God, bless with food and labor those who are poor. Comfort those who mourn with the strength that you alone can give. Satisfy the hungry, and come to those who suffer estrangement for the sake of the faith. Lord, in your mercy,

hear our prayer.

HERE OTHER INTERCESSIONS MAY BE OFFERED.

As you raised Christ from the dead, so lead us with your gracious hands through death to the new and eternal Jerusalem, where we shall join the saints in light. Lord, in your mercy,

hear our prayer.

All these things and whatever else you see that we need, grant us, O God, for the sake of your Son, Jesus Christ our Lord.

Amen

IMAGES FOR PREACHING

You may have heard about a woman who functions as a lay eucharistic minister in her parish. The woman has an illness that requires her to use a cane, making it necessary for a second person to carry the eucharistic bread so that she can distribute it.

While ministering one day, the eucharistic minister's assistant was an elderly nun whose order was attached to the parish. In the course of communion, a few crumbs dropped on the floor, which worried the elderly sister, who immediately dropped to her knees and gathered the fragments with her fingers. She brought them to eye

111

level and examining them said, "I'm not sure if this is lint or Jesus!" Upon tasting them she said, "Lint!" and the distribution of the sacrament continued.

We might ask whether the people we often dismiss as the world's poor are "lint or Jesus." From our position of relative power, we may have the tendency to view the poor as if they did not matter. We scrutinize them and make our judgments.

To each and every one of us—no matter how rich or how poor—come the words we hear as the sacrament of communion is distributed, "The body of Christ, given for you. The blood of Christ, shed for you."

We are all poor in that none of us is deserving of any of God's graces on our own merit. But we are also rich in that we are given the best gift we could ever hope for—God's own precious Son. In receiving this gift, we share in God's very self.

WORSHIP MATTERS

Our standing in worship—to sing, to pray, to hear the gospel—is a sign of our being raised with Christ. Throughout the centuries standing has been the most regular posture for worship, even though contemporary worshipers may be more accustomed to sitting. Standing to receive communion (especially during the Easter season) is a sign of the resurrection. Do not be timid about asking worshipers to stand. Of course, those whose health does not permit it may be seated (and should be given the option of sitting toward the front, rather than only behind other standing worshipers). Standing is also a sign of our activity in worship. Worship is our corporate work, so it requires a posture more suited for work than for relaxation.

LET THE CHILDREN COME

Let's stand and stretch! Singers stand to straighten their posture and make a big air space for breath to sing. Standing straightens our posture, and it gets us ready for an important activity. We often stand in worship for singing and praying and hearing about Jesus' life in the gospel. As we stand, we are also reminded that like Jesus, we too are raised to new life.

MUSIC FOR WORSHIP

GATHERING

| LBW 248 | Dearest Jesus, at your word |
| WOV 760 | For the fruit of all creation |

PSALM 1

Haas, David. "Happy Are They" in PCY, vol. 3.

Howard, Julie. *Sing for Joy: Psalm Settings for God's Children.* LTP.

Howard, Julia/arr. Vera Lyons. "Like a Tree" in LS.

Kallman, Daniel. PW, Cycle C.

Kline, Patsy Hilton. "Psalm 1: Planted by the Waters" in *Renew*. HOP.

Schoenbachler, Tim. "Psalm 1: Happy Are They" in STP, vol. 2.

See proper 18.

HYMN OF THE DAY

| WOV 764 | Blest are they |
| | BLEST ARE THEY |

VOCAL RESOURCES

Haas, David. "Blest Are They." GIA G-2958. U/SAB, cong, 2 C inst, gtr.

INSTRUMENTAL RESOURCES

Cotter, Jeannie. "Blest Are They" in *After the Rain*. GIA. G-3390. Pno.

Keesecker, Thomas. "Partita on 'Blest Are They.'" CPH 97-6546. Org.

ALTERNATE HYMN OF THE DAY

| LBW 232 | Your Word, O Lord, is gentle dew |
| LBW 562 | Lift every voice and sing |

COMMUNION

| LBW 316 | Jesus, the very thought of you |
| WOV 668 | There in God's garden |

SENDING

| LBW 221 | Sent forth by God's blessing |
| WOV 671 | Alleluia, alleluia, give thanks |

ADDITIONAL HYMNS AND SONGS

DH 86	Blessed are you
NCH 313	Like a tree beside the waters
TFF 147	I shall not be moved
W&P 18	Bind us together

MUSIC FOR THE DAY

CHORAL

Ashdown, Franklin. "Jesus, the Very Thought of You." AFP 11-10886. SATB, org, C inst.

de Victoria, Tomas Luis. "Jesu, the Very Thought of Thee" in *The Oxford Easy Anthem Book* OXF.

Hillert, Richard. "Happy Are Those Who Delight." GIA G-4259. U, org, fl, opt str qrt.

Nicholson, Paul. "He Comes to Us as One Unknown." AFP 11-10736. SATB, cong, org, vc or hrn.

112

Ratcliff, Cary. "See the Silent Ones Who Wait." KAI K-15.
SATB, kybd.

Willcock, Christopher. "Give Us a Pure Heart." OCP 4529.
SATB, org.

CHILDREN'S CHOIRS

Erickson, John. "The Lord Is Great!" in LS.

Haas, David. "Blest Are They." GIA G-2958. U/SATB, cong, kybd,
2 C inst, gtr.

Leavitt, John. "Blessed Are They." CG CGA-425. U/2 pt, kybd.

Medema, Ken. "Tree Song." SHW E-212. 2 pt, kybd, opt hb.

KEYBOARD/INSTRUMENTAL

Cherwien, David. "Your Word, O Lord, Is Gentle Dew" in *Interpretations, Book 2*. AMSI OR-3. Org.

Ferguson, John. "Shall We Gather at the River." AFP 11-10824. Org.

HANDBELL

Greer, Bruce. "River Medley." Ringing Word RW8108. 3-4 oct.

Sherman, Arnold B. "Shall We Gather at the River?" AG 2098. 3-6 oct.

PRAISE ENSEMBLE

Harrah, Walt, and John Schreiner. "I Will Delight" in W&P.

Ylvisaker, John. "We Shall Not Be Moved" in *Borning Cry*. NGP.

WEDNESDAY, FEBRUARY 14
CYRIL, MONK, 869; METHODIUS, BISHOP, 885;
MISSIONARIES TO THE SLAVS

These two brothers from a noble family in Thessalonika in northeastern Greece were priests and missionaries. After some early initial missionary work by Cyril among the Arabs, the brothers retired to a monastery. They were later sent to work among the Slavs, the missionary work for which they are most known. Since Slavonic had no written form at the time, the brothers established a written language with the Greek alphabet as its basis. They translated the scriptures and the liturgy using this Cyrillic alphabet. The Czechs, Serbs, Croats, Slovaks, and Bulgars regard the brothers as the founders of Slavic literature. The brothers' work in preaching and worshiping in the language of the people are honored by Christians in both East and West.

113

FEBRUARY 18, 2001
SEVENTH SUNDAY AFTER THE EPIPHANY

INTRODUCTION

The promise and its fulfillment may not look at all alike, even though they are intimately connected. Paul speaks about seeds and plants as he tries to picture resurrection life. Joseph's brothers never thought they would see him alive again, so how shocking he must have appeared to them as an Egyptian leader! Jesus invites us to sow seeds of new life by loving enemies. Today we also remember Martin Luther, who saw in the gospel the heart of the matter—a seed to be planted for new life.

PRAYER OF THE DAY

God of compassion, keep before us the love you have revealed in your Son, who prayed even for his enemies; in our words and deeds help us to be like him through whom we pray, Jesus Christ our Lord.

READINGS

Genesis 45:3-11, 15

A central theme in the Joseph story emphasizes the hidden nature of many of God's activities in human history. Joseph recognized the brothers who sold him into slavery. He repeatedly tested them to see if they had changed. Now Joseph must decide how he will treat them: with vengeance or with the love God has shown him.

Psalm 37:1-12, 41-42 (Psalm 37:1-11, 39-40 [NRSV])

The lowly shall possess the land; they will delight in abundance of peace. (Ps. 37:12)

1 Corinthians 15:35-38, 42-50

In this chapter on the resurrection of the dead, Paul responds to the objection that bodies may decay before they are raised. Jesus' resurrection, says Paul, sets the pattern for ours. As the living plant is wondrously transformed from the seed that was sown, so will those who are raised to life receive new bodies more glorious than flesh and blood.

Luke 6:27-38

Jesus teaches his disciples how to live in accord with his proclamation of the kingdom of God. They should treat others— even their enemies—as they themselves wish to be treated, that is, with the same kindness and mercy that God graciously shows to all.

COLOR Green

THE PRAYERS

Let us pray for all people upon whom the light of Christ shines with grace and mercy.
A BRIEF SILENCE.
For the church's schools, daycare centers, and all places of learning, that they may help people to establish their lives in Christ. Lord, in your mercy,
hear our prayer.
For local government and mayors, managers and planning officers, that life in community may be well and safely ordered. Lord, in your mercy,
hear our prayer.
For all who are ill and for those receiving medical treatment, we ask for your healing power (especially…). Lord, in your mercy,
hear our prayer.
For our own community of the baptized, that in our daily serving the love of Christ may be seen. Lord, in your mercy,
hear our prayer.
HERE OTHER INTERCESSIONS MAY BE OFFERED.
We offer thanks for those we have released to your keeping. Bring us with Martin Luther and all your saints to the glory of resurrection. Lord, in your mercy,
hear our prayer.
All these things and whatever else you see that we need, grant us, O God, for the sake of your Son, Jesus Christ our Lord.
Amen

IMAGES FOR PREACHING

Most of us are quite familiar with the golden rule: "Do unto others as you would have them do unto you." It is something that many people have learned, whether they are Christians or have ever read the Bible. While the golden rule is a part of our gospel for the day, you could say that it is not really an accurate summary of the whole passage from Luke 6.

"If you love those who love you, what credit is that to you? For even sinners love those who love them. If you do good to those who do good to you, what credit is that to you? For even sinners do the same…. But love your enemies, do good, and lend, expecting nothing in return."

What Jesus commands in this passage is really to go beyond the requirements of the law. What Jesus suggests here is that members of the Christian community are not to follow the social and economic status quo. Jesus calls the believing community to be more than a community of equals.

Jesus leads us beyond "Do unto others as you would have them do to you" to "Do to others as God has done and is doing with both you and them." Of course, this golden rule taken in context is not easy, but we do have the support of the entire Christian community in carrying it out.

WORSHIP MATTERS

It may be a shock to many people that the Christian community actually lives out forgiveness. We enact this practice of forgiving every week when we offer signs of peace to one another and when communicants are reconciled to one another. But do we really live out what happens in our worship, or do we merely give lip service to God's love? Genuine Christian communities are marked by their ability to love everyone without any discrimination. It is hard work, to be sure, but it is also God's work. When God forgives us our sins, they are forgiven. Congregations need to be encouraged in living out this forgiveness as well.

LET THE CHILDREN COME

Bread is one of the most important foods of life. In many places throughout the world, when bad times came, people survived if they had bread. When the people had no bread, governments were overthrown. In the Middle East, where our faith began, people have a special reverence for bread. Our breaking of bread in communion reminds us of Jesus' last supper with his disciples. Encourage children to bring an item of food to church to share with a food pantry, where people in need can go for supplies.

MUSIC FOR WORSHIP

GATHERING

LBW 470	Praise and thanks and adoration
WOV 716	Word of God, come down on earth

PSALM 37

Cox, Joe. "Be Still before the Lord" in *Psalms for the People of God*. SMP 45/1037 S.

Marshall, Jane. "Psalm 37" in *Psalms Together*. CG CGC-18.

See proper 22.

HYMN OF THE DAY

LBW 307	Forgive our sins as we forgive
	Detroit

VOCAL RESOURCES

Busarow, Donald R. "Detroit" in *Thirty More Accompaniments for Hymns in Canon*. AFP 11-10163.

Hobby, Robert A. "Forgive Our Sins as We Forgive." CPH 98-2870. SAB.

INSTRUMENTAL RESOURCES

Dorian, Mark. "Detroit" in *Around the World*. AFP 11-10618. Pno.

Held, Wilbur. "Detroit" in *Seven Settings of American Folk Hymns*. CPH 97-5829. Org.

Marcus, Mary. "Detroit" in *Ten Hymn Enhancements*. MSM 10-817. Kybd.

ALTERNATE HYMN OF THE DAY

LBW 422	O God, empower us
WOV 739	In all our grief

COMMUNION

LBW 309	Lord Jesus, think on me
WOV 765	Jesu, Jesu, fill us with your love

SENDING

LBW 527	All creatures of our God and King
WOV 796	My Lord of light

ADDITIONAL HYMNS AND SONGS

LLC 462	When we are living
PH 530	O Lord of life, where'er they be
TFF 190	God has smiled on me
W&P 52	Good soil
W&P 132	Step by step

MUSIC FOR THE DAY

CHORAL

Bender, Jan. "O God, O Lord of Heaven and Earth." AFP 11-10481. Also in *The Augsburg Choirbook*. AFP 11-10817. SATB, org.

Hopson, Hal H. "When We Are Living/ *Pues si vivimos.*" AFP 11-10966. SATB, kybd.

Howells, Herbert. "My Eyes for Beauty Pine" in *The Oxford Easy Anthem Book*. OXF 42.008. SATB, org.

Proulx, Richard. "Psalm 133." HOP FPC 126. SATB, org.

Schalk, Carl. "Fill My Cup, Lord." CPH 98-3071. SATB, org.

Schulz-Widmar, Russell. "We Are Not Our Own." AFP 11-10913. SATB, kybd.

CHILDREN'S CHOIRS

Eltringham, Susan. "Love Your Neighbor" in LS.

Hopson, Hal H. "Love One Another." CG CGA741. U/2 pt, kybd.

Wagner, Douglas E. "For Love Shall Be Our Song." CG CGA-389. U, kybd, opt fl.

KEYBOARD/INSTRUMENTAL

Howells, Herbert. "Prelude II" in *Three Psalm Preludes, Set One*. NOV 14853. Org.

Sadowski, Kevin. "Partita on 'When in Our Music.'" CPH 97-6478. Org.

Wold, Wayne L. "Father of Mercies/ Forgive Our Sins" in *Boundless Grace*. AMSI OR-26. Org.

HANDBELL

Moklebust, Cathy. "Meditation on Beautiful Savior." CG CGB175. 3-5 oct.

Sherman, Arnold B. "What Wondrous Love Is This." RRM HB0020A 2-3 oct, HB0020B 4-5 oct.

PRAISE ENSEMBLE

Espinosa, Eddie. "Change My Heart, O God" in W&P.

Larsen, Lloyd. "Come Share This Feast of Love." BEC BP1460. SATB, kybd.

Ylvisaker, John. "Brother Joseph" in *Borning Cry*. NGP.

SUNDAY, FEBRUARY 18
MARTIN LUTHER, RENEWER OF THE CHURCH, 1546

For those in the habit of remembering the work of Martin Luther on Reformation Day, this commemoration may seem out of place. But it is a custom to remember saints on the day of their death, their "heavenly birthday." On this day Luther died at the age of 62. For a time, he was an Augustinian monk, but it is his work as a biblical scholar, translator of the Bible, reformer of the liturgy, theologian, educator, and father of German vernacular literature, which holds him in our remembrance. In Luther's own judgment, the greatest of all of his works was his catechism written to instruct people in the basics of faith. And it was his baptism that sustained him in his trials as a reformer.

If a congregation has catechumens who will be baptized at the Easter Vigil, they might receive the catechism during the Enrollment of Candidates on the first Sunday in Lent. If there are no catechumens, a congregation might study the catechism during Lent to renew its own baptismal faith.

TUESDAY, FEBRUARY 20
RASMUS JENSEN, THE FIRST LUTHERAN PASTOR IN NORTH AMERICA, 1620

Jensen came to North America in 1619 with an expedition sent by King Christian IV of Denmark and Norway. The expedition took possession of the Hudson Bay area, naming it Nova Dania. Within months of their arrival, most of the members of the expedition died, including Jensen. After this expedition, much Danish missionary activity was concentrated in India and the Virgin Islands.

Today would be an appropriate time to give thanks for the church in Canada, which flourished even after its early struggles. It would also be an opportunity to pray for missionaries who face difficulty in their tasks.

FRIDAY, FEBRUARY 23
POLYCARP, BISHOP OF SMYRNA, MARTYR, 156

Polycarp was bishop of Smyrna and a link between the apostolic age and the church at the end of the second century. He is said to have been known by John, the author of Revelation. In turn he was known by the Iranaeus, bishop of Lyon in France, and Ignatius of Antioch. At the age of eighty-six was martyred for his faith. When urged to save his life and renounce his faith, Polycarp replied, "Eighty-six years I have served him, and he never did me any wrong. How can I blaspheme my king who saved me?" The magistrate who made the offer was reluctant to kill a gentle old man, but he had no choice. Polycarp was burned at the stake.

In preaching on the upcoming Transfiguration Sunday, one might use the example of Polycarp to underscore what Paul is saying in 2 Corinthians: "Therefore, since it is by God's mercy that we are engaged in this ministry, we do not lose heart."

FRIDAY, FEBRUARY 23
BARTHOLOMAEUS ZIEGENBALG, MISSIONARY TO INDIA, 1719

Bartholomaeus Ziegenbalg was a missionary to the Tamil's of Tranquebar on the southeast coast of India. The first convert to Christianity was baptized about ten months after Ziegenbalg began preaching. His missionary work was opposed both by the local Hindus and also by Danish authorities in that same area. Ziegenbalg was imprisoned for his work on a charge of converting the natives. The Copenhagen Mission Society that opposed him wanted an indigenous church that did not reflect European patterns or show concern for matters other than the gospel. Ziegenbalg, in contrast, argued that concern for the welfare of others is a matter of the gospel. Today, the Tamil Evangelical Lutheran Church carries on his work.

With Ash Wednesday a week away, consider Isaiah 58:1-12 for the first reading, "Is not this the fast that I choose…to share your bread with the hungry." Ziegenbalg's missionary work can lead us into Lent with the reminder that we are called to live in service to others.

SATURDAY, FEBRUARY 24
ST. MATTHIAS, APOSTLE

After Christ's ascension, the apostles met in Jerusalem to choose a replacement for Judas. Matthias was chosen over Joseph Justus by the casting of lots. Little is known about Matthias, and little is reported about him in the account of his election in Acts 1:15-26. Matthias had traveled among the disciples from the time of Jesus' baptism until his ascension. His task, after he was enrolled among the eleven remaining disciples, was to bear witness to the resurrection.

During the weeks of Lent, congregations with catechumens will have a chance to learn stories of how people have been called, some in unusual ways like Matthias.

FEBRUARY 25, 2001

INTRODUCTION

Things are not always what they seem! Bread and wine can become a place where we meet God. We, too, are changed in our encounter with grace. When Moses came back from speaking with God, no one could look at him the same. Deaconess Elizabeth Fedde, whom we commemorate today, worked for God by serving others. Her work was a reflection of God's transfiguring love.

PRAYER OF THE DAY

Almighty God, on the mountain you showed your glory in the transfiguration of your Son. Give us the vision to see beyond the turmoil of our world and to behold the king in all his glory; through your Son, Jesus Christ our Lord, who lives and reigns with you and the Holy Spirit, one God, now and forever.

or

O God, in the transfiguration of your Son you confirmed the mysteries of the faith by the witness of Moses and Elijah, and in the voice from the bright cloud you foreshadowed our adoption as your children. Make us with the king heirs of your glory, and bring us to enjoy its fullness, through Jesus Christ our Lord, who lives and reigns with you and the Holy Spirit, one God, now and forever.

READINGS

Exodus 34:29-35

Moses' face shone with the reflected glory of God after he received the Ten Commandments. The sight caused the Israelites to be afraid. Moses wore a veil to mask the radiance of God's glory while allowing direct communication with the people.

Psalm 99

Proclaim the greatness of the LORD; worship upon God's holy hill. (Ps. 99:9)

2 Corinthians 3:12—4:2

In his debates with the Corinthians, Paul contrasts the glory of Moses with the glory of Christ. The Israelites could not see Moses' face because of the veil. But in Christ we see the unveiled glory of God and are transformed into his likeness.

Luke 9:28-36 [37-43]

Today's reading offers a remarkable conclusion to the Epiphany season and turns us toward Lent. The transfiguration of Jesus is itself a great epiphany or manifestation. But in the very midst of this event is talk of what will happen in Jerusalem, where Jesus must suffer and die.

COLOR White

THE PRAYERS

Let us pray for all people upon whom the light of Christ shines with grace and mercy.

A BRIEF SILENCE.

Let us pray for all who have been sent into the world as heralds of Christ's victory over death and the powers of destruction. Lord, in your mercy,

hear our prayer.

Let us pray for nations and regions of the world clouded by violence and social strife (especially...), that Christ's reign of justice and peace will transfigure them with the splendid light of hope. Lord, in your mercy,

hear our prayer.

Let us pray for those in our midst whose lives are overshadowed by sickness (especially...). As Christ's servants, may we respond with gentle care to their needs. Lord, in your mercy,

hear our prayer.

Let us pray for this community of faith, where the holy gospel brings illumination and Christ's supper is a foretaste of the feast to come. Lord, in your mercy,

hear our prayer.

HERE OTHER INTERCESSIONS MAY BE OFFERED.

Let us pray for God to strengthen our hearts in times of uncertainty so that with Elizabeth Fedde and all the saints we may follow Christ in faithful trust through death to the glorious transfiguration of eternal life. Lord, in your mercy,

hear our prayer.

All these things and whatever else you see that we need, grant us, O God, for the sake of your Son, Jesus Christ our Lord.

Amen

117

IMAGES FOR PREACHING

Peter, John, and James were in a fog when Jesus led them up the mountain. They were tired, and they had just seen a spectacular vision of Jesus talking with Moses and Elijah about upcoming events. But then a cloud came and overshadowed them, and as do most of us who enter a patch of fog, they became terrified.

Just about all of us can relate to this scene. We have all had those experiences where things seem to be less clear for us. We may find ourselves going through life with a lot more questions than we used to have. People who used to comfort us have either moved away or died. The old neighborhood does not look the same as it used to, either. It is as if we have entered into a cloud along with Peter, John, and James. And like them we are terrified about the way things seem to be. What are we to do?

Only Christ can lead us in those times. Only Jesus can provide us with a sense of constancy. Yes, the neighborhood is changing. Yes, the people we have always known grow old, die, or move away. Yes, even our church changes from time to time. We will always be inclined to look back over our shoulders, trying to remember the safer places where we have been, places where the light seemed brighter.

If we are honest, we have probably all wanted to build some booths like Peter, John, and James were inclined to do, in order to preserve the glory days forever. It is then that God's voice speaks to us in the same way God spoke to Peter, John, and James, "This is my Son, my Chosen; listen to him!"

WORSHIP MATTERS

Festivals and seasons on our liturgical calendar named for Christ use the color white (or gold). How do white vestments and hangings dazzle in our worship spaces? Dull or dirty white paraments do nothing to proclaim the brilliance of this and other festivals of our Lord. The brightness of worship leaders' clothing and chancel furnishings for this festival is a sign of Christ's brightness.

LET THE CHILDREN COME

Make a large poster or banner with the children: print "Alleluia" in bright colors and decorative items. Hide the "Alleluia" word somewhere in the church. Explain that no "Alleluias" are used in worship during Lent.

Carry the Alleluia out of the worship space during the singing of the last hymn. Make the connection to the joy of Easter, when the children will find the Alleluia poster and bring back the banner.

MUSIC FOR WORSHIP
SERVICE MUSIC

The level of festivity in the service music today parallels that of the Sundays after Christmas and the Baptism of Our Lord. Certainly the Gloria and musical alleluias are worthy of special treatment before these elements are set aside for Lent.

GATHERING

LBW 552	In thee is gladness
WOV 797	O God beyond all praising

PSALM 99

TFF 11　Bow down before the holy mountain of God

Hobby, Robert. PW, Cycle C.

Hopson, Hal H. TP.

HYMN OF THE DAY

LBW 315	Love divine, all loves excelling
	HYFRYDOL

VOCAL RESOURCES

Pelz, Walter. "Love Divine, All Loves Excelling." CPH 98-3185. SATB, kybd, inst.

INSTRUMENTAL RESOURCES

Carlson, J. Bert. "Hyfrydol" in *A New Look at the Old.* AFP 11-11009. Org.

Ferguson, John. "Hyfrydol" in *Festival Hymns for Organ, Brass, and Timpani, Set III.* GIA G-4124.

Honoré, Jeffrey. "Hyfrydol" in *Classical Embellishments.* AFP 11-11005. Org, opt inst.

Sedio, Mark. "Hyfrydol" in *Let Us Talents and Tongues Employ.* AFP 11-10718. Org.

ALTERNATE HYMN OF THE DAY

LBW 80	Oh, wondrous type! Oh, vision fair
WOV 651	Shine, Jesus, shine

COMMUNION

LBW 518	Beautiful Savior
WOV 649	I want to walk as a child of the light

SENDING

| LBW 514 | O Savior, precious Savior |
| WOV 654 | Alleluia, song of gladness |

ADDITIONAL HYMNS AND SONGS

NCH 183	Jesus, take us to the mountain
TFF 63	We are marching in the light of God
VU 104	We have come, at Christ's own bidding
W&P 32	Come to the mountain

MUSIC FOR THE DAY

CHORAL

Bach, J. S. "Transcendent, Holy God" in BAS. SATB, kybd.

Bouman, Paul. "Christ upon the Mountain Peak." CPH 98-2856. SATB, org.

Helman, Michael. "Go Up to the Mountain of God." AFP 11-10961. SATB, pno, opt fl.

Mendelssohn, Felix. "And Then Shall Your Light Break Forth" in *Elijah*. Pro Art 1381.

Schalk, Carl. "Jesus, Take Us to the Mountain." MSM 50-2601. SATB, opt cong, org.

White, David Ashley. "This Glimpse of Glory." AFP 11-10201. SATB, org, opt tpt.

CHILDREN'S CHOIRS

Bach, J. S./arr. K. Lee Scott. "Come with Hearts and Voices Sounding." MSM-50-9402. 2 pt trbl, kybd.

Hughes, Pamela L. "Come to the Mountain" in LS.

Knowles, Julie. "Beautiful Saviour." JEN 417-02013. SSA, pno.

KEYBOARD/INSTRUMENTAL

Keesecker, Thomas. "Oh, Wondrous Type! Oh, Vision Fair" in *Piano Impressions for Epiphany*. CPH 97-6806. Pno.

Near, Gerald. "Deo Gracias" in *Deo Gracias*. AUR AE104. Org.

Vaughan Williams, Ralph. "Hyfrydol" in *Three Preludes Founded on Welsh Hymn Tunes*. Stainer and Bell 2155 Org.

HANDBELL

Kinyon, Barbara B. "A Gift of Joy." CG CGB202. 2-3 oct.

Honoré, Jeffrey. "Shine, Jesus, Shine." CPH 97-6633. 3-5 oct.

Mathis, William H. "Alleluia!" ("In Thee Is Gladness") SMP 20/1167 S. 3 oct; 20/1168 S. 4-5 oct.

PRAISE ENSEMBLE

Davis, Geron, and Paul Ferrin. "Holy Ground." WRD 301 0302 169. SATB, kybd, opt gtr, electric bass, drms.

Jacobs, Hanneke. "Spirit Of God" in *Praise & Worship*. MAR.

Smiley, Bill, Mark Gersmehl, and Bob Farrell. "Shine Down" in *Hosanna! Music*, #3. INT.

SUNDAY, FEBRUARY 25
ELIZABETH FEDDE, DEACONESS, 1921

Fedde was born in Norway and trained as a deaconess. In 1882, at the age of thirty-two, she was asked to come to New York to minister to the poor and to Norwegian seamen. Her influence was wide ranging, and she established the Deaconess House in Brooklyn and the Deaconess House and Hospital of the Lutheran Free Church in Minneapolis. She returned home to Norway in 1895 and died there.

Fedde was an example of selfless service to those in need. How does your congregation reach out to those who are sick, in need, or forgotten? Perhaps ways to reach out that have been overlooked can easily be incorporated in your congregation's ministry.

LENT

The cross is eternal

IMAGES OF THE SEASON

God is a mystery. To say that God is a mystery is to admit that our words can never grasp the fullness of God, that God remains elusive. Words about God are fragile and imperfect. Words serve to point and to evoke images of God, but they cannot wrap around God in a definitive way. The eighteenth-century Protestant thinker, counselor, and hymnwriter Gerhard Tersteegen said, "Any God who can be grasped is not God."

That said, we continue to speak of God and to proffer God to others in proclamation and in ritual. We have no alternative, for we have been chosen for the task. The liturgical year is one of the principal aids to the task of proclaiming and imaging God. In *Letters and Papers from Prison*, Dietrich Bonhoeffer spoke of engaging the world through righteous action that is born in the hidden disciplines of prayer, at the center of which lies the liturgical year.

The word *Lent* comes from an old English word meaning "to lengthen," and it names the time of the year when (in the Northern Hemisphere) the days begin to get longer in the spring. After the cold, dark, and often dismal months of the year come the signs of renewal. The calendar year thus aids the liturgical year. As people begin to feel renewal and recreation again following the hibernation and somnolent days of winter, even so the church stirs into action for renewal in the season of Lent.

Two concerns drive the Lenten season. Lent is driven by our need for renewal in both mind and spirit. The former need gives the season a catechetical dynamic, the latter need, a penitential dynamic.

The two themes of Lent come together in various ways. To be led where God's glory flashes out is to undergo both repentance and training in the school of prayer. We turn around to face the Holy One and, having confronted God's majesty and mercy, we then examine the mystery of God. This mystery leads to the profundity of the cross and the exaltation of the resurrection.

The church constructed its catechetical process over the course of the early centuries. The hidden discipline, so precious to Bonhoeffer in his last days in prison, was in the church's early history a time for catechumens to receive instruction in scripture, prayer, and the creed. These precious gifts of the church were transmitted to the catechumens, "handed over" (see 1 Cor. 11:24-26; 15:3-8) by the teachers. Eventually came the night of baptism, the night when the heavenly angels "celebrate the divine mysteries with exultation," in the words of the Easter proclamation *(Exsultet)* from the Easter Vigil. On this night we are plunged into the death of Christ in the water of baptism and raised again with Christ to new life (Romans 6). All our senses are engaged as we move from sight and hearing to touch and taste and feel the presence of the Risen One active in our lives. This entry into the divine mystery is the heart of Lent, even as it is the message of Easter.

Erik Davis, in his book *TechGnosis* (Harmony Books, 1999), thinks about our technological explosion from a philosophical perspective. He proposes that much of the technological drive toward utopian cyberspace is, in fact, a move in the wrong direction, because technology is a search for an elite state that escapes the body. The bodily disciplines of Lent—prayer, fasting, and almsgiving—may be penitential practices, but they are also powerful learning tools. We learn in and through the body. We do not seek to escape the body in utopia, but to discover how we may offer body and mind to others in the servant-spirit of Christ. We bend to the training of the season in order that we might become seasoned athletes of faith (1 Cor. 9:24-27).

The mysterious transaction between God and world that takes place on the cross is beyond our comprehension. The cross is eternal. The cross was raised in history, but its meaning is eternal. Thus the cross is always now and here, and the cross is always for us. It is never behind us or distant from us. We behold the cross with the mother who stands weeping, "at the cross her station keeping." At the end of a magnificent ancient hymn we sing:

> Jesus, may her deep devotion
> stir in me the same emotion,
> Source of love, redeemer true.

—LBW 110, stanza 5

Indeed, the pathway of Lent draws us with both heart and mind into the same emotion that Mary knew when she stood at the cross. Mary, the mother of our Lord, knows him also as the mysterious presence of God's love among us. She is the model for our contemplation. Throughout the forty days of Lent, we learn by penitence and through catechesis to see Christ both as one of us and at the same time as the One who comes from God in love for us.

ENVIRONMENT AND ART FOR THE SEASON

Environmental considerations for the season of Lent are determined by understanding its place in the Easter or paschal cycle. The Three Days are at the heart of this cycle. Lent is the time of preparation for Maundy Thursday, Good Friday, and the Resurrection of Our Lord.

At Easter the paschal experience of Jesus is celebrated in the dying and rising of the newly baptized. Lent is a season of baptismal preparation for those who will be baptized as well as all who will affirm their baptism. Spatial and visual arrangements for Lent, therefore, need to be based on the baptismal nature of the season. Lent's penitential character is secondary.

Environmental attention to the place of baptism is a primary responsibility of a seasonal planning team. *Where We Worship* (Philadelphia: Board of Publication, Lutheran Church in America, 1987) and other guidebooks on liturgical space provide rationale for the placement, size, and arrangement of the place of baptism. Placing the font near the entrance to the worship space speaks of each baptized person's origin in Christ. This placement also speaks to worshipers as they are sent each week into ministry.

To accommodate baptismal liturgies and portions of the eucharistic liturgy, make a generous space around the font. In some places, entire congregations may be able to stand around the font for the order for confession and forgiveness. Fresh water in the baptismal bowl invites worshipers to touch and remember their baptism. Running or living water was an ancient requirement for baptism and an evocative aural and visual sign. Baptismal hangings and green plants are effective ways to draw attention to the place of baptism.

If a congregation has a catechumenal ministry,

Lent becomes a time of intensified preparation for Easter baptisms. In that case, the great baptismal gospels from cycle A are appropriate every year. The dialogues between Jesus and Satan, Nicodemus, the woman at the well, the man born blind, and Mary, Martha and Lazarus could be read or dramatized from the place of baptism.

Lent is a spiritual journey for the whole congregation on its way to affirming baptism. One prepares for an arduous journey by packing only the basic necessities. "Pack light" is the advice we give to ourselves and to others. So it is with Lent. As church, we pack the liturgical basics for our journey toward Easter. Environmental simplicity allows us to focus on the primary symbols of our Lenten worship.

"'Tis a gift to be simple," goes the Shaker hymn. Simplicity *is* a gift to bring to our worship spaces during Lent. Store or eliminate the superficial and secondary, so that the assembly can concentrate on what is important in our worship and in our faith. Chancels should be cleared of flags, candelabra, musical furniture, unnecessary credence tables or chairs. All we need on the chancel platform is a place for proclaiming the word (an ambo, reading desk, or pulpit), the altar table, and seating for the liturgical ministers. Ideally the font has its own place elsewhere (perhaps near the entrance). Freestanding candle stands (torches) and a processional cross are useful to indicate special attention to one liturgical center or another. Everything else is superfluous and potentially distracting.

Emphasis on the cross during Lent gives a mixed message. The cross *is* central to the Good Friday liturgy, but we should not make Lent into an extended Good Friday by drawing undue attention to a cross. On the other hand, a central symbol of the Ash Wednesday liturgy is the imposition of ashes in the form of a cross on each believer's forehead. This cross symbolizes cleansing as well as a remembrance of our mortality. After the service worshipers go home, to work, or school, wearing a key visual symbol. Creating the appropriate Lenten environment is not so much a matter of decorating walls or chancels as it is facilitating the liturgical themes and ritual actions.

Shrove Tuesday has occasioned congregational dinners and social events. An effective ending to a Shrove Tuesday event is burning dried palms as ritual preparation for the imposition of ashes on Ash Wednesday. After the social event, people may gather outside around a fire bowl. A fire bowl may be purchased from an ecclesiastical arts company, or inexpensive ones can be made. One only needs a metal or earthenware bowl, a stone or metal stand, and dried palms or plants. After the strains of carnival have ended, all gather in silence to burn branches saved from the previous Palm Sunday.

A tradition in some congregations is to drape a hanging or wall-mounted cross with purple or black cloth. Black is a traditional color for Ash Wednesday, the solemn day of the liturgical year. Purple, the color of Lent, also has a somber message. Fixed colors for days and seasons of the liturgical year were only established 400 years ago at the counterreformation Council of Trent. Although common ecumenical patterns are desirable, so is a sense of freedom and flexibility concerning such matters. An alternative tradition is to use coarse, natural fabrics with neutral colors. Unadorned vestments and altar cloths reflect the simplicity of Lent. Our Lenten fast is a fast from ornamentation, embellishment, and excess. Large bare branches may be "planted" around the chancel or congregational space. They recall the spareness of trees in the winter without their leaves or flowers. They increase our yearning for a new springtime in nature and our lives.

Passion Sunday preferably begins outside with a procession with palms. In some Mediterranean countries such as Spain, Italy, and Greece, worshipers are given four-foot-long fronds. These generous symbols give participants a fuller sense of participation in the procession. Other palm branches may be strewn down the main aisle, extending the liturgy that began outside. Like receiving ashes on our forehead on Ash Wednesday, carrying a large palm home is part of our public liturgy in the community.

A conundrum of our desire to be faithful to Lent and its meanings is the fact that Sunday is always the celebration of the resurrection of Christ. According to one way of reckoning, the forty days of Lent are technically forty weekdays and do not include the Sundays. Because most Christians only worship publicly on Sunday, how do we celebrate Lent and Easter at the same time? It is best to approach the liturgical environment holding both themes in tension without feeling the need to resolve the apparent contradiction. The celebration of Lent can be serious but not mournful; the celebration of Sunday as Easter can be one of solemn joy.

PREACHING WITH THE SEASON

Water—so gentle, yet so powerful—washes and shapes us. The gestures,

words, art, and faithful gathering of God's people for the sacramental liturgies

of Lent, along with the great Three Days and the

unfolding mysteries of the Easter season, cascade

over our lives of faith like rivers, great and small. From the Colorado River that over the centuries has carved out the Grand Canyon in Arizona, to the twisting and turning waters of the Gooseberry River of Minnesota that has shaped its five waterfalls, to the churning waters of the Chattooga River as it leaves North Carolina to form the border between South Carolina and Georgia and gives joy to whitewater rafters, we see the transformational power of water. Similarly, the liturgical cycle of Lent, the great Three Days, and Easter has the power to conform the lives of God's people to the image of Christ.

Certainly the gospel has the power to shape us throughout the year, but it does so in a focused way as we celebrate the saving mystery of Jesus' death and resurrection. In a practical sense, as people participate in the liturgy week after week, year after year, through the cycles of the liturgical year and through the cycles of their own lives, they will come to experience the profound shaping power of the gospel as it cascades over them in the liturgical year's fullest expressions. We are shaped so that we become what we celebrate.

We may diminish the power of the gospel to conform us to Christ by our own worship practices that try to confine the risen Lord to a once-upon-a-time story. First-person Lenten dramas portraying biblical characters dressed in full costume, or Palm Sunday parades with live donkeys, or passion plays staged to reenact the last supper may be entertaining to some, but they keep the gospel at arm's length. Must we leave the twentieth century in a flight of imagination to experience the power of the gospel story? No! Rather, we must take seriously Luther's theology of the Holy Spirit. In his memorable phrasing, Luther says that "the Holy Spirit has called me through the gospel," just as the Holy Spirit "calls, gathers, enlightens, and makes holy the whole Christian church on earth and keeps it with Jesus Christ in the one common, true faith" (from the third article of the Apostles' Creed, *A Contemporary Translation of Luther's Small Catechism*, Timothy J. Wengert, trans., Augsburg Fortress, 1994). Luther insisted that in communion the promise of the gospel is "for you." Similarly, the promise of the gospel that cascades over us through the abundant riches of sacramental liturgical celebrations during the Lent-Easter cycle has the power to do what it says, conform us to Christ. The Holy Spirit, calling us through the gospel, helps us to be faithful to Jesus' word, "Do this for the remembrance of me," and keeps us united, in our twenty-first-century lives, with the risen Lord.

For preaching, use the waters of baptism at the center of the Lent-Easter cycle as the dominant homiletical image. Preaching during Lent may be shaped by the anticipation of these baptismal waters. The renunciations and affirmations of baptism (see *LBW*, p. 123) may then set a pattern for Lenten preaching. In some ancient baptismal rites the renunciation of the devil was quite dramatic. In the text of the eighth-century rite of Constantinople, at the moment of the renunciation of the devil, the candidates faced the west, where the devil was said to be standing and gnashing his teeth. By the ritual act of blowing, they were to throw to the devil anything in their hearts that belonged to him, and anything still remaining was to be spit out. After the renunciation candidates turned to the east and were asked to adhere to Christ. This strong image of renouncing the devil and adhering to Christ may be helpful to the preacher during Lent, calling us to strip away the ragged, old clothes of self-centered living with which we cover our mortal nakedness, so that we might prepare to be clothed with the garments of resurrection life.

We are reminded of our mortality on Ash Wednesday as we receive an ashen cross on our foreheads. We hear the words "Remember that you are dust, and to

125

dust you shall return." These are sobering words for pastors who apply the ashes, conscious that during the next year they may be making the sign of the cross on some of these same people at their funerals. Being so starkly reminded of our naked mortality, we begin to name and strip off the garments covering our mortal fear. The sign of mortality is also made in the form of hope, the sign of the cross.

The gospel for Ash Wednesday calls us to strip off the garment which we wear to seek the approval of others and instead store up treasure in heaven. On the first Sunday in Lent we see how Jesus responded to the temptations to be clothed with fulfillment, power, and control. On the next Sunday we note our resistance to being gathered up and clothed in the body of Christ as we hear the longing of our Lord to gather us as a hen gathers her chicks under her wing. The third Sunday in Lent presents Jesus' parable of the barren fig tree

and the promise of God's graciousness as we turn toward Christ, who nurtures us, so that we may bear the fruit of the gospel. The gospel for the fourth Sunday in Lent shows us the prodigal son after finding himself among the pigs, stripped down to his naked mortality, making his way home to be robed in the graciousness of his father. The next Sunday's gospel reading calls us to strip away phony concern for the poor and points us to the expensive fragrance of love, as Mary anoints Jesus' feet while Judas complains. And on the Sunday of the Passion we follow our Lord as he begins his passover that will strip him of all dignity but his faith, as he says in his last moments on the cross, "Father, into your hands I commend my spirit." During Lent the Holy Spirit calls us through the proclamation of the gospel to just this point, where we too have been made ready to be immersed and conformed to the risen Lord.

SHAPE of WORSHIP for the SEASON

BASIC SHAPE OF THE EUCHARISTIC RITE

- Confession and Forgiveness: see alternate worship text for Lent in *Sundays and Seasons*

GATHERING

- Greeting: see alternate worship text for Lent in *Sundays and Seasons*
- Use the Kyrie during Lent
- Omit the hymn of praise during Lent

WORD

- For dramatic readings based on lectionary passages, use *Scripture Out Loud!* (AFP 3-3964) for Ash Wednesday and the first Sunday in Lent
- For contemporary dramas based on lectionary passages, use *Can These Bones Live?* (AFP 3-3965) for Ash Wednesday, first Sunday in Lent, and Passion Sunday
- Use the Nicene Creed
- The Prayers: see alternate forms and responses for Lent in *Sundays and Seasons*

MEAL

- Offertory Prayer: see alternate worship text for Lent in *Sundays and Seasons*
- Use the proper preface for Lent
- Use the proper preface for Passion beginning with Passion Sunday
- Eucharistic prayer: in addition to four main options in *LBW*, see "Eucharistic Prayer D: The Season of Lent" in *WOV* Leaders Edition, p. 68
- Invitation to communion: see alternate worship text for Lent in *Sundays and Seasons*
- Post-communion prayer: see alternate worship text for Lent in *Sundays and Seasons*

SENDING

- Benediction: see alternate worship text for Lent in *Sundays and Seasons*
- Dismissal: see alternate worship text for Lent in *Sundays and Seasons*

OTHER SEASONAL POSSIBILITIES

- Ash Wednesday liturgy: see *LBW* Ministers Edition, pp. 129–31; congregational leaflets available from Augsburg Fortress (AFP 3-5325)
- Enrollment of Candidates for Baptism (for First Sunday in Lent): see *Welcome to Christ: Lutheran Rites for the Catechumenate*, pp. 18–21
- Midweek Lenten worship: see order for evening prayer services in seasonal rites section
- Blessing of Candidates for Baptism (for third,

fourth, and fifth Sundays in Lent): see *Welcome to Christ: Lutheran Rites for the Catechumenate*, pp. 22–34

- Procession with Palms liturgy for Passion Sunday: see *LBW* Ministers Edition, pp. 134–35; congregational leaflets available from Augsburg Fortress (AFP 3-5326)
- Blessing of oil: for synodical gatherings (and other groupings of congregations wishing to celebrate this order), see "Dedication of Worship Furnishings" in *Occasional Services*, pp. 176–77

LECTIONARY OPPORTUNITY FOR HEALING SERVICES

- Wednesday in Holy Week (second reading)

ASSEMBLY SONG FOR THE SEASON

Lent is the springtime for our souls, a time of growth and renewal. Focus the song of the assembly on growth into God's way of life, on prayer, on the need for repentance and change, and on baptismal transformation. Make the Lenten season a time of growth.

Morning and evening prayer sung during the middle of the week give people an opportunity to come together to pray and reflect (in addition to *LBW*, see the settings of daily prayer in the list that follows). Consider praying these offices without a sermon and with generous use of psalmody and silence. Vary the psalmody by singing some psalms unaccompanied, with and without antiphons. When using two additional psalms, use a paraphrase for one psalm. Reclaim the use of some of the traditional office hymns as listed in *Lutheran Book of Worship* Ministers Edition, page 499. These hymn texts are strong, and many are appropriate to the season of Lent. Pick one or two that are unfamiliar and learn them this season.

GATHERING

The Litany (*LBW*, p. 168) can be a prayerful way to begin the discipline of Lent. Sing the Litany on the first Sunday in Lent as the entrance hymn. Begin the service in silence. See the Advent "Assembly Song" for suggestions.

Sundays in Lent can also begin with a Kyrie or litany instead of an entrance hymn. Try using a different Kyrie each week, such as the two paraphrases in *LBW*, "Kyrie, God Father" (LBW 168) or "Your heart, O God, is grieved" (LBW 96), or use one of the Kyrie settings in *With One Voice* (WOV 601–605) for the entire season. These Kyries offer a variety of styles and cultures from which to choose. The use of "Kyrie" (WOV 604) with phrases punctuated by a few handbells can be especially contemplative. Have a cantor or choir lead, singing phrase by phrase, with the assembly repeating the phrases after them.

WORD

A seasonal psalm refrain and tone is "I will call upon the name of the Lord" (TFF 14). A setting of the Lenten verse *Return to the Lord* is "Turn back to God" (LLC 202). An alternative to the proper verse, if not sung by the choir, is "Return to the Lord" (WOV 615). Another seasonal gospel acclamation is "Everyone who calls upon the name of the Lord" (Ray Makeever, DH 17), with its text drawn from the second reading for the first Sunday in Lent.

MEAL

Two strong choices for the offertory exist. The gospel of Luke has a strong emphasis on Jerusalem. "What shall I render to the Lord" is a fitting choice for an offertory canticle during the Lenten season. "Create in me a clean heart" is also appropriate.

"O Christ, thou Lamb of God" (LBW 103) can be sung throughout the season as an alternative to the *LBW* setting. "Lamb of God" (WOV 621) has a lyrical melody that can be sung in canon.

SENDING

Use a seasonal post-communion hymn such as "On my heart imprint your image" (LBW 102) or "I want Jesus to walk with me" (WOV 660 and TFF 66).

MUSIC FOR THE SEASON

VERSE AND OFFERTORY

Busarow, Donald. *Verses and Offertory Sentences, Part III—Ash Wednesday through Maundy Thursday.* CPH 97-5503. Acc. 97-5509. SATB, org.

Cherwien, David. *Verses for the Sundays in Lent.* MSM 80-300. U/2 pt, org.

Farlee, Robert Buckley. *Verses and Offertories for Lent.* AFP 11-10065. U/SATB.

Haydn, Franz Joseph/arr. Austin C. Lovelace. "God So Loved the World." AFP 11-2147. SATB, kybd.

LBW 13   Keep in mind that Jesus Christ has died for us (Offertory)

Moore, Dom Andrew. "First Sunday of Lent" in *Gospel Acclamations.* Kevin Mayhew 1400050. U, org.

Nelson, Ronald. "Whoever Would Be Great Among You." AFP 11-1638. U/SAB, kybd/gtr.

Norris, Kevin. *Verses and Offertories (Lent).* AFP 11-9545. U, kybd.

Schramm, Charles. *Verses for the Lenten Season.* MSM 80-301.

WOV 611b Gospel Acclamation: Lent

WOV 614   Praise to you, O Christ, our Savior

WOV 615   Return to the Lord

W&P 34   Create in me a clean heart

CHORAL

Biery, James. "Communion Antiphons for the Lenten Season." MSM 80-835. SATB/SSAA, cant, cong, org.

de Victoria, Tomas Luis. "Hosanna to the Son of David" in *A First Motet Book.* CPH 97-4845.

Farrant, Richard. "Call to Remembrance." ECS 1639.

Ferguson, John. "Psalm 130." AFP 11-10749. SATB, org.

Parker, Alice. "We Will March Thro' the Valley." GIA G-4242. SSATB, solo.

Purcell, Henry. "Remember Not, Lord, Our Offences." GSCH 1146. SSATB.

Purcell, Henry. "Thou Knowest, Lord, the Secrets of Our Hearts." HWG 1665.

Schalk, Carl. "Out of the Depths." MSM 50-3410. SAB, org.

Sedio, Mark. "Rich in Promise." AFP 11-10924. 2 pt, kybd.

CHILDREN'S CHOIRS

Christopherson, Dorothy. "Followers of the Lamb." CG CGA-672. U, pno, fl, xyl, tamb, fc.

Cox, Joe. "We Are Climbing Jacob's Ladder." CG CGA-604. U, kybd.

Hopson, Hal H. "I Want Jesus to Walk with Me." CG CGA-701. 2 pt trbl/mxd, kybd.

Kemp, Helen. "A Lenten Love Song." CG CGA-486. U, kybd.

Pooler, Marie. "A Song for Lent." AFP 11-10361. U/2 pt, kybd.

KEYBOARD/INSTRUMENTAL

Augsburg Organ Library: Lent. AFP 11-11036.

Behnke, John. *Wondrous Cross.* CPH 97-6643. Org.

Hancock, Gerre. *Air.* HWG GSTC 897. Org.

Near, Gerald. *Two Preludes for the Evening Service* (St. Clement & Ar hyd y Nos). AUR AE 40/1. Org.

Perera, Ronald. *Five Meditations on "Wondrous Love."* ECS #4145. Org.

Sandresky, Margaret Vardell. "Agnus Dei" from "L'homme Armé Organ Mass" in *Organ Music Volume I.* ECS WL600031. Org.

HANDBELL

Kinyon, Barbara B. "Throned upon That Awful Tree." BEC HB143. 3 oct.

Larson, Katherine Jordahl. "I Lay My Sins on Jesus." Art Masters Studios HB-29. 3-5 oct.

McKlveen, Paul. "Lenten Meditation." CPH 97-6257. 2-3 oct.

Mozart/Keller. "Lachrymosa." AGEHR AG45033. 4-5 oct.

Nelson, Susan T. "Elegy." AFP 11-10554. 2 oct, opt sop sax.

Pennington, Vicki. "Near the Cross." RRM BL5002. 2-3 oct.

PRAISE ENSEMBLE

Carter, John. "For Love of You." HOP JC 293. SATB, kybd.

Courtney, Craig. "The Cross." BEC BP1507. SATB, kybd.

Mengel, Dana. "Lord, Throughout These Forty Days." CPH 98-3343. SATB, kybd.

MUSICAL SETTINGS OF DAILY PRAYER

Haugen, Marty. *Holden Evening Prayer.* GIA G-3460.

Haugen, Marty. *In the Morning I Will Sing.* GIA G-4493.

Makeever, Ray. *Joyous Light Evening Prayer.* AFP 11-11070.

Weber, Paul. *Music for Morning Prayer.* AFP 11-10928.

Worship & Praise. Full Music Edition. AFP 3-851. *See the appendix for outlines of daily prayer using songs from this resource.*

ALTERNATE WORSHIP TEXTS

CONFESSION AND FORGIVENESS

In the name of the Father, and of the ✛ Son, and of the Holy Spirit.
Amen

Trusting in the steadfast, sure love of God,
let us return to the Lord, confessing our sins.

Silence for reflection and self-examination.

Most merciful God,
**you desire to gather your children together,
yet we are not always willing.
We squander your gifts,
misuse our power,
and turn away from your love.
We spend ourselves for what does not satisfy
and neglect those in sorrow and in need.
Spare us, O Lord,
and forgive us our sins,
that we may turn from evil ways
and find shelter beneath your wings. Amen**

God is generous to all who ask for help.
Almighty God have mercy on you,
forgive you all your sins through Jesus Christ,
and by the power of the Holy Spirit
keep you in eternal life.
Amen

GREETING

From our God who loves us with an everlasting love,
who brings forth a new creation in Christ,
who leads us by the Spirit in the wilderness:
grace and abundant mercy be with you all.
And also with you.

OFFERTORY PRAYER

God our provider,
**you have not fed us with bread alone,
but with words of grace and life.
As our ancestors offered the first fruits of harvest,
so we bring what is precious
for sharing as there is need.
Bless us and these your gifts,
which we receive from your bounty. Amen**

INVITATION TO COMMUNION

Sons and daughters who were dead are alive again.
Come, let us eat, for now the feast is spread.

POST-COMMUNION PRAYER

God our strength, in this holy meal
you spread a table with the richest of food;
you send rivers in the desert.
May the life you give us in this feast so nourish us
that our own lives may extend your welcome to all;
through Jesus Christ our Lord.
Amen

BENEDICTION

The God who formed us in love,
renews us through grace,
and will transform us into glory,
✛ bless you this day and always.
Amen

DISMISSAL

Reconciled to God through Christ,
let us go out into the world in peace.
Thanks be to God.

130

SEASONAL RITES

SERVICE OF THE WORD FOR HEALING IN LENT

An order for Service of the Word for Healing is presented in the seasonal materials for autumn. It may also be adapted for use during Lent in the following ways:

DIALOG

Behold, now is the acceptable time;
now is the day of salvation.
Return to the Lord, your God,
who is gracious and merciful, slow to anger,
and abounding in steadfast love.
God forgives you all your sins
and heals all your infirmities.
God redeems your life from the grave
and crowns you with mercy and lovingkindness.
God satisfies you with good things,
and your youth is renewed like an eagle's.
Bless the Lord, O my soul,
and all that is within me bless God's holy name.

FIRST READING: Isaiah 53:3-5
PSALM: Psalm 138
GOSPEL: Matthew 8:1-3, 5-8, 13-17

THE PRAYERS

HYMNS

Either of these hymns may be used when the Service of the Word for Healing occurs during Lent:
LBW 93   Jesus, refuge of the weary
LBW 104   In the cross of Christ I glory

MIDWEEK EVENING PRAYER FOR LENT

This flexible order of evening prayer may be celebrated as a midweek service during Lent. It is an adaptable form of vespers with readings and music that highlight five of the readings from the Easter Vigil. These stories are among the most prominent of passages that announced hope and salvation to the ancient Hebrew people. For Christians these readings are regarded as "types" of the salvation brought to us through the death and resurrection of Christ. Because of their traditional use in the Easter Vigil, the primary liturgy for baptism, these readings also have a strong baptismal association for Christians.

Contemporary dramatizations of these same five readings are available in Can These Bones Live? Contemporary Dramas for Lent and Easter *by David Kehret (AFP 3-3965).*

OVERVIEW: MIDWEEK THEMES BASED ON READINGS FROM THE EASTER VIGIL

FIRST WEEK
Genesis 1:1–2:4a
Creation

SECOND WEEK
Genesis 7:1-5, 11-18; 8:6-18; 9:8-13
The Flood

THIRD WEEK
Genesis 22:1-18
The Testing of Abraham

FOURTH WEEK
Exodus 14:10-31; 15:20-21
Israel's Deliverance

FIFTH WEEK
Ezekiel 37:1-14
The Valley of the Dry Bones

SERVICE OF LIGHT

A lit vesper candle may be carried in procession during the following versicles and placed in its stand near the altar.

These versicles may be sung to the tones given in Evening Prayer, LBW, p. 142.

Behold, now is the accept- | able time;
now is the day of sal- | vation.
Turn us again, O God of | our salvation,
that the light of your face may shine on | us.
May your justice shine | like the sun;
and may the poor be lifted | up.

HYMN OF LIGHT

One of the following hymns may be sung.

LBW 248   Dearest Jesus, at your word
WOV 728   O Light whose splendor thrills
WOV 729   Christ, mighty Savior
TFF 262   I heard the voice of Jesus say

THANKSGIVING FOR LIGHT

This is set to music in LBW, p. 144.

The Lord be with you.
And also with you.
Let us give thanks to the Lord our God.
It is right to give our thanks and praise.
Blessed are you, O Lord our God, king of the universe,
who led your people Israel by a pillar of cloud by day
and a pillar of fire by night:
Enlighten our darkness by the light of your Christ;
may his Word be a lamp to our feet and a light to our path;
for you are merciful, and you love your whole creation,
and we, your creatures, glorify you, Father, Son, and Holy Spirit.
Amen

PSALMODY

The first psalm may be Psalm 141, as printed in LBW, pp. 145–46; or another setting of this psalm may be used.

An additional psalm or canticle may be used for each of the weeks during Lent (see Psalter for Worship):

FIRST WEEK
Ps. 136:1-9, 23-26
SECOND WEEK
Ps. 46
THIRD WEEK
Ps. 16
FOURTH WEEK
Exodus 15:1b-13, 17-18 (Song of Moses and Miriam)
FIFTH WEEK
Ps. 143

HYMN

Possibilities for hymns related to the readings for each of the weeks follow.

FIRST WEEK
LBW 515   How marvelous God's greatness
WOV 799   When long before time
TFF 222   God the sculptor of the mountains

SECOND WEEK
LBW 351   Oh, happy day when we shall stand
WOV 741   Thy holy wings
TFF 199   'Tis the old ship of Zion

THIRD WEEK
LBW 313   A multitude comes from the east and the west
WOV 746   Day by day
TFF 190   God has smiled on me

FOURTH WEEK
WOV 670   When Israel was in Egypt's land
LBW 358   Glories of your name are spoken
TFF 114   Wade in the water

FIFTH WEEK
LBW 315   Love divine, all loves excelling
WOV 658   The Word of God is source and seed
TFF 73   Jesus, keep me near the cross

OTHER HYMN OPTIONS INCLUDE:

LBW 194   All who believe and are baptized

LBW 325   Lord, thee I love with all my heart

LBW 338   Peace, to soothe our bitter woes

WOV 698   We were baptized in Christ Jesus

WOV 695   O blessed spring

TFF 260   A wonderful Savior is Jesus

READINGS FOR EACH OF THE WEEKS OF LENT

FIRST WEEK

Genesis 1:1--2:4a

SECOND WEEK

Genesis 7:1-5, 11-18; 8:6-18; 9:8-13

THIRD WEEK

Genesis 22:1-18

FOURTH WEEK

Exodus 14:10-31; 15:20-21

FIFTH WEEK

Ezekiel 37:1-14

A homily or meditation may follow the reading.

Silence is kept by all.

The silence concludes:

Long ago, in many and various ways,

God spoke to our ancestors by the prophets;

but in these last days God has spoken to us by the Son.

GOSPEL CANTICLE

LBW 180   My soul now magnifies the Lord

WOV 730   My soul proclaims your greatness

TFF 168   My soul does magnify the Lord

LITANY

The music for the litany in LBW, p. 148, may be used with the following.

In peace, let us pray to the Lord.

Lord, have mercy.

For the peace from above, let us pray to the Lord.

Lord, have mercy.

For the peace of the whole world, for the well-being of the church of God, and for the unity of all, let us pray to the Lord.

Lord, have mercy.

For those who are preparing for the Easter sacraments, let us pray to the Lord.

Lord, have mercy.

For the baptized people of God and for their varied ministries, let us pray to the Lord.

Lord, have mercy.

For those who are poor, hungry, homeless, or sick, let us pray to the Lord.

Lord, have mercy.

Help, save, comfort, and defend us, gracious Lord.

Silence is kept by all.

Rejoicing in the fellowship of all the saints, let us commend ourselves, one another, and our whole life to Christ, our Lord.

To you, O Lord.

133

PRAYER OF THE DAY

From the previous Sunday if a service is held during the week.

THE LORD'S PRAYER

BLESSING

For a musical setting, see LBW, p. 152.

Let us bless the Lord.

Thanks be to God.

The almighty and merciful Lord, the Father, the Son, and the Holy Spirit, bless and preserve us.

Amen

FEBRUARY 28, 2001

ASH WEDNESDAY

INTRODUCTION

Ash Wednesday marks the beginning of Lent with ash on our foreheads. This cross is an echo of our baptismal anointing, when we were buried with Christ. The ash is a chilling reminder of our mortality, but because our death is now in Christ, our endings are beginnings. The Lenten disciplines of acts of kindness, prayer, and fasting are tools of discipleship that can lead us to renewal as we bury all that is holding us back from being truly alive.

PRAYER OF THE DAY

Almighty and ever-living God, you hate nothing you have made and you forgive the sins of all who are penitent. Create in us new and honest hearts, so that, truly repenting of our sins, we may obtain from you, the God of all mercy, full pardon and forgiveness; through your Son, Jesus Christ our Lord, who lives and reigns with you and the Holy Spirit, one God, now and forever.

READINGS

Joel 2:1-2, 12-17

The context of this reading is a community liturgy of sorrow over sin. The prophet has called the people to mourn a devastating plague and to announce a day of darkness, the day of the Lord. The people are called to repent and to return to God, who is gracious and merciful.

or Isaiah 58:1-12

The fast that God chooses

Psalm 51:1-18 (Psalm 51:1-17 [NRSV])

Have mercy on me, O God, according to your lovingkindness. (Ps. 51:1)

2 Corinthians 5:20b–6:10

Out of love for humankind, Christ experienced sin and suffering, so that the saving power of God could penetrate the most forbidding and tragic depths of human experience. No aspect of human life is ignored by the presence of God's grace. Because of this, Paul announces that this day is a day of God's grace, an acceptable time to turn toward God's mercy.

Matthew 6:1-6, 16-21

In this passage Matthew sets forth a vision of genuine righteousness illustrated by three basic acts of Jewish devotion: almsgiving, prayer, and fasting. Jesus does not denounce these acts—in the New Testament they are signs of singular devotion to God. Rather, he criticizes those who perform them in order to have a sense of self-satisfaction or to gain public approval. Care for the poor, intense prayer, and fasting with a joyous countenance are signs of loving dedication to God.

COLOR   Black *or* Purple

THE PRAYERS

As we mark this holy season with repentance and forgiveness, let us pray for the renewal of the church and the restoration of the world to the life of God.
A BRIEF SILENCE.

For the church, that the people God recreated in baptism may be strengthened through their Lenten disciplines of almsgiving, prayer, fasting, and works of love. Let us pray to the Lord.

Lord, have mercy.

For all nations, that the peace and hope revealed in Jesus Christ may lead people to repent from the ways of bloodshed and war. Let us pray to the Lord.

Lord, have mercy.

For those who are poor, hungry, or afflicted by illness (especially . . .), that they may know God's steadfast love. Let us pray to the Lord.

Lord, have mercy.

For all preparing for baptism, that shaped by the word of the Lord, they will be made ready to be reborn in the waters of new life. Let us pray to the Lord.

Lord, have mercy.

HERE OTHER INTERCESSIONS MAY BE OFFERED.

Remembering all who have died in the promise of Easter hope, we pray that we may receive with them the eternal salvation prepared for us through Christ. Let us pray to the Lord.

Lord, have mercy.

Gracious God, hear us as we pray, and sustain us with your hope, through Jesus Christ our Lord.

Amen

IMAGES FOR PREACHING

Ashes, a sign of our humanity, together with the cross, a sign of our hope, set us on our Lenten pilgrimage. We receive this sign on our forehead, hearing the words that recall Genesis 3:19, "Remember that you are dust, and to dust you shall return." Ashes are a reminder of our mortality. Like Adam, our bodies are created from the same chemical elements as the earth. When we die, we will be returned to the earth.

Ashes are a powerful reminder of our naked mortality. This Wednesday draws attention to the meaning of that cross-shaped smudge on our forehead. Yet throughout the year we try to cover up this naked truth with the garments of our self-centered living.

Jesus exposes our schemes. He names the ragged garment that must be removed, that is, the belief that the approval of others will quell the fear of mortality. That fear takes many forms. Do we fear poverty? Do we fear holy relationships? Do we fear emptiness? Do we fear to be alone? He sees those who use their piety to seek the approval of others, and says, "So whenever you give alms, do not sound a trumpet before you." He notices how some people pray or fast in order to be noticed by others. Instead, Jesus teaches that we are to practice our piety in secret. Certainly, our faith takes on a public character. Yet, in this scripture reading for Ash Wednesday, our Lord is stripping us of a false garment, so that we might be ready to wear the garment of resurrection life.

For now, our Lord gives us the gifts of almsgiving, prayer, and fasting. By using these gifts during Lent, we allow our lives of faith to be conformed to Christ and his cross.

WORSHIP MATTERS

Strange, is it not, to look at the children kneeling before you, so full of life, and to announce to them, "You are dust and to dust you shall return!" Yet from the beginning it is a paradoxical sign of both death and life. The first man and woman have the sign *proclaimed* to them—a cross they must bear. Their son, Cain, on the other hand, was *marked* with a sign—for protection. Does not the same word judge in order to save?

The proclamation to each person on Ash Wednesday is the word of the cross. Ashes rubbed into the sign placed on our foreheads in baptism are a sign of our mortality. A burdensome word, it reminds us of what

our just desserts would be apart from the Lord. Simultaneously, it is a reminder of the promise of eternal life and the means by which we are protected. The cross of ashes on our foreheads is simply preliminary, however, and would amount to nothing without the benefits of the word and the sign fully realized in the sacraments.

LET THE CHILDREN COME

"Where did the pastor get the ashes?" If children can see the burning of the palms from last Passion Sunday or smell the smoke (always do this outdoors!), they will better remember. Ashes on the forehead remind us of Jesus. Ashes are for all who want to remember Jesus' story. Ashes mark us as followers of Jesus and are for all the children of God, regardless of age. We are marked with the sign of the cross on our foreheads at the time of baptism. Today the ashes remind us of our death with Christ, just as Easter will remind us of our resurrection with Christ.

MUSIC FOR WORSHIP

SERVICE MUSIC

The Ash Wednesday liturgy customarily begins with the singing of Psalm 51. A single voice coming out of silence to intone the refrain or first psalm verse makes a powerful beginning. (If another psalm is desired after the first reading, Psalm 103:8-14 may be used.) The penitential note of Ash Wednesday may be reinforced through the use of subdued accompaniments, introductions, and instrumental music, as well as a generous use of silence. Optional sections of the service are best omitted on this day, using the liturgy in its simple form.

PSALM 51

Cox, Joe. "Create in Me a Clean Heart, O God" in *Psalms for the People of God.* SMP 45/1037S.

Hurd, David. "Psalm 51: Create in Me" in STP, vol. 1.

Kogut, Malcolm. "Psalm 51: Create in Me a Clean Heart" in PCY, vol. 10.

Kreutz, Robert. *Psalms and Selected Canticles.* OCP.

Makeever, Ray. "Be Merciful, O God" in DH.

Schwarz, May. PW, Cycle C.

See proper 19.

HYMN OF THE DAY

WOV 659   O Sun of justice

JESU DULCIS MEMORIA

135

A SUGGESTION FOR THE HYMN OF THE DAY

Handbells work well to set the tone for this hymn.
Ring "A" at the beginning and after each phrase.

INSTRUMENTAL RESOURCES

Callahan, Charles. "Jesu dulcis memoria" in *Chant, Volume I.*
CPH 97-6765. Org.

Glick, Sara. "O Sun of Justice" in *Piano Arrangements for Worship.*
AFP 11-11013. Pno.

ALTERNATE HYMN OF THE DAY

| LBW 91 | Savior, when in dust to you |
| LBW 295 | Out of the depths I cry to you |

COMMUNION

LBW 99	O Lord, throughout these forty days
LBW 296	Just as I am, without one plea
WOV 733	Our Father, we have wandered

SENDING

| LBW 276 | Now all the woods are sleeping |
| WOV 734 | Softly and tenderly Jesus is calling |

ADDITIONAL HYMNS AND SONGS

LLC 442	Create in me a clean heart
NCH 186	Dust and ashes touch our face
REJ 104	God be merciful to me
TFF 216	Give me a clean heart
W&P 34	Create in me a clean heart

MUSIC FOR THE DAY

CHORAL

Bach, J. S. "Bring Low Our Ancient Adam" in BAS. SATB, kybd.

Byrd, William. "Miserere mei, Deus." OXF TCM 26. SATBB.

di Lassus, Orlando. "Miserere mei, Domine." AFP 11-10267. SATB.

James, Layton. "Create in Me." MSM 50-3043. SATB, S solo, pno/hp.

Oldham, Kevin. "Out of the Depths Have I Cried to Thee."
KJO ED. J11. SATB, org, hp.

Schalk, Carl. "Have Mercy on Me, O God." AFP 11-10937. SATB.

Schütz, Heinrich. "The Blood of Jesus Christ" in CC. SAB, org.

Scott, K. Lee. "Out of the Depths I Cry to Thee." AFP 11-4644.
2 pt, kybd.

CHILDREN'S CHOIRS

Grieg, Edvard/arr. Hal H. Hopson. "Prayer to Jesus." AFP 11-2407.
U, pno/org.

Marshall, Jane. "Create in Me, O God." CG CGA750. U antiphonal,
kybd.

KEYBOARD/INSTRUMENTAL

Organ, Anne Krentz. "Savior, When in Dust to You" in *Christ, Mighty
Savior.* AFP 11-10819. Pno.

Reger, Max. "Aus tiefer Not" in *Thirty Short Chorale Preludes.*
CFP 3980. Org.

Vaughan Williams, Ralph/arr. Bayard. *Variations on Aberystwyth.*
OXF 31.158. Org.

HANDBELL

Afdahl, Lee J. "St. Clement." AFP 11-10986. 3 or 5 oct.

Nystrom, Martin/arr. Cota. "As the Deer." HOP AG 2-56. 3-5 oct.

Rogers, Sharon Elery. "Nearer My God to Thee." MSM 30-301.
2-3 oct.

PRAISE ENSEMBLE

Dufford, Bob. "Return to the Lord Your God" in *Glory & Praise.* OCP.

Espinosa, Eddie, and Mary Rice Hopkins/Tom Fettke. "Change My
Heart, O God/Create in Me." MAR 25986-6198-7. SATB,
kybd, opt gtr.

Haugen, Marty. "Let Justice Roll Like a River" in W&P.

Haugen, Marty. "Be Merciful, O Lord" (Psalm 51) in PCY, vol. 1.
U/SATB, kybd, solo, opt cong, gtr.

THURSDAY, MARCH 1

GEORGE HERBERT, PRIEST, 1633

As a student at Trinity College, Cambridge, George
Herbert excelled in languages and music. He went to
college with the intention of becoming a priest, but his
scholarship attracted the attention of King James I. Herbert served in parliament for two years. After the death
of King James and under the influence of a friend, Herbert's interest in ordained ministry was renewed. He was
ordained a priest in 1630 and served the little parish of
St. Andrew Bremerton until his death. He was noted for
unfailing care for his parishioners, bringing the sacraments to them when they were ill, and providing food
and clothing for those in need.

Herbert was also a poet and hymnwriter. One of
his hymns, "Come, my way, my truth, my life" (LBW
513), invites an intimate encounter with Christ through
a feast that "mends in length" and could be included on
the first Sunday in Lent as an assurance that Christ is
with us in the temptations we face.

FRIDAY, MARCH 2
JOHN WESLEY, 1791; CHARLES WESLEY, 1788;
RENEWERS OF THE CHURCH

The Wesleys were leaders of a revival in the Church of England. Their spiritual discipline of frequent communion, fasting, and advocacy for the poor earned them the name "Methodists." The Wesleys were missionaries in the American colony of Georgia for a time but returned to England discouraged. Following a conversion experience while reading Luther's *Preface to the Epistle to the Romans*, John was perhaps the greatest force in eigh-

teenth-century revival. Their desire was that the Methodist Societies would be a movement for renewal in the Church of England, but after their deaths the societies developed a separate status.

Charles wrote more than six hundred hymns, twelve of which are in *Lutheran Book of Worship* and one of which is in *With One Voice*. Three of Charles's hymns are especially appropriate for Lent: "Christ, whose glory fills the skies" (LBW 265), "Love divine, all loves excelling" (LBW 315), and "Forth in thy name, O Lord, I go" (LBW 505).

MARCH 4, 2001

FIRST SUNDAY IN LENT

137

INTRODUCTION

The Lenten discipline is a spiritual struggle. In the confession of sins we acknowledge that we struggle and seek God's strength. Jesus struggles with us, and so we are sustained. Help is as close as a prayer and a confession that we cannot do it on our own. God gives life and its fruit, and so all we offer in worship is giving back what was first given us by grace.

PRAYER OF THE DAY

Lord God, you led your ancient people through the wilderness and brought them to the promised land. Guide now the people of your Church, that, following our Savior, we may walk through the wilderness of this world toward the glory of the world to come; through your Son, Jesus Christ our Lord, who lives and reigns with you and the Holy Spirit, one God, now and forever.

or

Lord God, our strength, the battle of good and evil rages within and around us, and our ancient foe tempts us with his deceits and empty promises. Keep us steadfast in your Word and, when we fall, raise us again and restore us through your Son, Jesus Christ our Lord, who

lives and reigns with you and the Holy Spirit, one God, now and forever.

READINGS

Deuteronomy 26:1-11

The annual harvest festival called the feast of weeks provides the setting for this reading. This festival celebrates the first fruits of the produce of the land offered back to God in thanks. In this text, worshipers announce God's gracious acts on behalf of Israel.

Psalm 91:1-2, 9-16

God shall charge the angels to keep you in all your ways. (Ps. 91:11)

Romans 10:8b-13

Paul reminds the Christians at Rome of the foundational affirmation of those who are saved: the confession of faith in the risen Jesus as Lord.

Luke 4:1-13

After being filled with the Holy Spirit at his baptism, Jesus is tempted by the devil and defines what it means to be called "the Son of God."

COLOR   Purple

THE PRAYERS

As we mark these forty days with repentance and forgiveness, let us pray for the renewal of the church and the restoration of the world to the life of God.

A BRIEF SILENCE.

For all the baptized, that led through the wilderness of this world, we may resist temptation to sin and evil through reliance upon the divine bread of God. Let us pray to the Lord.

Lord, have mercy.

For the church, that it may witness to God's love in the parched lands of depression, loneliness, and fear that fill the lives of many. Let us pray to the Lord.

Lord, have mercy.

For all who wander as refugees and exiles in this world, that they may find an everlasting home with God. Let us pray to the Lord.

Lord, have mercy.

For those who are imprisoned, persecuted for their faith, or burdened by illness (especially…), that they may be delivered and protected from harm to body and soul. Let us pray to the Lord.

Lord, have mercy.

For those who will soon confess the faith of the church through baptism, that they may grasp that word of faith and so repel temptation with confidence. Let us pray to the Lord.

Lord, have mercy.

HERE OTHER INTERCESSIONS MAY BE OFFERED.

Remembering those who called upon the name of Christ in this life, we pray that we may abide with them in the shelter of the Most High. Let us pray to the Lord.

Lord, have mercy.

Gracious God, hear us as we pray, and sustain us with your hope, through Jesus Christ our Lord.

Amen

IMAGES FOR PREACHING

"If" is a tempting word. Three times (verses 3, 7, 9) the devil says, "If." The word *if* is a conditional word that creates a world of possibilities. The devil invites Jesus to enter his world and live by its assumptions. Jesus' mission as the Son of God, "full of the Holy Spirit," would have ended in the wilderness if he had accepted the premise of the devil's world of possibilities. He would not have made his way to his cross and resurrection.

On this day, in some congregations, candidates will be enrolled for baptism at the Vigil of Easter or Easter Sunday. The presiding minister will say to them, "By God's grace you have been drawn to this congregation. You have heard the word of God and prayed with us. Do you desire to be baptized?" (*Welcome to Christ: Lutheran Rites for the Catechumenate,* p. 19.) The season of Lent becomes for them a time of final preparation for their baptism. Like the journey of Jesus to his cross and resurrection, this period of preparation is endangered by a world that does not belong to Christ.

Jesus responds to the devil by asserting that he, and all who are his followers, live in another world, the world of faith. The central confession of Deuteronomy was not far from Jesus' lips, "Hear, O Israel: The Lord is our God, the Lord alone" (see Deut. 6:4-9). Jesus responded to the three temptations by quoting Deuteronomy 8:3, 6:13, and 6:16. Notice that the devil also quoted scripture, turning a psalm of trust (Ps. 91:11-12) into an instrument of doubt.

We, too, are tempted to cover our naked mortality with schemes to achieve fulfillment, power, and control. By these schemes we turn in on ourselves, attempting to cover our fear. Jesus is showing us the way through that wilderness, where we become starkly aware of our mortality. He calls us to the way of faith.

WORSHIP MATTERS

We have a choice before us: traditional or contemporary. No, this choice is not about worship style but rather the Lord's Prayer. The decision about which version is prayed may be rooted in comfort, tradition, or relevancy. Note, however, that each version also presents a teaching opportunity, especially with regard to the sixth petition: Lead us not into temptation/Save us from the time of trial.

Whereas the traditional version recalls the story of Jesus' baptism, after which the Spirit drove him into the wilderness to be tempted, the contemporary version recalls Easter and the protection afforded to those who call upon the Lord's name. Both provide the possibility for a fascinating biblical and theological excursus. If your congregation has only used the traditional version of the prayer, is it possible to introduce the newer ecumenical version for a given season or occasion?

LET THE CHILDREN COME

In the Lord's Prayer we pray that we will be saved from the time of trial (or we use the traditional words: "lead us not into temptation"). As Lent begins, we ask that the victory Jesus gives us in the resurrection be able to protect us at all times. With the children, think of the many ways God protects us. How do we pray for this protection?

MUSIC FOR WORSHIP

SERVICE MUSIC

This is a good day to use the Litany (*LBW*, p. 168) at the entrance, replacing confession and forgiveness, entrance hymn, and Kyrie. Its rhythmic, almost hypnotic cadence is best realized when the bids and responses are sung with a steady pulse, overlapping one another slightly. As the Litany is sung, cross and ministers process slowly through the aisles, the people either following to their places or kneeling (standing) at their seats. After a brief silence, the liturgy continues with greeting and prayer of the day.

GATHERING

LBW 99   O Lord, throughout these forty days
WOV 657   The glory of these forty days

PSALM 91:1-2, 9-16

Haas, David. "Lord, Be with Me" in PCY, vol. 9.

Joncas, Michael. "Psalm 91: Be with Me, Lord" in STP, vol. 1.

Keesecker, Thomas. PW, Cycle C.

Marshall, Jane. *Psalms Together II*. CGC-18.

W&P 110 (WOV 779) On Eagle's Wings

HYMN OF THE DAY

LBW 228/9   A mighty fortress is our God
            Ein feste Burg

VOCAL RESOURCES

Bisbee, B. Wayne. "A Mighty Fortress Is Our God." CPH 98-2821. SATB, br, kybd, cong.

Busarow, Donald. "Ein feste Burg" in *Thirty More Accompaniments for Hymns in Canon*. AFP 11-10163.

Hassler, Hans Leo. "A Mighty Fortress" in CC. SATB.

INSTRUMENTAL RESOURCES

Albrecht, Timothy. "A Mighty Fortress Is Our God" in *Grace Notes V* (AFP 11-10764) and *Grace Notes VI* (AFP 11-10825). Org.

Diemer, Emma Lou. "A Mighty Fortress Is Our God" in *Laudate!* vol. 4; ed. James W. Kosnik. CPH 97-6665. Org.

Ferguson, John. "Ein feste Burg" in *Festival Hymns for Organ, Brass and Timpani*, Set 4. GIA G-4217.

Moklebust, Cathy. "A Mighty Fortress Is Our God" in *Hymn Stanzas for Handbells*. AFP 11-10722 (4-5 oct) and 11-10869 (2-3 oct). Hb.

Wellman, Samuel. "A Mighty Fortress Is Our God" in *Keyboard Hymn Favorites*. AFP 11-10820. Pno.

ALTERNATE HYMN OF THE DAY

LBW 341   Jesus, still lead on
WOV 660   I want Jesus to walk with me

COMMUNION

LBW 212   Let us break bread together
LBW 225   Lord Jesus Christ, we humbly pray
WOV 748   Bind us together

SENDING

LBW 562   Lift every voice and sing
WOV 614   Praise to you, O Christ, our Savior

ADDITIONAL HYMNS AND SONGS

RS 548   Jesus, tempted in the desert
RS 557   Jesus walked this lonesome valley
TFF 183   I must tell Jesus
W&P 115   Out in the wilderness
W&P 117   Praise the name of Jesus

MUSIC FOR THE DAY

CHORAL

Erickson, Richard. "By the Babylonian Rivers." AFP 11-10814. SATB, org.

Gibbons, Orlando. "Almighty and Everlasting God." OXF TCM 36.

Hopson, Hal H. "A Lenten Walk." AFP 11-10568. 2 pt mxd, org, opt timp, hb.

Isaac, Heinrich. "O Bread of Life from Heaven" in CC. SATB.

Kitson, C. H. "Jesu, Grant Me This, I Pray." OXF 42-041. SATB, org.

Near, Gerald. "A Lenten Prayer." AUR (MSM) AE91. 2 pt, org.

Schütz, Heinrich. "We Offer Our Praise and Thanks" in CC. SATB.

Walter, Johann. "I Build on God's Strong Word Alone" in CC. SATB.

CHILDREN'S CHOIRS

African American spiritual. "I Want Jesus to Walk with Me" in LS.

Burkhardt, Michael. "Thy Holy Wings/I Lift My Soul." MSM 50-5552. U/2 pt, pno, opt ob, cl, vc.

Joncas, Michael. "On Eagle's Wings." Cant, cong, desc, pno, gtr, opt vc, opt C inst.

KEYBOARD/INSTRUMENTAL

Billingham, Richard. "I Want Jesus to Walk with Me" in *Seven Reflections on African American Spirituals.* AFP 11-10762. Org.

Inniss, Carleton. "Invocation—I Want Jesus to Walk with Me" in *A Spiritual Service.* CFI 05395. Org.

HANDBELL

Polley, David J. "Two Lenten Hymns for Handbells." MSM 30-300. 3 oct.

Wood, Dale. "Aria for Handbells." AGEHR AG34005. 3-5 oct.

PRAISE ENSEMBLE

Hooker, John Leon. "Now Let Us All with One Accord" in *Gather.* GIA.

Nelson, Marc. "I Believe in Jesus" in *Praise Hymns and Choruses,* 4th ed. MAR.

WEDNESDAY, MARCH 7
PERPETUA AND FELICITY AND COMPANIONS, MARTYRS AT CARTHAGE, 202

In the year 202 the emperor Septimius Severus forbade conversions to Christianity. Perpetua, a noblewoman, Felicity, a slave, and other companions were all catechumens at Carthage in North Africa. They were imprisoned and sentenced to death. Perpetua's father, who was not a Christian, visited her in prison and begged her to lay aside her Christian convictions in order to spare her life and spare the family from scorn. Perpetua responded and told her father, "We know that we are not placed in our own power but in that of God."

During the weeks of Lent, congregations that do not have catechumens can pray for those who do as they approach their own death and rebirth in the waters of baptism at the Easter Vigil and are clothed with the new life of Christ.

WEDNESDAY, MARCH 7
THOMAS AQUINAS, TEACHER, 1274

Thomas Aquinas was a brilliant and creative theologian of the thirteenth century. He was first and foremost a student of the Bible and profoundly concerned with the theological formation of the church's ordained ministers. As a member of the Order of Preachers (Dominicans), he worked to correlate scripture with the philosophy of Aristotle, which was having a renaissance in Aquinas's day. Some students of Aristotle's philosophy found in it an alternative to Christianity. But Aquinas immersed himself in the thought of Aristotle and worked to explain Christian beliefs in the philosophical culture of the day. The contemporary worship cultural studies done by the Lutheran World Federation resonate with Aquinas's method.

Aquinas was also a hymnwriter. His hymn "Thee we adore, O hidden Savior" (LBW 199) is traditionally sung on Maundy Thursday and might also be sung this Sunday as a communion hymn.

MARCH 11, 2001
SECOND SUNDAY IN LENT

INTRODUCTION

Baptism is the compass that guides us through life. And Lent is a season for immersing ourselves in a new identity—reminding us who we are and calling us to what we are to be doing. The miracle of grace is as amazing as starting a family in your old age, as Abraham and Sarah did, or being reminded that our true citizenship lies beyond this world.

PRAYER OF THE DAY

Eternal God, it is your glory always to have mercy. Bring back all who have erred and strayed from your ways; lead them again to embrace in faith the truth of your Word and to hold it fast; through Jesus Christ your Son our Lord, who lives and reigns with you and the Holy Spirit, one God, now and forever.

READINGS

Genesis 15:1-12, 17-18

God promises a childless and doubting Abram that he will have a son, that his descendants will be as numerous as the stars, and that the land will be their inheritance. Abram's trust in God's promise is sealed with a covenant-making ritual, a sign of God's promise.

Psalm 27

In the day of trouble, the LORD shall keep me safe.
(Ps. 27:7)

Philippians 3:17—4:1

Although Paul's devotion to Christ has caused him to be persecuted, he does not regret the course he has taken. Writing from prison, he expresses confidence in a glorious future and encourages other Christians to follow in his footsteps.

Luke 13:31-35

Jesus likens the tyrant Herod to a murderous fox. He speaks of himself as a mother hen who would sacrifice her own life to shield her children from danger.

COLOR   Purple

THE PRAYERS

As we mark these forty days with repentance and forgiveness, let us pray for the renewal of the church and the restoration of the world to the life of God.

A BRIEF SILENCE.

For all those making the pilgrimage through Lent, that they may fervently seek the Lord in prayer. Let us pray to the Lord.

Lord, have mercy.

For those gathered into the house of God, that they might remain firm in hope and proclaim God's name to others. Let us pray to the Lord.

Lord, have mercy.

For all nations, that they may care for their land as a trust from God and learn to employ its resources wisely. Let us pray to the Lord.

Lord, have mercy.

For those confronted with difficult times, persecuted for the faith, or weakened by sickness (especially...), that they may see and taste God's goodness. Let us pray to the Lord.

Lord, have mercy.

For those longing for baptism, that the church may show them the way to God. Let us pray to the Lord.

Lord, have mercy.

HERE OTHER INTERCESSIONS MAY BE OFFERED.

Remembering all the saints, martyrs, and faithful people who stood firm in the Lord, we pray that we may imitate their example and obtain with them the fulfillment of your covenant promise. Let us pray to the Lord.

Lord, have mercy.

Gracious God, hear us as we pray, and sustain us with your hope, through Jesus Christ our Lord.

Amen

IMAGES FOR PREACHING

In order to express his desire to gather and nurture God's children, Jesus calls to mind the image of a mother hen protecting her chicks by gathering them under her wing. (See also Deut. 32:10-14.) In the gospel reading for today, he is on his way to Jerusalem, where he will be welcomed as king (Luke 19:38) and crucified under an inscription, "This is the King of the Jews" (Luke 23:38). While still on his journey he anticipates his fate as he laments, "Jerusalem, Jerusalem, the city that kills the prophets and stones those who are sent to it."

Carolina Sandell-Berg illuminates this image with her hymn text: "Thy holy wings, O Savior, spread gently over me, and let me rest securely through good and ill in thee. Oh, be my strength and portion, my rock and hiding place, and let my every moment be lived within thy grace" (WOV 741).

To whom or what do we turn for nurture? Do we respond to the allure of the kingdoms of this world, with their stories of success and power? Are we not tempted quite literally to put on the garments of success, with the logo of our favorite sports team? Jesus calls us to the world of faith where he brings healing by "casting out demons and performing cures." Within the season of Lent, Jesus strips us of another ragged garment with which we cover our mortal fear, thus preparing us to put on the garments of resurrection life.

We are invited to be gathered and nurtured under the Savior's holy wings and fed at the table of the Lord, where we sing, "Holy, holy, holy Lord, God of power and might: Heaven and earth are full of your glory. Hosanna in the highest. Blessed is he who comes in the name of the Lord. Hosanna in the highest" (*LBW,* p. 69).

141

WORSHIP MATTERS

Evildoers assail us, Satan's armies encamp against us, and wars rise up around us…and so we fear. The good news that is constantly proclaimed to us, however, is "Do not fear!"

Therefore the Lord's house ought to be the quintessential place where security and peace *obviously* reign! What do visitors actually *see* that announces this place as one of refuge? Are children present during the liturgy, or are they sent off to a nursery or Sunday school where they will not be a bother? Do bulletins and signs clearly indicate a desire to accommodate newcomers? Ultimately, is the proclamation of the word one that comforts? Are people made to feel that they are the brood gathered under the wings of the Almighty?

LET THE CHILDREN COME

We gather most often in a building, surrounded by friends to share our worship experience. The building is strong, and the love of the members for one other reflects how God loves and cares for us. We are safe in that secure place. We share that caring for one other when we pass the peace, "The peace of the Lord be with you." As our churches become a place where children are welcomed, nurtured, and cared for, everyone will understand that God loves deeply.

MUSIC FOR WORSHIP

GATHERING

LBW 496	Around you, O Lord Jesus
WOV 656	By the Babylonian rivers

PSALM 27

DeBruyn, Randall. "The Lord Is My Light" in STP, vol. 4.

Howard, Julie. *Sing for Joy: Psalm Settings for God's Children.* LTP.

Keesecker, Thomas. PW, Cycle C.

Kreutz, Robert. *Psalms and Selected Canticles.* OCP.

Zimmerman, Heinz Werner. "The Lord Is My Light." CPH 98-2174. SATB, org.

HYMN OF THE DAY

WOV 663	When twilight comes
	DAPIT HAPON

INSTRUMENTAL RESOURCES

Organ, Anne Krentz. "Dapit Hapon" in *Global Piano Reflections.* AFP 11-10932. Pno.

ALTERNATE HYMN OF THE DAY

LBW 421	Lord Christ, when first you came to earth
LBW 427	O Jesus Christ, may grateful hymns be rising

COMMUNION

LBW 496	Around you, O Lord Jesus
WOV 741	Thy holy wings

SENDING

LBW 343	Guide me ever, great Redeemer
WOV 699	Blessed assurance

ADDITIONAL HYMNS AND SONGS

H82 149	Eternal Lord of love, behold your church
PH 179	God is my strong salvation
TFF 67	By the waters of Babylon
W&P 1	A song of unity (As a mother hen)

MUSIC FOR THE DAY

CHORAL

Distler, Hugo. "For God So Loved the World" in CC. SAB.

Helgen, John. "That Priceless Grace." AFP 11-10992. SATB, kybd.

Owens, Sam Batt. "Hide Me under the Shadow of Your Wings." MSM 50-9207. 2 pt, org.

Sadowski, Kevin J. "God So Loved the World," in *Three Motets from the Gospel of John.* CPH 98-3472. SATB.

Schütz, Heinrich. "God So Loved the World" in CC. SATTB.

Stainer, John. "God So Loved the World." NOV 29.0234.06. SATB, kybd.

CHILDREN'S CHOIRS

Christopherson, Dorothy. "The Lord Is My Light." AFP 11-4683. U, pno, fc, opt choregraphy.

Hopson, Hal H. "We Are Singing, for the Lord Is Our Light." AG HH 3949. U/SATB, kybd.

Jennings, Carolyn. "My Song Is Love Unknown." CG CGA-559. U, kybd.

KEYBOARD/INSTRUMENTAL

Cherwien, David. "Thy Holy Wings" in *Rejoice in God's Saints.* AFP 11-10713. Org.

Distler, Hugo. "Mit Freuden Zart" in *Short Chorale Arrangements.* Masters Music Publications M 1466. Org.

Haan, Raymond H. *Canonic Variations on "With High Delight."* CPH 97-6167. Org.

Moklebust, Cathy. "Thy Holy Wings." CPH 97-6518. 3-4 oct.

Morris, Hart. "I'm Just a Poor Wayfaring Stranger." RRM HB0017.
3-5 oct, opt alto sax.

PRAISE ENSEMBLE

Cornell, Garry. "Trusting You For All." Celebrations Unlimited CU
155. SATB, kybd.

Hanson, Handt. "Psalm 27" in *Spirit Touching Spirit*. CCF.

Jernigan, Dennis, and Bruce Greer. "You Are My All in All."
WRD 301 0937 164. SATB, kybd, 2 fl.

Ylvisaker, John. "You're My Light and My Salvation" in *Borning Cry*.
NGP.

MONDAY, MARCH 12
GREGORY THE GREAT, BISHOP OF ROME, 604

Gregory was born into a politically influential family. At one time he held political office, and at another time he lived as a monk, all before he was elected to the papacy. Gregory's work was extensive. He influenced public worship through the establishment of a lectionary and prayers to correlate with the readings. He established a school to train church musicians, and Gregorian chant is named in his honor. He wrote a treatise underscoring what is required of a parish pastor serving a congrega-tion. He sent missionaries to preach to the Anglo-Saxons who had invaded England. And at one time he organized distribution of grain during a shortage of food in Rome.

Gregory's life serves as an example of the link between liturgy and social justice. His Lenten hymn, "O Christ, our king, creator, Lord" (LBW 101), sings of God's grace flowing out from the cross to all creation.

SATURDAY, MARCH 17
PATRICK, BISHOP, MISSIONARY TO IRELAND, 461

At sixteen, Patrick was kidnapped by Irish pirates and sold into slavery in Ireland. He himself admitted that up to this point he cared little for God. He escaped after six years, returned to his family in southwest Britain, and began to prepare for ordained ministry. He later returned to Ireland, this time to serve as a bishop and missionary. He made his base in the north of Ireland and from there made many missionary journeys with much success. In his autobiography he denounced the slave trade, perhaps from his own experience as a slave.

Patrick's famous baptismal hymn to the Trinity, "I bind unto myself today" (LBW 188), can be used as a meditation on Lent's call to return to our baptism.

143

MARCH 18, 2001

THIRD SUNDAY IN LENT

INTRODUCTION

Can we take the news to heart? Each story we encounter in this season is really about us. Lent began as we were reminded by an ashen cross that we do not have forever. The clock is ticking; the forty days are unwinding. We have now! If we take this day seriously, we may discover that our deepest hungers can be filled. When we know that we are heading toward a forgiving God, the news becomes good news.

PRAYER OF THE DAY

Eternal Lord, your kingdom has broken into our troubled world through the life, death, and resurrection of your Son. Help us to hear your Word and obey it, so that we become instruments of your redeeming love; through your Son, Jesus Christ our Lord, who lives and reigns with you and the Holy Spirit, one God, now and forever.

READINGS

Isaiah 55:1-9

To those who have experienced long years in exile, the return to their native land seems like an unbelievable promise of free food and drink for all who come to the celebration. What is more, those who return to the Lord also enjoy new life and forgiveness, because God's ways are not our ways.

Psalm 63:1-8

O God, eagerly I seek you; my soul thirsts for you. (Ps. 63:1)

1 Corinthians 10:1-13

Paul uses images from Hebrew story and prophecy to speak the truth of Jesus Christ: He is our rock, our water, our food, and our drink. Christ is the living sign of God's faithfulness.

Luke 13:1-9

Jesus addresses the age-old question of whether people deserve the seemingly random calamities that happen to them. The short answer is no. But the key to our peace is using the present moment to throw ourselves upon God's grace.

COLOR   Purple

THE PRAYERS

As we mark these forty days with repentance and forgiveness, let us pray for the renewal of the church and the restoration of the world to the life of God.

A BRIEF SILENCE.

For all believers, that through daily repentance we may return to God. Let us pray to the Lord.

Lord, have mercy.

For the body of Christ, that we may remain with God in every word and deed. Let us pray to the Lord.

Lord, have mercy.

For all parents, that they may give thanks for their children, nurturing them with self-giving love and devotion. Let us pray to the Lord.

Lord, have mercy.

For all who thirst for God, those facing death, those persecuted for their faith, those who are sick (especially...), that God may uphold them through all trials. Let us pray to the Lord.

Lord, have mercy.

For those soon to be baptized into Christ's body, that they may hear God's voice as they journey to new life. Let us pray to the Lord.

Lord, have mercy.

HERE OTHER INTERCESSIONS MAY BE OFFERED.

We remember with thanks all those now satisfied by the eternal feast of heaven. May we unite our voices with the praise of their lips. Let us pray to the Lord.

Lord, have mercy.

Gracious God, hear us as we pray, and sustain us with your hope, through Jesus Christ our Lord.

Amen

IMAGES FOR PREACHING

Fertilizing is an important means by which an experienced gardener brings out the best in her or his plants and trees. Fruit trees and vineyards cannot grow without the right soil conditions, water, and sun. Neither can we grow in our life of faith without the care and nurture of our Lord Jesus Christ. The call to repentance is placed within this care and nurture. The repentant life bears fruits. (See, for example, Col. 3:12-17.) We need the gardener's care, and we need the grace of more time. Yet, we do not bear fruit on our own.

Martin Luther wrote: "I believe that by my own understanding or strength I cannot believe in Jesus Christ my Lord or come to him, but instead the Holy Spirit has called me through the gospel, enlightened me with his gifts, made me holy, and kept me in the true faith, just as he calls, gathers, enlightens, and makes holy the whole Christian church on earth and keeps it with Jesus Christ in the one common, true faith" (third article of the Apostles' Creed, *A Contemporary Translation of Luther's Small Catechism*, Study Edition, p. 29). The Holy Spirit calls us to life in Christ, nurtures and sustains us in faith, and helps us to bear the fruits of faithfulness.

In some congregations during this season of Lent, adults are preparing to be baptized. On this Sunday they gather along with their sponsors before the congregation, which recites the Apostles' Creed to them, thus ritually giving them the gift by which we make our affirmation of faith. The presiding minister says, "As the barren fig tree required the gardener's care in order to thrive and bear fruit, so the church confesses its need of Christ and its trust in God's mercy. We invite you whom God has chosen for baptism to join all the people of God in confessing the faith of the church" (*Welcome to Christ: Lutheran Rites for the Catechumenate,* p. 23).

WORSHIP MATTERS

The ease of travel, technological wizardry, and the multitude of opportunities afforded by this society quickly consume our time if we are not careful. A superficial chat during the drive from school to the athletic event replaces the family conversation. Computers and video games devour our family time. Sundry opportunities compete with Sunday worship. As our time is consumed, our spiritual thirst and hunger increase. How can we slake such thirst?

Look to the body of Christ. Begin the exercise of daily prayer. Personally receive the Lord's various words of comfort proclaimed throughout the liturgy. Read and study the scriptures as well as the lives of the saints.

LET THE CHILDREN COME

We need food and drink for our bodies. In baptism, our bodies receive life-giving water. In communion, we receive bread and wine to feed our bodies and our souls. Baptismal fonts that are open and filled with water can help children to be more aware of the power in this sacrament. Children are also interested in seeing the bread and wine used in communion. The more senses involved, the better the understanding and remembering will be.

MUSIC FOR WORSHIP
GATHERING

| LBW 446 | Whatever God ordains is right |
| WOV 782 | All my hope on God is founded |

PSALM 63:1-8

Haugen, Marty. "Your Love Is Finer Than Life," in PCY, vol. 1.

Keesecker, Thomas. PW, Cycle C.

Schutte, Daniel. "My Soul Thirsts" in STP, vol. 4.

Walker, Christopher. "Psalm 63: O Lord, I Will Sing" in STP, vol. 2.

Psalms for All Seasons: An ICEL Collection. NPM.

HYMN OF THE DAY

| LBW 326 | My heart is longing |
| | PRINCESS EUGENIE |

INSTRUMENTAL RESOURCES

Ferguson, John. "My Heart Is Longing" in *Behold a Host.* AFP 11-5183. Org.

Sedio, Mark. "Princess Eugenie" in *Dancing in the Light of God.* AFP 11-10793. Pno.

ALTERNATE HYMN OF THE DAY

| LBW 343 | Guide me ever, great Redeemer |
| WOV 662 | Restore in us, O God |

COMMUNION

| LBW 197 | O living Bread from heaven |
| WOV 707 | This is my body |

SENDING

| LBW 341 | Jesus, still lead on |
| WOV 723 | The Spirit sends us forth to serve |

ADDITIONAL HYMNS AND SONGS

HS98 890	When aimless violence takes those we love
NCH 586	Come to tend God's garden
TFF 290	Praised be the rock
UMH 340	Come, ye sinners, poor and needy
W&P 161	You are the rock of my salvation

MUSIC FOR THE DAY
CHORAL

Benson, Robert. "Wondrous Love." AFP 11-10993. SATB, org.

Christiansen, Paul. "Wondrous Love." AFP 11-1140. SATB.

Farlee, Robert Buckley. "O My People, Turn to Me" in *Three Biblical Songs.* AFP 11-10604. U, kybd.

Gerike, Henry V. "Create in Me." AFP 11-10746. SAB, org.

Goudimel, Claude. "As the Deer, for Water Yearning" in CC. SATB.

Mendelssohn, Felix. "O Come, Every One That Thirsteth." AFP 11-10334. SATB, kybd.

CHILDREN'S CHOIRS

Cherubini, Luigi/arr. Hal H. Hopson. "Come, All Who Thirst." SAB/3 pt trbl, pno/org.

Handel, G. F./arr. Hal H. Hopson. "Blest Are They Whose Spirits Long." CG CGA-183. 2 pt mxd, org/pno.

Haydn, Joseph/arr. Hal H. Hopson. "Lord, You Are My God." CG CGA-431. U, pno/org.

Sleeth, Natalie. "Fear Not for Tomorrow" in LS.

KEYBOARD/INSTRUMENTAL

Albrecht, Timothy. "Guide Me Ever, Great Redeemer/God of Grace and God of Glory" in *Grace Notes VIII.* AFP 11-10970. Org.

Cherwien, David. "As the Sun with Longer Journey" in *Organ Plus One.* AFP 11-10758. Org, inst.

Mahnke, Allan. "Guide Me Ever, Great Redeemer/God of Grace and God of Glory" in *Thirteen Pieces for Treble Instruments and Organ.* CPH 97-6030. Inst, org.

145

HANDBELL

Dobrinski, Cynthia. "Great Is Thy Faithfulness." AG 1280. 3-5 oct.

Seibert, Roberta. "What Wondrous Love Is This?" AGEHR AG4028. 4 oct.

PRAISE ENSEMBLE

Carter, John. "Seek the Lord." HOP JC 287 SATB, kybd.

Founds, Rick. "Jesus, Draw Me Close" in *Praise Hymns and Choruses*, 4th ed. MAR.

MONDAY, MARCH 19
JOSEPH, GUARDIAN OF OUR LORD

The gospels are silent about much of Joseph's life. We know that he was a carpenter or builder by trade. The gospel of Luke shows him acting in accordance with both civil and religious law by returning to Bethlehem for the census and by presenting the child Jesus in the temple on the fortieth day after his birth. The gospel of Matthew tells of Joseph's trust in God, who led him through visionary dreams. Because Joseph is not mentioned after the story of a young Jesus teaching in the temple, it is assumed that he died before Jesus reached adulthood.

Congregations might consider a Sicilian tradition to commemorate Joseph that combines the three Lenten disciplines of fasting, almsgiving, and prayer. The poor are invited to a festive buffet called "St. Joseph's Table." Lenten prayers and songs interrupt the course of the meal. What other ways can a congregation's almsgiving and charity be increased during Lent?

THURSDAY, MARCH 22
JONATHAN EDWARDS, TEACHER, MISSIONARY TO THE AMERICAN INDIANS, 1758

Edwards was a minister in Connecticut and has been described as the greatest of the New England Puritan preachers. One of Edwards's most notable sermons has found its way into contemporary anthologies of literature. In this sermon, "Sinners in the Hands of an Angry God," he spoke at length about hell. Throughout the rest of his works and his preaching, however, he had more to say about God's love than God's wrath. His personal experience of conversion came when he felt overwhelmed with a sense of God's majesty and grandeur rather than a fear of hell. Edwards served a Puritan congregation. He believed that only those who had been fully converted ought to receive communion; his congregation thought otherwise. Edwards left that congregation and carried out mission work among the Housatonic Indians of Massachusetts. He became president of the College of New Jersey, later to be known as Princeton.

SATURDAY, MARCH 24
OSCAR ARNULFO ROMERO, BISHOP OF EL SALVADOR, MARTYR, 1980

Romero is remembered for his advocacy on behalf of the poor in El Salvador, though it was not a characteristic of his early priesthood. After being appointed as bishop he preached against the political repression in his country. He and other priests and church workers were considered traitors for their bold stand for justice, especially defending the rights of the poor. After several years of threats to his life, Romero was assassinated while presiding at the eucharist. During the 1980s thousands died in El Salvador during political unrest.

Romero is remembered as a martyr who gave his life in behalf of the powerless in his country. Our Lenten journey of conversion calls us to be bold in our witness to Christ, work on behalf of the powerless, and speak on behalf of justice and equality for all people, who are created in the image of God.

MARCH 25, 2001

FOURTH SUNDAY IN LENT

INTRODUCTION

Lent is the time for coming home. In the ancient church it was the season for reconciling lapsed Christians to the community of the faithful. Today's readings provide images of homecoming—Israel's entry into the land of promise, a prodigal son who returned to his waiting father. In this week, nine months before Christmas, the church also celebrates the Annunciation. The angel Gabriel announced to a surprised Mary that God would make a home within her, as she became the mother of Jesus. Welcome home!

PRAYER OF THE DAY

God of all mercy, by your power to heal and to forgive, graciously cleanse us from all sin and make us strong; through your Son, Jesus Christ our Lord, who lives and reigns with you and the Holy Spirit, one God, now and forever.

READINGS

Joshua 5:9-12

By celebrating the Passover and eating the produce of the promised land instead of the miraculous manna that had sustained them in the desert, the Israelites symbolically bring their forty years of wilderness wandering to an end at Gilgal.

Psalm 32

Be glad, you righteous, and rejoice in the LORD. (Ps. 32:12)

2 Corinthians 5:16-21

In Jesus' death on the cross, God works to persuade us of divine love, so that we might be reconciled to God. As part of God's new creation, we are challenged to share with others the good news of our reconciled relationship to God.

Luke 15:1-3, 11b-32

Jesus tells a story about a son who discovers his father's love only when he walks away from it. But the father's grace is also a crisis for an older brother, who thought that by his obedience he had earned a place in the father's home.

COLOR   Purple

THE PRAYERS

As we mark these forty days with repentance and forgiveness, let us pray for the renewal of the church and the restoration of the world to the life of God.

A BRIEF SILENCE.

For the church in its Lenten journey, that it may give generously from the blessings it has received to those who are thirsty, hungry, and without home or money. Let us pray to the Lord.

Lord, have mercy.

For the nations and those who guide their affairs, that they may devote themselves to the plight of those neglected throughout the world. Let us pray to the Lord.

Lord, have mercy.

For those weighed down by sin, longing for companionship, or stricken by illness (especially...), that they may find comfort in God's love. Let us pray to the Lord.

Lord, have mercy.

For those who give their time to assist those in need, that others might see the reconciling love of God through them. Let us pray to the Lord.

Lord, have mercy.

For those preparing for baptism, that they might joyfully anticipate their rebirth by water and the Spirit. Let us pray to the Lord.

Lord, have mercy.

HERE OTHER INTERCESSIONS MAY BE OFFERED.

That we may be united with all those who have departed this life and have been welcomed home to God, Mary, the renewers of the church, and all the blessed dead, for whom we give thanks. Let us pray to the Lord.

Lord, have mercy.

Gracious God, hear us as we pray, and sustain us with your hope, through Jesus Christ our Lord.

Amen

IMAGES FOR PREACHING

An embrace says more than words. On April 20, 1999, parents waited in terror while the high school in Littleton, Colorado, was under siege. Twelve students and one teacher were killed by two young men who then took

147

their own lives. As students fled the school and came to the place where their parents waited, a daughter could be seen running into the waiting arms of her tearful mother, and there in the makeshift waiting room they embraced. This scene, as we recall, is neither a mere illustration nor an allegory of Jesus' parable of the prodigal son. These youth were running from evil into the arms of grace.

The power of this embrace can be told well in a song like "Amazing grace, how sweet the sound." "Through many dangers, toils, and snares I have already come; 'tis grace has brought me safe thus far, and grace will lead me home" (LBW 448).

In some congregations where adults are preparing for baptism, they gather along with their sponsors before the congregation, following the hymn of the day, and hear the presiding minister say, "As the prodigal son abandoned his life of sin and returned to the joy of the father, so the church, empowered by the Spirit, renounces the power of evil in the world. Let us join with saints and angels to pray that God will expose the devil's empty promises and flood the world with light" (*Welcome to Christ: Lutheran Rites for the Catechumenate,* p. 28).

The embrace of the father in Jesus' parable shows unrestrained grace as he held, kissed, and feasted his younger son. His older son, however, was blinded to mercy by his own sense of fairness. Yet, he too received a gracious word from his father, who said, "Son, you are always with me, and all that is mine is yours. But we had to celebrate and rejoice. . . ."

WORSHIP MATTERS

Is that a person with whom you had a run-in last week? Is not that . . . a foreigner . . . my gay neighbor . . . a convicted felon . . . a never-married mother of four? Do not regard them from "a human point of view. . . . If anyone is in Christ, there is a new creation" (2 Cor. 5:16-17).

Consider yourself. Where would you be if you were judged on your own merits and not on those of Jesus Christ? Would you ever be worthy to come to the table of the Lord? But if we are in Christ—baptized, believing, and hoping in him—we are a new creation, pure and sinless, able to drink of the fruit of the vine. "Happy are those whose transgression is forgiven, whose sin is covered" (Ps. 32:1).

LET THE CHILDREN COME

Pass out paper plates to each child present. "Anyone need a plate? You have all been invited to supper, and no matter how many people come, there is a plate for you and a place at this table." This is the wonderful news for us: God has a place for each of us at the banquet table. . . Sing a song about an invitation to communion, such as "Come, let us eat" (LBW 214). Have a soloist sing each phrase, and then have the group echo.

MUSIC FOR WORSHIP
GATHERING

LBW 499	Come, thou Fount of every blessing
WOV 736	By gracious powers

PSALM 32

Cooney, Rory. "I Turn to You" in PCY, vol. 4.

Howard, Julie. "Psalm 32" in *Sing for Joy: Psalm Settings for God's Children.* LTP.

Isele, David Clark. TP.

Keesecker, Thomas. PW, Cycle C.

See proper 6 and proper 26.

HYMN OF THE DAY

WOV 734	Softly and tenderly Jesus is calling THOMPSON

VOCAL RESOURCES

Bertalot, John. "Softly and Tenderly." AFP 11-10212. SAB, org.

INSTRUMENTAL RESOURCES

Carlson, J. Bert. "Softly and Tenderly Jesus Is Calling" in *Blessed Assurance.* AFP 11-10935. Pno.

Ferguson, John. "Thompson" in *Three Nineteenth-Century Revival Hymns.* AFP 11-10976. Org.

Hassell, Michael. "Thompson" in *Jazz Sunday Morning.* AFP 11-10212. Pno.

ALTERNATE HYMN OF THE DAY

LBW 448	Amazing grace, how sweet the sound
WOV 733	Our Father, we have wandered

COMMUNION

LBW 298	One there is, above all others
WOV 746	Day by day

SENDING

LBW 341   Jesus, still lead on
WOV 781   My life flows on in endless song

ADDITIONAL HYMNS AND SONGS

ASG 19   Let this season be
TFF 73   Jesus, keep me near the cross
W&P 160   You are my hiding place (Ps. 32:7)

MUSIC FOR THE DAY

CHORAL

Bach, J. S. "Lord, Thee I Love with All My Heart" in BAS. SATB.

Cherwien, David. "How Can I Keep from Singing." AFP 11-10963.
    U, kybd.

Kellam, Ian. "Dear Lord, Who Bore Our Weight of Woe." GIA G-4474.
    SATB, kybd.

Pinkham, Daniel. "Thou Hast Turned My Laments into Dancing."
    PET 66568.

Powell, Robert J. "Remember Your Lord God." AFP 11-10776.
    U, kybd.

Ratcliff, Cary. "God of the Sparrow." KAI K-12. U, kybd.

Thompson, J. Michael. "Taste and See the Lord Is Good."
    AFP 11-10842. SATB, org, ob.

Viadana, Lodovico. "Shout for Joy, Ye Righteous/Exsultate justi" in Eu-
    ropean Sacred Music. OXF 0-19-343695-7. SATB.

CHILDREN'S CHOIRS

Cherubini, Luigi/arr. Austin Lovelace. "Like as a Father."
    CG CGA-156. 3 pt canon, pno.

Edwards, Rusty. "God Be with You" in LS. Use as a benediction.

Wold, Wayne. "Rejoice! I Found the Lost." AFP 11-10463. U/2 pt,
    kybd.

KEYBOARD/INSTRUMENTAL

Biery, James. "The Prodigal Son" in Three Gospel Scenes. MSM-10-317.
    Org.

Lovelace, Austin C. "Fughetta on 'You Are the Way; to You Alone'"
    from Four Organ Pieces for Lent. CPH 97-6029. Org.

Sedio, Mark. "Jesus Sinners Will Receive" in Organ Tapestries, vol. 1.
    CPH 97-6812. Org.

HANDBELL

Morris, Hart. "Amazing Grace." AGEHR AG35076. 3-5 oct.

Thompson, Martha Lynn. "Come, Thou Fount of Every Blessing."
    Fred Bock Music BG0798. 4-5 oct.

PRAISE ENSEMBLE

Keesecker, Thomas. "Jesus, Keep Me Near the Cross." AFP 11-10744.
    SATB, pno.

Landry, Carey. "Come Home" in Glory & Praise. OCP.

Makeever, Ray, and John Helgen. "Brighter Than the Sun." AFP 11-
    11054. SATB, kbd.

MONDAY, MARCH 26
THE ANNUNCIATION OF OUR LORD (TRANSFERRED)

Nine months before Christmas we celebrate the annunciation. In Luke we hear how the angel Gabriel announced to Mary that she would give birth to the Son
of God and she responded, "Here am I, the servant of
the Lord." Ancient scholars believed that March 25 was
also the day on which creation began and the date of
Jesus' death on the cross. Thus from the sixth to eighth
centuries, March 25 was observed as New Year's Day in
much of Christian Europe.

Set within Lent, Mary's openness to the will of
God is an example of faithful discipleship and leads us
to the work of God in our own lives. In worship today,
sing "The angel Gabriel from heaven came" (WOV
632). Or, as a canticle after communion, sing a setting of
the Magnificat, such as the paraphrase "My soul proclaims your greatness" (WOV 730).

THURSDAY, MARCH 29
HANS NIELSEN HAUGE, RENEWER OF THE CHURCH, 1824

Hans Nielsen Hauge was a layperson who began
preaching about "the living faith" in Norway and Denmark after a mystical experience that he believed called
him to share the assurance of salvation with others. At
the time itinerant preaching and religious gatherings
held without the supervision of a pastor were illegal,
and Hauge was arrested several times. He also faced
great personal suffering: his first wife died, and three of
his four children died in infancy.

Some might remember Hauge by singing the Norwegian hymn "My heart is longing" (LBW 326), with
its devotional response to the death of Christ.

SATURDAY, MARCH 31
JOHN DONNE, PRIEST, 1631

This priest of the Church of England is commemorated for his poetry and spiritual writing. Most of his poetry was written before his ordination and is sacred and secular, intellectual and sensuous. He saw in his wife, Anne—a marriage that resulted in his imprisonment—glimpses of the glory of God and a human revelation of divine love. In 1615 he was ordained, and seven years later he was named dean of St. Paul's Cathedral in London. By that time his reputation as a preacher was firmly in place.

In his poem "Good Friday, 1613. Riding westward" he speaks of Jesus' death on the cross: "Who sees God's face, that is self life, must die; What a death were it then to see God die?"

APRIL 1, 2001

FIFTH SUNDAY IN LENT

INTRODUCTION

The Lenten preparation is almost at an end. Something new is about to happen! Mary's act of anointing Jesus is extravagant, but when we know that grace has come to us, it is time for lavishness. Our old values get re-arranged when we realize how deeply we are loved.

PRAYER OF THE DAY

Almighty God, our redeemer, in our weakness we have failed to be your messengers of forgiveness and hope in the world. Renew us by your Holy Spirit, that we may follow your commands and proclaim your reign of love; through your Son, Jesus Christ our Lord, who lives and reigns with you and the Holy Spirit, one God, now and forever.

READINGS

Isaiah 43:16-21

This prophet of the exile declares that long ago the Lord performed mighty deeds and delivered Israel from Egyptian bondage. Now, the Lord is about to perform another act of deliverance. This salvation leads the people to praise God.

Psalm 126

Those who sowed with tears will reap with songs of joy. (Ps. 126:6)

Philippians 3:4b-14

Writing to Christians in Philippi, Paul admits that his heritage and reputation could give him more reason than most people to place confidence in his spiritual pedigree. But the overwhelming grace of God in Jesus calls Paul to a new set of values.

John 12:1-8

Judas misunderstands Mary's extravagant act of anointing Jesus' feet with a costly perfume. Jesus recognizes the true significance of her beautiful expression of love and commitment as an anticipation of his burial.

COLOR   Purple

THE PRAYERS

As we mark these forty days with repentance and forgiveness, let us pray for the renewal of the church and the restoration of the world to the life of God.

A BRIEF SILENCE.

For the whole people of God, that we may drink deeply of the refreshing waters that come to us through baptism into Jesus Christ. Let us pray to the Lord.

Lord, have mercy.

For artisans and artists of the church, that God might bless the efforts of their craft and so guide others to experience Christ more completely. Let us pray to the Lord.

Lord, have mercy.

For those in the world who do not know the life of God, that they may learn of the new things God is doing in Christ. Let us pray to the Lord.

Lord, have mercy.

For those suffering from unemployment, persecution for the faith, or illness (especially...), that they may have their needs supplied in the Lord and through this Christian community. Let us pray to the Lord.

Lord, have mercy.

For those who prepare to affirm their faith and to respond to the call of God in Christ Jesus, that they may grow in trust and understanding. Let us pray to the Lord.

Lord, have mercy.

HERE OTHER INTERCESSIONS MAY BE OFFERED.

Remembering those who have died in Christ, we ask that we may press on to know God in glory as they now do. Let us pray to the Lord.

Lord, have mercy.

Gracious God, hear us as we pray, and sustain us with your hope, through Jesus Christ our Lord.

Amen

IMAGES FOR PREACHING

"What a waste!" That was Judas's attitude. "Why was this perfume not sold for three hundred denarii and the money given to the poor?" The anointing was, in fact, an extraordinary gesture of devotion by Mary. Three hundred denarii represented nearly a year's wages for a common laborer. Mary of Bethany (not to be confused with the woman who anointed Jesus' feet in Luke 7, nor, Mary Magdalene), her sister, Martha, and brother, Lazarus (whom Jesus had already raised from the dead), were friends of Jesus. They had invited him to dine at their home. Judas, on the other hand, was expressing a phony concern for the poor. Mary and Judas represent two responses to Jesus. In this gospel reading we hear Jesus strip us of phony concern for the poor, so that our hearts might be opened to true love.

Mary showed true love as she anointed Jesus' feet. Her act of love is mirrored by Jesus himself as he washes his disciples' feet. In that story Peter complains that the Lord should not wash his feet. But Jesus says, "Unless I wash you, you have no share with me." In John's gospel, Jesus is the love of God sent into the world. For Peter to receive the love of God, he had to be open to receiving a sign of that love. Before Jesus washed the feet of his disciples, he opened himself to receive the act of Mary's love. Mary, who at her brother's death had been inarticulate in comparison to her sister, Martha, became a disci-

ple in her own right by this extravagant act of love, done in exquisite and fragrant silence. Is love ever a waste?

Candidates preparing for baptism hear the presiding minister say, "As Mary of Bethany honored Jesus with her love and concern, so the church prays for you and for all the needs of the world, confident in the life-giving presence and mercy of Christ" (*Welcome to Christ: Lutheran Rites for the Catechumenate,* p. 32). They may also hear the congregation pray or sing the Lord's Prayer to them, receiving it as a gift from the Lord.

WORSHIP MATTERS

Looking toward the Easter Vigil, this day provides a wonderful opportunity to teach about chrismation—anointing with oil in the baptismal liturgy—as a proclamation of the visible word. The anointing of Jesus by Mary is a visible proclamation (interpreted by Jesus) of his death. As this death comes to the one who has no death in him, however, this oil of death is also the oil of gladness!

Likewise, as Mary anointed Jesus, so also in baptism we are anointed by one who is called to proclaim the word. This visible word of anointing is exactly the same one proclaimed to Jesus—it proclaims *his* death, not our own. Having been given his death in baptism, we are also given his life, being sealed by the Holy Spirit and marked with the cross of Christ forever! Thus the mortality proclaimed to us on Ash Wednesday is healed by the one who is anointed to give eternal life.

LET THE CHILDREN COME

"The house was filled with the fragrance of the perfume." This text offers a rare opportunity to involve our sense of smell in worship. With Mary, children can discover a new way to honor their Lord. Consider burning some incense during the service. Or the children could assemble some potpourri in advance, to distribute as "fragrant gifts" for people's homes, a reminder of Mary's generous gift to Jesus. Package the following in small plastic bags:

2 sticks cinnamon (broken in pieces)
¼ cup whole cloves
2 bay leaves
A few pieces dried orange peel

At home, add 2 tablespoons of lemon juice and 2 cups of water, and simmer on the stovetop.

151

MUSIC FOR WORSHIP

GATHERING

LBW 107	Beneath the cross of Jesus
WOV 785	Weary of all trumpeting

PSALM 126

Haugen, Marty. "God Has Done Great Things for Us" in PCY, vol. 2.

Keesecker, Thomas. PW, Cycle C.

Roff, Joseph. *Psalms for the Cantor*, vol. 3. WLP.

Stewart, Roy James. "The Lord Has Done Great Things" in PCY, vol. 5.

HYMN OF THE DAY

LBW 336	Jesus, thy boundless love to me
	RYBURN

INSTRUMENTAL RESOURCES

Sedio, Mark. "Ryburn" in *Organ Tapestries*, vol. 1. CPH 97-6812. Org.

ALTERNATE HYMN OF THE DAY

LBW 482	When I survey the wondrous cross
WOV 655	As the sun with longer journey

COMMUNION

LBW 316	Jesus, the very thought of you
WOV 706	Eat this bread, drink this cup

SENDING

LBW 97	Christ, the life of all the living
WOV 778	O Christ the same

ADDITIONAL HYMNS AND SONGS

OBS 100	Holy woman, graceful giver
TFF 233	I'd rather have Jesus
W3 644	Said Judas to Mary
W&P 41	Give thanks

MUSIC FOR THE DAY

CHORAL

Ferguson, John. "Lord, in All Love." AFP 11-10788. SATB, org, opt cong.

Mozart, W. A. "Adoramus te." AMC 112. SATB, opt kybd.

Proulx, Richard. "Weary of All Trumpeting." AFP 11-10897. SAB, cong, org, brass.

Schütz, Heinrich. "Praise to You, Lord Jesus" in CC. SATB.

Scott, K. Lee. "Jesu, Our Hope, Our Heart's Desire." CPH 98-2951. SATB, org.

Sedio, Mark. "Take My Life, That I May Be/ *Toma, oh, Dios, mi voluntad.*" AFP 11-10967. SATB, pno, fl, opt perc.

CHILDREN'S CHOIRS

Owens, Sam Batt. "Take My Life, and Let It Be." CG A-268. 2 pt, org.

Paraguayan. "On the Poor" in LS. Use in place of Kyrie.

Pooler, Marie. "Wondrous Love." AFP 1385. U, kybd.

Voohaar, Richard E. "Sing Out to God." SMP S-7434. SAB, kybd.

KEYBOARD/INSTRUMENTAL

Bijster, Jacob. "Partita on 'When I Survey the Wondrous Cross'" (Rockingham Old). Ars Nova 339. Org.

Martinson, Joel. "Partita on the Lenten Chorale 'A Lamb Goes Uncomplaining Forth.'" PAR PPMO9207. Org.

Near, Gerald. "Rockingham" in *Deo Gracias*. AUR AE104. Org.

HANDBELL

Linker/McFadden. "Deep River." AGEHR AG35087 (hb) AG35086 (kybd). 3-5 oct, kybd.

Mathis, William H. "Beneath the Cross of Jesus." SMP 20/1172S (3 oct) 20/1173 S (4-5 oct).

PRAISE ENSEMBLE

Horness, Joe. "To Know You More" in *Praise Hymns and Choruses*, 4th ed. MAR.

Kendrick, Graham. "Knowing You (All I Once Held Dear)" in *Praise Hymns and Choruses*, 4th ed. MAR.

Kendrick, Graham/David T. Clydesdale. "Amazing Love." WRD 310 0557 166. SATB, kybd.

Ylvisaker, John. "Praising the Lord" in *Borning Cry*. NGP.

WEDNESDAY, APRIL 4
BENEDICT THE AFRICAN, CONFESSOR, 1589

Born a slave on the island of Sicily, Benedict first lived as a hermit and labored as a plowman after he was freed. When the bishop of Rome ordered all hermits to attach themselves to a religious community, Benedict joined the Franciscans, where he served as a cook. Although he was illiterate, his fame as a confessor brought many visitors to the humble and holy cook, and he was eventually named superior of the community. A patron saint of blacks in the United States, Benedict is remembered for his patience and understanding when confronted with racial prejudice and taunts.

Use the story of Benedict's ministry as a confessor to revisit Martin Luther's advocacy of mutual consolation and conversation among the community.

FRIDAY, APRIL 6
ALBRECHT DÜRER, PAINTER, 1528;
MICHELANGELO BUONARROTI, ARTIST, 1564

These two great artists revealed through their work the mystery of salvation and the wonder of creation. Dürer's work reflected the apocalyptic spirit of his time, when famine, plague, and social and religious upheaval were common. He was sympathetic to the reform work of Luther but remained Roman Catholic. At his death, Luther wrote to a friend, "Affection bids us mourn for one who was the best." Michelangelo was a sculptor, painter, poet, and architect. His works such as the carving of the Pieta and the statue of David reveal both the tenderness and the grandeur of humanity.

With Good Friday one week away, consider the ways in which the art of these two people might highlight the church's celebration of the mystery of Christ's passion.

APRIL 8, 2001

SUNDAY OF THE PASSION
PALM SUNDAY

INTRODUCTION

The procession with palms brings us into Holy Week and the celebration of the mystery of our salvation. We enter the week by hearing the story of Jesus' passion— his suffering and death. In baptism we have been fused to this story; in Holy Week we make our way through it again, because it brings us to life with Christ.

READINGS FOR PROCESSION WITH PALMS

Luke 19:28-40

Psalm 118:1-2, 19-29

Blessed is he who comes in the name of the LORD. (Ps. 118:26)

PRAYER OF THE DAY

Almighty God, you sent your Son, our Savior Jesus Christ, to take our flesh upon him and to suffer death on the cross. Grant that we may share in his obedience to your will and in the glorious victory of his resurrection; through your Son, Jesus Christ our Lord, who lives and reigns with you and the Holy Spirit, one God, now and forever.

READINGS FOR LITURGY OF THE PASSION

Isaiah 50:4-9a

This text, the third of the Servant Songs that arose in the last years of Israel's exile in Babylon, speaks of the servant's obedience in the midst of persecution. Though the servant has been variously understood as the prophet himself or a remnant of faithful Israel, Christians have often recognized the figure of Christ in these poems.

Psalm 31:9-16

Into your hands, O LORD, I commend my spirit. (Ps. 31:5)

Philippians 2:5-11

Paul quotes from an early Christian hymn that describes Jesus' humble obedience, even to death, and his exaltation as Lord of all.

Luke 22:14—23:56 *or* Luke 23:1-49

The passion story in Luke's gospel is filled with human and cosmic images of what God is doing through the death of Jesus: restoring all creation to the grace and peace of paradise.

COLOR   Scarlet *or* Purple

THE PRAYERS

As we mark these forty days with repentance and forgiveness, let us pray for the renewal of the church and the restoration of the world to the life of God.

A BRIEF SILENCE.

For all who have sojourned through Lent, that in this holy week they may feast upon the Savior, who entered into suffering and death. Let us pray to the Lord.

Lord, have mercy.

For pastors and all who witness to the gospel of Christ, that in their proclamation they may boldly confess Christ's obedience to death on a cross for the world's life and salvation. Let us pray to the Lord.

153

Lord, have mercy.

For those throughout the world who long and work for peace, that they may be sustained by the word of God that proclaims the humility of Christ Jesus. Let us pray to the Lord.

Lord, have mercy.

For those in distress and those who are sick (especially…), that your face may shine upon them and that they may receive help and healing from God. Let us pray to the Lord.

Lord, have mercy.

For those to be baptized at Easter, that they might be raised to new life in Christ.

HERE OTHER INTERCESSIONS MAY BE OFFERED.

Join us in praise and prayer with those who now confess Christ as Lord in the eternal glory of God, and move us to imitate their witness. Let us pray to the Lord.

Lord, have mercy.

Gracious God, hear us as we pray, and sustain us with your hope, through Jesus Christ our Lord.

Amen

IMAGES FOR PREACHING

Even though a full reading of the appointed gospel for this Sunday may overshadow the sermon, the proclamation of this gospel is heady stuff, worthy of full treatment in the sermon. The passion story stands on its own but may be interpreted through a couple lenses.

One lens is provided by the appointed offertory from John 12:24, 26, which understands Jesus' death as a prelude to life. We follow our Lord into the events of this coming week, so that where our Lord is, we shall be also. Thus we anticipate our own passion and passover from death to life eternal, both now and eternally. Our suffering and death is placed into the larger context of Jesus' death and resurrection.

Another interpretive lens is the second reading, Philippians 2:5-11. "Let the same mind be in you that was in Christ Jesus." We are to be conformed to the mind of Christ and incorporated into the pattern of his life. By entering into the liturgical life of the congregation during Holy Week, we may ritually let the mind of Christ be in us. "Having this mind" does not mean that we make a mental return to a "once-upon-a-time" story of the first century. Christ is eucharistically present to us here and now, by the power of the Holy Spirit that "calls, gathers, enlightens, and sanctifies" us and that keeps us united with

the resurrected Christ. The resurrection even invades Passion Sunday. It calls us through, not around, the cross and its sufferings and calls us into the mind of Christ, where our suffering and death can be transcended.

WORSHIP MATTERS

All verbal communication is accompanied by body language. Even when the second party cannot see the first, as during a telephone conversation, both parties still gesture. Examples of body language are replete throughout the scriptures: bowing, lifting hands, kneeling, and prostration. Use of body language in worship is helpful in avoiding mindless, rote worship!

Be mentally alert to participate bodily in worship: making the sign of the cross at every invocation of the Trinity, recalling our baptism; kneeling in humility to receive the sacrament of the altar; standing during the reading of the gospel and singing of hymns to honor the Lord. Once we admit that such body language is natural, our worship will become less passive and more active—physically and mentally!

LET THE CHILDREN COME

On Passion Sunday we often overlook the obvious: Luke's gospel says nothing of palm branches but mentions people "throwing their cloaks on the colt" and "spreading their cloaks on the road." It might be an appropriate day to donate used coats and other clothing for someone else's use. During the Palm Sunday procession, children could carry donated items of clothing into the worship space, placing them in appropriate containers and even scattering a few on the floor at the front of the church. A prayer of thanks for clothing shared for reuse by others may be read by the children.

MUSIC FOR WORSHIP

SERVICE MUSIC

"All glory, laud, and honor" (LBW 108) is the time-honored hymn at the procession with palms. Careful planning, such as interspersing choir members in the procession, using handbells or hand-held instruments, or using an extended instrumental introduction until the first singers enter the nave, will help this festive moment to be musically satisfying. An extended procession can include other hymns, a setting of processional Psalm 118 (using the Palm Sunday refrain, not the Easter refrain), and instrumental fanfares/interludes.

GATHERING

LBW 121 Ride on, ride on in majesty
WOV 631 Lift up your heads, O gates

PSALM 118:1-2, 19-29 (PROCESSION)

Hommerding, Alan J. "Psalm 118" in *Sing Out! A Children's Psalter.*
WLP 7191.

Hopson, Hal H. "Praise the Lord: Service Music." CG CGA 530.
U, opt inst.

Hruby, Dolores. *Seasonal Psalms for Children with Optional Orff.*
WLP 7102.

Smith, Timothy R. "Give Thanks to the Lord" in STP, vol. 4.

PSALM 31:9-16

DeBruyn, Randall. "Father, I Put My Life in Your Hands" in
STP, vol. 4.

Farlee, Robert Buckley. PW, Cycle C.

HYMN OF THE DAY

LBW 97 Christ, the life of all the living
JESU, MEINES LEBENS LEBEN

VOCAL RESOURCES

Cherwien, David. "Christ, the Life of All the Living." MSM 60-3001.
SATB, cong, org.

INSTRUMENTAL RESOURCES

Bisbee, B. Wayne. "Jesu, meines Lebens Leben" in *From the Serene to the
Whimsical.* AFP 11-10561. Org.

Burkhardt, Michael. "Christ, the Life of All the Living" in *Easy Hymn
Settings—Lent.* MSM 10-315. Org.

Organ, Anne Krentz. "Christ, the Life of All the Living" in *Christ,
Mighty Savior.* AFP 11-10819. Pno.

ALTERNATE HYMN OF THE DAY

LBW 105 A lamb goes uncomplaining forth
WOV 661 My song is love unknown

COMMUNION

LBW 115 Jesus, I will ponder now
WOV 740 Jesus, remember me

SENDING

LBW 116/7 O sacred head, now wounded
WOV 668 There in God's garden

ADDITIONAL HYMNS AND SONGS

LLC 333 Filled with excitement
PH 89 Hosanna, loud hosanna

TFF 72 Down at the cross
UMH 425 O crucified redeemer
W&P 12 At the name of Jesus
W&P 106 Now we remain

MUSIC FOR THE DAY
CHORAL

Friedell, Harold. "Jesus, So Lowly." HWG GCMR 02018.

Gerike, Henry. "Guide Me, Savior, through Your Passion." GIA G-2767.
U, opt 2 pt, org.

Gesius, Bartholomäus. "Hosanna to the Son of David" in CC. SATB.

Gibbons, Orlando. "Hosanna to the Son of David." OXF 352078-8.
SATB div.

Niedmann, Peter. "Lift Up Your Heads, Ye Mighty Gates" in *The Augsburg Choirbook.* AFP 11-10817. SATB, org.

Rogner, James. "O Sacred Head." AFP 11-10994. SATB, org.

Shute, Linda Cable. "What Language Shall I Borrow." AFP 11-10844.
SATB, org.

CHILDREN'S CHOIRS

Brahms, Johannes/arr. Hal H. Hopson. "Let All the Gates Be Opened
Wide." CG CGA736. U/2 pt (trbl or mxd), kybd.

Horman, John. "Sing Hosanna! Hosanna!" ABI 061776. U/opt 2 pt,
kybd.

Horman, John. "We Sang Our Glad Hosannas." ABI 024099.
U/SATB, kybd.

Kemp, Helen. "Hosanna! The Little Children Sing" in LS.

Quintana, Ariel. "Hosanna! Filled with Excitement." AFP 11-10995.
U or 2 pt, kybd, perc.

KEYBOARD/INSTRUMENTAL

Fruhauf, Ennis. "Prelude on 'My Song Is Love Unknown/Our Father,
by Whose Name'" in *Welsh Hymn Tunes.* CPH 97-6671. Org.

Post, Piet. *Partitas for Advent and Christmas.* Ars Nova #402. Org.

Vaughan Williams, Ralph. "Rhosymedre" in *Three Preludes Founded on
Welsh Hymn Tunes.* Stainer and Bell 2155. Org.

Willan, Healey. "Epilogue on 'St. Theodulph'" in *Festal Voluntaries.*
NOV 18246. Org.

HANDBELL

Bedford, Michael. "Triumphal Entry." AGEHR AG3038. 3 oct.

Mathis, William H. "Pie Jesu." H. T. FitzSimons F0703. 3-5 oct.

Morris, Hart. "Entrata Exsultate." RRM HB0009. 3-5 oct.

PRAISE ENSEMBLE

Armstrong, Matthew. "Hosanna." CPH 98-3486. SATB, kybd.

Kauflin, Bob. "You Have Been Given" in *Come & Worship.* INT.

Pote, Allen. "Hosanna." CG CGA-596. SATB, kybd.

155

MONDAY, APRIL 9
MONDAY IN HOLY WEEK
DIETRICH BONHOEFFER, TEACHER, 1945

Bonhoeffer was a German theologian who, at the age of twenty-five, became a lecturer in systematic theology at the University of Berlin. In 1933, and with Hitler's rise to power, Bonhoeffer became a leading spokesman for the confessing church, a resistance movement against the Nazis. He was arrested in 1943. He was linked to a failed attempt on Hitler's life and sent to Buchenwald, then later to Schoenberg prison. After leading a worship service on April 8, 1945, at Schoenberg, he was taken away to be hanged the next day. His last words as he left were, "This is the end, but for me the beginning of life."

A hymn written by Bonhoeffer shortly before his death includes the line, "By gracious powers so wonderfully sheltered, and confidently waiting come what may, we know that God is with us night and morning, and never fails to greet us each new day" (WOV 736). Bonhoeffer's courage is a bold witness to the paschal mystery of Christ's dying and rising celebrated in the upcoming three days.

TUESDAY, APRIL 10
TUESDAY IN HOLY WEEK
MIKAEL AGRICOLA, BISHOP OF TURKU, 1557

Agricola was consecrated as the bishop of Turku in 1554 without papal approval. As a result, he began a reform of the Finnish church along Lutheran lines. He translated the New Testament, the prayerbook, hymns, and the mass into Finnish and through this work set the rules of orthography that are the basis of modern Finnish spelling. His thoroughgoing work is particularly remarkable in that he accomplished it in only three years. He died suddenly on a return trip after negotiating a treaty with the Russians.

During these finals days of the Lenten journey the Finnish hymn "Lord, as a pilgrim" (LBW 485) can be sung at parish gatherings. Its emphasis on God's faithful presence through the offenses and suffering of life can lead us to the foot of the cross.

WEDNESDAY, APRIL 11
WEDNESDAY IN HOLY WEEK

THE THREE DAYS

The tomb is empty, for Christ is risen!

IMAGES of the SEASON

Life involves crossing various boundaries: from childhood to adolescence,

adolescence to adulthood, single life to married life for some, and ultimately

life to death. Salvation also involves crossing

boundaries. For Israel, the exodus meant journeying

from slavery to freedom. From its earliest days, the church has celebrated Christ's journey from death to life with a liturgical observance known as the Triduum or Three Days, which begins Maundy Thursday evening and concludes on the evening of Easter Sunday—the liturgical day being reckoned from sundown to sundown. In one continuous celebration encompassing three consecutive days, the church remembers Christ's salvific acts and experiences his presence in the sacraments of baptism and the eucharist. In a sense, these liturgical celebrations together constitute a three-act play.

In act one (Maundy Thursday) Jesus' actions reveal that discipleship means crossing the boundary from selfishness to servanthood. While the plot against him begins to unfold, Jesus has a meal with his disciples and afterwards washes their feet. The latter action is more than a mere nicety. The humility and self-denial of the footwashing foreshadow the cross, where Jesus washes the whole world in his blood. It is in this context that Jesus gives his disciples a "new commandment" (*mandatum*), to love one another "just as I have loved you" (John 13:34).

In the Maundy Thursday liturgy, we wash feet as a reminder that we follow the path of Christ's humble love for others. We share the meal of bread and wine so that, having become one with Christ, we might share ourselves with others in love and service. We strip the altar as a further reminder that Christ was stripped of his dignity on the cross and that our servanthood involves humility and self-denial.

In act two (Good Friday) our Lord's servanthood reaches its zenith. On the cross Jesus became the lamb who was slain for sinners. There he was wounded for our transgressions and bruised for our iniquities (Isa. 53:4). There he revealed the Father's love and became the living way into the "sanctuary" (Heb. 10:19-20) that is communion with God the Father.

Good Friday is hardly a funeral service for Jesus. Rather, it is a celebration of the triumph of the cross. In the St. John Passion (always appointed for Good Friday) Christ goes to the cross wearing the purple robe, unlike the gospels of Matthew and Mark in which the robe is removed from Jesus before his journey to Calvary. In John's gospel, Jesus is the king on his way to enthronement, for it is on the cross that God's power is revealed and God's enemies (sin and death) are defeated. The hymn "Sing, my tongue, the glorious battle" (LBW 118) extols Christ, who "as a victim won the day," and proclaims the cross to be a "trophy" and "symbol of the world's redemption." Because God raised the crucified One, the cross is now a symbol of how God triumphs in and through our acts of service and self-sacrifice. The Good Friday liturgy thus aids us in our ongoing struggle to live as people who have crossed the boundary from selfishness to servanthood.

Act three of the Three Days, the Great Vigil, is the expression par excellence of our spiritual boundary crossing. Each of the four scenes of this act points to some facet of our passage from death to life with Christ.

Scene 1. The setting is the new fire, a symbol of Christ's glorious resurrection from the dead. But we quickly begin a procession to the place of reading, led by the paschal candle. This action symbolizes Christ's leading us from the darkness of sin to the light of forgiveness and righteousness. The Easter proclamation images Christ's light as purging away the darkness of sin, breaking the chains of death, and giving light to all humanity.

Scene 2. The focal point is now the ambo. The readings contain images that prefigure our baptismal passage from death to life. The creation story prefigures our journey from the spiritual chaos of sin and death to eternal life in Christ. The flood story from Genesis 7–9 reminds us that we, like Noah, have been preserved from God's condemnation, having been brought safely through the waters of baptism. Like Noah, we who have been saved are a new humanity. The exodus story suggests that we have been rescued from the slavery of sin and brought to the promised land of righteousness in Christ. Ezekiel's prophecy of the valley of dry bones points to our baptismal reception of the life-giving Holy Spirit. The story of the three men in the furnace is an image of our baptismal salvation from the fiery ordeal of sin and death.

Scene 3. The focus shifts to the font, as the church celebrates the central act of crossing the boundary from sin and death to new life with Christ: baptism. Tonight candidates for baptism are adopted as God's newest sons and daughters and are made members of the body of Christ, the church. This celebration of baptism reminds all of us that in baptism we die and rise again with Christ, are cleansed from sin, and are "sealed by the Holy Spirit and marked with the cross of Christ forever" (*LBW*, p. 124).

Scene 4. The focus once again shifts, this time to the Lord's table. In the eucharistic meal, we remember how Christ, our Passover Lamb, was slaughtered to gain our freedom from sin and death. In this act of remembrance, the risen Christ himself comes to be our food, filling us with faith, hope, and love. We anticipate the day "when Christ will come again in beauty and power to share with us the great and promised feast" (*LBW* Ministers Edition, p. 223). That is, we look toward our final transition from this world to the next.

On Easter Sunday, the paschal journey continues with an extended epilogue of sorts. The tomb is empty, for Christ is risen! Like Mary Magdalene, we experience the risen Lord. Sadness and weeping come to an end. We now begin a fifty-day feast that lasts until the day of Pentecost. On that day we will commemorate the fulfillment of Christ's promise to send the Holy Spirit, the one who guides and sustains us until we pass from this world to the next.

159

ENVIRONMENT AND ART FOR THE SEASON

Maundy Thursday begins a liturgy that continues on Good Friday and culminates in the Resurrection of Our Lord. Each one of the Three Days has one or more ritual acts and symbols that direct our setting of the liturgical environment. Rather than simply decorating the church, the best approach for environmental ministers is to study the liturgies and scripture readings proper for each day to determine the best settings for worship. On Maundy Thursday, for instance, a primary indicator of the environment is the foot washing. The gospel for the day tells that Jesus washed the feet of his disciples as a symbolic enactment of his new command, "to love one another as I have loved you."

Congregations are at different stages in the introduction of the foot washing ritual. For some, foot washing remains a text to be read; in others the pastor washes the feet of a symbolic twelve members. Still others invite all worshipers to come forward for foot washing. Like the imposition of ashes on Ash Wednesday, we are relearning the power of ancient rituals. Setting the environment for this experience becomes a visual prelude and invitation to the congregation. Two chairs at each station are set so that one person may change footwear while another participates in the footwashing. A wash basin, a ewer of water, and towels are placed near the chairs. Each station should be visible to the congregation but not in a way to cause participants to be self-conscious. A credence table displaying extra towels and warm water is placed to one side. Narrow banners or torches may be positioned behind each station. A simple white fair linen may grace the altar in preparation for the sacrament.

The liturgy for Maundy Thursday ends with a ritual

stripping of the altar, which serves as a provocative intersection of physical furnishings and liturgical actions. As a reminder that Jesus was stripped before he was beaten and crucified, this simple action should be a moving drama. The altar guild and other liturgical ministers assist the presiding minister. Slow, deliberate movements should lead to a procession in which everything movable in the chancel is removed except altar, ambo desk, and ministers' chairs. As the lights are dimmed, Psalm 22 may be read or sung.

The tone of Good Friday is one of prayer and reflection. It is a solemn celebration of our Lord's victory on the cross. The focus of the Good Friday liturgy is on the passion reading from St. John, an ancient bidding prayer, and the veneration of the cross. The long passion narrative may be divided among three or four readers and the congregation. Placement of these readers is an environmental consideration. Does the space lend itself to a particular arrangement? Can all readers be seen and heard? How far apart should they stand? Do they face one another at certain points in the narrative?

Readers for Passion Sunday, Good Friday, and the Easter Vigil need to have folders for texts rather than loose pages or Bibles of differing sizes and shapes. Handsome liturgical folders for these readers can be purchased from ecclesiastical arts stores. Effective, matching folders can be purchased at any stationary or office store. Often overlooked, this folder is another visual contribution to overall worship environment and facilitates the liturgical experience. Visually it speaks of a skilled, intentional proclamation of the text.

For some communities, Good Friday has been the occasion for a Tenebrae service emphasizing the interplay of light and darkness. This theme, however, is more appropriate as the opening act of the Easter Vigil in lighting the new fire and paschal candle. The "veneration of the cross" or "adoration of the crucified" is the historic ritual experience for Good Friday. For this occasion, a large rough-hewn cross is constructed. The wood should not be treated or fastened with metal bolts; it should look like a crude instrument of death. Placed in front of the congregation or propped on the chancel stairs, the congregation is invited to contemplate it as an instrument of Christ's death and our salvation. This contemplation may take place in silence or during the quiet singing of a hymn.

Anciently, Christians venerated the cross by kissing it. Another form of reverence and respect is to touch the cross during silent prayer. In some congregations, worshipers hammer nails into the cross, around which flowers are woven on Easter Day. Many other possibilities provide symbolic action. Our purpose in these moments is stated in the versicles sung or said by the presiding minister: "Behold, the life-giving cross on which was hung the salvation of the whole world." Our response to this sign too big for words is "Oh, come, let us worship him."

The congregation's worship space may remain open as a place for prayer and meditation during Holy Week. Before and after major liturgies, individuals, small groups, and prayer chains may use the space. Signs of the great liturgies of the Three Days may be left in place to prompt the prayer of those who visit the otherwise empty space: the palms of Passion Sunday, a basin and ewer on a credence table after Maundy Thursday, the large cross from Friday until the Easter Vigil. Part of the visual prelude to each of these liturgies might be the physical changing of symbols. Prayer folders with appropriate readings and prayers for Holy Week may be available on a small table for people to use as they see fit. Lighting and noise from choir and liturgy rehearsals should all be considered as environmental ministers try to maintain this space as one conducive to prayer.

No other Christian liturgy compares with the Vigil of Easter. The four major acts of the vigil suggest four different venues. The service of light, the service of readings, the service of baptism, and the eucharistic meal have distinctive symbols and environmental requirements. In fact, this great liturgy lives in symbols that generously express the gospel in word and sacrament. Every Christian should have the opportunity to participate in this annual feast under the auspices of the local congregation or a partnership of congregations.

The liturgy begins outside after dark. Worshipers gather in the darkness around a bonfire. A brazier with a smaller fire could be used to accommodate fire codes in a particular area, but it is best to experience the evocative power of a larger fire against the darkness. The paschal candle is lit as a symbol of Christ, the light of the world. This candle should be of a substantial size. The size and natural beauty of the candle are more important than numbers and other symbols placed upon it.

160

The procession with this great light is a public liturgical act. The candle may lead the worshipers around the church building to the place of readings. A fellowship hall may serve as an oratory for the service of readings with accompanying silence, song, and prayer. Flexible seating might allow for an antiphonal or other seating arrangement. Readers may stand at the end points of cruciform aisles, providing a sense of variety and proximity. The open space between the two major seating areas needs to be large enough for liturgical dance or dramatic presentations of one of the texts. A raised platform or stage behind one of the stations could be used for slides of creation during the reading of Genesis 1. In other words, a fellowship hall may provide maximum possibilities for creatively rendering the readings and saving this part of the liturgy from tedium. Note, however, it is easy to get carried away with the possibilities; it is liturgy, not performance.

Led by the paschal candle, the congregation then moves to the place for the service of baptism or affirmation of baptism. Fresh flowers brought by worshipers could form a perimeter around the font. Chairs or pews can be removed to make room for people standing around the baptismal pool or font. The paschal candle on its stand completes the furnishing for this space.

Martin Luther encouraged baptism by immersion as the best way to express the meaning of this sacramental act. Guides to sacramental practices (especially *The Use of the Means of Grace*, principle 26) encourage congregations to consider this possibility. A growing number of congregations are building larger fonts containing enough water for the immersion of infants. A growing trend, however, is the conversion of adults to Christianity. Baptism for adults invites the use of baptismal pools where the candidates stand or kneel while water is poured on their heads.

As a premonition of this direction in our sacramental life, some congregations are creating temporary baptismal pools for the Easter Vigil. Simple materials, such as concrete blocks, plastic pool liners, or wading pools can be used. Natural rocks and plants may be arranged to conceal the plastic container. In three or four hours, an attractive place of water can be created and later drained and disassembled.

Following the baptisms and affirmation of baptism, the assembly moves to the eucharistic table. This movement may be accompanied with hymn and song as liturgical ministers and people vest the altar table, take flowers from the place of baptism to surround the altar, and generally prepare the space for a festive meal. The transition from the place of baptism to the place of the meal is a spatial and psychological arranging of the liturgical landscape. The movements themselves are important parts of worship.

For those who attend the Vigil of Easter, the usual Easter Day service may be a bit anticlimactic. The challenge for worship planners is to bring the spirit of resurrection celebration into Easter Day and throughout the Easter season.

PREACHING with the SEASON

Baptismal immersion is a powerful image for preaching during the Three Days—from Maundy Thursday through the Resurrection of Our Lord, whether or not it is common practice in the congregation's life. Some who will be baptized at the Vigil of Easter will in fact be baptized by immersion. There are multiple meanings to this immersion. We are immersed into the life of Christ through baptism, immersed into the death and resurrection of Christ, and immersed into a rebirth as children of God. Baptism is not a private affair but is celebrated by the whole church and as such shapes the liturgies of this time of the year.

Immersion is an important image for preaching

about how Christians are united to the saving death and resurrection of Christ. Two dominant symbols are the cross and the empty tomb. They cannot be pulled apart. We are called to follow our Lord's way of the cross. His way leads through the cross to resurrection life. By faith we entrust ourselves to the one who said, "I am the way, the truth, and the life." During the Three Days the church tells the story that shapes our individual Christian lives. The death and resurrection of Christ gives meaning to those who suffer, and gives hope to those who have nothing to hold onto but faith. This immersion is a matter of life and death!

Immersion, in still another dimension of baptismal meaning, may be experienced by those who are already baptized as they participate fully in the liturgies of the Three Days. Invite members of the congregation to attend all of the worship services of this time: Maundy Thursday, Good Friday, Vigil of Easter, Resurrection of Our Lord, and Easter Evening. Some people will, of course, want to only dip politely into this celebration, making an annual pilgrimage to church on Easter Sunday morning. But others may respond well to such an invitation to be immersed in the gospel waters through which the Holy Spirit calls us and conforms us to Christ.

Printing one bulletin that contains all the liturgies for this time may be a helpful way to invite worshipers to experience the Three Days as an immersion in the passover of Jesus Christ. If the congregation's worship practice does not include one or more of these liturgies, consider inviting members to attend another congregation's worship service as a group (even offering to help out in advance). Certain worship practices, such as abbreviating the full reading of the passion according to St. John on Good Friday or shortening the Vigil of Easter so that it may be more convenient for worshipers, only diminish the experience of being immersed in the gospel.

It is important not to overscript the work of the Spirit during these days. Preaching should not be highly didactic. The best opportunities for a traditional sermon are Maundy Thursday and Easter morning. The gospel may also be experienced in a variety of ways. The gospel shapes us as we have our feet washed, reverently

process the cross, follow the newly lit paschal candle into a darkened church, settle in for a full hearing of the story of salvation, sing joyful hymns of exaltation, enjoy a dramatic visual change of colors and flowers in the worship space, and joyfully but simply proclaim "Alleluia. Christ is risen!"

The gospel reading for Maundy Thursday reminds us that if we are to have life in the name of Jesus and enter into his passover, we must be washed in his love. Even if the washing of feet is not part of the congregation's worship practice on Maundy Thursday, the preacher may use it as a powerful image. Foot washing was part of the ancient baptismal practice of Milan, and according to Ambrose it was regarded as sacramental. Good Friday calls for a full reading of the passion according to St. John. A traditional sermon on Good Friday may diminish the impact of such a reading. Follow the gospel reading with a brief sermon amplifying the self-giving sacrificial love of Christ into which we, in our life of faith, have been immersed. Through the readings of the Vigil of Easter we are immersed into God's story of salvation. These readings take us from creation to redemption. Here too, a traditional sermon may have a hard time competing with the impact of the readings themselves. Following the readings a brief homily may proclaim that the risen Lord has now brought us into this story of salvation, and like the women at the tomb we are amazed.

Easter morning worship services bring many to church who have not shared in a full immersion in the gospel of the Three Days. Among them will be many who seldom take part in the weekly sacramental life of the congregation. Easter morning worship is an opportunity to give them the best that the congregation has to offer (like the hospitality in *Babbette's Feast*), an immersion in grace, so that they may leave saying, "I have seen the Lord." Easter Evening, like other liturgies of the Three Days, may not call for a traditional sermon as much as a homiletical moment to recollect the congregation's immersion in the gospel that has taken place through this time and how through word and sacramental meal hearts of faith have burned and eyes of faith have been opened.

SHAPE of WORSHIP for the SEASON

BASIC SHAPE OF THE MAUNDY THURSDAY LITURGY

- See Maundy Thursday Liturgy in *LBW* Ministers Edition, pp. 137–38; also available as a congregational leaflet from Augsburg Fortress (AFP 3-5327)

GATHERING

- The sermon may begin the liturgy
- An order for corporate confession and forgiveness may be used (*LBW*, pp. 193–95)
- The peace follows the order for confession and forgiveness

WORD

- The washing of feet may follow the reading of the gospel
- For a dramatic reading based on the gospel use *Scripture Out Loud!* (AFP 3-3964)
- For a contemporary drama based on the second reading, use *Can These Bones Live?* (AFP 3-3965)
- No creed is used on Maundy Thursday
- The Prayers: see Maundy Thursday in *Sundays and Seasons*

MEAL

- Offertory prayer: see alternate worship texts for the Three Days in *Sundays and Seasons*
- Use the proper preface for Passion
- Eucharistic prayer: in addition to the four main options in *LBW*, see "Eucharistic Prayer D: The Season of Lent" in *WOV* Leaders Edition, p. 68
- Invitation to communion: see alternate worship texts for the Three Days in *Sundays and Seasons*
- Post-communion prayer: see alternate worship texts for the Three Days in *Sundays and Seasons*
- No post-communion canticle
- Stripping of the altar follows post-communion prayer
- No benediction on Maundy Thursday
- No dismissal on Maundy Thursday

BASIC SHAPE OF THE GOOD FRIDAY LITURGY

- See Good Friday liturgy in *LBW* Ministers Edition, pp. 139–43; also available as a congregational leaflet from Augsburg Fortress (AFP 3-5328). See an alternate order in the seasonal rites section.

WORD

- The passion according to St. John is read; a version involving readers and congregation may be used (AFP 3-5166)
- For a reading based of the passion interspersed with choral music, use *St. John Passion* (AFP 11-10991)
- The bidding prayer for Good Friday may be used (*LBW* Ministers Edition, pp. 139–42)
- Adoration of the Crucified may be used (*LBW* Ministers Edition, p. 142)
- No communion for Good Friday
- No benediction for Good Friday
- No dismissal for Good Friday

BASIC SHAPE OF THE RITE FOR THE EASTER VIGIL

- See Vigil of Easter in *LBW* Ministers Edition, pp. 143–53; *WOV* Leaders Edition, pp. 88–89; *Vigil of Easter—Music Edition* (AFP 3-5330); also see congregational leaflet from Augsburg Fortress (AFP 3-5329)

LIGHT

- The service of light may begin outside at the lighting of a new fire
- The congregation processes into the darkened nave following the lit paschal candle
- A cantor sings the Easter proclamation (*Exsultet*)

WORD

- Twelve readings appointed for the Easter Vigil (each of which may be followed by a sung response and a prayer) are listed in *WOV* Leaders Edition, pp. 88–89
- Canticle of the Sun (a version is printed in the autumn seasonal rites) may conclude the service of readings
- For dramatic readings based on two of the appointed passages see *Scripture Out Loud!* (AFP 3-3964)
- For contemporary dramas based on five of the passages see *Can These Bones Live?* (AFP 3-3965)

163

BAPTISM

- If no candidates will be baptized, a congregational renewal of baptism may be used; notes for this portion of the liturgy are printed in *LBW* Ministers Edition, p. 152

MEAL

- The "Litany of the Saints" in the seasonal rites section may be sung during movement from font to the place of the meal
- Hymn of praise (traditionally "Glory to God")
- During the hymn of praise, lights may be turned on, accompanied by the ringing of bells
- Prayers: see Vigil of Easter in *Sundays and Seasons*
- Offertory prayer: see alternate worship texts for the Three Days in *Sundays and Seasons*
- Use the proper preface for Easter
- Eucharistic prayer: in addition to four main options in *LBW*, see "Eucharistic Prayer E: The Season of Easter" in *WOV* Leaders Edition, p. 69
- Invitation to communion: see alternate worship texts for the Three Days in *Sundays and Seasons*
- Post-communion prayer: see alternate worship texts for the Three Days in *Sundays and Seasons*
- Benediction: see alternate worship texts for the Three Days in *Sundays and Seasons*
- Dismissal: see alternate worship texts for the Three Days in *Sundays and Seasons*

BASIC SHAPE OF THE RITE FOR EASTER DAY

- Confession and Forgiveness: see alternate worship text for the Easter season in *Sundays and Seasons*

GATHERING

- Greeting: see alternate worship texts for the Three Days in *Sundays and Seasons*
- Use the Kyrie
- Use the hymn of praise ("This is the feast of victory")

WORD

- For a dramatic reading based on the gospel according to John use *Scripture Out Loud!* (AFP 3-3964)
- Use Nicene Creed
- The prayers: see Easter Day in *Sundays and Seasons*

MEAL

- Offertory prayer: see alternate worship texts for the Three Days in *Sundays and Seasons*
- Use the proper preface for Easter
- Eucharistic prayer: in addition to four main options in *LBW*, see "Eucharistic Prayer E: The Season of Easter" in *WOV* Leaders Edition, p. 69
- Invitation to communion: see alternate worship texts for the Three Days in *Sundays and Seasons*
- Post-communion prayer: see alternate worship text for the Three Days in *Sundays and Seasons*

SENDING

- Benediction: see alternate worship texts for the Three Days in *Sundays and Seasons*
- Dismissal: see alternate worship texts for the Three Days in *Sundays and Seasons*

OTHER SEASONAL POSSIBILITIES

PASCHAL VESPERS

- If you are able to gather for worship on Easter Sunday evening, a festival form of evening prayer may be desired. Consider appending the paschal blessing to evening prayer (*LBW*, pp. 138–41) anytime in the Easter season, even though it is printed as a part of morning prayer. See notes for this order in *LBW* Ministers Edition, page 16, and *Manual on the Liturgy*, pages 294–95. A hymn, such as "We know that Christ is raised" (LBW 189), "I bind unto myself today" (LBW 188), or "O blessed spring" (WOV 695), may replace the canticle "Te Deum," which is customarily associated with morning prayer.

ASSEMBLY SONG FOR THE SEASON

The Three Days is the center of the church's communal life. During this time we journey as pilgrims from death to resurrection. The journey involves actions in which we participate; readings to hear and ponder; and songs, hymns, and responses to sing.

MAUNDY THURSDAY

GATHERING

The order of these three days is different from that of typical Sunday liturgies. *Lutheran Book of Worship* Ministers Edition suggests that a hymn begin the service and be followed by the sermon. An appropriate entrance hymn is "Lord, who the night you were betrayed" (LBW 206).

WORD

During the foot washing keep the assembly music simple and memorable by using "Ubi caritas et amor/Where true charity and love abide" (WOV 665). This refrain is easily memorized. Have a cantor/choir sing the verses as printed in *Music from Taizé* (GIA Publications, Inc., 1981). Simple accompaniments and instrumental descants are also available. Additional hymns are "Great God, your love has called us" (WOV 666), "Where charity and love prevail" (LBW 126), and "Love consecrates the humblest act" (LBW 122).

MEAL

Use "What shall I render to the Lord" as the offering canticle.

STRIPPING OF THE ALTAR

Have a single voice, representing the voice of Christ, chant Psalm 22 unaccompanied during this ritual. A simple antiphon such as "Into your hands, O Lord, I commend my spirit" (*LBW*, Prayer at the Close of the Day, p. 156) could be sung by the assembly.

GOOD FRIDAY

The song of the assembly on this day is simple, unadorned song, with as little instrumental accompaniment as possible and mixed with generous amounts of silence. *Lutheran Book of Worship* Ministers Edition suggests the order and hymns used on Good Friday. Use the choir to sing some stanzas of hymns, and allow the congregation to reflect on the text. Stanza 2 of "Ah, holy Jesus" (LBW 123) is especially effective when sung in canon at an interval of one measure by the choir, or the assembly if able. The dissonances help point out the final line of text "I crucified thee."

"There in God's garden" (WOV 668) is an appropriate final hymn extolling the victory of the cross of Christ.

165

VIGIL OF EASTER

READINGS

The appointed responses and refrains are available for each reading in *Psalter for Worship, Cycle C* (Augsburg Fortress, 1997). "When Israel was in Egypt's land" (WOV 670) is especially appropriate for the Exodus reading if hymns are used as responses to some of the readings.

BAPTISM

Welcome to Christ: Lutheran Rites for the Catechumenate has a number of appropriate responses for baptism and also a litany, which may be used for concluding the rite. "You have put on Christ" (WOV 694) or "Celtic Alleluia" (WOV 613) are responses that can be used within the rite immediately after each person is baptized. Have children lead the response and punctuate the cadences with handbells.

Let the song of the eucharist be joyful. Sing Easter hymns, but reserve some of the festive music for Easter Day. Purchase some small bells. Distribute them and have people ring them when they sing an "alleluia."

EASTER DAY

The Resurrection of Our Lord is one of the festivals for which the sequence hymn *Victimae Paschali*, "Christians, to the paschal victim" (LBW 137), may be sung before the reading of the gospel. Have the choir sing LBW 137 alternately by sections, with the assembly singing "Christ is arisen" (LBW 136). Divide these hymns into three sections each as follows:

LBW 137

Section 1: "Christians, to the paschal…The prince of life, who died, reigns immortal"

Section 2: '"Speak, Mary, declaring…to Galilee he goes before you'"

Section 3: "Christ indeed from death…"to the end of the hymn, omitting the amen

LBW 136

Section 1: "Christ is arisen…alleluia"

Section 2: "Were Christ not arisen…We praise the Father of our Lord. Alleluia"

Section 3: "Alleluia, alleluia, alleluia! Now let our joy…"to the end

An effective way of leading this antiphonal singing is to have the choir sing its part unaccompanied and to use a full organ sound to accompany the assembly.

MUSIC FOR THE SEASON

VERSE AND OFFERTORY

See the Lent and Easter seasonal listings.

CHORAL

Billings, William. "When Jesus Wept." PRE 352-00102.

Christiansen, F. M., arr. "Lamb of God." AFP 11-0133. SATB.

Dengler, Lee. "Saw Ye My Savior." CPH 98-3247. SATB.

Ferguson, John. *St. John Passion.* AFP 11-10991. SATB, org, opt cong.

Frahm, Frederick. "Crux Fidelis." CPH 98-3478. SAB.

Gerike, Henry. "Guide Me, Savior, through Your Passion." GIA G-2767. U, opt 2 pt, org.

Rhein, Robert. "Crucifixion." MSM 50-3033. SATB, vla.

Schütz, Heinrich. "Christ, Be Thine the Glory." GSCH 10123.

CHILDREN'S CHOIRS

Anderson, Norma S. "The Walk to Calvary." CG CGA739. U, kybd.

Johnson, Ralph M. "As Moses Lifted Up." CG CGA-550. U, fl, org.

Leaf, Robert. "At Gethsemane." AFP 10143. U, kybd.

Miller, John D. "What a Friend/Lonesome Valley." CG CGA-518. 2 pt mxd, pno, fl/synth.

Pote, Allen. "On the Third Day." HOP F1000. SATB, opt hb, brass, timp.

KEYBOARD/INSTRUMENTAL

Cherwien, David. "There in God's Garden" in *O God, Beyond all Praising.* AFP 11-10860. Org.

Powell, Robert. "Jesu, Jesu, Fill Us with Your Love" in *Three New Hymn Settings for Organ.* HOP 1948. Org.

Sedio, Mark. "Great God, Your Love Has Called Us" in *Organ Tapestries,* vol. 1. CPH 97-6812. Org.

Sedio, Mark. "Jesu, Jesu, Fill Us with Your Love" in *Dancing in the Light of God.* AFP 11-10793. Pno.

Young, Jeremy. "There in God's Garden" in *At the Foot of the Cross.* AFP 11-10688. Pno.

HANDBELL

Bizet/Wagner. "Agnus Dei." AG 1452. 3 oct.

Hopson, Hal H. "Solemn Passacaglia." AG 1374. 3-5 oct.

Kauffmann, Ronald. "When I Survey the Wondrous Cross." AG 1226. 3 oct.

Wagner, Douglas E. "Prelude on the Passion Chorale." SMP S-HB49. 3-4 oct.

PRAISE ENSEMBLE

Haas, David. "Alive in Christ Jesus" (Romans 8:3-11). GIA G-4871. SATB, solo, kybd, opt cong, C inst, gtr.

Smith, Michael W. "Agnus Dei." HAL 40326298. SAB, kybd.

Yannerella, Charles. "Lest We Forget." HOP A 561. SATB, kybd.

Ylvisaker, John and John Helgen. "I Was There to Hear Your Borning Cry." KJO Ed. 8826. SAATB, kybd, rec or C inst.

ALTERNATE WORSHIP TEXTS

GREETING (EASTER DAY)

Alleluia! Christ is risen!

Christ is risen indeed! Alleluia!

The grace and peace of our Lord Jesus Christ,
who was raised from the dead to bring everlasting hope,
be with you all.
And also with you.

OFFERTORY PRAYER
(MAUNDY THURSDAY, EASTER VIGIL/DAY)

God of glory,
receive these gifts and the offering of our lives.
As Jesus was lifted up from earth,
draw us to your heart in the midst of this world,
that all creation may be brought from bondage to freedom,
from darkness to light, and from death to life;
through Jesus Christ our Lord. Amen

INVITATION TO COMMUNION
(MAUNDY THURSDAY)

This is the food and drink of remembrance.
Let all who hunger for grace come and eat.
Let all who thirst for salvation take of the cup.

INVITATION TO COMMUNION (EASTER VIGIL/DAY)

Alleluia! Christ our Passover is sacrificed for us.
Therefore, let us keep the feast. Alleluia!

POST-COMMUNION PRAYER (MAUNDY THURSDAY)

Lord God, in a wonderful sacrament
you have left us a memorial of your suffering and death.
May this sacrament of your body and blood
so work in us that the way we live
will proclaim the redemption you have brought;
for you live and reign with the Father and the Holy Spirit,
one God, now and forever.
Amen

POST-COMMUNION PRAYER (EASTER VIGIL/DAY)

God, our strength and our salvation,
in this eucharistic feast
we have entered a paradise
of sweet honey and flowing milk,
where death no longer has dominion.
Empower us to tell the good news of the risen Christ,
through whom we praise you now and forever.
Amen

BENEDICTION (EASTER VIGIL/DAY)

May the Almighty, who shaped earth
and kindled the lights of heaven,
renew in you the image of God.

May Christ, who shattered the chains of death,
lead you forward in freedom.

May the Spirit, who breathes forth resurrection power,
fill your hearts with boundless joy.

The blessing of almighty God, Father, ✝ Son, and Holy Spirit,
be among you and remain with you always.
Amen

DISMISSAL (EASTER VIGIL/DAY)

Go in peace. Serve the Lord. Alleluia, alleluia!
Thanks be to God. Alleluia, alleluia!

167

SEASONAL RITES

LITANY OF THE SAINTS

Lord, have mercy.
Lord, have mercy.
Christ, have mercy.
Christ, have mercy.
Lord, have mercy.
Lord, have mercy.

Be gracious to us.
Hear us, O God.
Deliver your people.
Hear us, O God.

You loved us before the world was made:
Hear us, O God.
You rescued the people of your promise:
Hear us, O God.
You spoke through your prophets:
Hear us, O God.
You gave your only Son for the life of the world:
Hear us, O God.

For us and for our salvation he came down from heaven:
Great is your love.
And was born of the virgin Mary:
Great is your love.
Who by his cross and suffering has redeemed the world:
Great is your love.
And has washed us from our sins:
Great is your love.
Who on the third day rose from the dead:
Great is your love.
And has given us the victory:
Great is your love.
Who ascended on high:
Great is your love.
And intercedes for us at the right hand of God:
Great is your love.

For the gift of the Holy Spirit:
Thanks be to God.
For the one, holy, catholic, and apostolic church:
Thanks be to God.
For the great cloud of witnesses into which we are baptized:
Thanks be to God.

For Sarah and Abraham, Isaac and Rebekah:
Thanks be to God.

For Gideon and Deborah, David and Esther:
Thanks be to God.
For Moses and Isaiah, Jeremiah and Daniel:
Thanks be to God.
For Miriam and Rahab, Abigail and Ruth:
Thanks be to God.
For Mary, mother of our Lord:
Thanks be to God.
For John, who baptized in the Jordan:
Thanks be to God.
For Mary Magdalene and Joanna, Mary and Martha:
Thanks be to God.
For James and John, Peter and Andrew:
Thanks be to God.
For Paul and Apollos, Stephen and Phoebe:
Thanks be to God.
Other names may be added
For all holy men and women, our mothers and fathers in faith:
Thanks be to God.
For the noble band of the prophets:
Thanks be to God.
For the glorious company of the apostles:
Thanks be to God.
For the white-robed army of martyrs:
Thanks be to God.
For the cherubim and seraphim, Michael and the holy angels:
Thanks be to God.

Be gracious to us.
Hear us, O God.
Deliver your people.
Hear us, O God.

Give new life to these chosen ones by the grace of baptism:
Hear us, O God.
Strengthen all who bear the sign of the cross:
Hear us, O God.
Clothe us in compassion and love:
Hear us, O God.
Bring us with all your saints to the river of life:
Hear us, O God.

Lord, have mercy.
Lord, have mercy.
Christ, have mercy.
Christ, have mercy.
Lord, have mercy.
Lord, have mercy.

APRIL 12, 2001

MAUNDY THURSDAY

INTRODUCTION

Maundy Thursday is the beginning of the Three Days—the ancient observance of the mystery of our salvation, which plunges the faithful into the death of Jesus and brings them with him to resurrection life. The Three Days are really one liturgy extending from Thursday evening through Easter Sunday evening.

The Maundy Thursday liturgy focuses on three significant actions. First, the confession of sins and announcement of forgiveness brings to a conclusion the Lenten discipline of repentance that began on Ash Wednesday. Second, the church obeys Jesus' command (in Latin, *mandatum*, from which this day receives its name) to follow his example and wash one other's feet. And third, we celebrate our meal of deliverance, taking our place at the supper Jesus shared with his disciples on this night.

PRAYER OF THE DAY

Holy God, source of all love, on the night of his betrayal, Jesus gave his disciples a new commandment: To love one another as he had loved them. By your Holy Spirit write this commandment in our hearts; through your Son, Jesus Christ our Lord, who lives and reigns with you and the Holy Spirit, one God, now and forever.

or

Lord God, in a wonderful Sacrament you have left us a memorial of your suffering and death. May this Sacrament of your body and blood so work in us that the way we live will proclaim the redemption you have brought; for you live and reign with the Father and the Holy Spirit, one God, now and forever.

READINGS

Exodus 12:1-4 [5-10] 11-14

Israel celebrated its deliverance from slavery in Egypt by keeping the festival of Passover. This festival included the slaughter, preparation, and eating of the Passover lamb, whose blood was used to protect God's people from the threat of death. The early church described the Lord's supper using imagery from the Passover, especially in portraying Jesus as the lamb who delivers God's people from sin and death.

Psalm 116:1, 10-17 (Psalm 116:1-2, 12-19 [NRSV])

I will take the cup of salvation and call on the name of the LORD. (Ps. 116:11)

1 Corinthians 11:23-26

In all of Paul's letters, the only story from the life of Jesus that he recounts in detail is this report of the last supper. His words to the Christians at Corinth are reflected today in the liturgies of churches throughout the world.

John 13:1-17, 31b-35

The story of the last supper in John's gospel presents a remarkable event not mentioned elsewhere. Jesus performs the duty of a slave, washing the feet of his disciples and urging them to do the same for each other.

COLOR Scarlet *or* White

THE PRAYERS

As we mark these forty days with repentance and forgiveness, let us pray for the renewal of the church and the restoration of the world to the life of God.

A BRIEF SILENCE.

O God, as Jesus washed the feet of his disciples, cleanse the church by your love and lead it to kneel in service for others. Lord, in your mercy,

hear our prayer.

O God, as you once delivered Israel from bondage, deliver all oppressed people into your life-giving presence in Christ Jesus. Lord, in your mercy,

hear our prayer.

O God, hear the prayers of all who cry to you. Protect those suffering for your name. Heal those who are ill (especially...). Comfort those surrounded by the snares of death. Lord, in your mercy,

hear our prayer.

O God, unite this community, especially those preparing for baptism, that as one body we may pass from death to life with Christ. Lord, in your mercy,

169

hear our prayer.

O God, you have led us to repent and to seek reconciliation with you and with one another. May our reception of your forgiveness proclaim that we are fully reconciled to you in your church. Lord, in your mercy,

hear our prayer.

HERE OTHER INTERCESSIONS MAY BE OFFERED.

O God, gathered in the remembrance of Jesus, your church is united with the faithful of all ages. Clothe us in your love, that we may follow their example of faith. Lord, in your mercy,

hear our prayer.

Gracious Lord, listen to the cry of mercy that comes from our lips, and sustain us with your hope, through Jesus Christ our Lord.

Amen

IMAGES FOR PREACHING

John writes that Jesus, "having loved his own who were in the world…loved them to the end" (vs. 1b). The gospel for the beginning of the Three Days calls us to be immersed in this love. Some congregations will share in an experience of footwashing that is described in this gospel text. Members of these congregations will have the added advantage of reflecting on the experience of having their feet washed.

Many North American Christians, accustomed to being in control of their own personal space, may at first feel awkward at the experience of having their feet washed. They may feel vulnerable when taking off their shoes and stockings. The actual washing of feet is a highly sensory experience as the warm water is poured. Some people give little attention to this part of their body and may be surprised to feel, in addition to their awkwardness, that they are being cared for at a deep level.

How many times a day do we wash? Probably more than we might guess. We wash our hands before eating. We have been taught by health care professionals to wash after visiting each patient in the hospital. We wash after a workout. We wash our hair. We wash our babies, and for many children bathtime becomes a favorite time of the day. The common experience of washing is an image that allows us to connect with Peter and the disciples, as well as those in hospice and nursing homes who need to be bathed by others. Jesus said to Peter, "Unless I wash you, you have no share with me." Are we ready to be washed in the warm waters of Jesus' love?

Our Lord bids us to follow his example, which includes his own experience of having his feet washed by Mary of Bethany. Before we can give love, must we not also be open to receive love?

WORSHIP MATTERS

DaVinci was wrong! It was not the *last* supper, it was the *first*; it was not the end of an era, it was the beginning! This distinction is what makes this celebration of the Lord's supper radically different from that of Easter. Whereas Easter is a time to recollect what God *had done*, the Lord's supper is a time to remember what God *is doing*—here and now! Indeed, both events have related elements: sin and death, blood and protection, bread and deliverance…and a lamb. However in the Lord's supper, it is not our death—it is Jesus'; it is not just any sacrificial lamb from the flock—it is Jesus; it is not *just* unleavened bread—it is Jesus' promise that *this is my body given for you.*

LET THE CHILDREN COME

During the reading of the foot-washing gospel, children may participate in the actions of the gospel by placing an alb on a chair, then carrying a pitcher of water, a basin, and a towel into the midst of the congregation. After the gospel, these items may be placed in front of the altar. If foot washing is included in the service, children may be among the participants who have their feet washed as well as assist in the washing. The new commandment may be spoken for each footwashing: "As Jesus has loved us, we also should love one another."

MUSIC FOR WORSHIP
GATHERING

LBW 377	Lift high the cross
WOV 666	Great God, your love has called us

PSALM 116

Farlee, Robert Buckley. PW, Cycle C.

Haas, David. "Psalm 116: The Name of God" in PCY, vol. 3.

Kendzia, Tom. "In the Presence of God" in STP, vol. 4.

Joncas, Michael. "Psalm 116: Our Blessing Cup" in STP, vol. 2.

Schalk, Carl. "Now I Will Walk at Your Side" in *Sing Out! A Children's Psalter.* WLP 7191.

HYMN OF THE DAY

WOV 663   When twilight comes
           DAPIT HAPON

INSTRUMENTAL RESOURCES

See Lent 2.

ALTERNATE HYMN OF THE DAY

LBW 126   Where charity and love prevail
LBW 199   Thee we adore, O hidden Savior

COMMUNION

LBW 203   Now we join in celebration
WOV 711   You satisfy the hungry heart

ADDITIONAL HYMNS AND SONGS

DH 62   Take off your shoes
RS 566   Jesus took a towel
TFF 69   What can wash away my sin?
W&P 24   Broken in love
W&P 150   We bring the sacrifice of praise

MUSIC FOR THE DAY

CHORAL

Aston, Peter. "I Give You a New Commandment." GIA G-4331.
    2 pt, org.
Baser, Paul. "Ubi caritas." PLY PJMS-121. SATB, pno, horn.
Benson, Robert. "Wondrous Love." AFP 11-10993. SATB, org.
Candlyn, T. Frederick H. "Thee We Adore." CFI C.M.492. SATB, org.
Duruflé, Maurice. "Ubi caritas." DUR 312-41253. SATTBB.

Farlee, Robert Buckley. "Mandatum." AFP 11-10535. SATB.
Mendelssohn, Felix. "See What Love" in CC. SATB, org.

CHILDREN'S CHOIRS

Christopherson, Dorothy. "Jesu, Jesu." CPH 98-3177. SAB, kybd,
    congas.
Hruby, Dolores. "Go Now to Love and Serve the Lord." CG CGA-354.
    U, kybd, fl, signing.
Pote, Allen. "The Last Supper." CG CGA-532. SATB, kybd, opt gtr,
    opt bass.

KEYBOARD/INSTRUMENTAL

Hobby, Robert A. "Love Consecrates the Humblest Act/Where
    Charity and Love Prevail" in Three Lenten Hymn Settings.
    MSM 10-311. Org.
Owens, Sam Batt. "Adoro te devote" in Six Meditations on Plainsong
    Melodies. MSM-10-531. Org.

HANDBELL

Kinyon, Barbara B. "An Upper Room Did Our Lord Prepare."
    LOR 20/1059L. 3-5 oct.
Wagner, Douglas E. "Meditation on 'Let Us Break Bread Together.'"
    AG 1232. 3 oct.

PRAISE ENSEMBLE

Johnston, Cindy, arr. "Jesu, Jesu, Fill Us with Your Love." GIA G-3000.
    2 pt, kybd, fl.
Keesecker, Thomas. "Remember." AFP 11-10743. SATB, kybd,
    2 trbl inst, opt cong.
Lovelace, Austin C. "I Come with Joy" in Hymnal Supplement 1991. GIA.
Whitfield, Frederick. "O How I Love Jesus" in Praise Hymns & Cho-
    ruses, 4th ed. MM.
Willard, Kelly. "Make Me a Servant" in W&P.

171

APRIL 13, 2001

GOOD FRIDAY

INTRODUCTION

This day is the second portion of the liturgy of the
Three Days, which extends from Maundy Thursday to
Easter Evening. As the church gathers to remember the
death of Jesus, we focus not only upon the agony of the
cross but especially upon God's victory through the
crucified. Even more, we "lift high the cross" as the sign
of God's triumph over sin, death, and evil.

PRAYER OF THE DAY

Almighty God, we ask you to look with mercy on your
family, for whom our Lord Jesus Christ was willing to
be betrayed and to be given over to the hands of sinners
and to suffer death on the cross; who now lives and
reigns with you and the Holy Spirit, one God, forever
and ever.

or

Lord Jesus, you carried our sins in your own body on the tree so that we might have life. May we and all who remember this day find new life in you now and in the world to come, where you live and reign with the Father and the Holy Spirit, now and forever.

READINGS

Isaiah 52:13—53:12

The prophet weaves a vision of the suffering servant, whose agony is not a sign of God's rejection, but points to the God who brings healing out of suffering.

Psalm 22

My God, my God, why have you forsaken me? (Ps. 22:1)

Hebrews 10:16-25

The writer to the Hebrews uses the Hebrew scriptures to understand the meaning of Christ's death on the cross. Like a great priest, Jesus offered his own blood as a sacrifice for our sins, so that now we can worship God with confidence and hope.

or Hebrews 4:14-16; 5:7-9

Jesus is our merciful high priest.

John 18:1—19:42

On Good Friday, the story of Jesus' passion—from his arrest to his burial—is read in its entirety from the gospel of John. For John, the death of Jesus is the sign of God's victory, and the cross is the throne from which the new king reigns.

THE PRAYERS

Bidding Prayer, *LBW* Ministers Edition, pages 139–42; or *Book of Common Worship*, pages 283–87.

IMAGES FOR PREACHING

A seven-year-old daughter of a faithful Christian couple left the Good Friday service weeping, asking her father, "Why did they kill Jesus?" What is "good" about this Friday? A sermon, following the full reading of the passion according to St John, may have a hard time competing with the experience of this solemn worship service. Yet, important words are waiting to be said to people who bring their own experience of suffering and death to this day that we call "good." Many, on this day, will keep a grief-stricken fast.

Psalm 22, the appointed psalm for today, may be a point of departure. We hear Jesus reciting this psalm from the cross, "My God, my God, why have you forsaken me?" (see Matt. 27:46 and Mark 15:34). Psalm 22 is a lament of one who places his or her entire trust in

God, not of an existentialist who is waiting for a god who never shows up. Jesus Christ, through his death on the cross, has taken on the suffering of humanity and has transformed death into life. Therefore, speaking in the language of the psalmist (vs. 29-31), those who have died and "a people yet unborn" will hear of his victory.

Those who preach from the passion according to John may point to Christ's glorification on the cross, where he is "lifted up" and enthroned as king. He is Word made flesh (John 1:14) and the great "I am" (John 18:5-6). Christ made the cross a sign of his glory. The image of the cross was described by Martin Luther as the only side of God we are allowed to see (see Exod. 33). By faith we are immersed into the death and resurrection of Christ, so that even our own suffering and death finds its meaning and ultimate transformation through the cross of Jesus Christ. Today is a day to speak a word of good news that brings hope to those who know suffering and grief.

WORSHIP MATTERS

Worshiping today is not unlike repeatedly watching your favorite movie—we know the ending! That is why it is called *Good* Friday after all. Sure, it holds the graphic and gory details of our Lord's death, yet it is by this death that our sins are forgiven. This death will once again make us worthy to enter the garden. And so we do what we sing at Christmas: we come and adore him. We give him that love and adulation that is worthy only of God.

LET THE CHILDREN COME

At an evening service, the reading of the lengthy Good Friday gospel might effectively be accompanied by the showing of a series of color slides, which, with a little imagination, could be locally produced. These visuals, including children's art showing highlights of the Passion narrative, would help to maintain the children's interest. A fade-in, fade-out feature, if available, would be preferable and less disruptive than the quick changing of slides.

MUSIC FOR WORSHIP
SERVICE MUSIC

At the procession with the cross, the versicles may be sung three times to a reciting tone, dropping the interval of a minor third:

Behold, the life-giving cross on which was hung the salvation of the whole | world.

Oh, come, let us wor- | ship him.

GATHERING

The liturgy begins in silence.

PSALM 22

Farlee, Robert Buckley. PW, Cycle C.

Haugen, Marty. PCY, vol. 1.

Kogut, Malcolm. "I Will Praise You, Lord" in PCY, vol. 10.

Schiavone, John. "Psalm 22: My God, My God, Why Have You Abandoned Me" in STP, vol. 3.

See Proper 7.

HYMN OF THE DAY

LBW 92   Were you there
         WERE YOU THERE

VOCAL RESOURCES

Proulx, Richard. "Were You There." AFP 11-10571. SATB, sop solo.

INSTRUMENTAL RESOURCES

Larson, Katherine Jordahl. "Tallis' Canon and Were You There." AFP 11-10353. Hb.

Nicholson, Paul. "Were You There." AFP 11-10528. Org, fl.

Owens, Sam Batt. "Were You There" in *Three Meditations on Spirituals.* MSM-10-895. Org.

Young, Jeremy. "Were You There" in *At the Foot of the Cross.* AFP 11-10688. Pno.

ALTERNATE HYMN OF THE DAY

LBW 118   Sing, my tongue
          (*alternate tune:* PICARDY)

WOV 668   There in God's garden

ADDITIONAL HYMNS AND SONGS

CHA 213   Who would ever have believed it?

TFF 68   That priceless grace

TWC 475   Hark! The voice of love and mercy

W&P 11   At the foot of the cross

W&P 83   Lamb of God

MUSIC FOR THE DAY

CHORAL

Bach, J. S. "Crucifixus" in BAS. SATB, kybd.

Carnahan, Craig. "Bright Joining: Meditations on the Cross." AFP 11-10996. SATB, org.

Ferguson, John. "St. John Passion." AFP 11-10991. SATB, org, opt cong.

Nelson, Ronald A. "Is It Nothing to You?" SEL 405-451. SATB, org.

Niedmann, Peter. "The Earth Did Tremble." AFP 11-10922. SATB, org.

Pergolesi, Giovanni. "Surely He Has Borne Our Griefs." AFP 11-10587. SATB, kybd.

Rickard, Jeffrey H. "Let Thy Blood in Mercy Poured." CFI C.M. 447. SAATB.

Shute, Linda Cable. "Thirty Years among Us." AFP 11-10997. SATB, org.

CHILDREN'S CHOIRS

Christopherson, Dorothy. "There Was a Man." AFP 11-10843. 2 pt, pno, ob.

Horman, John. "God So Loved the World." CG CGA-447. U/2 pt, kybd, opt fl, opt vln.

McIver, Robert H. "Pie Jesu." CG CGA814. 2 pt, pno, fl, ob/cl, opt str.

KEYBOARD/INSTRUMENTAL

Decker, Pamela. "Herzlich tut mich verlangen" in *A New Liturgical Year,* ed. John Ferguson. AFP 11-10810. Org.

Langlais, Jean. "Mon âme cherche une fin paisible" (Herzlich tut mich verlangen) in *Neuf Pieces.* BOR S.B. 5337. Org.

HANDBELL

Nelson, Susan T. "Give Me Jesus." AFP 11-10983. 3 oct.

Sticha, Paul. "Ah, Holy Jesus/Nine Tailors." PRE 114-40478. 3 oct.

PRAISE ENSEMBLE

Batstone, Bill. "Abba, Father, We Approach You" in *Praise Hymns and Choruses,* 4th ed. MM.

Dengler, Lee. "Christ's Sacrifice." SMP S-524. SATB, kybd.

Edwards, Rusty, and Frederick Whitfield. "By Grace We Have Been Saved" in W&P.

Moen, Don. "All We like Sheep" in *Hosanna! Music #3.* INT.

173

APRIL 14, 2001

INTRODUCTION

The Easter Vigil is the ancient and powerful celebration of the new creation that springs from Jesus' open tomb. The striking of the Easter fire; the lighting of the paschal candle; the singing of the ancient Easter proclamation, which calls the faithful to join the universe in new creation; the baptismal washing that buries us with Christ and raises us to life—all these powerful actions draw us into the wonder of resurrection. The church gathers to hear the whole story, from creation through exodus and the prophets, to bring us to the edge of the resurrection celebration.

PRAYER OF THE DAY

O God, who made this most holy night to shine with the glory of the Lord's resurrection: Stir up in your Church that Spirit of adoption which is given to us in Baptism, that we, being renewed both in body and mind, may worship you in sincerity and truth; through Jesus Christ our Lord, who lives and reigns with you, in the unity of the Holy Spirit, one God, now and forever.

174

READINGS

Creation: Genesis 1:1—2:4a

> Response: Psalm 136:1-9, 23-36
>
> *God's mercy endures forever. (Ps. 136:1b)*

The Flood: Genesis 7:1-5, 11-18; 8:6-18; 9:8-13

> Response: Psalm 46
>
> *The Lord of hosts is with us; the God of Jacob is our stronghold. (Ps. 46:4)*

The Testing of Abraham: Genesis 22:1-18

> Response: Psalm 16
>
> *You will show me the path of life. (Ps. 16:11)*

Israel's Deliverance at the Red Sea: Exodus 14:10-31; 15:20-21

> Response: Exodus 15:1b-13, 17-18
>
> *I will sing to the Lord who has triumphed gloriously. (Exod. 15:1)*

Salvation Freely Offered to All: Isaiah 55:1-11

> Response: Isaiah 12:2-6
>
> *With joy you will draw water from the wells of salvation. (Isa. 12:3)*

The Wisdom of God: Proverbs 8:1-8, 19-21; 9:4b-6

or Baruch 3:9-15, 32—4:4

> Response: Psalm 19
>
> *The statutes of the Lord are just and rejoice the heart. (Ps. 19:8)*

A New Heart and a New Spirit: Ezekiel 36:24-28

> Response: Psalm 42 and Psalm 43
>
> *My soul is athirst for the living God. (Ps. 42:2)*

The Valley of the Dry Bones: Ezekiel 37:1-14

> Response: Psalm 143
>
> *Revive me, O Lord, for your name's sake. (Ps. 143:11)*

The Gathering of God's People: Zephaniah 3:14-20

> Response: Psalm 98
>
> *Lift up your voice, rejoice and sing. (Ps. 98:5)*

The Call of Jonah: Jonah 3:1-10

> Response: Jonah 2:1-3 [4-6] 7-9
>
> *Deliverance belongs to the Lord. (Jonah 2:9)*

The Song of Moses: Deuteronomy 31:19-30

> Response: Deuteronomy 32:1-4, 7, 36a, 43a
>
> *The Lord will give his people justice. (Deut. 32:36)*

The Fiery Furnace: Daniel 3:1-29

> Response: Song of the Three Young Men 35-65
>
> *Sing praise to the Lord and highly exalt him forever. (Song of the Three Young Men 35b)*

NEW TESTAMENT READING

Romans 6:3-11

> *Christians are baptized into the death of Christ and are also joined to Christ's resurrection.*

Response: Psalm 114

> *Tremble, O earth, at the presence of the Lord. (Ps. 114:7)*

GOSPEL

Luke 24:1-12

> *The women who followed Jesus take the lead in proclaiming the resurrection.*

COLOR   White *or* Gold

THE PRAYERS

In the light of Christ's resurrection, let us pray for the church, the world, and all who long for the grace of new life.

A BRIEF SILENCE.

On this night, O God, enlighten your church to proclaim that in Christ all shall be made alive. Lord, in your mercy,

hear our prayer.

Scatter the light of Christ's resurrection to the ends of the earth, that all your creation may be jubilant at his rising. Lord, in your mercy,

hear our prayer.

Restore hope and joy through the life of the risen Christ to those who are depressed, imprisoned, homeless, sick, and dying (especially…). Lord, in your mercy,

hear our prayer.

Give to the newly baptized, and all who have affirmed their baptism, the joy to proclaim that they are alive to God in Christ. Lord, in your mercy,

hear our prayer.

HERE OTHER INTERCESSIONS MAY BE OFFERED.

Surround us with the cloud of witnesses who live in your eternal light. Bring us also to the day of resurrection. Lord, in your mercy,

hear our prayer.

Hear our prayers, O God, and grant us what we truly need, in the name of our risen Savior, Jesus Christ.

Amen

IMAGES FOR PREACHING

"This is the night!" is the repeated phrase of the Easter Proclamation (the *Exsultet*), which is sung when the newly lit paschal candle has been placed on its stand at the beginning of the Vigil of Easter.

> This is the night in which, in ancient times, you delivered our forebears, the children of Israel, from the land of Egypt.… This is the night in which all who believe in Christ are rescued from evil and the gloom of sin, are renewed in grace, and are restored to holiness. This is the night in which, breaking the chains of death, Christ arises from hell in triumph.
>
> *LBW* Ministers Edition, page 145

On this night the Holy Spirit, calling us through the gospel, brings us into the presence of our resurrected Lord. This is the night to be immersed in this story of salvation.

This is the night to take off your watch. It will take time to hear twelve readings (or whatever you select from these possibilities), plus a New Testament reading and a gospel reading. The story of salvation begins with God's act of creation when the Spirit of God swept over the waters. This story continues as God saved Noah and his family from the waters of the flood. We hear how God tested Abraham, delivered Israel at the Red Sea, and through the prophet Isaiah freely offered salvation to all. The wisdom of God is celebrated, and the promise of a new heart and a new spirit is heard. The Spirit of God brings life to dry bones, and God's people are gathered together anew. The grace of God is heard through the call of Jonah, the justice of God in the song of Moses, and the salvation of God in the story of the fiery furnace. This is the night that we are brought anew into this story.

Some will be baptized on this night. Others will affirm their baptism. Like the women who come to the tomb (Luke 24:1-12), we will be amazed. Like Mary Magdalene (John 20:1-18) we will say, "I have seen the Lord."

WORSHIP MATTERS

"Blessed are you, O Lord our God,…who led your people Israel by a pillar of cloud by day and a pillar of fire by night" (Evening Prayer, *LBW,* p. 144). It should be no surprise that a wax pillar is found at the great baptismal festival where the people are led through the water of baptism. Yet the pillars in both contexts are simply symbols of God's promise fulfilled in the person of Jesus Christ. We name this pillar the *paschal* candle, for it symbolizes the one who leads people out of bondage through the waters into the freedom of the promised land. In the Easter proclamation, we pray that the candle, and thus the Christ, "will continue to vanquish the darkness of this night and be mingled with the lights of heaven" (*LBW* Ministers Edition, p. 145).

LET THE CHILDREN COME

The service of light during the Easter Vigil communicates profoundly to children. They must not be overlooked in the distribution of candles, but good supervision must be provided for their safety. A child alongside

175

an adult could share in two or three of the readings. For example, in the creation reading, a child might read key words that mark the passage of time: "And there was evening and there was morning," or the words of God's approval, "And God saw that it was good." In the testing of Abraham a child might read the words that pertain to Isaac. Of course, be sure the child is well rehearsed and comfortable with the words.

MUSIC FOR WORSHIP

SERVICE MUSIC

AROUND THE GREAT FIRE

Berthier, Jacques. "Within Our Darkest Night" in *Songs and Prayers from Taizé*. GIA.

Biery, James. "Easter Sequence." MSM 80-404. U/brass qrt or org.

Schutte, Dan. "Holy Darkness." OCP 9906CC. Cong, kybd, gtr, vl, vla, vc, hrn.

AROUND THE LIGHT OF CHRIST

Batastini, Robert. "Exsultet" (Easter Proclamation). GIA G-2351. U chant.

"Rejoice Now, All Heavenly Choirs" in *Music for the Vigil of Easter*. AFP 3-5330. Cant, cong.

Tamblyn. "Lumen Christi." OCP 7235CC. Presider, cant, SATB, org, perc.

"The Exsultet" in TP.

AROUND THE READINGS

Reponses to all readings in PW, Cycle C.

Trapp, Lynn. "Responses for the Triduum." MSM 80-305. Cant/cong/kybd, opt solo/C inst.

FIRST READING

Carmona. "A Canticle of Creation." OCP 9973. U/cant, desc, org, tr.

Hopson, Hal. "O Praise the Lord Who Made All Beauty." CG CGA 143. U, kybd.

Smith, Alan. "God's Love Is Forever!" in PS, vol. 2.

SECOND READING

Cherwien, David. "God Is Our Refuge and Strength." MSM 80-800. U, org.

TFF 6   The Lord of hosts is with us

THIRD READING

Inwood, Paul. "Centre of My Life" in PS, vol. 2.

FOURTH READING

Barker, Michael. "Miriam's Song." CG CGA 740. U, kybd, opt tamb.

Cherwien, David. "Go Down, Moses." Evangel/AMSI. U, kybd.

Daw, Carl, Jr. "Metrical Canticles 25 and 26" in *To Sing God's Praise*. HOP 921. Cong, kybd.

Gibbons, John. "Canticle of Moses" in PS, vol. 2.

FIFTH READING

DeLong, Richard. "Seek Ye the Lord" in *Five Sacred Songs*. ECS 4759. Solo, kybd.

Lindh, Jody. "Behold, God Is My Salvation." CPH 98-3193. U/2 pt, org.

Rusbridge, Barbara. "Sing a Song to the Lord" in PS, vol. 1.

WOV 635   Surely it is God who saves me

SIXTH READING

Cox, Joe. "Psalm 19" in *Psalms for the People of God*. SMP 45/1037S. Cant, choir, cong, kybd.

Ogden, David. "You, Lord, Have the Message of Eternal Life" in PS, vol. 2.

SEVENTH READING

Goudimel, Claude. "As the Deer, for Water Yearning" in CC. SATB.

Howells, Herbert. "Like as the Hart." OXF 42.066. SATB, org.

Hurd, Bob. "As the Deer Longs" in PS, vol. 2.

LBW 452   As pants the hart for cooling streams

W&P 9   As the deer

NINTH READING

Johnson, Alan. "All the Ends of the Earth" in PS, vol. 1.

Jothen, Michael. "O Sing Ye!" BEC BP1128. U, kybd.

Martinson, Joel. "Psalm 98." CPH 98-3225. SATB, cong, tr, org.

TENTH READING

WOV 752   I, the Lord of sea and sky

TWELFTH READING

Daw Jr., Carl. "Metrical Canticles 13 and 14" in *To Sing God's Praise*. HOP 921. Cong, kybd.

Proulx, Richard. "Song of the Three Children." GIA G-1863. U, opt 2 pt, cant, cong, perc, org.

HS98 914   All you works of God, bless the Lord

AROUND THE FONT

"A Litany of the Saints" and "Springs of Water, Bless the Lord" in *Welcome to Christ: Lutheran Rites for the Catechumanate*. AFP 3-142.

Cherwien, David, and Susan Palo Cherwien. "Life Tree." CPH 98-3190. SAB, org, opt fl.

Cooney, Rory/arr. Gary Daigle. "Glory to God/Sprinkling Rite." GIA G-4020. Choir, cong, gtr, kybd, fl.

Farlee, Robert Buckley. "O Blessed Spring." AFP 11-10544. SATB, ob, org, opt cong.

Keesecker, Thomas. "Washed Anew." AFP 11-10676. SAB/SATB, opt 2 oct hb, opt cong.

Palmer, Nicholas. "Cleanse Us, O Lord: Sprinkling Rite." GIA G-4064. Cant, SATB, cong, gtr, org, opt inst.

Taylor-Howell, Susan. "You Have Put on Christ." CG CGA 325. U/3 pt, opt orff.

Trapp, Lynn. "Music for the Rite of Sprinkling." MSM 80-901. SATB, org.

WOV 694   You have put on Christ

PSALM 114

Farlee, Robert Buckley. *PW*, Cycle C.

Hopson, Hal H. *Psalm Refrains and Tones.* HOP 425.

The Psalter-Psalms and Canticles for Singing. WJK.

HYMN OF THE DAY

LBW 189   We know that Christ is raised
ENGELBERG

VOCAL RESOURCES

Wolff, Drummond. "We Know That Christ Is Raised." CPH 98-2609.
SATB, tpts.

INSTRUMENTAL RESOURCES

Cherwien, David. "We Know That Christ Is Raised" in *Gotta Toccata.*
AFP 11-11008. Org.

Cherwien, David. "When in Our Music God Is Glorified: Suite for
Organ." AFP 11-10765. Org.

Moklebust, Cathy. "We Know That Christ Is Raised" in *Hymn Stanzas
for Handbells.* AFP 11-10722 (4-5 oct) or 11-10869 (2-3 oct).

Wolff, S. Drummond. "Engelberg" in *Hymn Descants, Set III.*
CPH 97-6197. Org, inst.

ALTERNATE HYMN OF THE DAY

LBW 210   At the Lamb's high feast
WOV 679   Our Paschal Lamb, that sets us free

COMMUNION

LBW 135   The strife is o'er, the battle done
WOV 669   Come away to the skies

SENDING

LBW 527   All creatures of our God and King
WOV 671   Alleluia, alleluia, give thanks

ADDITIONAL HYMNS AND SONGS

NCH 308   At the font we start our journey
TFF 89   The Lamb
W&P 21   Blessing, honor, and glory

MUSIC FOR THE DAY

CHORAL

Dirksen, Richard. "Christ, Our Passover." HWG CMR 2874. SATB,
brass qrt, org, timp.

Erickson, Richard. "Come Away to the Skies." AFP 11-10816. SATB,
fl, fc.

Gesius, Bartholomäus. "Today in Triumph Christ Arose" in CC.
SATB.

Leaf, Robert. "Saints of God, Wake the Earth." AFP 11-2308.
SATB, org.

Hobby, Robert A. "Now All the Vault of Heaven Resounds."
AFP 11-10998. SAB, 2 tpt, org, opt cong.

Proulx, Richard. "Two Easter Carols." AFP 11-10683. 2 pt, org, hb,
perc.

Scott, K. Lee. "The Tree of Life." MSM 50-3000. SATB, opt cong, org,
opt brass qrt, opt hb.

Sedio, Mark. "O Night More Light Than Day." SEL 405-531. SATB,
solo.

CHILDREN'S CHOIRS

Rutter, John. "All Things Bright and Beautiful." HIN HMC-663.
2 pt, kybd.

Schalk, Carl. "See This Wonder in the Making." MSM-50-8400.
U/solo, opt C inst, org.

Taylor-Howell, Susan. "You Have Put On Christ." CG CGA-325.
U/3 pt trbl, opt orff inst.

KEYBOARD/INSTRUMENTAL

Billingham, Richard. "When Israel Was in Egypt's Land" in *Seven Reflections on African American Spirituals.* AFP 11-10762. Org.

Handel, G. F./arr. Sue Mitchell-Wallace and John Head. "Let the
Bright Seraphim" in *From Humility to Hallelujah.* HOP 299.
Org, tpt.

Organ, Anne Krentz. "Partita on 'Sonne der Gerechtigkeit'" in *Reflections on Hymn Tunes for Holy Communion.* AFP 11-10621. Pno.

HANDBELL

Afdahl, Lee J. "Gethsemane." AFP 11-10485. 3-5 oct.

Wagner, Douglas E. "Easter Joy." FBM BG0770. 3-5 oct.

Young, Philip M. "Good Christian Friends, Rejoice and Sing!"
AFP 11-10767. 2-3 oct.

PRAISE ENSEMBLE

Haugen, Marty. "All You Works of God" (Daniel 3:1-29). GIA 3481.
U/SATB, kybd, opt gtr, perc, electric bass, children, cong.

Kogut, Malcom. "Like a Deer That Longs for Flowing Streams" (Psalm
42, 43) in *PCY*, vol. 10. U, kybd, solo, opt cong, gtr.

Mullins, Rich. "Awesome God" in W&P.

Nystrom, Martin, and Tom Fettke. "As the Deer" in *With One Voice a
Cappella Moments of Praise for the Volunteer Choir.* LIL MB-638.
SATB.

177

APRIL 15, 2001

THE RESURRECTION OF OUR LORD
EASTER DAY

INTRODUCTION

The Lord is risen indeed! The open tomb of Jesus is the door to a new way of being in the world. Easter is not one day but fifty. For a week of weeks—fifty days—the church will explore the dimensions of this new life and raise a joyful alleluia!

PRAYER OF THE DAY

O God, you gave your only Son to suffer death on the cross for our redemption, and by his glorious resurrection you delivered us from the power of death. Make us die every day to sin, so that we may live with him forever in the joy of the resurrection; through Jesus Christ our Lord, who lives and reigns with you and the Holy Spirit, one God, now and forever.

or

Almighty God, through your only Son you overcame death and opened for us the gate of everlasting life. Give us your continual help; put good desires into our minds and bring them to full effect; through Jesus Christ our Lord, who lives and reigns with you and the Holy Spirit, one God, now and forever.

READINGS

Acts 10:34-43

Peter's sermon, delivered at the home of Cornelius, a Roman army officer, is a summary of the essential message of Christianity. Everyone who believes in Jesus, whose life, death, and resurrection fulfilled the words of the prophets, receives forgiveness of sins through his name.

or Isaiah 65:17-25

God promises a new heaven and a new earth

Psalm 118:1-2, 14-24

On this day the LORD has acted; we will rejoice and be glad in it. (Ps. 118:24)

1 Corinthians 15:19-26

Paul describes the consequences of the resurrection, including the promise of new life in Christ to a world that has been in bondage to death. He celebrates the destruction of the forces of evil and the establishment of God's victorious rule over all.

or Acts 10:34-43

See above.

John 20:1-18

Easter morning began with confusion: the stone was moved and the tomb was empty. Disciples arrive, then angels, and finally Jesus himself. Out of the confusion, hope emerges, and a weeping woman becomes the first to confess her faith in the risen Lord.

or Luke 24:1-12

The women who followed Jesus take the lead in proclaiming the resurrection.

COLOR White *or* Gold

THE PRAYERS

In the light of Christ's resurrection, let us pray for the church, the world, and all who long for the grace of new life.

A BRIEF SILENCE.

Almighty God, your church exults that Christ has broken the bonds of death. Inspire all Christians to testify to the freedom won for us in Christ. Lord, in your mercy,

hear our prayer.

God of heaven and earth, you are the ruler of all that you have made. Enable people everywhere to be witnesses to your gracious providence. Lord, in your mercy,

hear our prayer.

Merciful God, lead all who suffer (especially...) to call upon you, so that the power of Christ's resurrection might raise them to new life and hope. Lord, in your mercy,

hear our prayer.

Gracious God, you have given the newly baptized the gift of new life in Christ. Strengthen their desire to live faithfully and to witness to your grace. Lord, in your mercy,

hear our prayer.

HERE OTHER INTERCESSIONS MAY BE OFFERED.

Glorious God, you have opened the gates of righteousness to those who have died in faith. May we also enter

with them to the eternal joys of heaven. Lord, in your
mercy,
hear our prayer.
Hear our prayers, O God, and grant us what we truly
need in the name of our risen Savior, Jesus Christ.
Amen

IMAGES FOR PREACHING

"This is the day," proclaims the psalmist, on which the
Lord has acted. "We will rejoice and be glad in it" (Ps.
118:24).

Jesus asked Mary, "Woman, why are you weeping?"
She mistook him for the gardener, but she was not so
wrong, because he was the one whom Paul would call
the New Adam. Indeed, it was a moment of new creation. He calls her by name, like the good shepherd
who knows his own (John 10:3). She calls him Rab-
bouni, and resurrection faith is born in her. She is sent
to tell the others, "I have seen the Lord." As Luke tells
the story of the resurrection of our Lord, he says that
the women went into the empty tomb. Suddenly, in
their midst, two men in dazzling clothes stood by them.
The small dark space suddenly filled with angelic light.
Heaven had opened before them. The angels said, "Why
do you look for the living among the dead? He is not
here. He has risen."

In the spirituality of the Greek Orthodox Church,
icons tell the gospel story. A resurrection icon has been
called the "Harrowing of Hell." It shows Christ standing
on the cross that is floating on a sea of death. You can
see the wounds on his hands and feet. Christ is reaching
out and pulling Adam from the grave. Eve is also looking up to him. Behind the two of them are the prophets
of the Old Testament. What confidence! Christ has
taken the wounds of death and turned them into marks
of victory as he marches into the capital city of the
enemy and sets free the prisoners of war.

This is the day the Lord has made for all who, like
Mary Magdalene, hear him call them by name. This is
the day the Lord has descended into the place of death
in our lives and has set us free. This is the day the Lord
has sent us to proclaim, "I have seen the Lord."

WORSHIP MATTERS

Consider that the Three Days are one single event, and
today is the conclusion of that event, beginning with an
ominous foreboding and plunging from there into the
quagmire of death and finally rising to transformation
into the great and glorious news, "He lives!" Can we
even begin to imagine the confusion of emotions these
events must have caused among Jesus' disciples? Probably not. But no matter, such a finale simply cannot be
explained. Not even by the disciples. It can only be proclaimed; the resurrection, Jesus' as well as our own, is
not concerned with proof but with trust in the promise
of God. Thus the pure proclamation of that promise becomes the very basis of Christian hope—hope for our
own resurrection as well as for those whom we love.

LET THE CHILDREN COME

Let the children be responsible for the alleluias in one of
the hymns for Easter Sunday. With rehearsal, the children
can help the congregation bring back the alleluias with
enthusiasm, following the long Lenten season. Help children understand that *alleluia* is a universal word for
"Praise the Lord" and that it is something like a cheer
done at school or sporting events. This cheer is directed
to God, to celebrate God's raising Jesus from the dead
and promising us life everlasting.

MUSIC FOR WORSHIP
SERVICE MUSIC

Several embellished versions of the liturgy are available
for festive use on this day:

Cherwien, David. *Alternatives Within.* AFP 11-10611. Org, opt inst.

Farlee, Robert Buckley. *Great and Promised Feast.* AFP 11-11069.
Org, SATB, opt brass, opt str.

Ferguson, John. *Festival Setting of the Communion Liturgy* (*LBW,* setting
2). Full score CPH 6127. Choir 98-2994. Org, SATB, opt brass.

Hillert, Richard. *Festival Setting of the Communion Liturgy* (*LBW,* setting 1). Full score CPH 97-5939. Choral desc 97-2755; hb 97-
5958. U with desc, org, brass, ob, timp, 3 oct hb.

GATHERING

LBW 151	Jesus Christ is risen today
WOV 674	Alleluia! Jesus is risen

PSALM 118:1-2, 14-24

Haas, David. "Alleluia! Let Us Rejoice!" in PCY, vol. 3.

Roth, John. "Give Thanks Unto the Lord." CPH 98-3277.

Schalk, Carl. PW, Cycle C.

Shields, Valerie. "Psalm for Easter." MSM 80-405.

Smith, Timothy R. "Give Thanks to the Lord" in STP, vol. 4.

Soper, Scott. "Psalm 118: This Is the Day" in STP, vol 2.

See Second Sunday of Easter.

HYMN OF THE DAY

| LBW 129 | Awake, my heart, with gladness |
| | AUF, AUF, MEIN HERZ |

INSTRUMENTAL RESOURCES

Bisbee, B. Wayne. "Auf, auf, mein Herz" in *Hymn Introductions for Lent, Easter and Trinity.* MSM 10-868. Org.

Burkhardt, Michael. "Partita on 'Awake My Heart With Gladness.'" MSM 10-407. Org.

Keesecker, Thomas. "Auf, auf, mein Herz" in *Piano Impressions for Easter.* CPH 97-6695. Kybd.

Wolff, S. Drummond. "Auf, auf, mein Herz" in *Hymn Descants, Set II.* CPH 97-6068. Org, inst.

ALTERNATE HYMN OF THE DAY

| LBW 134 | Christ Jesus lay in death's strong bands |
| WOV 676 | This joyful Eastertide |

COMMUNION

| LBW 352 | I know that my Redeemer lives! |
| WOV 678 | Christ has arisen, alleluia |

SENDING

| LBW 145 | Thine is the glory |
| WOV 673 | I'm so glad Jesus lifted me |

ADDITIONAL HYMNS AND SONGS

DH 65	Good news, alleluia!
RS 600	Christ the Lord is risen
TFF 94	Low in the grave he lay
W&P 94	Majesty

MUSIC FOR THE DAY

CHORAL

Bach, J. S. "Alleluia" in BAS. SATB, kybd.

Farlee, Robert Buckley. "*Cristo Vive*/Christ Is Living!" AFP 11-11021. SATB, org, perc.

Fedak, Alfred V. "Begin the Song of Glory Now." MSM 50-4014. SATB, org, opt brass.

Gesius, Bartholomäus, "Today in Triumph Christ Arose" in CC. SATB.

Hillert, Richard. "Alleluia! This Is the Day." CPH 98-2924. SATB.

Hobby, Robert. "Now All the Vault of Heaven Resounds." AFP 11-10998. SAB, org, 2 tpt, opt hb, cong.

Hopp, Roy. "Christ the Lord Is Risen Today." AFP 11-10999. SATB, pno.

Mendelssohn, Felix. "Alleluia" in CC. SATB.

Near, Gerald. "Arise, My Love, My Fair One" in *The Augsburg Choirbook.* AFP 11-10817. SATB.

Proulx, Richard. "Our Paschal Lamb, That Sets Us Free." AFP 12-106. SATB, org.

Ratcliff, Cary. "Lift Your Voice Rejoicing, Mary." KAI. SATB, org, perc.

Vulpius, Melchior. "Arisen Is Our Blessed Lord" in CC. SATB/SATB or SATB and inst.

CHILDREN'S CHOIRS

Arguello/arr. Florindez. "Resucito, Resucito." CPH 98-3278. SA, kybd, opt 2 tpt, opt gtr.

Powell, Robert J. "Concertato on 'Thine Is the Glory.'" CG CGA-457. U, SA(T)B, cong, org, 2 tpt, opt 2 oct hb.

Holbert, Diana. Choreography for "Thine Be the Glory" in *Our Heritage of Hymns.* CG CGBK-49. p 48-49.

Proulx, Richard. "Easter Carol." GIA G-4465. U/2 pt, fl, org.

Ziegenhals, Harriet. "Now Let the Heavens Be Joyful." HOP JR 220. U/3pt trbl, kybd, opt fl/vln.

KEYBOARD/INSTRUMENTAL

Webster, Richard. "Paschal Suite for Organ and Trumpet." AFP 11-10831. Org, Tpt.

Wetzler, Robert. "Death to Life." AMSI B-5. Brass, org, perc.

Young, Gordon, "Christ the Lord Is Risen Today" (Easter Hymn) in *Twelve Toccatas.* HOP 1946. Org.

HANDBELL

Handel/Martha Lynn Thompson. "Hallelujah." FLA HP5104. 3-5 oct.

Moklebust, Cathy, and David Moklebust. "Lift High the Cross." CG CGB192. 3-5 oct, org, cong.

Morris, Hart. "Lift High the Cross." RRM. 3-5 oct, org, opt choir.

Sherman, Arnold B. "The Strife Is O'er." AG 1847. 3-5 oct.

PRAISE ENSEMBLE

Bullock, Geoff, David Reidy, and Gary Rhodes. "Blessing, Honor, and Glory with Were You There? and I See the Lord." WRD 301 0915 160. SATB, kybd, opt orch.

Carter, Sydney. "I Danced in the Morning" in *Hymnal Supplement 1991.* GIA.

Herring, Anne. "Easter Song" in *Spirit Touching Spirit.* CCF.

APRIL 15, 2001

THE RESURRECTION OF OUR LORD
EASTER EVENING

INTRODUCTION

The excitement of Easter morning has ended, but the adventure of the resurrection is only beginning. In the twilight of that hectic day, weary disciples try to piece the chaos together. We, too, pause to reflect on the magnitude of the events which we have celebrated this day.

PRAYER OF THE DAY

Almighty God, you give us the joy of celebrating our Lord's resurrection. Give us also the joys of life in your service, and bring us at last to the full joy of life eternal; through your Son, Jesus Christ our Lord, who lives and reigns with you and the Holy Spirit, one God, now and forever.

READINGS

Isaiah 25:6-9

This section of Isaiah seems to come from a time after the exile. The prophet looks forward to a day beyond death. Israel's pagan neighbors knew a god of death whose mouth was an open grave. The prophet knows that God will one day swallow death.

Psalm 114

Hallelujah. (Ps. 114:1)

1 Corinthians 5:6b-8

Paul discerns the implications of Jesus' resurrection. There is an interesting similarity between bread and Easter people: both rise!

Luke 24:13-49

Luke tells a story about distraught disciples who cannot piece together the puzzle of this new day. A stranger consoles them and begins to unlock the mystery.

COLOR   White

THE PRAYERS

In the light of Christ's resurrection, let us pray for the church, the world, and all who long for the grace of new life.

A BRIEF SILENCE.

Holy God, you offer us fullness of life as we share in your Son's resurrection. As we eat and drink with the risen Lord, nourish us with the power of your unending life, so that we may be signs of hope in this joyful Easter time. Lord, in your mercy,
hear our prayer.

In his victory over death, your Son vanquished the power of evil and brought the dawn of peace. Lead us and strengthen us to spread the light of his justice and work for peace in our troubled world. Lord, in your mercy,
hear our prayer.

Your Son emptied himself to become one of us and share our suffering. Lift the burdens of all who are sick (especially...). Come with healing to all who call upon you. Lord, in your mercy,
hear our prayer.

Through the waters of baptism you bring new life to your people. Help the newly baptized discover your grace in the living word and sacraments of Christ's love. Lord, in your mercy,
hear our prayer.

HERE OTHER INTERCESSIONS MAY BE OFFERED.

You raised Christ Jesus from the dead to sit at your right hand. On the last day, draw us to yourself, and welcome us with all the faithful departed to the wedding feast of the Lamb. Lord, in your mercy,
hear our prayer.

Hear our prayers, O God, and grant us what we truly need, in the name of our risen Savior, Jesus Christ.
Amen

IMAGES FOR PREACHING

Word and sacrament have been celebrated in their fullness during the great Three Days. We have been immersed in the gospel story of God's salvation, immersed in God's love through Christ's washing of feet, immersed in the death and resurrection of Christ who brings us hope and lets us call his death "good," immersed in the great story of God's salvation so that we know it is also our story, and immersed in Christ's victory over hell, so that we know that the powers of death and sorrow in our lives have been defeated.

181

Through word and sacrament we have been immersed in the new day that the Lord has made. All things have been made new.

The risen Lord has been made known to us in the breaking of bread. We say with Cleopas and his companion, "Were not our hearts burning within us... while he was opening the scriptures to us" on the way? (Luke 24:32).

Easter evening is a moment of fulfillment. Yet, this evening does not turn in on itself, but points us forward. Jesus says, "You are witnesses of these things" (Luke 24:48). He told his first disciples to wait for the promised Holy Spirit. The great fifty days of the Easter season is a celebration of that gift unfolding within our lives of faith.

MUSIC FOR WORSHIP

SUGGESTED HYMNS

LBW 154	That Easter day with joy was bright
LBW 263	Abide with us, our Savior
WOV 743	Stay with us
WOV 674	Alleluia! Jesus is risen

ADDITIONAL HYMNS AND SONGS

CW 146	His battle ended there
LLC 362	As I walked home to Emmaus
OBS 54	Day of arising
TLH 194	Abide with us, the day is waning
W&P 113	Open our eyes, Lord

MUSIC FOR THE DAY

CHORAL

De Majo, Gian Francesco/ed. Ronald A. Nelson. "Alleluia." CPH 98-3474. U, kybd.

Hovland, Egil. "Stay with Us." AFP 11-11019. SATB, org.

Larson, Lloyd. "Lift Your Voice and Sing, He Is Risen." BEC BP1541. SATB, kybd.

Pelz, Walter. "Stay with Us." CPH 98-2920. SATB, fl, org.

Praetorius, Michael. "Stay with Us" in CC. SATB.

Shute, Linda Cable. "This Joyful Eastertide." AFP 11-10750. 2 pt, hb, perc.

Thompson, Randall. "Alleluia." ECS 1786.

KEYBOARD/INSTRUMENTAL

Keesecker, Thomas. "Stay with Us" in *Piano Impressions for Easter.* CPH 97-6695. Pno.

Powell, Robert. "Earth and All Stars" in *Sing a New Song.* AFP 11-10766. Org.

THURSDAY, APRIL 19
OLAVUS PETRI, PRIEST, 1552;
LAURENTIUS PETRI, ARCHBISHOP OF UPPSALA, 1573;
RENEWERS OF THE CHURCH

These two brothers are commemorated for their introduction of the Lutheran movement to the Church of Sweden after studying at the University of Wittenberg. They returned home and, through the support of King Gustavus Vasa, began their work. Olavus published a catechism, hymnal, and a Swedish version of the mass. He resisted attempts by the king to gain royal control of the church. Laurentius was a professor at the university in Uppsala. When the king wanted to abolish the ministry of bishops, Laurentius persuaded him otherwise, and the historic episcopate continues in Sweden to this day. Together the brothers published a complete Bible in Swedish and a revised liturgy in 1541.

This week the Church of Sweden can be remembered in prayer. The Easter hymn "Praise the Savior, now and ever" (LBW 155) uses a Swedish folk tune and can be sung to commemorate the contributions of the Petris and the Swedish church to our worship life.

SATURDAY, APRIL 21
ANSELM, ARCHBISHOP OF CANTERBURY, 1109

This eleventh-century Benedictine monk stands out as one of the greatest theologians between Augustine and Thomas Aquinas. He is counted among the medieval mystics who emphasized the maternal aspects of God. Of Jesus Anselm says, "In sickness you nurse us and with pure milk you feed us." He is perhaps best known for his theory of atonement, the "satisfaction" theory. In this theory he argued that human rebellion against God demands a payment, but because humanity is fallen, it is incapable of making that satisfaction. Therefore, God takes on human nature in Jesus Christ in order to make the perfect payment for sin.

In preaching this Sunday, Anselm's theory of atonement may be used to underscore the message of the second reading, which describes Jesus as one "who loves us and freed us from our sins by his blood."

EASTER

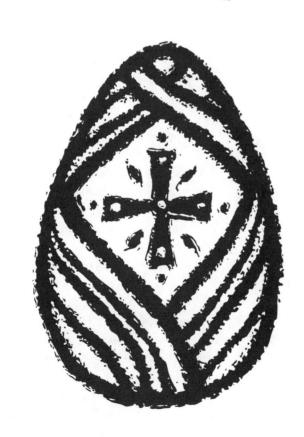

Alleluia, indeed!

IMAGES OF THE SEASON

Easter is the surprising happy ending to the story of Jesus. Happy endings, which are so difficult to achieve in our own space and time, are woven into God's future. The resurrection of Jesus seems to be the only way to resolve the contradictions in the story of God's chosen one. What is even more important, the resurrection of the Crucified seems to be the only way to resolve the paradox of a fallen world loved by a holy God. So, Easter is more than a remembrance of the Jesus story or a coronation of "ever-recurrent spring." Easter is, in fact, a celebration of God's victory over sin, death, and the devil—and more! Easter is the church's passage with Jesus by way of his cross and through his open tomb into God's new age.

We need this understanding if we are to grasp the images of the season. As John Updike says so eloquently in his "Seven Stanzas at Easter":

> Let us not mock God with metaphor,
> analogy, sidestepping, transcendence,…
> let us walk through the door.
> John Updike, *Collected Poems 1953–1993*

Because the door through which we walk at Eastertide is the door to Jesus' open tomb, it matters profoundly which direction we are walking. The danger is that we might limit the good news of Easter to the meeting of religious needs in the present. People want hope; Jesus' open tomb gives it. People hunger for security and stability; Christianity offers it. Postmodern masses yearn for a sense of meaning in the midst of the culture's chaotic noise; Easter faith gives something to believe in.

Unfortunately, this trajectory cheats us by taking us backwards through the open door—from the new day back into the tomb. Without a radical critique of the world in which we find ourselves, we end up using the ancient story merely as a commodity for coping with present-day problems. The world-as-it-is stays ultimately in control, calling the shots, defining our needs, laying out the blueprint for salvation.

A better use of Easter symbols is to let the images move us out from the tomb into God's new day. The open tomb, the paschal candle, the flowers and trumpets are much more than gimmicks to answer something lacking in our present. They are, rather, windows to a new world. They transport us in two directions at once—backwards to the story of the Crucified and his empty tomb, and forward to a future reality that is breaking in even now.

The three major images for the season are the same three that propel our worship every season through the liturgical year: the story, the bath, and the table.

We need to pay close attention to how the story of Jesus' death and resurrection works. Why should the resurrection of a man who died on a cross have anything to offer people living nearly two millennia after the event? For that matter, why does Jesus' resurrection have any significance for his own contemporaries? Where is the cosmic recipe book that declares that by this dying and rising, anything at all gets fixed?

Jesus' resurrection means salvation for this reason: because Jesus died and was raised in such a way as to *bring others with him.* Disciples, too, die with Jesus and are raised from the dead: Peter, as he denies him and is forgiven; Thomas, as he discovers the willingness of Jesus to offer what he needs for faith; murderous Saul, when he discovers that the man whose story he wants to destroy is calling him to a new life.

Easter is not a spectator sport; you "get it" when you engage in the dying and rising. Jesus is alive and well and working to bring you and me and our own contemporaries with him to new life.

What about the bath at Eastertide? The Easter Vigil, the great climax of the Three Days, was the place of the great washing. But the font is a strange bath! The only real way to get clean is to drown, to be plunged into the story with the Crucified and rise from the dead. Baptism, then, is the doorway through which we go to die and be raised. Easter is a great baptismal season, the time of myst-

184

agogy—the days in which the ancient church educated the newly baptized into the mysteries of the faith.

In our post-Christian world, an orientation toward life in God's new world is essential. Hit-and-run baptisms will prove to be insufficient for instilling the faith that leads to new life. Baptism is not a magic trick but rather the beginning of life with God. Each baptism has a future. Lent has brought us to a paschal affirmation of our watery beginnings celebrated in the Three Days; Easter is the season to unpack the implications of our death and resurrection for our future. Congregations that celebrate confirmation at Pentecost have a wonderful opportunity to live and affirm this reality.

And the table? Ah, the eucharistic table at Eastertide is the place where the faithful meet the risen Lord! Meals in the Easter readings are places for epiphanies: a revelatory lakeside breakfast that is a feast of forgiveness, a strange picnic of unclean beasts that points to a new age. But most importantly, at the table here in the present, the Risen Lord is with us in bread and wine, filling us with resurrection life and more! We who receive the Lord's body and blood also have his Spirit breathed into us. We are now his body, and our communion together is his incarnation uniting with our own flesh and blood.

Although Easter resurrection appears to come at the end, it is really a beginning. It is the season to tell the story in such a way that we are slain and raised to life. It is the season to remember that the baptismal bath commits us to a future and compels us to plan for new life, for the form of this world is passing away. It is the season to greet each other at the table, knowing that in our eating and drinking and community the risen Lord is unfolding the next chapter of his story in and through us. Alleluia, indeed!

185

ENVIRONMENT AND ART FOR THE SEASON

Ceremonial festivity is often expressed in quantitative terms—*more* flowers, *more* anthems, *longer* sermons and liturgies. Festivity, however, may better be expressed in qualitative ways. Rather than more of everything, give more attention to the liturgical essentials of worship. Look for quality and appropriateness in vestments, vessels, artwork, music, and the spatial environment. Here, good taste means a work of art used with liturgical and theological integrity. Art can be a powerful and convincing way to proclaim the gospel. Therefore, we need to choose it well.

Baptism is preeminent during Lent. Easter is the season to celebrate the continuation and culmination of baptism in the eucharist. The newly baptized have communed for the first time at the Vigil of Easter. Easter may also be an appropriate season for children to begin communing, as a congregation studies alternatives for its sacramental life. Worship planners should try to create a favorable climate for the developing eucharistic practices of the congregation.

New attention to sacramental practices has potential implications for the Easter season. Because of our renewed stress on the eucharist as a meal of the people of God, congregations are encouraged to use freestanding altar tables. To preserve the appearance of a table, less emphasis is placed on paraments that cover the entire altar. The use of real bread and a common cup are sensate reminders of this meal motif and our oneness in Christ. Eucharistic vestments and full eucharistic prayers are celebratory signs of joyful participation. In dealing with these new directions in eucharistic practice, planners should ask a simple question: How would we prepare to give a festive meal in our own home? What makes for a hospitable and celebrative environment? Answers given in such ordinary situations may also provide guidance for the arrangement of communion in your congregation.

In some churches the newly baptized lead the community to the holy table at the Vigil of Easter and throughout the Easter season. Newly baptized persons are given a place of honor in the worship space and may wear their baptismal garments every Sunday. Congregations may wish to make a baptismal vestment for infants and provide simple albs for the adults.

The paschal or Easter candle was lighted from the new fire in the liturgy for the Vigil of Easter. It led the congregational procession to the place for the readings, baptism, and the eucharist. The paschal candle is lighted for each liturgy during the fifty days of Easter, through the end of the liturgy on Pentecost Day.

White and gold paraments are appropriate for the Easter season. In some congregations, amateur and professional artists create special festival paraments with matching eucharistic vestments. As the meal image of the eucharist is recovered in our day, we are moving away from making the holy table a box-like canvas for textile art. A simple but elegant white cloth is always appropriate. The fabric, texture, design as well as color of this "table cloth" are important considerations.

In Orthodox churches, an icon appropriate to the day or season may be a center of devotional attention. We can take advantage of the stained glass windows and other art pieces that grace our worship space. Place flowers or candles beneath a resurrection window. If other artwork in the space relates to one or more readings for a given day, find a way for the art to enhance the liturgical experience.

A narthex or gathering space might be the venue for visual art that relates to a textual theme for a Sunday. Such art may be borrowed from local galleries, libraries, universities, or taken from offices or walls of the church building. Possibilities abound: *Risen Christ* by Michelangelo, *Doubting Thomas* by Rembrandt, *The Supper at Emmaus* by Velazquez, *Festival of Lights* by Swanson.

Artists in the congregation could be invited to create original art based on the Sunday lectionary. Children are capable of producing arresting and beautiful art. Each piece should be framed or matted. It may be hung in a place of honor or placed on an easel with special lighting. This artwork could provide an attractive visual on the cover of a bulletin or newsletter. Sometimes it becomes an engaging visual for a sermon or children's story.

Hymns and liturgical music offer cues for the work of the environmental minister. The Easter proclamation, sung during the Vigil of Easter, invites all of heaven and earth to join in one everlasting song of praise and gratitude. In this and other Easter texts, we celebrate the new creation in Christ with elemental images of earth, sea, sky, night, days, stars, plants, animals, and all living things. These creation themes can find expression in the liturgical art of Easter.

Lilies and flower bouquets often decorate our spaces during Easter. Explore the idea of plants and flowers that connect to Easter themes. If bare branches have been used during the season of Lent, let them give way to a mass of forsythia or dogwood. Members of the congregation could cover the rough cross of Good Friday with flowers before the Easter service begins. Instead of using professional florists all of the time, invite members of the congregation to contribute flowers from their gardens. Break the predictable patterns of floral bouquets by placing living plants or flowers in groupings near font or altar.

Pentecost, the Feast of Weeks, was based on a spring harvest festival. This agricultural origin may influence our choice of visual images. Mobiles of votive candles and red strip banners have been typical Pentecost art. Other images of harvest not only respect the origins of this season but emphasize gospel themes. Pentecost is a time of sending laborers into the fields and calls us to renewed ministry. It speaks of the final days, the coming of the Spirit, the end time harvest. It evokes images of eucharistic bread given to satisfy the hungry heart and to feed us for ministry and mission.

PREACHING WITH THE SEASON

Put on the garments of resurrection life. Colossians 3:12 says, "As God's chosen ones, holy and beloved, clothe yourselves with compassion, kindness, humility, meekness, and patience." In the Eastern churches the newly baptized are welcomed with the chanted words of Galatians 3:27, "As many of you as were baptized into Christ have clothed yourselves with Christ." Gospel preaching during the Easter season wraps us in baptismal garments.

During the season of Lent the proclamation of the gospel stripped us of the ragged garments of self-centered living so that we might be immersed in the saving mystery of Jesus Christ's death and resurrection. Now, for seven weeks, gospel preaching enfolds us in the garments of resurrection life. In many ancient baptismal rites, the adult baptismal candidate was immersed naked into a pool of water. Men and women were baptized separately and were attended by a baptismal deacon, male or female depending upon the gender of the baptismal candidate. As each newly baptized person emerged from the font, she or he was anointed with oil as a sign of the Holy Spirit's presence and then dressed in a new garment. In our contemporary society the choice of clothing for many is merely an expression of style, not status. Baptismal garments, however, are a sign that in baptism "we are made members of the Church which is the body of Christ" (*LBW*, p. 121).

Following baptism a white garment may be given to the newly baptized as a representative of the congregation says, "Put on this robe, for in baptism you have been clothed in the righteousness of Christ, who calls you to his great feast" (*Welcome to Christ: Lutheran Rites for the Catechumenate*, p. 47). The season of Easter, lasting for a week of weeks and ending Pentecost Sunday, has a single character. The story of the giving of the Holy Spirit is told both at the beginning of this season, as Jesus breathes on his disciples (John 20:22), and at its fulfillment, as the Holy Spirit is poured out upon the disciples as wind and fire and speech (Acts 2:1-4).

Throughout the Easter season the gift of the Holy Spirit wraps us anew in the garments of resurrection life. This character of "being robed" will be explored in the "Images for Preaching" for the Easter season. We are robed in these garments when the risen Lord meets us, just as Mary Magdalene, Thomas, and Peter were transformed as Christ encountered them.

Preaching that is formed by the season of Easter may be characterized by this baptismal image of being clothed in newness of life. Easter preaching on the second Sunday of Easter will clothe the people of God in the garment of resurrection peace, which we need because too many circumstances in life take our breath away. On the third Sunday of Easter we are wrapped in the garments of reconciling love as we hear Jesus call Peter, the one who denied knowing the Lord, to "feed my lambs." The baptismal garment that enfolds us on the fourth Sunday of Easter is trust. We entrust our lives to the Good Shepherd, who says, "My sheep hear my voice; I know them, and they follow me." On the fifth Sunday of Easter the preacher will clothe the faithful with our Lord's new commandment to love one another, for in this love we are given our identity. A new set of relationships is the baptismal robe that is given by our Lord on the sixth Sunday of Easter as he comes to make his home with us. Unity in Christ is the garment for the seventh Sunday of Easter, as we hear Jesus pray, "I ask...that they may all be one."

The season of Easter includes the celebration of Ascension and Pentecost. While the historical framework of the Acts of the Apostles has tended to shape our liturgical season, with Ascension forty days after the resurrection and Pentecost on the fiftieth day, the whole season of Easter may be seen as the outpouring of the Holy Spirit. This gift of the Spirit empowers us to be witnesses to Christ in the world, until that time when he comes again.

SHAPE of WORSHIP for the SEASON

BASIC SHAPE OF THE EUCHARISTIC RITE

- Confession and Forgiveness: see alternate worship text for Easter in *Sundays and Seasons*

GATHERING

- Greeting: see alternate worship text for Easter in *Sundays and Seasons*
- Use the Kyrie throughout Easter
- As the hymn of praise, use "This is the feast of victory"

WORD

- For dramatic readings based on lectionary passages, use *Scripture Out Loud!* (AFP 3-3964) for the second Sunday of Easter and Pentecost Day
- For contemporary dramas based on lectionary passages, use *Can These Bones Live?* (AFP 3-3965) for the second and fourth Sundays of Easter and Pentecost Day
- Use the Nicene Creed
- The prayers: see alternate forms and responses for Easter in *Sundays and Seasons*

BAPTISM

- Consider observing Pentecost Day (June 3) as a baptismal festival

MEAL

- Offertory prayer: see alternate worship text for Easter in *Sundays and Seasons*
- Use the proper preface for Easter; use proper preface for Pentecost on Pentecost Day
- Eucharistic Prayer: in addition to four main options in *LBW*, see "Eucharistic Prayer E: The Season of Easter" in *WOV* Leaders Edition, p. 69; and "Eucharistic Prayer F: The Day of Pentecost" in *WOV* Leaders Edition, p. 70
- Invitation to communion: see alternate worship text for Easter in *Sundays and Seasons*
- Post-communion prayer: see alternate worship text for Easter in *Sundays and Seasons*

SENDING

- Benediction: see alternate worship text for Easter in *Sundays and Seasons*
- Dismissal: see alternate worship text for Easter in *Sundays and Seasons*

OTHER SEASONAL POSSIBILITIES

BLESSING OF FIELDS AND GARDENS

- See seasonal rites section; may be used to conclude worship on the sixth Sunday of Easter or at another time when such a blessing is appropriate

VIGIL OF PENTECOST

- A celebration for this evening could be modeled on the Easter Vigil, but using these elements:
  - Service of Light (from *LBW,* pp. 142–44)
  - Service of Word (from the prayer of the day through the hymn of the day)
  - Service of Baptismal Affirmation (from *LBW,* pp. 199–201, with the congregation gathering around the font, space permitting; water may be sprinkled from the font during the recitation of the creed)
  - Service of Communion (from the offering through the dismissal)

LECTIONARY OPPORTUNITIES FOR HEALING SERVICES

- Easter 6 (alternate gospel from John 5) on May 20
- Easter 7 (first reading) on May 27

ASSEMBLY SONG FOR THE SEASON

Easter is the "eighth day"—the symbol of eternal life. The Easter season is one day made up of fifty days full of alleluias and resounding praise. Let the assembly song reflect this "queen of feasts" even as the season moves toward Pentecost.

GATHERING

After Easter Day is over, do not let the next six Sundays of Easter be lifeless. Prepare instrumentalists and choirs to play and sing hymn descants. Keep the bells ringing on the psalms and verses. Plan to sing an Easter entrance hymn every Sunday of Easter, even if it means repeating some hymns during the season.

If you are preparing to use a new setting for the hymn of praise, begin it on the second Sunday of Easter (Easter Day is not usually the best time to introduce something unfamiliar). "This is the feast of victory" (WOV 608) is a setting composed in a jazz idiom by Michael Hassell. The refrain could easily be learned by the assembly, with a choir or cantor singing the sections marked "I" and "II." Teach the refrain to the assembly ahead of time.

Take advantage of a popular interest in chant and use "This is the feast of victory" in *LBW,* setting 3. It can express a serene, confident joy in the resurrection, complementing the exuberant outbursts of joy during this season. Prepare the choir to lead the chant well and with a flowing style.

Hymn texts based on Revelation 5 such as "Al-abaré" (WOV 791) are also appropriate for the hymn of praise. Teach children to play simple percussion instruments to accompany this hymn.

WORD

Alleluias should abound at the psalmody. Use the alleluias from "The strife is o'er, the battle done" (LBW 135) as a psalm refrain. "Let the heavens rejoice" (TFF 10) is an appropriate refrain and psalm tone for the season.

The "Celtic Alleluia" (WOV 613) can be sung by the assembly, with the choir singing the proper verse(s) included in *WOV* Accompaniment Edition. Repeat the alleluias after the reading of the gospel. Ring handbells freely and accompany a gospel procession, or have children ring bells from their places in the pews.

A sequence hymn may be sung on Pentecost. Alternate the odd-numbered stanzas of "Come, Holy Ghost, our souls inspire" (LBW 472) sung by a cantor or choir with the assembly singing the even-numbered stanzas of "Come, Holy Ghost, our souls inspire" (LBW 473).

MEAL

"Let us talents and tongues employ" (WOV 754) can be sung as an offertory hymn. Teach this hymn to Sunday school children, and have them sing the first stanza. Gather children in or near the choir space at the conclusion of the peace, so that they may sing as a group. They could return to their pews during the remaining stanzas or at the beginning of distribution.

Use sung acclamations throughout the season at the eucharistic prayer. "Acclamations and Amen" (WOV 618b or 619b) are especially appropriate for this season, especially when used with the respective settings of "Holy, holy, holy Lord."

To continue the spirit of baptismal celebration, sing "You have put on Christ" (WOV 694) as the final hymn during distribution, especially if it was used at baptism at the Vigil of Easter. Accompany it with bells.

On Pentecost Day sing "Come, O Holy Spirit, come" (TFF 106 and WOV 681) during distribution. You can begin on the sixth Sunday of Easter and continue through the day of Pentecost.

SENDING

"Thank the Lord" ("Thankful hearts") is certainly appropriate for this season. Consider a rousing hymn such as "Good Christian friends, rejoice and sing!" (LBW 144) or "Thine is the glory" (LBW 145) as the post-communion canticle, especially on Easter Day. Stanzas 1 and 4 of "Christ has arisen, alleluia" (WOV 678 and TFF 96) offer another possibility.

MUSIC FOR THE SEASON

VERSE AND OFFERTORY

Cherwien, David. *Verses for the Sundays of Easter.* MSM-80-400. U, org.

Cherwien, David. *Verses for Ascension, Pentecost, and Trinity.* MSM-80-540. U, org.

Jennings, Carolyn. "Creator Spirit, by Whose Aid" (Gospel acclamation for Pentecost). AFP 11-2387 (score). SATB, 3 tpts, timp.

Pelz, Walter L. *Verses and Offertories: Easter–The Holy Trinity.* AFP 11-9546. SATB, org.

Running, Joseph. "I Will Not Leave You Comfortless." AFP 11-10150. SATB.

Schalk, Carl. *Verses and Offertory Sentences, Part IV: Easter Day through Easter 7.* CPH 97-5504. Acc. 97-5509.

Trapp, Lynn. "Psalm 19 and Gospel Acclamation." MSM-80-903. U, cant, org, cong, opt SATB, opt 2 tpts.

Verses and Offertory Sentences, Part V: Vigil of Pentecost through Pentecost 9 (Settings through Proper 11). CPH 97-5505. Acc ed 97-5510. U/2 pt.

Willan, Healey, arr. Timothy Guenther. *Verses for the Easter Season.* CPH 98-3057. SATB

WOV 612   Halle, halle, hallelujah

WOV 677   Alleluia Canon

WOV, p. 48   Word of life, Jesus Christ

CHORAL

Ellingboe, Bradley. "Mary at the Tomb." AFP 11-10833. SATB, pno.

Erickson, Richard. "Come Away to the Skies." AFP 11-10816. SATB, fl, fc.

Gouzes, Andre. "Christ Is Risen from the Dead." GIA G-4612. SATB.

Handel, G. F. "Since by Man Came Death" in *Messiah.* GSCH. SATB, kybd.

Handel, G. F. "Worthy Is the Lamb" in *Messiah.* GSCH. SATB, kybd.

Shute, Linda Cable. "This Joyful Eastertide." AFP 11-10750. 2 pt, hb, perc.

Thiman, Eric H. "The Strife Is O'er." NOV 1153. SATB, org.

CHILDREN'S CHOIRS

Artman, Ruth. "I Never Touched a Rainbow." CG CGA-355. U/2 pt, opt hand signs, fl, hb.

Christopherson, Dorothy. "Nature Sings in Celebration." AFP 11-10547. 2 pt trbl, kybd, rec/fl.

Hopson, Hal H. "Christ the Lord Is Risen Again." FLA A7263. SATB, org, opt brass, hb, hd.

Lovelace, Austin C. "Let Us Talents and Tongues Employ." CG CGA619. 2 pt mxd, pno, opt gtr and bng.

McRae, Shirley W. "Now the Green Blade Rises." CG CGA795. 2 pt, fl, 2 oct hb, tamb, kybd.

Schalk, Carl. "The Whole Bright World Rejoices Now." CG CGA-560. U, org, opt fl, opt 1 oct hb.

Telemann, Georg Philipp/ed. Joan Conlon. "Come, Enjoy God's Festive Springtime." AFP 11-2443. U, vln, kybd.

KEYBOARD/INSTRUMENTAL

An Album of Praise. OXF. Org.

Augsburg Organ Library: Easter. AFP 11-11075.

Diemer, Emma Lou. *Suite of Easter Hymns.* SMP KK322. Org.

Fedak, Alfred V. *A Lenten/Easter Suite.* SEL 160-123. Org.

HANDBELL

Bock, Almon C., II. "This Joyful Eastertide." AFP 11-10392. 2 oct.

Geschke, Susan. "This Day of Gladness." CG CGB208. 2-3 oct.

Gramann, Fred. "O Sons and Daughters, Let Us Sing." AGEHR AG45038. 4-5 oct.

McChesney, Kevin. "Now the Green Blade Riseth." AG 1892. 3-5 oct.

McFadden, Jane. "Blessing and Honor" and "Hallelujah! Jesus Lives!" AFP 11-10573. 3-5 oct.

Stephenson, Valerie. "Crown Him." ALF AP 18565. 3-6 oct.

Thompson, Martha Lynn. "Hymn of Promise." AG 1519. 3-5 oct.

PRAISE ENSEMBLE

Haas, David. "Open the Gates." GIA G-5007. U w/desc, solo, pno, opt cong, gtr, tpt.

Hassell, Michael. "This Is the Feast of Victory." AFP 11-10677. SATB, pno, opt cong.

Hayes, Mark. "And the Father Will Dance." HIN HMC-637. SATB, kybd.

Shaw, Kirby. "Glory to God." HAL 08595448. SAB, kybd.

ALTERNATE WORSHIP TEXTS

CONFESSION AND FORGIVENESS

In the name of the Father, and of the ✚ Son, and of the Holy Spirit.
Amen

God has given to all nations the repentance that leads to life.
Let us come with repentant hearts
to the God who makes all things new.

Silence for reflection and self-examination.

Gracious God,
we confess to you all the ways
in which we dismiss the resurrection news.
Foolish and slow of heart to believe,
we turn from others and retreat in fear.
Come into our locked rooms
and breathe into us your forgiving Spirit.
Reawaken our trust and strengthen our hope,
that we may be witnesses to your saving power.
Amen

Peace be with you, my sisters and brothers.
In baptism you have received a spirit of adoption;
you are God's beloved children.
In the name of Christ your sins are forgiven.
Rejoice, and welcome this freedom as a gift.
Amen

GREETING

Alleluia! Christ is risen!
Christ is risen indeed! Alleluia!
The grace and peace of our Lord Jesus Christ,
who was raised from the dead to bring everlasting hope,
be with you all.
And also with you.

OFFERTORY PRAYER

God of blessing and glory,
with people of every language and nation
we bring the first fruits of our labor.
Let the sharing of these gifts
proclaim our joyful hope in Jesus Christ,
the first fruits of the resurrection.
Thanksgiving and honor be to you, O God,
forever and ever. Amen

INVITATION TO COMMUNION

Alleluia! Christ our Passover is sacrificed for us.
Therefore, let us keep the feast. Alleluia!

POST-COMMUNION PRAYER

Living God,
as the disciples ate and drank with their risen Lord,
we have been nourished with the very presence of Christ.
Through this meal may we be strengthened to keep your word
and to proclaim the power of your saving love
in Jesus Christ our Lord.
Amen

BENEDICTION

The God of life,
who raised Jesus from the bonds of death,
who sends forth the Spirit to renew the face of the earth,
be merciful to you and ✚ bless you, now and forever.
Amen

DISMISSAL

Rejoicing in the power of the Spirit,
go in peace to love and serve the Lord.
Thanks be to God.

191

SEASONAL RITES

CONFESSION AND FORGIVENESS WITH SPRINKLING

The order may be used before the entrance hymn or in conjunction with the entrance hymn (in procession). People are invited to turn and face the baptismal font or the place where the sprinkling bowl is located. All stand.

St. Paul writes, "As many of you as were baptized into Christ have clothed yourselves with Christ" (Gal. 3:27). As we are clothed with Christ, we are clothed with God's mercy. Standing under that mercy, we freely confess that we have sinned and fallen short of the glory of God.

Silence for self-examination.

In the waters of Holy Baptism
God liberated us from sin and death,
joining us to the death and resurrection
of our Lord Jesus Christ.
**Our life in Christ is nothing more
than a constant return to our baptism.
We daily die to sin and rise to newness of life.**

THANKSGIVING OVER THE WATER
Gracious God,
from age to age
you made water a sign of your presence among us.
In the beginning your Spirit brooded over the waters,
calling forth life that was good.
You led the people of Israel safely through the Red Sea
and into the land of promise.
In the waters of the Jordan,
you proclaimed Jesus Beloved,
the One upon whom your favor rests.

By water and the Spirit
you adopted us as your daughters and sons,
making us heirs of the promise,
and laborers for the Reign of God.

In the sprinkling of this water,
remind us of our baptism.
Shower us with your Spirit ✛,

so that we may experience anew
your forgiveness,
your grace,
and your love.
Amen

An ordained minister sprinkles the people with water, in silence or during the entrance hymn (in procession). The singing of Psalm 51 in Lent and Psalm 117 in Easter, with an appropriate antiphon, may be used in place of the entrance hymn. After the sprinkling, the liturgy of Holy Communion continues with the greeting (Kyrie or hymn of praise), and prayer of the day.

Reprinted by permission from *Worship '99* (January) Chicago: Division for Congregational Ministries, Evangelical Lutheran Church in America.

BLESSING OF ROGATION ELEMENTS

PRAYER FOR SEEDS
Hold seeds aloft.
Creating God, you have given seed to the sower and bread to the people. Nourish, protect, and bless the seeds which your people have sown in hope. By your loving and bountiful giving, may they bring forth their fruit in due season, through Jesus Christ our Lord. Amen

PRAYER FOR THE SOIL
Hold soil aloft.
Giver of life, we give you thanks that in the richness of the soil, nature awakens to your call of spring. We praise you for the smell of freshly tilled earth, the beauty of a cleanly cut furrow, and a well-plowed field. We ask that you help us to be good stewards of this land. In the name of the one who gives us new life, Jesus Christ our Lord. Amen

PRAYER FOR WATER AND RAIN
Hold water aloft.
Sustaining God, we receive the fruits of the earth from you. We give you thanks for the smell of the earth after rain, for its welcome cooling, and its necessary hydration for the land. We ask that the rain come as often as it is needed so that the crops may flourish and the coming harvest be indeed bountiful. Amen

From *Worship from the Ground Up: A Worship Resource for Town and Country Congregations.* Dubuque, Iowa: Center for Theology and Land, University of Dubuque and Wartburg Theological Seminaries, 1995. Contact 319/589-3117 for reprint permission.

APRIL 22, 2001

SECOND SUNDAY OF EASTER

INTRODUCTION

These first weeks of Easter focus our attention on appearances of the risen Lord. It is not always easy to see Jesus after his resurrection. The gospel will remind us that Jesus has a new body in which he now lives: As we gather this day to greet each other and share the peace of the Lord, may our eyes be opened to discern that we are looking at the risen body of Christ!

PRAYER OF THE DAY

Almighty God, with joy we celebrate the festival of our Lord's resurrection. Graciously help us to show the power of the resurrection in all that we say and do; through your Son, Jesus Christ our Lord, who lives and reigns with you and the Holy Spirit, one God, now and forever.

READINGS

Acts 5:27-32

Peter has been arrested for proclaiming the good news of Jesus' death and resurrection. His response to the charges of the high priest summarizes the early church's proclamation of forgiveness of sin through repentance.

Psalm 118:14-29

This is the LORD'S doing and it is marvelous in our eyes. (Ps. 118:23)

or Psalm 150

Let everything that has breath praise the LORD. (Ps. 150:6)

Revelation 1:4-8

The book of Revelation recounts a vision of the risen Christ experienced by a Christian prophet named John. Here he describes Christ as the faithful witness, or martyr; firstborn of the dead; ruler in a kingdom of priests; the one who comes; the beginning and the end of all time.

John 20:19-31

The proclamation of Easter continues in John's gospel as Jesus appears to his disciples. Jesus' words to Thomas assure us that the blessings of the resurrection are also for those who "have not seen and yet believe."

COLOR White

THE PRAYERS

In the light of Christ's resurrection, let us pray for the church, the world, and all who long for the grace of new life.

A BRIEF SILENCE.

Gracious God, in our every doubt give us peace and assurance through Christ's death and resurrection. By your Spirit breathe into us the forgiveness of sins and harmony with you. God of our salvation,

hear our prayer.

Gracious God, violence, hatred, and the misuse of drugs threaten many people in our world. May our world's leaders work to curb these threats to peace. God of our salvation,

hear our prayer.

Gracious God, continue to make yourself known to the newly baptized in this congregation, that they may hear your voice and confess you as Lord. God of our salvation,

hear our prayer.

Gracious God, we thank you for the steadfast love you show to those who are persecuted for the faith and to those who are sick (especially...). Be their strength and their might. God of our salvation,

hear our prayer.

HERE OTHER INTERCESSIONS MAY BE OFFERED.

Gracious God, we bless you for all the faithful who have lived according to your will and have died in the faith. May we be joined with them in your eternal home. God of our salvation,

hear our prayer.

Hear our prayers, O God, and grant us what we truly need, in the name of our risen Savior, Jesus Christ.

Amen

IMAGES FOR PREACHING

What takes your breath away? Is it a phone call telling of the death of a loved one? Is it news of a drive-by shooting? Or is it TV coverage of the atrocities of war? All you can say is, "Oh, no! Oh, no!"

Jesus Christ, in an act of new creation, stood among his disciples and breathed on them, giving them the

193

Holy Spirit (see also Gen. 2). This breath of new life is meant for all who have had their breath taken away. The Easter gospel wraps us in the garment of peace.

During the communion service, following the prayers and before we come to the table of our Lord, we greet one another with the words of Jesus, "Peace be with you." This greeting is not an intermission, but a solemn moment to speak Jesus' words and thus use his breath. Throughout our worship his word of peace is on our lips. In the Kyrie we pray "in peace." With the angels we sing of peace at the birth of Jesus in the hymn of praise. We pray "grant us peace" in the Lamb of God. We recall the song of Simeon as we sing, "Lord, now let your servant go in peace." And we are blessed and sent forth with the words, "Go in peace. Serve the Lord."

In our lives of faithfulness we have the opportunity to be instruments of peace, extending the peace of Christ from our worship to the world. The prayer attributed to St. Francis says, in part, "Lord, make us instruments of your peace. Where there is hatred, let us sow love; where there is injury, pardon; where there is discord, union; where there is doubt, faith; where there is despair, hope; where there is darkness, light; where there is sadness, joy" (LBW, p. 48).

WORSHIP MATTERS

The part of the liturgy called "the peace" is a formalized use of the greeting used by Jewish people: Shalom! That one word is so full of meaning: May you have peace, joy, rest, fullness of life; may you live to see your children and your children's children. The peace has been variously located within the liturgy. In the transitional position between the prayers and the offering it is both a response to the proclaimed word and a preparation for communion. Located after the words of institution, it proclaims that the Lord's sacrifice alone provides shalom. A third location with sound theological basis immediately follows the absolution in the order for confession and forgiveness. Support for this placement can be found in the liturgies for corporate and individual confession. Consider using the peace in its various liturgical locations as a tool for teaching and preaching.

LET THE CHILDREN COME

The sharing of the peace is a rather stiff, artificial moment in some churches. But when Jesus came into a locked room and said, "Peace be with you," it was not a formality. He breathed on his disciples and said, "Receive the Holy Spirit." Jesus made his sharing of the peace a life-giving, community-creating moment. The peace might include the joining of hands within each row and across the aisles, while singing, "Bind us together" (WOV 748). A child, seeing the congregation joining hands in this way, was heard to exclaim, "Wow!"

MUSIC FOR WORSHIP

GATHERING

LBW 131	Christ is risen! Alleluia!
LBW 139	O sons and daughters of the King

PSALM 118:14-29

Hruby, Dolores. *Psalms for All Seasons: An ICEL Collection.* NPM.

Kreutz, Robert. *Psalms and Selected Canticles.* OCP 8311.

Shields, Valerie. "Psalm for Easter." MSM 80-405.

Smith, Timothy R. "Give Thanks to the Lord" in STP, vol. 4.

Walker, Christopher. "Psalm 118: This Day Was Made by the Lord" in STP, vol. 3.

See Easter Day.

HYMN OF THE DAY

LBW 148	Now the green blade rises
	NOËL NOUVELET

VOCAL RESOURCES

Fleming, Larry L. "Now the Green Blade Rises." AFP 11-10658. SATB, inst.

Zgodava, Richard. "Noël nouvelet." AFP 11-0520. SATB.

INSTRUMENTAL RESOURCES

Dorian, Mark. "Noël nouvelet" in *Around the World.* AFP 11-10618. Pno.

Hyslop, Scott. "Noël nouvelet" in *Six Chorale Fantasias for Solo Instrument and Piano.* AFP 11-10799. Pno, inst.

Manz, Paul. "Noël nouvelet" in *Varied Hymn Accompaniments for Easter.* MSM 10-410. Org.

Uhl, Dan. "Now the Green Blade Rises" in *Easter Suite for Trumpet, Organ and Optional Timpani.* AFP 11-10692. Org, tpt, timp.

ALTERNATE HYMN OF THE DAY

LBW 145	Thine is the glory
WOV 675	We walk by faith and not by sight

COMMUNION

LBW 315	Love divine, all loves excelling
WOV 774	Dona nobis pacem

SENDING

LBW 260	On our way rejoicing
WOV 721	Go, my children, with my blessing

ADDITIONAL HYMNS AND SONGS

NCH 255	Jesus, sovereign savior, once for sinners slain
OBS 109	Rise, O church, like Christ arisen
TFF 228	I love to tell the story
W&P 113	Open our eyes, Lord

MUSIC FOR THE DAY

CHORAL

Bach, J. S. "Dona nobis pacem" in BAS. SATB, kybd.

Hopp, Roy. "Let Us Sing God's Praise, Rejoicing: Alleluia!" AFP 11-10959. SATB. pno.

Keesecker, Thomas. "We Walk by Faith." CPH 98-3327. SATB, kybd.

Marenzio, Luca. "Quia vidisti me, Thoma." CPH 98-2617. SATB.

Proulx, Richard. "Easter Carol." GIA G-4465. 2 pt, fl, org.

Young, Gordon. "My Master from a Garden Rose." FLA A-6087.

CHILDREN'S CHOIRS

African American spiritual. "Come and See" in LS.

Ferguson, John. "Jesus, My Lord and God." AFP 11-2246. U, org.

Leaf, Robert. "Come with Rejoicing." AFP 11-1598. U, org/pno.

Lindh, Jody W. "Praise the Lord Who Reigns Above." CG CGA-583. U, pno, opt xyl, 3 oct hb, tamb, bass.

Oliver, Curt. "Wounded Healer." MSM-50-4408. SAB, narr, kybd.

KEYBOARD/INSTRUMENTAL

Bender, Jan. "Come, You Faithful, Raise the Strain" in *Five Festive Preludes on Easter Hymns.* CPH 97-5495. Org.

Biery, James. *We Walk by Faith.* MSM-10-526. Org.

Demessieux, Jeanne. "O Filii et Filiae" in *Twelve Chorale Preludes on Gregorian Chant Themes.* SMP 0603. Org.

HANDBELL

Larson, Katherine Jordahl. "Easter Resonance." CPH 97-6624. 2-3 oct.

Laurence, Eileen. "Shalom." AG 1858. 3-5 oct.

Mozart/McChesney. "Ave Verum Corpus." JEF JHS9247. 3-4 oct.

PRAISE ENSEMBLE

British traditional/arr. David Haas. "Singing Praise to God" (Psalm 150) in PCY, vol. 9. U/2 pt, kybd, solo/duet, opt cong, gtr.

Bullock, Geoff, Gail Dunshea, and Daniel Smith. "You Are My God." WRD 301 0606 257. SATB, kybd, opt gtr, electric bass, drms, opt orch.

Post, Marie J. "Psalm 150: Hallelujah, Praise The Lord" in *Renew.* HOP.

Unknown. "Jesus Is My Lord" in *Praise & Worship.* MAR.

SUNDAY, APRIL 22
DAY OF THE CREATION (EARTH DAY)

This day calls us to attend to the glories of creation that surround us. Especially in the Northern Hemisphere, creation springs green again after the death of winter, and we are mindful of our stewardship of the earth as our God-given home. The great hymn of Francis of Assisi, "Canticle of the Sun" (see LBW 527 or the version in the autumn seasonal rites), might be sung today both for its Easter alleluias and its rejoicing in the gift of creation.

MONDAY, APRIL 23
TOYOHIKO KAGAWA, RENEWER OF SOCIETY, 1960

Toyohiko Kagawa was born in 1888 in Kobe, Japan. Orphaned early, he was disowned by his remaining extended family when he became a Christian. Kagawa wrote, spoke, and worked at length on ways to employ Christian principles in the ordering of society. His vocation to help the poor led him to live among them. He established schools, hospitals, and churches. He also worked for peace and established the Anti-War League. He was arrested for his efforts to reconcile Japan and China after the Japanese attack of 1940.

In celebration of his witness, recognize those people in your parish who work on behalf of the poor and oppressed and who, through their work, reveal the peace of Christ that is a gift of the resurrection.

WEDNESDAY, APRIL 25
ST. MARK, EVANGELIST

Though Mark himself was not an apostle, it is likely that he was a member of one of the early Christian communities. The gospel attributed to him is brief and direct. It is considered by many to be the earliest gospel. Tradition has it that Mark went to preach in Alexandria, Egypt, where he was martyred.

Mark's story of the resurrection ends with women at the tomb, who say nothing to anyone because of their fear. Though their witness faltered, the good news of the resurrection, the good news of these fifty days, has reached out to include us.

APRIL 29, 2001

INTRODUCTION

Resurrection also means reconciliation. In today's gospel, Peter's denials are trumped by a threefold commissioning from Jesus. We, too, are reconciled to one another and to God as we join in the hymn of all creation with angels and archangels and all the company of heaven: "Worthy is the Lamb who was slain!" Catherine of Siena was a fourteenth-century saint who experienced that vision in powerful ways; we remember her with thanksgiving this day.

PRAYER OF THE DAY

O God, by the humiliation of your Son you lifted up this fallen world, rescuing us from the hopelessness of death. Grant your faithful people a share in the joys that are eternal; through your Son, Jesus Christ our Lord, who lives and reigns with you and the Holy Spirit, one God, now and forever.

READINGS

Acts 9:1-6 [7-20]

Saul (later called Paul) appears for the first time in Acts at the stoning of Stephen. He becomes an ardent persecutor of the Christian church. This reading recounts his blinding and conversion experiences on the way to Damascus.

Psalm 30

You have turned my wailing into dancing. (Ps. 30:12)

Revelation 5:11-14

The vision of John recorded in Revelation offers a glimpse of cosmic worship on the Lord's Day. At its center is "the Lamb who was slain."

John 21:1-19

The risen Christ blesses his followers, especially Peter, and welcomes them to a meal of fellowship and forgiveness.

COLOR   White

THE PRAYERS

In the light of Christ's resurrection, let us pray for the church, the world, and all who long for the grace of new life.

A BRIEF SILENCE.

Ruler of all, through Jesus you fed those called to be your disciples. Bless the labors of all missionaries as they feed others with the bread of heaven. God of our salvation,

hear our prayer.

Ruler of all, guide leaders and peoples of the world to pursue peace and equality for all in the midst of chaotic changes. God of our salvation,

hear our prayer.

Ruler of all, you blessed the work of your people Israel and of Christ's disciples. Guide and bless our labors, that we may glorify your name in all we do. God of our salvation,

hear our prayer.

Ruler of all, countless saints and angels serve around your eternal throne. Assist us and all who minister in this assembly, that our praise may rise to you. God of our salvation,

hear our prayer.

Ruler of all, be gracious to those who cry for help, particularly those who face death for loving you, those who are starving, and those who are ill (especially...). God of our salvation,

hear our prayer.

HERE OTHER INTERCESSIONS MAY BE OFFERED.

Ruler of all, we praise you for the faithful departed who fed your sheep with your word, especially Catherine of Siena (and those we remember now...). God of our salvation,

hear our prayer.

Hear our prayers, O God, and grant us what we truly need, in the name of our risen Savior, Jesus Christ.

Amen

IMAGES FOR PREACHING

"Weeping may spend the night, but joy comes in the morning" (Ps. 30:6). The psalmist's insight was true for Ananias as well as Saul, and it was true for Peter. Peter is invited to a "power breakfast" with important business to transact. In what may have been eyeball-to-eyeball questioning, the Lord asks him, "Do you love me?" (John 18:12-18, 25-27). This powerful and personal encounter brings to Peter the resurrection gift of forgiveness as a call to ministry; "feed my sheep," but know that your life is no longer your own. During this Easter season we are enfolded in the garment of reconciling love.

Peter received the gift of reconciling love. This love builds the church through its ministry of outreach, as we are called to "go fishing" and to cast the net in places where we have not previously been working. Too often congregations have been described as communities of like-minded people. The mission field is the next door neighbor, just on the other side of the boat. Where else do we cast our nets to the other side of the boat?

WORSHIP MATTERS

Our two hymns of praise bracket the high points of the Jesus story. The traditional Gloria is the proclamation of the heavenly host regarding the birth of Christ, "Glory to God in the highest. . . ." The contemporary hymn of praise, extracted from the book of Revelation, is frequently assigned to the Easter season. In this canticle people sing of the feast of victory that is provided by the crucified and risen Christ.

LET THE CHILDREN COME

Nearly everyone, including children, can relate to a good fishing story. The gospel offers that—and more. At their point of discouragement, Jesus tells the disciples to cast their net on the right side of the boat. They obey and get such a large catch they are barely able to haul it in. A contemporary fishing story might be intertwined with the gospel, to show how the risen Jesus brings blessing to disciples who obey his word (and notice, he calls them *children*). Small, inexpensive fish stickers could be distributed, to be placed on a right-side window in the family car, reminding everyone of this story.

MUSIC FOR WORSHIP
GATHERING

LBW 143	Now all the vault of heaven resounds
WOV 789	Now the feast and celebration

PSALM 30

Daigle, Gary. "I Will Praise You, Lord" in PCY, vol. 4
Haas, David. PCY, vol. 3. GIA.

Ridge, M. D. "Psalm 30: I Will Praise You, Lord" in STP, vol. 3.
Schalk, Carl. PW, Cycle C.

W&P 99	Mourning into dancing

HYMN OF THE DAY

LBW 525	Blessing and honor
	AMERICAN HYMN

INSTRUMENTAL RESOURCES

Langlois, Kristina. "American Hymn" in *Three Hymns of Thanksgiving*. MSM 10-721. Org.

McFadden, Jane. "Blessing and Honor and Hallelujah, Jesus Lives!" AFP 11-10573. Hb.

Weitzel, Thomas. "American Hymn" in *Hymn Preludes and Free Accompaniments*, vol. 23. AFP 11-9422. Org.

ALTERNATE HYMN OF THE DAY

LBW 154	That Easter day with joy was bright
WOV 791	Alabaré

COMMUNION

LBW 385	What wondrous love is this
WOV 801	Thine the amen, thine the praise

SENDING

LBW 210	At the Lamb's high feast we sing
WOV 754	Let us talents and tongues employ

ADDITIONAL HYMNS AND SONGS

ASG 8	Feed my lambs
HS98 910	Splendor and honor
RS 807	You walk along our shoreline
TFF 282	Let all that is within me cry, "Holy!"
W&P 21	Blessing, honor, and glory

MUSIC FOR THE DAY
CHORAL

Bullard, Alan. "Come, Let Us Join Our Cheerful Songs." GIA G-4312. SAB, org.

Cherwien, David, and Susan Palo Cherwien. "Blessing Be and Glory to the Living One." AFP 11-10918. U/2 pt, org, 2 inst.

de Prez, Josquin. "O Mighty Word from God Come Down" in CC. SATB.

Handel, G. F. "Worthy Is the Lamb" in *Messiah*. GSCH. SATB, kybd.

Hopp, Roy. "Let Us Sing God's Praise Rejoicing: Alleluia." AFP 11-10959. SATB, pno.

Willan, Healey. "O Sacred Feast." HWG GCMR 715.

197

CHILDREN'S CHOIRS

Folkening, John. "Feed Us, Jesus" in LS.

Nelson, Ronald A. "Alabaré." AMSI H658. 2 pt mxd, kybd.

Ramseth, Betty Ann. "Do You Love Me?" in *Have You Seen My Lord?* AFP 11-9226. U/SATB, pno, gtr, str bass.

Sleeth, Natalie. "Feed My Lambs." CFI CM 7777. U, kybd, 2 fl.

KEYBOARD/INSTRUMENTAL

Billingham, Richard. "I've Just Come from the Fountain" in *Seven Reflections on African American Spirituals.* AFP 11-10762. Org.

Couperin, François. "Elevation" from *Mass for the Convents.* KAL K03315. Org.

HANDBELL

Maggs, Charles. "All Creatures of Our God and King." Genesis Press GP1013. 3-4 oct.

McChesney, Kevin. "Awake, My Soul." Ringing Word RW8099. 4-6 oct.

Tucker, Sondra. "Come Away to the Skies." CPH 97-6739. 3-5 oct.

PRAISE ENSEMBLE

Cull, Bob, and Tom Fettke. "Open Our Eyes, Lord" in *The Lord Is My Song.* LIL MB-609. SATB.

White, Phil. "Glory, Glory to the King" in *Hosanna! Music, #3.* INT.

SUNDAY, APRIL 29
CATHERINE OF SIENA, TEACHER, 1380

Catherine of Siena was a member of the Order of Preachers (Dominicans), and among Roman Catholics she was the first woman to receive the title Doctor of the Church. She was a contemplative and is known for her mystical visions of Jesus. Catherine was a humanitarian who worked to alleviate the suffering of the poor and imprisoned. She was also a renewer of church and society and advised both popes and any uncertain persons who told her their problems.

Catherine's life is a reminder that prayer and activism belong together and that the glorious vision in today's second reading from Revelation can lead to Jesus' commission to Peter in the gospel, "Feed my sheep."

TUESDAY, MAY 1
ST. PHILIP AND ST. JAMES, APOSTLES

Philip, one of the first disciples of Jesus, after following Jesus invited Nathanael to "come and see." According to tradition, he preached in Asia Minor and died as a martyr in Phrygia. James, the son of Alphaeus, is called "the less" to distinguish him from another apostle named James, commemorated July 25. Philip and James are commemorated together because the remains of these two saints were placed in the Church of the Apostles in Rome on this day in 561.

During these fifty days of Easter, how can your community invite others to come and see the new life of Christ?

WEDNESDAY, MAY 2
ATHANASIUS, BISHOP OF ALEXANDRIA, 373

Athanasius attended the Council of Nicea in 325 as a deacon and secretary to the bishop of Alexandria. At the council and when he himself served as bishop of Alexandria, he defended the full divinity of Christ against the Arian position held by emperors, magistrates, and theologians. Because of his defense of the divinity of Christ he was considered a troublemaker and was banished from Alexandria on five separate occasions.

Athanasius is an appropriate saint to be remembered at Easter. His name means "deathless one," though he himself lived in threat of death because of his theological stands. We are made in God's likeness, Athanasius affirmed. By the resurrection we are remade in the likeness of the Son, who has conquered death.

FRIDAY, MAY 4
MONICA, MOTHER OF AUGUSTINE, 387

Monica was married to a pagan husband who was illtempered and unfaithful. She rejoiced greatly when both her husband and his mother became Christian. But she is best known because she is the mother of Augustine. Monica had been a disciple of Ambrose, and eventually Augustine came under his influence. Almost everything we know about Monica comes from Augustine's *Confessions,* his autobiography. Her dying wish was that her son remember her at the altar of the Lord, wherever he was.

Monica's life bore witness to the vital role that parents play in the faith formation of their children. Consider how the church supports parents in that task.

MAY 6, 2001

FOURTH SUNDAY OF EASTER

INTRODUCTION

With the fourth Sunday of Easter the gospel readings turn away from resurrection appearances of Jesus and begin to focus on echoes of Jesus' earlier words that had pointed toward his death and resurrection during his ministry. He meant to go this path all along. As we listen to Jesus' words from the tenth chapter of John's gospel, we learn that Jesus is both shepherd as well as the victorious Lamb. Peter is a shepherd like Jesus as he leads one of Jesus' sheep from death to life.

PRAYER OF THE DAY

God of all power, you called from death our Lord Jesus, the great shepherd of the sheep. Send us as shepherds to rescue the lost, to heal the injured, and to feed one another with knowledge and understanding; through your Son, Jesus Christ our Lord, who lives and reigns with you and the Holy Spirit, one God, now and forever.

or

Almighty God, you show the light of your truth to those in darkness, to lead them into the way of righteousness. Give strength to all who are joined in the family of the Church, so that they will resolutely reject what erodes their faith and firmly follow what faith requires; through your Son, Jesus Christ our Lord, who lives and reigns with you and the Holy Spirit, one God, now and forever.

READINGS

Acts 9:36-43

When Dorcas, faithful minister to the widows of Joppa, fell ill and died, Peter raised her back to life through the power of prayer.

Psalm 23

The Lord is my shepherd; I shall not be in want. (Ps. 23:1)

Revelation 7:9-17

Christ is the shepherd who leads his faithful to springs of the water of life. Christ is also the lamb who vanquishes sin and suffering, in whose blood the saints have washed their robes and made them white.

John 10:22-30

Three times Jesus says that his sheep are secure; no one will snatch them from Jesus' or the Father's hands. The sheep have eternal life and so shall never perish.

COLOR White

THE PRAYERS

In the light of Christ's resurrection, let us pray for the church, the world, and all who long for the grace of new life.

A BRIEF SILENCE.

Watchful Shepherd, allow your church, the sheep of your flock, to hear your voice through the pastors, bishops, and other leaders you have given to tend to your church. God of our salvation,

hear our prayer.

Watchful Shepherd, as we look to the heavenly Jerusalem where people of every tribe and nation gather, establish peace among the diverse ethnic groups that live throughout our world. God of our salvation,

hear our prayer.

Watchful Shepherd, give increase to the fields tended by all farmers. Increase in us gratitude for those who grow the land's crops and who produce the food that nourishes us. God of our salvation,

hear our prayer.

Watchful Shepherd, instill in us devotion to serve all people in your name. Strengthen the service ministries of our congregation and synod. God of our salvation,

hear our prayer.

Watchful Shepherd, gather under your protective care all who feel neglected or shunned in our society, all who are oppressed by persecution, and all who suffer physical ailments (especially…). God of our salvation,

hear our prayer.

HERE OTHER INTERCESSIONS MAY BE OFFERED.

Watchful Shepherd, wipe away the tears of those who mourn the death of loved ones. May we one day sing with all whose robes have been washed in the blood of the Lamb. God of our salvation,

199

hear our prayer.

Hear our prayers, O God, and grant us what we truly need, in the name of our risen Savior, Jesus Christ. **Amen**

IMAGES FOR PREACHING

Whom do we trust? Whose voice calls us? A mother calls her children to get ready for bed. A teacher calls his students to gather around him and listen to a poem. A firefighter's voice calls more urgently, "Get out now!" A doctor says, "You need to come in to see me, soon." A lover asks, "Will you marry me?" A child calls her puppy to come and eat. These voices are heard and trusted. This entrustment, this faith, is more than an intellectual assent. It is an affirmative response. Today we are clothed with the resurrection garment of trust.

The image of the good shepherd dominates this Sunday in the Easter season. During this year, in the three-year cycle of texts from John 10, the emphasis is on the protection of the shepherd, that is, the resurrected Jesus Christ who says, "My sheep hear my voice. I know them, and they follow me." "No one will snatch them out of my hand." We have heard the stories of Mary Magdalene, Thomas, and Peter. All of them heard the good shepherd call them. And they followed.

Each week, the congregation gathers for worship and hears the pastor proclaim the gospel in the form of a sermon. The sermon, simple or eloquent, is a moment when the people of God's pasture are listening for the good shepherd's voice that calls them by name. The sermon, for many faithful Christians, is a time of entrustment to the Word who is spoken.

Nurtured by the word of the good shepherd, faithful Christians go each week into the routines of their daily lives to reflect the image of the good shepherd. Perhaps few Christians will face the "great ordeal" of first-century martyrs. Yet the witness of these martyrs may strengthen our faith during the times when we need to be guided "to springs of the water of life" and know that "God will wipe away every tear from [our] eyes."

WORSHIP MATTERS

One of Luke's unifying theological themes can be found at the beginning of the gospel (Luke 2:37) when the prophet Anna does exactly what the disciples do at the conclusion: "and they were continually in the temple blessing God" (24:53). Is this behavior a concern or an interest for the faithful of this age? Have we been taught to understand the importance of daily prayer and devotion? Do we yearn to be fed on the word of the Lord? These texts encourage us to become familiar with and to use the church's daily prayer offices, devotional scripture reading, table blessings, and other prayers throughout the day. Acknowledgment of the corporate nature of daily prayer—even when one is alone—helps to underscore the glorious gathering in the reign of God.

LET THE CHILDREN COME

Even without looking, children can recognize the voice of their mother or father, their teacher or pastor, their friends. Jesus says, "My sheep hear my voice. I know them, and they follow me." The quality of the preacher's voice is important. Harsh, strident voices declaring God's love will sound inappropriate, even if the words are true. Be conscious of your voice quality, and practice speaking the words of Jesus as he may have said them—with warmth, sincerity, and gentleness. Hearing the shepherd's voice ought to be a pleasant, reassuring experience, never ponderous or intimidating.

MUSIC FOR WORSHIP

GATHERING

LBW 175 Ye watchers and ye holy ones
WOV 691 Sing with all the saints in glory

PSALM 23

Haas, David. "You Are My Shepherd" in PCY, vol. 9.

Schalk, Carl. PW, Cycle C.

Smith, Timothy R. "The Lord Is My Shepherd" in STP, vol. 4.

Young, Jeremy. PW, Cycle B.

LBW 451 The Lord's my shepherd

LBW 456 The King of love my shepherd is

HYMN OF THE DAY

LBW 456 The King of love my shepherd is
       St. Columba

VOCAL RESOURCES

Bouman, Paul. "The King of Love My Shepherd Is." MSM 60-9009. SATB, cong, ob, org.

Busarow, Donald. "St. Columba" in *All Praise to You, Eternal God*. AFP 11-9076. 2 pt canon, org.

INSTRUMENTAL RESOURCES

Cherwien, David. "St. Columba" in *Organ Plus One*. AFP 11-10758.
Org, inst.

Herald, Terry. "St. Columba" in *Hymn Accompaniment for Instrumental
Ensembles*. CPH 97-6263. Inst.

Kane, Daniel Q. "St. Columba" in *Selectable Delectables*. AFP 11-10619.
Kybd.

Sedio, Mark. "St. Columba" in *Music for the Paschal Season*.
AFP 11-10763. Org.

ALTERNATE HYMN OF THE DAY

LBW 371   With God as our friend
WOV 673   I'm so glad Jesus lifted me

COMMUNION

LBW 476   Have no fear, little flock
WOV 711   You satisfy the hungry heart

SENDING

LBW 196   Praise the Lord, rise up rejoicing
WOV 671   Alleluia, alleluia, give thanks

ADDITIONAL HYMNS AND SONGS

ASG 23   My good shepherd is the Lord
RS 699   You, Lord, are both lamb and shepherd
TFF 180   Oh, when the saints go marching in
W&P 130   Spirit song
W&P 15   Be bold, be strong

MUSIC FOR THE DAY

CHORAL

Bach, J. S. "Flocks in Pastures Green Abiding" in *The Oxford Easy Anthem Book*. OXF. SATB, org.

Bell, John, and John Ferguson. "We Will Lay Our Burden Down."
GIA G-4221. SATB, solo or cong, fl.

Boumann, Paul. "The Lord Is My Shepherd." CPH 98-2911. U, kybd.

Ellingboe, Bradley. "Jesus, Good Shepherd." AFP 11-10969.
SATB, pno/harp.

Schalk, Carl. "Thine the Amen, Thine the Praise." AFP 11-2173.
SATB, opt cong, org.

Schütz, Heinrich. "O Lord, I Trust Your Shepherd Care" in CC.
SATB, org.

Thomson, Virgil. "My Shepherd Will Supply My Need."
HWG GCMR 2046.

CHILDREN'S CHOIRS

Archer, Malcolm. "The Lord's My Shepherd." GIA G-4645. 2 pt, org.

Christopherson, Dorothy. "The Lord Is My Shepherd." AFP 11-4691.
U, hb, kybd, opt sign language.

Pote, Allen. "The Lord Is My Shepherd." CG CGA-551, SAT, SAB, or
SATB, pno.

Traditional. "The Lord Is My Shepherd" in LS.

Wienhorst, Richard. "The King of Love My Shepherd Is."
CG CGA-602. U/2 pt trbl/SATB, org, opt 2 fl.

Wold, Wayne. "Jesus, Shepherd Us" in LS.

KEYBOARD/INSTRUMENTAL

Held, Wilbur. *The Lord Is My Shepherd: Six Hymn Settings on Psalm 23*.
MSM-10-420. Org.

Uehlein, Christopher. "Pastorale No.1" and "Pastorale No.2" in *Blue
Cloud Abbey Book*. AFP 11-10394. Org.

Wright, Searle. "Prelude on 'Brother James' Air.'" OXF 93-103. Org.

HANDBELL

Larson, Katherine Jordahl. "Beautiful Savior." AFP 11-10516. 3-4 oct.

Lichlyer, Mary. "My Shepherd Will Supply My Need." CG CGB191.
3 oct.

Starks, Howard F. "Beside Still Waters." AG 1047. 3 oct.

PRAISE ENSEMBLE

Dresie, Deborah. "Gentle Shepherd." BEC BP1469. SATB, kybd.

Haugen, Marty. "Shepherd Me, O God" in PCY, vol. 2. U/SATB,
kybd, solo/duet, opt cong, gtr.

TUESDAY, MAY 8
VICTOR THE MOOR, MARTYR, 303

Known also as Victor Marus, this native of the African
country of Mauritania was a Christian from his youth.
He served as a soldier in the Praetorian Guard. Under
the persecution of Maximian, Victor died for his faith at
Milan. Few details are known about his life, but many
churches in the diocese of Milan are dedicated to him.

MAY 13, 2001

INTRODUCTION

Visions of the end time work their way into our Easter worship. A strange and wondrous vision from God instructs Peter about how wide the new fellowship in Christ might be. John's vision of a new Jerusalem suggests that beginnings and endings are tied to Jesus. And in the gospel, Jesus begins to prepare his disciples for his departure. We, too, gather this day as Jesus' end-time community, with one foot planted in this world and the other in the world to come.

PRAYER OF THE DAY

O God, form the minds of your faithful people into a single will. Make us love what you command and desire what you promise, that, amid all the changes of this world, our hearts may be fixed where true joy is found; through your Son, Jesus Christ our Lord, who lives and reigns with you and the Holy Spirit, one God, now and forever.

READINGS

Acts 11:1-18

In defense of his earlier baptism of pagan believers, Peter demonstrates to the members of the Jerusalem church that God's intention to save Gentiles as well as Jews is revealed in Jesus' own testimony. In this way the mission to the Gentiles is officially authorized.

Psalm 148

The splendor of the LORD is over earth and heaven.
(Ps. 148:13)

Revelation 21:1-6

John's vision shows us that in the resurrection the new age has dawned; God dwells with us already. Yet we wait for the time when the tears that cloud our vision will be wiped away. Then we will see the new heaven, new earth, and new Jerusalem.

John 13:31-35

Jesus speaks of his glorification on the cross. As Jesus loves, even to death on the cross, so ought his disciples love one another. Indeed, love will be the distinctive mark of Jesus' community.

COLOR White

THE PRAYERS

In the light of Christ's resurrection, let us pray for the church, the world, and all who long for the grace of new life.

A BRIEF SILENCE.

Alpha and Omega, you have promised us a new heaven and a new earth. Prepare us to live forever in the place where you will dwell with us as our God. God of our salvation,

hear our prayer.

Alpha and Omega, the pressure of growing populations and cultural changes challenges the leaders of many cities and countries in our world. Encourage them with your wisdom to pursue what is right and just. God of our salvation,

hear our prayer.

Alpha and Omega, we honor you for the gift of mothers. Shower them with such charity that they continue to love as Christ has loved them. God of our salvation,

hear our prayer.

Alpha and Omega, awaken our community to your love and cast away our prejudices, so that we may welcome those whom you have welcomed. God of our salvation,

hear our prayer.

Alpha and Omega, defend from harm those who suffer for being your disciples. Strengthen those who are weak and sick (especially...). God of our salvation,

hear our prayer.

HERE OTHER INTERCESSIONS MAY BE OFFERED.

Alpha and Omega, give the vision of your new Jerusalem to all who are dying. Even in the midst of death, may they praise you with the hosts of heaven. God of our salvation,

hear our prayer.

Hear our prayers, O God, and grant us what we truly need, in the name of our risen Savior, Jesus Christ.

Amen

IMAGES FOR PREACHING

The resurrection garment that we are given today is the commandment to love. Many will notice that this text, appointed for the Fifth Sunday of Easter, fits well with a

202

celebration of life in Christian families and Mother's Day. In John's gospel, love flows from God to humankind (John 3:16; 15:9). This love is defined by Christ: "No one has greater love than this, to lay down one's life for one's friends" (John 15:13).

When congregations assemble for Sunday worship, members come prepared to give an offering. In the worship practice of Christians in the African country of Cameroon, the offering is not received in offering baskets that are passed from person to person as they sit in a pew. People bring their offering forward, singing and dancing as they make their way, one person following another in procession. Their offerings are not monetary, but consist mostly of food offerings. These offerings are received and blessed, and then distributed to those in need or sold. This kind of direct care for those in need has its counterpart in the United States as congregations support local food shelves and the World Hunger Appeal. With creativity, this sharing of love can be brought into the congregation's worship life at the offering.

Martin Luther and Katherine von Bora were married on June 13, 1525, and built a life together. Their story is worth telling on this day. When the university at Wittenberg was closed because of the plague, they chose to stay and turn their home into a hospital. Martin came to understand that marriage is a Christian vocation in which the fruits of faith may be expressed. Marriage "even provides men with the ethical power to meet all the daily demands of life—including even the washing of diapers to the glory of God!" He also spoke of raising children as "the noblest and most precious work of them all," and the role of parents as being "the children's apostles, bishops, and pastors" (see William Lazareth, *Luther on the Christian Home* [Philadelphia: Muhlenberg Press, 1960], pp. 217–20).

WORSHIP MATTERS

Having addressed the importance of a regular prayer life last week, it might be helpful to examine one particular way we address God. Jesus teaches us to pray, "Our Father. . . ." Sensitivity to the plight of those abandoned or abused by their fathers has caused serious questions to be raised about the use of this name, though. One answer seems to be total abandonment of the name; a second is to use other names. A third solution allows us to exercise the name revealed to us by Jesus and still address the contemporary concern. That solution is to

teach the faithful that earthly fatherhood is derived from the heavenly fatherhood, not vice versa. Fathers of this world need to be encouraged to uphold the honor of this name and to accept the responsibility that comes with bearing it.

LET THE CHILDREN COME

Jesus tells the disciples ("little children") that they are to love one another as he has loved them. Examples of love within a family might be highlighted. Children learn to share by the simple formula, "One for you, one for me." When we pray "Our Father in heaven," we claim the family to which Jesus invites us. What we ask for ourselves, we also seek for others: daily bread, forgiveness of sins, saving from trial, deliverance from evil. Praying the Lord's Prayer is a profound expression of love for our brothers and sisters for whom we pray.

MUSIC FOR WORSHIP

GATHERING

LBW 140 With high delight let us unite
WOV 674 Alleluia! Jesus is risen

PSALM 148

Hobby, Robert A. PW, Cycle C.

Hopson, Hal H. TP.

Schalk, Carl. PW, Cycle C.

Smith, J. "Let All Praise the Name of the Lord." GIA G-2989.

LBW 540 Praise the Lord! O heavens

LBW 541 Praise the Lord of heaven!

See first Sunday after Christmas.

HYMN OF THE DAY

LBW 143 Now all the vault of heaven resounds
LASST UNS ERFREUEN

VOCAL RESOURCES

Hobby, Robert A. "Now All the Vault of Heaven Resounds."
AFP 11-10998. SAB, org, 2 tpt, opt hb, cong.

INSTRUMENTAL RESOURCES

Albrecht, Timothy R. "Lasst uns erfreuen" in *Grace Notes VII.*
AFP 11-10856. Org.

Dahl, David P. "Lasst uns erfreuen" in *Hymn Interpretations for Organ.*
AFP 11-10972. Org.

Porter, Rachel Trelstad. "Lasst uns erfreuen" in *Day by Day.*
AFP 11-10772. Pno.

Rose, Richard. "Lasst uns erfreuen" in *Hymnal Companion for Woodwinds, Brass and Percussion, Series 1.* CPH 97-6714. Inst.

ALTERNATE HYMN OF THE DAY

| LBW 363 | Christ is alive! Let Christians sing |
| WOV 666 | Great God, your love has called us |

COMMUNION

| LBW 331 | Jerusalem, my happy home |
| WOV 664 | A new commandment |

SENDING

| LBW 533/4 | Now thank we all our God |
| WOV 742 | Come, we that love the Lord |

ADDITIONAL HYMNS AND SONGS

H82 286	Who are these like stars appearing
PH 453	O holy city, seen of John
TFF 41	I want to be ready
W&P 154	We will glorify

MUSIC FOR THE DAY

CHORAL

Aston, Peter. "I Give You a New Commandment." GIA G-4331. 2 pt, org.

Bainton, Edgar L. "And I Saw a New Heaven." NOV 29 0342 03. SATB, org.

Benson, Robert. "Wondrous Love." AFP 11-10993. SATB, org.

Duruflé, Maurice. "Ubi caritas." DUR 312-41253. SATTBB.

Farlee, Robert Buckley. "Mandatum." AFP 11-10535. SATB.

Laster, James H. "Ubi caritas." CPH 98-3338. SATB, org.

Sedio, Mark. "Each New Day/*Al despuntar en la loma el día.*" AFP 11-10968. SATB, 2 C inst, perc, pno.

CHILDREN'S CHOIRS

Hruby, Dolores. "Help Us Accept Each Other." CG CGA713. U, kybd, opt fl, opt gtr.

Traditional. "Love God and Your Neighbor" in LS.

Wold, Wayne L. "Build New Bridges." AFP 11-10879. U, opt 2 pt, kybd.

KEYBOARD/INSTRUMENTAL

Albrecht, Timothy. "Christ Is Alive! Let Christians Sing" in *Grace Notes VIII.* AFP 11-10970. Org.

Kerr, J. Wayne. *Theme and Variations on "Jesus Loves Me."* CPH 97-6788. Org.

Weyrauch, Johannes. "Nun bitten wir" in *An Eternity of Praise: Thirty Chorale Preludes from Present-Day Germany,* compiled by John A. Behnke. CPH 97-6782. Org.

HANDBELL

Kerr, J. Wayne. "A Joyous Song." AGEHR AG 35047. 3-5 oct.

McCleary, Mary G. "Psalm 148." AGEHR AG 35030. 3-5 oct.

Stephenson, Valerie. "Joyous Spirit." RRM. 3-5 oct.

PRAISE ENSEMBLE

Haas, David. "Praise in the Heights" in PCY, vol. 9. U with desc, kybd, solo, opt cong, gtr.

Haugen, Marty. "Gathered in the Love of Christ." GIA G-5066. 2 pt, solo, cong, gtr, kybd, opt fl, ob, cello.

Hayford, Jack. "Praise the Name of Jesus, Praise the Son of God" in *Hosanna! Music,* #10. INT.

Ryder, Dennis. "Beloved, Let Us Love One Another" in *All God's People Sing.* CPH.

MONDAY, MAY 14
PACHOMIUS, RENEWER OF THE CHURCH, 346

Pachomius was born in Egypt about 290. He became a Christian during his service as a soldier. In 320 he went to live as a hermit in Upper Egypt, where other hermits lived nearby. Pachomius organized them into a religious community in which the members prayed together and held their goods in common. His rule for monasteries influenced both Eastern and Western monasticism through the Rule of Basil and the Rule of Benedict respectively.

The Egyptian (Coptic) church may be unfamiliar to many Western Christians. Use the commemoration of Pachomius to teach about the Egyptian church at parish gatherings this week.

FRIDAY, MAY 18
ERIK, KING OF SWEDEN, MARTYR, 1160

Erik, long considered the patron saint of Sweden, ruled there from 1150 to 1160. He is honored for efforts to bring peace to the nearby pagan kingdoms and for his crusades to spread the Christian faith in Scandinavia. He established a protected Christian mission in Finland that was led by Henry of Uppsala. As king, Erik was noted for his desire to establish fair laws and courts and for his concern for those who were poor or sick. Erik was killed by a Danish army that approached him at worship on the day after the Ascension. He is reported to have said to them, "Let us at least finish the sacrifice. The rest of the feast I shall keep elsewhere." As he left worship he was killed.

The commemoration of Erik could be the beginning of a discussion on the relationship between civil rule and the place of faith in the public sphere.

SATURDAY, MAY 19
DUNSTAN, ARCHBISHOP OF CANTERBURY, 988

By Dunstan's time, Viking invaders had wiped out English monasticism. Dunstan played an important role in its restoration. He was commissioned by King Edmund to reestablish monastic life at Glastonbury, which became a center for monasticism and learning.

He was exiled by a later king, Edwy, whom he had publicly rebuked. After Edwy's death Dunstan was made Archbishop of Canterbury and carried out a reform of church and state. He corrected abuses by the clergy, encouraged laity in their devotional life, and was committed to concerns of justice. He was also well known as a musician and for his painting and metal work.

MAY 20, 2001

SIXTH SUNDAY OF EASTER

INTRODUCTION

Visions are the distinctive mark of this day. Paul receives a vision from God telling him that he needs to leap from one continent to another to take the good news abroad. John the Seer shares his vision of the new Jerusalem—an image of what it means to live with God. Jesus is the reflection of God's plan for the world and for our lives.

PRAYER OF THE DAY

O God, from whom all good things come: Lead us by the inspiration of your Spirit to think those things which are right, and by your goodness help us to do them; through your Son, Jesus Christ our Lord, who lives and reigns with you and the Holy Spirit, one God, now and forever.

READINGS

Acts 16:9-15

A vision compels Paul to move his ministry into Greece. There he meets Lydia, an important person in the business community, whose heart has been opened by God to receive the gospel. Her conversion and baptism provide the impetus for the founding of the church at Philippi.

Psalm 67

Let the nations be glad and sing for joy. (Ps. 67:4)

Revelation 21:10, 22—22:5

John's vision of a new Jerusalem coming out of heaven provides continuity with God's past actions. Yet in this new city, God's presence replaces the temple, and the glory of God and the Lamb supplant sun and moon.

John 14:23-29

Jesus promises to send the Advocate to teach and remind us of all Jesus taught. Under this Spirit's guidance, we shall gain a deepened understanding of what Jesus has told us, and we shall experience Jesus' gift of peace that overcomes fear.

or John 5:1-9

Jesus heals on the Sabbath.

COLOR White

THE PRAYERS

In the light of Christ's resurrection, let us pray for the church, the world, and all who long for the grace of new life.

A BRIEF SILENCE.

God, source of all good, through your generous gifts move us to give of ourselves. Lead us to offer such hospitality to all people. God of our salvation,

hear our prayer.

God, source of all good, you bless all the ends of the earth. May all the world's people praise and revere your goodness. God of our salvation,

hear our prayer.

God, source of all good, make your home with every family facing the struggles of life. Strengthen parents and children with your peace and confidence. God of our salvation,

hear our prayer.

God, source of all good, bring contentment to the troubled hearts of those who feel unloved, who are persecuted, and who are ill (especially…). God of our salvation,

hear our prayer.

God, source of all good, we thank you for those called to public vocations of ministry. Lead each one of us in paths of service. God of our salvation,

hear our prayer.

HERE OTHER INTERCESSIONS MAY BE OFFERED.

God, source of all good, your servants who have gone before us now live in the radiance of your face. May we also see the light of your glory forever. God of our salvation,

hear our prayer.

Hear our prayers, O God, and grant us what we truly need, in the name of our risen Savior, Jesus Christ.

Amen

IMAGES FOR PREACHING

What makes a house "a home"? Asking various people that question brings differing answers. It is relationships, personal space, orderliness, beauty, my stuff that reflects my character, safety, nurture, calmness, and many other things. When you move into a new house, what is the first thing you bring? Jesus promises that he will come and make a home with us. A trinitarian character enters into this homemaking: the promise of a relationship that brings us into the sacred life of God; love makes this house a home; and peace is the first thing that Jesus brings in his homemaking.

What new relationships, characterized by love and peace, are given to us as a garment of resurrection life? Certainly, they include those with whom we share life in Christian community. Our being "in Christ" means that we see each other in a new light. (See 2 Cor. 5:16-21 for this theme of being in Christ.) As the congregation gathers for worship each Sunday, a transformation takes place. We come from our many individual lives, and through the celebration of word and sacrament we are made the church of Christ, a new being.

Just as the entrance to the church is a place of gathering where we prepare to enter into new relationships that have been created by the homemaking of Jesus Christ, so too may our homes become places of love and peace. A prayer in "Blessing of a Dwelling" says, "O God, we pray that you will bless this home and *those* who *live* here with your gracious presence, that your love may be *their* inspiration, your wisdom *their* guide,

your truth *their* light, and your peace *their* benediction; through Jesus Christ our Lord. Amen" (*Occasional Services,* p. 190).

WORSHIP MATTERS

What is God's name? Is it simply *Father*? Of course not. Where would that leave the other two persons of the Trinity? The best place to find God's name is to look at God's signature on a contract. For instance, what signature is found on the binding contract of holy baptism? More like a simple mark than a signature, it is the signing of a cross of Christ, the signing by which God has chosen to be present in our lives. But that is not all, for as God's name is signed, so also it is spoken for all to hear, that this signing is done "In the name of the Father and of the Son and of the Holy Spirit." As an emblem on our forehead, we forever carry a full and complete name for God: Father, Son, and Holy Spirit.

LET THE CHILDREN COME

We know a lot about many products by their labels: Coca-Cola, McDonald's, Disney. Imagine if people were "labeled." We *are*, and we *can be!* Nametags may be worn by all in church this Sunday to help people know one another by name. But in the second reading (Rev. 22:4) we discover we wear another "nametag," the name of Christ the Lamb upon our foreheads. This Sunday would be a good opportunity for all the baptized to retrace the cross on their foreheads with water from the font. We are labeled with the name of Christ to be his disciples forever.

MUSIC FOR WORSHIP
SERVICE MUSIC

Echoing today's gospel, sing "Dona nobis pacem" (WOV 774) at the breaking of the bread. Sing in unison once through, then begin in canon with the congregation, adding the choir and an instrument for the second and third parts.

GATHERING

| LBW 393 | Rise, shine, you people! |
| WOV 745 | Awake, O sleeper |

PSALM 67

Gieseke, Richard. "May the People Praise You, O God." CPH 98-3428.

Haas, David. "May God Bless Us with Mercy" in PCY, vol. 8.

Kogut, Malcolm. "May God Bless Us in His Mercy" in PCY, vol. 10.

Makeever, Ray. "Let All the People Praise You" in DH.

Schalk, Carl. PW, Cycle C.

LBW 335   May God bestow on us his grace

HYMN OF THE DAY

WOV 674   Alleluia! Jesus is risen!
EARTH AND ALL STARS

INSTRUMENTAL RESOURCES

Cook, Larry. "Earth and All Stars/Rise, Shine, You People."
AFP 11-10712. Org, brass, timp, cong.

Manz, Paul. "Earth and All Stars" in *Nine Hymn Improvisations*.
MSM 10-875. Org.

Organ, Anne Krentz. "Earth and All Stars/Alleluia! Jesus Is Risen."
AFP 11-10987. Hb.

Organ, Anne Krentz. "Earth and All Stars" in *On Eagle's Wings: Piano Reflections*. AFP 11-10711.

Uhl, Dan. "Alleluia! Jesus Is Risen" in *Easter Suite for Trumpet, Organ and Optional Timpani*. AFP 11-10692.

ALTERNATE HYMN OF THE DAY

LBW 166   All glory be to God on high
LBW 358   Glories of your name are spoken

COMMUNION

LBW 508   Come down, O Love divine
WOV 690   Shall we gather at the river

SENDING

LBW 386   Christ is the king!
WOV 781   My life flows on in endless song

ADDITIONAL HYMNS AND SONGS

PH 486   When the morning stars together
TFF 258   I've got peace like a river
W3 643   For the healing of the nations
W&P 88   Lift up your heads
W&P 158   You are mine

MUSIC FOR THE DAY

CHORAL

Harris, William H. "Come Down, O Love Divine." NOV 29 0470 05.
SATB, org.

Proulx, Richard. "Our Paschal Lamb, That Sets Us Free." AFP 12-106.
SATB, org.

Schalk, Carl. "Thine the Amen, Thine the Praise." AFP 11-2173.
SATB, opt cong, org.

Schulz-Widmar, Russell. "Jerusalem, Jerusalem." AFP 11-10646.
2 pt, kybd.

Scott, K. Lee. "The Tree of Life." MSM 50-3000. SATB, org, opt cong.

Shephard, Richard. "The Secret of Christ." GIA G-4186. SATB, org.

CHILDREN'S CHOIRS

Christopherson, Dorothy. "Let All the Peoples Praise God."
CPH 98-3453. SSA, kybd.

Exner, Max V. "Wade in the Water." CG CGA-572. U, kybd.

Litz, Helen. "Prayer of St. Francis." CG CGA-242. U/2 pt, hp/kybd.

Praetorius, Michael. "God Gave to Me a Life to Live" in LS.

KEYBOARD/INSTRUMENTAL

Burkhardt, Michael. "Like the Murmur of the Dove's Song" in *Eight Improvisations on Twentieth-Century Hymn Tunes*. MSM-10-707.
Org.

Wold, Wayne L. "Glorious Things of Thee Are Spoken" in *Songs of Thankfulness and Praise, Set 1*. MSM-10-711. Org.

Young, Jeremy. "How Can I Keep From Singing" in *At the Foot of the Cross*. AFP 11-10688. Pno.

HANDBELL

Peel, Deborah. "Tapestry on 'St. Anne.'" AGEHR AG 45016. 4-5 oct.

Wood, Dale. "Shall We Gather at the River." CG CGB47. 3 oct.

PRAISE ENSEMBLE

Haas, David. "Peace I Leave With You." GIA G-4869. SAB, kybd, opt cong, gtr.

Routledge, Keith. "My Peace" in *Praise Hymns and Choruses*, 4th ed.
MAR.

207

MONDAY, MAY 21

JOHN ELIOT, MISSIONARY TO THE AMERICAN INDIANS, 1690

John Eliot was born in England, and his first career was as a schoolteacher. In 1631 he came to New England to preach to the Puritan settlers. In New England he developed an interest in the Algonkian Indians and learned their language and customs. He published a catechism in 1654 and in 1658 translated the scriptures into Algonkian, preparing the first complete Bible printed in the colonies. Eliot also established towns for Indians who had converted to Christianity. These towns were away from Puritan colonies and were established so that the Algonkians could preserve their own culture and live according to their own laws. Eliot also trained indigenous leaders to serve as missionaries to their own people.

As we pray for greater respect and justice for indigenous peoples, use this commemoration as an opportunity to learn of various American Indian and native Alaska tribal spiritualities and traditions.

WEDNESDAY, MAY 23
LUDWIG NOMMENSEN, MISSIONARY TO SUMATRA, 1918

Ludwig Ingwer Nommensen was born in Schleswig-Holstein, Germany. In the early 1860s he went to Sumatra to serve as a Lutheran missionary. His work was among the Batak people, who had previously not seen Christian missionaries. Though he encountered some initial difficulties, the missions began to succeed following the conversion of several tribal chiefs. Nommensen translated the scriptures into Batak while honoring much of the native culture and did not seek to replace it with a European one. At the time of World War II all missionaries were driven out, and the Batak people took over leadership of their own church.

MAY 24, 2001

THE ASCENSION OF OUR LORD

INTRODUCTION

Why did Jesus leave just when the disciples were beginning to understand his resurrection? The readings for this day point us toward an answer: Jesus' visible absence makes possible a new way for him to be in the world through his Spirit. Christ is with us through the community that gathers around the baptismal washing, the table of grace, and the living word of his forgiving and empowering love.

This day is also the occasion to commemorate Nicolaus Copernicus, who proposed the modern model of the solar system, and Leonhard Euler, remembered for his advancements in mathematical theory.

PRAYER OF THE DAY

Almighty God, your only Son was taken up into heaven and in power intercedes for us. May we also come into your presence and live forever in your glory; through your Son, Jesus Christ our Lord, who lives and reigns with you and the Holy Spirit, one God, now and forever.

READINGS

Acts 1:1-11

Before he ascends into heaven, Jesus promises that the missionary work of the disciples will spread from Jerusalem to all the world. Jesus' words provide an outline of the book of Acts.

Psalm 47

God has gone up with a shout. (Ps. 47:5)

or Psalm 93

Ever since the world began, your throne has been established. (Ps. 93:3)

Ephesians 1:15-23

After giving thanks for the faith of the Ephesians, Paul prays that they might also see the power of God, who in the ascension has now enthroned Christ as head of the church, his body.

Luke 24:44-53

At the time of his ascension, Jesus leaves the disciples with the promise of the Holy Spirit and an instruction that they should await the Spirit's descent.

COLOR White

THE PRAYERS

In the light of Christ's resurrection, let us pray for the church, the world, and all who long for the grace of new life.

A BRIEF SILENCE.

Almighty God, Christ has ascended to the heavenly places as Lord of all. Bless your church with trust and confidence in your merciful reign. God of our salvation, **hear our prayer.**

Almighty God, all power in heaven and on earth is granted by you. Enlighten all leaders to recognize the source of their authority and to use it to serve others. God of our salvation,

hear our prayer.
Almighty God, shield those tried for their faith and heal those who are sick (especially . . .). God of our salvation,
hear our prayer.
Almighty God, you have opened the minds of those who will make public affirmation of their baptism. Continually fulfill your promise to them, enlightening their hearts by your great power. God of our salvation,
hear our prayer.

HERE OTHER INTERCESSIONS MAY BE OFFERED.

Almighty God, Christ Jesus has ascended to prepare a glorious inheritance for all the saints. We praise you for the witness of your saints, especially Nicolaus Copernicus and Leonhard Euler. God of our salvation,
hear our prayer.
Hear our prayers, O God, and grant us what we truly need, in the name of our risen Savior, Jesus Christ.
Amen

IMAGES FOR PREACHING

The color for Ascension is white, a fact that may go unnoticed within the Easter season. White is used to associate this day with the risen Christ. The story of the ascension as told by Luke is like a window frame, not unlike other "white" frames such as Christmas, through which we also see our risen Lord. While the frame of the ascension helps us see Christ in a unique way, our focus is still drawn to the death and resurrection of Christ as God's saving mystery. The focus of Ascension Day is the lordship of Jesus Christ, his intercession for us, our living with the expectation of his return and during this time as his witnesses.

The Acts of the Apostles tells of this witnessing. Peter, Stephen, James, Paul, Barnabas and Silas, Priscilla and Aquila are a few of the witnesses. Often their witness was in a public place, before a magistrate or someone with public authority to impose a sentence of imprisonment or death. It was not long before the word for witness, *martyr,* came to mean one who died for his or her faith.

At the beginning of the second century, Ignatius, the elderly bishop of Antioch, was condemned to death. Before his martyrdom in Rome he wrote seven letters to the churches of Asia Minor, including one to Bishop Onesimus, who perhaps was the slave mentioned in Paul's letter to Philemon. In one letter Ignatius wrote, "I am God's wheat, to be ground by the teeth of beasts, so that I may be offered as pure bread of Christ." (See Justo

L. Gonzalez, *The Story of Christianity,* vol. 1 [New York: HarperCollins Publishers, 1984], chapter 6.)

We too "have been clothed with power from on high" (Luke 24:49). Our lives take on the cruciform pattern of Christ through our imitation of him. We are promised the gift of the Holy Spirit to strengthen us as our lives are conformed to Christ.

WORSHIP MATTERS

Luke begins the story of Jesus as he ends it. As the infant Jesus is brought to the temple for dedication, we are told that the Prophet Anna "never left the temple but worshiped there with fasting and prayer night and day" (2:37). At the end of the story, having seen the resurrected Messiah ascend into heaven, the disciples returned with great joy to Jerusalem, where "they were continually in the temple blessing God." Where were Simeon and the disciples but in church! Do you suppose Luke was trying to make a point? Is not the assembly where the faithful are to be found? Is not the actual act of going to worship the ultimate witness to our friends and neighbors? If people do not take us seriously as Christians, perhaps it is because we ourselves do not take seriously enough the public worship of our Lord.

LET THE CHILDREN COME

"They were continually in the temple blessing God." Sometimes we expect children to be quiet in church, but Psalm 47 begs for sound effects: "Clap your hands, all you peoples." "God has gone up with a shout, the Lord with the sound of the trumpet." "Sing praises, to God, sing praises." Let the Ascension of Our Lord be an occasion for applause, not for the sermon or the anthem, but for the goodness of Christ our Lord, who is with us forever. Shouts (not whispers) of "Alleluia" and the sound of a great trumpet fanfare might accompany at least one Ascension hymn of praise.

MUSIC FOR WORSHIP
GATHERING

| LBW 158 | Alleluia! Sing to Jesus |
| LBW 170 | Crown him with many crowns |

PSALM 47

LLC 363   Clap your hands, all you people

Bell, John L. "Clap your hands all you nations" in *Psalms of Patience, Protest and Praise.* GIA G-4047.

Hopson, Hal H. *Psalms for All Seasons: An ICEL Collection*. NMP.

Howard, Julie. *Sing for Joy: Psalm Settings for God's Children*. LTP.

Sterk, Valerie Stegink. "Psalm for Ascension." SEL 24-1047. Cong, choir, org, tamb.

HYMN OF THE DAY

WOV 756   Lord, you give the great commission
            ABBOT'S LEIGH

INSTRUMENTAL RESOURCES

Burkhardt, Michael. "Abbot's Leigh" in *Improvisations for the Lenten Season, Set 1*. MSM 10-707. Org.

Burkhardt, Michael. "God of Life." MSM 60-8702. Brass, hb, opt inst, org, cong.

Cherwien, David. "Abbot's Leigh" in *Two Hymntune Preludes*. GIA G-4477. Org.

Manz, Paul. "Abbot's Leigh" in *Three Hymn Improvisations*. MSM 10-867. Org.

Moklebust, Cathy. "Lord, You Give the Great Commission" in *Hymn Stanzas for Handbells*. AFP 11-10722 (4-5 oct) and 11-10969 (2-3 oct). Hb.

ALTERNATE HYMN OF THE DAY

LBW 157   A hymn of glory let us sing!
LBW 159   Up through endless ranks of angels

COMMUNION

LBW 518   Beautiful Savior
WOV 669   Come away to the skies

SENDING

LBW 363   Christ is alive! Let Christians sing
WOV 682   Praise the Spirit in creation

ADDITIONAL HYMNS AND SONGS

CW 173   On Christ's ascension I now build
H82 214   Hail the day that sees him rise
TFF 95   He is Lord
W&P 55   He is exalted
W&P 94   Majesty

MUSIC FOR THE DAY

CHORAL

Busarow, Donald. "O Lord, You Are My God and King." AFP 11-10892. SAB, org, tpt, hb, opt cong.

Cherwien, David. "Up Through Endless Ranks of Angels." AFP 11-11020. SAB, org, opt tpt, opt cong.

Powell, Robert J. "King of Glory." GIA G-4771. SATB, org.

Riegal, F.S. "See God to Heaven Ascending" in CC. SATB.

Vaughan Williams, Ralph. "At the Name of Jesus." OXF 40.100. SATB, org.

CHILDREN'S CHOIRS

Hallock, Peter. "O Clap Your Hands." WAL 2194. 2 pt, cong, hand-clapping, hb, tri, tamb.

Reilly, Dadee. "Resurrection." AFP 11-2370. 2 pt, kybd, opt rhythm bells.

Sleeth, Natalie. "Go Into the World" in LS.

Tucker, Margaret R. "Christ's Own Body." CG CGA801. U/2 pt, kybd, opt cong, opt 2 oct hb.

KEYBOARD/INSTRUMENTAL

Nixon, June. "March on 'Lasst uns erfreuen'" in *Festival Finales*. Kevin Mayhew 1405599. Org.

Schack, David. "Ye Watchers and Ye Holy Ones" in *Nine Chorale Preludes*. CPH 97-5045. Org.

Vaughan Williams, Ralph. "Bryn Calfaria" in *Three Preludes Founded on Welsh Hymn Tunes*. Stainer and Bell 2155. Org.

HANDBELL

Sewell, Gregg. "Alleluia" in *Bells and Ivories*. BEC HBC3. 3 oct, pno.

Tucker, Sondra. "Come Away to the Skies." CPH 97-6739. 3-5 oct.

PRAISE ENSEMBLE

Kee, Ed. "Come, Give Glory to the Lord" in *Sing & Rejoice*. BNT.

Kogut, Malcom. "God Mounts His Throne to Shouts of Joy" (Psalm 47) in PCY, vol. 10. SATB/U, kybd, solo, opt cong, gtr.

Owens, Jimmy. "Clap Your Hands" in *Master Chorus Book*. LIL.

THURSDAY, MAY 24

NICOLAUS COPERNICUS, 1543;
LEONHARD EULER, 1783; TEACHERS

Scientists such as Copernicus and Euler invite us to ponder the mysteries of the universe and the grandeur of God's creation. Copernicus is an example of a renaissance person. He formally studied astronomy, mathematics, Greek, Plato, law, medicine, and canon law. He also had interests in theology, poetry, and the natural and social sciences. Copernicus is chiefly remembered for his work as an astronomer and his idea that the sun, not the earth, is the center of the solar system. Euler is regarded as one of the founders of the science of pure mathematics and made important contributions to mechanics, hydrodynamics, astronomy, optics, and acoustics.

The commemoration coincides this year with Ascension Day, offering an opportunity to juxtapose the insights of scientific cosmology with the spiritual insights of Christ's ascension.

MAY 27, 2001

SEVENTH SUNDAY OF EASTER

INTRODUCTION

"Come, Lord Jesus!" John the Seer shares the ancient prayer of the early church in today's second reading. Echoes of the prayer occur as the church gathers for the eucharist, and some of us use those ancient words at our own dinner tables. The "threefold truth" propels us into this day: "Christ has died. Christ is risen. Christ will come again."

Swiss reformer John Calvin, who died on this day in 1564, spent his life systematically describing and organizing the theology of a Reformation theology. We remember him today with thanksgiving.

PRAYER OF THE DAY

Almighty and eternal God, your Son our Savior is with you in eternal glory. Give us faith to see that, true to his promise, he is among us still, and will be with us to the end of time; who lives and reigns with you and the Holy Spirit, one God, now and forever.

or

God, our creator and redeemer, your Son Jesus prayed that his followers might be one. Make all Christians one with him as he is one with you, so that in peace and concord we may carry to the world the message of your love; through Jesus Christ our Lord, who lives and reigns with you and the Holy Spirit, one God, now and forever.

READINGS

Acts 16:16-34

The owners of a young woman who used her powers to tell fortunes threw Paul and Silas into jail for "healing" her and consequently ruining their business. But God used their imprisonment to bring the jailer and his family to Christ.

Psalm 97

Rejoice in the LORD, you righteous. (Ps. 97:12)

Revelation 22:12-14, 16-17, 20-21

The ascended Christ, hidden from our sight, promises to come again. We eagerly pray, "Come, Lord Jesus," with all who respond to this invitation.

John 17:20-26

In the life of the church is a unity of mission: to proclaim in word and deed that God loves all people. The unity of this mission finds its source in our union with Christ through word and meal.

COLOR White

THE PRAYERS

In the light of Christ's resurrection, let us pray for the church, the world, and all who long for the grace of new life.

A BRIEF SILENCE.

Righteous God, we bless you as the Holy One. Give the church an undivided oneness in you. God of our salvation,
hear our prayer.

Righteous God, you desire all people to experience your love. Direct the leaders of the world, especially of this country, to use their power to promote peace among nations. God of our salvation,
hear our prayer.

Righteous God, many are imprisoned and feel isolated from your mercy. Surround those who are ill (especially . . .). May your word of life free and strengthen them. God of our salvation,
hear our prayer.

Righteous God, in the waters of life you invited us to come to you. Enliven this congregation to invite others to join us in satisfying our thirst in you. God of our salvation,
hear our prayer.

HERE OTHER INTERCESSIONS MAY BE OFFERED.

Righteous God, we remember those who have renewed and strengthened your people, especially John Calvin and all who have died in defense of liberty. May we join all the saints in your heavenly glory. God of our salvation,
hear our prayer.

Hear our prayers, O God, and grant us what we truly need in the name of our risen Savior, Jesus Christ.
Amen

IMAGES FOR PREACHING

In Christ we are given the resurrection garment of unity. This purpose of this unity (John 17:23), which is expressed in the constitution of the Evangelical

Lutheran Church in America, 4.01: "The Church is a people created by God in Christ, empowered by the Holy Spirit, called and sent to bear witness to God's creative, redeeming, and sanctifying activity in the world." Unity is not an end in itself, but it is the Easter gift of the Holy Spirit for witness in the world.

How are we still divided, as a church, as families, as a nation, as people of the world? Paul's vision of unity is well known: "There is no longer Jew or Greek...slave or free...male and female; for all of you are one in Christ Jesus" (Gal. 3:28). Perhaps by naming our divisions, as did Paul, we can visualize our unity in Christ.

As we gather for worship in our congregational life, this unity is symbolized well in communion. Although practices vary from one congregation to the next, common symbols of unity may be the altar, one chalice, one loaf of bread, kneeling together with others at the altar, receiving the bread and wine in a continuous procession, receiving a common blessing, or even taking eucharistic elements directly from the church's worship service to those who are absent because of illness or disability.

In our daily lives this unity may be expressed as local churches work together to serve the needs of the poor in their community, run local hunger programs, provide after-school tutoring, organize housing projects, and in many other specific ways express the unity we find in Christ.

WORSHIP MATTERS

We often conclude prayers to God "through Jesus Christ." Do not assume that everyone knows why we do so. Apart from Jesus, the God of mystery may inspire fear and trembling. When God is revealed to us through Jesus, however, God's love, compassion, and mercy are known. Thus it is through Jesus that we come to know the true nature of God.

Conversely, when we pray through Jesus, this beloved Son stands alone before the throne of God on our behalf. Our prayers come before God through the one who has reconciled us to God.

LET THE CHILDREN COME

Worship is a time for us not only to pray, but to listen to Jesus' prayer for us. Jesus is the one who takes our simple prayers and delivers them most effectively to the Father. Our words may be "the simplest form of speech that infant lips can try...," as the hymn "Prayer is the

soul's sincere desire" states (*Service Book and Hymnal* 458). Even as parents and other adults speak up for their child's needs, so Jesus speaks up for us to God. When we pray "through Jesus Christ our Lord," Jesus prays for us. Make sure that children hear prayers for them as part of this service and thereby experience Jesus' blessing.

MUSIC FOR WORSHIP
GATHERING

LBW 545/6	When morning gilds the skies
LBW 555	When in our music God is glorified
WOV 802	When in our music God is glorified

PSALM 97

Cooney, Rory. "The Lord Is King" in STP, vol. 4.

Haas, David. "Our God Is Here/The Lord Rules Above" in PCY, vol 9.

Schalk, Carl. PW, Cycle C.

See Christmas Dawn.

HYMN OF THE DAY

| LBW 76 | O Morning Star, how fair and bright! |
| | WIE SCHÖN LEUCHTET |

VOCAL RESOURCES

Busarow, Donald. "O Morning Star, How Fair and Bright." CPH 98-2819. SAB, kybd, cong.

Pelz, Walter. "O Morning Star, How Fair and Bright." MSM 60-2001. SATB, cong, org.

Praetorius, Michael. "O Morning Star, How Fair and Bright" in CC. SATB.

INSTRUMENTAL RESOURCES

Albrecht, Timothy. "O Morning Star, How Fair and Bright" in *Grace Notes VII.* AFP 11-10856. Org.

Hobby, Robert A. "O Morning Star, How Fair and Bright." MSM 60-2000. Inst, org, SAB.

Manz, Paul. "O Morning Star, How Fair and Bright" in *A New Liturgical Year,* ed. John Ferguson. AFP 11-10810. Org.

Rose, Richard. "Wie schön leuchtet" in *Hymnal Companion for Woodwinds, Brass and Percussion, Series 1.* CPH 97-6710. Inst.

ALTERNATE HYMN OF THE DAY

| LBW 364 | Son of God, eternal Savior |
| WOV 801 | Thine the amen, thine the praise |

COMMUNION

| LBW 225 | Lord Jesus Christ, we humbly pray |
| WOV 695 | O blessed spring |

SENDING

| LBW 363 | Christ is alive! Let Christians sing |
| WOV 750 | Oh, praise the gracious power |

ADDITIONAL HYMNS AND SONGS

NCH 47	O Christ Jesus, sent from heaven
NCH 390	Eternal Christ, who kneeling
TFF 264	To God be the glory
W&P 140	There is a Redeemer
W&P 18	Bind us together

MUSIC FOR THE DAY

CHORAL

Goudimel, Claude. "Father, We Thank Thee." GIA G-2725.

Joule, Anthony. "I Will Not Leave You Comfortless." GIA G-4492. SATB, org.

Manz, Paul. "E'en So, Lord Jesus, Quickly Come." MSM 50-0001. SATB.

Sadowski, Kevin J. "I Will Not Leave You Desolate" in *Three Motets from the Gospel of John*. CPH 98-3472. SATB.

Schütz, Heinrich. "Psalm 97" in *Four Psalms*. AFP 12-205980. SATB.

CHILDREN'S CHOIRS

Brazzeal, David. "Blessed Be the Name of the Lord." CG CGA810. U/2 pt, pno.

Patterson, Mark. "With One Heart." CG CGA804. U, kybd, opt fl.

Sleeth, Natalie. "In the Bulb There Is a Flower" in LS.

KEYBOARD/INSTRUMENTAL

Albrecht, Mark. "Communion Meditation on Three Tunes" (Grace Church, The Ash Grove, Cleansing Fountain) in *Three for Piano and Sax* (or other instrument). AFP 11-10929. Inst/pno.

Organ, Anne Krentz. "Thine the Amen, Thine the Praise" in *Reflections on Hymn Tunes for Holy Communion*. AFP 11-10621. Pno.

Rohlig, Harald. "Lord Jesus Christ, We Humbly Pray" in *Hymn Preludes for Holy Communion, Vol. 2*. CPH 97-5487. Org.

HANDBELL

Dobrinski, Cynthia. "Praise, My Soul, the King of Heaven." AG 1974. 3-5 oct.

Helman, Michael. "There Is a Balm in Gilead." ALF AP 18559. 3-5 oct.

Stephenson, Valerie W. "Crown Him." ALF. AF 18565. 3-6 oct, opt hc/windchimes.

PRAISE ENSEMBLE

Haas, David. "As the Grains of Wheat" in W&P.

Sabolick, Joseph. "Come Just As You Are" in *Praise Hymns and Choruses*, 4th ed. MAR.

Schaefer, Marty. "That Christ Be Known" in W&P.

Stradwick, Dan. "The Lord Reigns" in *Praise Hymns and Choruses*, 3rd ed. MAR.

SUNDAY, MAY 27
JOHN CALVIN, RENEWER OF THE CHURCH, 1564

John Calvin began his studies in theology at the University of Paris when he was fourteen. In his mid-twenties he experienced a conversion that led him to embrace the views of the Reformation. His theological ideas are systematically laid out in his *Institutes of the Christian Religion*. He is also well known for his commentaries on scripture. He was a preacher in Geneva, was banished once, and then later returned to reform the city with a rigid, theocratic discipline.

Calvin is considered the father of the Reformed churches. In today's gospel, as Jesus prays that all his followers may be one, hold up the ecumenical agreement the Evangelical Lutheran Church in America shares with churches of the Reformed tradition as an example of the unity we share in Christ.

213

TUESDAY, MAY 29
JIRI TRANOVSKY, HYMNWRITER, 1637

Tranovský is considered the "Luther of the Slavs" and the father of Slovak hymnody. Trained at the University of Wittenberg in the early seventeenth century, Tranovský was ordained in 1616 and spent his life preaching and teaching in Prague, Silesia, and finally Slovakia. He produced a translation of the Augsburg Confession and published his hymn collection *Cithara Sanctorum* (Lyre of the Saints), the foundation of Slovak Lutheran hymnody.

Use the commemoration to pray for the Slovak church and to give thanks for the gifts of church musicians. Sing Tranovský's Easter hymn, "Make songs of joy" (LBW 150), at parish gatherings today.

THURSDAY, MAY 31
THE VISITATION

The Visitation marks the occasion of Mary visiting her cousin Elizabeth. Elizabeth greeted Mary with the words, "Blessed are you among women," and Mary responded with her famous song, the Magnificat. Luke tells us that even John the Baptist rejoiced and leapt in his mother's womb when Elizabeth heard Mary's greeting. Today we are shown two women: one too old to have a child bears the last prophet of the old covenant, and the other, still quite young, bears the incarnate Word and the new covenant.

In what ways does the church bear the good news of Christ to others and remain faithful to God's call?

FRIDAY, JUNE 1
JUSTIN, MARTYR AT ROME, C. 165

Justin was born of pagan parents. At Ephesus he was moved by stories of early Christian martyrs and came under the influence of an elderly Christian man he had

met there. Justin described his conversion by saying, "Straightway a flame was kindled in my soul and a love of the prophets and those who are friends of Christ possessed me." Justin was a teacher of philosophy and engaged in debates about the truth of Christian faith. He was arrested and jailed for practicing an unauthorized religion. He refused to renounce his faith and he and six of his students, one of them a woman, were beheaded.

Justin's description of early Christian worship around the year 150 is the foundation of the church's pattern of worship, East and West. His description of it is in *With One Voice* (p. 6) and helps reveal the deep roots our contemporary shape of the liturgy has in the ancient worship of the church.

JUNE 2, 2001

VIGIL OF PENTECOST

INTRODUCTION

Every major festival has a vigil to accompany it, and so does Pentecost. Even though the Holy Spirit has already come among us, the church always eagerly awaits and anticipates further outpouring of the Spirit's power. God is not done with us yet!

PRAYER OF THE DAY

Almighty and ever-living God, you fulfilled the promise of Easter by sending your Holy Spirit to unite the races and nations on earth and thus to proclaim your glory. Look upon your people gathered in prayer, open to receive the Spirit's flame. May it come to rest in our hearts and heal the divisions of word and tongue, that with one voice and one song we may praise your name in joy and thanksgiving; through your Son, Jesus Christ our Lord, who lives and reigns with you and the Holy Spirit, one God, now and forever.

READINGS

Exodus 19:1-9

After having escaped the Egyptian armies at the Red Sea, Israel gathers at the base of Mount Sinai, and Moses climbs

the peak to meet God. God's word is clear and stirring: "You are my people! I am coming to you!"

or Acts 2:1-11

The disciples are filled with the Spirit to tell God's deeds.

Psalm 33:12-22

The LORD is our help and our shield. (Ps. 33:20)

or Psalm 130

There is forgiveness with you. (Ps. 130:3)

Romans 8:14-17, 22-27

Paul says even though we are God's people and led by God's Spirit, we do not always know how to express this reality in words. The apostle reminds us, however, that this struggle for speech is really part of an entire universe groaning in labor as it awaits God's redemption.

John 7:37-39

Jesus says that our ultimate thirst will be quenched by streams of water that flow from human hearts. The Holy Spirit, poured into God's people, is the source of that stream.

COLOR Red

THE PRAYERS

In the light of Christ's resurrection, let us pray for the church, the world, and all who long for the grace of new life.

A BRIEF SILENCE.

Spirit of God, you are the spring of the living water that flows from our hearts. By your power may your living water continue to flow through us to others. Come, Holy Spirit:

Renew the face of the earth.

Spirit of God, the whole creation groans to be adopted as the children of God. Fill your world with hope, and strengthen all people who wait for the fulfillment of your promises. Come, Holy Spirit:

Renew the face of the earth.

Spirit of God, many thirst for your presence: those searching for you, those suffering for you, and those who await your healing (especially...). Comfort them and give them patience as you dwell within them. Come, Holy Spirit:

Renew the face of the earth.

Spirit of God, you lead your people into all truth. Teach us how to speak your words and obey them. Come, Holy Spirit:

Renew the face of the earth.

HERE OTHER INTERCESSIONS MAY BE OFFERED.

Spirit of God, we bless you for all those who suffered with Christ and now are glorified. May their witness strengthen us to live in your light. Come, Holy Spirit:

Renew the face of the earth.

Hear our prayers, O God, and grant us what we truly need, in the name of our risen Savior, Jesus Christ.

Amen

IMAGES FOR PREACHING

Affirmation of the Vocation of the Baptized in the World, a rite available to all Christians but especially designed for newly baptized adults, may be set within the service of Holy Communion after the post-communion canticle. (See *Welcome to Christ: Lutheran Rites for the Catechumenate,* pp. 59–61.) The blessing that concludes this rite says, "Go out into the world in peace; be of good courage; hold to what is good; return no one evil for evil; strengthen the faint-hearted; support the weak; help the suffering; honor all people; love and serve our God, rejoicing in the power of the Holy Spirit."

Jesus says in the gospel for this vigil, "Out of the believer's heart shall flow rivers of living water." This river is the outpouring of the Holy Spirit. These living waters are seen as the fruits of faithfulness mentioned in the blessing. During this rite of affirmation a sponsor presents the newly baptized and describes the area of service that will be affirmed. Each person being presented may then comment on the significance of their choice.

By faith we are able to say with Jesus that this Christian service is a gift from him. For our Lord says, "Let anyone who is thirsty come to me, and let the one who believes in me drink." The ministry of the church of all the baptized is a gift from the risen and ascended Lord.

WORSHIP MATTERS

"But Pastor, I don't know how to pray!" We must not forget—neither did the disciples. In fact, even after our Lord taught them how to pray, we find that at least ten years later, Paul still maintained that "we do not know how to pray as we ought" (Rom. 8:26). How we pray and what we pray for may be less important than that we just do it. Jesus comforts us with the knowledge that "your Father knows that you need [food and drink]" (Luke 12:30). Paul affirms this knowledge in other words when he teaches that "the Spirit intercedes for the saints according to the will of God" (Rom. 8:27). Even more comfort may we take in knowing that it is God's will to care for us!

LET THE CHILDREN COME

This evening vigil offers another opportunity for the liberal use of candles. The references to receiving the Spirit's flame (prayer of the day) and setting hearts on fire with the Spirit's love (verse) provide strong images of the Spirit's power among us. The gospel provides other powerful images: "Let anyone who is thirsty come to me," and "Out of the believer's heart shall flow rivers of living water." The reading of this short gospel might be accompanied by a pouring of water from a pitcher into the font, amplified, if necessary, by a nearby microphone. Pentecost is an action-filled, powerful event of the Spirit, growing, watering, warming, and enlightening us.

MUSIC FOR WORSHIP

GATHERING

| LBW 161 | O day full of grace |
| WOV 686 | Veni Sancte Spiritus |

PSALM 33

Farlee, Robert Buckley. PW, Cycle C.

Foley, John. "Psalm 33: God, Let Your Mercy" in PCY, vol. 7.

HYMN OF THE DAY

| WOV 685 | Like the murmur of the dove's song |
| | BRIDEGROOM |

VOCAL RESOURCES

Burkhardt, Michael. "Like the Murmur of the Dove's Song." MSM-60-5000. 2 pt, cong, ob, org.

INSTRUMENTAL RESOURCES

Biery, James. "Bridegroom" in *Tree of Life*. AFP 11-10701. Org.

Dahl, David P. "Bridegroom" in *Hymn Interpretations for Organ*. AFP 11-10972. Org.

Meyer, Edward. "Bridegroom" in *Easy Hymn Accompaniments for Organ or Piano*. CPH 97-6608. Kybd.

Sedio, Mark. "Bridegroom" in *How Blessed This Place*. AFP 11-10934. Org.

ALTERNATE HYMN OF THE DAY

| LBW 472/3 | Come, Holy Ghost, our souls inspire |
| WOV 684 | Spirit, Spirit of gentleness |

COMMUNION

| LBW 508 | Come down, O Love divine |
| WOV 693 | Baptized in water |

SENDING

| LBW 358 | Glories of your name are spoken |
| WOV 773 | Send me, Jesus |

ADDITIONAL HYMNS AND SONGS

ASG 31	Enter, Holy Spirit!
LLC 370	Holy Spirit, our fount of love
NCH 64	Fire of God, undying flame
PH 323	Loving Spirit, Holy Spirit
TFF 101	Spirit of the living God
W&P 127	Song over the waters

MUSIC FOR THE DAY

CHORAL

Hassell, Michael. "Spirit, Spirit of Gentleness." AFP 11-10850. SATB, pno, sax/cl.

Manalo, Ricky. "By the Waking of Our Hearts." OCP 10981. U, cong, desc, kybd, gtr, C inst.

Sateren, Leland B. "Come, Holy Ghost, in Love." AFP 1283. SATB, org.

Tallis, Thomas. "If Ye Love Me." HWG GCMR 1629.

Way, Tony. "The Spirit of the Lord." AFP 12-107. 2 pt, org.

CHILDREN'S CHOIRS

Cherubini, Luigi/arr. Hal H. Hopson. "Come, All Who Thirst." SAB/3 pt trbl, pno/org.

Christopherson, Dorothy. "As the Water Sings." AFP 11-10476. U, 2 cl, tba/bass.

KEYBOARD/INSTRUMENTAL

Bender, Jan. "Four Variations for Organ on 'Down Ampney.'" AFP 11-00807. Org.

Pepping, Ernst. "Komm, Gott Schöpfer" in *Hymnen für Orgel*. Bärenreiter 2747. Also in *Hymns for Organ*. KAL K-09968. Org.

HANDBELL

McChesney, Kevin. "Dona Nobis Pacem." Cantabile CP 6058. 2 oct, quartet.

McChesney, Kevin. "Every Time I Feel the Spirit." Cantabile CP 6065. Quartet.

PRAISE ENSEMBLE

Batstone, Bill. "My Soul Waits (Psalm 130)" in *Praise & Worship*. MAR.

Hanson, Handt. "Spirit Touching Spirit" in *Spirit Touching Spirit*. CCF.

Mengel, Dana. "Holy Ghost, Dispel Our Sadness." CPH 98-3396. SATB, kybd.

JUNE 3, 2001

THE DAY OF PENTECOST

INTRODUCTION

An ancient Hebrew harvest festival that came to be associated with the giving of God's law at Mount Sinai, Pentecost became for Christians the occasion for the gift of the Holy Spirit to the church. The Spirit is the power of the resurrected Jesus in our midst, claiming us in baptism, feeding us at the eucharist, and sending us into the world to be bearers of that divine word that can raise the dead to new life.

Pope John XXIII, who died on this day in 1963, convened the Second Vatican Council, which became a powerful tool for the Holy Spirit's renewal of the church in the latter third of the twentieth century.

PRAYER OF THE DAY

God, the Father of our Lord Jesus Christ, as you sent upon the disciples the promised gift of the Holy Spirit, look upon your Church and open our hearts to the power of the Spirit. Kindle in us the fire of your love, and strengthen our lives for service in your kingdom; through your Son, Jesus Christ our Lord, who lives and reigns with you in the unity of the Holy Spirit, one God, now and forever.

or

God our creator, earth has many languages, but your Gospel announces your love to all nations in one heavenly speech. Make us messengers of the good news that, through the power of your Spirit, everyone everywhere may unite in one song of praise; through your Son, Jesus Christ our Lord, who lives and reigns with you in the unity of the Holy Spirit, one God, now and forever.

READINGS

Acts 2:1-21

Before Jesus ascended into heaven, he told his disciples they would be filled with the Holy Spirit and become witnesses for him to the ends of the earth. As the people spoke in many languages, the all-encompassing nature of the church and its mission were revealed.

or Genesis 11:1-9

God scatters those who were building the tower of Babel.

Psalm 104:25-35, 37 (Psalm 104:24-34, 35b [NRSV])

Alleluia, or *Send forth your Spirit and renew the face of the earth. (Ps. 104:31)*

Romans 8:14-17

Here Paul speaks about the mystery of baptism: through the Spirit we are adopted, gathered, and welcomed into Christ's body, the church. And we receive new names: brother, sister, child of God.

or Acts 2:1-21

See above.

John 14:8-17 [25-27]

On the night he was betrayed, in his final address to his disciples, Jesus promises that though he must now leave them, they will soon receive the presence of an Advocate, the Spirit of truth, whom God will send to comfort and enlighten them.

COLOR   Red

THE PRAYERS

In the light of Christ's resurrection, let us pray for the church, the world, and all who long for the grace of new life.

A BRIEF SILENCE.

Pour out your words into the hearts of your faithful people, that they may do the great work of bearing witness to Christ in the world. Come, Holy Spirit:

Renew the face of the earth.

Pour out your peace upon the leaders and peoples of every continent, that they may receive every good thing that comes from you. Come, Holy Spirit:

Renew the face of the earth.

Pour out your grace into our hearts that we may give thanks for the wonders of your creation and may use them responsibly. Come, Holy Spirit:

Renew the face of the earth.

Pour out your presence into the bodies and spirits of those who suffer for you, those who are sick or dying (especially...), and any in need. Come, Holy Spirit:

Renew the face of the earth.

Pour out confident trust upon all who are baptized, all who affirm their faith, and all who receive Christ's body and blood. Come, Holy Spirit:

217

Renew the face of the earth.

HERE OTHER INTERCESSIONS MAY BE OFFERED.

Pour out your love upon people who grieve, that they might stand in the last day with the faithful from every nation. Come, Holy Spirit:

Renew the face of the earth.

Gracious Spirit, intercede for us with sighs too deep for words; keep us in true faith; and gather us with the whole church on earth, into the communion of the triune God.

Amen

IMAGES FOR PREACHING

Do you know parents who have spent thousands of dollars to free their child from addiction; or Christians who give thousands of hours of volunteer service at hospitals, nursing homes, and in hospice service; or doctors who travel to medical missions in developing countries and give their services freely? We may name and describe many more examples. On this day we celebrate the outpouring of the Holy Spirit that follows Jesus' death and resurrection. We also celebrate that God has drawn all the baptized into God's saving work in the world until the day when our Lord will come again.

If this work were the result of a manifesto for action or a program of mercy, it would not have lasted the centuries. Rather, Christian ministry is the gift of our Lord's presence. Jesus redefined sabbath, so that now he is Lord of the sabbath. "Come to me, all you who are weary and are carrying heavy burdens, and I will give you rest" (Matt. 11:28). He is the sabbath year and the jubilee, the "year of the Lord's favor" fulfilled now in our hearing (Luke 4:16-21). Jesus is the presence of God-with-us. He is with us in baptismal water and holy bread and wine. He is with us as the word is broken open and our hearts burn within us. He is with us where two or three gather in his name. He is with us when we roll up our sleeves and love our neighbor in his name. How do we know these things? We have his word of promise and the gift of his presence. What more can we ask? Jesus says that we will do greater works than these.

WORSHIP MATTERS

Out of judgment God works blessing. One might suppose that if, in the land of Shinar, the people had not tried to make a name for themselves and had not thus been scattered over the face of all the earth, then what was intended as judgment—the multiplication of languages—could not have been transformed into blessing. However, a blessing it is! As difficult as it may be for us as individuals to communicate with people of a different tongue, what a blessing it is that virtually every person on this earth is able to hear the word of God proclaimed in his or her own language. We therefore perceive the multitude of languages not as a threat, but with eyes of faith as a miracle and blessing for all God's children.

LET THE CHILDREN COME

It is important on Pentecost to hear many voices, both young and old, both male and female, "speaking about God's deeds of power." During the psalm it would be appropriate for children to speak or sing the words of the refrain: "Send forth your Spirit and renew the face of the earth."

MUSIC FOR WORSHIP

GATHERING

LBW 478	Come, oh, come, O quickening Spirit
WOV 688	O Holy Spirit, root of life

PSALM 104

Haugen, Marty. "Lord, Send Out Your Spirit" in PCY, vol. 1.

Hunnicutt, Judy. "Lord, Send Out Your Spirit" in *Sing Out! A Children's Psalter*. WLP.

Makeever, Ray. "When You Send Forth Your Spirit" in DH.

Schalk, Carl. PW, Cycle C.

Schoenbachler, Tim. "Psalm 104: Send Out Your Spirit" in STP, vol. 2.

LBW 548   Oh, worship the King

HYMN OF THE DAY

LBW 523   Holy Spirit, ever dwelling

IN BABILONE

INSTRUMENTAL RESOURCES

Albrecht, Timothy. "In Babilone" in *Grace Notes VI*. AFP 11-10825. Org.

Burkhardt, Michael. "In Babilone" in *Five Hymn Accompaniments for Brass Quartet and Organ, set 2*. MSM 20-843.

Kolander, Keith. "In Babilone" in *Hymn Tune Preludes in Trio Style*. CPH 97-6614. Org.

Langlois, Kristina. "In Babilone" in *Eight Miniatures for the Seasons of Lent, Easter and Pentecost*. MSM 10-345. Org.

218

ALTERNATE HYMN OF THE DAY

| LBW 284 | Creator Spirit, heavenly dove |
| WOV 687 | Gracious Spirit, heed our pleading |

COMMUNION

| LBW 508 | Come down, O Love divine |
| WOV 680 | O Spirit of life |

SENDING

| LBW 475 | Come, gracious Spirit, heavenly dove |
| WOV 682 | Praise the Spirit in creation |

ADDITIONAL HYMNS AND SONGS

H82 224	Hail this joyful day's return
TFF 104	Holy Spirit, light divine
W&P 130	Spirit song
W&P 157	Wind of the Spirit

MUSIC FOR THE DAY

CHORAL

Bach, J.S. "Come, Holy Ghost, God and Lord" in BAS. SATB.

Callahan, Charles. "Creator Spirit, by Whose Aid." MSM 50-5400. U, opt desc, org.

Distler, Hugo. "Come Holy Ghost, God and Lord" in CC. SATB.

Schwarz, May. "Come, Holy Spirit, Blow across the Waters." AFP 11-10920. SATB, org, opt brass, opt cong.

Steffens, Mark C. "To God the Holy Spirit, Let Us Pray." CPH 98-2877. SAB, C inst, org.

Vulpius, Melchior. "O Spirit of God, Eternal Source" in CC. SATB.

CHILDREN'S CHOIRS

Cox-Johnson, J. Philip. "Pentecost Joy." AFP 11-10018. U, kybd.

Horman, John. "Spirit Falling Like a Dove." ABI 503310. U, opt fl, kybd.

Manley, James. "Spirit, Spirit of Gentleness" in LS.

Ramseth, Betty Ann. "Spirit Boundless." AFP 11-0327. U, kybd, fl, fc.

KEYBOARD/INSTRUMENTAL

Demessieux, Jeanne. "Veni Creator" in *Twelve Chorale Preludes on Gregorian Chant Themes*. SMP 0602. Org.

Larsen, Libby. "Veni Creator Spiritus" in A *New Liturgical Year;* ed. John Ferguson. AFP 11-10810. Org.

Tournemire, Charles. "In Festo Pentecostes" from *Petites Fleurs Musicales, Opus 66*. Universal Organ Editions UE 17465. Org.

HANDBELL

Bartsch, John. "Descending Dove." FBM BG0875. 4-5 oct.

Larson, Katherine Jordahl. "O Day Full of Grace." CPH 97-6774. 3-5 oct, opt hc.

Wagner, Douglas E. "Beautiful Savior." LOR HB 366. 3 oct.

PRAISE ENSEMBLE

Cherwien, David M. "Filled with the Spirit's Power." U/2 pt, org, opt fl.

Edwards, Rusty, and Linda Cable Shute. "Here and Now God" in ASG.

Fry, Steve. "Abba Father" in *Sing & Rejoice*. BNT.

Makeever, Ray. "Spirit of the Living God" in DH.

SUNDAY, JUNE 3
JOHN XXIII, BISHOP OF ROME, 1963

In his ministry as a bishop of Venice, John was well loved by his people. He visited parishes and established new ones. He had warm affection for the working class—he himself was the child of Italian peasants—and he worked at developing social action ministries. At age seventy-seven he was elected bishop of Rome. Despite the expectation that he would be a transitional pope, he had great energy and spirit. He convened the Second Vatican Council in order to open the windows of the church and "let in the fresh air of the modern world." The council brought about great changes in the church's worship, changes that have influenced Lutherans and many other Protestant churches as well.

219

TUESDAY, JUNE 5
BONIFACE, ARCHBISHOP OF MAINZ, MISSIONARY TO GERMANY, MARTYR, 754

Boniface (his name means "good deeds") was born Wynfrith in Devonshire, England. He was a Benedictine monk who at the age of thirty was called to missionary work among the Vandal tribes in Germany. He led large numbers of Benedictine monks and nuns in establishing churches, schools, and seminaries. Boniface was also a reformer. He persuaded two rulers to call synods to put an end to the practice of selling church offices to the highest bidder. Boniface was preparing a group for confirmation on the eve of Pentecost when he and the others were killed by Vandal warriors.

THURSDAY, JUNE 7
SEATTLE, CHIEF OF THE DUWAMISH CONFEDERACY, 1866

Noah Seattle was chief of the Suquamish tribe and later became chief of the Duwamish Confederacy, a tribal alliance. When the tribes were faced with an increase in white settlers, Seattle chose to live and work peacefully with them rather than engage in wars. After Seattle became a Roman Catholic, he began the practice of morning and evening prayer in the tribe, a practice that continued after his death. On the centennial of his birth, the city of Seattle—named for him against his wishes—erected a monument over his grave.

When parish groups gather today, remember Chief Seattle and his work as a peacemaker. Consider beginning or ending parish events with a simple form of morning or evening prayer, not only today, but as a regular part of the parish life.

SATURDAY, JUNE 9
COLUMBA, 597; AIDAN, 651; BEDE, 735; CONFESSORS

Today we commemorate three monks from the British Isles who kept alive the light of learning and devotion during the Middle Ages. Columba founded three monasteries, including one on the island of Iona, off the coast of Scotland. That monastery was left in ruins after the Reformation but today is home to an ecumenical religious community. Aidan was known for his pastoral style and ability to stir people to charity and good works. Bede was a Bible translator and scripture scholar. He wrote a history of the English church and was the first historian to date events *anno domini* (A.D.). Bede is also known for his hymns, including "A hymn of glory let us sing!" (LBW 157).

SUMMER

A time to discover anew the extraordinary gospel

for our ordinary lives

IMAGES of the SEASON

Summer is a time of creating memories as we take vacations or arrange our

schedules to do new and different things. We may also pause longer during

these weeks to hear the stories people share with

us, drawing us into the web of community memory.

The lectionary texts read in worship during these weeks create memory for some people and refresh the memory of others. The biblical story is the memory bank of the Christian church that gives us a history, a present, and a future. Today many people are researching their family histories and trying to discover where they come from and the people who are part of their genealogy. The biblical texts are our Christian family's faith genealogy, the story that informs us whose we are and who we are, where we come from and where we are going.

Our story includes skeletons in the Jewish and Christian closets. David's adultery with Bathsheba is exposed. The word of God brings King David to repentance, and we remember that sin is to be confessed and amendment of life is to follow. We remember that in Christ we live by grace. A sinful woman dares to weep at Jesus' feet and wipe his feet with her hair. This emotional outburst would embarrass many of us, but she was overwhelmed because Jesus said to her: "Your sins are forgiven" (Luke 7:48). These persons remind us that "as many of you as were baptized into Christ have clothed yourselves with Christ" (Gal. 3:27). As the memory of the church recounts this diverse group drawn into the life of God, we discover God has a diverse and surprising family that includes us.

But the story also reminds us that living in Christ and walking in the Spirit does oppose the sin in our life. Works of the flesh are opposed to the fruit of the Spirit. So Paul recalls the baptismal gift of the Holy Spirit and reminds us, "If we live by the Spirit, let us also be guided by the Spirit" (Gal. 5:25).

Even so, when we discover around us sinners like King David or the anonymous woman, we are to restore them "in a spirit of gentleness" (Gal. 6:1). Summer is a time to remember and also to make amends. It is a time to discover anew the extraordinary gospel for our ordinary lives. The prophet Jeremiah jars our memory, "Is not my word like fire, says the Lord, and like a hammer that breaks a rock in pieces?" (Jer. 23:29). The texts of this season bring us fully into the story, so that we are part of the continuation of God's story.

Memory helps re-member us into communities. Class reunions often happen in summertime, and old memories that were part of our development come back as people share stories and memories. Sunday morning is reunion time for the Christian community. We remember the central things of our faith and are re-membered with the hosts of heaven and the church on earth. The lectionary provides the worshiping community with the stories that brought it into being and have nourished it toward today and a new future.

We see how important memory is to human community and our individual being. The retelling of the old, old story keeps reminding us of the touchstones of our faith. These are the creative, life-giving memories that infuse the community with its living faith and a word of new life. The church nurtures and embraces these stories, which constantly feed its faith and life.

If we dispense with the church's liturgy or scriptures, our memory as a church shrivels, and we become isolated from the great story and from many people over the centuries. This story needs to be nurtured, embraced, told again and again, and passed onto future generations. We add our little bit to this great story and then pass it along. We take time to create a community of memory in our worship.

Important texts of the Christian faith were handed over to early church converts to the Christian faith. The Lord's Prayer and the Apostles' Creed were taught to and memorized by converts, so that they could perform their part as members of a community with its collective memory. From earliest times, the community's memory has been cultivated through the retelling of key stories and the recitation of certain prayers and creeds.

Summer is a time to create memories and savor stories of generations of our families. On Sundays celebrating the church's collective memory is an integral part of celebrating the eucharist. Some Christians speak of summer as the season of "ordinary time." As the gospel of Lent, Easter, and Pentecost has centered us in the core of our faith and life, we now see our ordinary days filled with the extraordinary gospel. As our birthright as Christians, this extraordinary life in the Holy Spirit is in fact the ordinary experience of Christians. We discover and look for the ex-

traordinary gift of each day. Like the psalmist, we can say of summer, "This is the day that the Lord has made; let us rejoice and be glad in it" (Ps. 118:24). Or with Jeremiah we discover anew that God's "mercies are new every morning" (Lam. 3:23). It is a time to center our lives more deeply in what God has given us and made of us. These texts deepen and expand our horizons. And so our summer worship in ordinary time can reform, renew, refresh, restore, and recreate us. Rejoice that we share a community with a long and glorious memory!

ENVIRONMENT AND ART FOR THE SEASON

After Pentecost Sunday the church moves into the second half of the liturgical year: the time of the church, ordinary time, or simply, the days after Pentecost. During these ordinary days, God's people are called upon to reflect on how to be the church, how to be the body of

Christ, how to live out the Pentecost gift, and how to be God's people in the world. From Advent to Pentecost the gathered people of God have stepped into the story of Christ. Now the emphasis changes, and the guiding question becomes: since God has come to us, since Christ has raised us, since the Spirit dwells in us, how are we to live?

Ordinary time tends to be simpler than the first half of the church year. The first half is rich with festivals, while the days after Pentecost embrace but a few principal festivals in a sea of simple days. The time of the church is somewhat like everyday existence. Now that the bells and trumpets and clouds of incense have faded, we are given time to weigh whom we have become and whom God calls us to be, as individuals and as a community. The season's predominant color is a vibrant green, the color of life and of growth.

The days after Pentecost begin and end with principal festivals of the church: the Sunday of the Holy Trinity and Christ the King Sunday. Holy Trinity is a fitting beginning for these days, for it draws the church once again into the mystery of the God who has called

us to be a holy people. This festival is a wonderful opportunity to use incense, for we are told that when Isaiah saw his vision and heard the winged creatures singing, "Holy, holy, holy," "the house filled with smoke" (Isa. 6:4). The worship environment can invite worshipers to encounter the beauty, majesty, and mystery of God using all their senses. Perhaps an old custom, such as that of ringing a bell three times at the moment of the Sanctus (Holy, holy, holy), could be returned to this day with renewed meaning.

White is the liturgical color for Holy Trinity: white, the sum of all colors. Banners for the day could be as simple as three equal and overlapping lengths of tulle.

Icons are an Orthodox tradition that may enrich the celebration of Holy Trinity. One in particular is the icon of the Trinity portrayed as the three angels who appeared to Abraham at Mamre (Gen. 18:1-2). The three sit at the table prepared for them, vessels and food before them. Such an icon might be placed along with a votive candle on a stand or small table at the main entrance to the church. Icons appropriate to the day's liturgy hold a place of honor in Orthodox churches.

Christian church buildings are replete with trinitarian symbolism: triangles, the three fish, trefoils, three steps to the altar. Perhaps this would be a good occasion to point out these symbols to the congregation in some way. It is said that St. Patrick lifted up the shamrock to illustrate the Trinity. Pots of shamrocks, wood sorrel, or other three-leafed plants could adorn the worship space for the day. Also, the Japanese art of flower arranging called *ikebana* is based on three focal points; such an arrangement would be suitable for the festival.

The environment for worship in ordinary time is simple without being austere, subdued without being drab. Finely crafted earthenware or pewter communion vessels might be used rather than those of silver. Incense could be burned in a pottery bowl partly filled with sand, rather than in an ornate thurible. Flowers and greens to grace the sanctuary might be offered by parish gardeners as the season permits. Whatever is used, whether earthenware or silver, crafted or gathered, should be of the highest quality and invite people into the mystery of God.

Parishes might want to consider creating or commissioning a set of paraments and vestments for the days after Pentecost different from those used in the days after Epiphany. The time after Epiphany is more a time of revelation, with auxiliary colors of blue, white, and silver tying the days into the entire Advent/Christmas/Epiphany cycle, whereas the time after Pentecost is more a time of growth, with rich colors of gold and yellow augmenting a palette of green.

With the shift from the life of Christ to the life of the church at the half-year comes an emphasis on community. Vines and tree-of-life symbolism richly portray the community's relationship with Christ and one another (John 15:5 and Rev. 22:2). A vine could be potted and trellised and brought inside for the liturgies. Black-eyed Susan vine (thunbergia), cardinal climber, hyacinth bean, cypress vine, scarlet runner bean, mandevilla, and glory vine are all rampant climbers whose growth might actually be visible from week to week. A grapevine grows more slowly but is richer in symbolism. One living ficus tree might be brought into the worship space during these days, perhaps to be replaced by a larger vase of bare branches as the days after Pentecost draw to a close.

Vine wreaths can be made for the outer church doors by filling wire wreath forms with Spanish or sphagnum moss and inserting ivy plants into the center of the moss. The vines are then attached to the form with florist's pins to take the shape of the wreath.

If your nave is in a traditional cruciform style, a finely appliquéd banner of a cross in the intertwined tracery of the Book of Kells could well depict the vining of a community growing in Christ. If you have a modern space, a banner bearing a fractal cross might be more suitable. Fractals are mathematical patterns formed of the shape they form, like a branch made of many small branches, a cross formed of many crosses, Christ formed of many Christs. Fractal designs can be drawn using computer programs such as *FractaSketch* and *Mandelzot,* many of which are available in school and college math departments.

Tree-of-life and vine images for banners may be found in books about medieval stained glass windows, medieval and Renaissance religious paintings, cathedral sculpture, and many other sources. Banners really need not include words or text. The imaginative and marvelous human mind will contemplate an image much longer than a word, will puzzle much longer over a mystery than a thing named and categorized.

The disciple said to the teacher, "Why do you teach us stories and stories and do not teach us what they mean?"

The teacher replied, "How would you like it if I offered you a ripe fruit and chewed it for you first?"

Twice this year during the summer months, lesser festivals step onto our calendar of Sundays, breaking the orderly march of days: the Nativity of St. John the Baptist on June 24 and St. Mary Magdalene on July 22.

The Nativity of John the Baptist takes place close to the summer solstice, opposite the Nativity of Our Lord, which occurs close to the winter solstice. The six-month separation of the nativity festivals of John and Jesus is based on Luke's account that the angel Gabriel announced the conception of Jesus to Mary "in the sixth month" of Elizabeth's pregnancy (Luke 1:26).

John's day is one of the oldest festivals honoring a saint, and since early times it has been a tradition to light a bonfire on the eve of John's nativity. If no evening vigil is planned prior to the festival, perhaps the tradition could be continued by placing a grouping of candles in the worship space, or by lining the path to the church's building with torches. Zechariah prophesied in the Benedictus that John would be a prophet to prepare the way for the "dawn from on high" (Luke 1:78).

Bunches of St. John's wort (hypericon) and daisies ("day's eyes"—for their resemblance to the sun), both of which are associated with St. John's day, would be appropriate as bouquets or shaped into floral arches above the doors. The color for this festival being white, the daisies would fit doubly well.

Banners for the Nativity of St. John the Baptist might incorporate a simple baptismal shell, or a rising sun and a setting sun, a sun and a moon (which reflects the sun's light), a winged figure (messenger), or even an axe laid to the root of a tree, for John's preaching (Matt. 3:10). Another suitable sign for this saint's day is the depiction of living water, such as the Jordan River, along which John baptized and preached. John is often portrayed in traditional iconography wearing animal skins and carrying a long staff topped by a cross. The font might be prominently placed on this day, open and filled with clear, fresh water (if it is not already).

On July 22, the church honors St. Mary Magdalene, known as "the apostle to the apostles." An apostle is one who is sent out with authority on behalf of the one who sends. Mary Magdalene, first witness to the resurrected Christ, was sent by Christ to announce the glad news to the other disciples.

What we actually know of Mary of Magdala from the gospel accounts is that she was delivered of seven "devils" by Jesus. Precisely what devils is not known. The gospels also relate that Mary was a woman of some means who was able to help support the ministry of Jesus. She was a friend and a disciple, present at the cross, present at the empty tomb.

Tradition in the Eastern church says that Mary, being of noble rank, traveled to Rome to vilify Pilate before Caesar. In her audience with the emperor, Mary picked up a hen's egg to portray the resurrection. Caesar scoffed and said a dead person had as much likelihood of living again as a hen's egg had of turning red. The egg in Mary's hand turned red, the story goes, and that is why Orthodox Christians give red-dyed eggs at Easter. Mary is said to have then traveled around the Mediterranean, preaching and witnessing to the resurrection.

White is the color for this lesser festival, and perhaps a bowl of red eggs or a single red-dyed egg on a stand could represent Mary's gift to the community: the astonishing news of the resurrected Christ. Mary is also portrayed in traditional icons as one of the three myrrh-bearing women approaching the tomb at early dawn. For her festival day, this icon might be displayed in a prominent place, lit by a votive candle.

Sunflowers are in bloom in many latitudes at this time of year, and large bouquets would be appropriate for celebrating the saint who was the first to encounter the risen Son. Sweet cicely is related to the shrub from which myrrh is derived and could be added to floral arrangements for the day.

As the summer months draw to a close, the changing of the season may be apparent in the environment for worship. The ivy wreaths on the doors could have late summer flowers added to them. Gladiolas, sunflowers, and other seasonal blooms could brighten the space. The liturgical year grows out of the natural seasons of the Northern Hemisphere, and it is fitting to acknowledge this link to the natural world around us in our prayer and praise, as in our ordinary days.

225

PREACHING WITH THE SEASON

The desert Southwest of the United States is a land of a thousand shades of browns and blues. Mountain shadows created by light, clouds, and crags paint a variegated palette of colors as the sun makes its way across the broad skyline. Every minute of the day, the hues in one place subtly change from the minute before. In the midst of this desert magnificence people from other regions may miss the oozing saturation of green.

Even for those living in more arid climes, green is the primary color of life as we know it. The presence of green is usually evidence of a healthy organism that is flourishing in its environment. Healthy growth does not take place overnight, but is the result of a slow maturation process that builds upon the days, weeks, months, and sometimes years. The green season after Pentecost is that time of the liturgical year that provides the preacher with a wealth of opportunity to use the teachings and themes of Jesus' ministry as a kind of growth fertilizer that can be applied to the roots of everyday life.

Whether preachers face a congregation from the elevated position of the pulpit or from the chancel floor, we do well to hold a mirror mentally to our faces, as if we were preaching to ourselves and to our own strengths and shortcomings. In doing so, we provide a reality check for ourselves to ensure that our words will have practical relevance for that middle-aged couple in the second pew who find themselves in marital crisis, or for the single mom preoccupied with whether the support check will be in the mail Monday morning, or for the restless teen anxious to get home and tune in again to the images and rhythms of MTV.

The ability to make the connection between gospel and listener, using images, examples, and personal stories, must be cultivated if changed lives and congregational renewal are to happen. Standing before a congregation with warmed-over notes from a seminary class in historical criticism is unlikely to help people connect the gospel message of Jesus Christ to the difficult circumstances of their lives.

The lectionary for this time of the year provides great preaching latitude for the one who proclaims the word each week. The preacher can handle each Sunday as a self-contained unit or identify several broad themes to use over several weeks. Given the reality of sporadic summer attendance in many congregations, it is probably wise for the preacher to choose the former approach over the latter.

Finally, some of the most vital elements of effective proclamation are one's personal commitment to the gospel being proclaimed and one's willingness to be honest and genuine about personal struggles and triumphs in daily life. Dogs, children, and everyday people in the pews can spot a phony from a mile away. For the message to ring true, the messenger must be true. Never should the preacher use a congregation as a cheap collective therapist, but never should honest proclamation be avoided in order to maintain a façade of moral superiority or righteousness.

The kerygmatic proclamation of the gospel of Jesus Christ is perhaps the greatest privilege a Christian minister can possess. It also carries with it great responsibility. Let this summer be a time for all who respond to the call of preaching to seek out effective tools needed for this task: a study of the word, frequent prayer, worldly wisdom, frequent filling by the Spirit, humility, honesty, and humor. Blended together in the right amounts, these ingredients will result in a proclamation that has authenticity, boldness, and power. Enjoy the task! Count it an honor. And leave the results of your proclamation to the Lord.

226

SHAPE OF WORSHIP FOR THE SEASON

BASIC SHAPE OF THE EUCHARISTIC RITE

- Confession and Forgiveness: see alternate worship text for summer in *Sundays and Seasons*

GATHERING

- Greeting: see alternate worship text for summer in *Sundays and Seasons*
- Omit the Kyrie during the summer (except on the festival of the Holy Trinity)
- Omit or use the hymn of praise during the summer (use for the festival of the Holy Trinity; also consider using the hymn of praise for the festivals of the Nativity of John the Baptist on June 24 and St. Mary Magdalene on July 22)

WORD

- Nicene Creed for Holy Trinity and for the two lesser festivals (Nativity of St. John the Baptist and St. Mary Magdalene); Apostles' Creed for remaining Sundays in this season
- The prayers: see alternate forms and responses for summer in *Sundays and Seasons*

MEAL

- Offertory prayer: see alternate worship text for summer in *Sundays and Seasons*
- Use the proper preface for Holy Trinity on the festival of the Holy Trinity; use the preface for Advent on the Nativity of St. John the Baptist, June 24; use the preface for Easter or All Saints on the festival of St. Mary Magdalene, July 22; use the proper preface for Sundays after Pentecost for the remainder of the season
- Eucharistic prayer: in addition to four main options in *LBW*, see "Eucharistic Prayer G: Summer" in *WOV* Leaders Edition, p. 71

- Invitation to communion: see alternate worship text for summer in *Sundays and Seasons*
- Post-communion prayer: see alternate worship text for summer in *Sundays and Seasons*

SENDING

- Benediction: see alternate worship text for summer in Sundays and Seasons
- Dismissal: see alternate worship text for summer in *Sundays and Seasons*

OTHER SEASONAL POSSIBILITIES

BLESSING FOR TRAVELERS

- See seasonal rites; use before the benediction whenever groups from the congregation set out to travel

FAREWELL AND GODSPEED

- See *Occasional Services,* pp. 151–52, for whenever people are leaving the congregation; it may be used either after the prayers or following the post-communion prayer

LECTIONARY OPPORTUNITY
FOR HEALING SERVICES

- Proper 9 (alternate first reading from 2 Kings) on July 8

227

ASSEMBLY SONG FOR THE SEASON

The lectionary during this season recounts to us the stories of Jesus as the journeying prophet, the one who instructs, heals, and turns the world around and upside down. Jesus calls us to discipleship and to witness to God's reign. How shall we sing of Jesus' story and our mission?

GATHERING

Plan some hymn singing sessions as the prelude. If you are working with only one hymnal, use it to the fullest. It is a rare congregation that knows or has even sung all the hymns in its worship book. Think about the hymn repertoire of your congregation. Every assembly has its natural preferences and backgrounds that affect its hymn repertoire. Which style(s) of hymnody does the assembly know well? Into what new style of hymnody can you pastorally stretch the assembly? Pick a different style of hymn, or choose from another culture. Make a plan to teach and learn these hymns. Intersperse the new hymns with the assembly's favorites. Sing the new hymns at the next hymn sing with more assembly favorites. Sing the new hymns during worship more than once during the season. "Come, I invite you to sing praises" (LLC 588) can work well as an introduction to the hymn sing and can be accompanied by guitar. Use it to begin every hymn sing.

Be aware that some people will be absent some of this time. Plan slowly but intentionally. Repeat hymns as often as needed to learn them. Use new hymns as instrumental music at the offering, distribution, and postlude, to get the hymn tune into worshipers' ears.

The gathering rite can omit the Kyrie and the hymn of praise during summer months. Choose a well-known entrance hymn, so that it can serve as a strong beginning.

WORD

Sing the psalms during the summer months. Make a refrain from a hymn phrase. Use a phrase (usually the first phrase) from a well-known hymn, so that the congregation can easily sing the opening phrase from memory. First phrases of hymns such as "Praise to the Lord, the Almighty" (LBW 543), "All glory be to God on high" (LBW 166) or "Come, thou Fount of every blessing" (LBW 499) work well. Select a psalm tone. Transpose the key of the tone, if necessary, to make sure that the tone and antiphon are complementary.

"Gospel Acclamation: General" (WOV 611a) is a good summer alleluia verse and is easily learned. *With One Voice* Accompaniment Edition has a melodic formula that can be used for the proper verse. Other choices include "Alleluia" (WOV 610 and TFF 26), and "Aleluya" (LLC 197).

MEAL

"What shall I render" is a fitting choice for an offertory hymn during this season, because of the strong emphasis on Jerusalem in Luke's gospel. Or learn a new offertory hymn such as "Accept, O Lord, the gifts we bring" (WOV 759) or "Now we offer" (WOV 761).

SENDING

Learn a new post-communion canticle/sending hymn for the season. "Amen, we praise your name" (WOV 786 and TFF 279) and "Praise, praise, praise the Lord" (TFF 278) are easily learned. Those wanting a traditional hymn might choose one with a focus on discipleship.

MUSIC FOR THE SEASON

VERSE AND OFFERTORY

Bender, Mark. "O Lord, I Love the Habitation of Your House."
CPH 98-2859. 2 pt, org.

Berger, Jean. "The Eyes of All Wait upon Thee." AFP 11-1264. SATB.

Cherwien, David. *Verses for the Season of Pentecost, Set 1.* MSM-80-541.
U, kybd.

Cherwien, David. *Verses and Offertories for the Season of Pentecost, Set 2.*
MSM-80-542.

Lovelace, Austin C. "How Lovely Is Thy Dwelling Place."
AFP 11-10207. SATB, kybd.

Powell, Robert. *Verses and Offertory Sentences, Part 6.* CPH 97-5506;
acc ed 97-5510. U, kybd.

Scott, K. Lee. "God Shall the Broken Heart Repair." AFP 11-10530.
SATB, kybd.

WOV, p. 47 Salvation belongs to our God

WOV 783 Seek ye first the kingdom of God

CHORAL

Berger, Jean. "The Eyes of All Wait upon Thee." AFP 11-1264. SATB.

Hanson, Jeremy. "An Irish Blessing." AFP 11-10802. SATB.

Jeffrey, Richard C. "You Are Redeemed." CPH 98-3491. U/SATB,
cong, kybd.

Meyer, Daniel C. "Psalm 100: The Lord Is Good." GIA G-4436.
U, opt cong, kybd.

Parry, C. Hubert H. "Dear Lord, and Father of Mankind."
NOV 29 0247. SATB, org.

Proulx, Richard. "Though We Are Many, in Christ We Are One."
MSM 80-834. U, opt SATB, cong, org.

Schulz-Widmar, Russell. "God Remembers." AFP 11-10882.
SATB, org.

Willan, Healy, arr. "Lord of All Hopefulness." PET 6985. SATB, kybd.

Zimmermann, Heinz Werner. "Psalm 100." AFP 11-0640. SATB, org,
bass.

CHILDREN'S CHOIRS

Boyce, William/arr. Jane McFadden and Janet Linker. "Psalm of Joy."
CG CGA760. 2 pt, kybd, opt 2 oct hb.

Caldara, Antonio/arr. Michael Burkhardt. "Filled with the Spirit."
MSM-50-7402. 3 pt canon, opt hb/kybd.

Ferguson, John. "All Things Bright and Beautiful." GIA G-3104.
SATB/2 pt, alto and bass xyl, fl/picc.

Purcell, Henry/arr. Dolores Hruby. "Celebrate This Happy, Holy
Day." CG CGA-587. U, kybd, opt C inst.

Ziegenhals, Harriet. "You Shall Have a Song." HOP A 577. 2 pt,
(opt 3 pt), kybd, opt fl.

KEYBOARD/INSTRUMENTAL

Boyce, William/arr. Don Andrew Moore. *Eight Symphonies for Organ.*
Kevin Mayhew 1400029. Org.

Keller, Hermann. *Eighty Chorale Preludes.* CFP 4448. Org or kybd.

Micheelsen, Hans Friedrich. *The Holstein Little Organ Book.*
Bärenreiter 1679. Org.

Peeters, Flor. *Aria.* Heuwekemeijer 265. Org.

HANDBELL

Gramann, Fred. "An American Folk Hymn Sampler." LOR 20/1019L.
3-6 oct.

Hentz, Phyllis Treby. "Meditation on Morecambe." MSM-30-801.
4-6 oct.

McChesney, Kevin. "Jubilant Fanfare." CG CGB 141. 2-3 oct.

McCleary, Mary G. "Fanfare for Bells." CG CGB14. 4 oct.

Rogers, Sharon Elery. "God, Who Stretched the Spangled Heavens."
AFP 11-10873. 3-5 oct, opt hc.

Vaughan Williams, Ralph, arr. Douglas E. Wagner. "Rhosymedre." AG
1318. 3-4 oct.

Wagner, Douglas E. "Chant and Celebration." AGEHR AG 2011.
2 oct.

PRAISE ENSEMBLE

Fisher, Bobby, and Mark Friedman. "All the Earth Proclaim God's
Glory." GIA G-3726. U/SATB, kybd, opt cong, gtr, 2 C inst.

Keesecker, Thomas. "Washed Anew." AFP 11-10676. SAB/SATB,
kybd, opt hb, cong.

Shaw, Kirby. "Gonna Sing!" HAL 08666033. SAB.

Smith, Michael W,. and Deborah D. Smith, arr. Ed Lojeski. "Great Is
the Lord." HAL 08307232. SAB, kybd.

229

ALTERNATE WORSHIP TEXTS

CONFESSION AND FORGIVENESS

In the name of the Father, and of the ✝ Son, and of the Holy Spirit.
Amen

Let us confess our sin to God,
who promises to comfort us
as a mother comforts her children.

Silence for reflection and self-examination.

Compassionate God,
we confess that we are a rebellious people,
following our own desires rather than your call.
We have counted ourselves better than others,
failing to seek justice for the neighbor in need.
We have sought earthly treasures,
neglecting your gifts of word and sacrament.
For the sake of Jesus Christ,
forgive our sins,
strengthen our faith,
and lead us by your Holy Spirit
to joyful service in your name. Amen

In the mercy of God,
I declare to you the forgiveness of your sin.
In baptism, you have been crucified with Christ;
it is no longer you who live,
but Christ who lives in you.
Amen

GREETING

Sisters and brothers, called to freedom in Christ:
grace, mercy, and peace be with you all.
And also with you.

OFFERTORY PRAYER

Gracious God,
you open your hand,
filling our lives with all good things
and renewing the face of the earth.
We offer these gifts in thanksgiving
for all that we have received from your bounty.
Accept them for the sake of him
who offered his life for us,
Jesus Christ our Lord. Amen

INVITATION TO COMMUNION

Come, all has been prepared;
eat and drink with delight, and be satisfied.

POST-COMMUNION PRAYER

Giver of all good gifts,
we give you thanks
for the great mystery of Christ's body and blood
in which we have shared.
Through this meal strengthen our faith,
so that our lives may reflect your love and grace
until we come to your heavenly city,
to the banquet prepared for all your people;
through Jesus Christ our Lord.
Amen

BENEDICTION

Continue to walk in Christ Jesus,
rooted and built up in him.
Almighty God, Father, ✝ Son, and Holy Spirit,
bless you now and forever.
Amen

DISMISSAL

Go in peace and declare how much God has done for you.
Thanks be to God.

230

SEASONAL RITES

BLESSING FOR TRAVELERS

Use this prayer before leaving on a journey.

O God,
our beginning and our end,
you kept Abraham and Sarah in safety
throughout the days of their pilgrimage,
you led the children of Israel through the midst of the sea,
and by a star you led the magi to the infant Jesus.
Protect and guide us now as we [or substitute the names
of travelers] set out to travel.
Make our ways safe and our homecomings joyful,
and bring us at last to our heavenly home,
where you dwell in glory with our Lord Jesus Christ
and the life-giving Holy Spirit,
one God, now and forever.
Amen

231

Adapted from *Lutheran Book of Worship*, page 167.

JUNE 10, 2001

THE HOLY TRINITY
FIRST SUNDAY AFTER PENTECOST

INTRODUCTION

Early Christians began to speak of the one God in three persons in order to fully describe the wonder of salvation. God is above us, beside us, within us. God is our loving Father, our savior Jesus, our companion Spirit. To be baptized in this name is to enter into God's community.

PRAYER OF THE DAY

Almighty God our Father, dwelling in majesty and mystery, renewing and fulfilling creation by your eternal Spirit, and revealing your glory through our Lord, Jesus Christ: Cleanse us from doubt and fear, and enable us to worship you, with your Son and the Holy Spirit, one God, living and reigning, now and forever.

or

Almighty and ever-living God, you have given us grace, by the confession of the true faith, to acknowledge the glory of the eternal Trinity and, in the power of your divine majesty, to worship the unity. Keep us steadfast in this faith and worship, and bring us at last to see you in your eternal glory, one God, now and forever.

READINGS

Proverbs 8:1-4, 22-31

In the Bible, wisdom has many faces. It is portrayed in terms sometimes human and sometimes divine. Often, it is personified as feminine. In this passage, wisdom is depicted not only as a creation of God, but also as part of God's creative activity.

Psalm 8

Your majesty is praised above the heavens. (Ps. 8:2)

Romans 5:1-5

Paul describes the life of faith with reference to God, Jesus, and the Holy Spirit. Even now, we have peace with God through Jesus, and our hope for the future is grounded in the love of God that we experience through the Spirit.

John 16:12-15

The Spirit, sent by the Father, reveals God's truth by glorifying the Son and making him known.

COLOR White

THE PRAYERS

Freed by Christ and led by the Spirit, let us offer our prayers to God for the world, the church, and all those in need.

A BRIEF SILENCE.

That the mystery of the triune God may continue to call us into wholeness of life. God of truth,

hear our prayer.

That leaders of nations and people everywhere may be guided by justice. God of truth,

hear our prayer.

That all who suffer in any way may experience the love of God (especially...). God of truth,

hear our prayer.

That the ministry of this congregation may reach out in love for those who are broken. God of truth,

hear our prayer.

HERE OTHER INTERCESSIONS MAY BE OFFERED.

That as we remember the faithful departed with joy, we too may journey in the faith of the Holy Trinity. God of truth,

hear our prayer.

Receive the prayers of our hearts, O God, and grant that we may forever trust in your promises, through Jesus Christ our Lord.

Amen

IMAGES FOR PREACHING

When attending a conference, reading a good book, or participating in a seminar, many of us consider the time well spent if we can take from that experience at least one useful piece of information, a newly discovered piece of wisdom or inspiration that will be of use to us in everyday life.

A first day in seminary, nearly twenty-five years ago, was such an experience for one seminarian. During that orientation day, a professor was speaking on the nature of truth. He spoke an unforgettable phrase: "Ladies and gentlemen, welcome to the world of graduate school. The academic demands we will place upon you will be as rigorous as any demands of any other profes-

232

sional school. But the education you are embarking on is essentially different from that of other professions. Whereas students in other schools seek to master the subject matter of their discipline, you are here that you may be mastered *by* the subject matter of this place, Jesus Christ, who is the Way, the Truth, and the Life."

For Christians, ultimate truth is not simply a collection of stories bound in genuine Moroccan leather, nor a set of societal laws and prescriptions. Rather, ultimate truth is only discovered as one acknowledges the embodiment of that truth, Jesus Christ. In other words, we discover truth in a relational journey we walk each day with the Lord and with our brothers and sisters who share the Christ experience. As we share our lives with one another, Christ will share his life with us. We learn truth in community as we rub shoulders with those whom we love or dislike, when we weep with those who suffer and rejoice with others in their blessings. We come to know truth experientially and then seek to understand that truth through study, prayer, and academic discipline.

Too often, from the intimidating heights of our pulpits, we preachers tend to convey truth as facts to be learned, confessions to be memorized, or denominational customs and behaviors to be followed. In today's first reading from Proverbs 8, Wisdom is personified throughout in relational terms. She is given gender, voice, and the ability to delight the creator. According to the writer, she was the first product of the Lord's creation, an idea that would someday find its fullest expression in John's gospel with the phrase, "And the Word became flesh and lived among us, and we have seen his glory" (John 1:14a). In today's gospel from John, it is clear that to understand this truth, one must be guided to it, as a seeing-eye dog gently guides a blind person across a crowded street. The guide in this case is the Holy Spirit of God. This Spirit will take you by the hand and lead you in the journey that all Christians must walk, a journey to be lived and experienced.

WORSHIP MATTERS

It is such a simple gesture, the sign of the cross. Touch head to heart, shoulder to shoulder (left to right, or right to left does not matter). It is such a simple gesture, and yet it conveys so much: Father, Son, and Holy Spirit; Creator, Redeemer, and Sustainer; baptism and blessing;

prayer and promise; a reminder of whose we are and of who we are to be. On Trinity Sunday, as we seek to put God into words and in so doing find just how inadequate our words are, we turn to something simpler: a gesture, a sign, a cross. It is in the cross that God speaks most clearly to us. In making the sign of the cross, we echo God's good news in ways that words cannot.

LET THE CHILDREN COME

Children admire and praise athletic heroes, singers, TV and movie stars, among others. Worship reminds us that God, above all, is worthy of our praise. Psalm 8 sets the tone: "Out of the mouths of infants and children your majesty is praised above the heavens." A simple hymn of praise to the Holy Trinity could be sung by the entire congregation, with at least a stanza or two by the children alone or a children's choir. For what specific things do we praise God? Let children prepare and display letters or drawings of praise for all that God has done.

MUSIC FOR WORSHIP

SERVICE MUSIC

This festival is an especially fitting time for the trinitarian hymn of praise, "Glory to God." If "This is the feast of victory" has been used throughout Eastertide, this shift will also signal the transition to a new season of the church year.

GATHERING

| LBW 535 | Holy God, we praise your name |
| WOV 717 | Come, all you people |

PSALM 8

Cooney, Rory. "How Glorious Is Your Name" in PCY, vol. 4.

Cox, Joe. "O Lord, Our Lord, How Majestic Is Your Name" in *Psalms for the People of God*. SMP 45/1037S.

Hanson, Handt. "Psalm 8" in *Spirit Touching Spirit*. CCF.

Hopson, Hal H. "Psalm 8" in TP.

Shields, Valerie. PW, cycle C.

HYMN OF THE DAY

| WOV 796 | My Lord of light |
| | BARBARA ALLEN |

A SUGGESTION FOR THE HYMN OF THE DAY

A guitar with flute or recorder would offer a suitable accompanying instrumentation.

233

INSTRUMENTAL RESOURCES

Cherwien, David. "Barbara Allen" in *O God Beyond All Praising.*
AFP 11-10860. Org.

Keesecker, Thomas. "Barbara Allen" in *Come Away to the Skies.*
AFP 11-10794. Pno.

ALTERNATE HYMN OF THE DAY

| LBW 164 | Creator Spirit, by whose aid |
| LBW 169 | Father most holy |

COMMUNION

| LBW 205 | Now the silence |
| WOV 687 | Gracious Spirit, heed our pleading |

SENDING

| LBW 260 | On our way rejoicing |
| WOV 787 | Glory to God, we give you thanks |

ADDITIONAL HYMNS AND SONGS

HS98 895	Voices raised to you we offer
LW 437	Alleluia! Let praises ring!
TFF 142	In the name of the Father
TWC 693	We believe in God almighty
W&P 60	Holy, holy

MUSIC FOR THE DAY

CHORAL

Britten, Benjamin. "Te Deum." OXF 42.141. SATB, org, S solo.

Erickson, Richard. "When Long Before Time." AFP 11-10815. SATB,
fl, org.

Hassell, Michael. "How Exalted Is Your Name." AFP 11-10854.
SATB, pno.

Proulx, Richard. "You Are God: We Praise You." GIA G-4577.
U, cong, hb.

Sowerby, Leo. "All Hail, Adored Trinity." OXF A165. SATB, org.

CHILDREN'S CHOIRS

Christopherson, Dorothy. "God of the Universe." CG CGA821. 2 pt,
perc, pno/orff inst.

Erickson, John. "The Lord Is Great" in LS.

Hopson, Hal H. "Lord, O Lord, Your Name Is Wonderful."
CG CGA762. U, kybd, opt 6 hb.

Marcello, Benedetto/arr. Dale Grotenhuis. "O God, Creator."
MSM-50-9420. 2 pt, kybd.

Nelson, Ronald A. "Children's Praise." CG CGA-574. U/2 pt, inst.

KEYBOARD/INSTRUMENTAL

Attaingnant, Pierre. "Kyrie Fons" in *Second Organ Book of 1531.*
KAL 4473. Org.

Bach, J. S. "Kyrie, Gott Vater" BWV 669-674 in *Clavierübung, Part 3.*
Various ed. Org.

Hampton, Calvin. "Nicaea" in *Music for Organ.* Warner Brothers
DM00266. Org.

HANDBELL

Dobrinski, Cynthia. "Holy, Holy, Holy." AG 1905. 3-5 oct, opt narr.

Harlan, Benjamin. "Fantasy on 'Come, Thou Almighty King.'"
Ring Out Press. 3-5 oct.

Morris, Hart. "Canticle of Creation." RRM HB0023. 3-5 oct,
opt perc.

PRAISE ENSEMBLE

Daigle, Gary, and Rory Cooney. "Way, Truth and Life." U/SATB,
cong, gtr.

Jacobs, Peter. "How Excellent Your Name (Psalm 8)" in *Praise & Worship.* MAR.

LeBlanc, Lenny. "Come and See" in W&P.

Makeever, Ray. "Who Are We (Psalm 8)" in DH.

Smith, Michael, W. "How Majestic Is Your Name" in W&P.

MONDAY, JUNE 11
ST. BARNABAS, APOSTLE

The Eastern church commemorates Barnabas as one of the seventy commissioned by Jesus. Though he was not among the twelve mentioned in the gospels, the book of Acts gives him the title of apostle. His name means "son of encouragement." When Paul came to Jerusalem after his conversion, Barnabas took him in over the fears of the other apostles, who doubted Paul's discipleship. Later, Paul and Barnabas traveled together on missions.

At the Council of Jerusalem, Barnabas defended the claims of Gentile Christians regarding the Mosaic law. How can his work on behalf of others and his support of other Christians serve as a model for contemporary Christians and churches?

THURSDAY, JUNE 14
BASIL THE GREAT, BISHOP OF CAESAREA, 379; GREGORY OF NAZIANZUS, BISHOP OF CONSTANTINOPLE, C. 389; GREGORY, BISHOP OF NYSSA, C. 385

These three are known as the Cappadocian fathers, and all three of them explored the mystery of the Holy Trinity. Basil was influenced by his sister Macrina to live a monastic life, and he settled near his home.

Basil's Longer Rule and Shorter Rule for monastic life are the basis for Eastern monasticism to this day. In his rule, he establishes a preference for communal, rather than eremetical monastic life by making the case that Christian love and service are by nature communal. Gregory of Nazianzus was sent to preach on behalf of the orthodox faith against the Arians in Constantinople, though the orthodox did not have a church there at the time. He defended orthodox trinitarian and christological doctrine, and his preaching won over the city. Gregory of Nyssa was the younger brother of Basil the Great. He is remembered as a writer on spiritual life and the contemplation of God in worship and sacraments.

JUNE 17, 2001

SECOND SUNDAY AFTER PENTECOST
PROPER 6

INTRODUCTION

Confession and forgiveness frequently serve as a doorway to worship. We come into God's presence not because we earn it, but purely as an act of grace. Today's readings introduce us to some of the world's great sinners, and we take our place among them, hungry to taste the wonderful love of God.

PRAYER OF THE DAY

God, our maker and redeemer, you have made us a new company of priests to bear witness to the Gospel. Enable us to be faithful to our calling to make known your promises to all the world; through your Son, Jesus Christ our Lord.

READINGS

2 Samuel 11:26—12:10, 13-15

King David has misused his royal power by taking advantage of his neighbor, Bathsheba, and is responsible for killing her husband, Uriah, by sending him into battle without proper support to defend him. God sends the prophet Nathan to confront the king with his guilt.

Psalm 32

Then you forgave me the guilt of my sin. (Ps. 32:6)

Galatians 2:15-21

Paul explores the dynamics of grace. We are made right with God through Jesus and are crucified with Christ. We trade the old life of sin for a new life with God.

Luke 7:36—8:3

A forgiven sinner expresses great love for Jesus. This humble

act reveals what is lacking in the self-righteous who feel no need to be forgiven.

ALTERNATE FIRST READING/PSALM

1 Kings 21:1-10 [11-14] 15-21a

Ahab and Jezebel ruled Israel in the days of Elijah. After they cheated Naboth out of the vineyard that was his family inheritance, God sent the prophet to confront them with their sin.

Psalm 5:1-8

Lead me, O Lord, in your righteousness; make your way straight before me. (Ps. 5:8)

COLOR   Green

THE PRAYERS

Freed by Christ and led by the Spirit, let us offer our prayers to God for the world, the church, and all those in need.

A BRIEF SILENCE.

That leaders of a world longing for peace come to recognize the need for justice, and that each of us commit ourselves to lives of justice and peace. God of truth,

hear our prayer.

That the church may be strengthened in its commitment to mission, and that we who have received God's forgiveness might extend forgiveness to others. God of truth,

hear our prayer.

That fathers everywhere may be supported and encouraged as they care for their families. God of truth,

hear our prayer.

That all who are mourning or discouraged may know your comfort and that all who are ill may experience your healing (especially . . .). God of truth,
hear our prayer.

HERE OTHER INTERCESSIONS MAY BE OFFERED.

That we, like all your saints who have gone before us, may one day share in your feast that has no end. God of truth,
hear our prayer.

Receive the prayers of our hearts, O God, and grant that we may forever trust in your promises, through Jesus Christ our Lord.
Amen

IMAGES FOR PREACHING

The "drugs" of authority and power can be dangerous for many of us. With ever-increasing success and experience, we are given ever-larger doses of them. In the beginning we start out using them according to label directions. Over time, however, we may develop a tolerance to the prescribed dosage and discover that an additional pill or two are needed to effect the desired outcome. If left unchecked, the effects can be euphoric and dangerous both to oneself and to others.

Old Nathan aimed his finger a few inches from the center of King David's forehead and shouted, "You are the man!" Nathan knew this admonition might be his last act as the king's prophet, but the situation demanded a response. David, the all-powerful king, was out of control. He had slipped into the royal medicine cabinet and swallowed the entire bottle of divine power and authority the Lord had prescribed for him as king. The euphoric gods of power and authority had gained control over David's servant heart and now held it a hostage. No longer was he serving the people of Judah. They were becoming tools of flesh and blood that would serve his own selfish needs and desires. At the visible tip of this out-of-control iceberg were the sins of adultery with Bathsheba and David's premeditated murder of her husband, Uriah, a calculated act meant only to cover his political tracks.

In today's gospel Simon the Pharisee was unknowingly addicted to the same drugs as David. It was certainly a more subtle form of the addiction, but he was seduced nonetheless. Such a state had produced a pride in Simon that had over time blinded him to the qualities of holiness that being a Pharisee was meant to witness: hospitality, love, and mercy. Simon possessed a kind of righteousness that prevented him from seeing the true poverty of his own condition. In the second reading Paul spoke of the danger in possessing knowledge that "puffs up."

A prophet's finger aimed in the king's face produced the desired result. David saw the light and repented, and Nathan lived to see another day on this earth. Simon never quite "got it" and held on to his indignity at the woman's waste of good perfume.

WORSHIP MATTERS

Go in peace! With these words we conclude our worship. We can go in peace each week because God has forgiven us. In the assurance of the absolution, in the proclamation of Jesus' suffering, death, and resurrection, and in Christ's gift of himself in bread and cup, we receive God's unconditional forgiveness and love. No matter what difficult choices we must make—and despite the fact that we fail to love God and neighbor—God claims us as God's own, always giving us yet another chance. Though we leave worship to deal with challenges in our lives, jobs, and families, these realities cannot destroy us because of the true peace that God gives.

LET THE CHILDREN COME

The gospel highlights a woman who served Jesus. Children have heard many stories about the men in the Bible. Preachers and teachers must be sure that the discipleship of women serving Jesus is not overlooked. For example, Jesus affirms to a woman: "Your faith has saved you; go in peace." Though it is Father's Day, it may be a good time to highlight the importance of how parents (male and female) work together to raise children. We may also highlight the importance of males and females of all ages respecting and cooperating with one another at home and school, at work and play.

MUSIC FOR WORSHIP
GATHERING

| LBW 524 | My God, how wonderful thou art |
| WOV 719 | God is here! |

PSALM 32

Cooney, Rory. "Forgive the Wrong I Have Done," in PCY, vol. 4.

Haas, David. "God, I Confess My Wrong" in PCY, vol. 9.

Howard, Julie. *Sing for Joy: Psalm Settings for God's Children.* LTP.

Isele, David Clark/Hal H. Hopson. "Psalm 32" in TP.

Shields, Valerie. PW, Cycle C.

Stewart, Roy James. "I Turn to You, Lord," in PCY, vol. 5.

See fourth Sunday in Lent and proper 26.

HYMN OF THE DAY

LBW 356   O Jesus, joy of loving hearts

             WALTON

INSTRUMENTAL RESOURCES

Albrecht, Timothy. "Walton" in *Grace Notes VIII*. AFP 11-10970. Org.

Cherwien, David. "Walton" in *Interpretations, vol. 3*. AMSI OR-6. Org.

Sadowski, Kevin. "Walton" in *Six Hymn Preludes*. CPH 97-6044. Org.

ALTERNATE HYMN OF THE DAY

LBW 396   O God, O Lord of heaven and earth

WOV 738   Healer of our every ill

SUGGESTION FOR THE ALTERNATE HYMN OF THE DAY

Violin or other C instrument on obligato part for "Healer of Our Every Ill" by Marty Haugen. GIA G3478.

COMMUNION

LBW 327   Rock of Ages, cleft for me

WOV 671   Alleluia, alleluia, give thanks

SENDING

LBW 479   My faith looks up to thee

WOV 771   Great is thy faithfulness

ADDITIONAL HYMNS AND SONGS

ASG 16   Heal this old heart

BH 268   The love of Christ, who died for me

OBS 100   Holy woman, graceful giver

TFF 184   Wonderful grace of Jesus

W&P 83   Lamb of God

MUSIC FOR THE DAY

CHORAL

Hilton, John. "Lord, for Thy Tender Mercy's Sake" in *The Oxford Easy Anthem Book*. OXF.

Kosche, Kenneth T. "When All Your Mercies, O My God." CPH 98-3445. SAB, kybd.

Weelkes, Thomas. "Let Thy Merciful Ears, O Lord." ECS 1018.

Wood, Dale. "Rise, Shine!" AFP 11-10737. SATB, org.

CHILDREN'S CHOIRS

Nichols, Jean. "Come to Me, Savior." MSM-50-6014. 2 pt/duet, kybd.

KEYBOARD/INSTRUMENTAL

Hassell, Michael. "He Leadeth Me" in *Jazz Sunday Morning*. AFP 11-10700. Pno.

Kosnik, James W. "Healer of Our Every Ill" in *Laudate! vol 4*. CPH 97-6665. Org.

Whitlock, Percy. "Allegro Risoluto" in *Plymouth Suite*. OXF 0193758938. Org.

HANDBELL

Dobrinski, Cynthia. "Blessed Assurance." LAK HB 90018. 3-5 oct.

Downey, Erin, and Gail Downey. "Praise Medley." JEF JHS 9015. Solo hb and pno.

Page, Anna Laura. "Fairest Lord Jesus." ALF 8659. 2-3 oct.

PRAISE ENSEMBLE

Dyer, Scott, and Joe Horness. "Everything I Am" in *Praise Hymns and Choruses*, 4th ed. MAR.

Hanson, Handt. "Go in Peace and Serve the Lord" in W&P.

Shaw, Kirby. "Sing Praise to God." HAL 08596585. SATB, solo, kybd, opt electric bass, gtr, drms.

Ylvisaker, John. "Steadfast Love Surrounds You" in *Borning Cry*. NGP.

THURSDAY, JUNE 21

ONESIMOS NESIB, TRANSLATOR, EVANGELIST, 1931

Onesimos was born in Ethiopia. He was captured by slave traders and taken from his Galla homeland to Eritrea, where he was bought, freed, and educated by Swedish missionaries. He translated the Bible into Galla and returned to his homeland to preach the gospel there. His tombstone includes a verse from Jeremiah 22:29, "O land, land, land, hear the word of the Lord!"

Does your congregation support mission work through synod or churchwide offerings, or do you support a specific missionary? Let the commemoration of Onesimos Nesib be a way for your congregations to focus on missions during the summer months.

JUNE 24, 2001

INTRODUCTION

We are now on the far side of the sun from Christmas and the celebration of Jesus' birth. In the Northern Hemisphere the days now begin to grow shorter as we celebrate the birth of John the Baptist, the forerunner of Messiah. In comparing himself to Jesus, John once said, "He must increase, but I must decrease." John was eager to see his ministry eclipsed.

PRAYER OF THE DAY

Almighty God, you called John the Baptist to give witness to the coming of your Son and to prepare his way. Grant to your people the wisdom to see your purpose and the openness to hear your will, that we too may witness to Christ's coming and so prepare his way; through your Son, Jesus Christ our Lord, who lives and reigns with you and the Holy Spirit, one God, now and forever.

READINGS

Malachi 3:1-4

The prophet Malachi announces the coming of one who will prepare a way for God's arrival. His burning program of reform will make God's people ready for salvation.

Psalm 141

My eyes are turned to you, Lord GOD. (Ps. 141:8)

Acts 13:13-26

In Antioch of Pisidia, Paul preaches in the synagogue and recalls the ministry of John the Baptist, showing how John was the pivot point between history and the new acts God was performing through Jesus.

Luke 1:57-67 [68-80]

The birth and naming of John ends his father Zechariah's silence. He announces the child's name given by the angel and speaks a prophesy about the newborn infant.

COLOR   White

THE PRAYERS

Freed by Christ and led by the Spirit, let us offer our prayers to God for the world, the church, and all those in need.

A BRIEF SILENCE.

That leaders and nations may strive to bring peace and harmony to a world longing for wholeness. God of truth, **hear our prayer.**

That like John the Baptist, bishops, pastors, associates in ministry, deaconesses, diaconal ministers, and all the baptized may have the courage to bear the good news of Christ. God of truth, **hear our prayer.**

That all who are awaiting the birth of a child may, like Elizabeth and Zechariah, be filled with hope and the Holy Spirit. God of truth, **hear our prayer.**

That your healing love may be felt by those whose lives are broken in any way (especially...). God of truth, **hear our prayer.**

HERE OTHER INTERCESSIONS MAY BE OFFERED.

That as we remember those who have gone before us, we may also remember your holy covenant made in our baptism. God of truth, **hear our prayer.**

Receive the prayers of our hearts, O God, and grant that we may forever trust in your promises, through Jesus Christ our Lord. **Amen**

IMAGES FOR PREACHING

When a child is born, those who gather around to celebrate the joyous event often imagine the infant coming to greatness later on in life. Usually we do not imagine the greatness that our children might achieve through their association with someone else. But in the case of John the Baptist, his greatness is known through his association with the life and ministry of Jesus.

The reason we know John is because the gospel reveals that at significant turning points in Jesus' life, the life of John the Baptist intersected with Jesus' own. At Jesus' baptism, John was there. Even before they were born, the lives of John and Jesus were interwoven. The baby John is said to have leapt in the womb when Elizabeth heard the greeting of her relative, Mary, who was pregnant with Jesus.

John's role may be difficult for us to understand,

especially in a world that celebrates stardom. But in the world of John the baptizer, the person of faith gives way to the light of God. John bore the task of giving himself for someone greater. He did not seek his own glory but God's.

Named from his mother's womb to be the instrument to prepare the way for the kingdom of God and for Christ, John called Israel to be a servant people. Israel would show the light of God's salvation in order to lighten all the peoples.

We are not called to point to ourselves, but to Christ. Each of us is named at our baptism, so that God may be glorified. The baptismal liturgy in *Lutheran Book of Worship* quotes Matthew 5:16: "Let your light so shine before others that they may see your good works and glorify your Father in heaven." Just as John yielded to Jesus, so we are to yield to Jesus' light as well. We do not need to be the stars. We just need to carry the light, so that others may see Christ shining in their midst.

WORSHIP MATTERS

"Blessed be the Lord, the God of Israel." With these words of morning prayer and praise, the church blesses God each day. These words remind us that this day—every day—is a part of God's continuing work of redemption, another chapter in the still unfolding history of salvation. As God swore to make Abraham and Sarah a great nation, so God makes great and precious promises to us. As God brought Israel through the sea, freeing it from bondage in Egypt, so God brings us through the waters of baptism, freeing us from all that would enslave us. As God fed Israel with manna in the wilderness, so God feeds us in our wilderness with the life of God's Son. As Israel waited for the coming of the Messiah, so we wait for the Messiah's return. From this perspective, every day is truly a gift from God. In praise and thanksgiving the church sings, "Blessed be the Lord, the God of Israel!"

LET THE CHILDREN COME

"What then will this child become?" is the question people ask regarding the infant John the Baptist. This is a question to be pondered regarding every child, and the answer is a mystery. But we have the opportunity to affirm that God has a purpose for every child. Now may be a time to dream with children and parents about what each one can become, and to pray that, above all, our children, like John, will grow and become strong in spirit.

MUSIC FOR WORSHIP

GATHERING

| LBW 36 | On Jordan's banks the Baptist's cry |
| LBW 265 | Christ, whose glory fills the skies |

PSALM 141

Haugen, Marty. "Psalm 141" in *Holden Evening Prayer*. GIA.

Makeever, Ray. "We Lift Our Hands in Prayer" in *Joyous Light Evening Prayer*. AFP.

Turner, Ronald. PW, Cycle C.

LBW, p. 145 Let my prayer rise before you as incense

TFF 18   Let my prayer arise before you

HYMN OF THE DAY

| WOV 725 | Blessed be the God of Israel |
| | FOREST GREEN |

INSTRUMENTAL RESOURCES

Carter, Andrew. "A Christmas Canon on 'Forest Green'" in *Seasons*, vol. 1. PVN P7001. Org.

Fruhauf, Ennis. "Forest Green" in *Ralph Vaughan Williams and the English School*. AFP 11-10826. Org/kybd.

Haan, Raymond. "Prelude on Forest Green." MSM 20-197A. Org, inst.

Hildebrand, Kevin. *Triptych on "Forest Green" for Violin and Organ*. MSM-20-165. Inst, org.

Leavitt, John. "Forest Green" in *Christmas Suite*. AFP 11-10857. Org.

Sedio, Mark. "Forest Green" in *Dancing in the Light of God*. AFP 11-10793. Pno.

ALTERNATE HYMN OF THE DAY

| LBW 177/8 | By all your saints in warfare (st. 15) |

COMMUNION

| LBW 390 | I love to tell the story |
| WOV 766 | We come to the hungry feast |

SENDING

| LBW 507 | How firm a foundation |
| WOV 689 | Rejoice in God's saints |

ADDITIONAL HYMNS AND SONGS

H82 272	The great forerunner of the morn
LW 187	When all the world was cursed
TFF 225	I believe I'll testify
W&P 147	We are called

239

MUSIC FOR THE DAY

CHORAL

Farlee, Robert Buckley. "Song of Zechariah" in *Three Biblical Songs.*
AFP 11-10604. U, kybd.

Ferguson, John, arr. "Comfort, Comfort." AFP 11-2381. SATB opt
picc, 2 cl, tamb.

Ferguson, John. "Comfort, Comfort." AFP 11-2381. Also in *The Augs-burg Choirbook.* AFP 11-10817. SATB, opt picc, opt 2 cl, opt
tamb, opt kybd.

Gibbons, Orlando. "This Is the Record of John." LAW 550. SAATB,
T solo, org.

CHILDREN'S CHOIRS

Larson, Sonia. "Come to the River Jordan" in *Three for the Children.*
AMSI CC-8. U/2 pt, kybd.

Ramseth, Betty Ann. "Sent from God" in *Give Praises with Joy.*
BRD 4591-05. U, autoharp/dulcimer.

KEYBOARD/INSTRUMENTAL

Fields, Tim. "All Hail the Power of Jesus' Name." AFP 11-11006. Org.

Heschke, Richard. "O God of Earth and Altar" in *Twenty-two Hymn
Settings.* CPH 97-6063. Org.

Muffat, Georg. "Ciacona" in *Apparatus musico-organisticus,* vol. 4.
Doblinger. Org.

HANDBELL

Behnke, John. "Fantasy on 'St. Columba.'" JEF JHS9227. 3-5 oct,
opt hc.

Maggs, Charles. "How Firm a Foundation." HOP CP 6088. Quartet.

PRAISE ENSEMBLE

Armstrong, Matthew. "On Jordan's Bank." CPH 98-3227. SATB,
C inst, pno.

Sappington, Ralph C. "Blessed Be the Lord God of Israel" in W&P.

Schutte, Dan. "Let the Valleys Be Raised" in *Glory & Praise.* OCP.

JUNE 24, 2001

THIRD SUNDAY AFTER PENTECOST
PROPER 7

INTRODUCTION

Before God saves us in baptism, we are held prisoner to
hostile spiritual forces. Some of them are known to us, and
some are of our own making. Often we do not see or recognize the spirits that trouble us. As we come into God's
presence today, a word of liberation is announced to us.

Today the church remembers with thanksgiving
the Nativity of John the Baptist, the forerunner of Jesus
who called God's people to leave the past and enter
God's future.

PRAYER OF THE DAY

O God our defender, storms rage about us and cause us
to be afraid. Rescue your people from despair, deliver
your sons and daughters from fear, and preserve us all
from unbelief; through your Son, Jesus Christ our Lord.

READINGS

Isaiah 65:1-9

*The prophet announces God's impatience. The people's self-
absorption is idolatry, and images from pagan worship fill this
reading. Like a vintner who crushes the grape to release the
wine, God will use Israel's exile to establish a new community
of the faithful.*

Psalm 22:18-27 (Psalm 22:19-28 [NRSV])

In the midst of the congregation I will praise you. (Ps. 22:21)

Galatians 3:23-29

*For Paul, baptism is a powerful bond that unites people in
faith. Those who are baptized experience a radical equality that
removes distinctions based on race, social class, or gender.*

Luke 8:26-39

*In response to being healed, the Gerasene indicated his willing-
ness to be Jesus' disciple by sitting at Jesus' feet. Unlike the rest
of the Gerasenes who, in their fear, ask Jesus to leave, the man
who has been healed testifies to what Jesus has done for him.*

ALTERNATE FIRST READING/PSALM

1 Kings 19:1-4 [5-7] 8-15a

*In the previous chapter, Elijah had triumphed over the
prophets of Ba'al through the power of the Lord. Now, terrified
by Queen Jezebel's threats, Elijah flees into the wilderness,
where he seeks refuge at Horeb (Sinai), the mountain of God.*

God addresses Elijah's dejection by sending him on to Damascus to anoint Elisha as his successor.

Psalm 42 and 43

Send out your light and truth that they may lead me.
(Ps. 43:3)

COLOR Green

THE PRAYERS

Freed by Christ and led by the Spirit, let us offer our prayers to God for the world, the church, and all those in need.

A BRIEF SILENCE.

That leaders of nations and all citizens may strive to bring peace and harmony into a world longing for wholeness. God of truth,

hear our prayer.

That in Christ the walls of race, gender, and class may no longer divide us. God of truth,

hear our prayer.

That enlivened by our worship and the gift of God's saving grace, we may return to our homes and workplaces eager to declare how much you have done for us. God of truth,

hear our prayer.

That all who are in need of healing of any kind (especially…) may be comforted and empowered by your love. God of truth,

hear our prayer.

HERE OTHER INTERCESSIONS MAY BE OFFERED.

That as we give thanks for the faithful who have gone before us, we may live graciously toward those around us. God of truth,

hear our prayer.

Receive the prayers of our hearts, O God, and grant that we may forever trust in your promises, through Jesus Christ our Lord.

Amen

IMAGES FOR PREACHING

The man was undoubtedly a scary sight: naked, wild-eyed, and smeared with dirt. He was certainly not the greeting party the disciples expected as they pulled their boat from the water onto the shore of the Gerasenes. His home had appropriately been the tombs outside the city gates, for he had become an animated corpse,

owned and inhabited by forces not his own. These forces would someday lead to his total destruction, only to inhabit and possess another.

One characteristic of our human makeup is our receptivity to being controlled by another. Paul would later speak of this human tendency as the difference between being a slave and being free. Jesus' response was to take control over this controlling other and to expel it from the one who had been held captive for so many years.

We sophisticates of the twenty-first century are still vulnerable. The voices that call out to us are many and varied and are not limited to the type that possessed the Gerasene demoniac. Other voices include unchecked greed, selfishness, and pride, along with the behaviors of an addictive or otherwise destructive nature.

Our only way out of this dilemma is in being released by Jesus and filled with his indwelling Spirit. It is in being claimed by Christ that we discover true release and freedom. In Galatians, Paul says that we are now "clothed with Christ" (Gal. 3:27). It is in his gracious covering that we find perfect freedom and peace.

WORSHIP MATTERS

Whether the context is a congregational meeting or a churchwide assembly, we often mistakenly think that in order for the church to be united we must all agree. Because there is no longer Jew or Greek, slave or free, male or female (Gal. 3:28), we think that we must agree in all things. In so thinking we mistake differences for divisions. Christ has not done away with our differences. Christ has overcome the power of our differences to divide us. The church is united not by our agreement, not by the fact that we are all the same, but because Christ Jesus has made us all children of God through faith (Gal. 3:26). Clothed in Christ through baptism, our differences become opportunities to creatively live out our calling as heirs according to God's promise (Gal. 3:29) within the one, catholic church.

LET THE CHILDREN COME

Children like to wear nice clothes and sometimes think they must have certain brand names and styles, so they can be like their friends. On some occasions, families dress alike. The baptized have clothed themselves with Christ (Gal. 3:27) and can be like Christ in some ways. What does it mean for a child to be clothed with

241

Christ? Part of the answer is suggested in today's alleluia verse. God's Spirit in our hearts causes us to cry, "Abba! Father!" Like Jesus, we are intimately connected to a loving parent. Clothed with Christ, we are united with Jesus and share his mission to the world.

MUSIC FOR WORSHIP

GATHERING

| LBW 545/6 | When morning gilds the skies |
| WOV 682 | Praise the Spirit in creation |

PSALM 22

Guimont, Michel. "Psalm 22: I Will Praise You, Lord" in *RitualSong*. GIA.

Hopson, Hal H. *Psalm Refrains and Tones*. HOP 425.

Hughes, Howard. *Psalms for all Seasons: An ICEL Collection*. NMP.

Shields, Valerie. PW, Cycle C.

See Good Friday.

HYMN OF THE DAY

| LBW 415 | God of grace and God of glory |
| | CWM RHONDDA |

VOCAL RESOURCES

Kohrs, Jonathan. "God of Grace and God of Glory" in *Hymn Stanzas for Choirs, Set I*. CPH 97-6755. SAB.

INSTRUMENTAL RESOURCES

Albrecht, Timothy. "Cwm Rhondda" in *Grace Notes VIII*. AFP 11-10970. Org.

Carlson, J. Bert. "Cwm Rhondda" in *A New Look at the Old*. AFP 11-11009. Org.

Moklebust, Cathy. "Cwm Rhondda" in *Hymn Stanzas for Handbells*. AFP 11-10722 (4-5 oct) or 11-10869 (2-3 oct). Hb.

Pelz, Walter L. "Cwm Rhondda" in *Hymn Settings for Organ and Brass*, set 2. AFP 11-10272.

ALTERNATE HYMN OF THE DAY

| LBW 393 | Rise, shine, you people! |
| WOV 750 | Oh, praise the gracious power |

COMMUNION

| LBW 560 | Oh, that I had a thousand voices |
| WOV 710 | One bread, one body |

SENDING

| LBW 520 | Give to our God immortal praise! |
| WOV 724 | Shalom |

ADDITIONAL HYMNS AND SONGS

TFF 207	Satan, we're going to tear your kingdom down
TFF 214	In Christ there is no east or west
TWC 340	Amid the thronging worshipers (Ps. 22)
W&P 131	Stand in the congregation
W&P 137	The summons

MUSIC FOR THE DAY

CHORAL

Bach, J. S. "All Who Believe and Are Baptized" in BAS.

Carter, John. "I Will Arise and Go to Jesus." Roger Dean CD-105.

Keesecker, Thomas. "Washed Anew." AFP 11-10676. SAB/SATB, kybd, opt hb, opt cong.

Weelkes, Thomas. "Early Will I Seek Thee." BRD 931.

Wood, Dale. "Rise, Shine!" AFP 11-10737. SATB, org.

CHILDREN'S CHOIRS

Lord, Suzanne. "Faith That's Sure" in LS.

Sleeth, Natalie. "Go into the World." CG A-209. 3 pt (SAB/SSA) or 2 pt (SA/mxd), pno.

Ziegenhals, Harriet. "Oh, Sing to the Lord." CG CGA640. U/2 pt, kybd, opt maracas.

KEYBOARD/INSTRUMENTAL

Cherwien, David. *Rise, Shine, You People*. AFP 11-10523. Org.

Rorem, Ned. "Elms" in *Views from the Oldest House*. B&H. Org.

Wold, Wayne L. "Suite on 'Oh, Praise the Gracious Power'" in *Child of the Light: Preludes on Hymntunes by Women*. AFP 11-10938. Org.

HANDBELL

Linker/McFadden. "Rise, Shine, You People." AFP 11-10629. 3-5 oct, org.

Satie/arr. Wright. "Gymnopedie #1." HOP CP 6015. 2 oct. Qrt.

PRAISE ENSEMBLE

Hesla, Bret. "Let Us Put on the Clothes of Christ" in *Global Songs 2*. AFP 11-10813.

Hurd, Bob. "Pan de vida" in *Glory & Praise*. OCP.

Kogut, Malcom. "I Will Praise You, Lord" (Psalm 22) in PCY, vol. 7. U/SATB, kybd, solo, opt cong, gtr.

SUNDAY, JUNE 24
THE NATIVITY OF ST. JOHN THE BAPTIST

The Nativity of St. John the Baptist is celebrated exactly six months before Christmas Eve. For Christians in the Northern Hemisphere, these two dates are deeply symbolic. John said that he must decrease as Jesus increased. John was born as the days are longest and then steadily decrease. Jesus was born as the days are shortest and then steadily increase. In many countries this day is celebrated with customs associated with the summer solstice. Midsummer is especially popular in northern European countries that experience few hours of darkness at this time of year.

At this time of year, parishes could consider having a summer festival shaped by the pattern of the liturgical year. Consider a church picnic on or near this date, and use John's traditional symbols of fire and water in decorations and games.

MONDAY, JUNE 25
PRESENTATION OF THE AUGSBURG CONFESSION, 1530; PHILIPP MELANCHTHON, RENEWER OF THE CHURCH, 1560

The University of Wittenberg hired Melanchthon as its first professor of Greek, and there he became a friend of Martin Luther. Melanchthon was a popular professor—even his classes at six in the morning had as many as six hundred students. As a reformer he was known for his conciliatory spirit and for finding areas of agreement with fellow Christians. He was never ordained. On this day in 1530 the German and Latin editions of the Augsburg Confession were presented to Emperor Charles of the Holy Roman Empire. The Augsburg Confession was written by Melanchthon and endorsed by Luther. In 1580 when the *Book of Concord* was drawn up, the unaltered Augsburg Confession was included as the principal Lutheran confession.

In the spirit of Melanchthon's work, consider a summer ecumenical study group with a nearby Roman Catholic parish. Use the Augsburg Confession and the Joint Declaration on the Doctrine of Justification as study documents.

THURSDAY, JUNE 28
IRENAEUS, BISHOP OF LYONS, C. 202

Irenaeus believed that the way to remain steadfast to the truth was to hold fast to the faith handed down from the apostles. He believed that only Matthew, Mark, Luke, and John were trustworthy gospels. Irenaeus was an opponent of gnosticism and its emphasis on dualism. As a result of his battles with the gnostics he was one of the first to speak of the church as "catholic." By "catholic" he meant that congregations did not exist by themselves, but were linked to one another throughout the whole church. He also maintained that this church was not contained within any national boundaries. He argued that the church's message was for all people, in contrast to the gnostics who emphasized "secret knowledge."

What do we mean when we say that the church is catholic and apostolic? How is the apostolic faith passed down through the generations?

FRIDAY, JUNE 29
ST. PETER AND ST. PAUL, APOSTLES

These two are an odd couple of biblical witnesses to be brought together in one commemoration. It appears that Peter would have gladly served as the editor of Paul's letters: in a letter attributed to Peter, he says that some things in Paul's letters are hard to understand. Paul's criticism of Peter is more blunt. In Galatians he points out ways that Peter was wrong. One of the things that unites Peter and Paul is the tradition that says they were martyred together on this date in A.D. 67 or 68. What unites them more closely is their common confession of Jesus Christ. In the gospel reading Peter declares that Jesus is the Christ through whom the foundation of the church is established. In the second reading Paul tells the Corinthians that they are the temple of Christ. Together Peter and Paul lay a foundation and build the framework for our lives of faith through their proclamation of Jesus Christ.

SATURDAY JUNE 30

JOHAN OLOF WALLIN, ARCHBISHOP OF UPPSALA,
HYMNWRITER, 1839

Wallin was consecrated archbishop of Uppsala and primate of the Church of Sweden two years before his
death. He was considered the leading churchman of his
day in Sweden, yet his lasting fame rests upon his poetry
and his hymns. Of the five hundred hymns in the
Swedish hymnbook of 1819, 130 were written by
Wallin, and approximately two hundred were revised or
translated by him. For more than a century the Church
of Sweden made no change in the 1819 hymnbook.

Take a look at the three Wallin hymns in *Lutheran
Book of Worship:* "All hail to you, O blessed morn!" (73),
"We worship you, O God of might" (432), and "Christians, while on earth abiding" (440). Which of these
hymns might be included in worship tomorrow when
two other hymnwriters, Catherine Winkworth and John
Mason Neale, are also remembered?

JULY 1, 2001

FOURTH SUNDAY AFTER PENTECOST
PROPER 8

244

INTRODUCTION

As we are called by Jesus, we leave one life behind and
take up another. The readings for this day invite us to
take the bold step that brings us into a new world.

Today the church commemorates two translators
who made hymns accessible to English-speaking worshipers: Catherine Winkworth, who died on this day in
1878 and who translated many German hymn texts; and
John Mason Neale, who translated ancient Greek and
Latin hymns. Often treasures from the past can open
God's people to the future.

PRAYER OF THE DAY

O God, you have prepared for those who love you joys
beyond understanding. Pour into our hearts such love
for you that, loving you above all things, we may obtain
your promises, which exceed all that we can desire;
through your Son, Jesus Christ our Lord.

READINGS

1 Kings 19:15-16, 19-21

*In the story preceding today's reading, the prophet Elijah flees
for his life to the security of God's mountain. There the Lord
reveals to Elijah the work that is to be done and promises to
be present wherever God's people are faithful in their work.*

Psalm 16

I have set the LORD always before me. (Ps. 16:8)

Galatians 5:1, 13-25

*For Paul, the freedom Christ gives is not permission to do
whatever we want. It is the ability to be what we could not be
otherwise. The power and guidance of the Spirit produce a different kind of life, one marked by the qualities Paul lists in
this reading.*

Luke 9:51-62

*Luke's gospel describes a long journey to Jerusalem during
which Jesus teaches his followers about the costs of discipleship.
Today's reading describes the outset of this journey and the resolute action needed for travel.*

ALTERNATE FIRST READING/PSALM

2 Kings 2:1-2, 6-14

*Elijah's ministry comes to a successful conclusion, and a new
chapter of the story begins as Elisha accepts the spirit of his
teacher to carry on God's ministry.*

Psalm 77:1-2, 11-20

By your strength you have redeemed your people. (Ps. 77:15)

COLOR   Green

THE PRAYERS

Freed by Christ and led by the Spirit, let us offer our
prayers to God for the world, the church, and all those
in need.

A BRIEF SILENCE.

That the world, and especially this country, may be blessed by leaders anointed with the qualities of wisdom, justice, and compassion. God of truth,

hear our prayer.

That the church might not use the freedoms it has as excuses for self-indulgence, but as opportunities for service to others. God of truth,

hear our prayer.

That those who suffer brokenness in spirit, mind, or body (especially . . .) may be empowered and filled with hope by your healing love. God of truth,

hear our prayer.

That along with those of hymnwriters Catherine Winkworth and John Mason Neale, our words and songs may echo beyond our earthly life. God of truth,

hear our prayer.

HERE OTHER INTERCESSIONS MAY BE OFFERED.

That as you help us in our grief for those who have died, we will know the certainty of your grace for all who believe in you. God of truth,

hear our prayer.

Receive the prayers of our hearts, O God, and grant that we may forever trust in your promises, through Jesus Christ our Lord.

Amen

IMAGES FOR PREACHING

Children see the future as a blank check: anything is possible, and no barrier is too difficult to overcome. As we grow and mature in this life, we quickly discover that there is no blank check, but only the cash we have on deposit. That account is further diminished as we say yes to some choices (and therefore by default, say no to other possibilities).

The gospel for today recounts that pivotal moment in Jesus' life when "he set his face to go to Jerusalem" (Luke 9:51b). At that precise moment, he said no to all the other possibilities. He said no to settling down with a wife at his side and children in his lap. He said no to developing his skills as a carpenter and bringing the joy of his craft to others. He said no to experiencing that first gray hair, the birth of his first grandchild, or to the respect that would someday be his as a wise elder of the village of Nazareth.

In setting his face, Jesus said yes to a certain and premature death on a cross. He said yes to humiliation and suffering. He said yes to placing his life and death in the hands of another, not being at all certain of the consequences of that act.

Elisha was also confronted with tough choices, for in accepting Elijah's mantle, Elisha committed his life to the call of God. From that day forward, Elisha would say no to tilling the ground but yes to the dangerous occupation of tilling the human conscience. In slaughtering the oxen that had provided his livelihood, Elisha burned the bridges to his past and took a road not of his own design or personal choosing.

WORSHIP MATTERS

When we think of gifts of the Spirit, we usually think of extraordinary things—prophesy, healing, speaking in tongues. In our second reading we find a list of the Spirit's gifts that, though less extraordinary, are much more important for everyday life. Paul counts as gifts of the Spirit "love, joy, peace, patience, kindness, generosity, faithfulness, gentleness, and self-control" (Gal. 5:22-23). These gifts remind us that in Christ every one of us is guided by the Spirit, and all of us are called to live by the Spirit. Free in Christ and equipped by the Spirit, we use our gifts to love others as ourselves. In so doing we put an end to competition and envy and live as heirs of the kingdom of God.

LET THE CHILDREN COME

Children like to go grocery shopping with their parents. During the summer, the produce section offers an abundance of tasty, colorful fruits, such as strawberries, peaches, grapes, and watermelon. We consider "fruits of the Spirit" in the second reading. Fresh fruit is as important in our spiritual lives as it is in a healthy, appealing diet. Let worship leaders envision and create a "shopping expedition," in which children may consider some of the beautiful, sweet fruits of the Spirit to share with others.

MUSIC FOR WORSHIP

GATHERING

| LBW 459 | O Holy Spirit, enter in |
| WOV 703 | Draw us in the Spirit's tether |

PSALM 16

Haas, David. "Show Me the Path" in PCY, vol. 8.

Inwood, Paul. "Psalm 16: Center of My Life" in STP, vol. 1.

245

Makeever, Ray. "You Show Us the Path of Life" in *Joyous Light Evening Prayer*. AFP.

Shields, Valerie. PW, Cycle C.

Soper, Scott. "Psalm 16: The Path of Life" in STP, vol. 3.

HYMN OF THE DAY

LBW 503   O Jesus, I have promised
                MUNICH

INSTRUMENTAL RESOURCES

Albrecht, Timothy. "Munich" in *Grace Notes V*. AFP 11-10764. Org.

Tryggestad, David. "Munich" in *Deo Gracias*. AFP 11-10471. Org.

Wellman, Samuel. "Munich" in *Keyboard Hymn Favorites*. AFP 11-10820. Pno.

ALTERNATE HYMN OF THE DAY

LBW 455   "Come, follow me," the Savior spake

WOV 777   In the morning when I rise

COMMUNION

LBW 501   He leadeth me: oh, blessed thought!

WOV 711   You satisfy the hungry heart

SENDING

LBW 552   In thee is gladness

WOV 782   All my hope on God is founded

ADDITIONAL HYMNS AND SONGS

TFF 146   I can hear my Savior calling

VU 691   Though ancient walls may still stand proud

W&P 103   Now God our Father

W&P 137   The summons

MUSIC FOR THE DAY

CHORAL

Callahan, Charles. "In Your Mercy, Lord, You Called Me." CPH 98-2861. U, kybd.

Cherwien, David "God Has Called Us." CPH 98-3357. SATB, cong, opt brass, opt timp, org.

Fleming, Larry. "Give Me Jesus" in *The Augsburg Choirbook*. AFP 11-10817. SATB.

Friedell, Harold. "Draw Us in the Spirit's Tether." HWG GCMR 2472. SATB, org.

Handel, G. F. "Jesus, Sun of Life, My Splendor." CPH 98-1445. SATB, org.

CHILDREN'S CHOIRS

Dietterich, Philip R. "Come One, Come All, Come Follow." CG CGA-553. U antiphonal vcs, kybd.

Eltringham, Susan. "Love Your Neighbor" in LS.

Sleeth, Natalie. "The Kingdom of the Lord." AMSI 301. 2 pt, opt fl, pno/hpd/org.

KEYBOARD/INSTRUMENTAL

Biery, James. "Air and Canon on 'Draw Us in the Spirit's Tether'" in *Tree of Life*. AFP 11-10701. Org.

Billingham, Richard. "Give Me Jesus" in *Seven Reflections on African American Spirituals*. AFP 11-10762. Org.

Callahan, Charles. "In the Beginning: A Biblical Poem." MSM 20-923. Org, tba, vc.

HANDBELL

Anderson and Page. "Be Still My Soul." HOP 1983. Solo.

Stephenson, Valerie. "O Jesus, I Have Promised." AG 1894. 3-5 oct, opt hc.

Wagner, Douglas E. "Springs of Joy." AGEHR AG-2012. 2 oct.

PRAISE ENSEMBLE

Bullock, Geoff, and Gail Dunshea. "You Are My God" in W&P.

Goodine, Wayne. "I'm Free" in *Sing & Rejoice*. BNT.

Haugen, Marty. "Eye Has Not Seen." GIA G-3726. U/SATB, kybd, opt cong, gtr.

Muller, Teresa. "Draw Me into Your Presence" in *Praise Hymns and Choruses,* 4th ed. MAR.

SUNDAY, JULY 1

CATHERINE WINKWORTH, 1878;
JOHN MASON NEALE, 1866; HYMNWRITERS

Neale was an English priest associated with the movement for church renewal at Cambridge. Winkworth lived most of her life in Manchester, where she was involved in promoting women's rights. These two hymnwriters translated many hymn texts into English. Catherine Winkworth devoted herself to the translation of German hymns, and John Mason Neale specialized in ancient Latin and Greek hymns. Winkworth has thirty hymns in *LBW,* and Neale has twenty-one. In addition, two texts by Neale are in *WOV.* Use the indexes at the back of both books to discover some of their most familiar translations. Include hymns by those two hymnwriters in worship today.

FRIDAY, JULY 6
JAN HUS, MARTYR, 1415

Jan Hus was a Bohemian priest who spoke against abuses in the church of his day in many of the same ways Luther would a century later. He spoke against the withholding of the cup at Holy Communion and because of this stance was excommunicated, not for heresy but for insubordination toward his archbishop. He preached against the selling of indulgences and was particularly mortified by the indulgence trade of two rival claimants to the papacy who were raising money for war against each other. He was found guilty of heresy by the Council of Constance and burned at the stake.

The followers of Jan Hus became known as the Czech Brethren and later became the Moravian Church. The Evangelical Lutheran Church in America and the Moravian Church in America have recently inaugurated a relationship of full communion.

JULY 8, 2001

FIFTH SUNDAY AFTER PENTECOST
PROPER 9

INTRODUCTION

We are nurtured; we are nurturing. Today's readings remind us how God cares for us. We are called to adopt God's sustaining ways. We are fed at the table, and we are sent into the world to care for others.

PRAYER OF THE DAY

God of glory and love, peace comes from you alone. Send us as peacemakers and witnesses to your kingdom, and fill our hearts with joy in your promises of salvation; through your Son, Jesus Christ our Lord.

READINGS

Isaiah 66:10-14

Those who returned from the exile found that the hopes and expectations for the glorious restoration of Judah were not fulfilled. For these disappointed people, the prophet envisions salvation in the image of a nursing woman. Mother Jerusalem and a mothering God remind the community how they are sustained and supported.

Psalm 66:1-8 (Psalm 66:1-9 [NRSV])

God holds our souls in life. (Ps. 66:8)

Galatians 6:[1-6] 7-16

In this letter, Paul insists that all people are made right with God through faith in Jesus Christ. Here Paul offers practical advice about how people who believe this truth will live, exercising common concern for one another in "the family of faith."

Luke 10:1-11, 16-20

Jesus commissions his followers to go where he would go and do what he would do. Risking hardship and danger, they offer peace and healing as signs that the reign of God is near.

ALTERNATE FIRST READING/PSALM

2 Kings 5:1-14

Naaman, a Syrian general, suffers from leprosy. In this passage Elisha miraculously cures his illness, but only after Naaman realizes, with the help of his servants, that his real problem lies in his pride.

Psalm 30

My God, I cried out to you, and you restored me to health. (Ps. 30:2)

COLOR Green

THE PRAYERS

Freed by Christ and led by the Spirit, let us offer our prayers to God for the world, the church, and all those in need.

A BRIEF SILENCE.

Rouse all people to speak and act for justice, and inspire our leaders to guide us into peace. God of truth,
hear our prayer.
Bless all the baptized, and grant strength to all servants of the church who have gone to work in your harvest. God of truth,
hear our prayer.
Energize and uphold us in bearing the burdens of those weighed down by poverty, hunger, loneliness, abuse, anxiety, and illness (especially...). God of truth,
hear our prayer.

HERE OTHER INTERCESSIONS MAY BE OFFERED.

Comfort us with the certainty that we will be united with the saints who walked among us and now rest in your presence. God of truth,
hear our prayer.
Receive the prayers of our hearts, O God, and grant that we may forever trust in your promises, through Jesus Christ our Lord.
Amen

IMAGES FOR PREACHING

A modern-day preacher who prepares for the task of writing a sermon sits down with a Bible, a notebook, a laptop computer, a mechanical pencil, glasses, and a mug of hot coffee. Has she forgotten anything? Yes, probably. But all these things are considered essential ingredients for many preachers if they are to produce quality work.

This week, as we wait for computers to boot, we read Jesus' words to the seventy he sends out into the towns and villages of the region. "Go on your way. I am sending you out like lambs into the midst of wolves. Carry no purse, no bag, no sandals; and greet no one on the road" (Luke 10:3-4). Might those words apply to us? "Preacher, set aside your laptop, your books, the reading glasses, and your hot coffee, that stuff you think so essential to spreading the word. Leave it all, and then come follow me."

Occasionally we realize that the stuff we use to aid in the spread of the gospel can become a source of distraction and preoccupation that prevents the real work from being accomplished. The computer confuses us or freezes, the coffee must be constantly refilled, and pencil leads break frequently. We spend so much time tending to the trappings and the tools that the primary tasks themselves can often be neglected.

Jesus knew that if the proclamation of his message was to be effective, the messengers of that good news must not be encumbered by the cares and distractions caused by the possession of extraneous stuff. He also wanted to demonstrate that the faithful proclamation of the gospel message would in and of itself provide for the physical, emotional, and spiritual needs of those who faithfully proclaim it.

In Isaiah, the Lord promises that even in the midst of captivity and despair God's people will be sustained even as a hungry child is completely nourished at a mother's breast. Such a promised consolation was difficult for God's chosen people to believe as they languished in a foreign land. But the Lord is faithful in every work and word.

WORSHIP MATTERS

Go in peace. Serve the Lord. With these words we, like the seventy, are sent from our encounter with Christ into the world. The harvest is plentiful and the laborers are few. So, more than asking the Lord of the harvest to send laborers into his harvest, we need to allow our prayer to lead to action and become laborers ourselves. Jesus warns us to be careful, for he is sending us as lambs in the midst of wolves (Luke 10:3). But Jesus also assures us that we need not worry about being successful. Our task is not to save souls but to bring the good news to others so that, whether people hear or refuse to hear, they will "know this: that the kingdom of God has come near" (Luke 10:6). We rejoice not in numbers and not in our success, but in the good news that our names are written in heaven (Luke 10:20).

LET THE CHILDREN COME

Jesus sent the seventy out in pairs. Large numbers can overwhelm children, but when they are paired up with a partner or as part of a team, they feel more secure. Tasks that seem impossible for one child to do become feasible and even fun when two can work together. Jesus' idea of pairing people, two by two, might be emphasized by asking people at the end of the service to exit hand-in-hand with spouse or significant other, with another child, or another adult. God does not ask us to play or to work alone!

MUSIC FOR WORSHIP
GATHERING

| LBW 519 | My soul, now praise your maker! |
| WOV 781 | My life flows on in endless song |

PSALM 66

Cooney, Rory. "Let All the Earth Cry Out" in STP, vol. 4.

Haugen, Marty, and David Haas. "Let All the Earth" in PCY, vol. 10.

Marshall, Jane. *Psalms Together.* CGC-21.

Shields, Valerie. PW, Cycle C.

Warner, Steven C. "Psalm 66: Cry Out to the Lord" in STP, vol. 2.

HYMN OF THE DAY

| WOV 755 | We all are one in mission |
| | KUORTANE |

A SUGGESTION FOR THE HYMN OF THE DAY

Intonation	C instrument plays cantus firmus; key-board joins on third phrase
Stanza 1	All
Stanza 2	Choir in canon, a cappella
Stanza 3	All; keyboard uses accompaniment from LBW 339; choir could also sing in harmony using LBW 339

INSTRUMENTAL RESOURCES

Below, Robert. "Suite for Organ" in *Organ Music for the Seasons*, vol. 2. AFP 11-10101. Org.

Cherwien, David. "Kuortane" in *Organ Plus One*. AFP 11-10758. Org, inst.

Keesecker, Thomas. "Kuortane" in *Come Away to the Skies*. AFP 11-10794. Pno.

Sedio, Mark. "Kuortane" in *How Blessed This Place*. AFP 11-10934. Org.

ALTERNATE HYMN OF THE DAY

| LBW 381 | Hark, the voice of Jesus calling |
| LBW 384 | Your kingdom come, O Father |

COMMUNION

| LBW 379 | Spread, oh, spread, almighty Word |
| WOV 769 | Mothering God, you gave me birth |

SENDING

| LBW 221 | Sent forth by God's blessing |
| WOV 754 | Let us talents and tongues employ |

ADDITIONAL HYMNS AND SONGS

DH 40	Dancing at the harvest
PH 415	Come, labor on
TFF 222	God the sculptor of the mountains
TH 584	Go, labor on
W&P 43	Glory and praise to our God

MUSIC FOR THE DAY
CHORAL

Cotter, Jean. "Let All the Earth." GIA G-4633. U, cong, pno, gtr.

Jennings, Kenneth. "With a Voice of Singing." AFP 11-1379. Also in *The Augsburg Choirbook.* AFP 11-10817. SATB.

Johnson, David N., arr. "O God, Eternal Source of Love" in *Gloria Deo 1.* AFP 11-9160. SAB, kybd.

Rhein, Robert. "Come, Let Us Eat." CPH 98-3092. 2 pt, pno.

CHILDREN'S CHOIRS

Handel, George F./arr. Jane McFadden. "Let My Heart and Soul Praise the Lord." CG CGA650. U, kybd.

Helms, Judith A. "Let Me Be Your Servant, Jesus" in LS.

Marshall, Jane. "Psalm 66" in *Psalms Together.* CG CGC-18. U, cong, kybd.

Ramseth, Betty Ann. "Making Happy Noises" in *Making Happy Noises.* AFP 11-9280. U, drum set, fl.

Sleeth, Natalie. "God Is Calling Us." AMSI 610. 2 pt mxd, kybd, opt cong.

KEYBOARD/INSTRUMENTAL

Diemer, Emma Lou. "Battle Hymn" and "National Hymn" in *God and Country.* SMP 70/1141S. Org.

Haan, Raymond H. "Gott Sei Dank—Partita for Organ." NPH OL 27-0010. Org.

Wesley, Charles. "Variations on 'God Save the King' (America)." ECS WL700018. Org/kybd.

HANDBELL

Afdahl, Lee J. "Abbot's Leigh." AG 2103. 3-5 oct.

Kinyon, Barbara. "God of Our Fathers." HOP 1670. 2-3 oct.

McChesney, Kevin. "Blessed Assurance." HOP CP 6024. Quartet.

PRAISE ENSEMBLE

Bond, Derek. "At the Foot of the Cross" in W&P.

Cook, Steve, and Vikki Cook. "Jesus, You Reign Over All" in *Praise Hymns and Choruses,* 4th ed. MAR.

Rathmann, Dawn. "Go Forth." CPH 98-3332. U, kybd.

249

WEDNESDAY, JULY 11
BENEDICT OF NURSIA, ABBOT OF MONTE CASSINO, C. 540

Benedict is known as the father of Western monasticism. He was educated in Rome but was appalled by the decline of life around him. He went to live as a hermit, and a community of monks came to gather around him. In the prologue of his rule for monasteries he wrote that his intent in drawing up his regulations was "to set down nothing harsh, nothing burdensome." It is that moderate spirit that characterizes his rule and the monastic communities that are formed by it. Benedict encourages a generous spirit of hospitality in that visitors to Benedictine communities are to be welcomed as Christ himself.

Benedictine monasticism continues to serve a vital role in the contemporary church. A summer reading group might choose *A Share in the Kingdom* by Benet Tvedten, OSB (Liturgical Press, 1989) to learn about Benedict's Rule and hear this ancient voice speak to the church today.

THURSDAY, JULY 12
NATHAN SÖDERBLOM, ARCHBISHOP OF UPPSALA, 1931

In 1930, this Swedish theologian, ecumenist, and social activist received the Nobel Prize for peace. He saw the value of the ancient worship of the catholic church and encouraged the liturgical movement. He also valued the work of liberal Protestant scholars and believed social action was a first step on the path toward a united Christianity. He organized the Universal Christian Council on Life and Work, which was one of the organizations that in 1948 came together to form the World Council of Churches.

As you commemorate Söderblom, discuss the ecumenical situation in the church now in this new millennium. What are some of the achievements of the past century? What hopes of Söderblom's might still wait to be achieved?

JULY 15, 2001

SIXTH SUNDAY AFTER PENTECOST
PROPER 10

INTRODUCTION

God can be as near as a neighbor, and our opportunities to share God's love are as close as the words that leave our lips. The peace of Christ we exchange in this community we also take with us into the world to share with others.

Today we remember Vladimir, who died on this day in 1015, and also his grandmother, Olga—the first Christian rulers of Russia. We commend to God's care our Russian sisters and brothers who have become neighbors to us in Christ.

PRAYER OF THE DAY

Almighty God, we thank you for planting in us the seed of your word. By your Holy Spirit help us to receive it with joy, live according to it, and grow in faith and hope and love; through your Son, Jesus Christ our Lord.
or

Lord God, use our lives to touch the world with your love. Stir us, by your Spirit, to be neighbor to those in need, serving them with willing hearts; through your Son, Jesus Christ our Lord.

READINGS

Deuteronomy 30:9-14

Moses calls the people to renew the covenant God made with their ancestors. Through this covenant God gives life and asks obedience. God's word is brought near to the people, so that they may remain true to the covenant.

Psalm 25:1-9 (Psalm 25:1-10 [NRSV])

Show me your ways, O LORD, and teach me your paths. (Ps. 25:3)

Colossians 1:1-14

The letter to the Colossians was written to warn its readers of various false teachings. The first part of the letter is an expres-

sion of thanks for the faith, hope, and love that mark this com-
munity. It concludes with a prayer for continued growth in
understanding.

Luke 10:25-37

In this well-known parable, Jesus shifts the focus of concern
from speculation concerning who is one's neighbor to the treat-
ment of one's neighbor with mercy.

ALTERNATE FIRST READING/PSALM

Amos 7:7-17

Amos, a shepherd from the southern village of Tekoa, is called
by God to preach against Israel, the Northern Kingdom, in a
time of economic prosperity. Today's reading illustrates how
Amos's stinging criticism of those in authority alienated him
from both king and priest.

Psalm 82

Arise, O God, and rule the earth. (Ps. 82:8)

COLOR   Green

THE PRAYERS

Freed by Christ and led by the Spirit, let us offer our
prayers to God for the world, the church, and all those
in need.

A BRIEF SILENCE.

Prosper the work of peace in the world, that all people
may be freed from the bonds of hunger, war, abuse, and
every form of injustice. God of truth,

hear our prayer.

We turn to you with all our hearts and souls, praying
for those who are hospitalized, suffering long-term illness, or in need of any form of healing (especially...).
God of truth, .

hear our prayer.

Strengthen our prayers for the welfare of others, that
they may be filled with the knowledge of your will.
God of truth,

hear our prayer.

Join us in solidarity with neighbors and all who are in
need. God of truth,

hear our prayer.

HERE OTHER INTERCESSIONS MAY BE OFFERED.

We give thanks for those who have set an example of
faithful living and who now rest from their labors: those
dear to us, as well as members of the great company of
faith, including Vladimir and Olga. God of truth,

hear our prayer.

Receive the prayers of our hearts, O God, and grant
that we may forever trust in your promises, through
Jesus Christ our Lord.

Amen

IMAGES FOR PREACHING

As the pastor stands in the narthex, greeting each
parishioner by name and with a handshake, the pastor
sees the man waiting his turn at the end of the line.
Each person takes the pastor's hand, smiles, and shares a
comment such as, "That was a wonderful sermon, pastor," or "I want to talk with you about my getting my
child baptized." The pastor sees the man at the end of
line still waiting amid an island of empty space created
by the respectable members of the parish.

As the line shrinks the pastor thinks how wonderful it will soon be to shed the hot vestments, get into a
car, and drive to a favorite restaurant for a quiet and re-
laxing lunch with the family. Perhaps the man at the
end of the line will get tired of waiting and leave. If the
pastor speaks to some favorite members of the parish
for a while, he will surely get the message. Ninety-year-
old Mrs. Jones squeezes the pastor's hand as she talks
about her failing husband at the nursing home.

The next-to-the-last person shakes the pastor's hand
and thanks him for announcing the men's group meeting on Tuesday. The pastor is tired and anxious to run to
the sacristy. But the man at the end of line is now here,
standing face to face with the pastor. The air is suddenly
mixed with the stale odor of whiskey mixed with sweat.
His eyes are glazed and distant, his clothing tattered and
ill fitting. "Preacher, I really need your help," he says.

How easy it is for a preacher to stand in the pulpit
and expound upon the Christian's call to serve brothers
and sisters in need. How easy it is for those in padded
pews to nod in agreement and place a sacrificial five
dollars in the plate as it is passed. The Christian's response to need gets tough when we are forced to smell
it, talk to it, touch it, and change our schedules because
of it. The miracle of the good Samaritan is not that a
lowly Samaritan responded to the needs of another, but
that one human being actually went against the tendency we have to ignore the need of our neighbor
when a response to it would be inconvenient, expensive, or an offense to our sensibilities.

251

WORSHIP MATTERS

How do we pray without ceasing (Col. 1:9)? Many of us find it difficult to slow the pace of our lives in order to find time to pray. The truth is that prayer is like exercise. We stay in shape by incorporating physical activity into our way of living. So Paul hints at some of the exercises we can do that will make for prayer-filled living. Always thank God, especially for faith. Seek God's will in all things. Lead lives worthy of the Lord. Be prepared to endure everything with patience. Even a few minutes of this kind of serious exercise every day will drive us to our knees, turn us to our God, and fill our lives with prayer.

LET THE CHILDREN COME

Seeing a child spontaneously comfort a crying baby teaches us. God's commandments are neither too hard for us nor too far away. What the Good Samaritan did was not too hard but fairly easy and natural for a compassionate heart, and it was near him—just across the road from where he walked. Children often inspire adults by doing quickly and well what compassion requires, helping someone who is close at hand. A childlike innocence characterizes the Samaritan, who does not rationalize neglect (as adults often do), but in his pity rushes to help the injured man. The spontaneous hug or kiss of a child is in the spirit of this gospel.

MUSIC FOR WORSHIP

GATHERING

LBW 423	Lord, whose love in humble service
WOV 666	Great God, your love has called us

PSALM 25

Artman, Ruth. "Teach Me Your Ways, O Lord" in *Sing Out! A Children's Psalter.* WLP.

Haugen, Marty. "To You, O Lord" in *PCY,* vol. 10.

Kreutz, Robert. "Come, O Lord" in *Psalms and Selected Canticles.* OCP.

Shields, Valerie. *PW,* Cycle C.

Soper, Scott. "Psalm 25: To You, O Lord" in *STP,* vol. 1.

See first Sunday in Advent.

HYMN OF THE DAY

LBW 551	Joyful, joyful we adore thee
	HYMN TO JOY

VOCAL RESOURCES

Wolff, Drummond. "Joyful, Joyful, We Adore Thee." CPH 98-3076. SATB, tpt, kybd.

INSTRUMENTAL RESOURCES

Cherwien, David. "Hymn to Joy" in *Postludes on Well-Known Hymns.* AFP 11-10795. Org.

Honoré, Jeffrey. "Hymn to Joy" in *Classic Embellishments.* AFP 11-11005. Org, opt inst.

Moklebust, Cathy. "Hymn to Joy" in *Hymn Stanzas for Handbells.* AFP 11-10722 (4-5 oct) or 11-10869 (2-3 oct). Hb.

Uehlein, Christopher. "Toccata on Hymn to Joy" in *Blue Cloud Abbey Organ Book.* AFP 11-10394. Org.

Wasson, Laura E. "Hymn to Joy" in *A Piano Tapestry, Book 2.* AFP 11-10978. Pno.

ALTERNATE HYMN OF THE DAY

LBW 505	Forth in thy name, O Lord, I go
WOV 765	Jesu, Jesu, fill us with your love

COMMUNION

LBW 425	O God of mercy, God of light
WOV 665	Ubi caritas et amor

SENDING

LBW 505	Forth in thy name, O Lord, I go
WOV 763	Let justice flow like streams

ADDITIONAL HYMNS AND SONGS

ASG 2	Be a searchlight
BH 613	We are travelers on a journey
NCH 541	They asked, "Who's my neighbor?"
TFF 224	Help me, Jesus
W&P 70	I will call upon the Lord

MUSIC FOR THE DAY

CHORAL

Englert, Eugene. "I Lift Up My Soul." AFP 11-1797. SATB, fl, kybd.

How, Martin. "Day by Day." GIA G-4178. U/2 pt/3 pt, org.

Nelson, Ronald. "To You, O Lord, I Lift Up My Soul." CPH 98-2928. U, kybd.

Rorem, Ned. "Sing, My Soul, His Wondrous Love." PET 6386.

CHILDREN'S CHOIRS

Carter, Sydney. "When I Needed a Neighbor" in LS.

Christopherson, Dorothy. "Jesu, Jesu." CPH 98-3177. SAB, pno, congas.

Horman, John. "The Good Samaritan." CG CGA-281. 2 pt, kybd.

LeDoux, Joanne. "The Good Samaritan." KIR K131. U, hb, kybd.

KEYBOARD/INSTRUMENTAL

Stanford, Charles Villers. "On a Theme of Orlando Gibbons" (Song 34) in *English Romantic Classics,* ed. Barbara Owen. BEL DM 248. Org.

Rotermund, Donald. "Three Partitas on 'Donne Secours'" in *Seven Hymn Preludes,* Set 4. CPH 97-6573. Org.

HANDBELL

Freeman, Ardis. "Beside Still Waters." HOP CP 9002. Sextet.

Kinyon, Barbara B. "Joyful, Joyful" in *Let's All Ring the Classics.* BEC HB86. 2 oct.

Peterson, Merle. "Mother Earth, Spirit Sky." AGEHR AG 34019. 3-4 oct.

PRAISE ENSEMBLE

Caudhill, Susan. "My Eyes Are Ever on the Lord" (Psalm 25). FBM BG2177. SATB, kybd.

Makeever, Ray. "Someone in Need of Your Love" in DH.

Neaveil, Ryan. "In Christ There Is No East or West." CPH 98-3425. SATB, kybd.

SUNDAY, JULY 15
VLADIMIR, FIRST CHRISTIAN RULER OF RUSSIA, 1015; OLGA, CONFESSOR, 969

Princess Olga became a Christian about the time she made a visit to Constantinople, center of the Byzantine church. She had no success persuading her son or her fellow citizens to receive the gospel. Vladimir was Olga's grandson, and he took the throne at a ruthless time and in a bloodthirsty manner: he killed his brother for the right to rule. After Vladimir became a Christian he set aside the reminders of his earlier life, including pagan idols and temples. He built churches, monasteries, and schools, brought in Greek missionaries to educate the people, and was generous to the poor. Together Vladimir and Olga are honored as the first Christian rulers of Russia.

Today's second reading from Colossians urges the church to give thanks to God, who "has enabled you to share in the inheritance of the saints in the light." The work of Vladimir and Olga shows how that light came to the people of Russia.

TUESDAY, JULY 17
BARTOLOMÉ DE LAS CASAS, MISSIONARY TO THE INDIES, 1566

Bartolomé de las Casas was a Spanish priest and a missionary in the Western Hemisphere. He first came to the West while serving in the military, and he was granted a large estate that included a number of indigenous slaves. When he was ordained in 1513, he granted freedom to his servants. This act characterized much of the rest of de las Casas's ministry. Throughout the Caribbean and Central America he worked to stop the enslavement of native people, to halt the brutal treatment of women by military forces, and to promote laws that humanized the process of colonization.

In a time when churches continue to work for the rights of all people we can recall the words of de las Casas: "The Indians are our brothers, and Christ has given his life for them. Why, then, do we persecute them with such inhuman savagery when they do not deserve such treatment?"

253

JULY 22, 2001

ST. MARY MAGDALENE

INTRODUCTION

Bernard of Clairvaux affectionately called Mary of Magdala "the apostle to the apostles," because she was sent on Easter to bring them good news from Jesus' open tomb. Today we remember her with thanksgiving and recall other women of faith who by their actions and words gave witness to God's powerful new life.

PRAYER OF THE DAY

Almighty God, your Son Jesus Christ restored Mary Magdalene to health of body and mind, and called her to be a witness of his resurrection. Heal us now in body and mind, and call us to serve you in the power of the resurrection of Jesus Christ, who lives and reigns with you and the Holy Spirit, one God, now and forever.

READINGS

Ruth 1:6-18

After her husband and sons died, the widow Naomi lived in Moab for ten years. When Naomi decides to return to Israel, the powerful devotion of her Moabite daughter-in-law, Ruth, shows the deep affection between these two women of faith.

or Exodus 2:1-10

A child is saved by the daughter of Pharaoh and is named Moses.

Psalm 73:23-29 (Psalm 73:23-28 [NRSV])

I will speak of all your works in the gates of the city of Zion. (Ps. 73:29)

Acts 13:26-33a

Paul shares the apostolic witness to Jesus' resurrection—a message first brought to the apostles by Mary Magdalene.

John 20:1-2, 11-18

The fourth evangelist tells the story of Easter, relaying how Mary is surprised as she meets the risen Jesus and is chosen to be the first to share this good news with others.

COLOR White

THE PRAYERS

Freed by Christ and led by the Spirit, let us offer our prayers to God for the world, the church, and all those in need.

A BRIEF SILENCE.

United in our shared humanity, may all nations and their leaders have the commitment to work for justice and peace. God of truth,

hear our prayer.

May all the people of your church be led daily to serve others through the grace you have given us in baptism. God of truth,

hear our prayer.

Grant comfort to those who are in any emotional, spiritual, or physical need (especially…). God of truth,

hear our prayer.

Free us from outworn notions of mission to share the good news of the risen Christ in the world today. God of truth,

hear our prayer.

HERE OTHER INTERCESSIONS MAY BE OFFERED.

Certain with Mary Magdalene and all the saints of your eternal victory over death, we ask for grace to cling to you in all circumstances. God of truth,

hear our prayer.

254

Receive the prayers of our hearts, O God, and grant that we may forever trust in your promises, through Jesus Christ our Lord.

Amen

IMAGES FOR PREACHING

"And so, with Mary Magdalene and Peter and all the witnesses of the resurrection, with earth and sea and all their creatures, and with angels and archangels, cherubim and seraphim, we praise your name and join their unending hymn" (Easter preface, *Lutheran Book of Worship* Ministers Edition).

Mary Magdalene does not always get top billing as she does in this passage. But during Easter's great fifty days she is appropriately listed ahead of Peter and all the other witnesses to Christ's resurrection. She was there first after all (something that surely must have irked the sons of Zebedee to no end). She was certainly among the group that was closest to Jesus. She also was witness to Jesus' crucifixion, burial, and—as we read in today's gospel—his first appearance after the resurrection.

Mary Magdalene's reputation has frequently been questioned, though. The gospel accounts, however, give no evidence that Mary Magdalene was a prostitute nor even one of the women who anointed Jesus' feet. What we know is that she was a central character on Easter morning. She was the one who announced, "I have seen the Lord." The other disciples who were there merely went back to their homes.

Few churches seem to have been named in honor of Mary Magdalene, even though she is the only woman to be accorded the title "saint" in LBW's calendar. Be sure to use the proper preface for Easter today, because this first brave witness to the resurrection deserves to be remembered in the song of the church. Blessed are they who see.

WORSHIP MATTERS

Mary Magdalene was the first apostle. She was both the first witness to the resurrection and the first one sent by the risen Christ to proclaim the good news. According to her culture, Mary was suspect as a witness because she was a woman. So Mary reminds us that Jesus chooses unexpected, even questionable voices with which to proclaim the gospel. As the disciples received the good news of the resurrection from Mary, so the church today must discern what witnesses the risen Christ is sending to us. Then, let us listen to them.

LET THE CHILDREN COME

Children are no strangers to grief and death. They experience pain of loss, fear of separation, and hope in eternal life. Mary Magdalene weeps at her loss. When Jesus appears to her, she becomes a herald of this good news. "I have seen the Lord," she declares (John 20:18).

Some paintings show Mary Magdalene holding a red egg, a symbol of the resurrection. Celebrate by offering red-dyed hard-boiled eggs at coffee hour. Share memories of loved ones who have died in the faith. Tell their stories with tears of joy. Herald the good news that Jesus is risen.

MUSIC FOR WORSHIP

GATHERING

| LBW 182 | Rise, O children of salvation |
| WOV 745 | Awake, O sleeper |

PSALM 73

Jennings, Carolyn. PW, Cycle C.

"How Good God Is to Israel" in *The Grail Gelineau Psalter.* GIA G-1703.

HYMN OF THE DAY

| WOV 692 | For all the faithful women |
| | BARONITA |

ALTERNATE HYMN OF THE DAY

| LBW 147 | Hallelujah! Jesus lives! |

COMMUNION

| LBW 148 | Now the green blade rises |
| WOV 706 | Eat this bread, drink this cup |

SENDING

| LBW 533/4 | Now thank we all our God |
| WOV 690 | Shall we gather at the river |

ADDITIONAL HYMNS AND SONGS

H82 673	The first one ever, oh, ever to know
NEH 174	Mary, weep not, weep no longer
OBS 68	In the fair morning
TFF 90	They crucified my Savior
W&P 99	Mourning into dancing

MUSIC FOR THE DAY

CHORAL

Cherwien, David. "Blessing Be and Glory to the Living One." AFP 11-10918. U/2 pt, org, 2 inst.

Christiansen, Paul. "Easter Morning." AFP 11-1057. SATB.

Ellingboe, Bradley. "Mary at the Tomb." AFP 11-10833. SATB, pno.

Moore, Undine Smith, arr. "I Believe This Is Jesus." AFP 11-0559. SATB, div.

Owens, Sam Batt. "There Is a Balm in Gilead." MSM 50-8832. SATB, solo.

Shepperd, Mark. "Balm in Gilead." AFP 11-10923. SATB, kybd.

CHILDREN'S CHOIRS

James, Layton. "They Rolled the Stone Away." MSM-50-4036. SAB, kybd.

Ramseth, Betty Ann. "On the First Day of the Week" in *Have You Seen My Lord?* AFP 11-9226. U/SATB, A xyl, B xyl, timp.

KEYBOARD/INSTRUMENTAL

Bisbee, B. Wayne. "Hallelujah! Jesus Lives!" in *From the Serene to the Whimsical.* AFP 11-10561. Org.

Hytrek, Theophane. "Sequence for Easter" (Victimae Paschali) in *Laudate!* vol. 4, ed. James W. Kosnik. CPH 97-6665. Org.

HANDBELL

Anderson/Kramlich. "Jesus, Lover of My Soul." HOP 1729. Solo.

Moklebust, Cathy. "Staccato Giocoso." AFP 11-8352. 3 oct.

PRAISE ENSEMBLE

Hierro, Jude Del. "More Love, More Power" in *Come & Worship.* INT.

Priory, Weston, and Gregory Norbet. "Wherever You Go" in *Glory & Praise.* OCP.

Randolph, Jennifer. "Joy of My Desire" in *Come & Worship.* INT.

Vogt, Janet. "Rise Up with Him." OCP 10846. SATB, solo, kybd, opt cong, gtr.

JULY 22, 2001

INTRODUCTION

Stay alert! You might be entertaining God! Today we are introduced to people who hosted God in their homes, although they were not always aware of God's presence. God comes close to us—even within us, as Paul exclaims.

The church today remembers Mary Magdalene, who also was surprised by the risen Jesus and sent to share the good news of his resurrection with the disciples.

PRAYER OF THE DAY

O Lord, pour out upon us the spirit to think and do what is right, that we, who cannot even exist without you, may have the strength to live according to your will; through your Son, Jesus Christ our Lord.

or

O God, you see how busy we are with many things. Turn us to listen to your teachings and lead us to choose the one thing which will not be taken from us, Jesus Christ our Lord.

READINGS

Genesis 18:1-10a

The Lord visits Abraham and Sarah and promises the birth of a child even though they are too old to start a family.

Psalm 15

Who may abide upon your holy hill? Whoever leads a blameless life and does what is right. (Ps. 15:1-2)

Colossians 1:15-28

The great mystery of God is "Christ in you." Because Christ is present in his body, the church, Christians share in his life, suffering, and glory.

Luke 10:38-42

Jesus speaks with two disciples. One is very busy, but the other sits quietly and listens.

ALTERNATE FIRST READING/PSALM

Amos 8:1-12

Amos announces the coming of God's judgment upon the people of Israel, who have continued to oppress the poor, engage in unethical business practices, and break God's commands.

Amos's vision is based on a Hebrew wordplay: he sees a basket of summer fruit (qayits) that will ripen at the end (qets) of the summer. The end of Israel will come through a famine of hearing the word of the Lord.

Psalm 52

I am like a green olive tree in the house of God. (Ps. 52:8)

COLOR   Green

THE PRAYERS

Freed by Christ and led by the Spirit, let us offer our prayers to God for the world, the church, and all those in need.

A BRIEF SILENCE.

Grant that all rulers and powers throughout the world may discover the vision of your reign of peace. God of truth,

hear our prayer.

In the chaos of daily living, help all people of faith to hold fast to the promises of Jesus Christ. God of truth,

hear our prayer.

Enliven the hospitality of this congregation, that we would welcome all people in the manner of Christ. God of truth,

hear our prayer.

When we are distracted by many things, help us to center our lives on your word, that we may grow as disciples. God of truth,

hear our prayer.

Grant healing and strength to all who are in spiritual, emotional, or physical need (especially…). God of truth,

hear our prayer.

HERE OTHER INTERCESSIONS MAY BE OFFERED.

Certain with Mary Magdalene and all the saints of your eternal victory over death, we ask for grace to cling to you in all circumstances. God of truth,

hear our prayer.

Receive the prayers of our hearts, O God, and grant that we may forever trust in your promises, through Jesus Christ our Lord.

Amen

IMAGES FOR PREACHING

How many Marthas or Marys do you know? Many, perhaps. When you visit Martha's home you will dine on spotless china with freshly polished silverware laid out for a four-course meal. The bread will be warm and freshly baked. The roasted pork, marinated for days before your arrival, will melt in your mouth. Each course will follow seamlessly after the other as Martha quickly collects the dishes. .

In Mary's home you eat pizza ordered by calling the speed-dial on her phone. You dine on paper plates as you share a space on the couch with Tasha, her Persian cat. Mary informs you that she has a half-filled bottle of wine in the door of the refrigerator and invites you to help yourself to it. Mary sits on the floor next to the hearth, soaking in every word uttered by her guests. She only half hears the doorbell that marks the arrival of the pizza. One of the invited guests attends to it. Mary is present and animated as she enjoys the words spoken, stories shared, and laughs expressed.

Each woman offers a form of hospitality consistent with her personality. Jesus is welcomed by both forms, but he does note a problem that can occur with Martha's form of hospitality. The purpose of hospitality is to provide an environment and space where relationships can be nurtured without distraction. Providing that space can become such a complicated chore that souls fail to connect, and the hunger for fellowship remains long after the dishes have been washed and put away.

Hospitality in simplicity can be a profound experience. May we come to know that true hospitality is achieved when we share not only our things, but our very selves with one another.

WORSHIP MATTERS

Where would our worship be without the Marthas in our congregation? We need to thank those who prepare the altar, provide bread and wine, mark the Bible, light the candles, fill the font, pass out bulletins, greet visitors, sing, and chant. But sometimes we forget that these tasks are not ends in themselves, but are meant to help us receive God's gifts to us in word and sacrament. Sometimes we allow these tasks to become a burden that colors our whole experience of worship. Then we need to take a cue from Mary and sit at the Lord's feet,

for the focus of our worship is God's gift of word and sacrament, and we cannot allow our works in ministry to take this gift from us.

LET THE CHILDREN COME

Children readily focus on the here and now. Adults are filled with worries and are distracted by many things. At worship, we come to receive the gift of God through the word and the sacraments. When the gospel is read, invite members of the congregation to hold their hands out in front of them, palms upward, to receive the word as a gift. When communion is given, encourage the worshipers to place one hand on top of the other, palms upward, making a cross. The children can experience ways we give our attention to God's gift of word and sacrament.

MUSIC FOR WORSHIP

GATHERING

| LBW 544 | The God of Abraham praise |
| WOV 730 | My soul proclaims your greatness |

PSALM 15

Gelineau, Joseph. "Psalm 15" in RS.

Haas, David. "They Who Do Justice" in PCY, vol. 3.

Hopson, Hal H. *Psalm Refrains and Tones.* HOP 425.

Paradowski, John. PW, Cycle C.

HYMN OF THE DAY

| LBW 325 | Lord, thee I love with all my heart |
| | HERZLICH LIEB |

VOCAL RESOURCES

Bach, J. S. "Lord, Thee I Love with All My Heart" in BAS. SATB.

Ferguson, John. "Lord, in All Love." AFP 11-10788. SATB, org, opt cong.

Rotermund/Bach. "Lord, You I Love with All My Heart." CPH 98-2750. SAB, inst, kybd.

INSTRUMENTAL RESOURCES

Manz, Paul. "Herzlich lieb" in *Nine Hymn Improvisations.* MSM 10-875. Org.

Weber, S. "Herzlich lieb" in *Four Hymn Preludes.* CPH 97-6089. Org.

ALTERNATE HYMN OF THE DAY

| LBW 248 | Dearest Jesus, at your word |
| WOV 776 | Be thou my vision |

COMMUNION

| LBW 316 | Jesus, the very thought of you |
| WOV 777 | In the morning when I rise |

SENDING

| LBW 480 | Oh, that the Lord would guide my ways |
| WOV 778 | O Christ the same |

ADDITIONAL HYMNS AND SONGS

LW 277	One thing's needful
OBS 51	Christ, burning Wisdom
TFF 136	We have come into his house
TFF 140	Jesus, we are gathered
W&P 67	I love you, Lord

MUSIC FOR THE DAY

CHORAL

Ashdown, Fredrick. "Jesus, the Very Thought of You." AFP 11-10886.
SATB, org, opt C inst.

Candlyn, T. Frederick H. "Thee We Adore." CFI C.M.492. SATB, org.

Hopson, Hal H. "God, in Your Goodness." SEL 420-267. SATB, org,
opt solo.

Near, Gerald. "Jesu! The Very Thought of Thee." AUR AE47.
SATB, org.

Vaughan Williams, Ralph. "The Call." MSM 50-9912. U, kybd.

CHILDREN'S CHOIRS

Brokering, Lois. "What Does It Mean to Follow Jesus?" in LS.

Lord, Suzanne. "Do You Know Your Shepherd's Voice?" CG CGA673.
2 pt, kybd.

Scott, K. Lee. "Best of all Friends." MSM-50-9003. 2 pt trbl, pno.

KEYBOARD/INSTRUMENTAL

Krapf, Gerhard. "Chorale Partita for Manuals on 'Lord, You I Love
with All My Heart'" MSM-10-870. Org/kybd.

Willan, Healey. "At the Close of the Day" (Slane). CFP 66034. Org.

HANDBELL

Baker, Cheryl Sutton. "When Morning Gilds the Skies."
HIN HHB 15. 3-5 oct.

McChesney, Kevin. "When Morning Gilds the Skies." HOP CP 6067.
Qrt.

PRAISE ENSEMBLE

Blair, Rick. "By Him, for Him" in *America's 200 Favorite Praise Choruses & Hymns*. BNT.

Cook, Steve, and Vikki Cook. "Jesus, You Reign Over All" in *Praise
Hymns and Choruses*, 4th ed. MAR.

Farrar, Sue. "As Long as I Have Breath." BEC BP1298. SATB, kybd.

258

SUNDAY, JULY 22
ST. MARY MAGDALENE

The gospels report Mary Magdalene was one of the
women of Galilee who followed Jesus. She was present
at Jesus' crucifixion and his burial. When she went to
the tomb on the first day of the week to anoint Jesus'
body, she was the first person to whom the risen Lord
appeared. She returned to the disciples with the news
and has been called "the apostle to the apostles" for her
proclamation of the resurrection. Because John's gospel
describes Mary as weeping at the tomb, she is often
portrayed in art with red eyes. Icons depict her standing
by the tomb and holding a bright red egg.

This glimpse of Easter in the middle of summer invites us to keep our eyes open for the signs of Christ's
resurrection and new life that are always around us.

MONDAY, JULY 23
BIRGITTA OF SWEDEN, 1373

Birgitta was married at age thirteen and had four
daughters with her husband. She was a woman of some
standing who, in her early thirties, served as the chief
lady-in-waiting to the Queen of Sweden. She was wid-
owed at the age of thirty-eight, shortly after she and her
husband had made a religious pilgrimage. Following the
death of her husband the religious dreams and visions
that had begun in her youth occurred more regularly.
Her devotional commitments led her to give to the
poor and needy all that she owned while she began to
live a more ascetic life. She founded an order of monks
and nuns, the Order of the Holy Savior (Birgittines),
whose superior was a woman. Today the Society of St.
Birgitta is a laypersons' society that continues her work
of prayer and charity.

WEDNESDAY, JULY 25
ST. JAMES THE ELDER, APOSTLE

James is one of the sons of Zebedee and is counted as
one of the twelve disciples. He and his brother John had
the nickname "sons of thunder." One of the stories in
the New Testament tells of their request for Jesus to

grant them places of honor in the kingdom. They are also reported to have asked Jesus for permission to send down fire on a Samaritan village that had not welcomed them. Their nickname appears to be well deserved. James was the first of the twelve to suffer martyrdom and is the only apostle whose martyrdom is recorded in scripture.

James is frequently pictured with a scallop shell. It recalls his life as a fisherman, his call to fish for people, and the gift of our baptism into Christ.

SATURDAY, JULY 28
JOHANN SEBASTIAN BACH, 1750; HEINRICH SCHÜTZ, 1672; GEORGE FREDERICK HANDEL, 1759; MUSICIANS

These three composers have done much to enrich the worship life of the church. Johann Sebastian Bach drew on the Lutheran tradition of hymnody and wrote about two hundred cantatas, including at least two for each Sunday and festival day in the Lutheran calendar of his day. He has been called "the fifth evangelist" for the ways that he proclaimed the gospel through his music. George Frederick Handel was not primarily a church musician, but his great work, the *Messiah,* is a musical proclamation of the scriptures. Heinrich Schütz wrote choral settings of biblical texts and paid special attention to ways his composition would underscore the meaning of the words.

A musical gathering might be planned for this weekend to commemorate these and other great church composers. Remember to include a prayer of thanksgiving for organists, choir directors, composers, and all who make music in worship.

JULY 29, 2001

EIGHTH SUNDAY AFTER PENTECOST
PROPER 12

INTRODUCTION

We want to learn how to pray, and our prayers have many shapes. Jesus' model prayer shapes our own and leads us to a more full realization of God's presence in our lives and in the world—a vision shared by Paul as he proclaims Christ's new day. Today the church remembers Mary, Martha, and Lazarus of Bethany—Jesus' close friends; and Olaf, Christian king of Norway.

PRAYER OF THE DAY

O God, your ears are open always to the prayers of your servants. Open our hearts and minds to you, that we may live in harmony with your will and receive the gifts of your Spirit; through your Son, Jesus Christ our Lord.

READINGS

Genesis 18:20-32

In today's first reading, Abraham fulfills the commission given him by God, that all the nations of the earth should bless *themselves through him. Abraham's call is to teach God's way of justice and righteousness.*

Psalm 138

Your love endures forever; do not abandon the works of your hands. (Ps. 138:9)

Colossians 2:6-15 [16-19]

The letter to the Colossians warns about "the empty lure" of ideas that compromise the faith into which people are baptized. Through baptism, the church is rooted in Christ.

Luke 11:1-13

In Luke's gospel Jesus prays often and urges his disciples to do the same. Here, he teaches them to pray and encourages them to trust in God at all times.

ALTERNATE FIRST READING/PSALM

Hosea 1:2-10

Hosea's marriage to a faithless wife symbolizes Israel's faithless disregard of the covenant. Even the names of Hosea's children—Jezreel (where Israel's idolatrous kings had been killed), Lo-ruhamah ("she is not pitied"), and Lo-ammi ("not my

*people")—announce the nation's coming doom, countered by
the proclamation that sinful Israel remains a child of the living
God.*

Psalm 85

Righteousness and peace shall go before the LORD. (Ps. 85:13)

COLOR   Green

THE PRAYERS

Freed by Christ and led by the Spirit, let us offer our
prayers to God for the world, the church, and all those
in need.

A BRIEF SILENCE.

Grant that the world may awaken to your power and be
healed of all oppression, war, and injustice. God of
truth,

hear our prayer.

Thankful for having received Jesus Christ in our baptism, we ask for new energy in the task of sharing our
faith with others. God of truth,

hear our prayer.

Give us the wisdom to seek those things that are right
for us and to enter doors through which your Spirit is
leading us. God of truth,

hear our prayer.

Bless all who have encountered any form of brokenness
in their lives, especially those who are hospitalized,
homebound, lonely, or ill (especially...). God of truth,

hear our prayer.

HERE OTHER INTERCESSIONS MAY BE OFFERED.

Remembering your saints Mary, Martha, and Lazarus of
Bethany, and the martyr Olaf, we pray for faith to live
and die in the certainty of the resurrection you have
prepared for us. God of truth,

hear our prayer.

Receive the prayers of our hearts, O God, and grant
that we may forever trust in your promises, through
Jesus Christ our Lord.

Amen

IMAGES FOR PREACHING

How often have exhausted mothers responded to the
repeated question "Why?" from their children with the
phrase, "Because I am the mother! That's why!" We who
have children would gladly shout a loud "Amen" in
support of this mom if given the opportunity. Yet persis-

tent questioning is allowed and even condoned in
today's readings.

In Genesis we read of a spirited debate between
Abraham and the Lord over the fate of Sodom. This exchange provides a number of insights into the nature of
the God we worship. The primary issue is about the
merciful nature of the Lord and the influence we humans really do have in the divine outcome of earthly
events. While many people accuse the Lord of the Hebrew scriptures as vengeful and eager to punish, this
story demonstrates God's desire for a mercy-filled response to sin. Abraham's bold bargaining with the Lord
is only possible where a true relationship exists.

Abraham's repetitive "Lord, what if..." nature of
the exchange is the verbal equivalent of the man's rap,
rap, rapping on his neighbor's door in the middle of the
night, which we hear about in the gospel reading for
today. Rather than condemning him for being a nui-
sance, Jesus lauds this man's persistence, which finally
forced the neighbor to respond to his need. For Jesus,
prayer was a simple exercise. It is the give-and-take in
an exchange first made possible by the parties involved
living in relationship one with another.

Persistent prayer, however, is not the same thing as
whining or nagging to get one's way. To be persistent in
prayer is to be focused, but it is also to risk having one's
heart changed as an outcome of the experience.

WORSHIP MATTERS

Jesus says, "Ask, and it will be given you..." (Luke 11:9).
Does prayer really work that way? In prayer we do not
ask for what we want. We do not ask for what we like.
We ask for what we need. In the Lord's Prayer Jesus reminds us of our needs. We do not need a good life in
this world, but we do need the coming of God's kingdom. We do not need our will, but God's to be done.
We do not need wealth and affluence but daily bread.
We need forgiveness, yes, as we forgive others. In prayer
we ask for what we need, and God gives it.

LET THE CHILDREN COME

Jesus encourages his disciples to be bold in prayer, asking God for what they need. Ask the children to help
write the intercessory prayers this Sunday. What do they
want to ask of God? Who needs God's protection and
care? Where is God's creation in danger? For what are

260

they sorry? For what do they want to say, "Thank you, God?" Don't fuss about the difference between needs and wants. Accept all prayers with gratitude, and leave the sifting to God.

MUSIC FOR WORSHIP
SERVICE MUSIC

A sung version of the Lord's Prayer (for the assembly) can reinforce its presence in today's gospel reading. The versions in *LBW* (pp. 112–13) and TFF 33 may be used to sing the prayer at its place in the liturgy. Hymns that reflect on this prayer include LBW 442 and TFF 34.

GATHERING

| LBW 405 | Lord of light |
| WOV 795 | Oh, sing to the Lord |

PSALM 138

Cooney, Rory. "On the Day I Called" in STP, vol. 4.

Haas, David. "In the Presence of the Angels," in PCY, vol. 3.

Paradowski, John. PW, Cycle C.

Stewart, Roy James. "Lord, Your Love Is Eternal," in PCY, vol. 5.

See fifth Sunday after the Epiphany.

HYMN OF THE DAY

| LBW 442 | O thou, who hast of thy pure grace |
| | VATER UNSER |

INSTRUMENTAL RESOURCES

Johns, Donald. "Vater unser" in *Seven Binary Variations.* NPH OL-27-0017. Org.

Manz, Paul. "Vater unser" in *Improvisations on Classic Chorales.* MSM 10-843. Org.

Organ, Anne Krentz. "Vater unser" in *Organ Music for the Seasons.* AFP 11-10859. Org.

ALTERNATE HYMN OF THE DAY

| LBW 438 | Lord, teach us how to pray aright |
| WOV 746 | Day by day |

COMMUNION

| LBW 439 | What a friend we have in Jesus |
| WOV 775 | Lord, listen to your children praying |

SENDING

| LBW 440 | Christians, while on earth abiding |
| WOV 783 | Seek ye first |

ADDITIONAL HYMNS AND SONGS

PH 349	Let all who pray the prayer Christ taught
TFF 240	It's me, O Lord
TFF 242	Sweet hour of prayer
W&P 86	Let my prayer be a fragrant offering
W&P 91	Lord, listen to your children

MUSIC FOR THE DAY
CHORAL

Franck, Melchior. "Our Father, Thou in Heaven Above." GSCH 11174.

Gartner, Nancy. "Hymn of a Grateful Heart." GIA G-3716. SATB, S solo.

Hassell, Michael. "What a Friend We Have in Jesus." AFP 11-10919. SATB, S and T solo, pno.

Proulx, Richard. "The Eyes of All." AFP 12-109. U, org.

Schütz, Heinrich. "The Lord's Prayer" in CC. SATB.

CHILDREN'S CHOIRS

Barta, Daniel. "Ask and Seek and Knock." CG CGA683. 2 pt, kybd, opt C trbl inst.

Horman, John. "The Unexpected Guest." ABI 07255-7. U, kybd, narr, wb.

Lindh, Jody W. "I Give You Thanks." CG CGA-561. U, pno, perc, opt bass, opt synth.

KEYBOARD/INSTRUMENTAL

Buxtehude, Dietrich. Settings of "Vater unser." Various ed. Org.

Oliver, Curt. "Salvation unto Us Has Come." MSM 15-813. Pno.

HANDBELL

Beethoven/Crawford. "A Prayer." HOP CP 6046. Qrt.

Butler, Eugene. "Prayer and Finale." CG CGB15. 3-4 oct.

Linker and McFadden. "Prayer." BEC HB161. 3-5 oct, kybd.

PRAISE ENSEMBLE

Chapman, Morris. "Be Bold, Be Strong" in *Praise Hymns and Choruses,* 4th ed. MAR.

Medema, Ken, and Jack Schrader. "Lord, Listen to Your Children Praying." HOP GC 850. SATB, kybd, opt gtr, electric bass.

Nagy, Russell. "The Lord's Prayer." BEC JH511. U, kybd.

Smith, Scott V., and Malcolm du Plessis. "Stretch Out Your Hand" in *Praise Hymns and Choruses,* 4th ed. MAR.

Ylvisaker, John. "I Thank You Lord, For Love Unknown" in *Borning Cry.* NGP.

261

SUNDAY, JULY 29
MARY, MARTHA, AND LAZARUS OF BETHANY

Mary and Martha are remembered for the hospitality and refreshment they offered Jesus in their home. Following the characterization drawn by Luke, Martha represents the active life, and Mary, the contemplative. Mary is identified in the fourth gospel as the one who anointed Jesus before his passion and who was criticized for her act of devotion. Lazarus, Mary's and Martha's brother, was raised from the dead by Jesus as a sign of the eternal life offered to all believers. It was over Lazarus's tomb that Jesus wept for love of his friend. Congregations might commemorate these three early witnesses to Christ by reflecting on the role of hospitality in both home and church and the blessing of friendship.

SUNDAY, JULY 29
OLAF, KING OF NORWAY, MARTYR, 1030

Olaf is considered the patron saint of Norway. In his early career he engaged in war and piracy in the Baltic and in Normandy. It was there he became a Christian. He returned to Norway, declared himself king, and from then on Christianity was the dominant religion of the realm. He revised the laws of the nation and enforced them with strict impartiality, eliminating the possibility of bribes. He thereby alienated much of the aristocracy. The harshness that he sometimes resorted to in order to establish Christianity and his own law led to a rebellion. After being driven from the country and into exile, he enlisted support from Sweden to try to regain his kingdom, but he died in battle.

Olaf reminds the church of the temptation to establish Christianity by waging war, whether military or social. How might the church bear witness to the one who calls us to pray for enemies and persecutors?

262

AUGUST 5, 2001

NINTH SUNDAY AFTER PENTECOST
PROPER 13

INTRODUCTION

The church prays, "We offer with joy and thanksgiving what you have first given us—our selves, our time, and our possessions." We do much more than support the work of our congregation as we make our contributions. We actually reorient ourselves toward what we possess and what we value the most. God's word speaks to us about this fundamental realignment of our lives.

PRAYER OF THE DAY

Gracious Father, your blessed Son came down from heaven to be the true bread which gives life to the world. Give us this bread, that he may live in us and we in him, Jesus Christ our Lord.

or

Almighty God, judge of us all, you have placed in our hands the wealth we call our own. Give us such wisdom by your Spirit that our possessions may not be a curse in our lives, but an instrument for blessing; through your Son, Jesus Christ our Lord.

READINGS

Ecclesiastes 1:2, 12-14; 2:18-23

The teacher of wisdom who wrote Ecclesiastes sees that working for mere accumulation of wealth turns life into an empty game.

Psalm 49:1-11 (Psalm 49:1-12 [NRSV])

We can never ransom ourselves or deliver to God the price of our life. (Ps. 49:6)

Colossians 3:1-11

Life in Christ includes a radical reorientation of our values. Just as the newly baptized shed their old clothes in order to put on new garments, so Christians are called to let go of greed and take hold of a life shaped by God's love in Christ.

Luke 12:13-21

The gospel of Luke tells not only how Jesus brought good

news to the poor, but also how he sought to seek and save those who were rich. Here he warns against identifying the worth of one's life with the value of one's possessions.

ALTERNATE FIRST READING/PSALM

Hosea 11:1-11

The prophet compares God's love of Israel to the love parents have for their children. Whether teaching toddlers to walk or supporting them in the midst of rebellion, good parents continue to love their children as they try to lead them to life. In the same way, God's love will not let Israel go.

Psalm 107:1-9, 43

*Give thanks to the L*ORD*, all those whom the L*ORD *has redeemed. (Ps. 107:1-2)*

COLOR   Green

THE PRAYERS

Freed by Christ and led by the Spirit, let us offer our prayers to God for the world, the church, and all those in need.

A BRIEF SILENCE.

Send your spirit of wisdom, knowledge, and justice to leaders of all nations, that the world's people might live in peace. God of truth,

hear our prayer.

Renew us each day in your image, that we may live in unity with all people. God of truth,

hear our prayer.

Help us to trust that life does not consist in the abundance of possessions, in spite of powerful challenges that would have us believe otherwise. God of truth,

hear our prayer.

Bring healing to all who live without hope, including those who are hungry, homeless, oppressed, or ill (especially…). God of truth,

hear our prayer.

HERE OTHER INTERCESSIONS MAY BE OFFERED.

We give thanks for those who have gone before us in faith and with whom we share the eternal inheritance of your grace. God of truth,

hear our prayer.

Receive the prayers of our hearts, O God, and grant that we may forever trust in your promises, through Jesus Christ our Lord.

Amen

IMAGES FOR PREACHING

Someone who possesses a healthy stock portfolio recently asked, "Why does Jesus seem to dislike the wealthy so much?" Was Jesus truly against people simply for possessing wealth? Or rather, did he warn that those who have wealth face a particular danger?

Wealth can pose as an imposter. Its size and shape is deceptively similar to the contours of a hole that many of us carry deep within the core of our beings, a hole that can only be filled with the presence of the creator. It is in the act of filling this hole that we often grasp for this imposter, pushing, twisting, and turning it in ways that seem to provide a tight fit within this God-only-shaped cavity. Strangely enough this imposter provides us with feelings of security, which are remarkably akin to the security afforded us by the creator.

But where does our security come from? Does it come from that sense of well-being twice a month as we deposit a salary check into a checking account? Perhaps on those days we experience the feeling of "having enough" and feel a sense of security solely based on feelings akin to the rich man of today's parable.

In times of our greatest need, though, the security that wealth can provide quickly breaks down. Ask the millionaire who comes down with terminal cancer, or the wealthy parent who loses a child, or an entrepreneur who suddenly loses all in the deal of a lifetime gone bad. How reliable are possessions in these times of tragedy? The problem with wealth is not necessarily having it, but relying on it to provide things only the Lord can offer. May we learn to view wealth as a thing to use in the service of Christ, rather than a thing to rely on.

WORSHIP MATTERS

"Be on your guard against all kinds of greed," Jesus says, "for one's life does not consist in the abundance of possessions" (Luke 12:15). Possessions are not evil in and of themselves. Yet they can exercise a powerful hold. The more we have, the more we think we need. The more we think we need, the more afraid we are of losing what we have, and so we try even harder to get even more. Then something happens—our kids get in trouble, our parents get sick—and our possessions amount to nothing. The remedy for greed is generosity. The way to keep our possessions from having power over us is to use them for others, to work not to get more and more but to give more and more, and, in so doing, to find that we have more than enough.

LET THE CHILDREN COME

The life of a joyful disciple includes being a steward of all that God has given. Encourage the children to share their time, talents, and treasures. Have them fill shoeboxes with small toys, crayons, toothpaste, and tissue to send to children who have gone through a flood, fire, or tornado. Those with musical talents can lead the Kyrie or hymn of praise. Welcome their hand-drawn cards or greetings to be given to those receiving communion in their home or sent to those experiencing grief or illness. Affirm all ways that children are stewards.

MUSIC FOR WORSHIP

GATHERING

| LBW 358 | Glories of your name are spoken |
| WOV 718 | Here in this place |

PSALM 49

Hopson, Hal H. "Psalm 49" in TP.

Howard, Julie. *Sing for Joy: Psalm Settings for God's Children.* LTP.

Paradowski, John. PW, Cycle C.

Psalms for Praise and Worship: A Complete Liturgical Psalter. ABI.

HYMN OF THE DAY

| LBW 447 | All depends on our possessing |
| | ALLES IST AN GOTTES SEGEN |

INSTRUMENTAL RESOURCES

Bisbee, B. Wayne. "Alles ist an Gottes Segen" in *From the Serene to the Whimsical.* AFP 11-10561. Org.

Wolff, S. Drummond. "Alles ist an Gottes Segen" in *Hymn Descants, Set IV.* CPH 97-6275. Org, inst.

ALTERNATE HYMN OF THE DAY

| LBW 537 | O Jesus, king most wonderful! |
| WOV 782 | All my hope on God is founded |

COMMUNION

| LBW 209 | Come, risen Lord |
| WOV 710 | One bread, one body |

SENDING

| LBW 415 | God of grace and God of glory |
| WOV 776 | Be thou my vision |

ADDITIONAL HYMNS AND SONGS

ASG 9	For everything there is a time
NCH 563	We cannot own the sunlit sky
TFF 233	I'd rather have Jesus
W&P 84	Lead me, guide me
W&P 146	We are an offering

MUSIC FOR THE DAY

CHORAL

Bach, J. S. "Jesus, My Sweet Pleasure" in BAS.

Ferguson, John. "Be Thou My Vision." AFP 11-10925. SATB, org.

Hobby, Robert. "Beloved, God's Chosen" in OBS. AFP 11-10818. U.

Lovelace, Austin C. "Glory, Love, and Praise and Honor." CPH 98-2885. SAB, org.

Parker, Alice, arr. "Be Thou My Vision." HIN HMC-135.

Schalk, Carl. "All Things Are Yours, My God." MSM 50-9032. SATB, opt cong, org.

Schalk, Carl. "How Sweet the Name of Jesus Sounds." AFP 11-10678. SATB, org, fl, opt cong.

CHILDREN'S CHOIRS

Hopson, Hal H. "Simple Gifts." AG HH 3940. 2 equal vcs, kybd.

Sleeth, Natalie. "Consider the Lilies." CG A-195. U, pno/org, fl/vln.

Sleeth, Natalie. "Fear Not for Tomorrow" in LS.

KEYBOARD/INSTRUMENTAL

Haan, Raymond H. *Variations on "In Babilone."* FLA HH-5035. Org.

Schildt, Melchior. "Magnificat" in *Choralbearbeitungen.* F. Kistner, Nr. 24. Org.

HANDBELL

Anderson/Kramlich. "I Sing the Mighty Power of God." HOP 1669. Solo.

Behnke, John A. "Jesus, Priceless Treasure." CPH 97-6683. 3-5 oct.

Tucker, Sondra. "Beach Spring." LAK HB95043. 2-3 oct.

PRAISE ENSEMBLE

Booth, Tom. "I Will Choose Christ." OCP 10592. SAB, solo, kybd, opt cong, gtr.

Govenor, Deborah. "Jesus, Savior, Blessed Friend." BEC BP1321. SATB, kybd.

Ragsdale, Steve. "Hide Me in Your Holiness" in *Praise Hymns and Choruses,* 4th ed. MAR.

Ylvisaker, John. "I'm Not Afraid" in *Borning Cry.* NGP.

WEDNESDAY, AUGUST 8
DOMINIC, PRIEST, FOUNDER OF THE ORDER
OF THE DOMINICANS, 1221

Dominic was a Spanish priest who preached against the Albigensians, a heretical sect that held gnostic and dualistic beliefs. Dominic believed that a stumbling block to restoring heretics to the church was the wealth of clergy, so he formed an itinerant religious order, the Order of Preachers (Dominicans) who lived in poverty, studied philosophy and theology, and preached against heresy. The method of this order was to use kindness and gentle argument, rather than harsh judgment, when bringing unorthodox Christians back to the fold. Dominic was opposed to burning Christians at the stake. Three times Dominic was offered the office of bishop, which he refused so that he could continue his work of preaching.

FRIDAY, AUGUST 10
LAWRENCE, DEACON, MARTYR, 258

Lawrence was one of seven deacons of the congregation at Rome and, like the deacons appointed in Acts, was responsible for financial matters in the church and for the care of the poor. Lawrence lived during a time of persecution under the emperor Valerian. The emperor demanded that Lawrence surrender the treasures of the church. Lawrence gathered lepers, orphans, the blind and lame. He brought them to the emperor and said, "Here is the treasure of the church." This act enraged the emperor, and Lawrence was sentenced to death. Lawrence's martyrdom was one of the first to be observed by the church.

Amid the concerns for the institutional church, reflect on what we consider the treasures of the church today. If the people on the margins of life are treasured in God's eyes, consider ways a congregation can sharpen its vision for social ministry.

265

AUGUST 12, 2001

TENTH SUNDAY AFTER PENTECOST
PROPER 14

INTRODUCTION

"Faith is the conviction of things not seen," the second reading announces. "We've come this far by faith, leaning on the Lord," the hymn by Albert Goodson proclaims. This day we gather as a community of faith and seek renewed vision, so that we might make our way more boldly into the world as bearers of God's saving love.

PRAYER OF THE DAY

Almighty and everlasting God, you are always more ready to hear than we are to pray, and to give more than we either desire or deserve. Pour upon us the abundance of your mercy, forgiving us those things of which our conscience is afraid, and giving us those good things for which we are not worthy to ask, except through the merit of your Son, Jesus Christ our Lord.

READINGS

Genesis 15:1-6

God promises childless Abram that a child of his own will be his heir and that his descendants will number as many as the stars. Abram trusts God's promise and through this faith, he is considered righteous.

Psalm 33:12-22

Let your lovingkindness be upon us, as we have put our trust in you. (Ps. 33:22)

Hebrews 11:1-3, 8-16

Abraham and Sarah exemplify the vision of faith that people of God need in every age. Their hope and trust in God's promise allowed them to face an unknown future.

Luke 12:32-40

Jesus encourages his followers to recognize the true value of God's kingdom, so that their hearts may be where their real treasure lies. Instead of facing life with fear, those who know

God's generosity are always ready to receive from God and to give to others.

ALTERNATE FIRST READING/PSALM

Isaiah 1:1, 10-20

Isaiah announces God's displeasure with the offerings and sacrifices of a people who are without compassion and pleads with Judah, the Southern Kingdom, to return to the Lord that they might be cleansed.

Psalm 50:1-8, 22-23

To those who keep in my way will I show the salvation of God. (Ps. 50:2-4)

COLOR   Green

THE PRAYERS

Freed by Christ and led by the Spirit, let us offer our prayers to God for the world, the church, and all those in need.

A BRIEF SILENCE.

For a world longing to see peace, that its leaders might let your justice shine through them. God of truth,

hear our prayer.

For the church, that we may be faithful and obedient to your call. God of truth,

hear our prayer.

For all who face challenging decisions, that they may have the help of your wisdom. God of truth,

hear our prayer.

For the assurance that it is your pleasure to give us the kingdom, now and always. God of truth,

hear our prayer.

For those who live with chronic illness, and those who are hospitalized, homebound, or sick (especially…), that they might know the healing power of your love. God of truth,

hear our prayer.

HERE OTHER INTERCESSIONS MAY BE OFFERED.

Receive the prayers of our hearts, O God, and grant that we may forever trust in your promises, through Jesus Christ our Lord.

Amen

IMAGES FOR PREACHING

Many of us are impatient. We do not like to wait. We prefer immediate rather than deferred outcomes. Prefer-

ences for immediate outcomes can sometimes get us into trouble, however. If we choose to use a credit card to purchase nonessential items today, we run the risk of enslaving tomorrow's future with today's impulsivity.

Jesus' words in the gospel today go against our desire for an immediate outcome. He tells us to prepare today for something that will happen in an unknown tomorrow. We are told to "be dressed for action" and to have our "lamps lit" (Luke 12:35). We are to maintain a posture of diligent expectation that one day our master will return, and when he does, we must be ready. We might be tempted to pray: Lord, would it not be just as easy to tell us when you plan to invade our space and our lives? In that way we could take care of our present needs until such time as we need to prepare for your coming. As we look at calendars right now, we have other things to do, friends to see, money to invest, jobs to do, and families to support.

But Jesus invites us to prepare with patience. When our hearts are invested in the treasure of God's reigns, we can live with assurance in the midst of the unresolved. With Abram and Sarai, we journey in God's promise alone.

WORSHIP MATTERS

Abraham did not ask God where they were going: he trusted that God would guide them and he went. Abraham did not dismiss as ridiculous God's promise of descendants as numerous as the stars: he trusted that God would make it happen and waited. Abraham did not refuse to offer up his son. He did not doubt the promise's fulfillment. He trusted the Lord to provide. "Now faith is the assurance of things hoped for, the conviction of things not seen" (Heb. 11:1). We give thanks for Abraham, because he is for us a model of faith. Like Abraham, we are approved as righteous not because of who we are and what we do but because we trust God to be who God is and to do what God has promised to do.

LET THE CHILDREN COME

We need not be afraid. It is God's good pleasure to give us the kingdom. Abraham and Sarah saw the promises from a distance. We have seen the promises of God up close in Jesus. Choose songs and hymns that the children know by heart that speak about the great promises

266

of God. Include songs that are used in their educational opportunities. Pick songs that older people learned in their childhood that are engraved on their hearts. Sing about our promise-keeping God.

MUSIC FOR WORSHIP

GATHERING

LBW 477   O God of Jacob
WOV 725   Blessed be the God of Israel

PSALM 33

Cooney, Rory. "Happy the People You Have Chosen" in STP, vol. 4.

Dufford, Bob. "Lord, Let Your Mercy" in STP, vol. 4.

Foley, John. "Psalm 33: God, Let Your Mercy" in PCY, vol. 7.

Haugen, Marty. "Let Your Mercy Be on Us" in PCY, Vol. 2.

Inwood, Paul. "Psalm 33: The Lord Fills the Earth with His Love" in STP, vol. 3.

Paradowski, John. PW, Cycle C.

HYMN OF THE DAY

LBW 532   How great thou art
           O store Gud

INSTRUMENTAL RESOURCES

Dobrinski, Cynthia. "How Great Thou Art." HOP 1350. Hb.

Hassell, Michael. "How Great Thou Art" in *Jazz for All Seasons.* AFP 11-10822. Pno.

Held, Wilbur. "How Great Thou Art" in *Preludes and Postludes,* vol. 1. AFP 11-9318. Org.

Jones, Jack W. "How Great Thou Art." CPH 97-6808. Pno.

Langlois, Kristina. "How Great Thou Art" in *Five Hymns of Praise.* MSM 10-722. Org.

ALTERNATE HYMN OF THE DAY

LBW 463   God, who stretched the spangled heavens
WOV 794   Many and great, O God, are your works

COMMUNION

LBW 224   Soul, adorn yourself with gladness
LBW 476   Have no fear, little flock

SENDING

WOV 689   Rejoice in God's saints
WOV 771   Great is thy faithfulness

ADDITIONAL HYMNS AND SONGS

CW 404   Faith is a living power from heaven
TFF 197   We've come this far by faith
UMH 508   Faith while trees are still in blossom
W&P 55   He is exalted
W&P 133   That Christ be known

MUSIC FOR THE DAY

CHORAL

Haugen, Marty. "Let Your Mercy Be on Us." GIA G-3331. SATB, cong, gtr, kybd.

Mozart, W. A. "God Is Our Refuge." BRD 129.

Schalk, Carl. "Our Soul Waits for the Lord." CPH 98-3252. SATB.

Taverner, John. "Audivi" in *The Second Book of Chester Motets.* CHE.

Zimmermann, Heinz Werner. "Have No Fear, Little Flock" in *Five Hymns.* CPH 97-5131. U/SATB, kybd.

CHILDREN'S CHOIRS

Callahan, Mary David. "Ring Out Your Joy" in *God, Be Near Us.* AFP 11-4652. 2 pt, kybd/gtr.

Folkening, John. "One in a Hundred" in LS.

Sleeth, Natalie. "Everywhere I Go." CG CGA-171. U/2 pt, kybd.

Zimmerman, Heinz Werner/arr. Betty Ann Ramseth and Melinda Ramseth. "Have No Fear Little Flock" in *Take a Hymn.* AFP 11-2172. U, kybd, fl, cello, fc, wb.

KEYBOARD/INSTRUMENTAL

Albrecht, Mark. "God Who Stretched the Spangled Heavens" in *Early American Hymns & Tunes for Flute and Piano.* AFP 11-10830. Inst, pno.

Diemer, Emma Lou. "Many and Great" in *Eight Hymn Preludes.* AFP 11-10349. Org.

Hampton, Calvin. "Music for a Festival" in *Music for Organ.* Warner DM00266. Org.

Wallace, Sue Mitchell. "God Who Stretched the Spangled Heavens" in *Hymn Prisms.* HOP 270. Org.

HANDBELL

Anderson/Wagner. "Children of the Heavenly Father." HOP 1695. Solo.

Tucker, Sondra K. "All Things Bright and Beautiful" in *Hymn Preludes for Handbells.* CPH 97-6787. 2-3 oct.

PRAISE ENSEMBLE

Cortez, Jaime. "Rain Down" in *Glory & Praise.* OCP.

Lafferty, Karen, and John F. Wilson. "Seek Ye First." HOP CF 187. 3 pt, kybd.

Thomas, Donn, and Charles Williams. "A Shield About Me" in *Praise Hymns and Choruses,* 4th ed. MAR.

267

MONDAY, AUGUST 13
FLORENCE NIGHTINGALE, 1910; CLARA MAASS, 1901; RENEWERS OF SOCIETY

When Florence Nightingale decided she would be a nurse, her family was horrified. In the early 1800s nursing was done by people with no training and no other way to earn a living. Florence trained at Kaiserswerth, Germany, with a Lutheran order of deaconesses. She returned home and worked to reform hospitals in England. Nightingale led a group of thirty-eight nurses to serve in the Crimean War, where they worked in appalling conditions. She returned to London as a hero and there resumed her work for hospital reform. Clara Maass was born in New Jersey and served as a nurse in the Spanish-American War, where she encountered the horrors of yellow fever. She later responded to a call for subjects in research on yellow fever. During the experiments, which included receiving bites from mosquitoes, she contracted the disease and died. The commemoration of these women invites the church to give thanks for all who practice the arts of healing.

WEDNESDAY, AUGUST 15
MARY, MOTHER OF OUR LORD

The church honors Mary with the Greek title *theotokos,* meaning God-bearer. Origen first used this title in the early church, and the councils of Ephesus and Chalcedon upheld it. Luther upheld this same title in his writings. The honor paid to Mary as *theotokos* and mother of our Lord goes back to biblical times, when Mary herself sang, "from now on all generations will call me blessed" (Luke 1:48). Mary's life revealed the presence of God incarnate among the humble and poor. Mary's song, the Magnificat, speaks of reversals in the reign of God: the mighty are cast down, the lowly are lifted up, the hungry are fed, and the rich are sent away empty-handed.

Hymns to commemorate Mary as *theotokos* might include "Sing of Mary, pure and holy" (WOV 634) or a paraphrase of the Magnificat, such as "My soul proclaims your greatness" (WOV 730).

AUGUST 19, 2001

ELEVENTH SUNDAY AFTER PENTECOST
PROPER 15

INTRODUCTION

The candles that grace our worship seem like gentle lights, but fire is a powerful and purging force. Fire is used to purify molten ore and burn away the dross. In this day's worship, God's word comes among us like raging fire, consuming what is false and leaving behind pure gold.

PRAYER OF THE DAY

Almighty and ever-living God, you have given great and precious promises to those who believe. Grant us the perfect faith which overcomes all doubts, through your Son, Jesus Christ our Lord.

READINGS

Jeremiah 23:23-29

Because Jeremiah preaches the unpopular message of God's judgment, he suffers rejection. Today's reading speaks of the mistaken notion that God sees only what is happening in the temple. Rather, Jeremiah points out, God's distance allows for a panoramic view of all the universe, including the lies and deceptions of false prophets.

Psalm 82

Arise, O God, and rule the earth. (Ps. 82:8)

Hebrews 11:29—12:2

The author of Hebrews presents us with a long list of biblical heroes whose exemplary faith enabled them to face the trials of life. In addition to this "cloud of witnesses," we have Jesus, the perfect model of faithful endurance.

Luke 12:49-56

Today's gospel contains harsh words concerning the purifying and potentially divisive effects of God's call. People who follow the way of Christ often encounter hostility and rejection, even from those they love.

ALTERNATE FIRST READING/PSALM

Isaiah 5:1-7

The prophet begins to sing about a beautiful vineyard, but the beautiful song becomes chilling as Isaiah describes the vineyard's destruction and suggests it is a picture of Israel.

Psalm 80:1-2, 8-19

Look down from heaven, O God; behold and tend this vine. (Ps. 80:14)

COLOR   Green

THE PRAYERS

Freed by Christ and led by the Spirit, let us offer our prayers to God for the world, the church, and all those in need.

A BRIEF SILENCE.

Grant leaders of nations the wisdom to follow your guidance even when their decisions may be unpopular. God of truth,

hear our prayer.

Kindle within your church a fire for sharing the good news of Jesus Christ. God of truth,

hear our prayer.

In the midst of that which divides families, congregations, communities, and nations, bring us to the unity and wholeness only you can give. God of truth,

hear our prayer.

Comfort those who are living with depression, loneliness, and illness (especially . . .), that they may know the power of your presence. God of truth,

hear our prayer.

HERE OTHER INTERCESSIONS MAY BE OFFERED.

We give thanks for all who have served you in ages past and pray that we will be faithful until we join the great cloud of witnesses around your throne. God of truth,

hear our prayer.

Receive the prayers of our hearts, O God, and grant that we may forever trust in your promises, through Jesus Christ our Lord.

Amen

IMAGES FOR PREACHING

Bill awakens one morning with a scratchy throat. He brushes his teeth twice, gargles with an antiseptic mouthwash, swallows some extra vitamin C, and expects all will be well within the hour. Later that afternoon Bill's doctor suspects that he has a bad case of strep throat. The doctor takes a throat culture, places Bill on a strong antibiotic, and sends him home to bed. Under the covers Bill reads through a pamphlet explaining how to take the pills , and what the desired outcome of this medication would be. If Bill takes them, he should be back in the saddle within a few days. He is also warned that should he commingle this medication with any one of a long list of other medications or substances, the outcome could be disastrous!

When we search for evidence that humankind possesses a fallen nature, we need only observe decent peoples' reactions to the presence and ministry of Jesus. It seems that to hearts and minds of people unaffected by a fall, Jesus' message would be received with joy for the spiritual antibiotic it really is. Instead, those who hear the message of the gospel are likely to react, not in ways that produce spiritual health and personal reconciliation, but with behaviors that produce divisions between themselves and others.

This unfortunate although theologically predictable outcome suggests that within each of us is a tendency to react in rebellious ways when we ingest the message of the gospel into our systems. This discord is simply the symptom of a much deeper underlying problem. Instead of bringing life and hope, the gospel message sometimes creates misunderstanding, and estrangement.

For the gospel to bear its intended fruit in our lives, we must first honestly examine what it is within us that causes us to react in such negative ways. We must be willing to identify the elements in our lives that are incompatible with the gospel message. Do we really want to be healed? If we answer affirmatively, we must be willing to bring to Jesus any attitude, familiar behavioral pattern, or addictive behavior, which until now has been poisoning receptivity to the message and person of Jesus. Saying yes to Jesus may mean saying no to some treasured ways of life. What a challenging choice! But Jesus is willing and able to heal and transform us. What an incredible gift!

269

WORSHIP MATTERS

"We are surrounded by a great cloud of witnesses!" (Heb. 12:1). The author of Hebrews traces them through the Bible. We find even more witnesses if we just look at the people around us in worship: the couple that has been married for more than sixty years and now supports one another as they hobble to the rail for communion; the woman standing by her husband through a long period of unemployment, trusting the Lord to provide; the gay man trying to practice his faith without creating a crisis for others; the young parents teaching their kids how to behave in church. The cloud gets even denser when we think of the folks who have worshiped in that space before us: parents and grandparents, pastors and Sunday school teachers, friends who moved away and friends who died. "Since we are surrounded by so great a cloud of witnesses, . . . let us run with perseverance the race that is set before us" (Heb. 12:1). In so doing we become part of the great cloud that surrounds others—God's people.

LET THE CHILDREN COME

Create a "cloud of witnesses" balloon sculpture. Fill balloons with helium, tie them, and attach string. Write the names of the cloud of witnesses who are present and accounted for on balloons. Ask storytellers to tell the stories of the witnesses listed in Hebrews 11. Add stories of others who have shaped faith. Carry the balloons in a procession following the cross as Jesus leads the way in the great parade of witnesses. Secure the balloons in a free-form sculpture. Let children take a balloon home to encourage their marathon of faith.

MUSIC FOR WORSHIP

GATHERING

| LBW 231 | O Word of God incarnate |
| WOV 793 | Shout for joy loud and long |

PSALM 82

Paradowski, John. PW, Cycle C.

Williams, Kenneth E. "Psalm 82" in TP.

Psalms for Praise and Worship: A Complete Liturgical Psalter. ABI.

HYMN OF THE DAY

| LBW 508 | Come down, O Love divine |
| | DOWN AMPNEY |

VOCAL RESOURCES

Busarow, Donald. "Come Down, O Love Divine." CPH 98-2335. SAB, kybd.

Leavitt, John. "Come Down, O Love Divine." MSM 50-5401, Inst pts. 50-5401A. SATB, vln/fl, kybd.

Wolff, S. Drummond. "Come Down, O Love Divine." MSM 50-5500. SAB, tpt, kybd.

INSTRUMENTAL RESOURCES

Fruhauf, Ennis. "Down Ampney" in *Ralph Vaughan Williams and the English School.* AFP 11-10826. Org.

Sedio, Mark. "Down Ampney" in *Music for the Paschal Season.* AFP 11-10763. Org.

Stoldt, Frank. "Pastorale on Come Down, O Love Divine." MSM 20-540. Org, inst.

Wasson, Laura E. "Come Down, O Love Divine" in *A Piano Tapestry.* AFP 11-10821. Pno.

ALTERNATE HYMN OF THE DAY

| LBW 454 | If God himself be for me |
| WOV 785 | Weary of all trumpeting |

COMMUNION

| LBW 213 | I come, O Savior, to your table |
| WOV 649 | I want to walk as a child of the light |

SENDING

| LBW 495 | Lead on, O King eternal |
| WOV 736 | By gracious powers |

ADDITIONAL HYMNS AND SONGS

H82 601	O day of God, draw nigh
PH 419	How clear is our vocation, Lord
TFF 153	Guide my feet
W&P 15	Be bold, be strong
W&P 84	Lead me, guide me

MUSIC FOR THE DAY

CHORAL

Åhlén, Waldemar. "The Earth Adorned." WAL WH126. SATB, kybd.

Bell, John L. "The Love of God Comes Close." GIA G-5049. U, fl, kybd.

Gardner, John. "Fight the Good Fight." OXF. SATB, kybd.

Schütz, Heinrich. "Is God for Us." AFP 12-204920. SATB, kybd.

Thompson, J. Michael, and Barry L. Bobb. "He Came with His Love." AFP 11-10586. U, org.

CHILDREN'S CHOIRS

Lord, Suzanne. "Faith That's Sure." CG CGA695. U, pno, opt banjo/autoharp. Also in LS.

Shepherd, John. "A Living Faith." CG CGA-580. U/2 pt, kybd.

KEYBOARD/INSTRUMENTAL

Burkhardt, Michael. "Praise God. Praise Him" in *Eight Improvisations on Twentieth Century Hymn Tunes.* MSM-10- 707. Org.

Krebs, Johann Ludwig. "Herzlich lieb hab ich dich, O Herr" in *Sämtliche Orgelwerke, Band III.* Breitkopf 8415. Org.

Walcha, Helmut. "Ist Gott für mich so trete" in *Chorale Preludes I.* CFP 4850.Org.

HANDBELL

Anderson/Kramlich. "Classic Baroque Solos." HOP 1618. Solo.

Kinyon, Barbara B. "Lead On, O King Eternal." AG 1409. 2-3 oct.

Moklebust, Cathy. "Come, Let Us Eat." CG CGB 152. 3-5 oct, opt perc.

PRAISE ENSEMBLE

Haugen, Marty. "Send Down the Fire." GIA 3915. SATB, solo, kybd, gtr, opt perc.

Krippaehne, Dean. "Lord, My Strength" in W&P.

Soper, Scott. "One Lord" in Glory & Praise. OCP.

MONDAY, AUGUST 20
BERNARD, ABBOT OF CLAIRVAUX, 1153

Bernard was a Cistercian monk who became an abbot of great spiritual depth. He was a mystical writer deeply devoted to the humanity of Christ and consequently to the affective dimension of spirituality. He was critical of one of the foremost theologians of the day, Peter Abelard, because he believed Abelard's approach to faith was too rational and did not provide sufficient room for mystery. Bernard's devotional writings are still read today. His sermon on the Song of Solomon treats that book as an allegory of Christ's love for humanity. Bernard wrote several hymns, five of which are in *LBW.* Singing his hymn "Jesus the very thought of you" (316) could be a way to commemorate this monk at gatherings within the congregation today.

FRIDAY, AUGUST 24
ST. BARTHOLOMEW, APOSTLE

Bartholomew is mentioned as one of Jesus' disciples in Matthew, Mark, and Luke. The list in John does not include him but rather Nathanael, and these two are often assumed to be the same person. Except for his name on these lists of the twelve, little is known. Some traditions say Bartholomew preached in India or Armenia following the resurrection. In art, Bartholomew is pictured holding a flaying knife to indicate the manner in which he was killed.

In Bartholomew we have a model for the way many Christians live out their faith: anonymously. Like Bartholomew we are called by name to follow, though much of what we do in faith is quiet and unrecognized. Today we can look to the example of Bartholomew and pray for strength and guidance as we continue to live as disciples of Christ.

271

AUGUST 26, 2001

INTRODUCTION

Early Christians referred to Sunday as the Lord's Day, the eighth day of the week, the day beyond time in which a new creation is born. We gather this day for new beginnings, eager to be recreated by the Word who raises us to new life.

PRAYER OF THE DAY

God of all creation, you reach out to call people of all nations to your kingdom. As you gather disciples from near and far, count us also among those who boldly confess your Son Jesus Christ as Lord.

READINGS

Isaiah 58:9b-14

The Lord promises those who have returned from exile that where justice and mercy prevail, the ruins will be rebuilt and light will rise in the darkness. It is a day for new beginnings.

Psalm 103:1-8

The LORD crowns you with mercy and lovingkindness.
(Ps. 103:4)

Hebrews 12:18-29

The writer to the Hebrews presents a striking vision of the eternal dwelling place and the one who welcomes the righteous. It holds no fear, only forgiveness through Christ's blood.

Luke 13:10-17

Jesus heals a woman on the Sabbath, offering her a new beginning for her life. When religious leaders are angered because Jesus did work on the Sabbath, Jesus insists that new creation is not constrained by a legalistic reading of an ancient calendar.

ALTERNATE FIRST READING/PSALM

Jeremiah 1:4-10

The call of the prophet Jeremiah is a reminder that age is not an obstacle to being a witness for God. Jeremiah's difficult ministry in the years before the Babylonian exile is part of a plan God made before Jeremiah was born. God will give the prophet the words he needs to say.

Psalm 71:1-6

From my mother's womb you have been my strength. (Ps. 71:6)

COLOR Green

THE PRAYERS

Freed by Christ and led by the Spirit, let us offer our prayers to God for the world, the church, and all those in need.

A BRIEF SILENCE.

That you would raise up people in every nation who can restore broken lives and communities. God of truth,
hear our prayer.

That we may be gracious and compassionate to others who long for springs of living waters. God of truth,
hear our prayer.

That this community of faith may respect the sabbath you have created for us and pursue your will in all that we do. God of truth,
hear our prayer.

That those who are hungry, lonely, or ill (especially...) may be renewed and revived by your healing power. God of truth,
hear our prayer.

HERE OTHER INTERCESSIONS MAY BE OFFERED.

That in our time we will join all the saints and angels who continuously sing praises around your heavenly throne. God of truth,
hear our prayer.

Receive the prayers of our hearts, O God, and grant that we may forever trust in your promises, through Jesus Christ our Lord.
Amen

IMAGES FOR PREACHING

People often think of the desert as a wasteland, too hot for anything to grow and flourish. Yet heat is not the cause of a desert environment; a lack of available water is the culprit. Once a source of water is introduced to this "wasteland," incredible growth begins to occur. An unusual amount of rainfall can produce a wonderland of desert color, even from seeds that have lain dormant in the soil for decades.

Unfortunately, many churches are reminiscent of desert dryness. People with glassy stares and blank expressions sit as dormant seeds, neatly lined up in rows of straight-backed pews waiting for the water of the Spirit

272

to rain down on them. This parched environment may be caused by leaders who have substituted the law of religion and a demand for decency, order, and control, for the watering can of the Spirit.

Such a need to control is nothing new among leaders of the faithful. One need only observe the synagogue leader's reaction to Jesus' healing of the crippled woman on the Sabbath in today's gospel, "But the leader of the synagogue, indignant because Jesus had cured on the sabbath, kept saying to the crowd, 'There are six days on which work ought to be done; come on those days and be cured, and not on the sabbath day'" (Luke 13:14).

Once water enters a desert soil the results will be both startling and unpredictable. The one certainty is that new life will spring forth. One can never predict the kind of life that will emerge. It is this unpredictability that causes many leaders to opt for aridity and death. How often do leaders deny living water to God's people for fear of losing control?

We must learn from Isaiah that the Lord will inevitably quench the thirst of his people. God will even do it in spite of us, if necessary. The Lord promises that when the yoke is removed from them, "I will guide you continually, and satisfy your needs in parched places . . . and you shall be like a watered garden, like a spring of water, whose waters never fail" (Isa. 58:9b, 11). May preachers and leaders become water vessels in the hands of a gracious and life-giving God.

WORSHIP MATTERS

Sunday is the Christian sabbath. It is the new day that God has given us. On this day, the first day of the week, God raised Christ Jesus from the dead. If God rested from God's work of creation on the seventh day of the week, God fulfilled God's work of redemption on this eighth day of the week. When Jesus rose from death to new life, he inaugurated the ultimate sabbath rest: a rest from sin, fear, isolation and death. Through baptism we enter into the sabbath rest that the risen Christ brings. For this reason, many baptismal fonts are octagonal in shape: they point to the eighth day, God's new day of new life. We keep the Christian sabbath by gathering to worship on Sunday. We participate in the new day by returning to the font to be bathed in forgiveness. We hear the good news, share bread and cup, and receive the new life that is ours in Christ. Here is real rest.

LET THE CHILDREN COME

The days of summer are coming to a close. The daily routines of school and daycare will begin. We leave worship with the good news of the benediction, which blesses us on our way. Extend this blessing to the home. Encourage adults to lay their hands on their child's head and share words of blessing as leave-taking begins. Let the children reciprocate and bless their parents as they engage in their daily work. When Jesus laid hands on the crippled woman, she was healed, praised God, and moved into the new day.

MUSIC FOR WORSHIP

GATHERING

LBW 543	Praise to the Lord, the Almighty
WOV 719	God is here!

PSALM 103

Norbert, Gregory. "Psalm 103: O Bless the Lord" in *Morning Prayer–Evening Prayer.* OCP 10372.

Paradowski, John. PW, Cycle C.

Ziegenhals, Harriet Ilse. "The Lord Is Kind and Merciful" in *Sing Out! A Children's Psalter.* WLP.

LBW 519	My soul, now praise your maker!
LBW 543	Praise to the Lord, the Almighty
LBW 549	Praise, my soul, the King of heaven
WOV 798	Bless the Lord, O my soul

HYMN OF THE DAY

WOV 742	Come, we that love the Lord
	MARCHING TO ZION

INSTRUMENTAL RESOURCES

Carlson, J. Bert. "Marching to Zion" in *Blessed Assurance.* AFP 11-10935. Pno.

Ferguson, John. "Marching to Zion" in *Three Nineteenth Century Revival Hymns.* AFP 11-10976. Org.

Raney, Joel. "Marching to Zion" in *An Instrument of Your Peace.* HOP 1952. Pno.

ALTERNATE HYMN OF THE DAY

LBW 358	Glories of your name are spoken
LBW 507	How firm a foundation

COMMUNION

LBW 212	Let us break bread together
WOV 708	Grains of wheat

273

SENDING

| LBW 433 | The Church of Christ, in every age |
| WOV 722 | Hallelujah! We sing your praises |

ADDITIONAL HYMNS AND SONGS

NCH 538	Standing at the future's threshold
TFF 189	Heal me, O Lord
TFF 199	'Tis the old ship of Zion
W&P 26	Canticle of the turning
W&P 85	Let justice roll like a river

MUSIC FOR THE DAY

CHORAL

Bach, J. S. "Nun lob, mein Seel" in *Gottlob! Nun geht das Jahr zu Ende* (Cantata 28). BRE 4528. Str and ww double chorus in this movement and thus may be omitted.

Ippolitof-Ivanov, M. "Bless the Lord, O My Soul." GSCH 11100.

Owens, Sam Batt. "This Is the Day." MSM 50-4502. 2 pt, org.

Proulx, Richard. "O Lord, Your Word Be Always My Guide." GIA G-4301. 2 pt, org.

CHILDREN'S CHOIRS

Page, Sue Ellen. "Jesus' Hands Were Kind Hands." CG CGA-485. U, fl, kybd. Also in LS.

Pote, Allen. "Bless the Lord." AFP 3-75002. SATB, opt fl, bng, tamb, fl, pno.

KEYBOARD/INSTRUMENTAL

Held, Wilbur. "Foundation" in *Seven Settings of American Folk Hymns.* CPH 97-5829.

Jordan, Alice. "Partita on 'Foundation.'" FLA HH-5055. Org.

Lübeck, Vincent. "Praeludium und Fuge" in *Orgelwerke.* Various eds. Org.

HANDBELL

Bowen/Stone/Cortez. "Four Classic Handbell Duets." HOP 1866. Duet.

Hendricks, Ronnie. "A Joyful Noise." FBM BG 0882. 4 oct.

Maggs, Charles. "How Firm a Foundation." AG GP 1017. 3 oct.

PRAISE ENSEMBLE

Richards, Noel, and Tricia Richards. "Our Confidence Is in the Lord" in W&P.

Watanabe, Esther. "I Will Bless Thee, O Lord" in *Praise Hymns and Choruses,* 3rd ed. MAR.

TUESDAY, AUGUST 28
AUGUSTINE, BISHOP OF HIPPO, 430

Augustine was one of the greatest theologians of the Western church. Born in North Africa, he was a philoso- phy student in Carthage, where he later became a teacher of rhetoric. Much of his young life was a debauched one. As an adult he came under the influence of Ambrose, the bishop of Milan, and through him came to see Christian- ity as a religion appropriate for a philosopher. Augustine was baptized by Ambrose at the Easter Vigil in 387. He was ordained four years later and made bishop of Hippo in 396. Augustine was a defender of the Christian faith and argued, against the Donatists, that the holiness of the church did not depend on the holiness of its members, particularly the clergy, but that holiness comes from Christ, the head of the church. Augustine's autobiogra- phy, Confessions, tells of his slow move toward faith and includes the line, "Late have I loved thee."

TUESDAY, AUGUST 28
MOSES THE BLACK, MONK, C. 400

A man of great strength and rough character, Moses the Black was converted to Christian faith toward the close of the fourth century. Prior to his conversion he had been a thief and a leader of a gang of robbers. The story of his conversion is unknown, but eventually, he became a desert monk at Skete. The habit of his monastic com- munity was white, though Moses is reported to have said, "God knows I am black within." The change in his heart and life had a profound impact on his native Ethiopia. He was murdered when Berbers attacked his monastery.

FRIDAY, AUGUST 31
JOHN BUNYAN, TEACHER, 1688

John Bunyan had little schooling but became one of the most remarkable figures of seventeenth-century litera- ture. He was a lay preacher who made his living as a tinker. After the restoration in England he was ordered to stop preaching, but he refused and was jailed several times. His spiritual pilgrimage is revealed in his works, particularly *The Pilgrim's Progress.* It is an allegory of a person's experience from his first awareness of sin, through a personal conversion to Christ, then on to the life of faith and then finally to the "Celestial City," the true and eternal home. His commemoration and his own journey offer strength for people to continue their own quest for spiritual truth.

AUTUMN

God sees that love is, indeed, created

IMAGES of the SEASON

It is time to go back to work. The days of summer relaxation, vacations, and walks in the park begin to fade into distant memory as life returns to its often hectic pace. Labor Day really does seem to signal a return to the work of routine life. We buy for our children the new clothes and academic tools they need for another school year. Dance classes and music lessons, meetings and rehearsals appear again on the week's schedule.

The church is certainly not immune from this injection of renewed vigor. Church councils may hold annual retreats during these early autumn days, setting goals and objectives for the coming year. Committee chairs gather their volunteers and gear up for the coming festival season. Sunday schools rally with new teachers and students, and adolescents groan as confirmation classes begin yet again.

The energy renewed flows into the church, shaping the tenor and the focus of Christian life. Themes of work and discipleship emerge from this season's texts. In these next months, we hear the call to be workers in the vineyard, to seek out the lost sheep, to stand with the poor, to use our material abundance to make God's reign known. We are called like the widow who desires justice to be persistent and to pay careful attention to the character of our communities.

Deeply embedded in humans is the need for productive work, to toil for the maintenance of our bodies, our families, and our communities. When Jesus commands his disciples to pick up the cross, he does not intend to construct one more rigid rule for living life. Instead, he is calling us to be fully human, to invest through the sweat of our brow and the fire of our passion in God's work of redemption.

In this season, we take up our task of bearing the creative and redeeming work of God. As the Spirit has been poured out on us in Pentecost's fire, we become participants with God in the creation of compassion, love, and justice. And like Adam and Eve, we are called to go forth into the world to be fruitful in our commitment to justice and to multiply the love that has come to us in word and sacrament. Work is no longer a punishment for some ancient sin but, in grace, becomes a sign of God's own investment in the redemption of human life. In our work, even in the mundane tasks of church life, grace takes deeper root, and we glimpse a foretaste of the coming harvest. Can we come to see that setting goals and objectives on flip charts has the potential to transform our neighborhoods and our congregations? Can we trust that our work does, indeed, draw us into the life of God?

The rich green of the post-Pentecost season reminds us yet again that God has inexorably linked the experience of grace to the life and work of human beings. It is *ordinary* for the Christian church to be about the work of God's reign. It is *extraordinary* that this labor bears the very power of the resurrection. The last half of this season pushes us to see our work as sacramental, an incarnational expression of Christ's own life, death, and resurrection. In Western culture, we immediately consider the product of our labor. We count the cost, and we evaluate the outcome. The themes of the Sundays after Pentecost, however, suggest that the character of our work is as important as its product.

The gospel texts remind us again and again that our Christian task is to bring into being communities that are marked by sincere welcome and compassionate justice. Week after week, we are reminded that creating such communities is indeed work, for they contradict the common, cultural wisdom. In the church those on the margins are given priority. The outsider is invited to the party; the Samaritan is the one who comes back to thank Jesus for healing him; all work stops so that the lost sheep can be found. The poor, the rejected, and the lost become the cornerstone. We are called to take the low seats, so that those who have been denied seats altogether might have the higher place. Throughout this season, Jesus calls us to consider what kind of work we are doing, forcing us to compare the work of God's community with the ordinary ways our culture has taught us to think. The values of the green and growing commonwealth of God are often radically different from the cultural norms around us. Undoubtedly we have work to do.

Our work—picking up the cross, walking the path of suffering with the poor—is challenging and difficult. As we work together in new communities of grace, it is easy to become mired in tedious details. Teachers have to make lesson plans. Committee chairs have to produce agendas and place reminder calls to forgetful committee members. Altar care volunteers have to wash dishes. Ushers have to pick up discarded bulletins. At the same time we all realize that people's minds and hearts change ever so slowly; patterns of sin run deeply through all of us. Almost all members of faith communities come to a time when they wonder what happened to that rosy vision of God's grace. Like the persistent widow, we must return again and again, asking for

justice and grace, wondering when our request will be answered and when our harvest will be complete.

Yet even in the ambiguous, challenging context of our planning and our dreaming, the themes of this season remind us that our labor is held in the arms of God. In the end, growth does occur and patterns do change, despite our frailties and our weaknesses. Perhaps the heart of the message in these weeks of busy growth is that God stands in the midst of our work. God sees that love is, indeed, created. The fields bud into harvest before our eyes, and the food that sustains us is gathered into the granary. We come to the table with our lists of things to do and our faltering attempts to be faithful, and we are fed with grace, provided with a foretaste of the feast to come. Once again, the mystery of the resurrection opens new doors, filling us with new energy, and the work of God moves forward. The Spirit comes, and Pentecost continues in the bread and wine, in the water and the word, in our work and in our play.

277

ENVIRONMENT AND ART FOR THE SEASON

As the months move into autumn, thoughts naturally turn to harvest: harvest of the fruits of the earth, harvest of deeds, harvest of days, harvest of lives.

This focus becomes apparent from the many harvest festivals at this turning of the year. Sukkoth, the festival of booths, was originally an agricultural festival celebrating the harvest of the first vintage. Later use transformed the booths constructed for the harvest into commemorations of the dwellings of the Israelites in their forty years in the wilderness. Through such layering and transformation, the liturgical year has been distilled and passed on. Underlying the feast days of the Christian year are the Jewish festivals and the celebrations of the Romans and various nature religions, and beneath them all, as an ever-turning wheel, lie the cycles of God's blessed creation.

So it is good that in the shorter, darker days of winter, we light Advent candles. It is good that in the spare

and hungrier days of late winter, we fast. It is good that in the first rays of spring, we exchange eggs and sing alleluia at the joyful news of resurrection and new life. It is good that at the lengthening of days we see flame and hear wind and receive power for growth in the Spirit. And it is good, at the dwindling of days and the ingathering of harvest, that we remember and give thanks and lift up the good gifts of the earth.

Autumn does not bring the church into a new liturgical season: these are still the days after Pentecost, the days of the church, ordinary days, but the natural world surrounding the people of God is changing and should not be ignored. It is the wellspring for much of the imagery of the church's tradition and sacred writings.

During these harvest days of autumn, the environment for worship may reflect the maturing of the year. Gold, orange, brown, and scarlet may augment the green of the days after Pentecost, especially for churches in temperate climates. Grain wreaths or wreaths of grapevine or bittersweet (or pyracantha or pepperberry) could decorate the entrance doors of the church building, or arches of grain or vine could crown the lintels.

Wheat can be woven and hung on walls or gates. A bunch of wheat stalks could be bound to the processional cross with narrow satin ribbon in forest green, burnt orange, golden yellow, and brown. Large earthen vases or baskets filled with seasonal flowers—asters, goldenrod, black-eyed Susan—mixed with dried grasses and cattails or seed pods could replace the usual florist's arrangements. Wreaths and arrangements can also be constructed of nuts and pine cones, liquidamber pods, twigs, broom corn, dried flowers, dried herbs, locust pods, preserved autumn leaves, Chinese lanterns, dried hydrangeas, corn husks, honesty, curly willow, teasles, oats, foxtail, pepperberries, firethorn, pine needles, or any other harvested material from your area. What is important here is that the natural materials be selected and harvested with care, that they be crafted with skill and effort, and that the results be beautiful without dominating or detracting from the holy space and its furnishings.

One of the richest and most universal products of harvest is bread. Bread is an ancient symbol for life itself. The Egyptian hieroglyph for peace (*hotep*) is composed of bread on a reed mat. Many Middle Eastern weddings include the exchange of salt and bread by the bride and groom. Bread is also central to many biblical stories and images, as well as to the sacrament of communion.

Bread is composed of wheat, water, and salt, simple elements of life. When the wheat is ground, when the water and salt are kneaded in, when the loaf is placed in the hot oven, transformation occurs. The elements together, transformed by fire, become something they were not before and could not be by themselves: bread. Now, in this season of harvest, would be a good time to recover the use of bread in the sacramental meal: the gift of God, shaped by human hands, transformed into bread, broken and shared—just as those partaking in the meal will be transformed, broken, and shared.

Certainly at least one baker of bread, or someone waiting to be a baker, can be found in each congrega-

tion. Baking bread for communion is a wonderful project for Sunday school children or confirmation classes. Many recipes for eucharistic breads are available, and any recipes for pita work well. Perhaps a winemaker in the congregation would share first vintage, offered up in thanks and used for the sacramental wine this season. When we take the ordinary and offer it up in thanks for God's purpose, we may discern the truth that God often works through ordinary things—bread, wine, water, people—and begin to live out our ordinary days filled with the anticipation of encounter.

Parishes could consider including a blessing of the first fruits during the months of September or October. The eucharist might be followed by a chanting of Psalm 65 and a prayer of blessing over the fruits, herbs, grains, and flowers being harvested. Gertrud Mueller Nelson, in her fine book *To Dance with God,* relates that her parish then gathers outside around a table decorated with garden flowers, offerings of fruit and vegetables, and large wheels of seeded bread to be shared. The scripture readings for the Sunday of proper 20 (September 23, 2001) would support such a blessing ritual, and parishes could make a special collection for a food pantry as well.

In the midst of the ordinary days, ordinary tasks wait to be accomplished, and these green days are an opportunity to prepare for the approaching festivals and seasons. Altar guilds and those who take care of the accoutrements of worship can use this simpler time to make sure that all nongreen paraments, stoles, chasubles, and other vestments are cleaned and ready for the coming new cycle of the church year. Silver vessels may be cleaned and polished and stored in tarnish-free cloth bags. Altar cloths and fair linens that have been stored should be examined to see if they need to be cleaned or ironed. Now is a good time to order supplies: candles of the right size for the Advent wreath, baptismal candles for upcoming baptismal festivals, briquets and incense, sturdy stands and sufficient poles for banners, and so on.

At the end of October, many congregations celebrate Reformation Day. The color is red: red for the fire of transformation, red for the flame of the Spirit of God, red for the life-blood of the church, which is the grace of God. The paraments used are generally those from Pentecost Sunday, and it is good to tie Reformation in with the larger themes of the church's life.

PREACHING WITH THE SEASON

"You can become a Christian by going to church about as easily as you can become a car by sleeping in a garage," observed Garrison Keillor. We have returned from our vacations and our vacating of church for the summer, only to discover that we are still in ordinary time, this portion of the liturgical year when we look at texts on discipleship. How then do we live out our baptisms? We were hoping for a few familiar songs, joyful reunions with friends, some Sunday school classes for the kids, and a preacher filled with how-tos for living a successful life, like the coach in all those football huddles we will be watching this autumn. We would like some good pep talks, reminding us that God is on our side and is going to help us out.

The rhythm of the school year might have us as preachers longing to offer up exactly what our parishioners are hoping we will give them. They are back, after such spotty summer attendance, and we want to reward them, we want them to be happy that they returned. But the rhythm of the liturgical year calls us to a different place. Our gospel readings through autumn of this year of Luke are from the section (encompassing 9:51—19:28) that begins: "When the days drew near for him to be taken up, he set his face to go to Jerusalem." At the beginning of July, we began with gospel texts from this section of Luke. But now the church is full again, and we are still reading these challenging texts. These stories point us to Jerusalem, and we are being drawn into a journey, a pilgrimage with Jesus.

This season of texts offers us several possible thematic approaches. Our pilgrimage with Jesus could explore our lives as pilgrims, those who are on a journey of return, longing and learning, and grace. And the question for our pilgrimage is: Are we really interested in a God with power to transform us, or do we prefer one who helps us feel better about the way we are? These texts will lead us on a journey with Jesus, a journey of radical—or, at the very least, challenging—discipleship.

It is interesting to note that this autumn section of Lukan texts begins (proper 17) and ends (proper 25)

with these words of Jesus: "All who exalt themselves will be humbled, and those who humble themselves will be exalted." This saying is understood to be a teaching unique to Jesus. It frames these texts about radical reversals, radical changes in the status quo and standard expectations. This autumn will not strangely warm our hearts. Perhaps the theme for our fall preaching could be "Spending Our Lives," as we lift up the teachings of Jesus about how we spend our money, with whom we spend our time, how we spend our time. This theme might connect with a congregational focus on stewardship, as fall is often the time for pledging and budget preparations for the next year.

Our task as preachers with this section of texts, more than usual, is to step up to the prophetic dimensions of our calling. As Walter Brueggemann writes, "The task of prophetic ministry is to evoke an alternative community that knows it is about different things in different ways. And that alternative community has a variety of relationships with the dominant community" (*The Prophetic Imagination*, Minneapolis: Fortress Press, 1978, p. 111). How can we help our Christian communities understand themselves as alternative communities of solidarity, knowing that we cannot live out this kind of discipleship alone? Another thematic possibility for these autumn sermons is "Practicing Our Faith." Invite people to study the book *Practicing Our Faith* (ed. by Dorothy Bass, San Francisco: Jossey-Bass, 1997), which is a helpful way to lift up the communal dimensions of our learning and our living out of these "different ways."

Of course, it will be tempting or even easy to gloss over the good news of these texts, particularly if we are preaching to the comfortable. Challenging discipleship texts have often been preached as law that masquerades as gospel. Remind hearers that our baptism is a gift and that living it out is a gift; we *get to* discover the joy and transformation of following Jesus.

279

SHAPE OF WORSHIP FOR THE SEASON

BASIC SHAPE OF THE EUCHARISTIC RITE

- Confession and Forgiveness: see alternate worship text for autumn in *Sundays and Seasons*

GATHERING

- Greeting: see alternate worship text for autumn in *Sundays and Seasons*
- Omit the Kyrie during the autumn (except for Reformation Day)
- Omit or use the hymn of praise during the autumn (use for Reformation Day)

WORD

- Use the Apostles' Creed (Nicene Creed for Reformation Sunday or Day)
- The prayers: see alternate forms and responses for autumn in *Sundays and Seasons*

MEAL

- Offertory prayer: see alternate worship text for autumn in *Sundays and Seasons*
- Use the proper preface for Sundays after Pentecost
- Eucharistic prayer: in addition to four main options in *LBW,* see "Eucharistic Prayer H: Autumn" in *WOV* Leaders Edition, p. 72
- Invitation to communion: see alternate worship text for autumn in *Sundays and Seasons*
- Post-communion prayer: see alternate worship text for autumn in *Sundays and Seasons*

SENDING

- Benediction: see alternate worship text for autumn in *Sundays and Seasons*
- Dismissal: see alternate worship text for autumn in *Sundays and Seasons*

OTHER SEASONAL POSSIBILITIES

- Blessing of Teachers and Students (see seasonal rites section)
- See "Recognition of Ministries in the Congregation" in *Occasional Services,* pp. 143–46

DISTRIBUTION OF BIBLES

- If Bibles are distributed publicly to young readers, consider having their parents or sponsors involved in physically handing over the Bibles (as a follow-up to promises made at baptism)

BLESSING OF ANIMALS

- Traditionally celebrated on or near October 4 (Francis of Assisi, renewer of the church, 1226); see a possible order for this celebration in the seasonal rites section

HARVEST FESTIVAL OR HARVEST HOME

- Many congregations celebrate the harvest sometime each fall. While readings are appointed on page 39 of *LBW* for the occasion of harvest, the gospel for proper 23 (October 14) on the ten lepers speaks to the theme of thankfulness and may be a particularly suitable occasion to celebrate the harvest.

REFORMATION DAY

- One way to resolve the dilemma of whether to celebrate lesser festivals when they occur on Sundays or to observe the complete cycle of the Revised Common Lectionary would be to use lectionary readings for proper 25 on October 28, but to use the prayers of the day for both proper 25 and Reformation Day. While much of the music and the prayers could reflect the lectionary for proper 25, one or more of the hymns could be chosen to reflect the Reformation festival. The color for the day could also be red.

LECTIONARY OPPORTUNITY FOR HEALING SERVICE

- Proper 23 on October 14 (gospel)

ASSEMBLY SONG FOR THE SEASON

Jesus speaks to us in parables, giving us an image of the reign of God. Jesus tells us what we are to do—invite, give up, search, pray, be faithful. What faith will the song of the assembly proclaim? What song will help to form disciples?

The gospel of Luke is filled with many stories of Jesus' ministry of healing. Sing some of the many hymns of healing and wholeness, not only at this time, but also throughout the year of Luke. "Healer of our every ill" (WOV 738) would be appropriate to sing during anointing with oil in a service of healing or at the distribution of communion.

GATHERING

If the gathering rite has been streamlined during the summer, now is a time to add the Kyrie or hymn of praise or to alternate them weekly. The standard canticles of our worship books are always appropriate, and we need to keep them in our collective memory. Worship planners need to be aware of the richness and variety of familiar traditions, while enriching the assembly song with the music of other brothers and sisters in Christ. If the assembly has been singing the standard canticles, autumn might be a time to introduce variety by using alternate selections.

We often overlook the scriptural indexes at the back of worship books for hymn settings of canticles, such as the hymn of praise "Glory to God, we give you thanks" (WOV 787). Another setting is "All glory be to God on high" (LBW 166), which is especially appropriate on Reformation Sunday. Sing this hymn in a lively, duple meter, dance tempo, and judiciously add a tambourine.

WORD

The autumn parables are stories of mercy framed by passages on discipleship. The responses and hymns of the assembly should help to emphasize those stories. Sing "O Lord, let us see your kindness" (TFF 8) as a seasonal psalm refrain and tone.

"Alleluia. Lord, to whom shall we go?" (W&P 7) is an alternate setting of the standard alleluia verse for the season. The gospel reading might be framed by a gradual hymn such as "Word of God, come down on earth" (WOV 716), using selected stanzas or the refrain of "Listen, God is calling" (WOV 712). "Listen, God is calling" could also be used on Reformation Sunday, alternating with "Lord, keep us steadfast in your Word (LBW 230) as the hymn of the day.

MEAL

God's mercy is manifested in Jesus' table fellowship with sinners. He also calls us to give up our earthly possessions to follow him. These two themes are present in the lectionary this autumn. "We give thee but thine own" (LBW 410) is an old favorite of many and would be an appropriate offertory hymn for the season. Sing hymns of discipleship and stewardship during communion.

SENDING

As disciples, we pray that the reign of God would continue to come among us. For a different style of sending hymn, sing "Send me, Jesus" (WOV 773). Continue the singing after the dismissal as the people exit the nave. "The Spirit sends us forth to serve" (WOV 723) and "God, whose giving knows no ending" (LBW 408) are also appropriate seasonal sending hymns.

281

MUSIC FOR THE SEASON

VERSE AND OFFERTORY

Busarow, Donald. *Verses and Offertories.* AFP 11-9540. 2 pt, kybd.

Cherwien, David. *Verses for the Fall Festivals.* MSM-80-880. U/SATB, opt brass, org.

Cherwien, David. *Verses for the Season of Pentecost, Set 3.* MSM-80-543. Mxd vcs, org.

Hillert, Richard. *Verses and Offertories.* AFP 11-9543. U, org.

Neswick, Bruce. "O Taste and See." AFP 11-10592. SATB, sop solo.

Pelz, Walter, and Richard Wienhorst. *Verses and Offertory Sentences, Part VIII: Selected Lesser Festivals, Commemorations, and Other Occasions.* CPH 97-5508; acc ed 97-5510. U/2 pt.

Weber, Paul, Richard Gieseke, and David Schack. *Verses and Offertory Sentences, Part VII.* CPH 97-5507; full score 97-5510.

CHORAL

Burkhardt, Michael. "Filled with the Spirit." MSM 50-7402. 3 pt, opt hb/kybd.

Fauré, Gabriel. "Cantique de Jean Racine." BRO 801. SATB, kybd.

Fay, Peter. "O Sacred and Blessed Feast." AFP 11-10841. SATB.

Ferguson, John. "Be Thou My Vision." AFP 11-10925. SATB, org.

Pickard, John. "The King of Love." AFP 11-10910. U, desc, kybd.

Scott, K. Lee. "Christ Hath a Garden." MSM-50-9033. SATB div, org.

Willan, Healey, arr. "Sing to the Lord of Harvest." CPH 98-2013. SATB, org.

CHILDREN'S CHOIRS

Hopson, Hal H. "Planting and Harvesting." MSM-50-7400. U, pno.

Lindh, Jody W. "Come, Let Us Sing." CG CGA-478. U, kybd.

Pote, Allen. "I Lift Up Mine Eyes." HOP A 595. SATB, fl, ob, kybd.

Printz, Brad. "Gifts of Life." CG CGA775. 2 pt, fl, pno.

Wold, Wayne L. "God's Loving Call." CG CGA649. U, kybd.

KEYBOARD/INSTRUMENTAL

Helsel, Fanny Mendelssohn. *Prelude for Organ.* VIV 304. Org.

Pinkham, Daniel. *Versets for Small Organ.* ECS 4072. Org.

Vierne, Louis. *Twenty-four Pieces in Free Style, Books 1 & 2.* Master Organ Series M1705 & M1706. Org.

HANDBELL

Dobrinski, Cynthia. "Guide Me, O Thou Great Jehovah." AG 1364 (hb), 1365 (score). 3-5 oct, org, opt cong.

Honoré, Jeffrey. "Gift of Finest Wheat." CPH 97-6578. 3-5 oct.

Keller, Michael R. "Sing Praise to God Who Reigns Above." AG 1288. 2 oct.

Tucker, Margaret R. "With Timbrel and Dance." Composers Music BE 0436. 3 oct.

Wagner, Douglas E. "Fanfare Prelude on 'Nun Danket Alle Gott.'" CG CGB98. 3-4 oct.

Wagner, Douglas E. "Ring for Joy." AGEHR AG 3035. 3 oct.

Wiltse, Carl. "Deep River." Stained Glass Music SGM 3892. 3 oct.

PRAISE ENSEMBLE

African Traditional/arr. Roger Emerson. "O Sifuni Mungu." HAL 40326303. SAB/SATB, pno, opt gtr, electric bass, drms.

Green, Melody, and Doug Holck. "There Is a Redeemer." LIL AN-2592. SATB, kybd, opt orch.

Haas, David, and Herb Brokering. "God Has Done Marvelous Things." GIA G-4731. U, kybd, opt solo, cong, gtr.

ALTERNATE WORSHIP TEXTS

CONFESSION AND FORGIVENESS

In the name of the Father, and of the ✢ Son,
and of the Holy Spirit.
Amen

Have mercy on us, O God,
according to your lovingkindness;
in your great compassion
blot out our offenses.

Silence for reflection and self-examination.

God of grace,
we confess to you the ways
we have chosen death rather than life:
by trusting in ourselves rather than you;
by failing to follow your call;
by ignoring the cries of the poor;
by misusing your creation;
by seeking security through possessions;
by neglecting to give thanks for all your gifts.
Renew your salvation within us,
and hold us in your generous spirit. Amen

In great mercy, God abolished death
and brought life through our Savior Jesus Christ.
As a called and ordained minister of the church of Christ,
and by his authority, I declare to you
that you are forgiven by the grace of God
and empowered by the Holy Spirit to live a new life.
Amen

GREETING

The grace given to us in Christ Jesus,
the help of the Holy Spirit living in us,
and the power of God who calls us with a holy calling
be with you all.
And also with you.

OFFERTORY PRAYER

God of harvest,
to your table we bring wine and bread,
and gifts from the labor of our hands.
Receive the offering of our lives,
and feed us with your living bread from heaven,
that we may serve others in your name;
through Christ our Lord. Amen

INVITATION TO COMMUNION

Set your hope on God,
who richly provides us with every good thing.

POST-COMMUNION PRAYER

We give you thanks, faithful God,
for feeding us with this one heavenly food.
Transform us through this meal
into the likeness of your Son,
and unite us in love for one another,
that we may be your body in the world;
in Jesus' name we pray.
Amen

BENEDICTION

Almighty God, Father, ✢ Son, and Holy Spirit
watch over your going out and your coming in,
from this time forth and forevermore.
Amen

DISMISSAL

Go in peace, equipped by God for every good work.
Thanks be to God.

283

SEASONAL RITES

SERVICE OF THE WORD FOR HEALING

This service may be celebrated at any time. It may be especially appropriate on or near the festival of St. Luke, Evangelist (October 18).

Stand

HYMN

LBW 360	O Christ, the healer, we have come
WOV 716	Word of God, come down on earth
TFF 189	Heal me, O Lord

GREETING AND WELCOME

The grace of our Lord Jesus Christ, the love of God, and the communion of the Holy Spirit be with you all.
And also with you.

We gather to hear the word of God, pray for those in need, and ask God's blessing on those who seek healing and wholeness through Christ our Lord.

PRAYER OF THE DAY

The proper prayer of the day may be used, or the prayer for St. Luke (October 18), p. 118 in WOV Leaders Edition, or the following:

Great God, our healer,
by your power, the Lord Jesus healed the sick
and gave hope to the hopeless.
As we gather in his name,
look upon us with mercy, and
bless us with your healing Spirit.
Bring us comfort in the midst of pain,
strength to transform our weakness,
and light to illuminate our darkness.
We ask this in the name of Jesus Christ,
our crucified and risen Lord,
who lives and reigns with you and the Holy Spirit,
one God, now and forever.
Amen

Sit

READINGS

These readings, the readings listed for St. Luke, Evangelist (p. 118 in WOV Leaders Edition), or the readings listed on pp. 96–97 of Occasional Services may be used.

Isaiah 61:1-3a
Psalm 23
The LORD is my shepherd; I shall not be in want. (Ps. 23:1)
Luke 17:11-19

SERMON

HYMN

LBW 423	Lord, whose love in humble service
WOV 738	Healer of our every ill
WOV 798	Bless the Lord, O my soul
TFF 186	Come, ye disconsolate

Stand

THE PRAYERS

This litany or the prayers in Occasional Services (pp. 91–93) may be used.

God the Father, you desire the health and salvation of all people.
We praise you and thank you, O Lord.
God the Son, you came that we might have life
and might have it more abundantly.
We praise you and thank you, O Lord.
God the Holy Spirit,
you make our bodies the temples of your presence.
We praise you and thank you, O Lord.
Holy Trinity, one God,
in you we live and move and have our being.
We praise you and thank you, O Lord.
Lord, grant your healing grace to all who are sick, injured,
or disabled, that they may be made whole;
hear us, O Lord of life.
Grant to all who are lonely, anxious, or despondent
the awareness of your presence;
hear us, O Lord of life.
Mend broken relationships, and restore those in emotional distress
to soundness of mind and serenity of spirit;
hear us, O Lord of life.
Bless physicians, nurses, and all others who minister
to the suffering; grant them wisdom and skill,
sympathy and patience;
hear us, O Lord of life.

Grant to the dying a peaceful, holy death,
and with your grace strengthen those who mourn;
hear us, O Lord of life.
Restore to wholeness whatever is broken in our lives,
in this nation, and in the world;
hear us, O Lord of life.
Hear us, O Lord of life:
heal us, and make us whole.

Gracious God, in baptism you anointed us with the oil of salvation,
and joined us to the death and resurrection of your Son. Bless all
who seek your healing presence in their lives. In their suffering
draw them more deeply into the mystery of your love, that following Christ in the way of the cross, they may know the power of his
resurrection; who lives and reigns forever and ever.
Amen

Sit
LAYING ON OF HANDS AND ANOINTING
*Those who wish to receive the laying on of hands (and anointing)
come to the altar and, if possible, kneel. The minister lays both
hands on each person's head in silence, after which he or she
may dip a thumb in the oil and make the sign of the cross on the
person's forehead, saying:*

(Through this holy anointing) may God's love and mercy uphold
you by the grace and power of the Holy Spirit.
Amen

*During the anointing, the assembly may sing various hymns and
songs, instrumental music may be played, or a simple interval of
silence may be observed.*

Stand
PRAYER
After all have returned to their places, the minister may say:

As you are anointed with this oil,
may God bless you with the healing power of the Holy Spirit.
May God forgive you your sins,
release you from suffering,
and restore you to wholeness and strength.
May God deliver you from all evil,
preserve you in all goodness,
and bring you to everlasting life,
through Jesus Christ our Lord.
Amen

THE LORD'S PRAYER

BLESSING AND DISMISSAL

HYMN
LBW 263   Abide with us, our Savior
WOV 721   Go, my children, with my blessing
WOV 737
or TFF 185 There is a balm in Gilead

BLESSING OF TEACHERS AND STUDENTS

HYMN
LBW 558   Earth and all stars!

*If used on a Sunday morning the following prayer may be used
during or following the prayers.*

Let us pray for all who are beginning a new school year,
that both students and teachers will be blessed in their academic
endeavors.

Almighty God,
you give wisdom and knowledge.
Grant teachers the gift of joy and insight,
and students the gift of diligence and openness,
that all may grow in what is good and honest and true.
Support all who teach and all who learn,
that together we may know and follow your ways;
through Jesus Christ our Lord.
Amen

285

BLESSING OF ANIMALS

This service may be used entirely on its own, perhaps for an observance on or near the commemoration of Francis of Assisi, renewer of the church, 1226 (October 4). Various elements of this order may also be incorporated into another worship service, though this material is not intended to replace the customary Sunday worship of the congregation. Care should be used in adapting the service to the occasion and to the physical setting in which it is used. For practical reasons this service may be conducted outdoors or in a facility other than a congregation's primary worship space.

GREETING AND PRAYER
The grace of our Lord Jesus Christ, the love of God, and the communion of the Holy Spirit be with you all.
Amen

Let us pray.
O merciful Creator, your hand is open wide to satisfy the needs of every living creature. Make us always thankful for your loving providence; and grant that we, remembering the account that we must one day give, may be faithful stewards of your good gifts; through your Son, Jesus Christ our Lord.
Amen
OR
Almighty God, in giving us dominion over things on earth, you made us fellow workers in your creation: Give us wisdom and reverence so to use the resources of nature, that no one may suffer from our abuse of them, and that generations yet to come may continue to praise you for your bounty; through Jesus Christ our Lord.
Amen

Book of Common Prayer, prayer 41, p. 827

READINGS
Genesis 1:1, 20-28
Genesis 6:17-22
Psalm 8
Psalm 148
Other readings about God's creation and the care of animals may be used. A sermon or an address appropriate to the occasion may also be included.

HYMN OR CANTICLE
LBW 18	All you works of the Lord
LBW 409	Praise and thanksgiving
LBW 527	All creatures of our God and King
	or All creatures, worship God most high
	(see "Canticle of the Sun")
LBW 554	This is my Father's world
LBW 560	Oh, that I had a thousand voices
WOV 767	All things bright and beautiful

Song of the Three Young Men (*Psalter for Worship*, Cycle C, Vigil of Easter, response 12)

BLESSING OF ANIMALS
The leader may ask all who have brought pets or animals to the celebration to come forward for the following prayer.

The Lord be with you.
And also with you.
Let us pray.
Gracious God, in your love you created us in your image and made us stewards of the animals that live in the skies, the earth, and the sea. Bless us in our care for our pets and animals *[names of pets may be added here]*. Help us recognize your power and wisdom in the variety of creatures that live in our world, and hear our prayer for all that suffer over work, hunger, and ill-treatment. Protect your creatures, and guard them from all evil, now and forever.
Amen

THE LORD'S PRAYER

BLESSING
The Lord almighty order our days and our deeds in his peace.
Amen

CANTICLE OF THE SUN

All creatures, worship God most high!
Sound every voice in earth and sky: Alleluia! Alleluia!
Sing, brother sun, in splendor bright;
sing, sister moon and stars of night:
Alleluia, alleluia, alleluia, alleluia, alleluia!

Sing, brother wind; with clouds and rain
you grow the gifts of fruit and grain: Alleluia! Alleluia!
Dear sister water, useful, clear,
make music for your Lord to hear:
Alleluia, alleluia, alleluia, alleluia, alleluia!

O fire, our brother, mirthful, strong,
drive far the shadows, join the song: Alleluia! Alleluia!
O earth, our mother, rich in care,
praise God in colors bright and rare:
Alleluia, alleluia, alleluia, alleluia, alleluia!

All who for love of God forgive,
all who in pain or sorrow grieve: Alleluia! Alleluia!
Christ bears your burdens and your fears;
in mercy rest, sing through the tears:
Alleluia, alleluia, alleluia, alleluia, alleluia!

Come, sister death, your song release
when you enfold our breath in peace: Alleluia! Alleluia!
Since Christ our light has pierced your gloom,
fair is the night that leads us home.
Alleluia, alleluia, alleluia, alleluia, alleluia!

O sisters, brothers, take your part,
and worship God with humble heart: Alleluia! Alleluia!
All creatures, bless the Father, Son,
and Holy Spirit, Three in One:
Alleluia, alleluia, alleluia, alleluia, alleluia!

Text: Martin A. Seltz, based on a hymn of Francis of Assisi
Tune: LASST UNS ERFREUEN (LBW 143)

SEPTEMBER 2, 2001

THIRTEENTH SUNDAY AFTER PENTECOST
PROPER 17

INTRODUCTION

Who is welcome in your community of faith? And how would they know that they are? Today's readings ask us to think about hospitality, especially as it is practiced at the table. The feast of God's radical grace calls us into this place and connects friends and strangers with each other.

On this day in 1872, the great Danish bishop and theologian Nikolai Grundtvig died. He is remembered as a powerful intellect who insisted that ancient beliefs could find a home in modern culture.

PRAYER OF THE DAY

O God, we thank you for your Son who chose the path of suffering for the sake of the world. Humble us by his example, point us to the path of obedience, and give us strength to follow his commands; through your Son, Jesus Christ our Lord.

READINGS

Proverbs 25:6-7

The book of Proverbs is known as wisdom literature. It gave directions to Israel's leaders and people for the conduct of daily life. Today's reading is about humility.

or Sirach 10:12-18

Judgment rests upon the proud.

Psalm 112

The righteous are merciful and full of compassion. (Ps. 112:4)

Hebrews 13:1-8, 15-16

The conclusion of the letter to the Hebrews contains many suggestions for the conduct of life, all of which are shaped by God's love toward us in Jesus Christ.

Luke 14:1, 7-14

In Luke's gospel, Jesus often tells parables about meals in order to illustrate God's unexpected grace and to lead people to a faithful response. Here, we have two examples of these stories: one encourages humility, and in the other Jesus invites his listeners to review their guest list.

ALTERNATE FIRST READING/PSALM

Jeremiah 2:4-13

God, who has remained faithful despite Israel's rebellion, calls upon the heavenly council to witness the incredible foolishness of a people who, under the flawed leadership of priests, rulers, and prophets, willingly abandon God's life-giving water for leaky cisterns in the wilderness.

Psalm 81:1, 10-16

I feed you with the finest wheat and satisfy you with honey from the rock. (Ps. 81:16)

COLOR   Green

THE PRAYERS

With confidence in God's saving grace, let us pray for the church and for all God's creation in need.

A BRIEF SILENCE.

For all of us who serve you in our labor, that we may give of ourselves without expecting reward, we pray:

Lord, hear our prayer.

For all who show hospitality to strangers, who visit the imprisoned, and who proclaim the gospel, that they will know God's constant presence, we pray:

Lord, hear our prayer.

For this congregation, that we may minister to those who are poor and all those in need in our community, we pray:

Lord, hear our prayer.

For those living with despair, pain, addiction, or illness (especially…), that they may experience God's healing and compassion, we pray:

Lord, hear our prayer.

HERE OTHER INTERCESSIONS MAY BE OFFERED.

In thanksgiving for Nikolai Grundtvig and all the saints who have lived their lives as an offering to God, we pray:

Lord, hear our prayer.

Hear these and all our prayers, O God, in the name of our Savior, Jesus Christ.

Amen

IMAGES FOR PREACHING

This gospel text offers an image of movement. In the first half of this passage from Luke, the movement occurs at the table, from lower to higher places, from

288

Order next year's resources now!

Sundays and Seasons 2002

WORSHIP PLANNING GUIDE, CYCLE A

Order your copies today and you'll be ready for the next church year! The next edition of *Sundays and Seasons* will continue to supply you with all of the information you need to plan worship. Dated specifically for Advent through Christ the King Sunday.

0-8066-4084-7 $30.00
Three or more: $25.00 each

Worship Planning Calendar 2002

CYCLE A

You'll find this calendar an indispensible complement to *Sundays and Seasons*! Use this worship planning guide, daily devotional, and appointment calendar as your workbook. Each two-page spread includes propers, hymns, liturgical colors, and general rubrics for the Sunday, principal festivals, lesser festivals, and commemorations that occur during the week. You'll wonder how you managed without it!

0-8066-4085-5 $20.00

Words for Worship 2002

CYCLE A

This CD-ROM contains resources for use with the Revised Common Lectionary, Cycle A. The easy-to-use text and graphic files are organized by calendar date. Includes readings, prayers, introductions to the day, psalm refrains and tones, seasonal rites and texts, and the LBW Symbol font.

0-8066-4086-3
CD-ROM AND COPYRIGHT LICENSE $139.00

Kids Celebrate

WORSHIP BULLETINS FOR CHILDREN

This book of reproducible bulletins reinforces our Life Together Revised Common Lectionary-based curriculum by linking to key ideas from the Sunday school classroom.

Using the familiar "Gather, Hear, Celebrate, Send" pattern and containing more than 60 **reproducible** children's worship bulletins, this every Sunday (plus festivals) worship bulletin is ideal for lower elementary-age students with elements that can be appropriated for pre-readers and older elementary children, as well. It supports children's development by encouraging interaction, with elements of the worship setting—as well as the biblical texts—and begins with Advent 2001, (lectionary cycle A–Year of Matthew). May be used alone or to reinforce any lectionary-based curriculum.

136-pages; perfect bound; perforated.
0-8066-4090-1 $39.99

See back for more worship planning resources.
All prices are in U.S. dollars.

Shipping and Handling

Note: Prices and availability are subject to change without notice. **Shipping Charges:** Shipping charges are additional on all orders. For orders up through $10.00 add $2.50; $10.01–$20.00 add $4.00; $20.01–$35.00 add $5.50; $35.01 and above add $6.50. Actual shipping charges will be assessed for all orders over 35 lbs. in weight (bulk), and for expedited shipping service. Promotion orders are shipped separately from other orders. Additional shipping charges for international shipments. For Canadian orders, actual shipping costs will be charged. This policy is subject to change without notice. **Sales Tax:** Add appropriate state/province and local taxes where applicable. Tax exempt organizations must provide tax exempt numbers on all orders. **Return Policy:** All U. S. mail, fax and telephone order returns must be shipped postage prepaid to the Augsburg Fortress Distribution Center, 4001 Gantz Road, Suite E, Grove City, Ohio 43123-1891. Permission is not required for returns. Non-dated, in-print product in saleable condition may be returned for up to 60 days after the invoice date. Defective products, products damaged in shipment, or products shipped in error may be returned at any time and postage will be reimbursed. Special order or clearance items may not be returned. Canadian orders must be returned to the location from which the order was shipped.

Order Form

www.augsburgfortress.org

Worship Planning Resources 2002, Cycle A

Just complete this order card, affix postage, and drop it in the mail.
To order by phone: 1-800-328-4648 By fax: 1-800-722-7766

Send to: _____

Address: _____

City: _____ State: _____ Zip: _____

Phone: _____

Bill to: _____

Address: _____

City: _____ State: _____ Zip: _____

Method of Payment *(check one)*

☐ Augsburg Fortress Acct # _____

☐ Credit Card # _____

Exp. Date: _____
(Must be valid for Sept. 2001. Products ship August 2001.)

Signature: _____
(Required on all credit card orders.)

☐ Check *(Place check and order card in envelope and mail to address on reverse. Include applicable shipping charges and sales tax.)*

Qty.	Title	ISBN	Price
____	Sundays and Seasons	0-8066-4084-7	$30.00
____	Worship Planning Calendar	0-8066-4085-5	$20.00
____	Sunday & Seasons/calendar Combo Pack	0-8066-4091-X	$45.00
____	Words for Worship	0-8066-4086-3	$139.00
____	Children's Worship Bulletins	0-8066-4090-1	$39.99
____	Calendar of Word and Season	0-8066-4088-x	$8.95
____	Church Year Calendar	0-8066-4087-1	$1.95

Thank you for your order!

Calendar of Word and Season 2002

LITURGICAL WALL CALENDAR
CYCLE A

This beautiful full-color wall calendar will keep you on track at a glance. Identifies church festivals and U.S. and Canadian holidays. Large date blocks note Bible readings from the Revised Common Lectionary for Sundays and church festivals and identify the seasonal or festival color. They make great gift—and custom imprinting is available. Create a reference tool for each household or staff and committee members! 10⅞ x 8 ⅜". Spiral bound and punched for hanging. 28 pages. Call for details regarding custom imprinting.

0-8066-4088-x $8.95

Church Year Calendar 2002

CYCLE A

This simple sheet is a useful tool for anyone in your church: committee members, choir members, worship planners, the altar guild, teachers, and pastors. The full-color calendar gives dates, Bible readings, hymn of the day, and liturgical color for each Sunday and festival of the church year.

Two sides, 11 x 8½".

0-8066-4087-1 $1.95
12 FOR $9.96

humble to exalted positions. And in the second half of
the text, the movement is at the boundaries of our
usual world, from narrow to wide, from exclusive to
inclusive. The text is about our movement to some
degree, our seeking out the poor and excluded ones.
But mostly it is about the movement of God. God
lifts up the lowly, as Mary proclaimed in the Magnificat. Jesus seeks out sinners. God's movement changes
the shape of our feasts, our communities, our world,
and our lives.

How are we being called to be a part of God's
movement in the world? As North Americans celebrate
Labor Day, we can reflect on the meaning of our work.
Our gospel text offers us a vision of a different world
to serve. We glimpse this different world every time we
come to the feast shaped by Jesus' vision of a new
order. We glimpse it, we taste it, and we are gathered
into it. It is an amazing new order, the banquet that
reaches beyond the limited imagination of our usual
invitation list of friends, relatives, and most desirable
neighbors. What shall we do with this glimpse, besides
coming back to it over and over again, so that our vision can be changed by it? The good news is that we
do not labor alone. The new order is not dependent on
our movement. Jesus will keep teaching us about the
new world yet to come through the movement of our
God in our midst now.

WORSHIP MATTERS

In the eucharistic meal we are drawn to the Lord's table
and fed by Christ's body and blood. It is here that we
have our most intimate encounter with our God, as we
touch, taste, and see the reality of divine grace. It is here
that we receive the nourishment to live as people of the
word. It is here that we are fed, forgiven, and fortified
for our journey.

At the Lord's banquet, to all who answer his invitation God gives gifts in equal measure. Here we see a
model of the godly life that sees all God's children as
equal. How might this model change our congregations? How might it lead us to see our brothers and sisters simply as God's beloved children, children who
need God's grace and forgiveness no more and no less
than we ourselves do? How might it lead us to be more
welcoming to those who seek the Lord?

LET THE CHILDREN COME

I'm a-goin'-a eat at the welcome table,
I'm a-goin'-a eat at the welcome table,
some of these days.
                    —African American Spiritual (TFF 263)

The welcome table of Jesus receives the rich and
poor, the young and old, the outcast and the influential,
the distinguished and the disgraced. The wedding banquet of the Lamb has room for all. *The Use of the Means
of Grace* invites congregations to welcome the youngest
baptized among us to the Lord's table to hear the faith-
sustaining words, "for you."

MUSIC FOR WORSHIP
GATHERING

| LBW 424 | Lord of glory, you have bought us |
| WOV 797 | O God beyond all praising |

PSALM 112

Guimont, Michel. "Psalm 112: A Light Rises in the Darkness" in RS.

Hopson, Hal H. *Psalm Refrains and Tones.* HOP 425.

Paradowski, John. PW, Cycle C.

HYMN OF THE DAY

| LBW 211 | Here, O my Lord, I see thee |
| | FARLEY CASTLE |

VOCAL RESOURCES

Schalk, Carl. "Here, O My Lord, I See Thee." CPH 98-2493. SATB,
    inst, kybd.

INSTRUMENTAL RESOURCES

Farlee, Robert Buckley. "Farley Castle" in *Gaudeamus!* AFP 11-10693.
    Org.

Johnson, David N. "Farley Castle" in *Deck Thyself, My Soul, with Glad-
    ness,* vol. 2. AFP 11-9101. Org.

ALTERNATE HYMN OF THE DAY

| LBW 428 | O God of earth and altar |
| WOV 718 | Here in this place |

COMMUNION

| LBW 203 | Now we join in celebration |
| WOV 766 | We come to the hungry feast |

289

SENDING

| LBW 415 | God of grace and God of glory |
| WOV 723 | The Spirit sends us forth to serve |

ADDITIONAL HYMNS AND SONGS

OBS 107	O sacred River
TFF 263	I'm a-goin'-a eat at the welcome table
TWC 125	Praise the Savior, ye who know him
W3 623	We are your people
W&P 33	Come to the table
W&P 150	We bring the sacrifice of praise

MUSIC FOR THE DAY

CHORAL

Busarow, Donald, arr. "Come Down, O Love Divine." CPH 98-2335. SAB, org.

Carter, John. "We Come as Guests Invited." MSM 50-8312. SATB, kybd.

Toolan, Suzanne. "Jesus Christ, Yesterday, Today and Forever." OCP 10246. Cant, cong, kybd, opt SATB, opt inst.

Vaughan Williams, Ralph/arr. Brian Judge. "He That Is Down Need Fear No Fall." OXF 42.492. SATB, fl/ob.

White, David Ashley. "O Bread of Life from Heaven." AFP 11-10203. Also in *The Augsburg Choirbook*. AFP 11-10817. 2 pt, org.

CHILDREN'S CHOIRS

Nelson, Ronald A. "Whoever Would Be Great Among You." AFP 11-1638. SAB, kybd, opt gtr.

Ramseth, Melinda. "Lord, Whose Love in Humble Service" in *Take a Hymn*. AFP 11-2172. U, autoharp, rec.

Wold, Wayne. "To the Banquet Come" in LS.

KEYBOARD/INSTRUMENTAL

Behnke, John A. "Prelude on 'Gather Us In.'" CPH 97-6455. Org.

Leupold, A. W. "Jesu, meine Freude" in *An Organ Book*. AFP. Org.

Near, Gerald. "St. Agnes" in *Deo Gracias*. AUR AE-104. Org.

HANDBELL

Bach/Callahan. "Arioso." JEF JHS 883. Solo hb, pno.

Michael Helman. "Gift of Finest Wheat." AFP 11-10872. 3-5 oct.

PRAISE ENSEMBLE

Dearman, Kirk, and Deby Dearman. "We Are His Praise" in *America's 200 Favorite Praise Choruses & Hymns*. BNT.

Haugen, Marty. "Come to the Feast." GIA 3543. U/SATB, solo, kybd, opt cong, gtr, C inst, brass, hb.

Kogut, Malcolm. "Like a Lamp in the Darkness" (Psalm 112) in PCY, vol. 10. U, kybd, solo, opt cong, gtr.

Ylvisaker, John. "Anybody Ask You" in *Borning Cry*. NGP.

SUNDAY, SEPTEMBER 2
NIKOLAI FREDERIK SEVERIN GRUNDTVIG, BISHOP, RENEWER OF THE CHURCH, 1872

Grundtvig was one of two principal Danish theologians of the nineteenth century; the other was Søren Kierkegaard. Grundtvig's ministry as a parish pastor had a difficult start. He was officially censured after his first sermon, though he did receive approval a year later to be ordained. He served with his father for two years but was unable to receive a call for seven years after that. In 1826 he was forced to resign after he attacked the notion that Christianity was merely a philosophical idea rather than God's revelation made known to us in Christ and through word and sacrament. This belief would be a hallmark of Grundtvig's writing. He spent the last thirty-three years as a chaplain at a home for elderly women. From his university days he was convinced that poetry spoke to the human spirit better than prose, and he wrote more than a thousand hymns. Eight of his hymns are in *LBW*.

TUESDAY, SEPTEMBER 4
ALBERT SCHWEITZER, MISSIONARY TO AFRICA, 1965

Schweitzer was a philosopher, theologian, and an ordained Lutheran minister. He wrote *The Quest for the Historical Jesus*. He was also an organist who published a study of Johann Sebastian Bach. But he set aside careers as a university lecturer and musician, went to medical school, and became a missionary in the Gabon province of French Equatorial Africa. He believed that the solution to the world's problems was simple: have reverence for life. His style of practicing medicine shocked some, but he was a humanitarian who served Christ by serving his neighbors in need.

Now that school is resuming in many places, parishes can hold up Schweitzer as an example of someone who used vast knowledge for service and ministry to others.

SEPTEMBER 9, 2001

FOURTEENTH SUNDAY AFTER PENTECOST
PROPER 18

INTRODUCTION

In remembrance of baptism, many Christians make the sign of the cross. We are the people marked with Jesus' cross. But that cross is costly, and those who bear it must be prepared to let go of everything in order to take up the new life of the crucified and risen Christ.

PRAYER OF THE DAY

Almighty and eternal God, you know our problems and our weaknesses better than we ourselves. In your love and by your power help us in our confusion and, in spite of our weakness, make us firm in faith; through your Son, Jesus Christ our Lord.

READINGS

Deuteronomy 30:15-20

Life and blessing are the benefits of keeping the law God has given through Moses. In this passage, Moses presents the consequences of choosing between life and death.

Psalm 1

Their delight is in the law of the LORD. (Ps. 1:2)

Philemon 1-21

While Paul was in prison, he was aided by a runaway slave named Onesimus. The slave's master, Philemon, was a Christian friend of Paul. Paul told Onesimus to return to his master but encouraged Philemon to receive Onesimus back as a brother.

Luke 14:25-33

Jesus speaks frankly about the costs of discipleship. Those who follow him should know from the outset that they will have to renounce allegiance to all competing concerns.

ALTERNATE FIRST READING/PSALM

Jeremiah 18:1-11

God teaches Jeremiah a lesson at a potter's shop. Just as a potter is able to destroy an unacceptable vessel, starting over to refashion it into one of value, so God molds and fashions the nations, including Israel.

Psalm 139:1-6, 13-18

You have searched me out and known me. (Ps. 139:1)

COLOR   Green

THE PRAYERS

With confidence in God's saving grace, let us pray for the church and for all God's creation in need.
A BRIEF SILENCE.

For bishops, pastors, and all leaders of the church, that they may be faithful examples of Christian service, we pray:
Lord, hear our prayer.

For our schools, students, and teachers, that they may be filled with a love for learning as they begin this year, we pray:
Lord, hear our prayer.

For each of us, that we may abide in the abundant life you offer us in love, we pray:
Lord, hear our prayer.

For courage and strength, that we may follow freely in Jesus' steps, we pray:
Lord, hear our prayer.

For those who are grieving and those who are ill (especially . . .), that through our ministry they may experience God's grace and healing, we pray:
Lord, hear our prayer.

HERE OTHER INTERCESSIONS MAY BE OFFERED.

We give thanks for all the faithful departed who lived in the hope of Christ's resurrection. Help us to live in that same faith until we are once again reunited in your everlasting glory. We pray:
Lord, hear our prayer.

Hear these and all our prayers, O God, in the name of our Savior, Jesus Christ.
Amen

IMAGES FOR PREACHING

Jesus gives several ultimatums to the large crowds that were following him. He was on his way to Jerusalem, but why were all the rest of them there? They were looking for a big change in their lives; they wanted to be healed, to be fed, to have a better life. So, Jesus offers them several cautions for their unreflective enthusiasm for following him.

Many of us in this culture are looking for a big change in our lives. We sometimes sign up for expensive

291

seminars and workshops. Of course, we know that anything worthwhile may cost a great deal. Yet at the same
time, many seekers coming to the church looking for
help in changing their lives are not told very much
about the costs of discipleship. We do not want to scare
them away, for many of our churches no longer have
"large crowds" like those following Jesus on his way to
Jerusalem.

How can we reclaim and renew the process of
entry into the Christian church? Christians in earlier
centuries invited unbaptized people into the catechumenate and a lengthy process of instruction. How shall
we be more honest about the rigors of discipleship with
those preparing to be baptized or to affirm their baptism? Perhaps we, the church, are the ones who must be
reminded of the costs of discipleship and the importance of truth-in-advertising. What shall it profit us to
fill our pews if we do not speak of discipleship?

People are yearning for a big change in their lives,
and we must help them to understand that following
Jesus redefines all the loyalties in our lives. Looking for
a big change? Jesus invites you not only to reorder
your own life, your own family, and your own possessions, but also your neighborhood, your town, and the
world that God has made and continues to redeem
through us. Looking for a big change? Then just keep
following Jesus.

WORSHIP MATTERS

Most congregations display a cross prominently in the
worship space. It may be to this cross that the eye is first
drawn upon hearing this morning's gospel. But what of
the cross that each of us already carries? Today it may be
well to remind the assembly of the cross traced on our
foreheads on the day of baptism. Perhaps the font can
be open and filled, and all encouraged to take water and
trace the cross on their foreheads.

We need not look for crosses to carry. Already we
have been marked with the Lord's cross, the cross that
calls us to discipleship in his name. We bear the sign of
the cross that calls us to work for justice, to feed the
hungry, and at times to bear the weight of oppression
and indifference. We have been claimed by Christ and
called to live out our lives in faithfulness and service.
We carry his cross, and it calls us to repentance, faith,
and action.

LET THE CHILDREN COME

Invite children and adults to cut out construction paper
crosses and footprints. Tape the crosses and footprints on
the floor where you gather for worship and learning.
Tape some in other rooms and even out into the park-
ing lot. Teach all to make the sign of the cross in remembrance of their baptism into Jesus' death and resurrection. Encourage them to place a cross and a footprint
at the front door of their homes. As they leave home,
ask them to make the sign of the cross and remember
Jesus' invitation to take up the cross and follow him.

MUSIC FOR WORSHIP
GATHERING

LBW 377	Lift high the cross
WOV 750	Oh, praise the gracious power
	alternate tune: OLD HUNDREDTH

PSALM 1

Bell, John. "Happy Is the One" in *Psalms of Patience, Protest and Praise.*
GIA G-4047.

Christopherson, Dorothy. PW, Cycle C.

Cooney, Rory. "Psalm 1: Roots in the Earth." GIA G-3969. U, cong,
gtr, kybd.

Howard, Julie. *Sing for Joy: Psalm Settings for God's Children.* LTP.

Schoenbachler, Tim, and Sheryl Soderberg. "Psalm 1: Happy Are
They" in STP, vol. 2.

TFF 1	Happy are they

See sixth Sunday after the Epiphany.

HYMN OF THE DAY

LBW 398	"Take up your cross," the Savior said
	NUN LASST UNS DEN LEIB BEGRABEN

ALTERNATE HYMN OF THE DAY

LBW 406	Take my life, that I may be
WOV 782	All my hope on God is founded

COMMUNION HYMNS

LBW 486	Spirit of God, descend upon my heart
WOV 746	Day by day

SENDING

LBW 487	Let us ever walk with Jesus
WOV 778	O Christ the same

292

ADDITIONAL HYMNS AND SONGS

NCH 350	Now in the days of youth
TFF 147	I shall not be moved
TFF 237	Must Jesus bear the cross alone
TWC 342	How blest are they who, fearing God
W&P 72	I will delight

MUSIC FOR THE DAY

CHORAL

Hopson, Hal. H. "Take Up Your Cross." AFP 11-10570. 2 pt, kybd.

Keesecker, Thomas. "Blessed Are They Who Trust in the Lord."
CPH 98-3462. SA or TB, kybd.

Loosemore, Henry. "O Lord, Increase Our Faith" in *The New Church Anthem Book*. OXF 0-19-353109-7. SATB.

Owens, Sam Batt. "To You, O Lord, I Lift Up My Soul." GIA G-3040.
SATB, org.

Pelz, Walter. "Show Me Thy Ways." AFP 11-0642. Also in *The Augsburg Choirbook*. AFP 11-10817. SATB, gtr, ob or fl.

Pfautsch, Lloyd. "Commitment." AFP 11-1596. SATB, fl.

Wesley, Samuel Sebastian. "Lead Me, Lord." HWG GCMR 3183.
SATB, org, S solo.

CHILDREN'S CHOIRS

Howard, Julie/arr. Vera Lyons. "Like a Tree" in LS.

Medema, Ken. "Tree Song." SHW E-212. 2 pt, kybd, opt hb.

Pearson, Brian, and Sherry Pearson. "Life Together" in LS.

Sleeth, Natalie. "The Kingdom of the Lord." AMSI 301. 2 pt, opt fl,
pno/hpd/org.

KEYBOARD/INSTRUMENTAL

Franck, César. "Cantabile" in *Complete Works for Organ,* vol. 3. KAL.
Org.

Manz, Paul. "Let Us Ever Walk with Jesus" in *Five Hymn Improvisations for Weddings and General Use*. MSM-10-850 (also old edition vol. 9,
CPH). Org.

Mahnke, Allan. "Patmos" in *Thirteen Pieces for Treble Instruments and Organ*. CPH 97-6030. Inst, org.

HANDBELL

Dobrinski, Cynthia. "Lift High the Cross." AG 1491. 3-5 oct.

Hopson, Hal H. "Fantasy on 'Westminster Quarters.' "
AGEHR AG35014. 3-5 oct.

PRAISE ENSEMBLE

Beebe, Hank. "I Follow the Thing That Good Is." BEC JH501. SAB,
kybd.

Haas, David. "Happy Are They" (Psalm 1) in PCY, vol. 3. U/SATB,
kybd, duet, opt cong, gtr.

Kline, Patsy Hilton. "Psalm 1: Planted By The Waters" in *Renew*. HOP.

Ylvisaker, John. "We Shall Not Be Moved" in *Borning Cry*. NGP.

SUNDAY, SEPTEMBER 9
PETER CLAVER, PRIEST, MISSIONARY TO COLOMBIA, 1654

Peter Claver was born into Spanish nobility and was persuaded to become a Jesuit missionary. He served in Cartagena (in what is now Colombia) by teaching and caring for the slaves. The slaves arrived in ships, where they had been confined in dehumanizing conditions. Claver met and supplied them with medicine, food, clothing, and brandy. He learned their dialects and taught them Christianity. He called himself "the slave of the slaves forever." Claver also ministered to the locals of Cartagena who were in prison and facing death.

Claver's advocacy on behalf of the rights of slaves is a witness to a gospel that is for all people. Pray for contemporary ministries and for persons who offer care and compassion to people living in substandard living conditions.

293

THURSDAY, SEPTEMBER 13
JOHN CHRYSOSTOM, BISHOP OF CONSTANTINOPLE, 407

John was a priest in Antioch and an outstanding preacher. His eloquence earned him the nickname "Chrysostom" ("golden mouth") but it also got him into trouble. As bishop of Constantinople he preached against corruption among the royal court. The empress, who had been his supporter, sent him into exile. His preaching style emphasized the literal meaning of scripture and its practical application. This interpretation stood in contrast to the common style at the time, which emphasized the allegorical meaning of the text.

Chrysostom's skill in the pulpit has led many to describe him as the patron of preachers. This week at gatherings of parish groups, include prayers for pastors and all who proclaim the gospel through preaching.

FRIDAY, SEPTEMBER 14
HOLY CROSS DAY

Helena, the mother of Constantine, made a pilgrimage to Israel to look for Christian holy sites. She found what she believed were the sites of the crucifixion and burial of Jesus, sites that modern archaeologists believe may be correct. Here Constantine built two churches.

The celebration of Holy Cross Day commemorates the dedication of the Church of the Resurrection in 335.

This day gives the church a chance to celebrate the victory of the cross with a festivity that would be out of place on Good Friday. Today alleluias are sung in thanksgiving for the tree of the cross, which Andrew of Crete described as "the trophy of God's victory." This week sing the hymn "Lift high the cross" (LBW 377).

SEPTEMBER 16, 2001

FIFTEENTH SUNDAY AFTER PENTECOST
PROPER 19

INTRODUCTION

Only the lost can be found. The confession of sins is our admission that we do not know the way to God. But God has been looking for us. This day we are surrounded by images of people who "once were lost." Those who are found enter the joy of the Lord.

PRAYER OF THE DAY

O God, you declare your almighty power chiefly in showing mercy and pity. Grant us the fullness of your grace, that, pursuing what you have promised, we may share your heavenly glory; through your Son, Jesus Christ our Lord.

READINGS

Exodus 32:7-14

Prior to this chapter, Moses receives instructions from God on Mount Sinai. Meanwhile, the people grow rebellious and decide to make a golden calf. Today's reading suggests a court setting in which God acts as prosecuting attorney and Moses serves as defense attorney in a lawsuit against the people.

Psalm 51:1-11 (Psalm 51:1-10 [NRSV])

Have mercy on me, O God, according to your lovingkindness. (Ps. 51:1)

1 Timothy 1:12-17

The letters to Timothy are called the pastoral epistles because they contain advice especially intended for leaders in the church. Here the mercy shown to Paul, who once persecuted the church, is cited as evidence that even the most unworthy may become witnesses to the grace of God.

Luke 15:1-10

Jesus tells two stories about repentance to indicate that God takes the initiative in finding us. We are precious to God, and our recovery brings joy in heaven.

ALTERNATE FIRST READING/PSALM

Jeremiah 4:11-12, 22-28

The sinfulness of the people will surely bring their destruction. God's searing wind of judgment, in the form of a massive army from the north, will reduce the land to its primeval state of waste and void.

Psalm 14

The LORD looks down from heaven upon us all. (Ps. 14:2)

COLOR   Green

THE PRAYERS

With confidence in God's saving grace, let us pray for the church and for all God's creation in need.
A BRIEF SILENCE.
Loving God, even when we are lost, seek us and carry us back to safety. We pray:
Lord, hear our prayer.
God of patience, even when we turn our backs on you and worship false gods, show us your mercy. We pray:
Lord, hear our prayer.
God of mercy, we ask for strength and reassurance for those who are ill and afraid (especially...). Continue to heal them with your loving care. We pray:

Lord, hear our prayer.

Steadfast God, give us leaders who want only what is good and just for all the people of the world. We pray:

Lord, hear our prayer.

Faithful God, help us to be your servants in this world, searching and reaching out to those who are lost or in need. We pray:

Lord, hear our prayer.

HERE OTHER INTERCESSIONS MAY BE OFFERED.

Everlasting God, you hold in your arms all the faithful who have gone before us. Bring us with them into the security and joy of everlasting life. We pray:

Lord, hear our prayer.

Hear these and all our prayers, O God, in the name of our Savior, Jesus Christ.

Amen

IMAGES FOR PREACHING

It is gathering time. As we continue to gather people who were away on vacations and those who may have taken other kinds of summer breaks, we reconstitute ourselves. For many congregations, the first Sundays of September can be like an extended family reunion.

So we welcome one another as friends and fellow pilgrims who may have been separated from one another for a time. We sense an aspect of our regrouping that is not unlike the experience of the people in today's parables from Luke who rejoiced in the return of the lost sheep and the lost coin. But what about the part that follows? Have we truly found what is lost? Or have we simply found the familiar, people we already knew? Who is lost?

The lost ones, now returned, are the reason for the party. When we gather to be the church in the autumn, we may feel at full strength because the already-found have returned. And the already-found are the ones who keep the church going, or so we think. Yet Jesus came to save the lost—lost sheep, lost coins, lost children, and lost sinners. In these two parables we are invited to imagine ourselves as the shepherd and the woman, not the lost. We are lost in many ways, but this time, the story is not really about us. It is about the absent ones, without whom there is no party. We were once lost and have already been found by the shepherd of the flock. Now we are called to go out as shepherds, so that we may rejoice at our reunion party for the same reason the angels of God rejoice.

WORSHIP MATTERS

Where do we fit into the story of the prodigal? Are we those who long to be welcomed back into the community of faith? Are some of us people who long to be embraced by another of God's children and received as a sister or brother in Christ? Are there those among us in the assembly who long for these things? Do we greet them with the love and compassion of the parent of the prodigal?

Perhaps we are on the other side of this story. When the time comes to share God's peace, to whom do we gravitate? To those who have just found their way back to God's house, to the prodigals among us? Or do we share the peace primarily with our family and friends? Do we stay in our comfort zone, or do we dare to reach out to the person with AIDS, the repentant adulterer, and the re-formed addict? This peace of the Lord, by its very nature, breaks down the walls between us, drawing us closer together as redeemed sons and daughters of the Holy One.

LET THE CHILDREN COME

The heart of God is filled with joy when we repent of our sins. In *Ninety-nine Plus One* by Gerald Pottebaum, a friend of the poor finds the one child out of ninety-nine who has become lost at the zoo. Finding the child, he shouts, "This sure is something to shout about!" Before the pastor pronounces the absolution, have the children picture God bursting with joy and cheering out loud to welcome us home. Invite them to look up and smile joyfully and hear the news that their sins are forgiven. This is something to shout about!

MUSIC FOR WORSHIP

GATHERING

| LBW 448 | Amazing grace, how sweet the sound |
| WOV 771 | Great is thy faithfulness |

PSALM 51

Bedford, Michael. "Be Merciful, O Lord" in *Sing Out! A Children's Psalter*. WLP.

Christopherson, Dorothy. PW, Cycle C.

Haugen, Marty. "Be Merciful, O Lord" in PCY, vol. 1.

Jenkins, Steve. "Create in Me." MSM 80-302. 2 pt, cong, kybd.

Marshall, Jane. *Psalms Together II*. CGC 21.

Walker, Christopher. "Give Me a New Heart, O God" in STP, vol. 3.

WOV 732   Create in me a clean heart

See Ash Wednesday.

HYMN OF THE DAY

LBW 499   Come, thou Fount of every blessing
              NETTLETON

VOCAL RESOURCES

Kosche, Kenneth T. "Come, Thou Fount of Every Blessing" in *Three American Hymn Tunes.* MSM 50-9830. SATB.

INSTRUMENTAL RESOURCES

Albrecht, Mark. "Nettleton" in *Three for Piano and Sax (or Other Instrument).* AFP 11-10929. Pno, inst.

Albrecht, Timothy. "Nettleton" in *Grace Notes V.* AFP 11-10764; and *Grace Notes VIII,* AFP 11-10970. Org.

Farlee, Robert Buckley. "Nettleton" in *Gaudeamus!* AFP 11-10693. Org.

ALTERNATE HYMN OF THE DAY

LBW 291   Jesus sinners will receive

WOV 734   Softly and tenderly Jesus is calling

COMMUNION

LBW 298   One there is, above all others

WOV 775   Lord, listen to your children praying

SENDING

LBW 196   Praise the Lord, rise up rejoicing

WOV 699   Blessed assurance

ADDITIONAL HYMNS AND SONGS

ASG 8   Feed my lambs

LLC 442   Create in me a clean heart

TFF 216   Give me a clean heart

VU 360   A woman and a coin—the coin is lost

W&P 34/35   Create in me a clean heart

W&P 151   We rejoice in the grace of God

MUSIC FOR THE DAY

CHORAL

di Lassus, Orlando. "Miserere mei, Domine." AFP 11-10267. SATB.

Terry, R. R. "Richard de Castre's Prayer to Jesus" in *The Oxford Easy Anthem Book.* OXF.

Wold, Wayne. "Rejoice! I Found the Lost." AFP 11-10463. U/2 pt, kybd.

CHILDREN'S CHOIRS

Folkening, John. "One in a Hundred" in LS.

Hopson, Hal H. "Gentle Shepherd, Kind and True." CG CGA687. U, kybd, 2 opt hb.

Horman, John. "The Lost Sheep." CG CGA-308. U, kybd.

Wold, Wayne. "Rejoice, I Found the Lost." AFP 11-10463. U/2 pt, kybd.

KEYBOARD/INSTRUMENTAL

Finzi, Gerald/arr. Robert Gower. "Carol" in *A Finzi Organ Album.* OXF 0193753685. Org.

Langlois, Kristina. "Pleading Savior" in *Five Hymns of Praise.* MSM-10-722. Org.

Young, Gordon. *Variations on an American Hymntune* (Nettleton). JFB 9288. Org.

HANDBELL

Linker, Janet, and Jane McFadden. "O Worship the King." BEC HB 170. 3-5 oct. org.

Sherman, Arnold B. "What a Friend We Have in Jesus." RRM HB0032. 3-6 oct, opt hc.

PRAISE ENSEMBLE

Kendrick, Graham. "The Trumpets Sound, the Angels Sing" in W&P.

Mengel, Dana. "Jesus, Refuge of the Weary." CPH 98-3421. SATB, kybd, opt fc.

Unknown. "1 Timothy 1:17" in *The Other Song Book.* WWP.

Ylvisaker, John. "Please Have Mercy on Me" in *Borning Cry.* NGP.

SUNDAY, SEPTEMBER 16

CYPRIAN, BISHOP OF CARTHAGE, MARTYR, C. 258

Cyprian worked for the unity of the church and cared for his flock in North Africa during a time of great persecution. During Cyprian's time as bishop many people had denied the faith under duress. In contrast to some who held the belief that the church should not receive these people back, Cyprian believed they ought to be welcomed into full communion after a period of penance. Cyprian insisted on the need for compassion in order to preserve the unity of the church. His essay *On the Unity of the Catholic Church* stressed the role of bishops in guaranteeing the visible, concrete unity of the church. Cyprian was also concerned for the physical well-being of the people under his care. He organized a program of medical care during a severe epidemic in Carthage.

TUESDAY, SEPTEMBER 18
DAG HAMMARSKJÖLD, PEACEMAKER, 1961

Dag Hammarskjöld was a Swedish diplomat and humanitarian who served as Secretary General of the United Nations. He was killed in a plane crash on this day in 1961 in what is now Zambia while he was on his way to negotiate a cease-fire between the United Nations and the Katanga forces. For years Hammarskjöld had kept a private journal, and it was not until that journal was published as *Markings* that the depth of his Christian faith was known. The book revealed that his life was a combination of diplomatic service and personal spirituality, a combination of contemplation on the meaning of Christ in his life and action in the world.

To commemorate Hammarskjöld, pray for the work of the United Nations and for all peacemakers. Here is an example of a person whose quiet contemplation led to visible action in the world.

THURSDAY, SEPTEMBER 20
NELSON WESLEY TROUT, BISHOP, 1996

Trout was born in Columbus, Ohio, and attended the Evangelical Lutheran Theological Seminary in Columbus. Ordained in 1952, he served parishes in Montgomery, Alabama; Los Angeles, California; and Eau Claire, Wisconsin. Trout also served in staff positions with the American Lutheran Church, Lutheran Social Services of Dayton, and the Columbus seminary. In 1983 Trout was elected bishop of the South Pacific District of the American Lutheran Church, the first African American to serve in such a capacity.

FRIDAY, SEPTEMBER 21
ST. MATTHEW, APOSTLE AND EVANGELIST

Matthew was a tax collector for the Roman government in Capernaum. Tax collectors were distrusted because they were dishonest and worked as agents for a foreign ruler, the occupying Romans. In the gospels, tax collectors are mentioned as sinful and despised outcasts, but it was these outcasts to whom Jesus showed his love. Matthew's name means "gift of the Lord."

In the gospels Jesus tells his disciples to treat notorious sinners as Gentiles and tax collectors. That has often been taken as a mandate for the church to avoid such people. But Jesus brought his ministry to these very people. In what ways might the church not shun "tax collectors" and sinners but extend its ministry to them and see them as gifts of the Lord?

SEPTEMBER 23, 2001

SIXTEENTH SUNDAY AFTER PENTECOST
PROPER 20

INTRODUCTION

Early in the academic year may seem a strange time to think about the final exam, but on this day Jesus reminds us that each of us needs to give an accounting of all that is entrusted to us. In the new logic of God's reign, knowing the riches of grace we possess demands resolute action from us; we risk it all for possessing the lavish love of God offered to us.

PRAYER OF THE DAY

Lord God, you call us to work in your vineyard and leave no one standing idle. Set us to our tasks in the work of your kingdom, and help us to order our lives by your wisdom; through your Son, Jesus Christ our Lord.

READINGS

Amos 8:4-7

Amos was called by God to prophesy in the Northern Kingdom for a brief period of time. Peace and prosperity in Israel led to corruption and an increased gap between rich and poor. The prophet declares that God will not tolerate such a situation.

Psalm 113

The LORD lifts up the poor from the ashes. (Ps. 113:6)

1 Timothy 2:1-7

The pastoral epistles offer insight into how early Christians understood many practical matters, such as church administration and worship. The church's focused prayer for others is an expression of the single-minded passion God has toward us in Jesus.

Luke 16:1-13

Jesus tells the story of a dishonest man who cheats his employer and then is commended by him for having acted so shrewdly. Jesus reminds his listeners that God will not stand to be merely one of many commitments.

ALTERNATE FIRST READING/PSALM

Jeremiah 8:18—9:1

Jeremiah's primary task as God's prophet was to announce the terrible destruction that awaited the people of Israel because of their sin. In this passage, a grief-stricken Jeremiah anguishes over the sadness of that message and weeps day and night for his people.

Psalm 79:1-9

Deliver us and forgive us our sins, for your name's sake. (Ps. 79:9)

COLOR Green

THE PRAYERS

With confidence in God's saving grace, let us pray for the church and for all God's creation in need.

A BRIEF SILENCE.

For the leaders of the world, that they may guide us into ways of peace for all the world, we pray:

Lord, hear our prayer.

For those who are poor or hungry, that we may be responsive to their needs, we pray:

Lord, hear our prayer.

For this community, that we will be faithful with what we have been given and learn to serve you all our days, we pray:

Lord, hear our prayer.

For all who are ill (especially…) and for all who need safekeeping, that we may reach out to comfort and protect them, we pray:

Lord, hear our prayer.

For those who spread the gospel throughout the world, that the truth of God's love through Jesus Christ might be proclaimed, we pray:

Lord, hear our prayer.

HERE OTHER INTERCESSIONS MAY BE OFFERED.

For all who have suffered for their faith and for those who have died peacefully, that we may one day join them in paradise, we pray:

Lord, hear our prayer.

Hear these and all our prayers, O God, in the name of our Savior, Jesus Christ.

Amen

IMAGES FOR PREACHING

Jesus speaks of a shrewdness that is simultaneously conversion of the heart, the head, and the wallet. The manager in this parable stewarded resources in an intelligent way. Many congregations are now beginning a period of stewardship education, a time when we have often focused only on the heart and how thankful we should feel. But stewardship is also a matter of the head.

Perhaps we should be talking more about the plans we are making for the transfer of our own wealth to another generation. Why should wealth only be left to family members when we die? Does not stewardship invite a wider vision? The kingdom of God surely consists of more than our blood heirs. Shrewdness includes maximizing the impact that our gifts can make for the sake of God's kingdom. Shrewdness invites planned giving.

To God, conversion is certainly also a matter of the wallet. Our hearts and heads might be converted, but in what ways does money continue to be our master? Jesus teaches us that it all begins with faithful stewardship of the daily things, which also forms us in the larger matters. The wallet confronts us every day. We must constantly confront the matters of tangible faithfulness in small things.

How shall we spend our lives? The Christian community is the place where we help each other ask that question, and where we follow a Lord who keeps teaching and loving us into the answer. The answer, simply, is that we are called to spend our lives serving God as faithful stewards.

298

WORSHIP MATTERS

The prayers of the people are an integral part of the assembly's worship. It is here that God's children offer their joys and concerns to the creator. For whom and for what does the assembly pray? Within any congregation, a myriad of prayer concerns is possible, which reflects the diversity among the people. Worship leaders must be aware of the community's needs, and the community must be encouraged to share prayer requests with the pastor and other leaders.

The Christian church, local congregations of like and different denominations, those who are sick or grieving, new and expectant parents—all must have a place within the assembly's prayers. In the second reading Paul encourages us to remember our political leaders in prayer. No matter what our political convictions may be, we recognize that our leaders need our spiritual support and God's wisdom as they do the work to which they have been called.

LET THE CHILDREN COME

We may be taught to pray for the tall (leaders, teachers, those in authority) and the small (the outcast, the powerless, the needy). The second reading urges us to pray for everyone, for kings and all who are in high positions, so that we may lead a quiet and peaceable life. Who are those leaders that children hear about on television or read about in the newspaper? As you pray for those leaders, a good resource is the "Petitions, Intercessions, and Thanksgivings" in *LBW*, pp. 42–53.

MUSIC FOR WORSHIP

GATHERING

LBW 383	Rise up, O saints of God!
WOV 776	Be thou my vision

PSALM 113

Christopherson, Dorothy. PW, Cycle C.

Joncas, Michael. "Psalm 113: Praise God's Name" in RS. GIA.

Marchionda, James V. "Psalm 113" in *Psalms for the Cantor*, vol. 4. WLP 2506.

The Psalter—Psalms and Canticles for Singing. WJK.

HYMN OF THE DAY

WOV 763	Let justice flow like streams
	ST. THOMAS

INSTRUMENTAL RESOURCES

Callahan, Charles. "St. Thomas" in *Advent Music for Manuals*. MSM 10-001. Kybd/org.

Johnson, David M. "St. Thomas" in *Deck Thyself, My Soul With Gladness, vol. 2*. AFP 11-9101. Org.

Wolff, S. Drummond. "St. Thomas" in *Hymn Descants, Set I*. CPH 97-6051. Org, inst.

ALTERNATE HYMN OF THE DAY

LBW 408	God, whose giving knows no ending
LBW 413	Father eternal, ruler of creation

COMMUNION

LBW 364	Son of God, eternal Savior
WOV 710	One bread, one body

SENDING

LBW 562	Lift every voice and sing
WOV 782	All my hope on God is founded

ADDITIONAL HYMNS AND SONGS

NCH 527	We offer Christ to all the world around us
TFF 210	I've got a robe
TFF 285	Praise him! Jesus, blessed Savior
W&P 40	From where the sun rises
W&P 85	Let justice roll like a river

MUSIC FOR THE DAY

CHORAL

Handel, G. F. "Laudate Pueri Dominum." NOV 07-0467. SSATB, org, str, 2 ob.

Rorem, Ned. "Praise the Lord, O My Soul" (Psalm 146). B&H OCTB6105. SATB div, org.

Rutter, John. "Thy Perfect Love." OXF 42.392. SATB, org.

Scott, K. Lee. "Gracious Spirit Dwell With Me." AFP 11-2198. Also in *The Augsburg Choirbook*. AFP 11-10817. 2 pt, org.

Young, Philip M. "With What Shall I Come before the Lord." MSM 50-9083. SATB, org.

Zimmermann, Heinz Werner. "Praise the Lord" in *Five Hymns*. CPH 97-5131. U/SATB, kybd.

CHILDREN'S CHOIRS

African traditional. "I Am Thanking Jesus" in LS.

Kemp, Helen. "From the Rising of the Sun" in *Psalms/Anthems*, Set 2. CPH 97-6041. U, orff inst.

Powell, Robert J. "From the Rising of the Sun." CG CGA-463. U, kybd.

Proulx, Richard. "Praise Ye the Lord, Ye Children." AFP 11-0322. U, hb.

KEYBOARD/INSTRUMENTAL

Bach, J.S. "Duettos" in *Four Easy Pieces for Manuals*. Kevin Mayhew.
Org/kybd.

Manz, Paul. "Praise the Lord, Rise Up Rejoicing" in *Hymn Preludes for
Holy Communion*, vol. 2. CPH 97-5487. Org.

Wold, Wayne L. "O God of Earth and Altar/For All Your Saints in
Warfare" in *Boundless Grace*. AMSI OR-26. Org.

HANDBELL

Moklebust, Cathy. "Children of the Heavenly Father." CG CGB-139.
3 oct, opt hc.

Tucker, Margaret R. "Staff of Faith." BEC HB-138. 3-5 oct, opt fl.

PRAISE ENSEMBLE

Haas, David. "Nations and Heavens" (Psalm 113) in PCY, vol. 8.
U w/desc, kybd, solo/trio, opt cong, gtr.

Hayford, Jack. "Praise the Name of Jesus" in *Praise & Worship*. MM.

Lowry, Robert. "Here Is Love" in *Praise Hymns and Choruses*, 4th ed.
MM.

Martin, W. S. "God Will Take Care of You" in *Borning Cry*. NGP.

300

TUESDAY, SEPTEMBER 25
SERGIUS OF RADONEZH,
ABBOT OF HOLY TRINITY, MOSCOW, 1392

The people of Russia honor Sergius as the most
beloved of all their saints and a model of Russian spiritual life at its best. At the age of twenty he began to live
as a hermit, and others joined him. From their
monastery in the forest, Sergius led the renewal of
Russian monastic life. His monastery, the Monastery of
the Holy Trinity, was a center for pilgrimage where
people came to worship and receive spiritual support.
Sergius was also a peacemaker whose influence stopped
four civil wars between Russian princes. Sergius left no
writings, but his disciples founded seventy-five monasteries and spread his teachings.

The commemoration of Sergius is an opportunity
to consider the Russian church and the traditions of
Russian Orthodoxy. For example, a discussion could
begin about the place of icons in Orthodox spirituality
and ways icons can find a home among other Christians.

FRIDAY, SEPTEMBER 28
JEHU JONES, MISSIONARY, 1852

A native of Charleston, South Carolina, Jones was ordained by the New York Ministerium in 1832, and was
the Lutheran church's first African American pastor.
Upon returning to South Carolina he was arrested
under a law prohibiting free blacks from reentering the
state, so was unable to join the group of Charlestonians
he had been commissioned to accompany to Liberia.
For nearly twenty years Jones carried out missionary
work in Philadelphia in the face of many difficulties.
There he led the formation of the first African American Lutheran congregation, St. Paul's, and the construction of its church building.

SATURDAY, SEPTEMBER 29
ST. MICHAEL AND ALL ANGELS

On this festival day we ponder the richness and variety
of God's created order and the limits of our knowledge
of it. The scriptures speak of angels who worship God
in heaven, and in both testaments angels are God's messengers on earth. They are remembered most vividly as
they appear to the shepherds and announce the birth of
the savior. Michael is an angel whose name appears in
Daniel as the heavenly being who leads the faithful dead
to God's throne on the day of resurrection. In Revelation, Michael fights in a cosmic battle against Satan.

Sing "Ye watchers and ye holy ones" (LBW 175)
today or in worship tomorrow. The hymn delights in
the presence of the whole heavenly host of seraphs,
cherubim, thrones, archangels, virtues, and angel choirs
all led in praise of God by Mary, the "bearer of the
eternal Word."

SEPTEMBER 30, 2001

SEVENTEENTH SUNDAY AFTER PENTECOST

PROPER 21

INTRODUCTION

The readings for this day continue the theme of the past several weeks asking God's people to consider their relationship to wealth. Our money can be a powerful tool for alleviating suffering in the world, but it can just as easily become a strong force that alienates us from the riches of God's love. We need to know where we place our deepest values.

On this day in 420, the great biblical scholar and translator Jerome died. He was largely responsible for making the riches of Christian texts written in Greek available to Latin readers in the Roman Empire.

PRAYER OF THE DAY

God of love, you know our frailties and failings. Give us your grace to overcome them; keep us from those things that harm us; and guide us in the way of salvation; through your Son, Jesus Christ our Lord.

READINGS

Amos 6:1a, 4-7

The prophet Amos announces that Israel's great wealth is not a cause for rejoicing but rather for sorrow, because God's people have forgotten how to share their wealth with the poor.

Psalm 146

The LORD gives justice to those who are oppressed. (Ps. 146:6)

1 Timothy 6:6-19

Timothy is reminded of the confession he made at his baptism and of its implications for daily life. His priorities will be different from those of people who merely want to be rich.

Luke 16:19-31

When Jesus taught that no one can serve both God and wealth, some of his hearers mocked him. He responded with the story of the rich man and Lazarus.

ALTERNATE FIRST READING/PSALM

Jeremiah 32:1-3a, 6-15

In the year before Israel fell to the Babylonians, while the attack had already begun, Jeremiah was prisoner in the palace of the king. He arranged to purchase a tract of land to express

hope in God's ultimate restoration of Israel after the tragedy of the exile.

Psalm 91:1-6, 14-16

You are my refuge and my stronghold, my God in whom I put my trust. (Ps. 91:2)

COLOR   Green

THE PRAYERS

With confidence in God's saving grace, let us pray for the church and for all God's creation in need.

A BRIEF SILENCE.

For those who are poor, homeless, or rejected, that we may overcome our fears and minister to their needs, we pray:

Lord, hear our prayer.

For all servant leaders in your church, that they may guide us in righteousness, gentleness, and love in all that we do together, we pray:

Lord, hear our prayer.

For all those in need of comfort (especially...), that God's touch will soothe them and bring them peace, we pray:

Lord, hear our prayer.

For this community, that we can recognize how you have blessed us, and thereby reach out in love to others, we pray:

Lord, hear our prayer.

HERE OTHER INTERCESSIONS MAY BE OFFERED.

Together with Jerome and all your saints who have fought the good fight of faith, we look forward to that day when we, too, shall rest in God's arms. We pray:

Lord, hear our prayer.

Hear these and all our prayers, O God, in the name of our Savior, Jesus Christ.

Amen

IMAGES FOR PREACHING

Consider a dialogue between fear and hope. Fear says that we are in a mess, loving money more than people (1 Tim.) and ignoring poor Lazarus. We will end up tormented in Hades just like the rich man. Hope says that we are more like the five brothers of the rich man, those who still have the opportunity to be convinced. We are learning to feel the pain of Lazarus. We are able to articulate and hear the grief of the suffering ones, thereby opening the way to newness. We are learning to follow the example of Jesus, who entered into pain and gave it voice.

Fear says that we learn too little too late. We are so busy climbing our ladders that we are numbed by our striving for status and possessions, numbed like the rich man. Hope remarks that Abraham said we would not listen to someone, even if the person rose from the dead. But Jesus did rise from the dead and has been spreading the word ever since. Jesus called another Lazarus out of the tomb, and Jesus keeps calling us forth to a new life.

Fear says that the poor man Lazarus is both a literal and metaphorical reminder of our numbness. A child dies of hunger somewhere in the world for every breath we take, day and night. And what about those who are dying of spiritual hunger every day? Hope says that even though the dominant culture of selfishness cannot tolerate or co-opt compassion (Brueggemann, *Prophetic Imagination*, Fortress Press, p. 88), we are not yet dead in our riches. We are hearing the cries of the oppressed that announce the end of the dominant social order. We are hearing Paul's call to us to take hold of the life that really is life for all people, not just for ourselves, and we are becoming agents of change and sustainable livelihood.

Fear and hope live together in these texts, in our congregations, and in each of us. We are eager to end the tension between them. Yet Jesus welcomes all people to his table so that rich and poor, fearful and hopeful, may find grace, forgiveness, and strength at the feast of the one who gives life to all things.

WORSHIP MATTERS

"Go in peace. Serve the Lord." "Thanks be to God!"

Thanks be to God for the transforming and revitalizing power of the word, the word that calls us to look beyond ourselves and our own needs. Thanks be to God that the liturgy calls us to justice and service. Thanks be to God that in our worship we are forgiven, taught, fed, and strengthened, so that we might go forth as ambassadors of God's love—God's love of people, as well as

God's love of justice for the world God created. Thanks be to God that the Spirit will lead us to places of need and empower us to ensure that those needs might be met. Thanks be to God for the opportunity to serve the Lord in so many diverse ways.

LET THE CHILDREN COME

Children know how we need kindness and service from others. They understand the importance of a bandage and a kiss, a friend to push them on the swing, and a drink of water at bedtime. Give each child a servant's cloth. Remind them that they are servants of the Lord. Give them ample and significant ways to serve at church—making the coffee, bringing flowers from the garden to adorn the altar, taking garden surplus to the food bank, serving communion, and sorting items to be recycled. We need the gifts that children bring to the family of faith.

MUSIC FOR WORSHIP

GATHERING

| LBW 429 | God, whose giving knows no ending |
| WOV 718 | Here in this place |

PSALM 146

Christopherson, Dorothy. PW, Cycle C.

Joncas, Michael. "Psalm 146: Lord, Come and Save Us" in STP, vol. 2.

Smith, H. Hamilton. "Psalm 146" in *Psalms for the Cantor*, vol. 3. WLP 2504.

Stewart, Roy James. "Praise the Lord" in PCY, vol. 5.

| LBW 538 | Oh, praise the Lord, my soul! |
| LBW 539 | Praise the Almighty |

HYMN OF THE DAY

| LBW 383 | Rise up, O saints of God! |
| | FESTAL SONG |

INSTRUMENTAL RESOURCES

Marcus, Mary. "Festal Song" in *Ten Hymn Enhancements*. MSM 10-817. Org.

Moklebust, Cathy. "Festal Song" in *Hymn Stanzas for Handbells*. AFP 11-10722 (4-5 oct) and 11-10869 (2-3 oct). Hb.

Schelat, David. "Festal Song" in *Hymn Enrichments, Set 3*. MSM 10-516. Org.

ALTERNATE HYMN OF THE DAY

| LBW 325 | Lord, thee I love with all my heart |
| WOV 730 | My soul proclaims your greatness |

COMMUNION

| LBW 429 | Where cross the crowded ways of life |
| WOV 766 | We come to the hungry feast |

SENDING

| LBW 415 | God of grace and God of glory |
| WOV 790 | Praise to you, O God of mercy |

ADDITIONAL HYMNS AND SONGS

TFF 235	All to Jesus I surrender
TWC 429	Let your heart be broken for a world in need
VU 465	Christ, be our host
W&P 85	Let justice roll like a river
W&P 90	Lord, I lift your name on high

MUSIC FOR THE DAY

CHORAL

Gibbons, Orlando. "Almighty and Everlasting God." OXF TCM 36.

O'Brien, Francis Patrick. "To the Poor a Lasting Treasure." GIA G-4523. SATB, cong, gtr, kybd, C inst, opt str qrt.

Ratcliff, Cary. "See the Silent Ones Who Wait." KAL K-15. SATB, kybd.

Schalk, Carl. "All Things Are Yours, My God." MSM 50-9032. SATB, opt cong, org.

Schalk, Carl. "Lord of Feasting and of Hunger." CPH 98-2863. SATB, org.

CHILDREN'S CHOIRS

Kemp, Helen. "Prayer Litany." CG CGA747. 2 pt, kybd, opt ob.

Niwagila, Wilson/arr. Egil Hovland. "Gracious Spirit, Heed Our Pleading" in LS.

Sleeth, Natalie. "A Canon of Praise." CG A-79. 3 pt trbl/SAB, org, opt hb.

KEYBOARD/INSTRUMENTAL

Albrecht, Mark. "Lord, Whose Love in Humble Service" in *Early American Hymns and Tunes for Flute and Piano*. AFP 11-10830. Inst, org.

Bull, John/arr. S. Drummond Wolff. "Rondo for Organ." MSM 10-905. Org.

Sedio, Mark. "All My Hope on God Is Founded" in *Organ Tapestries*, vol. 1. CPH 97-6812. Org.

HANDBELL

McChesney, Kevin. "Praise to the Lord, the Almighty." AG 1499. 2-3 oct.

Sherman, Arnold B. "Immortal, Invisible." RRM HB 0008. 3-4 oct.

PRAISE ENSEMBLE

Cooney, Rory. "Praise the Lord, My Soul" (Psalm 146) in PCY, vol. 4. U/SAB, kybd, solo, opt cong, gtr.

Haugen, Marty. "Gather Us In." GIA G-2651. U/SATB, kybd, opt solo, cong, gtr, 2 fl.

Meares, Virgil. "He Is the King of Kings" in *Hosanna! Music*, 4. INT.

SUNDAY, SEPTEMBER 30
JEROME, TRANSLATOR, TEACHER, 420

Jerome is remembered as a biblical scholar and translator. Rather than choosing classical Latin as the basis of his work, he translated the scriptures into the Latin that was spoken and written by the majority of people in his day. His translation is known as the Vulgate, which comes from the Latin word for "common." While Jerome is remembered as a saint, he could be anything but saintly. He was well known for his short temper and his arrogance, although he was also quick to admit to his personal faults.

Thanks to the work of Jerome, many people received the word in their own language and lived a life of faith and service to those in need.

THURSDAY, OCTOBER 4
FRANCIS OF ASSISI, RENEWER OF THE CHURCH, 1226

Francis was the son of a wealthy cloth merchant. In a public confrontation with his father he renounced his wealth and future inheritance and devoted himself to serving the poor. Francis described this act as being "wedded to Lady Poverty." Under his leadership the Order of Friars Minor (Franciscans) was formed, and they understood literally Jesus' words to his disciples that they should take nothing on their journey and receive no payment for their work. Their task in preaching was to "use words if necessary." Francis had a spirit of gladness and gratitude for all of God's creation. This commemoration has been a traditional time to bless pets and animals, creatures Francis called his brothers and sisters. A prayer attributed to St. Francis is included in *LBW* (p. 48) and could be used at gatherings in the congregation today.

303

THURSDAY, OCTOBER 4
THEODORE FLIEDNER, RENEWER OF SOCIETY, 1864

Fliedner's work was instrumental in the revival of the ministry of deaconesses among Lutherans. While a pastor in Kaiserswerth, Germany, he also ministered to prisoners in Düsseldorf. Through his ministry to prisoners he came in contact with Moravian deaconesses, and it was through this Moravian influence that he was convinced that the ministry of deaconesses had a place among Lutherans. His work and writing encouraged women to care for those who were sick, poor, or imprisoned. Fliedner's deaconess motherhouse in Kaiserswerth inspired Lutherans all over the world to commission deaconesses to serve in parishes, schools, prisons, and hospitals. At this motherhouse in Kaiserswerth, Florence Nightingale received her training as a nurse (see August 13).

SATURDAY, OCTOBER 6
WILLIAM TYNDALE, TRANSLATOR, MARTYR, 1536

William Tyndale was ordained in 1521, and his life's desire was to translate the scriptures into English. When his plan met opposition from Henry VIII, Tyndale fled to Germany, where he traveled from city to city and lived in poverty and constant danger. He was able to produce a New Testament in 1525. Nine years later he revised it and began work on the Old Testament, which he was unable to complete. He was tried for heresy and burned at the stake. Miles Coverdale completed Tyndale's work, and the Tyndale-Coverdale version was published as the "Matthew Bible" in 1537. The style of this translation has influenced English versions of the Bible such as the King James (Authorized Version) and the New Revised Standard Version for four centuries.

OCTOBER 7, 2001

EIGHTEENTH SUNDAY AFTER PENTECOST
PROPER 22

INTRODUCTION

Faith is the foundation of our worship. We adore the God who has brought us into loving relationship, and we receive God's grace that continues to build up our faith.

On this day we celebrate the ministry of Henry Melchior Muhlenberg, who died this day in 1787. Muhlenberg worked as a Lutheran pastor and missionary to transplant the Christian faith to the North American continent.

PRAYER OF THE DAY

Our Lord Jesus, you have endured the doubts and foolish questions of every generation. Forgive us for trying to be judge over you, and grant us the confident faith to acknowledge you as Lord.

READINGS

Habakkuk 1:1-4; 2:1-4

The injustices of the Judean king and the violence of the Chaldeans (Babylonians) move this prophet to write during the years leading up to the Babylonian exile of Judah. The central issue for the prophet is: How can a good and all-powerful God see evil in the world and seemingly remain indifferent?

Psalm 37:1-10 (Psalm 37:1-9 [NRSV])

Commit your way to the LORD; put your trust in the LORD. (Ps. 37:5)

2 Timothy 1:1-14

These words preserve a personal message to a prominent leader in the early Christian church. In the face of hardship and persecution, Timothy is reminded that his faith is a gift of God. He is encouraged to exercise that faith with the help of the Holy Spirit.

Luke 17:5-10

On the way to Jerusalem, Jesus instructs his followers concerning the duties of discipleship. He wants his disciples to exhibit mutual support and forgiveness, to realize the power of faith, and to adopt the attitude of servants who do what is right without thought of reward.

ALTERNATE FIRST READING/PSALM

Lamentations 1:1-6

Jeremiah's announcement of destruction had become a reality. Now Israel is in exile. The book of Lamentations contains five poems mourning the exile. In this passage, Jerusalem is portrayed as a widow with no one to comfort her.

Lamentations 3:19-26

Great is your faithfulness, O LORD. (Lam. 3:23b)

or Psalm 137

Remember the day of Jerusalem, O LORD. (Ps. 137:7)

COLOR Green

THE PRAYERS

With confidence in God's saving grace, let us pray for the church and for all God's creation in need.

A BRIEF SILENCE.

Wise and loving God, give us the patience to let things happen in your time and not our own. We pray:

Lord, hear our prayer.

Generous and giving God, you have entrusted us with the gift of your word. Be with all of us as we proclaim your gospel. We pray:

Lord, hear our prayer.

Faithful and steadfast God, nourish our faith so that it can grow and startle us with its beauty. We pray:

Lord, hear our prayer.

Merciful God, lay your healing hands on all who are suffering in body, mind, and spirit (especially...). Keep them safely in your care. We pray:

Lord, hear our prayer.

God of justice, inspire all nations to protect the earth and all its creatures for future generations. We pray:

Lord, hear our prayer.

HERE OTHER INTERCESSIONS MAY BE OFFERED.

With Henry Melchior Muhlenberg and all who have nurtured our faith (especially...), we await the day when we will all be reunited in your eternal home. We pray:

Lord, hear our prayer.

Hear these and all our prayers, O God, in the name of our Savior, Jesus Christ.

Amen

IMAGES FOR PREACHING

In the prayer of the day we pray, "Our Lord Jesus, you have endured the doubts and foolish questions of every generation." We are like the apostles, longing for the Lord to increase our faith. We have so many questions and doubts. But we must not confuse doubts with foolish questions. Is there such a thing as a foolish question? Just ask someone who has lived under the weight of having a teacher tell them when they were a child that they asked dumb questions. Ask that one how it felt to live under the shame of that label, and then ask them about their faith journey. What did they do with their questions of faith along the way? Are they yet liberated to affirm the faith they can claim and the faith yet forming within them?

Doubting Thomas is good news for such folks, and so is our Lord's response to the apostles in this passage from Luke. Perhaps we will preach *against* the prayer of the day. Jesus affirms the apostles for the faith they have. Faith that is the size of a mustard seed—even faith the size of the smallest of seeds—is faith that can make a difference, that can move a tree, that can change the world. A person with faith the size of a mustard seed can be a full participant in a study of faith, for that is what Jesus called the apostles to do in this text. Use your mustard seed faith, discover what you can do with the faith that you have, and practice using the faith that you have been given. For with God, nothing is impossible.

WORSHIP MATTERS

Prayer is about much more than the words we use to convey our joys, cares, and concerns to God. True, our words convey much, but our prayer posture and gesture are of similar importance.

As worship leaders write this week's prayers, consider the following: What does my tone of voice convey? Can I face the assembly as I lead them in prayer (whether from the chair, from the lectern, or from another suitable place)? Our voice, our posture, even our facial expressions allow the assembly to enter more fully into the experience of prayer as God's gathered children.

The leader should make the prayers her or his own. One way is for the leader to write them down and have them well in mind before the service. At the same time, the leader must be prepared to receive last minute petitions and be able to pray them with ease and with meaning. Planning as well as being open to spontaneity are important.

305

LET THE CHILDREN COME

Remember. Rekindle. Empower. Envision. These words come to mind from the second reading. Today is a day to celebrate baptismal identity. Encourage the telling of baptismal stories, and look at pictures or videos. Hear again the threefold promise of forgiveness, deliverance, and salvation. Let the words sink in that Jesus has saved you for an everlasting life that begins in this life today. Invite children to look in the mirror each morning, splash their face with water, and look again at their wet face and say, "I am a child of God."

MUSIC FOR WORSHIP

GATHERING

| LBW 433 | The Church of Christ, in every age |
| WOV 719 | God is here! |

PSALM 37

Christopherson, Dorothy. PW, Cycle C.
Hopson, Hal H. "Psalm 37" in TP.
Marshall, Jane. "Psalm 37" in *Psalms Together*. CG. CGC-18.
See Seventh Sunday after the Epiphany.

HYMN OF THE DAY

| LBW 524 | My God, how wonderful thou art |
| | DUNDEE |

A SUGGESTION FOR THE HYMN OF THE DAY

This hymn has a very singable four-part harmony. Assign the choir one or two stanzas in alternation.

INSTRUMENTAL RESOURCES

Ferguson, John. "Dundee" in *Three Psalm Preludes*. AFP 11-10823. Org.
Gabrielsen, Stephen. "Dundee" in *We Are Your Own Forever*. AFP 11-10473. Org.
Schultz, Robert. "Dundee" in *Instrumental Hymn Enhancements*. MSM 20-860. Inst.

ALTERNATE HYMN OF THE DAY

| LBW 503 | O Jesus, I have promised |
| WOV 680 | O Spirit of life |

COMMUNION

| LBW 423 | Lord, whose love in humble service |
| WOV 705 | As the grains of wheat |

SENDING

| LBW 533/534 | Now thank we all our God |
| WOV 722 | Hallelujah! We sing your praises |

ADDITIONAL HYMNS AND SONGS

DH 98	Keep the faith
LW 354	I know my faith is founded
TFF 159	Take the name of Jesus with you
W&P 9	As the deer
W&P 15	Be bold, be strong

MUSIC FOR THE DAY

CHORAL

Currie, Randolph. "Taste and See." GIA G-2824. U/2 pt, cong, org.
Gibbons, Orlando. "O Lord, Increase My Faith" in *A First Motet Book*. CPH 97-4845.
Jennings, Carolyn. "Climb to the Top of the Highest Mountain." KJO. SATB/trbl choir, kybd.
Near, Gerald. "They That Wait upon the Lord." AUR AE17. SATB, org.
Neswick, Bruce. "O Taste and See." AFP 11-10592. SATB, S solo.
Schalk, Carl. "Our Soul Waits for the Lord." CPH 98-3252. SATB.

CHILDREN'S CHOIRS

Arabic folk song. "The Tiny Seed" in LS.
Hopson, Hal H. "Song of the Mustard Seed." GIA G-2239. U, org.
Lord, Suzanne. "Faith That's Sure" in LS.

KEYBOARD/INSTRUMENTAL

Ferguson, John. "Dundee" in *Three Psalm Preludes*. AFP 11-10823. Org.
Oliver, Curt. *O Word of God Incarnate*. MSM-15-818. Pno.

HANDBELL

DeWell, Robert. "Finlandia." AGEHR AG3050. 3 oct.
Littleton, R. Lyndel. "Promised Land." Ringing Word RW 8085. 3-5 oct.

PRAISE ENSEMBLE

Dengler, Lee. "Look at the Birds of the Air." CPH 98-3125. SATB, kybd, opt fl.
Founds, Rick, and Gary Rhodes. "Lord, I Lift Your Name on High." WRD 301 0805 160. SATB, kybd, opt cong, gtr, electric bass, drms, orch.
Fry, Steve. "Jesus, You Are My Life" in *Praise Hymns and Choruses*, 4th ed. MM.
Somma, Bob, Phil Kristianson, and Bill Batstone. "He's Calling Out Your Name" in *Praise Hymns and Choruses*, 4th ed. MM.

SUNDAY, OCTOBER 7

HENRY MELCHIOR MUHLENBERG,
MISSIONARY TO NORTH AMERICA, 1787

Muhlenberg was prominent in setting the course for
Lutheranism in this country. He helped Lutheran
churches make the transition from the state churches of
Europe to independent churches of America. Among
other things, he established the first Lutheran synod in
America and developed an American Lutheran liturgy.
His liturgical principles became the basis for the Common Service of 1888, used in many North American
service books for a majority of the past century.

The commemoration of Muhlenberg invites congregations to look back on what has shaped their identity, worship, and mission in the past and to look ahead
to what might shape it in the future.

MONDAY, OCTOBER 8

DAY OF THANKSGIVING (CANADA)

See Day of Thanksgiving (U.S.A.), November 22, 2001.

WEDNESDAY, OCTOBER 10

MASSIE L. KENNARD, RENEWER OF THE CHURCH, 1996

Massie L. Kennard was a native of Chicago, Illinois. He
was a major figure in supporting and working toward
ethnic and racial inclusiveness in the former Lutheran
Church in America. Ordained in 1958, he served the
church in various staff positions, including work as the
director for Minority Concerns of the Division for
Mission in North America.

307

OCTOBER 14, 2001

NINETEENTH SUNDAY AFTER PENTECOST
PROPER 23

INTRODUCTION

"Kyrie, eleison," the church cries: "Lord, have mercy." In
Jesus, God *does* have mercy—mercy upon lepers who
are outcasts, mercy on apostles who are in chains. God
has mercy upon foreigners, breaking through boundaries of nationality and political alienation.

PRAYER OF THE DAY

Almighty God, source of every blessing, your generous
goodness comes to us anew every day. By the work of
your Spirit lead us to acknowledge your goodness, give
thanks for your benefits, and serve you in willing obedience; through your Son, Jesus Christ our Lord.

READINGS

2 Kings 5:1-3, 7-15c

Naaman, a Syrian general, suffers from leprosy. In this passage

*Elisha miraculously cures his illness but only after Naaman
realizes, with the help of his servants, that he also needs healing for his pride.*

Psalm 111

*I will give thanks to the LORD with my whole heart.
(Ps. 111:1)*

2 Timothy 2:8-15

*Though Paul is chained as a prisoner, he reminds Timothy
that the word of God is never shackled. He encourages his
young friend to proclaim that word of freedom in an honest
and upright life as well as in his teaching and preaching.*

Luke 17:11-19

*A Samaritan leper becomes a model for thanksgiving. This one
who was healed does not take for granted the kindness shown
to him but offers thanks to Jesus and glorifies God.*

ALTERNATE FIRST READING/PSALM

Jeremiah 29:1, 4-7

From Jerusalem during the years of exile, Jeremiah sends a letter to those in Babylon encouraging them, while they live in this strange and alien place, to be in ministry for the sake of their Babylonian neighbors.

Psalm 66:1-11 (Psalm 66:1-12 [NRSV])

God holds our souls in life. (Ps. 66:8)

COLOR Green

THE PRAYERS

With confidence in God's saving grace, let us pray for the church and for all God's creation in need.

A BRIEF SILENCE.

Good and generous God, help us to see that our blessings are your gift and not of our own making. We pray:

Lord, hear our prayer.

Merciful God, reach out to all who need to experience your healing: those who are lonely, alienated, or ill (especially...). We pray:

Lord, hear our prayer.

Faithful God, bring us back to the path of justice, and make this congregation a voice on behalf of all who suffer violence and oppression. We pray:

Lord, hear our prayer.

Amazing God, make us willing to listen to your voice in all things, especially when you call us to difficult tasks. We pray:

Lord, hear our prayer.

HERE OTHER INTERCESSIONS MAY BE OFFERED.

Remembering the saints who have entered into the salvation of Jesus Christ, may we one day join them in your eternal embrace. We pray:

Lord, hear our prayer.

Hear these and all our prayers, O God, in the name of our Savior, Jesus Christ.

Amen

IMAGES FOR PREACHING

Is it still foreign to give thanks? The NRSV retains the translation of *foreigner* in referring to the Samaritan in today's gospel. Those who work with global missions tell us that it is no longer appropriate global mission language to speak of international guests or visitors as foreigners. But in this Lukan text, we are reminded of another meaning of *foreign*: something that is not characteristic of a person. Is it foreign for us to give thanks?

Have you ever lived in another country for any length of time? You see things in a new way. You see how clearly we need one another and how many gifts and guides we have to be thankful for. It is hard work finding one's way in a strange land. Even knowing where to find things in a grocery store can be hard, and newcomers constantly need help with innumerable daily needs. It is easy to feel and express gratitude to helpful persons in a strange land.

The grateful Samaritan—doubly outcast as both a leper and a Samaritan—teaches us about returning to give thanks. How can our experiences as outsiders teach us about gratitude and returning thanks to one another and to God? How might thanksgiving as a way of life look? Whether it is a time of stewardship focus in the congregation or a time of harvest celebration, let the witness of the Samaritan call us back to the basics.

WORSHIP MATTERS

"Kyrie eleison!" "Lord have mercy!" It is the cry of the faithful as we bring the cares and concerns both of the past week and of our lives before God. These words are found in the gathering rite and are frequently included in the prayers of the church. *Kyrie eleison*...as we pray for the church, our world and ourselves. *Kyrie eleison*...as we confess to our brokenness and seek God's forgiveness. *Kyrie eleison*...as we ask for strength to face what may lie ahead.

The Bread of Life setting (setting five in *With One Voice*) provides a wonderful opportunity to use this simple yet powerful request for God's mercy. The Kyrie offers the chance to hear and sing both the Greek words and the English equivalent. Worship planners would do well to use the Greek—even if it means taking extra time to teach pronunciation.

LET THE CHILDREN COME

Gestures are a powerful way to communicate. A "thumb's up" or a "thumb's down" or a simple shake of the head speaks clearly. Add gestures as you sing the refrain from the Kyrie, "Lord, have mercy." Use gestures for the prayer petitions from the prayers of the church as you say "Lord, in your mercy, hear our prayer." Ask an American Sign Language interpreter to teach you how to sign the words through simple gestures. Use these gestures in worship in the coming weeks.

MUSIC FOR WORSHIP

GATHERING

| LBW 559 | Oh, for a thousand tongues to sing |
| WOV 795 | Oh, sing to the Lord |

PSALM 111

Cherwien, David. "I Will Give Thanks to the Lord." CPH 98-2930. U, hb.

Christopherson, Dorothy. PW, Cycle C.

Hopson, Hal H. TP.

Proulx, Richard. "My Heart Is Full Today." AFP 11-0645. 2 pt, kybd, hb, perc.

Psalms for Praise and Worship: A Complete Liturgical Psalter. ABI.

HYMN OF THE DAY

| WOV 693 | Baptized in water |
| | BUNESSAN |

INSTRUMENTAL RESOURCES

Albrecht, Timothy. "Morning Has Broken" in *Grace Notes III.* AFP 11-10457. Org.

McFadden, Jane. "Morning Has Broken." AFP 11-10552. Hb.

Powell, Robert. "Bunessan" in *Eight Hymn Tunes for Flute, Oboe and Organ.* CPH 97-5652. Org, inst.

Wasson, Laura E. "Morning Has Broken" in *A Piano Tapestry.* AFP 11-10821. Pno.

ALTERNATE HYMN OF THE DAY

| LBW 431 | Your hand, O Lord, in days of old |
| WOV 696 | I've just come from the fountain |

COMMUNION

| LBW 211 | Here, O my Lord, I see thee |
| WOV 668 | There in God's garden |

SENDING

| LBW 543 | Praise to the Lord, the Almighty |
| WOV 790 | Praise to you, O God of mercy |

ADDITIONAL HYMNS AND SONGS

NCH 201	An outcast among outcasts
PH 386	O for a world
TFF 293	Thank you, Lord
W&P 81	Kyrie eleison
W&P 106	Now we remain

MUSIC FOR THE DAY

CHORAL

Bach, J. S. "Now Thank We All Our God" in BAS. SATB, kybd.

Buxtehude, Dieterich. "Everything You Do" in CC. SATB, org.

Cherwien, David. "I Will Give Thanks to the Lord." CPH 98-2930. U, cong, org, opt hb.

Distler, Hugo. "Praise to the Lord" in CC. SATB.

Ferguson, John. "A Song of Thanksgiving." AFP 11-10505. SATB, org.

Powell, Robert J. "My Heart Is Steadfast, O God." CPH 98-3352. SATB, org.

Scarlatti, Alessandro. "Exsultate Deo." PRE MC71.

CHILDREN'S CHOIRS

Dyer, Max. "I Will Sing, I Will Sing" in LS.

Jothen, Michael. "I Will Give Thanks." BEC BP1101. U, pno, opt fl.

Mozart, Wolfgang A./arr. Walter Ehret. "Praise the Lord, Our God, Forever." FB B-GO464. 3 equal vcs.

KEYBOARD/INSTRUMENTAL

Drischner, Max. *Lobe den Herren: Choral Fantasie für Klavier oder Orgel.* CFP CLS177. Org/kybd.

Oliver, Curt. *Variations on "Praise to the Lord" for Piano.* MSM-15-816. Pno.

Proulx, Richard. "Two Versets on 'Bunessan'" in *Laudate!* vol. 4; ed. James W. Kosnik. CPH 97-6665. Also in *Six Hymn Preludes.* CPH 97-6641. Org.

HANDBELL

Larson, Katherine Jordahl. "Borning Cry." AFP 11-10517. 3-4 oct.

Tucker, Margaret R. "Prayer and Praise." RRM BL5004. 3 oct.

PRAISE ENSEMBLE

Schutte, Dan. "Glory and Praise to Our God." OCP 9491. SATB, pno, gtr, opt cong.

Smith, Henry, and Ken Barker. "Give Thanks." WRD 301 0548 168. SATB, kybd, opt gtr, electric bass, drms, orch.

Ylvisaker, John. "I'll Give Thanks to God Above" in *Borning Cry.* NGP.

MONDAY, OCTOBER 15

TERESA OF JESUS, TEACHER, RENEWER OF THE CHURCH, 1582

Teresa of Jesus is also known as Teresa of Avila. She is commemorated with John of the Cross on December 14. Teresa chose the life of a Carmelite nun after reading the letters of Jerome. She was frequently sick during her early years as a nun and found that when she was sick her prayer life flowered, but when she was well it withered. Steadily her life of faith and prayer deepened, and she grew to have a lively sense of God's presence with her. She worked to reform her monastic community in Avila, which she believed had strayed from its original purpose. Her reforms asked nuns to maintain life in the monastic enclosure without leaving it and also to identify with those who are poor by not wearing shoes. Teresa's writings on devotional life are widely read by members of various denominations.

WEDNESDAY, OCTOBER 17
IGNATIUS, BISHOP OF ANTIOCH, MARTYR, C. 115

Ignatius was the second bishop of Antioch in Syria. It was there that the name "Christian" was first used to describe the followers of Jesus. Ignatius is known to us through his letters. In them he encouraged Christians to live in unity sustained with love while standing firm on sound doctrine. Ignatius believed Christian martyrdom was a privilege. When his own martyrdom approached, he wrote in one of his letters, "I prefer death in Christ Jesus to power over the farthest limits of the earth.... [D]o not stand in the way of my birth to real life."

Ignatius and all martyrs are a reminder that even today Christians face death because of their faith in Jesus. Still, the apostle Paul reminded us in last Sunday's reading from 2 Timothy, "If we die with him, we shall also live with him."

THURSDAY, OCTOBER 18
ST. LUKE, EVANGELIST

Luke is identified as the author of both Luke and Acts. Luke is careful to place the events of Jesus' life in both their social and religious contexts. Some of the most loved parables, including the good Samaritan and the prodigal son, are found only in this gospel. Luke's gospel has also given the church some of its most beautiful songs: the Benedictus sung at morning prayer, the Magnificat sung at evening prayer, and the Nunc dimittis sung at the close of the day. These songs are powerful witnesses to the message of Jesus Christ.

Paul calls Luke the "beloved physician," and some congregations use the day of St. Luke to remember and pray for those in healing professions. The Service of the Word for Healing in *Occasional Services* may be used.

OCTOBER 21, 2001

TWENTIETH SUNDAY AFTER PENTECOST
PROPER 24

INTRODUCTION

The life of faith means that we might wrestle with God. Jesus commends to us the story of a widow who would not take no for an answer. And Paul commends to Timothy a life of persistence in proclaiming good news, even when the world may not be eager to hear it. We contend with God, and we find our peace when God assures us of our identity and blesses us.

PRAYER OF THE DAY

Almighty and everlasting God, in Christ you have revealed your glory among the nations. Preserve the works of your mercy, that your Church throughout the world may persevere with steadfast faith in the confession of your name; through your Son, Jesus Christ our Lord.

READINGS

Genesis 32:22-31

Returning to the home he had fled after stealing his brother's birthright and his father's blessing, Jacob wrestles all night long with an adversary who ultimately blesses him and changes his name to "Israel," a name that means "he wrestles with God."

Psalm 121

My help comes from the Lord, the maker of heaven and earth. (Ps. 121:2)

2 Timothy 3:14—4:5

Paul continues his instruction of Timothy, his younger colleague in ministry, by emphasizing the importance of faithful teaching despite opposition.

Luke 18:1-8

Jesus tells a story reminding his listeners they are to be persis-

tent in prayer, unceasing in their appeals. If an unethical judge will ultimately grant the plea of a persistent widow, how much more will our loving God hear those who call upon him!

ALTERNATE FIRST READING/PSALM

Jeremiah 31:27-34

Jeremiah announces a day when Israel and Judah will be bound to God in a new covenant written upon their hearts and sealed with God's forgiveness.

Psalm 119:97-104

Your words are sweeter than honey to my mouth.

(Ps. 119:103)

COLOR   Green

THE PRAYERS

With confidence in God's saving grace, let us pray for the church and for all God's creation in need.

A BRIEF SILENCE.

For all the leaders of the church, that as they preach the gospel they may equip us all for good service, we pray:

Lord, hear our prayer.

For each of us, that we may hold steadfast to our prayers and discover your answers in unexpected ways, we pray:

Lord, hear our prayer.

For every community struggling with the word of God, that they may grow to live it fully, we pray:

Lord, hear our prayer.

For the beauty of all your creation, that we may cherish and guard it as faithful stewards, we pray:

Lord, hear our prayer.

For those who need encouragement, those who are homeless, poor, discouraged, or ill (especially . . .), that we might reach out and lessen their suffering, we pray:

Lord, hear our prayer.

HERE OTHER INTERCESSIONS MAY BE OFFERED.

For all those who have shared their faith with us, that one day we may all rejoice together in you, we pray:

Lord, hear our prayer.

Hear these and all our prayers, O God, in the name of our Savior, Jesus Christ.

Amen

IMAGES FOR PREACHING

A call for persistence jumps out of the second reading and the gospel. For those who are preachers, 2 Timothy comes as a direct and timely exhortation: "[P]ro-claim the message; be persistent whether the time is favorable or unfavorable; . . . they will accumulate for themselves teachers to suit their own desires, and will turn away from listening to the truth and wander away to myths" (2 Tim. 4:2a, 3b-4).

Consider the time: autumn. If you are in the United States, one of the chief competing gods we face at this time is football, as well as other organized sports that gobble up so many hours in the lives of children and youth. While these activities certainly offer benefits, we are frequently forced to organize our congregational lives around them, so that everyone can place competitive sports commitments first. Worship, confirmation programs, special church gatherings—nearly everything else is subservient. We who would wish for a different ordering of priorities are often not persistent enough against these and other idolatries that shape our lives. Unlike Jacob, we wrestle a little bit, protest quietly, and then give in.

Paul knew that the powers and principalities would continue to swirl about us. So, he encourages us, "[c]arry out your ministry fully" (2 Tim. 4:5). Dare to help people to see the order of their priorities. And tell them about the power of redemptive love. Tell them about the persistent widow who teaches us about persistent prayer. Tell them about the love of Jesus Christ that has already redeemed us, regardless of how well we perform in competitive endeavors. And ask them: When the Son of Man returns, will he find faith still alive among us? How will he be able to tell?

WORSHIP MATTERS

Prayer. What an elemental piece of what it means to be a Christian! It is our line of communication to our God. It is the time when God listens to our joys and concerns, both for ourselves and others. It is often in this time that we find peace and the courage to go on, even if we do not receive direct, neat answers.

Prayer is not confined to the weekly worship service. It is to be a part of who we are each and every day. How is prayer encouraged in the congregation? Are people taught different forms of prayer, such as, centering prayer, imaging, lectio divina, prayer with the psalms? Are children and parents encouraged to pray together, and are daily, weekly, and seasonal resources made available to help? How does the church work to enlighten and enable the assembly, so that prayer might have a meaningful and steady impact on their lives?

LET THE CHILDREN COME

Not so long ago, children were to be "seen and not heard." In God's family system, children are to be seen and heard. When young children sit in the back of the church so as not to bother anyone, it is difficult for them to worship fully. Invite young families to sit in the front seats where they can smell the bread and wine, watch the movements, and hear the splashing water. Those in the chancel area will be blessed to hear children's voices join them in praise and feel the unity God creates in common prayer.

MUSIC FOR WORSHIP

GATHERING

| LBW 294 | My hope is built on nothing less |
| WOV 768 | He comes to us as one unknown |

PSALM 121

Bobb, Barry L. "Psalm 121." AFP 11-4656. U, opt cong, kybd.

Christopherson, Dorothy. PW, Cycle C.

Cotter, Jeanne. "Our Help Is from the Lord" in PCY, vol. 3.

Cox, Joe. "I Lift Up My Eyes to the Hills" in *Psalms for the People of God*. SMP 45/1037S.

Edwards, Rusty, and LaJuana Fiester. "We Lift Our Eyes" in ASG.

Lovelace, Austin. "Psalm 121." CGC 361. U, fl.

| LBW 445 | Unto the hills |

HYMN OF THE DAY

| LBW 439 | What a friend we have in Jesus |
| | CONVERSE |

VOCAL RESOURCES

Hassell, Michael. "What a Friend We Have in Jesus." AFP 11-10919. SATB, sop and tenor solo, kybd.

INSTRUMENTAL RESOURCES

Bisbee, B. Wayne. "Converse" in *From the Serene to the Whimsical*. AFP 11-10561. Org.

Callahan, Charles. "Prelude on Two American Folk Hymns." MSM 10-97-6070. Org, inst.

Cherwien, David. "What a Friend We Have in Jesus" in *Seasonal Interpretations: Trinity/Pentecost*. AMSI SP-111. Org.

Sedio, Mark. "What a Friend We Have in Jesus" in *A Global Piano Tour*. AFP 11-10977. Pno.

ALTERNATE HYMN OF THE DAY

| LBW 440 | Christians, while on earth abiding |
| WOV 746 | Day by day |

COMMUNION

| LBW 403 | Lord, speak to us, that we may speak |
| WOV 772 | O Lord, hear my prayer |

SENDING

| LBW 259 | Lord, dismiss us with your blessing |
| WOV 736 | By gracious powers |

ADDITIONAL HYMNS AND SONGS

H82 638/9	Come, O thou Traveler unknown
TFF 198	When the storms of life are raging
W&P 93	Lord, my strength
W&P 159	You are my God

MUSIC FOR THE DAY

CHORAL

Attwood, Thomas. "Teach Me, O Lord, the Way of Thy Statutes." ECS 169. SATB, org.

Berger, Jean. "I to the Hills Lift Up Mine Eyes." AFP 11-0678. Also in *The Augsburg Choirbook*. AFP 11-10817. SATB.

Bertalot, John. "Let Us with a Gladsome Mind." AFP 11-10754. SAB, org, opt 2 tpt.

Mendelssohn, Felix. "He, Watching Over Israel" in *Elijah*. ECS 779. SATB, kybd.

CHILDREN'S CHOIRS

Bouman, Paul. "I Lift My Eyes to the Hills." B&H OCTB6550. 2 pt trbl, org.

Cox, Joe, and Jody Lindh. "Jesus, Son of God Most High." CG CGA-377. U, opt desc, kybd, fl, gtr, bass.

Medema, Ken. "Lord, Listen to Your Children Praying" in LS.

KEYBOARD/INSTRUMENTAL

Cherwien, David. "Day by Day" from *Eight for Eighty-eight*. AFP 11-10868. Pno, opt inst.

Rotermund, Donald. "A Bicinium on 'Fang Dein Werk'" in *Seven Hymn Preludes*, Set 3. CPH 97-6243. Org.

HANDBELL

Dobrinski, Cynthia. "In God We Trust." Singspiration 7531. 3-5 oct.

Hascall, Nancy. "I Lift Up Mine Eyes to the Hills." Bel Canto Press BCC-3. 4-5 oct.

PRAISE ENSEMBLE

Barbour, Anne. "Protector of My Soul" in *Praise Hymns and Choruses*, 4th ed. MM.

Bray, Stephen, Don Moen, and Martin J. Nystrom. "My Help Comes from the Lord" in *Come & Worship*. INT.

O'Shields, Michael, and Doug Holck. "I Will Call Upon the Lord." LIL AN-8065. SATB, kybd, opt orch.

TUESDAY, OCTOBER 23
JAMES OF JERUSALEM, MARTYR

James became an early leader of the church in Jerusalem. He is described in the New Testament as the brother of Jesus, and secular historian Josephus calls James, the brother of Jesus, "the so-called Christ." Little is known about him, but Josephus reported that the Pharisees respected James for his piety and observance of the law. His enemies had him put to death.

Was James a blood brother of the Lord? It is difficult to answer that question because the Aramaic word for *brother* can also mean *cousin*. Jesus also said, "Whoever does the will of God is my brother and sister and mother." The commemoration of James and his connection to Jesus as "brother" can spark further discussion about how we all share Christ as our brother through baptism into his death and resurrection.

FRIDAY, OCTOBER 26
PHILIPP NICOLAI, 1608; JOHANN HEERMANN, 1647;
PAUL GERHARDT, 1676; HYMNWRITERS

These three outstanding hymnwriters all worked in Germany in the seventeenth century during times of war and plague. When Philipp Nicolai was a pastor in Westphalia, the plague killed thirteen hundred of his parishioners. One hundred seventy people died in one week. His hymns "Wake, awake, for night is flying" (LBW 31) and "O Morning Star, how fair, how bright" (LBW 76) were included in a series of meditations he wrote to comfort his parishioners during the plague. The style of Johann Heermann's hymns moved away from the more objective style of Reformation hymnody toward expressing the emotions of faith. Three of his hymns are in *LBW,* including his plaintive text, "Ah, holy Jesus" (123). Paul Gerhardt lost a preaching position at St. Nicholas's Church in Berlin, because he refused to sign a document stating he would not make theological arguments in his sermons. Some have called him the greatest of Lutheran hymnwriters.

313

OCTOBER 28, 2001
REFORMATION SUNDAY

INTRODUCTION

This day the church remembers with thanksgiving the events of the sixteenth-century Reformation. We rightly celebrate the Reformation not when we glory in the events of the past, but rather when we pray, "Come, Holy Spirit!" The church is always in need of reform, always in need of dying again in Christ and being raised from the dead, so that it might be truly free. We celebrate our apostolic faith as we also remember St. Simon and St. Jude.

PRAYER OF THE DAY

Almighty God, gracious Lord, pour out your Holy Spirit upon your faithful people. Keep them steadfast in your Word, protect and comfort them in all temptations, defend them against all their enemies, and bestow on the Church your saving peace; through your Son, Jesus

Christ our Lord, who lives and reigns with you and the Holy Spirit, one God, now and forever.

READINGS

Jeremiah 31:31-34

The exiles in Babylon blamed their captivity on their ancestors who had broken the covenant established at Mount Sinai. But the prophet envisions a future day when the people can no longer make such a complaint, for there will be no need to teach the law. Knowledge of God and of God's laws will be a gift from God, written on the heart.

Psalm 46

The LORD of hosts is with us; the God of Jacob is our stronghold. (Ps. 46:4)

Romans 3:19-28

Martin Luther and other leaders of the Reformation believed the heart of the gospel was found in these words of Paul written

to the Romans. *All people have sinned, but God offers forgiveness of sins through Christ Jesus. We are justified—put right with God—by the gift of God's grace, through faith in Jesus.*

John 8:31-36

The Reformation sought to emphasize that true freedom is not related to ethnic distinctions or social class. Only Jesus can free us from slavery to sin, which he does through the truth of the gospel.

COLOR Red

THE PRAYERS

With confidence in God's saving grace, let us pray for the church and for all God's creation in need.

A BRIEF SILENCE.

Life-giving God, though we try to free ourselves from evils that assail us, remind us that you have given us Jesus as the way to everlasting freedom. We pray:

Lord, hear our prayer.

God of justice, where people are enslaved to tyranny, poverty, and violence, make us your instruments for peace and freedom. We pray:

Lord, hear our prayer.

Loving and tender God, guide your church, that we may proclaim the truth of your word. We pray:

Lord, hear our prayer.

Healing and compassionate God, give refuge and strength to those in need of your help (especially…). Take away their fears and make them whole. We pray:

Lord, hear our prayer.

Almighty God, we remember all who have suffered for the faith and ask that they may be secure in your everlasting freedom. We pray:

Lord, hear our prayer.

HERE OTHER INTERCESSIONS MAY BE OFFERED.

In the company of St. Simon and St. Jude and all renewers of the church, may we anticipate that day when we will all feast together at your table. We pray:

Lord, hear our prayer.

Hear these and all our prayers, O God, in the name of our Savior, Jesus Christ.

Amen

IMAGES FOR PREACHING

In *Lake Wobegon Days*, Garrison Keillor offers a whimsical ninety-five theses (complaints) that an anonymous Wobegonian wrote about his upbringing. Those theses include references to quirks as well as deeply held traditions, such as the caution not to go overboard, the fear that God will slap you if you do not straighten out fast, and the fear of what the neighbors will say. He offers us a lighthearted and serious way of getting at the matter of how our beliefs can become tyranny in our lives.

The tyranny of having to do the right things in order to be accepted by parents can be close to the tyranny of trying to earn God's acceptance. We are justified by faith, wrote Paul. So do not boast about whatever you have done, and do not be tyrannized by what you have not done. In Jesus Christ, we are already loved, justified, and free. We are freed from the fear that we are too extreme or that God will slap us or that the neighbors will talk about us. Those tyrannies and all others need not hold us. We are freed from the chains of our fears and free to live as saved people.

And what shall we do with this freedom? How might we live out God's ongoing reformation in our church and in our world? The reforming movement in the church was born in examining church practices and doctrines against the gospel. Where are the things that need examination in our day? And how might we support those prophetic voices in our midst? We are *ecclesia reformata semper reformanda*—the reformed church ever in need of reformation. This understanding of the reformation freedom of the gospel led the reformers further in the work of ongoing reformation than they ever imagined. May that freedom, solely dependent on the grace of God, lead us in lives of courageous witness in our own day.

WORSHIP MATTERS

While we must be careful not to set up a "we vs. they" dynamic on Reformation Day, thereby separating ourselves from our sisters and brothers in the Roman Catholic church, this day does deserve to be celebrated. Today we celebrate the power of the Holy Spirit and the powerful effect on those who saw the need for reform in the church. We celebrate the presence of the Holy Spirit in the lives of the reformers and in our own lives of faith as touched by their witness.

The color for the day is red, symbolizing the fire of the Spirit and the flame of faith that burned in the hearts of the reformers. How might the color be made visible in the space, beyond the paraments themselves? Yet another witness to the Reformation would be to have copies of the Small Catechism available for all to take with them.

LET THE CHILDREN COME

Red is the appointed color for Reformation Sunday. Use it boldly in worship. Have the children teach the congregation a song about Christian freedom. "I will sing, I will sing" and "Baptized and set free" from *Worship & Praise,* or "Free at last" and "Freedom is coming" from *This Far by Faith* could be used. Tie red ribbon around embroidery hoops. The children could lead the congregation in a motion dance, waving their ribbons, as a response to the gospel reading.

MUSIC FOR WORSHIP

GATHERING

LBW 228/229 A mighty fortress is our God

WOV 750   Oh, praise the gracious power

PSALM 46

Burkhardt, Michael. *Three Psalm Settings.* MSM 80-705. U, cong, perc, org.

Cherwien, David. PW, Cycle C.

Cherwien, David. "Psalm 46: God Is Our Refuge." MSM 80-800. U, cong, org.

Folkening, John. *Six Psalm Settings with Antiphons.* MSM 80-700. SATB, U, cong, kybd.

Wood, Dale. PW, Cycle C.

Ziegenhals, Harriet Ilse. "God Is Our Help in Time of Trouble," in *Sing Out! A Children's Psalter.* WLP.

LBW 228/229   A mighty fortress is our God

HYMN OF THE DAY

WOV 712   Listen, God is calling
            Neno lake Mungu

ALTERNATE HYMN OF THE DAY

LBW 230   Lord, keep us steadfast in your Word

LBW 365   Built on a rock

COMMUNION

LBW 369   The Church's one foundation

WOV 701   What feast of love

SENDING

LBW 393   Rise, shine, you people!

WOV 790   Praise to you, O God of mercy

ADDITIONAL HYMNS AND SONGS

LW 351   By grace I'm saved,

PH 192   God, our help and constant refuge

TFF 46   Freedom is coming

TFF 213   We shall overcome

W&P 25   By grace we have been saved

W&P 114   Our confidence is in the Lord

MUSIC FOR THE DAY

CHORAL

Busarow, Donald. "The Church of Christ, in Every Age." AFP 11-10400. SATB, org, opt brass, opt cong.

Coleman, Gerald Patrick. "Christ Is with Me." CPH 98-3120. 2 pt, C inst, pno. Also CPH 98-3051. 2 pt/SATB, C inst, pno.

Distler, Hugo. "Salvation unto Us Has Come" in CC. SATB.

Ferguson, John. "Psalm 46." AFP 11-10748. SATB, org.

Hassler, Hans Leo. "A Mighty Fortress." CPH 98-1986.

Pachelbel, Johann. "On God and Not on Human Trust." CPH 98-1006.

Walter, Johann. "I Build on God's Strong Word Alone" in CC. SATB.

CHILDREN'S CHOIRS

Bertalot, John. "God Is Our Hope." CG CGA-444. 2 pt trbl, kybd.

Daniels, Bob. "He Set Me Free." AFP 11-1771. U, kybd/gtr.

Hayes, Mark. "Day by Day." AFP 11-10962. SATB, pno.

Lord, Suzanne. "Faith That's Sure" in LS.

Ramseth, Betty Ann, and Rudy Ramseth. "Lord, Keep Us Steadfast and Grant Peace, We Pray." in *Keep in Mind.* AFP 11-2291. U, adult choir and/or cong, org, spoken prayer.

KEYBOARD/INSTRUMENTAL

Bender, Jan. "Dear Christians, One and All, Rejoice" in *Festival Preludes on Six Chorales.* CPH 97-4608. Org.

Kee, Cor. *Een Vaste Burgt.* Ars Nova 184. Org/kybd.

Viderø, Finn. "Kirken den er et gammelt Hus" in *Tre Koralpartiter.* Engstrøm & Sødring 106 (CFP ENS). Org.

HANDBELL

Benton, Douglas. "Ein Feste Burg." AGEHR AG 35103 (score), AG 3075 (3 oct), AG 44049 (4-5 oct), 30/1182 AG (brass).

Dobrinski, Cynthia. "A Mighty Fortress." AG 1311. 3-5 oct.

Garee, Betty B. "A Mighty Fortress." CPH 97-5778. 4-5 oct.

PRAISE ENSEMBLE

Cook, Steve, Vicki Cook, and Keith Christopher. "We Rejoice in the Grace of God." WRD 301 0770 162. SATB, pno, gtr, electric bass, drms, opt orch.

Nelson, Greg, and Phil McHugh. "Only Jesus" in *Sing & Rejoice.* BNT.

Schultz, Timothy P. "God Is Our Refuge and Strength" (Psalm 46). CPH 98-3156. SATB.

315

OCTOBER 28, 2001

INTRODUCTION

Those who seem the farthest from God may be the closest to mercy. That is the theme of today's gospel, and it is echoed in the other readings. It is the dynamic that supports the dialogue in the first reading. We get close to God as we confess that we are in need of grace. This dynamic of grace is celebrated this week as we remember the sixteenth-century reformation of the church. It is also the heart of the apostolic witness we remember this day as we give thanks for St. Simon and St. Jude.

PRAYER OF THE DAY

Almighty and everlasting God, increase in us the gifts of faith, hope, and charity; and, that we may obtain what you promise, make us love what you command; through your Son, Jesus Christ our Lord.

READINGS

Jeremiah 14:7-10, 19-22

The prophet identifies with his people in this anguished prayer following the onslaught of the Babylonians and the destruction of Jerusalem.

or Sirach 35:12-17

God is impartial in justice and hears the powerless.

Psalm 84:1-6 (Psalm 84:1-7 [NRSV])

Happy are the people whose strength is in you. (Ps. 84:4)

2 Timothy 4:6-8, 16-18

The conclusion of this letter to a young minister offers a final perspective on life from one who is now facing death. Though others have let him down, Paul is sure of his faith in the Lord, who has stood by him and lent him strength.

Luke 18:9-14

At the time of Jesus, Pharisees were regarded as exceptionally religious persons, and tax collectors were treated as outcasts. In this parable Jesus contrasts the two in a surprising way to make a point about approaching God in humbleness.

ALTERNATE FIRST READING/PSALM

Joel 2:23-32

The prophet Joel uses the image of a plague of locusts as a reminder of Judah's destruction at the hands of hostile armies. Today's reading points beyond the judgment of the Day of the

Lord, when the Lord will repay "the years that the swarming locust has eaten" and everyone who calls on the Lord's name will be saved.

Psalm 65

Your paths overflow with plenty. (Ps. 65:12)

COLOR   Green

THE PRAYERS

With confidence in God's saving grace, let us pray for the church and for all God's creation in need.
A BRIEF SILENCE.

For understanding and unity among all believers, that when we wander from God's path, you will gently bring us back, we pray:

Lord, hear our prayer.

For this congregation, that we may know your presence whenever we feel alone, we pray:

Lord, hear our prayer.

For those in danger from war, violence, poverty, or oppression, that the church would assist in making your reign of justice known worldwide, we pray:

Lord, hear our prayer.

For those suffering from despair, fear, or illness (especially...), that they may be safe and comforted in God's care, we pray:

Lord, hear our prayer.

We bless you for the joy we receive when we sing praise for God's creation and all our blessings. We pray:

Lord, hear our prayer.

HERE OTHER INTERCESSIONS MAY BE OFFERED.

In the company of St. Simon and St. Jude and all renewers of the church, may we anticipate that day when we will all feast together at your table. We pray:

Lord, hear our prayer.

Hear these and all our prayers, O God, in the name of our Savior, Jesus Christ.

Amen

IMAGES FOR PREACHING

Welcome to Sinners Anonymous! That would be a more direct way, stripped of any extra words, of saying what we say at the beginning of the Brief Order for Confession and Forgiveness *(LBW)*: "If we say we have no sin, we deceive ourselves...." We are sinners, just like the Pharisee and the tax collector. The difference between them is that the Pharisee's hands were full of attempts to justify himself. His list of righteous acts was like a bunch of little gray stones of self-justification weighing him down, keeping his hands full and his heart closed and guarded with a stone wall. It takes energy to hold on to all those stones of moral virtue and achievement. The tax collector was one whose hands were empty: no long list of sins or virtues—simply hands that beat his breast with contrition.

Take some little gray stones with you into the pulpit. Hold them up as you list off ancient or modern ways we attempt to justify ourselves. And then invite your hearers to let go of those stones, one by one, and to enter the humility of the tax collector. Let the stones drop noisily from the pulpit to the floor. When we let go of our stones of self-righteousness, then and only then will our hands and hearts be open to receive the forgiveness and love of Jesus Christ. Then we are left with nothing to say other than, "God, be merciful to me, a sinner!"

To open our hands and let go of all justifications of ourselves means that we must also let go of our pride that we are not like the Pharisee. We are sinners, who brought nothing into this world and will take nothing out of this world. As Martin Luther is reported to have said on his deathbed, "We are beggars." Our hands are empty, and our only hope is the mercy of God. When a baby is baptized, its hands are empty, having had no time to accumulate any of life's little gray stones. When we come to the Lord's supper, our hands are empty, so that we might receive this meal of amazing grace. Our hands are empty, so that all who humble themselves may be exalted, through the mercy of the one who came to call sinners.

WORSHIP MATTERS

From where does the pastor lead the order for confession and forgiveness? If the arrangement of your church building permits, the font is an ideal place from which to lead the congregation in the confession of sin and to announce God's forgiveness.

Baptism, confession, and forgiveness are intrinsically linked. It is in the cleansing waters that we are reborn and raised to a new existence as God's forgiven children. A visual reminder of this connection will illustrate the tie between the waters and our need for continual cleansing. Ideally, then, the font should be in a visible location in the worship space. Perhaps it might be placed near the entrance, so that all could not help but notice it as they came to worship. The order for confession and forgiveness could then be led from this place, illustrating the rite as preparatory to the service, as an entrance to our corporate worship of God.

Another option would be to place the font front and center, so that all would pass by on their way to the Lord's table. Either way, the visible font filled with water, together with the powerful words of confession and absolution, will remind the assembly of our baptism into God's family and our rebirth in the Spirit.

LET THE CHILDREN COME

What do children understand when they hear the words "confession and forgiveness"? They may know that it has something to do with being sorry. They do know the reality of family arguments and playground squabbles, boasting bullies and painful put-downs. They also know how a hug or a handshake can bring together those who are divided. Invite the congregation to say the simple words "God, I am sorry" during the confession and to share handshakes of reconciliation during the peace.

MUSIC FOR WORSHIP

GATHERING

| LBW 401 | Before you, Lord we bow |
| WOV 782 | All my hope on God is founded |

PSALM 84

Cherwien, David. PW, Cycle C.

Haas, David. "How Lovely" (Psalm 84) in PCY, vol. 9.

Joncas, Michael. "Psalm 84: How Lovely Is Your Dwelling Place" in STP, vol. 1.

Mackie, Ruth E. "Psalm 84." CPH 98-3305. SATB, cong, inst, org.

Porter, Tom. "Happy Are They Who Dwell in Your House." GIA G-3026. Cong, choir, kybd, gtr, inst.

HYMN OF THE DAY

| LBW 417 | In a lowly manger born |
| | Mabune |

INSTRUMENTAL RESOURCES

Cherwien, David. "In a Lowly Manger Born" in *Interpretations,* vol. 7.
AMSI SP-104. Org.

ALTERNATE HYMN OF THE DAY

| LBW 310 | To you, omniscient Lord of all |
| WOV 739 | In all our grief |

COMMUNION

| LBW 309 | Lord Jesus, think on me |
| WOV 711 | You satisfy the hungry heart |

SENDING

| LBW 507 | How firm a foundation |
| WOV 763 | Let justice flow like streams |

ADDITIONAL HYMNS AND SONGS

H82 517	How lovely is your dwelling-place
LW 433	Come, my soul, with every care
TFF 153	Guide my feet
W&P 28	Change my heart, O God
W&P 90	Lord, I lift your name on high

MUSIC FOR THE DAY

CHORAL

Brahms, Johannes. "How Lovely Is Thy Dwelling Place." PET 3672.
Also in CC. SATB, kybd.

Clemens, James E. "Savior, Prince of Israel's Race." MSM 50-3041.
SATB.

Marshall, Jane. "How Lovely Is Your Dwelling Place." AFP 11-10884.
SATB, org.

Schütz, Heinrich. "The Pharisee and the Publican." GSCH 7473.
SATB, org, TB solos.

White, David Ashley. "Come, Ye Sinners." AFP 11-10362. 2 pt,
ob/C inst, kybd.

Wold, Wayne. "Kyrie Eleison: Lord, Have Mercy." MSM 80-303.
U, kybd.

CHILDREN'S CHOIRS

Brokering, Lois. "What Does It Mean to Follow Jesus" in LS.

Christopherson, Dorothy. "Come and Pray With Me." ABI 029627.
U, pno.

Medema, Ken/arr. J. Schrader, adapt. Cora Scholz. "Lord, Listen to
Your Children." MFS YS 500. SSA, kybd.

KEYBOARD/INSTRUMENTAL

Powell, Robert A. "Postlude on 'Fredericktown'" in *Sent Forth: Short
Postludes for the Day.* AFP 11-10612. Org.

Reger, Max. "Aus Tiefer Not" in *Thirty Short Chorale Preludes.*
CFP 3980. Org.

HANDBELL

Wagner, Douglas E. "The Ash Grove." JEF JHS9072. 2 oct.

Waldrop, Tammy. "Give Me Jesus." Ringing Word RW 8111.
3-5 oct, vocal solo.

PRAISE ENSEMBLE

Howard, Tom. "How Lovely Is Your Dwelling Place" in *Praise Hymns
and Choruses,* 4th ed. MM.

Mengel, Dana. "Blest Are the Pure in Heart." CPH 98-3450.
SATB, kybd.

SUNDAY, OCTOBER 28
ST. SIMON AND ST. JUDE, APOSTLES

We know little about Simon and Jude. In New Testament lists of the apostles, Simon the "zealot" or Cananean is mentioned, but he is never mentioned apart from these lists. Jude, sometimes called Thaddeus, is also mentioned in lists of the twelve. At the last supper Jude asked Jesus why he had chosen to reveal himself to the disciples but not to the world. A traditional story about Simon and Jude says that they traveled together on a missionary journey to Persia and were both martyred there.

The prayer of the day for this lesser festival asks that as Simon and Jude "were faithful and zealous in their mission, so we may with ardent devotion make known the love and mercy of our Lord and Savior Jesus Christ."

WEDNESDAY, OCTOBER 31
REFORMATION DAY

See Reformation Sunday, October 28, 2001.

NOVEMBER

We can rest assured that God will do

what God has promised

IMAGES OF THE SEASON

Here now we approach the end of the year, the turning of the calendar. We look back over the past, we analyze the present, we gaze into the future as we turn from the old to the new. Even though in most aspects of our lives we may experience this

reflection near December 31, the turning and deepening for the church happen in November as we move through the last Sundays of the year and approach the newness of another Advent.

Some distinct differences, though, distinguish ways we experience December 31 from the ways we experience the turning of the liturgical year. Mostly, these differences have to do with the scope and the scale of things. We perhaps each look over our own life choices, our careers, relationships, and dreams as we turn to January 1. The church's view, however, is wider and deeper. The church's view here at the end of the year is bigger than all of us.

Our view as the church here in November stretches wide to take in the past, present, and future, not only of each of us who gather, but the past, present, and future of God's whole universe. The last Sunday of the church year epitomizes the cosmic scope of this season. On the festival of Christ the King we hear, "He is the image of the invisible God, the firstborn of all creation; for in him all things in heaven and on earth were created, things visible and invisible, whether thrones or dominions or rulers or powers—all things have been created through him and for him. He himself is before all things, and in him all things hold together" (Col. 1:15-17). All that has ever been or ever will be, all that God has done and will do, all the great mystery of God's plan is held before us in this time.

We will hear this month of Daniel's terrifying dreams and visions, the burning of God's coming day, dreadful portents and great signs and coming persecutions. We will hear of the four great winds of heaven, four great beasts arising from the sea, wars and insurrections, the temple falling down. Jesus' own mouth will ring out "Woe!" in our ears. Doubts and questions arise in our hearts as we contemplate the coming day of

the Lord. It is all very big. It is all very frightening. It is all much more than we can take on our own.

And yet, amazingly, these Sundays are not days of doom and doubt, but rather this season offers peace and comfort, hope and joy. We confront God's mysterious and awesome future and God's even more awesome promise to us in Jesus Christ. Our ears are filled with the promise of an inheritance that will transcend all destruction. In the midst of dreadful portents, God offers a sure and certain hope.

We will hear this month that "the holy ones of the Most High shall receive the kingdom and possess the kingdom forever—forever and ever" (Dan. 7:18), and we know that in Christ we are numbered among these holy ones. We hear Job's triumphant cry: "I know that my Redeemer lives, and that at the last he will stand upon the earth. [T]hen in my flesh I shall see God," and we too can rest assured that "at the last" we will gaze with our own eyes on God.

While the coming day of the Lord is burning like an oven, on that same day our burns will be soothed as "the sun of righteousness shall rise with healing in its wings" (Mal. 4:2a). Paul, knowing full well the fear felt even by believers as we contemplate the coming of the Lord, tells the folks at Thessalonica (and us) "not to be quickly shaken in mind or alarmed" and urges us all to "stand firm and hold fast" (2 Thess. 2:2, 15).

In these days at the end of the year, we are also assured that it is not our own holding fast that will bring peace at the last. Faced with fearful portents, persecutions, and destruction, we are not the ones who will bring healing and fulfill all hope. No, indeed, it is "our Lord Jesus Christ himself and God our Father, who loved us and through grace gave us eternal comfort and good hope" who will "comfort your hearts and strengthen them in every good work and hope" (2 Thess. 2:16-17). We can rest assured that God will do what God has promised.

The deep mystery of God's mighty promise is shown forth most clearly by the major festivals of this season, which stand like bookends at its beginning and end. All Saints Day and the festival of Christ the King both speak of the cosmic power of Christ Jesus, but both also show that this power works through weakness and finally through death. As hard as it is for us to comprehend, we know in faith that the same one who hung dying with thieves on the cross is the one who is now seated "far above all rule and authority and power and dominion and above every name that is named" (Eph. 1:21). On All Saints Day we hear of this triumphant one who rules "not only in this age but also in the age to come." On Christ the King we hear how this one died under the dominion of others, refusing to save himself. As we gather here at the turning of the year, we know again God's mighty actions, God's deeply hopeful plan, and how all has been won by Jesus' death on the cross.

ENVIRONMENT AND ART FOR THE SEASON

The days of harvest continue into November but diminish, and the nights are becoming noticeably longer than the day. In temperate latitudes the bright hues of harvest bounty give way to fields plowed under, russet and rust; barren branches, gray on gray. In coastal areas, times of cloud cover and rain begin. The life-giving sun is less prominent. Thoughts turn to endings—end of the growing season, end of life, end of time, end and fulfillment of all creation.

In November the ordinary days after Pentecost draw to a close with a wise and prayerful look at endings. Death and change dance in the wheel of time as rightly as birth and being. Winter is as much a part of the cycle of seasons as summer. Dry seasons and wet seasons go hand in hand. All are woven into the fabric of creation, exceedingly good, and in the last days of the church year, the gathered people lift up the fullness of life and give thanks.

All Saints Day is November 1, six months from May Day, festival of spring and beginnings. A yearly commemoration of All Saints was originally held about May 12 to 13, but Rome was overfilled with pilgrims for the observance each year, and food supplies quickly ran out so early in the year. In A.D. 835 the church changed the commemoration to November 1, when food and wine from the recent harvest would be plentiful. This change also placed All Saints at the dying of the year in northern climes, where it now falls in with many other festivals honoring the dead around the world: Chung Yüan in China, I Morti in Sicily, Dia de los Muertos in Mexico, Samhain in Celtic lands.

At All Saints the church remembers not only the great cloud of witness who have gone before, but also the faith these saints modeled and taught. The church remembers that all the baptized are called to be a holy people. It is a time to remember those who in the last twelve months have crossed over to the other side of death. It is a time to remember ancestors in the faith and to remember our responsibility as heirs.

A part of that remembering might be served by placing a beautifully bound book of the dead at the entry to the nave, so that those who enter may inscribe the names of the people whose lives they wish to commemorate. The book may then be carried into the church and placed on a stand near the baptismal font and paschal candle. If a book of the dead is not used, the large volumes in which parishes have historically recorded baptisms and deaths could be placed at the entry to the nave for viewing and remembering.

If All Saints Sunday is observed as a baptismal festival, the paschal candle would be lit on this festival. Traditionally, Jewish families light a *Jahrzeit* candle on the anniversary of a loved one's death. Perhaps *Jahrzeit* candles or votives could be provided for the families of those who have died in the last twelve months. In some traditions Christians light thin tapers in remembrance of the saints and place them upright in basins of sand.

The base of the paschal candle could be encircled by sprigs of rosemary, which has long symbolized memory. Rosemary and evergreens could also be tucked into arrangements of white and yellow chrysanthemums, associated with the dead in both Central America and the Orient. Sprays might include palm branches, or palms could be formed into green arches above the doorways, for from Revelation 7 comes the image, "After this I looked, and there was a great multitude, ... standing before the throne and before the Lamb, robed in white, with palm branches in their hands" (7:9). Palms and sheaves of wheat might be bound to the processional cross with white cord or ribbons.

White is the color for All Saints, for celebration and joy, and banners or hangings could be made of rich white fabric like damask, brocade, or velvet. One image fitting for a banner would be silver stars on a white field (Dan. 12:3 and Wisdom 3:7). Other symbols appropriate for the festival are palm branches, the book (in which the names of the righteous dead are written), the angel blowing the trumpet or carrying the seal, or the new Jerusalem.

If your congregation has preserved altar furnishings such as cross and candles, altar cloths, communion vessels, Bibles, altar books or vestments from earlier days in the congregation's life, All Saints might be a perfect day on which to use them as a visual connection to past generations of worshipers.

Some congregations toll a bell at the reading of the names of the year's dead. Such a bell should be a tower bell or a large handbell of a deep and resonant quality, to evoke the solemnity of such a moment in the liturgy.

For two Sundays the liturgical color returns to the green of ordinary days, but the greenery, the wheat, the vines, the wreaths may be left in place from All Saints, for these last days in the church year are infused with those same themes of harvest, last days, the eschaton, last matters.

Culminating the days after Pentecost, and providing a bridge into the coming Advent season, is the last Sunday of the church year, the Sunday of the fulfillment, or Christ the King Sunday. It is a time for calling to mind that God's desire for all is wholeness—wholeness in individual lives, wholeness in communities, wholeness in creation—and that wholeness has its center in the Christ who was, who is, who is to come.

White, for purity and gladness, returns as the color for Christ the King Sunday. Images for Christ the King are similar to those for Transfiguration and Ascension: Christ upon a cloud, holding the gospel book, descends as Alpha and Omega, first and last, beyond time, beyond space. Sometimes in religious paintings Christ is shown seated on a rainbow, sign of covenant, hands offered in a gesture of blessing.

Another banner or hanging could be crafted by employing a medieval idea. Christ was often portrayed receiving a model of a city, a way of showing Christ's sovereignty over everyday existence and superiority over all worldly institutions. For Christ the King Sunday, a stylized or outlined Christ figure flanked by sun and moon, A and Ω, could hold an outline of the town or city in which the parish is located, or one or two recognizable buildings. In Christ, the city, the church, and the person find true and ultimate wholeness.

The harvest of lives, of time, has reached its culmination in the parousia—the coming of Christ—into history, into the world, into the hearts of humans. The harvest elements of wheat, vines, and grasses give way in the natural world to bare branches and fewer hours of daylight. After Christ the King, the harvest decorations cede to evergreens, just as the days after Pentecost, ordinary days, cede to the coming of Advent, days of expectation, becoming, and hope. What the church celebrated as fulfillment it now prays for with heartfelt sighs, but more deeply. The people of God in Christ enter again the cycle of the church year as changed persons, different from how they stepped into Advent just one year before.

322

PREACHING WITH THE SEASON

We are heading toward the end of the liturgical year, and in this home stretch the focus on ultimate realities is intensified. In these days, lectionary texts push us to put things in the perspective of the long view, the really long view. What is life and death and existence and God all about? Time is short; let us cut to the chase—the culminating liturgical year seems to say. Now is the time for summing up and being clear.

This also happens to be the call and expectation of so many of those who are considering a return or a first entry into our churches in these days of spiritual longing. Those who are the potentially rechurching are sitting figuratively on the steps of the church, having been exiled or wounded in their churched past. And every now and then, they get up and go to the window of the church and look in and wonder, "Is it safe to come back in yet? Are they still dabbling in distracting questions [Luke 20, proper 27]? Are they still spending all their time on solemn assemblies and little on learning to do good [Isaiah 1, proper 26]? Are they still worshiping their beautiful building and spending all their money on fortifying it, even as it is becoming more devoid of people [Luke 21, proper 28]?"

These lingering folks are not quite ready to forsake the spiritual home of their youth, because they long for a home for their hungry minds and souls. They are the children of the last millennium who are charting a path into this new millennium. They have looked for food for their souls on the spirituality shelves of countless bookstores and have tried to fashion their own eclectic, even idiosyncratic brand of spiritual meaning. But the endeavor has been lonely, unsatisfying, unnourishing. So they are giving their old home another chance.

"Blessed are you who are hungry now, for you will be filled." On All Saints Day, we begin this journey, guided by the inheritance we have received through the witness of the saints who know about deep hunger of many kinds. Yet even while we look to the past, we are inheriting the future, lifting our vision to a far horizon through these texts. We conclude this year and this November journey with the words of Christ the King, "Truly I tell you, today you will be with me in Paradise." Not only are we inheriting the future, but it is a *new* future, a different future, one that extends far beyond even this new millennium and that invites us into a new way of living *now*.

Those who are gathered outside on our steps hear this message as good news, but do we as insiders and proclaimers hear it that way?

Whether we focus in this November's preaching on hungry minds and souls, inheriting the future, being called into a new future, or new royalty for new days, don't forget about our sisters and brothers gathered on our steps. Their location may be different from ours, but their longings are the same as all of ours, whether we be baptized, confirmed, affirmed, reaffirmed, or yet to be baptized in the faith. By their honesty about their location, they are our teachers in this season.

SHAPE of WORSHIP for the SEASON

BASIC SHAPE OF THE EUCHARISTIC RITE

- Confession and Forgiveness: see alternate worship text for November in *Sundays and Seasons*

GATHERING

- Greeting: see alternate worship text for November in *Sundays and Seasons*
- Omit the Kyrie during November (except on the festivals of All Saints and Christ the King)
- Use the hymn of praise throughout November (or use "This is the feast of victory" just for the festivals of All Saints and Christ the King)

WORD

- Use the Nicene Creed for the festivals of All Saints and Christ the King, use the Apostles' Creed for the remainder of the month
- The prayers: see alternate forms and responses for November in *Sundays and Seasons*
- Incorporate the names of those who have died into one of the prayer petitions on All Saints Sunday

BAPTISM

- Consider observing All Saints Sunday (November 4) as a baptismal festival

MEAL

- Offertory prayer: see alternate worship text for November in *Sundays and Seasons*

- Use the proper preface for Sundays after Pentecost; for the festival of All Saints, use the proper preface for All Saints; *WOV* Leaders Edition provides a proper preface for Christ the King
- Eucharistic prayer: in addition to four main options in *LBW*, see "Eucharistic Prayer I: November" in *WOV* Leaders edition, p. 73
- Invitation to communion: see alternate worship text for November in *Sundays and Seasons*
- Post-communion prayer: see alternate worship text for November in *Sundays and Seasons*

SENDING

- Benediction: see alternate worship text for November in *Sundays and Seasons*
- Dismissal: see alternate worship text for November in *Sundays and Seasons*

LECTIONARY OPPORTUNITY FOR HEALING SERVICE

- Christ the King on November 25 (gospel)

ASSEMBLY SONG FOR THE SEASON

At the end of October the gospel asked the question, "When the Son of Man comes, will he find faith on earth?" (Luke 18:8). The saints of every time and place teach us and show us what faith is. The assembly needs to sing the songs of faith, so that we may be sustained on the journey as we wait for Christ's final appearing.

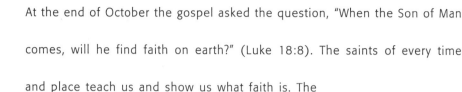

GATHERING

The Kyrie and hymn of praise are sung in the gathering rite on the festivals of All Saints Day and Christ the King. Either one of these alone is appropriate on the other two Sundays of November.

WORD

Between the two festivals the readings tell of the end times. But we need not fear persecution or our death for we know the end of the story: our redeemer lives and is the God of the living. Christ reigns and rules from the cross! Let many alleluias be sung this month. Link the alleluias that were sung with Easter psalmody to the psalmody of November. Do the same with the proper verse.

On All Saints Day use "For all the saints" (LBW 174) as the hymn of the day. Let the voices of choir, organ, cantors, and assembly alternate. Choose settings for these voices that are appropriate to the text.

MEAL

The standard canticle "Let the vineyards be fruitful" is appropriate as the offertory for this month. Also appropriate, especially on Christ the King Sunday, are "What feast of love" (WOV 701) or "The trumpets sound, the angels sing" (W&P 139).

"Holy, holy, holy Lord" (WOV 616a) and "Acclamations and Amen" (WOV 616b) are based on the tune LAND OF REST, "Jerusalem, my happy home" (LBW 331). Sing both of these on All Saints Day. If you have Orff instruments available, have the children accompany with ostinato patterns. Use a flute or other instrument to lead the tune.

"Santo" (LLC 225) as a Sanctus can be paired with "Cordero de Dios/O Lamb of God" (LLC 240) as an Agnus Dei. This music, sung very simply, can help to convey the surety of hope that we have in our living God and in victory over death.

SENDING

"Thank the Lord" is an appropriate post-communion canticle for the season. "Sing with all the saints in glory" (WOV 691), "Rejoice in God's saints" (WOV 689), and "Thine the amen, thine the praise" (WOV 801) are fitting sending hymns for All Saints Day. "Thine the amen, thine the praise" could also be used as a sending hymn for the month of November. Hymns with themes of harvest and general thanksgiving are also appropriate. Another hymn to consider is "Praised be the Rock" (TFF 290).

325

MUSIC FOR THE SEASON

VERSE AND OFFERTORY

Hillert, Richard. *Verses and Offertories (Lesser Festivals,* Vol. 1*).*
AFP 11-9542. U, org.

Hobby, Robert. "Offertory for All Saints Day." MSM-80-811.
2 pt, org.

Hobby, Robert. "Offertory for Day of Thanksgiving." MSM-80-600.
2 pt, org.

Hobby, Robert. "Offertory for the Transfiguration of Our Lord" (text
for Christ the King). MSM-80-225. Mxd vcs, hb, org.

Hobby, Robert. "Verse for All Saints Day." MSM-80-810. 2 pt, org.

Weber, Paul. "Praise the Name of the Lord" in *Oh, Sing to Our God.*
AFP 11-7544. U, org.

See also "Music for the Season" for Autumn.

CHORAL

Bainton, Edgar L. "And I Saw a New Heaven." NOV 29 0342 03.
SATB, org.

Bullard, Alan. "Come, Let Us Join Our Cheerful Songs." GIA G-4312.
SAB, org.

Candlyn, T. Frederick H. "King of Glory, King of Peace." HWG 2234.
SATB, org, S solo.

Compton, Michael. "The Promised Land." AFP 11-10732. SATB.

Holst, Gustav/arr. Paul Nicholson. "Jerusalem." AFP 11-10501. SATB,
org, tpt.

Martinson, Joel. "By All Your Saints." AFP 11-10300. 2 pt, org.

Weber, Paul. "I Will Sing the Story of Your Love." AFP 11-10839.
U/SATB, opt cong, org.

CHILDREN'S CHOIRS

Bedford, Michael. "Come Worship God This Holy Day."
CG CGA806. U, kybd, opt fl, opt tamb.

Christopherson, Dorothy. "God's Great Love." AFP 11-10421.
U (opt desc), cant, perc.

Christopherson, Dorothy. "O Praise the Lord, Hallelujah."
AFP 11-10550. U/2 pt, B flat cl, tamb, snare drm, pno 4 hands
(or pno and electronic kybd/glock.)

Davis, Katherine. "Let All Things Now Living." ECS 1819. U, desc,
pno.

Kosche, Kenneth T. "I Thank You, God." CG CGA651. U/2 pt, kybd.

Lindh, Jody W. "I Give You Thanks." CG CGA-561. U, pno, perc,
opt bass, opt synth.

Pote, Allen. "I Will Give Thanks." AFP 3-75001. SATB, pno, opt tpt.

KEYBOARD/INSTRUMENTAL

Augsburg Organ Library: November. AFP 11-11035. Org.

Fedak, Alfred V. *Fantasia on "St. Anne."* SEL 12-001. Org.

Fedak, Alfred V. *In Paradisum.* SEL 160-662. Org.

Martinson, Joel. *Rondeau Medievale.* CPH 97-6270. Org.

Schumann, Clara. *Prelude and Fugue, Op. 16, No. 3.* VIV 305. Org.

HANDBELL

Kinyon, Barbara B. "Glorious Things of Thee Are Spoken." AG 1774.
3-5 oct.

Klein, James. "Beautiful Savior." NMP HB-249. 2 oct.

Littleton, R. Lyndel. "Count Your Blessings." Ringing Word RW 8073.
3-5 oct.

Rogers, Sharon Elery. "Now Thankful People Come." AFP 11-10804.
2-3 oct.

PRAISE ENSEMBLE

Haas, David. "We Give You Thanks." GIA G-4973. U/SATB, solo,
kybd, opt cong, C inst, gtr, cello, hb.

Matsumura, Tom. "O That Will Be Glory." GS A-6270. SATB, kybd.

Smith, Michael W., and Fred Bock. "How Majestic Is Your Name."
FBM BG0488. SAB, kybd.

ALTERNATE WORSHIP TEXTS

CONFESSION AND FORGIVENESS

In the name of the Father, and of the ✚ Son,
and of the Holy Spirit.
Amen

In the presence of one another,
and before the church on earth and the hosts of heaven,
let us confess our sin and ask for God's boundless mercy.

Silence for reflection and self-examination.

Compassionate God,
we confess that we turn away
from whatever is true,
honorable, and pleasing to you.
Have mercy on us and forgive our sin.
Renew us and fill us with your love,
that we may walk in your ways,
to the glory of your holy name. Amen

God's steadfast love endures forever.
Through baptism into Christ your sin has been forgiven.
May the Spirit of hope strengthen you,
that you may know your glorious inheritance among God's saints.
Amen

GREETING

May the God of hope give you fullness of peace,
and may the Lord of life be with you all.
And also with you.

OFFERTORY PRAYER

God of our salvation,
all that we have comes from your hand.
We bring what you have already given us—
bread and wine for your table,
and gifts for the work of your kingdom.
Most of all we give you thanks
for your greatest gift to us
in Jesus Christ, our Lord. Amen

INVITATION TO COMMUNION

Blessed are all who hunger now,
for they shall be filled.

POST-COMMUNION PRAYER

God of the living,
you gather and shepherd your flock,
satisfying us with bread from heaven.
Sustain us through this meal
until the day of resurrection,
when we shall see you face to face;
in the name of our living redeemer, Jesus Christ.
Amen

BENEDICTION

May God who loves you,
and through the grace of Jesus Christ gives you good hope,
✚ bless you and comfort your hearts
by the power of the Holy Spirit.
Amen

DISMISSAL

Go in peace. Serve the Lord with gladness.
Thanks be to God.

327

SEASONAL RITES

VIGIL OF ALL SAINTS

This order of worship may be used on All Hallows Eve, October 31, or the evening before All Saints Sunday.

SERVICE OF LIGHT
PROCESSION
All stand as the lighted paschal candle is carried in procession to its stand in front of the assembly. The people may light handheld candles from its flame.

In the new Jerusalem there will be no need of | sun or moon,
for the glory of God will be its | light.
Before the Lamb is a multitude from | every nation,
and they worship God night and | day.
Surely he is | coming soon.
Amen. Come, Lord | Jesus.

HYMN OF LIGHT
As this hymn is sung, the candles on and near the altar are lighted from the flame of the paschal candle.

Joyous light of glory:
of the immortal Father;
heavenly, holy, blessed Jesus Christ.
We have come to the setting of the sun,
and we look to the evening light.
We sing to God, the Father, Son, and Holy Spirit:
You are worthy of being praised
with pure voices forever.
O Son of God, O Giver of light:
The universe proclaims your glory.

THANKSGIVING FOR LIGHT
The Lord be with you.
And also with you.
Let us give thanks to the Lord our God.
It is right to give our thanks and praise.
Blessed are you, O Lord our God, king of the universe,
who led your people Israel by a pillar of cloud by day
and a pillar of fire by night:
Enlighten our darkness by the light of your Christ;
may his Word be a lamp to our feet and a light to our path;
for you are merciful, and you love your whole creation,
and we, your creatures, glorify you, Father, Son, and Holy Spirit.
Amen

Sit

LITURGY OF THE WORD

FIRST READING
Genesis 12:1-8
Psalm 113

SECOND READING
Daniel 6:[1-15]16-23
Psalm 116

THIRD READING
Hebrews 11:32--12:2
Psalm 149

FOURTH READING
Revelation 7:2-4, 9-17

Stand
CANTICLE
This is the feast of victory

GOSPEL
Matthew 5:1-11

Sit
SERMON

Stand
HYMN OF THE DAY

THANKSGIVING FOR BAPTISM
If possible, the people may gather around the font. After the prayer each person may dip a hand in the water and make the sign of the cross in remembrance of baptism.

The Lord be with you.
And also with you.
Let us give thanks to the Lord our God.
It is right to give our thanks and praise.
Holy God and mighty Lord, we give you thanks,
for you nourish and sustain us and all living things
with the gift of water.
In the beginning your Spirit moved over the waters,
and you created heaven and earth.
By the waters of the flood you saved Noah and his family.
You led Israel through the sea out of slavery
into the promised land.

328

In the waters of the Jordan
your Son was baptized by John and anointed with the Spirit.
By the baptism of his death and resurrection
your Son set us free from sin and death
and opened the way to everlasting life.
We give you thanks, O God,
that you have given us new life in the water of baptism.
Buried with Christ in his death,
you raise us to share in his resurrection
by the power of the Holy Spirit.
Through it we are united to your saints
of every time and place
who proclaim your reign
and surround our steps as we journey
toward the new and eternal Jerusalem.
May all who have passed through the waters of baptism
continue in the risen life of our Savior.
To you be all honor and glory, now and forever.
Amen

Sit

LITURGY OF THE EUCHARIST

After all have returned to their places, the liturgy continues with the preparation of the altar and the presentation of the gifts.

NOTES ON THE SERVICE:

- The opening verses in the procession of the paschal candle may be sung using the musical setting found in LBW, p. 142.
- The hymn of light is found in LBW, p. 143. An alternate hymn is "O Light whose splendor thrills" (WOV 728).
- The thanksgiving for light (LBW, p. 144) may be sung or spoken by the leader.
- The psalm responses to the readings may be sung or spoken by the assembly.
- The canticle is sung using one of the available musical settings of this text.
- For the hymn of the day, one of the following hymns is suggested: "Sing with all the saints in glory" (WOV 691) or "Who is this host arrayed in white" (LBW 314).
- If the people cannot gather at the font, the worship leaders may process there during the singing of the hymn of the day.

THURSDAY, NOVEMBER 1
ALL SAINTS DAY

The custom of commemorating all of the saints of the church on a single day goes back at least to the third century. Our All Saints Day celebrates the baptized people of God, living and dead, who make up the body of Christ. Today, or on this upcoming All Saints Sunday, many congregations will remember the faithful who have died during the past year.

Our liturgy abounds with references to the saints and to our continual relationship with them. The preface for All Saints describes the relationship this way: "that moved by their witness and supported by their fellowship, we may run with perseverance the race that is set before us and with them receive the unfading crown of glory." Today and this week invite people to reflect on others—living and dead—who have moved and supported us in our lives of faith.

SATURDAY, NOVEMBER 3
MARTIN DE PORRES, RENEWER OF SOCIETY, 1639

Martin was the son of a Spanish knight and Ana Velázquez, a freed black slave from Panama. Martin apprenticed himself to a barber-surgeon in Lima, Peru, and was known for his work as a healer. Martin was a lay brother in the Order of Preachers (Dominicans) and engaged in many charitable works. He was a gardener as well as a counselor to those who sought him out. He was noted for his care of all the poor, regardless of race. His own religious community described him as the "father of charity." His work included the founding of an orphanage, a hospital, and a clinic for dogs and cats. He is recognized as an advocate for Christian charity and interracial justice.

NOVEMBER 4, 2001
ALL SAINTS SUNDAY

INTRODUCTION

"With the Church on earth and the hosts of heaven, we praise your name and join their unending hymn," proclaims the presiding minister in the eucharistic prayer. On the festival of All Saints we remember with thanksgiving those who have lived and died in the faith. They are the sign of our hope and an image of the glory we shall inherit. But even more, they are worshipers with us this day as we sing the praises of the God who brings life out of death.

PRAYER OF THE DAY

Almighty God, whose people are knit together in one holy Church, the body of Christ our Lord: Grant us grace to follow your blessed saints in lives of faith and commitment, and to know the inexpressible joys you have prepared for those who love you; through your Son, Jesus Christ our Lord, who lives and reigns with you and the Holy Spirit, one God, now and forever.

READINGS

Daniel 7:1-3, 15-18

During the second century before the birth of Jesus, the people of Israel suffered severe persecution at the hands of the Syrian king, Antiochus Epiphanes. The book of Daniel was written to support God's people during these dark and difficult days. His vision of the four beasts was meant to remind God's people that history was ultimately controlled by God and that this time of severe trial would pass.

Psalm 149

Sing the praise of the LORD in the congregation of the faithful. (Ps. 149:1)

Ephesians 1:11-23

After giving thanks for the faith of the Ephesians, Paul prays that they might also see the power of God, who has now enthroned Jesus as head of the church, which is his body.

Luke 6:20-31

Luke's recounting of Jesus' blessings and warnings suggest that God's standards and values may be quite different from those with which we are most familiar. They are the hallmark of the new life lived by God's saints.

COLOR   White

THE PRAYERS

Awaiting the fulfillment of God's reign, let us pray for the world, the church, and all people according to their needs.

A BRIEF SILENCE.

Loving God, inspire the leaders of all nations to put aside their hatred for old enemies and to see the possibilities for peace throughout the world. Lord, in your mercy,
hear our prayer.

Loving God, be with all of us as we proclaim your gospel of love and forgiveness for the world. Lord, in your mercy,
hear our prayer.

Loving God, continue to bless this congregation. Hear our songs of praise and thanksgiving for the saints of this congregation and your holy church. Lord, in your mercy,
hear our prayer.

Loving God, touch all our hearts, so that we may willingly share what we have with those in need. Lord, in your mercy,
hear our prayer.

Loving God, give comfort and reassurance to those who are grieving, hungry, lonely, or sick (especially...). Fill them with your love. Lord, in your mercy,
hear our prayer.

HERE OTHER INTERCESSIONS MAY BE OFFERED.

We give you thanks, loving God, for all your saints. Bind us to you until the day when all your faithful people will join in everlasting praise. Lord, in your mercy,
hear our prayer.

Hear our prayers, righteous God, as we await the coming of your great and glorious feast; through Christ, your beloved Son, our Messiah.
Amen

IMAGES FOR PREACHING

Have you ever seen a circular genealogical chart? Your name goes in the middle. One half of the chart holds your paternal ancestors, and the other half lists your maternal relatives. By the time you go out nine generations, your name is surrounded on the chart by 1022 people from whom you are directly descended. That is a

crowd much bigger than most of us find surrounding us in our churches on any Sunday. And the cloud of witnesses that we celebrate on this day is much bigger than that crowd of ancestors. When we sing the Sanctus, we can increase the volume on the organ, because we are singing with more than those we can see in the room. We are singing with "the church on earth and the hosts of heaven."

In many European countries on All Saints Day, cemeteries are filled with lit candles placed in front of every gravestone. On that night people go to cemeteries to soak up the light and to be reminded that we are surrounded by the light of those who have gone before us. "With the eyes of your heart enlightened, you may know what is the hope to which he has called you, what are the riches of his glorious inheritance among the saints..." (Eph. 1:18). We are surrounded by saints, famous and not so famous, dead and living.

The goodness that we see in the saints is different from the righteousness bestowed through Christ, for it is only God through Christ who can make us truly saints by forgiving sins. In other words, we are all made saints in baptism, and we exercise our sainthood by living out the gift of being forgiven. So look in the mirror. You will see not only a person shaped by generations of ancestral inheritance; you will see a person shaped by the glorious inheritance given to all the saints. You will see the face of a forgiven sinner and God's ability to make saints of us all.

WORSHIP MATTERS

How does the congregation remember those who have died since last All Saints Day? Many churches have the custom of including in the prayers of the people thanksgiving for those who have died . This list typically includes members of the congregation who have died in the past twelve months.

Worship leaders might consider extending an invitation to the congregation to include other family members, friends, and acquaintances who have died in the faith. For this purpose, a book with blank pages could be placed in an accessible place for one or two weeks prior to this day, so that people can write down the names of those whom they wish to have included in the prayers.

When the time comes for the names to be read on All Saints Sunday, the pastor(s) and assisting ministers may want to consider reading the names from the font. The connection between baptism and Christ's promise of eternal life would be reinforced by the visual image of the cleansing waters of rebirth.

LET THE CHILDREN COME

Oh, when the saints go marching in,
oh, when the saints go marching in,
O Lord, I want to be in that number
when the saints go marching in.

And on that hallelujah day,
and on that hallelujah day,
O Lord, I want to be in that number
on that hallelujah day.
African American spiritual

All Saints Sunday is a day to celebrate saints, baptized followers of Jesus both living and dead. Invite the children to come to the waters of the font and be marked with the sign of the cross. Help the children see God's claim on their lives through baptism.

MUSIC FOR WORSHIP

GATHERING

LBW 315   Love divine, all loves excelling
WOV 689   Rejoice in God's saints

PSALM 149

Cherwien, David. PW, Cycle C.

Hopson, Hal H. *Psalm Refrains and Tones.* HOP 425.

Hopson, Hal H. "Sing a New Song to the Lord." CG CGA 204. U, opt hb, kybd.

Wagner, Douglas. "Dance, Sing, Clap Your Hands." BEC BP1266. U, kybd.

Psalms for Praise and Worship: A Complete Liturgical Psalter. ABI.

HYMN OF THE DAY

LBW 369   The Church's one foundation
            Aurelia

VOCAL RESOURCES

Ferguson, John. "The Church's One Foundation." AFP 11-10965. SATB, org, brass qrt, opt cong.

Powell, Robert. "The Church's One Foundation." GIA G-2238. SATB, cong.

Schalk, Carl. "The Church's One Foundation." CPH 98-2344. SATB, 2 tr, org, opt cong. 98-2380 (inst pts).

INSTRUMENTAL RESOURCES

Albrecht, Timothy. "The Church's One Foundation" in *Grace Notes.* AFP 11-9925. Org.

Honoré, Jeffrey. "The Church's One Foundation" in *Classic Embellishments.* AFP 11-11005. Org, opt inst.

McChesney, Kevin. "The Church's One Foundation." AFP 11-10988. Hb.

Pelz, Walter L. "Aurelia" in *Hymn Settings for Organ and Brass, Set 1.* AFP 11-10184. Org, brass.

ALTERNATE HYMN OF THE DAY

LBW 175   Ye watchers and ye holy ones
WOV 764   Blest are they

COMMUNION

LBW 314   Who is this host arrayed in white
WOV 690   Shall we gather at the river

SENDING

LBW 553   Rejoice, O pilgrim throng!
WOV 691   Sing with all the saints in glory

ADDITIONAL HYMNS AND SONGS

ASG 14   Hallelujah! Sing to our God
H82 286   Who are these like stars appearing
TFF 174   Deep river
TFF 180   Oh, when the saints go marching in
W&P 22   Bring forth the kingdom

MUSIC FOR THE DAY

CHORAL

Bach, J. C. F. "In the Resurrection Glorious" in CC. SATB, org.

Bach, J. S. "O Jesus Christ, My Life, My Light" in BAS. SATB, org.

Bullock, Ernest. "Give Us the Wings of Faith." OXF 42.001. SATB, org.

Carr, Robert. "Blest Are the Pure in Heart." MSM 80-812. SATB, opt cong, org.

Kosche, Kenneth T. "Jerusalem, My Happy Home" in *Three American Hymn Tunes.* MSM 50-9830. SATB.

Shute, Linda Cable. "Who Are These Like Stars Appearing." AFP 11-10946. SATB, org.

Willan, Healey. "Te Deum laudamus." CPH 98-1126. SATB, org.

Wood, Dale. "O Fear the Lord, Ye His Saints." AFP 11-1486. SATB, org.

CHILDREN'S CHOIRS

Cool, Jayne Southwick. "Walk an Extra Mile." CG CGA-519. U, kybd, opt choral speaking.

Hassell, Michael. "I Sing a Song of the Saints of God." AFP 11-10945. 2 pt., pno, fl.

Peloquin, Alexander. "Gathering Song." GIA G-1947. U, org, perc.

Sleeth, Natalie. "In the Bulb There Is a Flower" in LS.

KEYBOARD/INSTRUMENTAL

Callahan, Charles. *Partita on "Laudate Dominum."* CPH 97-6768. Org.

Ferguson, John. "Behold a Host" in *Behold a Host.* AFP 11-5183. Org.

Hustad, Don "Jerusalem, My Happy Home" in *Early American Folk Hymns for Organ.* HOP 349. Org.

Kallman, Daniel. "Behold a Host" in *Two Hymns for Two Violins and Piano.* MSM 15-810. Pno, vln.

HANDBELL

Afdahl, Lee J. "Rejoice in God's Saints." AFP 11-10808. 3-5 oct, opt perc.

Garee, Betty B. "Sine Nomine." AGEHR AGC 021 (score), 46003 (4-6 oct), AGC 028 (choral).

Helman, Michael. "When the Saints Go Marching In." AGEHR AG35149. 3-5 oct.

PRAISE ENSEMBLE

Ducote, Darryl. "Beatitudes" in *Glory & Praise.* OCP.

Haas, David. "Blessed Are They." GIA G-2958. SAB, kybd, solo, opt cong, gtr, 2 C inst.

Young, Jeremy. "Eat This Bread, Drink This Cup." AFP 11-10651. U, kybd, opt cong.

NOVEMBER 4, 2001

333

TWENTY-SECOND SUNDAY AFTER PENTECOST
PROPER 26

INTRODUCTION

In today's gospel, Jesus invites himself to the home of a known sinner. This day God invites us into grace, even though we do not deserve it. "Today salvation has come to this house." Therefore, we always "enter God's courts with praise."

PRAYER OF THE DAY

Stir up, O Lord, the wills of your faithful people to seek more eagerly the help you offer, that, at the last, they may enjoy the fruit of salvation; through our Lord Jesus Christ.

READINGS

Isaiah 1:10-18

Isaiah announces God's displeasure with the offerings and sacrifices of a people who are sinful and without compassion. He pleads with Judah, the Southern Kingdom, to return to the Lord that they might be cleansed.

Psalm 32:1-8 (Psalm 32:1-7 [NRSV])

All the faithful will make their prayers to you in time of trouble. (Ps. 32:7)

2 Thessalonians 1:1-4, 11-12

The letters of Paul typically begin with a salutation, a blessing, and a few words of praise for what God is accomplishing among the recipients. By remaining faithful and growing spiritually during hardship, the Thessalonian Christians have become witnesses to the glory of God.

Luke 19:1-10

The story of Jesus and Zacchaeus illustrates well the central theme of Luke's gospel: Jesus is the Savior of all, especially those whom others reject.

ALTERNATE FIRST READING/PSALM

Habakkuk 1:1-4; 2:1-4

The injustices of the Judean king and the violence of the Chaldeans (Babylonians) move this prophet to write during the years leading up to the Babylonian exile of Judah. The central issue for the prophet is: How can a good and all-powerful God see evil in the world and seemingly remain indifferent?

Psalm 119:137-144

Grant me understanding, that I may live. (Ps. 119:144)

COLOR Green

THE PRAYERS

Awaiting the fulfillment of God's reign, let us pray for the world, the church, and all people according to their needs.

A BRIEF SILENCE.

For the people of all nations, that together we will put aside our differences and seek justice, rescue the oppressed, defend the orphan, and plead for the widow. Lord, in your mercy,

hear our prayer.

For those who are isolated, afraid, or suffering in body, mind, or spirit (especially...), that they will be comforted and made whole. Lord, in your mercy,

hear our prayer.

For the people of this congregation, that we will welcome Jesus into our homes and lives. Lord, in your mercy,

hear our prayer.

For God's forgiveness for those times when we have been quick to judge someone else as unworthy or sinful. Lord, in your mercy,

hear our prayer.

For the leaders of our church, that we will be open to their guidance and counsel. Lord, in your mercy,

hear our prayer.

HERE OTHER INTERCESSIONS MAY BE OFFERED.

We give you thanks, loving God, for all your saints. Bind us to you as we anticipate the day when all your faithful people will join in everlasting praise. Lord, in your mercy,

hear our prayer.

Hear our prayers, righteous God, as we await the coming of your great and glorious feast; through Christ, your beloved Son, our Messiah.

Amen

IMAGES FOR PREACHING

The prophet Isaiah tells us that the Lord cries out about our solemn assemblies. Surely these words were not only for the people of Israel. Our appointed festivals have become a burden to many who long for justice. Certainly this indictment is also a word for some of our religious assemblies. But we might ponder what other assemblies are devoid of justice. We live in countries where we have the right to assemble. Yet do we vote in order to choose those who will assemble on our behalf? In the United States, this time of year often brings an election. Perhaps this year it is a local election. How can we expect others to assemble on our behalf if we do not "seek justice, rescue the oppressed, defend the orphan, plead for the widow" through our right to vote? The Lord calls to us, in frustration and love: "Come now, let us argue it out..." (the RSV says "reason together").

It is as if Jesus is calling to Zacchaeus: "Hurry and come down." Jesus wanted Zacchaeus to quit observing only from a safe distance. Zacchaeus happily came down but still protected himself with his armor of money, responding to Jesus in terms of what preoccupied him. Jesus responded by calling him a son of Abraham, which moved Zacchaeus beyond his one-dimensional self-understanding into the perspective of eternity.

We are called to be more than observers and talkers. We are more than our money or our solemn assemblies or our political apathy. Jesus did not give up on Zacchaeus, and God did not give up on Israel. "Though your sins are like scarlet, they shall be like snow..." (Isa. 1:18). Surely, change will follow such mercy!

WORSHIP MATTERS

When we gather with those who are dear to us for a special meal, we want every detail of the meal to reflect its significance and importance. Perhaps we place the finest linens on the table and add candles to give a warm, inviting glow. Flowers may add to the special nature of the event, giving the eye something pleasant to gaze at while filling the nose with scent. Dishes are sparkling clean, as are glasses and utensils. Each piece is carefully laid out upon the table. The fellowship of the meal is what is most important, but attention to detail makes the experience even more enjoyable.

At the Lord's meal, all of God's family come together for fellowship and to receive forgiveness. The special nature of this event should be reflected by the care given to the preparation for the celebration.

LET THE CHILDREN COME

Jesus shared meals with people so they might come to know who Jesus is and what his will is for them. The communion meal is also for those who are lost, for those whom Jesus is seeking. Make available written instructions for making communion bread. Use recipes that are easy, so young children may be involved in the preparation. Have children bring the bread forward during the offertory. As Jesus eats a meal with Zacchaeus, so he graces our table with his presence.

MUSIC FOR WORSHIP

GATHERING

| LBW 499 | Come, thou Fount of every blessing |
| WOV 720 | In the presence of your people |

PSALM 32

Cherwien, David. PW, Cycle C.

Haas, David. "God, I Confess My Wrong" in PCY, vol. 9.

Howard, Julie. Sing for Joy: Psalm Settings for God's Children. LTP.

Stewart, Roy James. "I Turn to You, Lord" in PCY, vol. 5.

See Fourth Sunday in Lent and proper 6.

HYMN OF THE DAY

| LBW 312 | Once he came in blessing |
| | GOTTES SOHN IST KOMMEN |

VOCAL RESOURCES

Gieseke, Richard. "Once He Came in Blessing." CPH 98-2769. SAB.

INSTRUMENTAL RESOURCES

Burkhardt, Michael. "Gottes Sohn ist kommen" in Five Advent Hymn Improvisations, Set 1. MSM 10-004. Org.

Leavitt, John. "Gottes Sohn ist kommen" in Christmas Suite. AFP 11-10857. Org.

Meyer, Edward. "Gottes Sohn ist kommen" in Easy Hymn Accompaniments for Organ or Piano. CPH 97-6608. Kybd or org.

ALTERNATE HYMN OF THE DAY

| LBW 297 | Salvation unto us has come |
| WOV 793 | Shout for joy loud and long |

COMMUNION

| LBW 304 | Today your mercy calls us |
| WOV 706 | Eat this bread, drink this cup |

SENDING

| LBW 259 | Lord, dismiss us with your blessing |
| WOV 778 | O Christ the same |

ADDITIONAL HYMNS AND SONGS

TFF 150	Pass me not, O gentle Savior
TFF 184	Wonderful grace of Jesus
W&P 38	For by grace
W&P 160	You are my hiding place

MUSIC FOR THE DAY

CHORAL

Distler, Hugo. "Salvation unto Us Has Come" in CC. SATB.

Near, Gerald. "The Best of Rooms." AUR (MSM) AE7.

O'Brien, Francis Patrick. "To the Poor a Lasting Treasure." GIA G-4523. SATB, cong, gtr, kybd, C inst, opt str qrt.

Ratcliff, Cary. "Come to the Waters." KAL K-03. SATB, kybd.

Unruh, Eric W. "Kyrie eleison." AFP 11-10847. SAB, pno.

CHILDREN'S CHOIRS

African American spiritual. "I Want Jesus to Walk with Me" in LS. AFP 11-10939.

Leaf, Robert. "Come on Down, Zacchaeus." AFP 11-1654. U, pno, opt tamb, opt autoharp.

Weber, Paul D. "Psalm 32." AFP 11-0682. SST/SAB, opt cong, org.

KEYBOARD/INSTRUMENTAL

Buxtehude, Dietrich. "Praeludium" in Sämtliche Orgelwerke, Band I. BRE 6661. Org.

Kohrs, Jonathan. "Mississippi" in Four Tunes for Piano and Instruments. AFP 11-11011. Pno, 2 inst.

Sedio, Mark. "Today Your Mercy Calls Us" in How Blessed Is This Place. AFP 11-10934. Org.

HANDBELL

Sherman, Arnold B. "Our Great Redeemer's Praise." RRM HB0018. 3-5 oct.

Waits, Daniel. "Praise Almightily." AGEHR AG2015. 2 oct.

PRAISE ENSEMBLE

Carter, John, and Mary Kay Beall. "Love Like a Winter Rose." BEC BP1139. SATB, kybd.

Chapman, Morris. "Christ in Us Be Glorified" in Praise Hymns and Choruses, 4th ed. MAR.

Medema, Ken. "Come, Let Us Reason" in Renew. HOP.

Ragsdale, Steve. "Hide Me in Your Holiness" in Praise Hymns and Choruses, 4th ed. MAR.

335

WEDNESDAY, NOVEMBER 7

JOHN CHRISTIAN FREDERICK HEYER,
MISSIONARY TO INDIA, 1873

Heyer was the first missionary sent out by American Lutherans. He was born in Germany and came to the United States after his confirmation. He was ordained in 1820, established Sunday schools, and taught at Gettysburg College and Seminary. Heyer became a missionary in the Andhra region of India. During a break in his mission work he received the M.D. degree from what would later be Johns Hopkins University. He later served as chaplain of the Lutheran seminary at Philadelphia until his death.

Because of his work as a pastor, missionary, and medical doctor, his commemoration can lead us to be mindful of all who work for healing of both body and spirit.

NOVEMBER 11, 2001

TWENTY-THIRD SUNDAY AFTER PENTECOST

PROPER 27

INTRODUCTION

In these final weeks of the liturgical year, the church cries out, "Come, Lord Jesus!" We are always awaiting God's coming, and God does not disappoint us, making the divine presence known in water, bread, wine, and in this very human community of faith.

The church celebrates two people of faith who died on this date: Bishop Martin of Tours in 397, and Søren Kierkegaard in 1855. Martin helped Christianity come to rural France, and Kierkegaard in his philosophical writings helped to introduce the Christian faith to the modern era.

PRAYER OF THE DAY

Lord, when the day of wrath comes we have no hope except in your grace. Make us so to watch for the last days that the consummation of our hope may be the joy of the marriage feast of your Son, Jesus Christ our Lord.

READINGS

Job 19:23-27a

The dialogues of this book present Job in the midst of a tormenting problem. Job suffers the loss of family, physical health, and understanding friends yet knows himself to be innocent. Here, in the midst of his suffering, Job clings to the hope that one day he will be vindicated.

Psalm 17:1-9

Keep me as the apple of your eye; hide me under the shadow of your wings. (Ps. 17:8)

2 Thessalonians 2:1-5, 13-17

Paul writes to encourage the church at Thessalonica in a time of confusion and opposition. Here, the confusion concerned the return of Christ. Paul encourages those who had quit their jobs in anticipation of Jesus' imminent return to go back to work, secure in the salvation that is theirs in the gospel of God's grace.

Luke 20:27-38

The Sadducees, who do not believe in the resurrection of the dead, try to trap Jesus. They ask him about the marital status of a resurrected woman who had been married to a succession of seven brothers. The real issue, says Jesus, is not "Whose wife is she?" but rather "What is your relationship with God?"

ALTERNATE FIRST READING/PSALM

Haggai 1:15b—2:9

When Cyrus the Great defeated the Babylonians, his decree that exiles might return to Jerusalem and rebuild their temple brought an end to their homelessness. Upon returning, however, the people were more interested in rebuilding their own homes. The rebuilt temple paled in comparison with that of Solomon's. Haggai's message of encouragement and promise of future splendor invigorated the people and their leaders, Zerubbabel and Joshua.

Psalm 98

In righteousness shall the LORD judge the world. (Ps. 98:10)

COLOR   Green

THE PRAYERS

Awaiting the fulfillment of God's reign, let us pray for the world, the church, and all people according to their needs.
A BRIEF SILENCE.

For your holy church and all our leaders, that sanctified by the Spirit, we may proclaim the good news to the glory of Jesus Christ. Lord, in your mercy,

hear our prayer.

For the people of all nations, that in remembering those who have died in war, we may recommit ourselves to the cause of peace. Lord, in your mercy,

hear our prayer.

For all people who are in poverty or who are victims of violence, that you may protect them under your wings and give them shelter. Lord, in your mercy,

hear our prayer.

For those caught in doubt, despair, fear, or illness (especially...), that your steadfast love may break into their lives and give them comfort. Lord, in your mercy,

hear our prayer.

For each of us, that in knowing we are precious in your eyes, we may humbly serve all your creation. Lord, in your mercy,

hear our prayer.

HERE OTHER INTERCESSIONS MAY BE OFFERED.

Together with Martin of Tours, Søren Kierkegaard, and

all the faithful departed, welcome us to our place at the marriage supper of the Lamb. Lord, in your mercy,
hear our prayer.

Hear our prayers, righteous God, as we await the coming of your great and glorious feast; through Christ, your beloved Son, our Messiah.
Amen

IMAGES FOR PREACHING

The Sadducees tried to entangle Jesus with their questions. These cool interrogators wanted to make a case against the belief in the resurrection. It was a safe philosophical debate, and it enabled them to keep Jesus at a distance. They were most comfortable engaging in the kind of argument that kept them from getting emotionally involved in a life-changing way.

Do some of our congregational and denominational debates serve the same purpose, whether consciously or unconsciously, as we fill agendas and meetings with entanglements that keep us safely distant from the claims and calling of Jesus? Some truth can be pursued through debate, and some truth is available to us only through engagement, commitment, and risk.

Jesus reminds us here that God is God not of the dead but of the living. We are resurrected people, into eternity and also now. Dare we live like it? Dare we let go of debates and discussions that we think we can control and allow the gospel of Jesus Christ to make a claim on us, even to change us? "Now may our Lord Jesus Christ himself and God our Father, who loved us and through grace gave us eternal comfort and good hope, comfort your hearts and strengthen them in every good work and word" (2 Thess. 2:16-17).

WORSHIP MATTERS

What is the most commonly used method of communion distribution in your congregation? Some congregations commune by tables. Others offer a continuous communion. Some have seen the value and meaning of both and have adopted a rotating system of distribution.

Whichever method you use, an explanation of the method should be given and its significance or symbolism pointed out. For example, it is appropriate to stand for distribution during Easter, as standing is a more joyful posture than kneeling and reflects the nature of the season. Kneeling at tables might be better used in the reflective seasons of the year, such as Advent and Lent. Tables remind us of the meal aspect of the sacrament, while continuous communion can be illustrative of the unity of the Lord's supper.

LET THE CHILDREN COME

Children wonder where and how big heaven is. They ask if pets are there. Yet they trust that God is in heaven preparing a place for them. Marie Sundet, in her book *Come Right In—You're Home,* writes that "when we die on earth God will say 'Come right in. You're home.'" She makes the connection between baptismal adoption and eternal life with God. Help the children learn that by his death and resurrection Jesus has "set [them] free from the bondage to sin and death and has opened the way to the joy and freedom of everlasting life" (*LBW,* p. 122).

MUSIC FOR WORSHIP

GATHERING

LBW 331	Jerusalem, my happy home
WOV 742	Come, we that love the Lord

PSALM 17

Cherwien, David. *PW,* Cycle C.

Haas, David. "I Call to You, God" in PCY, vol. 8.

Honoré, Jeffrey. "Lord, Bend Your Ear" in *Sing Out! A Children's Psalter.* WLP.

Kogut, Malcolm. "Lord, When Your Glory Appears" in PCY, vol. 10.

Stewart, Roy James. "Lord, When Your Glory Appears" in PCY, vol. 5.

HYMN OF THE DAY

LBW 352	I know that my Redeemer lives!
	DUKE STREET

VOCAL RESOURCES

Beck, Theodore. "I Know That My Redeemer Lives." MSM 60-4000. SATB or SAB, 3 tpt, org, cong.

Behnke, John. "I Know That My Redeemer Lives." CPH 98-3197. SAB, cong, opt inst.

Bunjes, Paul. "I Know That My Redeemer Lives." CPH 98-2933. SATB, tpt, cong.

Hopson, Hal H. "I Know that My Redeemer Lives." GIA G-2344. SATB, cong, acc.

INSTRUMENTAL RESOURCES

Albrecht, Mark. "Duke Street" in *Festive Processionals.* AFP 11-10930. Org, tpt.

Albrecht, Timothy. "Duke Street" in *Grace Notes V.* AFP 11-10764. Org

Leavitt, John. "Duke Street" in *A Little Easter Suite*. CPH 97-6646. Org.

Rose, Richard. "Duke Street" in *Hymnal Companion for Woodwinds, Brass, and Percussion, Series 1*. Inst.

Sherman, Arnold. "Jesus Shall Reign." AG 1708. Hb.

ALTERNATE HYMN OF THE DAY

| LBW 340 | Jesus Christ, my sure defense |
| WOV 691 | Sing with all the saints in glory |

COMMUNION

| LBW 200 | For the bread which you have broken |
| WOV 702 | I am the Bread of life |

SENDING

| LBW 337 | Oh, what their joy |
| WOV 801 | Thine the amen, thine the praise |

ADDITIONAL HYMNS AND SONGS

LW 421	In God, my faithful God
TFF 181	To go to heaven
TFF 272	To God be the glory
W&P 131	Stand in the congregation
W&P 140	There is a Redeemer

MUSIC FOR THE DAY

CHORAL

Bach, J. C. F. "In the Resurrection Glorious" in CC. SATB, org.

Dressler, Gallus. "I Am the Resurrection" in CC. SATB.

Schulz-Widmar, Russell. "Jerusalem, Jerusalem." AFP 11-10646. 2 pt, org.

Schulz-Widmar, Russell. "Song of the Advents." AFP 11-10947. SAB or SATB, kybd.

Schütz, Heinrich. "We Offer Our Thanks and Praise" in CC SATB.

Svedlund, Karl-Erik. "There'll Be Something in Heaven." AFP 12-113. SATB.

Tyler, Edward. "St. Teresa's Bookmark." AFP 11-10964. SSATBB

CHILDREN'S CHOIRS

Kosche, Kenneth T. "Keep Me as the Apple of Your Eye." CG CGA800. U/2 pt, kybd.

Marshall, Jane. "Psalm 17" in *Psalms Together*. CG CGC-18. U, cong, kybd.

Riehle, Kevin R. "Song for Beginnings." CG CGA-493. U, opt desc, org.

KEYBOARD/INSTRUMENTAL

Albinoni, Thomaso/arr. S. Drummond Wolff. *Adagio in G Minor*. CPH 97-5779. Org.

Biery, James. "Thine" in *Tree of Life*. AFP 11-10701. Org.

Uehlein, Christopher. "Jesus, Thou Art Coming" in *Organ Music for the Seasons*, vol. 2. AFP 11-11010. Org.

HANDBELL

Afdahl, Lee J. "Thaxted." AFP 11-10982. 3 or 5 oct, opt brass, opt timp.

Mathis, William H. "Brother James' Air." SMP 20/1165 S (3 oct), 20/1166 S (4-5 oct).

PRAISE ENSEMBLE

Cook, Jerry. "The Lord Liveth" in *Praise & Worship*. MAR.

Dufford, Bob. "Songs of the Angels" in *Glory & Praise*. OCP.

Mullins, Rich, and Steven V. Taylor. "Awesome God." WRD 301 0468 164. SAB, kybd, opt gtr, electric bass, drms.

Ragsdale, Steve. "Hide Me in Your Holiness" in *Praise Hymns and Choruses*, 4th ed. MAR.

SUNDAY, NOVEMBER 11

MARTIN, BISHOP OF TOURS, 397

Martin's pagan father enlisted him in the army at age fifteen. One winter day, a beggar approached Martin for aid, and he cut his cloak in half and gave a portion to the beggar. Later, Martin understood that he had seen the presence of Christ in that beggar, and this ended his uncertainty about Christianity. He soon asked for his release from his military duties, but he was imprisoned instead. After his release from prison he began preaching, particularly against the Arians. In 371 he was elected bishop of Tours. As bishop he developed a reputation for intervening on behalf of prisoners and heretics who had been sentenced to death.

Today, at the same time as we remember this soldier turned peacemaker, we remember the end of World War I and veterans of all U.S. wars. Let these commemorations together move us to pray and work for peace in our families, congregations, and nation.

SUNDAY, NOVEMBER 11
SØREN AABYE KIERKEGAARD, TEACHER, 1855

Kierkegaard, a nineteenth-century Danish theologian whose writings reflect his Lutheran heritage, was the founder of modern existentialism. Though he was engaged to a woman he deeply loved, he ended the relationship because he believed he was called to search the hidden side of life. Many of his works were published under a variety of names, so that he could reply to arguments from his own previous works. Kierkegaard's work attacked the established church of his day. He attacked the church's complacency, its tendency to intellectualize faith, and its desire to be accepted by polite society.

Kierkegaard's work makes room for doubt in the life of faith. He also served as a prophetic challenge to churches that may want to set aside paradox for an easy faith and the gospel for cultural acceptability.

SATURDAY, NOVEMBER 17
ELIZABETH OF THURINGIA, PRINCESS OF HUNGARY, 1231

This Hungarian princess gave away large sums of money, including her dowry, for relief of the poor and sick. She founded hospitals, cared for orphans, and used the royal food supplies to feed the hungry. Though she had the support of her husband, her generosity and charity did not earn her friends within the royal court. At the death of her husband, she was driven out. She joined a Franciscan order and continued her charitable work, though she suffered abuse at the hands of her confessor and spiritual guide. Her lifetime of charity is particularly remarkable when one remembers that she died at the age of twenty-four. She founded two hospitals and many more are named for her.

339

NOVEMBER 18, 2001

TWENTY-FOURTH SUNDAY AFTER PENTECOST
PROPER 28

INTRODUCTION

Signs of the end time fill today's gospel. Christ will come again "to judge the living and the dead," we confess in the creed. How, then, shall we live, knowing that everything around us will one day pass away? We can live with hope if we know that history is heading toward the God who loves us. Yet we also live in the present moment ready for action, making the most of the time given to us as a gift.

PRAYER OF THE DAY

Lord God, so rule and govern our hearts and minds by your Holy Spirit that, always keeping in mind the end of all things and the day of judgment, we may be stirred up to holiness of life here and may live with you forever in the world to come, through your Son, Jesus Christ our Lord.
or

Almighty and ever-living God, before the earth was formed and even after it ceases to be, you are God. Break into our short span of life and let us see the signs of your final will and purpose, through your Son, Jesus Christ our Lord.

READINGS

Malachi 4:1-2a

Malachi, whose name means "my messenger," warns that the day of the Lord is coming and that it will bring doom to the evil but vindication to those who fear God.

Psalm 98

In righteousness shall the LORD judge the world. (Ps. 98:10)

2 Thessalonians 3:6-13

Some members of the community, because of their belief in the nearness of Christ's return, had ceased to work, preferring to live on the generosity of other members of the community. Paul warns them that if they want to eat, they need to work.

Luke 21:5-19

Luke's presentation of Jesus' teaching about the last days emphasizes the necessity for responsible behavior in the time between Jesus' ascension and the second coming.

ALTERNATE FIRST READING/PSALM

Isaiah 65:17-25

Isaiah 56–66 addresses the exiles who have returned to Jerusalem from exile in Babylon. The conditions in Jerusalem were discouraging, and the people were disillusioned. Into this gloomy situation the prophet proclaims a joyful message about a world fashioned in the designs of God's peace.

Isaiah 12

In your midst is the Holy One of Israel. (Is. 12:6)

COLOR Green

THE PRAYERS

Awaiting the fulfillment of God's reign, let us pray for the world, the church, and all people according to their needs.

A BRIEF SILENCE.

That all members of the body of Christ will proclaim the gospel boldly and without fear. Lord, in your mercy,

hear our prayer.

That leaders of all nations will not accept war as a way to resolve differences, but will work for peaceful solutions. Lord, in your mercy,

hear our prayer.

That we will have the courage to testify to our faith amid the hostilities of our world. Lord, in your mercy,

hear our prayer.

That those in pain and those who are sick (especially...) will find comfort and healing in your presence. Lord, in your mercy,

hear our prayer.

HERE OTHER INTERCESSIONS MAY BE OFFERED.

That we, with all the faithful departed, will share the fullness of God's victory in paradise. Lord, in your mercy,

hear our prayer.

Hear our prayers, righteous God, as we await the coming of your great and glorious feast; through Christ, your beloved Son, our Messiah.

Amen

IMAGES FOR PREACHING

Remember the end-time fever of 1999? Some Christians were sure that the end would arrive at the turning of the millennium. They pointed to scripture and the wars and insurrections, earthquakes, famines, and signs from heaven that filled our days. Now, in 2001, our days are not all that different, and we are still reading the same scripture passages. So, what shall we do now?

Those who teach our organizations about leadership development and change management advise us not to become complacent. Perhaps they have read today's passage from Luke, for Jesus cautions about admiring our churches too much. He tells us that many will want to predict the nearness of the end. We will be given signs, but we will also be afforded opportunities to give testimony. In other words, we cannot rest on the witness of those who have gone before us or on the greatness of their houses of worship.

We live in a time of continued upheavals of all sorts, which affect our values, societal structures, and spiritual communities in a time of materialistic idolatry. Our own witness and ability to build up the community of faith is needed, along with our courage to withstand persecution and attacks that threaten to shake the foundations of our faith and the future of the church. Our witness is needed, but we are not responsible to make the future come out right. That task is in God's hands. Our call is to bold faithfulness and bold testimony.

WORSHIP MATTERS

We do not know what the future will bring. We know who holds the future. We can live confidently today because our future is secure in God's wide embrace. In the rite of Holy Baptism in *LBW*, we are asked to "Let your light so shine before others that they may see your good works and glorify your Father in heaven." How does your congregation provide opportunities for that light to shine?

LET THE CHILDREN COME

Children have a natural curiosity, and for them to stand at the font on the day of a baptism is an excellent way for them to experience the sacrament of baptism. The presider might consider making baptism the focus on that day, explaining the significance of the sacrament and reminding everyone present that they too have been welcomed by God in this way. Children surrounding the font would further remind all present that each one of us is a part of God's family.

MUSIC FOR WORSHIP
GATHERING

| LBW 355 | Through the night of doubt and sorrow |
| WOV 782 | All my hope on God is founded |

PSALM 98

Cherwien, David. PW, Cycle C.

Haugen, Marty, and David Haas. "All the Ends of the Earth" in PCY.

Howard, Julie. *Sing for Joy: Psalm Settings for God's Children.* LTP.

Marshall, Jane. "Psalm 98." CG CGA-427. U, kybd.

Proulx, Richard. "The Lord Has Revealed to the Nations." GIA G-2306.

Smith, Timothy R. "The Lord Has Revealed" in STP, vol. 4.

HYMN OF THE DAY

| LBW 321 | The day is surely drawing near |
| | ES IST GEWISSLICH |

VOCAL RESOURCES

Beck, Theodore. "The Day Is Surely Drawing Near." CPH 98-2641. SATB, cong, opt tpt.

INSTRUMENTAL RESOURCES

Janson, P. "The Day Is Surely Drawing Near" in *Organ Music for the Seasons.* AFP 11-10859. Org.

Reger, Max. "Es ist gewisslich" in *Thirty Short Chorale Preludes, Op. 135a.* CFP 3980. Org.

ALTERNATE HYMN OF THE DAY

| LBW 418 | Judge eternal, throned in splendor |
| WOV 736 | By gracious powers |

COMMUNION

| LBW 198 | Let all mortal flesh keep silence |
| WOV 746 | Day by day |

SENDING

| LBW 332 | Mine eyes have seen the glory |
| WOV 762 | O day of peace |

ADDITIONAL HYMNS AND SONGS

H82 601	O day of God, draw near
TFF 194	When peace, like a river
TFF 198	When the storms of life are raging
W&P 17	Beauty for brokenness
W&P 73	I will sing, I will sing

MUSIC FOR THE DAY
CHORAL

Bach, J. S. "Lord, Thee I Love with All My Heart" in BAS. SATB, opt kybd.

Cherwien, David. "In Heavenly Love Abiding." CPH 98-3482. SATB, pno, opt fl.

Ferguson, John. "The Church's One Foundation." AFP 11-10965. SATB, org, brass qrt, opt cong.

Manz, Paul. "E'en So, Lord Jesus, Quickly Come." CPH 98-1054.

Owens, Sam Batt. "Sing to the Lord." GIA G-4714. U, cong, org, opt hb, opt desc.

Schütz, Heinrich. "Is God for Us." AFP 12-204920. SATB, kybd.

———. "Sing to the Lord" in CC. SATB.

White, David Ashley. "When Peace, Like a River." AFP 11-10575. SATB, kybd.

CHILDREN'S CHOIRS

Bach, J. S./arr. Hal H. Hopson. "With Songs of Rejoicing." CFI CM8086. 2 pt mxd, kybd/org.

Bedford, Michael. "Cantate Domino." CG CGA689. U/2 pt, kybd.

Traditional. "I've Got Peace Like a River" in LS.

KEYBOARD/INSTRUMENTAL

Couperin, François. "Elevation/Tierce en Taille" in *Two Masses for Organ.* DOV. Org.

Haan, Raymond A. "Prelude on 'Rhuddlan'" in *Welsh Hymn Tune Preludes.* SMP KK426. Org.

Pelz, Walter. "Triptych on 'Lord, Keep Us Steadfast in Your Word.'" MSM-10-808. Org.

Handbell

Hall, Jefferey A. "I Am the Bread of Life." CPH 97-6659. 3-5 oct, opt hc.

Kinyon, Barbara. "Lead on, O King Eternal." AG 1409. 2-3 oct.

McKechnie, Linda. "Lord, I Lift Your Name on High." AG 1977. 3-5 oct.

PRAISE ENSEMBLE

Haas, David. "God Has Done Marvelous Things" in W&P.

Kogut, Malcolm. "Lord, in Your Great Love." GIA G-5001. SATB, solo, kybd, opt cong, gtr.

Smith, Tim. "Our God Is Lifted Up" in *Come & Worship.* INT.

341

NOVEMBER 22, 2001

DAY OF THANKSGIVING (U.S.A.)

INTRODUCTION

One of the names for holy communion is *eucharist*. It comes from a Greek word meaning "to give thanks." Food and thanksgiving always go together, for life is a precious gift from God. Every meal, every harvest, is an occasion for giving thanks and for acknowledging that all God's gifts are on loan for us to use in acts of praise.

PRAYER OF THE DAY

Almighty God our Father, your generous goodness comes to us new every day. By the work of your Spirit lead us to acknowledge your goodness, give thanks for your benefits, and serve you in willing obedience; through your Son, Jesus Christ our Lord.

READINGS

Deuteronomy 26:1-11

The annual harvest festival called the feast of weeks provides the setting for today's reading. This festival celebrates the first fruits of the produce of the land offered back to God in thanks. In this text, worshipers announce God's gracious acts on behalf of Israel.

Psalm 100

Enter the gates of the LORD with thanksgiving. (Ps. 100:3)

Philippians 4:4-9

Because the Lord is near, Paul urges the Philippians to rejoice, include thanksgiving in their prayers, and take to heart whatever is worthy of praise.

John 6:25-35

The day after the feeding of the five thousand found the people still clamoring for bread. Jesus tells them that he is the bread of life and that faith in him will lead to eternal life.

COLOR White

THE PRAYERS

Awaiting the fulfillment of God's reign, let us pray for the world, the church, and all people according to their needs.

A BRIEF SILENCE.

Let us pray for bishops and leaders in the church, for teachers and evangelists, administrators and acolytes, social ministers and musicians, assisting ministers, greeters, ushers, musicians, artists, singers, and all who gather around Christ in word and sacrament. Lord, in your mercy,

hear our prayer.

Let us pray for those who struggle for justice and who work for peace among the nations, for public leaders and judges, diplomats and scholars of law, and for those who serve in the armed forces. Lord, in your mercy,

hear our prayer.

Let us pray for laborers, farmers, business people, and office workers, for those who bring us water, light, shelter, and food, and for those who guard our streets and protect the defenseless. Lord, in your mercy,

hear our prayer.

Let us pray for scientists and healthcare professionals, for those who study the universe, the earth, the body, and the mind, and illuminate the work of the divine creator. Lord, in your mercy,

hear our prayer.

Let us pray for those who wait for healing and strength (especially...). Let us pray for those who tend the sick, comfort us in our sorrow, and bury the dead. Let us pray for those who are lonely, fearful, anxious, confused, or weary. Lord, in your mercy,

hear our prayer.

HERE OTHER INTERCESSIONS MAY BE OFFERED.

Let us pray in thanksgiving for the faithful of every time and place who have witnessed to your generosity. Bring us with them to the banquet table of heaven. Lord, in your mercy,

hear our prayer.

Hear our prayers, righteous God, as we await the coming of your great and glorious feast; through Christ, your beloved Son, our Messiah.

Amen

IMAGES FOR PREACHING

One traditional mealtime prayer says, "Lord, make us grateful for this and all your bounty." Make us grateful. Gratitude does not seem to come naturally for us. Perhaps Bart Simpson does not overstate our mindset by much when he prays: "Hey God, we bought this food with our own money and we fixed it ourselves—so, thanks for nothing!" On this day we try to adjust our attitudes. It has been said that gratitude probably is the most accurate barometer of a person's spiritual maturity.

Our grounding in eucharistic living can become the focus of our proclamation. As we speak to those with hungry minds and souls, we recall this text from the gospel of John about hunger and thirst. Jesus offers us the bread of heaven. We are given daily bread in its broadest sense, the milk, honey, and sustenance of God's gracious hand (Deut. 26). We must not spiritualize this text to exclude physical bread. The images of bread in the gospel point us to a uniquely Christian reality, however. Jesus *is* the bread of life, and this food endures for eternal life.

In this month of looking to end things and in these days leading up to the festival of Christ the King, our thanksgiving is viewed from the perspective of eternity. Our soul's hunger is fed by a gracious God, one whose love and mercy come to us as gift, not as something we buy with our own money or fix ourselves. This love and mercy is offered to us as the body of Christ, a presence so real that we can taste it. It is a gift so life-changing that we become it, the body of Christ in the world.

WORSHIP MATTERS

A celebration of the eucharist is the most obvious way to observe this day, especially with the holiday's emphasis on food and sharing our bounty with others. In the eucharist we celebrate a joyful exchange, as Martin Luther described in his treatise about this sacrament in "The Blessed Sacrament of the Holy and True Body of Christ, and the Brotherhoods" in 1519:

> This fellowship consists in this, that all the spiritual possessions of Christ and his saints are shared with and become the common property of him who receives this sacrament. Again all sufferings and sins also become common property; and thus love engenders love in return and [mutual love] unites. (*Luther's Works,* 35, ed. Helmut T. Lehman and E. Theodore Bachmann (Philadelphia: Fortress Press, 1960), 51).

> When you have partaken of this sacrament…you must in turn share the misfortunes of the fellowship.…As love and support are given you, you in turn must render love and support to Christ in his needy ones. (*Luther's Works,* 54)

LET THE CHILDREN COME

Encourage children to join in contributing to the prayers by offering a phrase or a word about that for which they give thanks. In the weeks before Thanksgiving, written prayers and drawings could be gathered on posters. One or more children could be involved in offering prayers during the service itself. Thanksgiving Day is a time to remember all the things, big and small, for which we give thanks to God.

MUSIC FOR WORSHIP
GATHERING

LBW 407	Come, you thankful people, come
WOV 797	O God beyond all praising

PSALM 100

Cherwien, David. PW, Cycle C.

Gelineau, Joseph, S.J. "Psalm 100: Cry Out with Joy" in *Forty-one Grail/Gelineau Psalms.* GIA G-4402.

Haas, David. "Psalm 100: We Are His People" in PCY.

Howard, Julie. *Sing for Joy: Psalm Settings for God's Children.* LTP.

Marshall, Jane. *Sing Out! A Children's Psalter.* WLP 7191.

LBW 245	All people that on earth do dwell
LBW 256	Oh, sing jubilee to the Lord
LBW 531	Before Jehovah's awesome throne

HYMN OF THE DAY

LBW 409	Praise and thanksgiving
	BUNESSAN

VOCAL RESOURCES

Bisbee, B. Wayne. "Praise and Thanksgiving" in *Assist Us to Proclaim, Set 2.* AFP 11-10597. SATB.

Wolff, S. Drummond. "Praise and Thanksgiving." CPH 98-2514. SATB.

INSTRUMENTAL RESOURCES

See Proper 23, October 14, 2001.

ALTERNATE HYMN OF THE DAY

LBW 527	All creatures of our God and King
WOV 754	Let us talents and tongues employ

COMMUNION

| LBW 197 | O living Bread from heaven |
| WOV 702 | I am the Bread of life |

SENDING

LBW 278	All praise to thee, my God this night
LBW 412	Sing to the Lord of harvest
WOV 704	Father, we thank you

ADDITIONAL HYMNS AND SONGS

DH 99	Living thanksgiving
TFF 291	I will enter his gates
W&P 87	Let there be praise

MUSIC FOR THE DAY

CHORAL

Bach, J. S. "Now Thank We All Our God" in BAS. SATB, org.

Bell, John. "With Grace and Carefulness." GIA G-4670. SATB.

Ferguson, John. "A Song of Thanksgiving." AFP 11-10505. Also in *The Augsburg Choirbook.* 11-10817. SATB, org.

Haydn, Franz Joseph. "Fields Are Dancing with Ripened Corn." CPH 98-3523. SATB, kybd.

Jennings, Carolyn. "We Praise You, O God." AFP 11-10948. SATB, org, opt tpt.

Schütz, Heinrich. "We Offer Our Thanks and Praise" in CC. SATB.

Wood, Dale. "Jubilate Deo." AFP 11-1603. SATB, org, opt brass, opt perc. Also AFP 11-1646. U/2 pt, org, opt perc.

CHILDREN'S CHOIRS

Cherwien, David. "I Will Give Thanks to the Lord." CPH 98-2930. U, kybd.

Fleming, Tomas J. "For the Beauty of the Earth." MSM 50-9412. U, kybd.

Heck, Lyle. "Make a Joyful Noise unto the Lord." AFP 11-10601. 2 pt, kybd, fl.

Page, Sue Ellen. "Sing Alleluia" in LS.

KEYBOARD/INSTRUMENTAL

Cherwien, David. "Come, You Thankful People, Come" in *Interpretations,* vol. 10. AMSI SP-107. Org.

Organ, Anne Krentz. "Now We Offer" in *Woven Together.* AFP 11-10980. Pno, inst.

HANDBELL

Linker, Janet, and Jane McFadden. "Come, Ye Thankful People, Come." BEC BE HB95. 3-5 oct.

McChesney, Kevin. "All Things Bright and Beautiful." AFP 11-10687. 3-5 oct.

Rogers, Sharon Elery. "Now Thankful People, Come." AFP 11-10804. 2-3 oct.

PRAISE ENSEMBLE

Tarner, Evelyn. "Rejoice in the Lord Always" in *All God's People Sing!* CPH.

FRIDAY, NOVEMBER 23
CLEMENT, BISHOP OF ROME, C. 100

Clement was the third bishop of Rome and served at the end of the first century. He is best remembered for a letter he wrote to the Corinthian congregation still having difficulty with divisions in spite of Paul's canonical letters. Clement's writing echoes Paul's. "Love...has no limits to its endurance, bears everything patiently. Love is neither servile nor arrogant. It does not provoke schisms or form cliques, but always acts in harmony with others." Clement's letter is also a witness to early understandings of church government and the way each office in the church works for the good of the whole.

Clement's letter reminds us that divisions within the church are a sad part of our history and that pastoral love for people must be present amid our differing views of authority, scripture, and ministry.

FRIDAY, NOVEMBER 23
MIGUEL AGUSTÍN PRO, PRIEST, MARTYR, 1927

Miguel Pro grew up among oppression in Mexico, where revolutionaries accused the church of siding with the rich. He was a Jesuit priest who served during a time of intense anticlericalism, and therefore he carried out much of his ministry in private settings. He worked on behalf of the poor and homeless. Miguel and his two brothers were arrested, falsely accused of throwing a bomb at the car of a government official, and assassinated by a firing squad. Just before the guns fired he yelled, "Viva Christo Rey!" which means "Long live Christ the king!"

Make plans for work that can be done on behalf of the poor in the upcoming weeks. Raise questions about what long-term solutions may bridge the gap between rich and poor.

NOVEMBER 25, 2001

CHRIST THE KING
LAST SUNDAY AFTER PENTECOST
PROPER 29

INTRODUCTION

"Jesus shall reign where'er the sun does its successive journeys run," wrote the English hymnist Isaac Watts. He died on this date in 1748 but left a glorious legacy of English hymnody. On this last Sunday of the church year, we honor Christ, who reigns as king from the cross. All space and all time belong to the one who offers paradise to those who live and die with him.

PRAYER OF THE DAY

Almighty and everlasting God, whose will it is to restore all things to your beloved Son, whom you anointed priest forever and king of all creation: Grant that all the people of the earth, now divided by the power of sin, may be united under the glorious and gentle rule of your Son, our Lord Jesus Christ, who lives and reigns with you and the Holy Spirit, one God, now and forever.

READINGS

Jeremiah 23:1-6

Today's reading builds on the common ancient Near Eastern metaphor of the king as shepherd. The influence of an unjust ruler is about to bring disaster. Nevertheless, the Lord will raise up a new and righteous shepherd who will rule a restored Judah.

Psalm 46

I will be exalted among the nations. (Ps. 46:11)

Colossians 1:11-20

An early Christian hymn praises Christ as one who reigns in heaven and on earth.

Luke 23:33-43

On the cross, Jesus is revealed to be a type of ruler different from what many had anticipated. He has the power to welcome others to paradise but will not use that power to save himself from death.

COLOR   White

THE PRAYERS

Awaiting the fulfillment of God's reign, let us pray for the world, the church, and all people according to their needs.

A BRIEF SILENCE.

Shepherd of Israel, guide those who tend your flock. Be with the leaders of your church as they gather your people in safety. Lord, in your mercy,

hear our prayer.

Creator of the universe, we ask your forgiveness for all those times when we have been poor stewards of your world. Lord, in your mercy,

hear our prayer.

God of speech and song, give us courage in our words, that together with Isaac Watts and all who have written of your glory, we might forever proclaim your praises. Lord, in your mercy,

hear our prayer.

God, our help in trouble, bring healing and comfort to those who are sick (especially...). Lord, in your mercy,

hear our prayer.

HERE OTHER INTERCESSIONS MAY BE OFFERED.

King of glory, with the thief on the cross and all the holy saints who have gone before us, we look forward to that day when we will be with you in paradise. Lord, in your mercy,

hear our prayer.

Hear our prayers, righteous God, as we await the coming of your great and glorious feast; through Christ, your beloved Son, our Messiah.

Amen

IMAGES FOR PREACHING

Next Sunday is the start of a new liturgical year. At our New Year's parties we often only look ahead, and make resolutions for the year to come. But how do we mark the year's end?

Liturgically, we mark the end by looking to the end. Where do we find Jesus? Hanging on the cross, about to die, almost at his presumed end. But then, we hear his next-to-last words before he died, that amazing declaration to the criminal next to him: "Truly I tell you, today you will be with me in Paradise." That is quite a promise. Jesus points us beyond an earthly end, beyond the new year into God's end time.

345

In the Church of Sweden, this day is called *Domssöndagen*, which means Judgment Sunday. You can hear the "doom" in the word. It is a heavy day in a month filled with gloomy weather in that northern country with so little winter light. And our scene in Luke does not seem much lighter, with Jesus dying on the cross. But Jesus' words from that cross are words of light. Christ is king, and we are not! We are not doomed to languish in the shadows of our deeds.

Gerhard Frost shares an image for Christ's light: If I have two rooms, one dark, the other light, and I open the door between them, the dark room becomes lighter without the light one becoming darker. Jesus offers us his light for our darkness, but our darkness has not overcome him. Jesus, king of all creation, welcomes the dying criminal home. He also welcomes us at his eucharistic table and into an unending paradise.

WORSHIP MATTERS

Leaders, including presiding and assisting ministers, must take time to prepare, ensuring that each element of a worship service—from chanting to scripture readings and prayers—flows well. Worship leaders must also model service to others. The challenge worship leaders face is to be welcoming and helpful without being intrusive and overbearing.

While a well laid out service folder can be a helpful aid for visitors, simple, *concise* prompts can be given to the assembly by the worship leaders as well. An invitation, such as "We confess our faith in the words of the Apostles' Creed, as printed on page 85," can be used sparingly if the leader feels the need to direct people to an appropriate place in a printed worship resource. Frequent worshipers of the assembly can also be welcoming to newcomers. Members should be encouraged to help if someone "new" is obviously struggling to locate a place in a worship book or leaflet.

LET THE CHILDREN COME

Jesus' last action of his life was to serve others. On the cross we know him as the one who lays down his life for his friends. Those who are worship leaders in the congregation are given the opportunity to model servant leadership. Let the actions of worship be rich and bold, done with a sense of hospitality, honesty, and choreography. Let worship be done with care and en-

thusiasm, so that the central actions speak clearly. It is an awesome task to lead the people of God in their song, prayer, and proclamation.

MUSIC FOR WORSHIP

GATHERING

| LBW 377 | Lift high the cross |
| WOV 631 | Lift up your heads, O gates |

PSALM 46

See Reformation Sunday, October 28, 2001.

HYMN OF THE DAY

| WOV 778 | O Christ the same |
| | LONDONDERRY AIR |

INSTRUMENTAL RESOURCES

Albrecht, Mark. "Londonderry Air" in *Timeless Hymns of Faith,* vol. 2. AFP 11-11012. Pno.

McFadden, Jane. "The Londonderry Air." AFP 11-10769. 2-3 oct, hb, opt inst and hc.

ALTERNATE HYMN OF THE DAY

| LBW 172 | Lord, enthroned in heavenly splendor |
| LBW 328 | All hail the power of Jesus' name! |

COMMUNION

| LBW 514 | O Savior, precious Savior |
| WOV 740 | Jesus, remember me |

SENDING

| LBW 518 | Beautiful Savior |
| WOV 787 | Glory to God, we give you thanks |

ADDITIONAL HYMNS AND SONGS

DH 61	Strange king
REJ 348	Mighty God, while angels bless thee
TFF 267	All hail the power of Jesus' name!
W&P 94	Majesty
W&P 124	Shout to the Lord

MUSIC FOR THE DAY

CHORAL

Britten, Benjamin. "Festival Te Deum." B&H 15656. SATB, org, S solo.

Busarow, Donald. "O Lord, You Are My God and King." AFP 11-10892. SATB, org, opt cong.

Finzi, Gerald. "Lo, the Full Final Sacrifice." B&H 3036. SSAATTBB,
org, STB solos.

Joncas, Michael. "Exultate Justi." GIA G-4880. SATB, cong, org,
opt brass, opt timp.

Schalk, Carl. "Thine the Amen, Thine the Praise." AFP 11-2173.
SATB, opt cong, org.

Schütz, Heinrich. "Praise to You, Lord Jesus" in CC. SATB.

Sweelinck, Jan. "Sing to the Lord, New Songs Be Raising" in CC.
SATB.

Vaughan Williams, Ralph. "At the Name of Jesus." OXF 40.100.
SATB, org.

CHILDREN'S CHOIRS

Bertalot, John. "God Is Our Hope." CG CGA-444. 2 pt trbl, kybd.

Comer, Marilyn. "God Is Our Refuge and Strength" in LS.

Courtney, Craig. "Coronation." BEC BP1273. 2 pt mxd, kybd,
opt horn, opt ch.

Leaf, Robert. "To the Glory of Our King." CG CGA-173. U,
pno/org.

KEYBOARD/INSTRUMENTAL

Albrecht, Mark. "Duke Street" in *Festive Processionals.* AFP 11-10930.
Tpt, org.

Courtney, Mark. "Coronation." AMSI B-22. Brass, org, perc.

Schaffner, John Hebden. "Organ Motet for Christ the King" in *Organ
Music for the Seasons,* vol. 2. AFP 11-11010. Org.

Wold, Wayne L. *Partita on "Coronation."* SEL. Org.

HANDBELL

Callahan, Frances L. "Praise, My Soul, the King of Heaven."
MSM 30-802. 3 oct.

Gramann, Fred. "All Glorious Above." AGEHR AG370021. 3-7 oct.

McChesney, Kevin. "Canticle for a Festive Day." BEC BE HB182.
3-6 oct, opt ch.

McChesney, Kevin. "Sing Praise to God Who Reigns Above."
AGEHR AG23006. 2-3 oct.

Waldrop, Tammy. "Rejoice, the Lord Is King." WRD 3014065315.
2-3 oct.

PRAISE ENSEMBLE

Cook, Steve, and Vikki Cook. "Jesus, You Reign Over All" in *Praise
Hymns and Choruses,* 4th ed. MAR.

Hayford, Jack W., and Jack Schrader. "Majesty." HOP GC 868. SATB,
kybd.

SUNDAY, NOVEMBER 25
ISAAC WATTS, HYMNWRITER, 1748

Isaac Watts was born in England to a nonconformist
family, people who thought the Church of England had
not carried its reforms far enough. As a youth, Watts
complained to his father about the quality of hymnody
in the metrical psalter of his day. That was the start of his
hymnwriting career. He wrote about six hundred
hymns, many of them in a two-year period beginning
when he was twenty years old. Some of Watts's hymns
are based on psalms, a nonconformist tradition, but others are not. When criticized for writing hymns not taken
from scripture, he responded that if we can pray prayers
that are not from scripture but written by us, then surely
we can sing hymns that we have made up ourselves.

FRIDAY, NOVEMBER 30
ST. ANDREW, APOSTLE

Andrew was the first of the twelve. He is known as a
fisherman who left his net to follow Jesus. As a part of
his calling, he brought other people, including Simon
Peter, to meet Jesus. The Byzantine church honors Andrew as its patron and points out that because he was
the first of Jesus' followers, he was, in the words of John
Chrysostom, "the Peter before Peter." Together with
Philip, Andrew leads a number of Greeks to speak with
Jesus, and it is Andrew who shows Jesus a boy with five
barley loaves and two fish. Andrew is said to have died
on a cross saltire, an X-shaped cross.

We too are called to invite others to the life of
Christ that we will celebrate during Advent and Christ-
mas. In what ways will the church that bears the light of
Christ lead others to meet Jesus?

BIBLIOGRAPHY

CHOIRBOOKS

Augsburg Choirbook, The. Minneapolis: Augsburg Fortress, 1998. Kenneth Jennings, ed. Sixty-seven anthems primarily from twentieth-century North American composers.

Bach for All Seasons. Minneapolis: Augsburg Fortress, 1999. Richard Erickson and Mark Bighley, eds. Offers movements from cantatas and oratorios presented with carefully reconstructed keyboard parts and fresh English texts.

Chantry Choirbook. Minneapolis: Augsburg Fortress, 2000. Choral masterworks of European composers spanning five centuries, many with new English translations, and indexed for use in the liturgical assembly throughout the year.

100 Carols for Choirs. Oxford and New York: Oxford University Press, 1987. David Willcocks and John Rutter, eds. One hundred classic choral settings of traditional Christmas carols.

COMPUTER RESOURCES

Lutheran Resources for Worship Computer Series. *Lutheran Book of Worship Liturgies*; *With One Voice Liturgies*; *Words for Worship: 2001,* Cycle C; *Graphics for Worship*. Minneapolis: Augsburg Fortress, 1997 and ongoing. These CD-ROM resources enable worship planners to prepare weekly, seasonal, or occasional worship folders.

Worship Source. Augsburg Fortress, 2000 and ongoing. This series of CD-ROMs to assist with worship bulletin preparation includes *Stanza,* which contains over one thousand hymn texts and music graphics with multiple search functions, and *Icon,* with more than 250 graphic images for every Sunday and festival of the three-year cycle.

DAILY PRAYER RESOURCES

Book of Common Worship: Daily Prayer. Louisville, Ky.: Westminster John Knox Press, 1993. Presbyterian.

For All the Saints. 4 vols. Frederick Schumacher, ed. Delhi, N.Y.: American Lutheran Publicity Bureau, 1994.

Haugen, Marty. *Holden Evening Prayer.* Chicago: GIA Publications, Inc., 1990.

Makeever, Ray. *Joyous Light Evening Prayer.* Minneapolis: Augsburg Fortress, 2000.

Weber, Paul. *Music for Morning Prayer.* Minneapolis: Augsburg Fortress, 1999. Setting of liturgical music for morning prayer.

Welcome Home: Year of Luke. Minneapolis: Augsburg Fortress, 1997. Scripture, prayers, and blessings for the household.

ENVIRONMENT AND ART

Chinn, Nancy. *Spaces for Spirit: Adorning the Church.* Chicago: Liturgy Training Publications, 1998. Imaginative thinking about ways to treat visual elements in the worship space.

Clothed in Glory: Vesting the Church. Edited by David Philippart. Chicago: Liturgy Training Publications, 1997. Photos and essays about liturgical paraments and vestments.

Huffman, Walter C., S. Anita Stauffer, and Ralph R. Van Loon. *Where We Worship.* Minneapolis: Augsburg Publishing House, 1987. Written by three Lutheran worship leaders, this volume sets forth the central principles for understanding and organizing space for worship. Study book and leader guide.

Mauck, Marchita. *Shaping a House for the Church.* Chicago: Liturgy Training Publications, 1990. The author presents basic design principles for worship space and the ways in which the worship space both forms and expresses the faith of the worshiping assembly.

Mazar, Peter. *To Crown the Year: Decorating the Church through the Seasons.* Chicago: Liturgy Training Publications, 1995. A contemporary guide for decorating the worship space throughout the seasons of the year.

Stauffer, S. Anita. *Altar Guild and Sacristy Handbook.* Minneapolis: Augsburg Fortress, 2000. Revised and expanded edition of this classic on preparing the table and the worship environment.

HYMN AND SONG COLLECTIONS

As Sunshine to a Garden: Hymns and Songs. Rusty Edwards. Minneapolis: Augsburg Fortress, 1999. Forty-six collected hymns from the author of "We all are one in mission."

Borning Cry: Worship for a New Generation. Compiled by John Ylvisaker. Waverly, Iowa: New Generation Publishers, 1992.

Bread of Life: Mass and Songs for the Assembly. Minneapolis: Augsburg Fortress, 2000. Jeremy Young's complete eucharistic music based on *With One Voice* setting five together with twelve of his worship songs.

Dancing at the Harvest: Songs by Ray Makeever. Minneapolis: Augsburg Fortress, 1997. Over one hundred songs and service music items.

O Blessed Spring: Hymns of Susan Palo Cherwien. Minneapolis: Augsburg Fortress, 1997. New hymn texts set to both new and familiar hymn tunes.

Sound the Bamboo. Manila: Asian Institute for Liturgy and Music, 1990. Hymns from Asia.

Worship & Praise. Minneapolis: Augsburg Fortress, 1999. A collection of songs in various contemporary and popular styles, with helps for using them in Lutheran worship.

LEADING WORSHIP

Adams, William Seth. *Shaped by Images: One Who Presides*. New York: Church Hymnal Corporation, 1995. An excellent review of the ministry of presiding at worship.

Hovda, Robert. *Strong, Loving and Wise: Presiding in Liturgy*. Collegeville, Mn.: The Liturgical Press, 1981. Sound, practical advice for the worship leader from a beloved advocate of social justice and liturgical renewal.

Huck, Gabe. *Liturgy with Style and Grace*, rev. ed. Chicago: Liturgy Training Publications, 1984. The first three chapters offer a practical, well-written overview of the purpose of worship, the elements of worship, and liturgical leadership.

Huffman, Walter C. *Prayer of the Faithful: Understanding and Creatively Leading Corporate Intercessory Prayer*, rev. ed. Minneapolis: Augsburg Fortress, 1992. A helpful treatment of communal prayer, the Lord's Prayer, and the prayers of the people.

Singing the Liturgy: Building Confidence for Worship Leaders. Chicago: Evangelical Lutheran Church in America, 1996. A demonstration recording of the chants assigned to leaders in *LBW* and *WOV*.

LECTIONARIES

Lectionary for Worship, Cycle C. Minneapolis: Augsburg Fortress, 1997. The Revised Common Lectionary. Includes first reading, psalm citation, second reading, and gospel for each Sunday and lesser festival. Each reading is "sense-lined" for clearer proclamation of the scriptural texts. New Revised Standard Version.

Lectionary for Worship, Ritual Edition. Minneapolis: Augsburg Fortress, 1996. Large print, illustrated, hardbound edition that includes the complete three-year Revised Common Lectionary and lesser festival scriptural readings.

Readings and Prayers: The Revised Common Lectionary. Minneapolis: Augsburg Fortress, 1995. Scripture citations for the Revised Common Lectionary in use within the Evangelical Lutheran Church in America.

Readings for the Assembly, Cycle C. Gordon Lathrop and Gail Ramshaw, eds. Minneapolis: Augsburg Fortress, 1997. The Revised Common Lectionary. Emended NRSV with inclusive language.

LECTIONARY-BASED LEARNING RESOURCES

Life Together. Minneapolis: Augsburg Fortress, 2000–2001 (Year B/C). A new, comprehensive series of Revised Common Lectionary resources that integrates the primary activities of congregational life: worship, proclamation, and learning.

Faith Life Weekly. Reproducible weekly handouts to guide conversations, prayer, and activities in the home.

Kids Celebrate. Reproducible weekly children's worship bulletins.

LifeSongs (children's songbook, leader book, and audio CDs). A well-rounded selection of age-appropriate songs, hymns, and liturgical music that builds a foundation for a lifetime of singing the faith.

Life Together: Faith Nurturing Resources for Children. Quarterly teaching and learning resources for three age levels: pre-elementary, lower elementary, upper elementary.

Living and Learning. A quarterly guide for educational planning using the resources of Life Together.

Word of Life. Weekly devotional studies for adults based on the lectionary texts.

PERIODICALS

Assembly. Notre Dame Center for Pastoral Liturgy. Chicago: Liturgy Training Publications. Published five times a year. Each issue examines a particular aspect of worship practice. (800) 933-1800.

Catechumenate: A Journal of Christian Initiation. Chicago: Liturgy Training Publications. Published bimonthly with articles on congregational preparation of older children and adults for the celebration of baptism and eucharist. (800) 933-1800.

Cross Accent. Journal of the Association of Lutheran Church Musicians. Publication for church musicians and worship leaders in North America. (800) 624-ALCM.

Faith & Form. Journal of the Interfaith Forum on Religion, Art and Architecture. Editorial office, (617) 965-3018.

Grace Notes. Newsletter of the Association of Lutheran Church Musicians. (708) 272-4116.

Liturgy. Quarterly journal of The Liturgical Conference, Washington, DC Each issue explores a worship-related issue from an ecumenical perspective. (800) 394-0885.

Plenty Good Room. Chicago: Liturgy Training Publications. Published bimonthly. A magazine devoted to African American worship within a Roman Catholic context. Helpful articles on the enculturation of worship. (800) 933-1800.

Worship. Collegeville, Mn: The Order of St. Benedict, published through The Liturgical Press six times a year. Since the early decades of this century, the primary promoter of liturgical renewal among the churches. (800) 858-5450.

Worship 2000. Published periodically by the Office of Worship of the Evangelical Lutheran Church in America. Articles and annotated bibliographies on a range of worship topics. (800) 638-3522.

PLANNING TOOLS

Church Year Calendar 2001. Minneapolis: Augsburg Fortress, 2000. A one-sheet calendar of lectionary citations and liturgical colors for each Sunday and festival of the liturgical year. Appropriate for bulk purchase and distribution.

Choosing Contemporary Music: Seasonal, Topical, Lectionary Indexes. Minneapolis: Augsburg Fortress, 2000. *Indexes for Worship Planning: Revised Common Lectionary, Lutheran Book of Worship, With One Voice.* Minneapolis: Augsburg Fortress, 1996. *Choosing Contemporary Music* provides references to multiple collections of contemporary praise and liturgical songs; *Indexes for Worship Planning* indexes the hymns and songs in *Lutheran Book of Worship* and *With One Voice.* Both include extensive scripture and topic indexes.

Calendar of Word and Season 2001: Liturgical Wall Calendar. Minneapolis: Augsburg Fortress, 2000. Date blocks note Revised Common Lectionary readings for Sundays and festivals and identify seasonal or festival color. A reference tool for home, sacristy, office.

Worship Planning Calendar 2001. Minneapolis: Augsburg Fortress, 2000. A two-page per week calendar helpful for worship planners, with space to record appointments and notes for each day. Specially designed to complement *Sundays and Seasons.*

PREPARING MUSIC FOR WORSHIP

Cherwien, David. *Let the People Sing!: A Keyboardist's Creative and Practical Guide to Engaging God's People in Meaningful Song.* St. Louis: Concordia Publishing House, 1997. A practical and pedagogical approach to leading congregational singing and improvising at the organ.

Cotter, Jeanne. *Keyboard Improvisation for the Liturgical Musician.* Chicago: GIA Publications, Inc. Practical approach to keyboard improvisation.

Farlee, Robert Buckley, gen. ed. *Leading the Church's Song.* Minneapolis: Augsburg Fortress, 1998. Articles by various contributors, with musical examples and audio CD, giving guidance on the interpretation and leadership of various genres of congregational song.

Handbells in the Liturgy: A Practical Guide for the Use of Handbells in Liturgical Worship Traditions. St. Louis: Concordia Publishing House, 1996. Includes historical information on handbells in worship, ideas for structuring a bell program, and specific segments on the use of bells in the church year.

Haugen, Marty. *Instrumentation and the Liturgical Ensemble.* Chicago: GIA Publications, Inc., 1991. A resource for instrumental ensembles in liturgical settings.

Hopson, Hal H. *The Creative Use of Handbells in Hymn Singing.* Carol Stream: Hope Publishing Co. Resource contains specific handbell techniques to be used in accompanying congregational singing.

Rose, Richard. *Hymnal Companion for Woodwind, Brass and Percussion.* St. Louis: Concordia Publishing House, 1997.

Rotermund, Donald. *Intonations and Alternative Accompaniments for Psalm Tones.* St. Louis: Concordia Publishing House, 1997. (*LBW* and *LW* versions available separately.)

Weidler, Scott, and Dori Collins. *Sound Decisions.* Chicago: Evangelical Lutheran Church in America, 1997. Theological principles for the evaluation of contemporary worship music.

Westermeyer, Paul. *The Church Musician,* rev. ed. Minneapolis: Augsburg Fortress, 1997. Foundational introduction to the role and task of the church musician as the leader of the people's song in worship.

————. *Te Deum: The Church and Music.* Minneapolis: Fortress Press, 1998. An historical and theological introduction to the music of the church.

Wilson-Dickson, Andrew. *The Story of Christian Music.* Minneapolis: Fortress Press, 1996. An illustrated guide to the major traditions of music in worship.

Wold, Wayne. *Tune My Heart to Sing: Devotions for Choirs Based on the Three-Year Revised Common Lectionary.* Minneapolis: Augsburg Fortress, 1997.

PROCLAIMING THE WORD

Brown, Raymond E. *The Birth of the Messiah.* A volume in *The Anchor Bible Reference Library.* New York: Doubleday, 1993.

Brown, Raymond. *The Death of the Messiah.* Two volumes in *The Anchor Bible Reference Library.* New York: Doubleday, 1994.

Brueggemann, Walter, et al. *Texts for Preaching: A Lectionary Commentary Based on the NRSV.* Cycles A, B, C. Louisville, Ky.: Westminster John Knox Press, 1993–95.

Craddock, Fred, et al. *Preaching through the Christian Year.* Three volumes for Cycles A, B, C. Valley Forge, Pa.: Trinity Press International, 1992, 1993. In three volumes, various authors comment on the Sunday readings and psalms as well as various festival readings.

Days of the Lord: The Liturgical Year. 7 vols. Collegeville, Mn.: The Liturgical Press, 1991–94. Written by French biblical and liturgical experts, this series provides helpful commentary on the readings and seasons. Readily adapted to the Revised Common Lectionary.

Homily Service: An Ecumenical Resource for Sharing the Word. Silver Spring, Md.: The Liturgical Conference. A monthly publication with commentary on Sunday readings (exegesis, ideas and illustrations, healing aspects of the word, a preacher's reflection on the readings).

New Proclamation, Series C. Minneapolis: Augsubrg Fortress, 2000–2001. Various authors. A sound and useful series of commentaries on cycle C readings. In two volumes, Advent–Holy Week and Easter–Pentecost.

Reading the Lessons: A Lector's Guide to Pronunciation. Minneapolis: Augsburg Fortress, 1993.

PSALM COLLECTIONS

Anglican Chant Psalter, The. Alec Wyton, ed. New York: Church Hymnal Corporation, 1987.

Daw, Carl P., and Kevin R. Hackett. *A Hymn Tune Psalter.* New York: Church Publishing, 1999.

Grail Gelineau Psalter, The. Chicago: GIA Publications, Inc., 1972. 150 psalms and eighteen canticles.

Plainsong Psalter, The. James Litton, ed. New York: Church Hymnal Corporation, 1988.

Psalm Songs. David Ogden and Alan Smith, eds. Minneapolis: Augsburg Fortress, 1998.

    Psalm Songs 1 for Advent–Christmas–Epiphany.

    Psalm Songs 2 for Lent–Holy Week–Easter.

    Psalm Songs 3 for Ordinary Time.

Psalms for the Church Year. Various volumes by different composers. Chicago: GIA Publications, Inc., 1983–present.

Psalter, The. International Commission on English in the Liturgy (ICEL). Chicago: Liturgy Training Publications, 1995. A faithful and inclusive rendering from the Hebrew into contemporary English poetry, intended primarily for communal song and recitation.

Psalter for Worship. Martin Seltz, ed. Minneapolis: Augsburg Fortress, 1995 and continuing. Settings of psalm antiphons by various composers with *LBW* and other psalm tones. Psalm texts included. Prepared for psalms appointed in the Revised Common Lectionary for Sundays and festivals.

    Psalter for Worship, Cycle A.

    Psalter for Worship, Cycle B.

    Psalter for Worship, Cycle C. Includes all lesser festivals.

The Psalter: Psalms and Canticles for Singing. Louisville, Ky.: Westminster John Knox Press, 1993. Various composers.

Singing the Psalms. Various volumes with various composers represented. Portland: Oregon Catholic Press, 1995–present.

REFERENCE WORKS

Concordance to Hymn Texts: Lutheran Book of Worship. Robbin Hough, compiler. Minneapolis: Augsburg Publishing House, 1985.

New Dictionary of Sacramental Worship, The. Peter Fink, ed. Collegeville, Mn.: Michael Glazier/Liturgical Press, 1990.

New Westminster Dictionary of Liturgy and Worship, The. J. G. Davies, ed. Philadelphia: Westminster, 1986.

Praying Together. English Language Liturgical Consultation. Nashville: Abingdon Press, 1988. Core ecumenical liturgical texts with annotation and commentary.

Pfatteicher, Philip. *Festivals and Commemorations.* Minneapolis: Augsburg Publishing House, 1980.

———. Commentary on *Occasional Services.* Philadelphia: Fortress Press, 1983.

———. Commentary on *Lutheran Book of Worship.* Minneapolis: Augsburg Fortress, 1990.

Pfatteicher, Philip, and Carlos Messerli. *Manual on the Liturgy: Lutheran Book of Worship.* Minneapolis: Augsburg Publishing House, 1979.

Stulken, Marilyn Kay. *Hymnal Companion to the Lutheran Book of Worship.* Philadelphia: Fortress Press, 1981.

———. *With One Voice Reference Companion.* Minneapolis: Augsburg Fortress, 2000.

Van Loon, Ralph, and S. Anita Stauffer. *Worship Wordbook.* Minneapolis: Augsburg Fortress, 1995.

SEASONS AND LITURGICAL YEAR

Huck, Gabe. *The Three Days: Parish Prayer in the Paschal Triduum*, rev. ed. Chicago: Liturgy Training Publications, 1992. For worship committees, it is an excellent introduction to worship during the Three Days: Maundy Thursday, Good Friday, and Holy Saturday/Easter Sunday.

Hynes, Mary Ellen. *Companion to the Calendar.* Chicago: Liturgy Training Publications, 1993. An excellent overview of the seasons, festivals and lesser festivals, and many commemorations. Written from an ecumenical/Roman Catholic perspective, including commemorations unique to the Lutheran calendar.

Promise of His Glory: Services and Prayers for the Season from All Saints to Candlemas, The. Collegeville, Mn.: The Liturgical Press, 1991. And: Perham, Michael, et al., comps. *Enriching the Christian Year.* (Services and prayers from Lent through Pentecost). Collegeville, Mn.: The Liturgical Press, 1993. New liturgical texts, prayers, litanies, and complete services for congregational use.

WORSHIP BOOKS

Libro de Liturgia y Cántico. Minneapolis: Augsburg Fortress, 1998. A complete Spanish-language worship resource including liturgies and hymns, some with English translations.

Lutheran Book of Worship. Minneapolis: Augsburg Publishing House; Philadelphia: Board of Publication, Lutheran Church in America, 1978.

Lutheran Book of Worship, Ministers Edition. Minneapolis: Augsburg Publishing House; Philadelphia: Board of Publication, Lutheran Church in America, 1978.

Occasional Services: A Companion to Lutheran Book of Worship. Minneapolis: Augsburg Publishing House; Philadelphia: Board of Publication, Lutheran Church in America, 1982.

This Far by Faith. Minneapolis: Augsburg Fortress, 1999. A supplement of worship orders, psalms, service music, and hymns representing

African American traditions and developed by African American
Lutherans.

With One Voice: A Lutheran Resource for Worship. Minneapolis: Augsburg
Fortress, 1995. Pew, leader, and accompaniment editions; instrumental parts, organ accompaniment for the liturgy, and cassette.

WORSHIP STUDIES

Foley, Edward. *From Age to Age: How Christians Have Celebrated the Eucharist.* Chicago: Liturgy Training Publications, 1991. An excellent survey of Christian worship, music, environment, and theological concerns.

Gathered and Sent: An Introduction to Worship. Participant book by Karen
Bockelman. Leader guide by Roger Prehn. Minneapolis: Augsburg Fortress, 1999. Basic worship study course for inquirers and
general adult instruction in congregations.

Inside Out: Worship in an Age of Mission. Minneapolis: Fortress Press,
1999. Multiple authors writing on the mission of the church as
it pertains to various aspects of worship.

Open Questions in Worship. Gordon Lathrop, gen. ed. Minneapolis:
Augsburg Fortress.

   What are the essentials of Christian worship? vol. 1 (1994). The
scriptural, historical, and ecumenical consensus on essential elements of Christian worship.

   What is "contemporary" worship? vol. 2 (1995). Contemporary
church music, multiple services and diverse worship styles, and
the meaning of the word "contemporary."

   How does worship evangelize? vol. 3 (1995). Evangelism in American culture, liturgical leadership in evangelism, and the inclusive
nature of the liturgy.

   What is changing in baptismal practice? vol. 4 (1995). New develop-
ments in bringing adults to the faith, issues in infant baptism,
and the relationship between baptism and life stages.

   What is changing in eucharistic practice? vol. 5 (1995). Preaching,
the eucharistic prayer, and admission to the eucharist.

   What are the ethical implications of worship? vol. 6 (1996). Liturgy
serving social justice, worship and the cosmos/environment, and
liturgy in a secular world.

   What does "multicultural" worship look like? vol. 7 (1996). Worship
in North American culture, racial and ethnic-specific worship,
and culturally diverse worship.

   How does the liturgy speak of God? vol. 8 (1996). Images and
names for God in worship, women and men preaching, and the
trinitarian name invoked in the liturgy.

Ramshaw, Gail. *Every Day and Sunday, Too.* Minneapolis: Augsburg
Fortress, 1996. An illustrated book for parents and children.
Daily life is related to the central actions of the liturgy.

———. *1-2-3 Church.* Minneapolis: Augsburg Fortress, 1996. An illustrated rhyming primer and number book. For parents with
young children, this book presents the fundamental actions of
worship through numbered rhymes. A song for singing at home
or in church school is included.

———. *Sunday Morning.* Chicago: Liturgy Training Publications,
1993. A book for children and adults on the primary words of
Sunday worship.

Senn, Frank. *Christian Liturgy: Catholic and Evangelical.* Minneapolis:
Fortress Press, 1997. A comprehensive historical introduction to
the liturgy of the Western church with particular emphasis on
the Lutheran traditions.

*Use of the Means of Grace: A Statement on the Practice of Word and Sacrament,
The.* Chicago: Evangelical Lutheran Church in America, 1997. Also
available in Spanish and Mandarin versions.

Welcome to Christ: A Lutheran Catechetical Guide. Minneapolis, Augsburg
Fortress, 1997.

Welcome to Christ: A Lutheran Introduction to the Catechumenate. Minneapolis, Augsburg Fortress, 1997.

Welcome to Christ: Lutheran Rites for the Catechumenate. Minneapolis,
Augsburg Fortress, 1997.

What Do You Seek? Welcoming the Adult Inquirer. Minneapolis, Augsburg
Fortress, 2000. An introduction to a congregational process for
welcoming new members through affirmation of their baptism,
using the resources of catechumenal formation.